The Practice of Public Relations

eighth edition

Fraser P. Seitel

Managing Partner, Emerald Partners

Senior Counselor, Burson-Marsteller

Prentice Hall

Upper Saddle River, New Jersey 07458

To Uncle Howard, The Godfather

Acquisitions Editor: Leah Johnson
Editorial Assistant: Rebecca Calvert
Managing Editor (Editorial): Bruce Kaplan
Editor-in-Chief: Jim Boyd
Marketing Manager: Shannon Moore
Marketing Assistant: Kathleen Mulligan
Permissions Coordinator: Suzanne Grappi
Managing Editor (Production): John Roberts
Production Manager: Arnold Vila
Associate Director, Manufacturing: Vincent Scelta
Designer: Steven Frim
Design Manager: Patricia Smythe
Interior Design: Delgado Design
Cover Design: Steven Frim
Cover Illustration/Photo: Mark Hill/CNN
Composition: Carlisle Communications, Ltd.

Credits and acknowledgments for photographic materials borrowed from other sources and reproduced, with permission, in this textbook appear on pages 525–26. Credits and acknowledgments
for line art and textual materials borrowed from other sources and reproduced, with permission,
in this textbook appear on the appropriate page within text.

Library of Congress Cataloging-in-Publication Data

Seitel, Fraser P.
    The practice of public relations / Fraser P. Seitel.—8th ed.
        p. cm.
    Includes bibliographical references and index.
    ISBN 0–13–327679–0
    1. Public relations—United States   I. Title.
HM1221.S45 2001
659.2—dc21   00-032414

Printed in the United States of America
10 9 8 7 6 5 4 3 2 1
ISBN 0-13-327679-0

contents

Part II ▪ Validation

Part III ▪ Activation

Part V ▪ The Publics

Part VI · The Future

foreword

Unquestionably the major advance in the practice of public relations over the last quarter-century has been "reaction time," the speed at which PR practitioners can disseminate their messages. The fax machine provided the first big breakthrough, and now, with a network of computers and the Internet linking practitioners, clients, and the press, messages can be rocketed around the country (or the world) in a matter of seconds. In the 2000 election cycle, there were times when the spinmeisters for one political candidate reacted to a statement by the opposition candidate even before the statement was made, based on expectations or leaks.

Media guru Marshal McLuhan once stated that "instant information creates involvement in depth." True enough, but in hailing the technological advances that permit information to be flashed around the world in a split-second, we should not overlook one critical fact: Content is more important than speed. In other words, the message takes preference over the speed at which it is sent. It does the PR practitioner's client little good if he flashes a message to every news outlet known to man at the speed of light—unless it is the right message.

And that's the beauty of Fraser Seitel's book. He discusses not only how to communicate messages speedily but, more importantly, how to design and frame those messages. Anyone who knows how to use e-mail can send a message quickly; the real skill is knowing what message to send. This is what makes *The Practice of Public Relations* so valuable to everyone in our business—from the neophyte to the seasoned professional.

That Fraser Seitel is able to describe these techniques, complete with pertinent examples, in a way that is both profound and fun to read is a tribute to his own considerable communications skills. Like all good strategists, he can explain complex problems in language so simple it seems obvious, but those of us who do this for a living know just how difficult it really is.

So read, learn, enjoy, and prosper!

—*Joseph Napolitan*

Joseph Napolitan is a pioneer in the field of political counseling and is believed to be the first person ever to describe himself as a political consultant. He served on the campaign staffs of John F. Kennedy, Lyndon B. Johnson, and Hubert H. Humphrey. He was among the first Americans to serve as a consultant in foreign elections and has been a personal adviser to nine foreign heads of state. In 1999, he was chosen by PR Week *as "one of the 100 most influential PR people of the century," and in 2000 he was selected as one of the eight political consultants in the United States who have done the most to establish and maintain high standards in the industry. He is the author of* The Election Game and How to Win It *and* 100 Things I've Learned in 30 Years as a Political Consultant. *He maintains offices in New York City and Springfield, Massachusetts, where he lives.*

preface

In the last edition of this book, I opined, "The practice of public relations will never be replaced by a computer." I was right—sort of.

Public relations remains at base a personal, relationship-oriented practice demanding experienced judgment and finely honed interpersonal communications skills. *But . . .* the three years since the last edition of this book, the Internet has arrived with a vengeance in the practice of public relations, just as it has in every area of society. It is incumbent on public relations students and practitioners to understand the potential and pitfalls of the Internet and World Wide Web. Knowledge of the Web, in fact, has become a frontline public relations responsibility.

For example, a public relations vehicle as rudimentary as the news release has become a revitalized weapon on the Web. The Web enables corporations to communicate directly with investors, and a flurry of news releases indicates an aggressive company to many.

And so *The Practice of Public Relations,* Eighth Edition, places due emphasis on how every aspect of the field has been impacted by the growth of online communications.

From the chapter 1 ethical box feature on how Internet communications influenced the war in Kosovo to the chapter 20 discussion of how public relations positions are in high demand for the first time in history, thanks principally to the unbridled growth of the Internet, the clear bias of this book is the emerging cyberspace emphasis of the practice of public relations.

The purposes of this book remain the same: (1) to introduce readers to effective public relations and (2) to prepare students and professionals to deal with the situations and arrive at the solutions that distinguish the practice.

At the heart of public relations practice are real-life experiences—cases—that alter the communications landscape and redefine how we assess and handle communications challenges. The contemporary cases that dominate public relations discussion are the same ones that dominate the news of the day: Microsoft and its battle with the government, Coca-Cola's product contamination scare in Europe, Denny's rebound from race discrimination, the World Wrestling Federation's controversial rise to media prominence, the National Rife Association, John Rocker, JonBenet Ramsey, George W. Bush, Al Gore, Puff Daddy and Jennifer Lopez, the President and the intern. All play a part in public relations lore and learning, and they're all here.

So too are the Internet issues: Lockheed Martin's Internet employee ethics test, bogus Internet news releases, Beanie Baby Web warnings, rogue Web sites, investor Internet threads, intranet replacement of internal print publications.

The Practice of Public Relations, Eighth Edition, is different from other introductory texts in the field. Its premise is that public relations is a thoroughly engaging, constantly changing, Internet-influenced field. Although other texts may steer clear of the cases, the ethical challenges, the "how to" counsel, and the public relations conundrums that force students to think, this book confronts them all. It is, if you'll forgive the vernacular, an in-your-face textbook for an in-your-face profession.

This edition is divided into six discrete parts:

- ☑ Part I, "Evolution," deals with the field's antecedents and pioneers, definitions, and theoretical underpinnings.
- ☑ Part II, "Validation," deals with the concepts that separate the field from others— public opinion, ethics, research, and the law.
- ☑ Part III, "Activation," reviews the areas of expertise in which public relations practitioners must be knowledgeable, from the communications understanding that is the field's bedrock skill through general and crisis management through integrated marketing communications.
- ☑ Part IV, "Execution," reviews the primary technical skills that public relations professionals must possess—writing for the eye and ear and working in the on-line medium.
- ☑ Part V, "The Publics," discusses the field's most important constituencies, from employees and the media to consumers, investors, and diverse communities.
- ☑ Part VI, "The Future," discusses the challenges and opportunities presented to public relations in the new millennium.

The 40 case studies included here confront the reader with the most prominent and perplexing contemporary and legendary public relations problems: President Clinton and Monica Lewinsky, CNN and the Tailwind "exposé," the selling of the Blair Witch Project, Jesse Ventura's amazing gubernatorial victory, Exxon and the Gulf of Valdez, Dow Corning and the Tylenol murders, and many more.

Beyond this, a number of unique elements set this book apart:

- ☑ Wall-to-wall Internet application to public relations. Beyond the references in each chapter, chapter 13 offers the most comprehensive explanation of the practice of public relations on the Web.
- ☑ The prominence of ethics in the practice of public relations is highlighted with "A Question of Ethics" box features in every chapter, especially ethical issues surrounding Internet privacy.
- ☑ "Backgrounder" features complement the text with provocative examples of what's right, what's wrong, and what's wacky about public relations practice today.
- ☑ Chapter Summaries and Discussion Starter Questions highlight the key messages delivered in each chapter.
- ☑ Updated Suggested Readings, nourishing Appendices, and "Top of the Shelf" book reviews supplement the text with the field's most current literature. The vast majority of references cover 1997 to the present.
- ☑ "Over the Top" interviews air the views of the field's most prominent professionals—from President Clinton's White House Press Secretary Joe Lockhart to the most prominent public relations practitioner of the 20th century, Harold Burson— and the CEO newsmakers who presided over the field's most striking moments, from ValuJet CEO Lewis Jordan to PepsiCo CEO Craig Weatherup to Dow Corning CEO Richard Hazelton to the eminent management guru Dr. Peter Drucker.

All of these elements add to the excitement of this book. And the new features— Internet backgrounders and ethical questions, CEO interviews, 1999 to present cases, current readings, and so on—make this book particularly pertinent.

In that context, *The Practice of Public Relations,* Eighth Edition, is once again produced in a full-color format to underscore the liveliness, vitality, and relevance of a field that is built on the important personal relationships, judgmental skills, and on-line knowledge that will dominate the 21st century.

—Fraser P. Seitel

acknowledgments

The eighth edition of *The Practice of Public Relations* is dominated by the same force that has overtaken society in the 21st century: the Internet.

Notwithstanding this new cyberinfluence, the practice of public relations still depends on personal relationships. This public relations book therefore still depends for its inspiration on people, and there are many of them.

On the "front end" of the process, I am grateful to the top executives who sat with me for interviews. The CEOs of CBS, PepsiCo, Navistar, Madison Square Garden, and ACNielsen, Postmaster General Marvin Runyon, Air Force Secretary Sheila Widnall, management legend Peter Drucker, and the others originally were interviewed for *Public Relations Strategist* magazine, from which these interviews were excerpted. If public relations is to be accepted as a "management function," then public relations people must hear the views of top managers. We do that here because of the willingness of these CEOs.

I am indebted also to Ray Gaulke, president and cyclonic force behind the Public Relations Society of America, who was most kind to participate in this project and sit for the lead interview. Multitalented professional Paul Swift kindly prepared the bibliographic material and "Top of the Shelf" box features. Of course, the inestimable Jack O'Dwyer, who roars like a lion but is actually a teddy bear, was most kind to share photos from his industry magazine and sit for the final interview. Karen Randall, the pro's pro at Advantica Corp., the fine people at Historic Mount Vernon, and my old pal Bill Adams all pitched in with materials for the effort.

On the "back end" of the project, I am indebted to the finely tuned Prentice Hall team who patiently waited for the author to come through and then handled the new book effortlessly. Leah Johnson skillfully quarterbacked the project from her lofty perch north of the border. Closer to home, Rebecca Calvert did all the heavy lifting. And out there somewhere in the heartland, Arik Ohnstad and his copyediting staff sutured the broken syntax, patched up the factual errors, and nursed the failing grammar back to health. Meanwhile, managing editor John Roberts and permissions coordinator Suzanne Grappi kept the production team humming.

I also thank the public relations teachers whose insightful suggestions aided this eighth edition: Thomas Bivins at the University of Oregon, Charles Lubbers at Kansas State University, and Nancy Wolfe at Elon College all were quite helpful. They join in the Hall of Thanks those other distinguished professors who have reviewed past editions: Nickieann Fleener, Department of Communication, University of Utah; Mort Kaplan, Department of Marketing Communication, Columbia College (Chicago); Jack Mauch, Department of Communication, University of Idaho; Donnalyn Pompper, Department of Communication, Cabrini College; Cornelius B. Pratt, Department of Communications,

Michigan State University; J. D. Rayburn II, Department of Communication, Florida State University; Nancy Roth, Department of Communication, Rutgers, The State University (New Jersey); William C. Adams, School of Journalism and Mass Communications, Florida International University; John Q. Butler; Rachel L. Holloway, Department of Communications Studies, Virginia Tech; Diana Harney, Department of Communication and Theater, Pacific Lutheran University; Cornelius Pratt, Department of Advertising, Communications, and Public Relations, Michigan State University; Robert Cole, Pace University; Janice Sherline Jenny, College of Business, Herkimer County Community College, Craig Kelly, School of Business, California State University, Sacramento; Lyle J. Barker, Ohio State University; William G. Briggs, San Jose State University; E. Brody, Memphis State University; John S. Detweiler, University of Florida; Jim Eiseman, University of Louisville; Sandy Grossbart, University of Nebraska; Marjorie Nadler, Miami University; Sharon Smith, Middle Tennessee State University; Robert Wilson, Franklin University; Paul Brennan, Nassau Community College; Carol L. Hills, Boston University; George Laposky, Miami-Dade Community College; Mack Palmer, University of Oklahoma; Judy VanSlyke Turk, Louisiana State University; Roger B. Wadsworth, Miami-Dade Community College; James E. Grunig, University of Maryland; Robert T. Reilly, University of Nebraska at Omaha; Kenneth Rowe, Arizona State University; Dennis L. Wilcox, San Jose State University; Albert Walker, Northern Illinois University; Stanley E. Smith, Arizona State University; Jan Quarles, University of Georgia; Pamela J. Creedon, Ohio State University; Joel P. Bowman, Western Michigan University; Thomas H. Bivins, University of Oregon; Joseph T. Nolan, University of North Florida; Frankie A. Hammond, University of Florida; Bruce Joffe, George Mason University; Larissa Grunig, University of Maryland; Maria P. Russell, Syracuse University; and Melvin L. Sharpe, Ball State University.

Finally, the silent partners in this exercise remain critical to the effort. Architectural diva Rosemary, network mogul Raina, and Rose Bowl victor David Seitel are the real power behind the throne.

I thank you, one and all.

—Fraser P. Seitel
July 2000

about the author

Fraser P. Seitel is a veteran of close to three decades in the practice of public relations. In 1992, after serving for a decade as senior vice president and director of public affairs for Chase Manhattan Bank, Mr. Seitel formed Emerald Partners, a management and communications consultancy, and also became senior counselor at the world's largest public affairs firm, Burson-Marsteller. In his practice, Mr. Seitel continues to counsel corporations, nonprofits, associations, and individuals in the areas for which he had responsibility at Chase—media relations, speech writing, consumer relations, employee communications, financial communications, philanthropic activities, and strategic management consulting.

Mr. Seitel has supplemented his professional public relations career with steady teaching assignments at Fairleigh Dickinson University, Pace University, New York's Professional Development Institute, Chicago's Ragan Communications Workshops, and Colorado's Estes Park Institute. Over the course of his career, Mr. Seitel has taught thousands of public relations professionals.

After studying and examining many texts in public relations, he concluded that none of them "was exactly right." Therefore, in 1980, he wrote the first edition of The Practice of Public Relations "to give students a feel for how exciting this field really is." In nearly two decades of use at hundreds of colleges and universities, Mr. Seitel's book has introduced generations of students to the excitement, challenge, and uniqueness of the practice of public relations.

Chapter 1

What Is Public Relations?

In the closing days of 1999, as the world marched into the new millennium, a man named Steven A. Ballmer revealed to all the amazing power of public relations in the age of the Internet.

Mr. Ballmer, president of Microsoft Corporation and worth $23 billion himself, casually mentioned to a group of reporters trailing him at a Seattle conference, that he felt his company's stock was selling at too high a price. "There's such an overvaluation of tech stocks, it's absurd," he volunteered.[1] Within minutes, reports of the Microsoft executive's declaration spread across the nation and the world on the Internet. CNBC, the 24-hour financial cable network, broadcast it immediately. Radio news included it as a "breaking" development. And by day's end, Mr. Ballmer's offhanded comments had driven the Nasdaq stock index to its fourth worst point decline ever, torpedoed Microsoft stock by nearly five points—sending thousands of Microsoft shareholders into fits of rage—and reduced Mr. Ballmer's own holdings by more than $1 billion! (Microsoft's stock recovered shortly after its president's misguided ad lib.)

But the conclusion from this one-day tempest—besides the clear indication that the president of Microsoft, no matter how much money he has, is a knucklehead—is that there are few forces more impactful in our society in the new millennium than the power of communications.

Orchestrating communications, as well as managing how and what we say and through what media we say it, embodies the challenge of the practice of public relations. That challenge, like so many others in society, has been expanded, enhanced, and made more complex by the dominant role that the Internet now plays in society.

The practice of public relations, which has become a multibillion-dollar business employing hundreds of thousands of practitioners around the world, has always been difficult to define, measure, or explain. Consider the following, all examples of modern-day public relations.

  ◪ **In the realm of entertainment,** *one of the biggest-grossing movies in history—$48 million in the first week—is shot on a shoestring, features no big-name stars, and includes no sex and little on-screen* *violence. Instead,* The Blair Witch Project *relies on an overactive Web site to pump out details of the dreaded* Blair Witch *and the filmmakers who set out to track her down. The movie also produces a* Blair Witch *comic book, promotes a SciFi Channel* Blair Witch *Mockumentary, and furnishes a constant stream of publicity to general interest and entertainment magazines and TV shows. It is a huge hit.*

The flip side is The Walt Disney Company, one of the world's largest, most powerful and respected organizations. Largely through inept public relations, Disney wallows in a sagging stock price and a constant stream of criticism from all sides. One significant contributor to the company's unfortunate current state is a public relations approach built on caution, standoffishness, and arrogance.

◪ **In the field of politics,** *a sitting president, William Jefferson Clinton, admits lying to the American public about an illicit liaison with a White House intern, leaving his vice president, Albert Gore, to suffer the public relations fallout when he decides to compete for the presidency.*

On the other side of the aisle, Gore's presidential challenger George W. Bush, governor of Texas, stumbles miserably in trying to figure a public relations strategy to dispel nasty cocaine rumors.

We live in a day when name recognition and national publicity have become inestimable political assets; where political pundits of every stripe—from the ultraconservative radio dynamo Rush Limbaugh to the ultrahip former Clinton aide-turned-TV-analyst George Stephanopoulos—become household words (Figure 1-1; where a card-carrying World Wrestling Federation veteran, Jesse "The Body" Ventura, is elected governor of Minnesota; and where an egomaniacal megabuilder, Donald Trump, considers serving the "Trump constituency" by running for president on the Reform Party ticket.[2]

◪ **In business,** *a dowdy and out-of-touch retailer, Abercrombie & Fitch, recruits a hip new CEO, who uses public relations techniques to change the image and resurrect the company. Using buff advertising models, hip-hop music, on-the-edge quarterly magazine-catalogs, and college campus research visits, the company has become one of the nation's trendiest clothing chains.[3]*

An equally nontraditional public relations approach is adopted by perhaps the nation's most successful airline, Southwest, whose CEO, Herb Kelleher, has become revered primarily because of his candor and approachability. Southwest personnel are loose and friendly. The airline prides itself on first-come, first-served seating, on-time takeoff and no food—only nuts. Mr. Kelleher, whose biography is titled Nothing but Nuts, *even announced to the world in the summer of 1999 that he had prostate cancer and expressed great confidence it would affect neither him nor the company one little bit.*

FIGURE 1-1 **Media darlings.** On the left, former President Clinton "handler" and now TV pundit George Stephanopoulos. On the right, right-wing radio colossus Rush Limbaugh, reaching millions of people every day.

- ▨ **In the media,** *the consolidation of media giants—America Online, Time Warner, and Turner; Viacom and CBS; General Electric and NBC; and Disney and ABC—has meant that ratings, which mean profits, have become superior to "hard news," at least in the minds of those in charge. As a consequence, "soft" feature news has gained in importance in TV newscasts, and the opportunities for public relations publicity are profound.*

  Meanwhile, the proliferation of cable channels and the growing popularity of talk radio offer myriad additional public relations possibilities.

- ▨ **Finally, the Internet and World Wide Web** *have opened a new vista for public relations activity.*
  - *—Within organizations, e-mail has become the most dominant employee communications medium.*
  - *—The plethora of on-line newspapers and magazines and specialized e-zines has opened up brand new publicity channels. The growing number of reporters who research and communicate online has changed the face of media relations.*
  - *—Investors today daily, and even more frequently, check financial news and the fate of their own portfolios on-line, so that communicating with investors—investor relations—has changed dramatically.*

—Consumer relations has also changed, with organizations no longer requiring intermediaries to communicate with their key customers. Today, they can communicate directly via the Web.

As a consequence, public relations agencies devoted to creating Web sites, monitoring the Web, and orchestrating on-line communications programs have sprung up and become immensely successful. Classical public relations agencies and organizational public relations departments devote significant attention to dealing with constituents on the World Wide Web.

In the new millennium then, the communications revolution brought about by the growth of the Internet and World Wide Web has exponentially increased the power and value of the practice of public relations.

Doing the Right Thing

Public relations, simply defined, is the practice of doing the right thing—of performing—and communicating the substance of that performance. Public relations as a field has grown immeasurably in numbers and respect over the last three decades and today is clearly a *growth industry*.

- In the United States alone, public relations is a multibillion-dollar business practiced by nearly 200,000 professionals, according to the U.S. Bureau of Labor Statistics. Furthermore, the bureau ranks public relations as one of the fastest-growing industries, with job growth by 2005 projected at a nearly 47 percent increase.
- In a 1999 study by the Council of Public Relations Firms to assess the corporate communications spending patterns of Fortune 500 firms, a direct correlation was found between how much a company spends on public relations and how much it is respected.[4]
- Approximately 200 colleges and universities in the United States and many more overseas offer a public relations sequence or degree program. Many more offer public relations courses. In the vast majority of college journalism programs, public relations sequences rank first or second in enrollment.
- In the 21st century, while industries such as banking, utilities, and retailing are vulnerable to seismic movements, the public relations profession is expected to thrive, with more and more organizations interested in communicating their story.[5]
- The U.S. government has 9,000 communications workers employed by the U.S. Information Agency alone. Another 1,000 communications specialists work in the Department of Defense. The 20 largest public relations agencies generate in excess of $2 billion in fee income annually.[6]

The field's strength stems from its roots: "a democratic society where people have freedom to debate and to make decisions—in the community, the marketplace, the home, the workplace, and the voting booth. Private and public organizations depend on good relations with groups and individuals whose opinions, decisions, and actions affect their vitality and survival."[7]

So pervasive has the influence of public relations become in our society that some even fear it as a pernicious force; they worry about the power of public relations to exercise a kind of thought control over the American public.

The Curse of "Spin"

Which brings us to "spin."

The propensity in recent years for presumably respected public figures to lie in an attempt to deceive the public has led to the notion that "spinning" the facts is synonymous with public relations practice.

It isn't. Spin—outright lying to hide what really happened—is antithetical to the proper practice of public relations. In public relations, if you lie once, you will never be trusted again—particularly by the media.

Nonetheless, public relations spin has come to mean the twisting of messages to create the appearance of performance, which may or may not be true. Distortion, obfuscation, even downright lying is fair game as far as spin is concerned.

Consider the following:

- Democratic President Bill Clinton goes before the American public on national television and assures his constituents that he "did not have sexual relations" with a young intern as rumored. Six months later, the dismaying Monica Lewinsky saga (see "Case Study," chapter 4) would become well known in the land and reveal the president to have been a liar.
- Republican presidential candidate George W. Bush decries the lack of candor in politics but then refuses to divulge whether he took cocaine while a partying college student. Bush's silence on the drug issue is deafening, particularly in light of his background as a no-nonsense governor when it came to drug penalties.
- Newsweek journalist Joe Klein, who also rails against truth-defying politicians, is himself caught in a lie about his authorship of the anti-Clinton best-seller, *Primary Colors*. Klein and his editor, who also lied to protect his subordinate's anonymity, try to explain away their canard. Other reporters, most noticeably well-known *Boston Globe* columnist Mike Barnicle, fabricate or plagiarize without revealing the sources of their writings to their readers.
- Others are culpable when it comes to "spin": Clinton strategist Dick Morris, who allowed a prostitute to listen in on conversations with the president and revealed confidential secrets in a tell-all book; Ronald Reagan biographer Edmund Morris, who created a fictional character—himself—to travel through life with his famous subject; to famed sports announcer Marv Albert, who claimed he was innocent of charges of biting a lover and then reluctantly admitting his guilt to settle the case.

All of this has implications for the practice of public relations. Indeed the *New York Times* headlines its review of a popular book on the field, "How Public Relations Tries to Keep the World Spinning."[8] In such an era of spin and consequent unrelenting questioning by the media and the public, individuals and organizations must not only be sensitive to but also highly considerate of their actions and communication with many influential publics.

Prominence of Public Relations

In the dawn of the 21st century, the prominence of public relations has never been greater. On the other hand, the wave of downsizings, layoffs, mergers, and outright firings that have become standard business practice around the world has taken its toll on the public relations profession. The pervasive retrenchment of organizations has weighed heavily on public relations professionals. Many have lost their jobs, and the environment for the public relations people who remain employed has become decidedly less enjoyable or secure.

So the conundrum for public relations in the new century is that, on the one hand, the field has never been more accepted, respected, or high paying, but on the other hand, jobs are less plentiful, less predictable, and often less pleasant.

- President Clinton twice rode into office by deftly using the public relations techniques of town meetings, satellite press conferences, and message-rebuttal SWAT teams. Many consider communications and a deft knowledge of using the media Clinton's greatest assets.
- George W. Bush, the Republican governor of Texas, follows the Clinton media style to launch his presidential campaign. Meanwhile, a third political party in the United States—led by billionaire industrialist H. Ross Perot, wrestler-turned-governor Ventura, New York egomaniacal builder Trump, and similar main-stream political outcasts—has made miraculous strides, largely through public relations techniques such as using television talk shows to speak directly to the American public.
- Similarly, in Great Britain, Labour Party Prime Minister Tony Blair uses Clintonesque public relations approaches to give that perpetually losing party newfound life.
- In the business world, a new wave of media-savvy, techno-savvy, young high-tech leaders—from Dell Computer's Michael Dell to Amazon.com's Jeff Bezos to America Online's Steve Case and Bob Pittman—have deemed the public relations function to be a vitally important component in high-tech promotional thinking.
- Salaries for public relations executives continued to rise in both corporations and agencies, with the very top performers earning in the seven-figure range.
- In the nonprofit world, America's largest charity, United Way, has steadily regained its former respectability through sound public relations measures, after its chairman was fined and imprisoned in the wake of a stunning public relations scandal.

So public relations has made real progress in shedding old misconceptions, and it has acquired new responsibilities and inherited an increasing amount of power, prestige, and pay.

However, along with its new stature, the practice of public relations is faced with unprecedented pressure.

- The most difficult pressure on public relations professionals is the new job insecurity that afflicted the field in the 1990s and has carried over into the new millennium.

◪ Although public relations jobs are expected to grow in the years ahead, nonetheless organizations are becoming more rigorous in their scrutiny of the function. Just as public relations salaries have increased, so has the reality of decreasing job security.

◪ The very name *public relations* is being challenged by such euphemisms as *public affairs, corporate communications, integrated marketing, public information,* and a variety of other terms.

◪ The credibility of the field as a trusted source of contact among the public has been brought under question, with one study revealing that among 45 different occupations, public relations people were regarded among the "least credible" along with entertainers and television talk show hosts.[9]

◪ As public relations positions have achieved heightened stature, competition from other fields has become more intense. Today the profession finds itself vulnerable to encroachment by people with non–public relations backgrounds, such as lawyers, marketers, and general managers of every stripe. Ironically, among the most prominent public relations people in America are the chief lawyers of General Motors and Philip Morris, who serve as the overall heads of their powerful organizations' public relations offensives (see "Over the Top," chapters 6 and 19).

◪ The lack of leadership among public relations professionals continues to plague the field. Few practitioners are seen as leaders. No wonder cries of "PR for PR" are heard constantly.

◪ Many in public relations also are concerned about the preponderance of women in the field, the lack of equal pay for equal work among these women, and the paucity of minority practitioners.

◪ The field's focus on mastering the new technology of the Internet and World Wide Web is both a blessing and a curse. On the one hand, public relations professionals need to understand the implications and uses of cyberspace. On the other hand, working with the new technology is but one of many skill sets that practitioners should use.[10]

◪ Finally, public relations continues to be hampered by a general lack of understanding among senior managers of its purpose and value. Even today—nearly a century after the first American public relations professional rose to prominence—many in management still don't understand what public relations is all about.

Despite its considerable problems—in attaining leadership status, in finding its proper role in society, in disavowing spin and earning enduring respect—the practice of public relations has never been more prominent. Approaching its first 100 years as a formal, integrated, strategic thinking process, public relations has become part of the fabric of modern society.

Defining Public Relations

Leon Hess, who died in 1999 after successfully running one of the nation's largest oil companies and the New York Jets football team, used to pride himself on not having a public relations department. Mr. Hess, a very private individual, abhorred the limelight for himself or his company.

But times have changed. Today, the CEO who thunders, "I don't need public relations!" is a fool. He or she doesn't have a choice. Every organization has public relations, whether it wants it or not. The trick is to establish *good* public relations. That's what this book is all about—professional public relations, the kind you must work at.

Public relations affects almost everyone who has contact with other human beings. All of us, in one way or another, practice public relations daily. For an organization, every phone call, every letter, every face-to-face encounter is a public relations event.

To be sure, public relations is not yet a profession like law, accounting, or medicine, in which all practitioners are trained, licensed, and supervised. Nothing prevents someone with little or no formal training from hanging out a shingle as a public relations specialist. Such frauds embarrass professionals in the field and, thankfully, are becoming harder and harder to find.

As the field has increased in prominence, it also has grown in professional stature. The International Association of Business Communicators, a broad-based group that started with an internal communications focus, has 12,500 members. The Public Relations Society of America, with a national membership of nearly 18,500 in 109 chapters, has accredited about one-third of its members through a standardized examination. The society has also investigated legal licensing—similar to that of the accounting and legal professions—for public relations practitioners. The society's main objective is to increase the field's professionalism. It has a code of standards (see appendix A), which focuses strongly on the practitioner's ethical responsibilities.

Whereas marketing and sales have as their primary objective selling an organization's products, public relations attempts to sell the organization itself. Central to its concern is the public interest.

Advertising also generally aims to sell products through paid means. Good public relations, on the other hand, cannot be bought; it must be earned. The credibility derived from sound public relations work may far exceed that gained through paid advertising.

The earliest college teachers of public relations exhorted students to learn new ways of using knowledge they already had—a different viewpoint, as if one moved to one side and looked at everything from unfamiliar angles. Project yourself into the minds of people you are trying to reach and see things the way they do. Use everything you've learned elsewhere—English, economics, sociology, science, history—you name it.[11]

Three decades later, it is still widely thought that a broad background is essential to manage public issues effectively. Although specific definitions of public relations may differ, most who practice it agree that good public relations requires a firm base of theoretical knowledge, a strong sense of ethical judgment, solid communication skills including knowledge of the Internet, and, most of all, an uncompromising attitude of professionalism.

What, then, is public relations? Many people seem to have a pretty good idea, but few seem to agree. American historian Robert Heilbroner described the field as "a brotherhood of some 100,000, whose common bond is its profession and whose common woe is that no two of them can ever quite agree on what that profession is."[12]

The reason for the confusion is understandable. On the one hand, the scope of activities taken on by public relations professionals is limitless. The duties of a practitioner in one organization may be completely different from those of a colleague in another organization. Yet both are engaged in the practice of public relations. Beyond this, because public relations is such an amorphous, loosely defined field, it is vulnerable to entry to anyone self-styled as a "public relations professional."

In 1923, the late Edward Bernays described the function of his fledgling public relations counseling business as one of providing "information given to the public, persuasion directed at the public to modify attitudes and actions, and efforts to integrate attitudes and actions of an institution with its publics and of publics with those of that institution."[13]

Today, although a generally accepted definition of public relations still eludes practitioners, there is a clearer understanding of the field. One of the most ambitious searches for a universal definition was commissioned in 1975 by the Foundation for Public Relations Research and Education. Sixty-five public relations leaders participated in the study, which analyzed 472 different definitions and offered the following 88-word sentence:

> Public relations is a distinctive management function which helps establish and maintain mutual lines of communications, understanding, acceptance, and cooperation between an organization and its publics; involves the management of problems or issues; helps management to keep informed on and responsive to public opinion; defines and emphasizes the responsibility of management to serve the public interest; helps management keep abreast of and effectively utilize change, serving as an early warning system to help anticipate trends; and uses research and sound and ethical communication techniques as its principal tools.[14]

In 1980, the Task Force on the Stature and Role of Public Relations, chartered by the Public Relations Society of America, offered two definitions that have stood the test of time. Each projects an image of the field at the highest policy-making level and encompasses all its functions and specialties:

> Public relations helps an organization and its publics adapt mutually to each other.
> Public relations is an organization's efforts to win the cooperation of groups of people.[15]

BACKGROUNDER

Defining "Public Relations"

Still confused about the difference between public relations, publicity, advertising, and promotion? This will straighten you out.

Let's say the circus comes to town, and you want people to know about it.

1. **Advertising** Displaying a sign announcing that the circus is in town
2. **Promotion** Displaying the sign on an elephant and parading the animal through town
3. **Publicity** If the elephant carrying the sign tramples through the ornamental garden of the mayor and the newspaper reports it
4. **Public Relations** If you are able to get the mayor to laugh about the incident and ride in the circus parade with no hard feelings

Raleigh Pinskey, The Zen of Hype: An Insider's Guide to the Publicity Game, Carol Communications, Inc., New York, NY, 1998.

Defining by Functions

Communications professor John Marston suggested that public relations be defined in terms of four specific functions: (1) research, (2) action, (3) communication, and (4) evaluation.[16] Applying the R-A-C-E approach involves researching attitudes on a particular issue, identifying action programs of the organization that speak to that issue, communicating those programs to gain understanding and acceptance, and evaluating the effect of the communication efforts on the public.

Public relations professor Sheila Clough Crifasi has proposed extending the R-A-C-E formula into the five-part R-O-S-I-E to encompass a more managerial approach to the field. R-O-S-I-E prescribes sandwiching the functions of objectives, strategies, and implementation between research and evaluation. Indeed, setting clear objectives, working from set strategies, and implementing a predetermined plan is a key to sound public relations practice.

Both R-A-C-E and R-O-S-I-E echo one of the most widely repeated definitions of public relations, developed by Denny Griswold, public relations matriarch, who founded Public Relations News, a leading newsletter for practitioners:

> Public relations is the management function which evaluates public attitudes, identifies the policies and procedures of an individual or an organization with the public interest, and plans and executes a program of action to earn public understanding and acceptance.[17]

The key words in this definition are management and action. Public relations, if it is to serve the organization properly, must report to top management. Public relations must serve as an honest broker to management, unimpeded by any other group. For public relations to work, its advice to management must be unfiltered, uncensored, and unexpurgated. This can only be achieved if the public relations department reports to the CEO. Although marketing promotes a specific product, public relations promotes the entire institution.

Nor can proper public relations take place without appropriate action. No amount of communications—regardless of its persuasive content—can save an organization whose performance is substandard. Performance—that is, action—must precede publicity. Indeed, in 1993, when PepsiCo was accused of allowing syringes to be placed in its cans, the company was so certain of the integrity of its manufacturing process that it "cried foul" immediately and was promptly vindicated. Pepsi could never have responded so quickly or triumphed so convincingly if its performance had been at all suspect. The same was true in General Motors' rebuttal of NBC's *Dateline* charges of "exploding trucks." (Both the Pepsi and GM cases are included in this book.)

Public relations, then, boils down to a process, as educator Melvin Sharpe has put it, that "harmonizes" long-term relationships among individuals and organizations in society.[18] Professor Sharpe applies five principles to this process:

1. Honest communication for credibility
2. Openness and consistency of actions for confidence
3. Fairness of actions for reciprocity and goodwill
4. Continuous two-way communication to prevent alienation and to build relationships
5. Environmental research and evaluation to determine the actions or adjustments needed for social harmony

Stated yet another way, the profession is described by public relations professor Janice Sherline Jenny as "the management of communications between an organization and all entities that have a direct or indirect relationship with the organization, i.e. its publics."

The goal of effective public relations, then, is to harmonize internal and external relationships so that an organization can enjoy not only the goodwill of all of its publics, but also stability and long life.

Interpreting Management to the Public

Public relations practitioners are basically interpreters. On the one hand, they must interpret the philosophies, policies, programs, and practices of their management to the public; on the other hand, they must convey the attitudes of the public to their management.

To accomplish these tasks accurately and truthfully, practitioners must gain attention, understanding, acceptance, and, ultimately, action from target publics. But first, they have to know what management is thinking.

Good public relations can't be practiced in a vacuum. No matter what the size of the organization, a public relations department is only as good as its access to management. For example, it's useless for a senator's press secretary to explain the reasoning behind an important decision without first knowing what the senator had in mind. So, too, an organization's public relations staff is impotent without firsthand knowledge of the reasons for management's decisions and the rationale for organizational policy.

The public relations department in a profit-making or nonprofit enterprise can counsel management. It can advise management. It can even exhort management to take action. But management must call the shots on organizational policy. Practitioners must fully understand the whys and wherefores of policy and communicate these ideas accurately and candidly to the public. Anything less can lead to major problems.

Interpreting the Public to Management

The flip side of the coin is interpreting the public to management. Simply stated, this task means finding out what the public really thinks about the firm and letting management know. Regrettably, recent history is filled with examples of public relations departments failing to anticipate the true sentiments of the public.

- In the 1960s, General Motors paid little attention to an unknown consumer activist named Ralph Nader, who spread the message that GM's Corvair was unsafe at any speed. When Nader's assault began to be believed, the automaker assigned professional detectives to trail him. In short order, General Motors was forced to acknowledge its act of paranoia, and the Corvair was eventually sacked, at great expense to the company.

- In the 1970s, as both the price of gasoline and oil company profits rose rapidly, the oil companies were besieged by an irate gas-consuming public. When, at the height of the criticism, Mobil Oil purchased the parent of the Montgomery Ward department store chain, the company was publicly battered.

- In 1980, Ronald Reagan rode to power on the strength of his ability to interpret what was on the minds of the electorate. To his critics, President Reagan was a man of mediocre intellect and limited concentration. But to his supporters, Reagan was the "great communicator" who led the nation to eight years of unprecedented worldwide acclaim.

☑ In the 1990s, Reagan's successor in the White House, George Bush, turned out to be a less skillful communicator. Despite an overwhelming Gulf War victory and unprecedented popularity, President Bush suffered a stunning electoral defeat in 1992 at the hands of another savvy communicator, Governor Bill Clinton of Arkansas. While Bush stumbled, Clinton kept his candidacy focused on one single, unwavering message: "It's the economy, stupid." Candidate Clinton became President Clinton largely on the strength of correctly interpreting to the American public the importance of that key theme.

☑ As the century ended, Clinton's communications embarrassment in the Monica Lewinsky scandal (another case, alas, discussed in this book) tarnished those around him, most particularly his loyal Vice President Al Gore, who bore the brunt of public disaffection in his subsequent campaign for the presidency.

In the new millennium, the savviest institutions—be they government, corporate, or nonprofit—understand the importance of effectively interpreting their management and organizational philosophy, policies, and practices to the public and, even more important, interpreting how the public views their organization back to management.

The Publics of Public Relations

The term *public relations* is really a misnomer. Public*s* relations, or relations with the publics, would be more to the point. Practitioners must communicate with many different publics—not just the general public—each having its own special needs and requiring different types of communication. Often the lines that divide these publics are thin, and the potential overlap is significant. Therefore, priorities, according to organizational needs, must always be reconciled (Figure 1-2).

Technological change—particularly satellite links for television, the Internet, and World Wide Web, and the computer generally—has brought greater interdependence to people and organizations, and there is growing concern in organizations today about managing extensive webs of interrelationships. Indeed, managers have become interrelationship conscious.

Internally, managers must deal directly with various levels of subordinates, as well as with cross relationships that arise when subordinates interact with one another. Externally, managers must deal with a system that includes government regulatory agencies, labor unions, subcontractors, consumer groups, and many other independent—but often related—organizations. The public relations challenge in all of this is to manage effectively the communications between managers and the various publics, which often pull organizations in different directions.

Definitions differ on precisely what constitutes a public. One time-honored definition states that a public arises when a group of people (1) face a similar indeterminate situation, (2) recognize what is indeterminate and problematic in that situation, and (3) organize to do something about the problem.[19] In public relations, more specifically, a public is a group of people with a stake in an issue, organization, or idea.

Publics can also be classified into several overlapping categories:

1. **Internal and external.** Internal publics are inside the organization: supervisors, clerks, managers, stockholders, and the board of directors. External

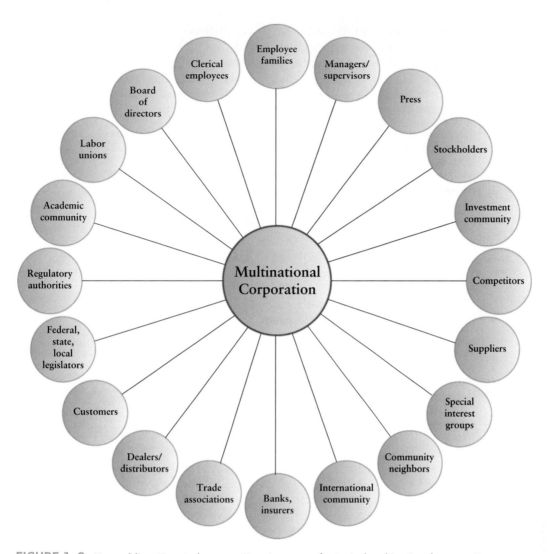

FIGURE 1-2 **Key publics.** Twenty key constituent groups of a typical multinational corporation.

publics are those not directly connected with the organization: the press, government, educators, customers, the community, and suppliers.

2. **Primary, secondary, and marginal.** Primary publics can most help—or hinder—the organization's efforts. Secondary publics are less important, and marginal publics are the least important of all. For example, members of the Federal Reserve Board of Governors, who regulate banks, would be the primary public for a bank awaiting a regulatory ruling, whereas legislators and the general public would be secondary. On the other hand, to the investing public, interest rate pronouncements of the same Federal Reserve are of primary importance.

3. **Traditional and future.** Employees and current customers are traditional publics; students and potential customers are future ones. No organization can afford to become complacent in dealing with its changing publics. Today, a firm's publics range from women to minorities to senior citizens to homosexuals. Each might be important to the future success of the organization.

4. **Proponents, opponents, and the uncommitted.** An institution must deal differently with those who support it and those who oppose it. For supporters, communications that reinforce beliefs may be in order. But changing the opinions of skeptics calls for strong, persuasive communications. Often, particularly in politics, the uncommitted public is crucial. Many a campaign has been decided because the swing vote was won over by one of the candidates.

Another way of segmenting publics—based on values and lifestyles—separates consumers into eight distinct categories:

1. Actualizers are those with the most wealth and power
2. Fulfilleds have high resources and are principle-oriented professionals or retirees
3. Believers are Fulfilleds without the resources
4. Achievers have high resources and are status oriented
5. Strivers lack the resources of Achievers but are equally status oriented
6. Experiencers have high resources and are action oriented and disposed toward taking risks
7. Makers also are action oriented but have low resources and
8. Strugglers have the lowest resources.[20]

A QUESTION OF ETHICS

The Internet and Kosovo Disclosure

Public relations has become a pervasive function throughout society, and that includes during wars. In the 21st century, wartime communications on the Internet rules.

The thirst of reporters for up-to-the-minute developments on the battlefield, coupled with the growth of the Internet, have led to ethical questions among military officials as to how much information to provide the public. Stated another way, "How much of a 'right to know' does the public have in a war?"

In the 1999 conflict in Kosovo, where the U.S.-supported NATO troops in intervening in the former Yugoslavia to protect ethnic Albanians, an all-out public relations effort was launched by the Pentagon to convince Americans to support a war in a country most couldn't find on a map.

In return, reporters from America and around the world insisted on being updated in daily, often stormy briefings. U.S. Defense Secretary William Cohen, fearing a breach of security, ordered a clampdown on releasing details to the news media. As a result, military spokespeople resorted to an oft-repeated phrase,

"I'm afraid I can't get into that level of detail." Reporters grumbled about "news management."

Complicating the issue, according to Pentagon spokespeople, was the fact that the enemy, Serbian Prime Minister Slobodan Milosevic's forces, had ready access to all U.S. information via the Internet—the first war affected by the growth of cyberspace.

As a consequence, U.S. officials were even more circumspect than usual in releasing information about troop deployments and war developments. Reporters argued that the government's "censure" of information would lead to questions about the veracity of what the government was communicating. Concluded one social psychologist, "Large portions of the populations need this information, otherwise they won't believe what they are being told."

The question is, Where are the limits to disclosure in a free society during wartime, when everyone in the world has access to the Internet?

For further information, see Chris Cobb, "The Role of Public Relations in the Kosovo Conflict," Tactics, June 1999, 29.

Applying such lifestyle characterizations to publics can help companies make marketing and public relations decisions to effectively target key audiences.

The typical organization is faced with a myriad of critical publics with whom it must communicate on a frequent and direct basis. It must be sensitive to the self-interests, desires, and concerns of each public. It must understand that self-interest groups today are themselves more complex. Therefore, the harmonizing actions necessary to win and maintain support among such groups should be arrived at in terms of public relations consequences.[21] Whereas management must always speak with one voice, its communications inflection, delivery, and emphasis should be sensitive to all its constituent publics.

S U M M A R Y

Ethics, truth, credibility—these values are what good public relations is all about. Cover-up, distortion, and subterfuge are the antitheses of good public relations.

Much more than customers for their products, managers today desperately need constituents for their beliefs and values. In the 21st century, the role of public relations is much more to guide management in framing its ideas and making its commitments. The counsel that management will need must come from advisers who understand public attitudes, public moods, public needs, and public aspirations.

Winning this elusive goodwill takes time and effort. Credibility can't be won overnight, nor can it be bought. If management policies aren't in the public's best interest, no amount of public relations can obscure that reality. Public relations is not effective as a temporary defensive measure to compensate for management misjudgment. If management errs seriously, the best—and only—public relations advice must be to get the story out immediately. One public relations leader summed up the responsibilities of public relations professionals as being the organization's "conscience."

There are others in the corporate hierarchy who may possess the same amount or even more of these attributes than the individuals responsible for public relations. But the fact is that being the professional corporate conscience is not part of the job description of other executives. It is part of the job description of the chief public relations officer.[22]

No less an authority than Abraham Lincoln once said: "Public sentiment is everything . . . with public sentiment nothing can fail. Without it, nothing can succeed. He who molds public sentiment goes deeper than he who executes statutes or pronounces decisions. He makes statutes or decisions possible or impossible to execute."

Stated another way, no matter how you define it, the practice of public relations has become an essential element in the conduct of relationships in the new millennium.

Discussion Starters

1. Why did the practice of public relations become so pervasive in the 1990s?
2. Why are others—lawyers, accountants, general managers, and so on—interested in doing public relations?
3. Why is the practice of public relations generally misunderstood by the public?
4. How important is the Internet in public relations?
5. Explain the approach toward defining public relations by the nature of its functions.
6. Explain the approach toward defining public relations as a harmonizing process.
7. Why is a public relations professional fundamentally an interpreter?
8. What are the four overlapping categories of publics?
9. What is the essence of proper public relations practice?
10. As the Internet grows as a communications medium, what kinds of ethical public relations issues does its pervasiveness raise?

Notes

1. Robert D. Hershey, "Stocks Plunge over Remark on Microsoft," *New York Times* (September 24, 1999): C1.
2. Adam Nagourney, "President? Why Not? Says a Man at the Top," *New York Times* (September 25, 1999): A12.
3. Adam Bryant, "Fashion's Frat Boy," *Newsweek* (September 13, 1999): 40–41.
4. Jack Bergen, "Corporate Communications Spending and Reputations of Fortune 500 Companies," *Ragan's Public Relations Journal* (July/August 1999): 9–32.
5. Ronald B. Liebert, "How Safe Is Your Job?" *Fortune* (April 1, 1996): 76.
6. Jack O'Dwyer, "1998 PR Fee Income of 50 Firms," *O'Dwyer's PR Services Report* (March 1999): 5.
7. "The Design for Undergraduate Public Relations Education," a study cosponsored by the public relations division of the Association for Education and Journalism and Mass Communication, the Public Relations Society of America, and the educators' section of PRSA, 1987, 1.
8. Deborah Stead, "How Public Relations Tries to Keep the World Spinning," *New York Times* (November 3, 1996): B8.
9. Jennifer Harper, "Supreme Court Justices Rank Highest in Credibility, Index Says," *The Washington Times* (July 8, 1999): A8.
10. Roger W. W. Baker, "Lurking and Seeding Within the Web," *The Public Relations Strategist* (Winter 1996): 42.
11. Berton J. Ballard, lecture at San Jose State University, San Jose, CA, 1948. Cited in Pearce Davies, "Twenty-Five Years Old and Still Growing," *Public Relations Journal* (October 1977): 22–23.
12. Cited in Scott M. Cutlip and Allen H. Center, *Effective Public Relations,* 6th ed. (Upper Saddle River, NJ: Prentice Hall, 1985): 5.
13. Edward L. Bernays, *Crystallizing Public Opinion* (New York: Liveright, 1961).

14. Rex F. Harlow, "Building a Public Relations Definition," *Public Relations Review* 2, no. 4 (Winter 1976): 36.

15. Philip Lesly, "Report and Recommendations: Task Force on Stature and Role of Public Relations," *Public Relations Journal* (March 1981): 32.

16. John E. Marston, *The Nature of Public Relations* (New York: McGraw-Hill, 1963): 161.

17. Denny Griswold, *Public Relations News,* 127 East 80th Street, New York, NY 10021.

18. This definition was developed by Dr. Melvin L. Sharpe, professor and coordinator of the Public Relations Sequence, Department of Journalism, Ball State University, Muncie, IN 47306.

19. John Dewey, *The Public and Its Problems* (Chicago: Swallow Press, 1927).

20. Linda P. Morton, "Segmenting Publics by Lifestyles," *Public Relations Quarterly* (Fall 1999), 46–47.

21. Sharpe, definition.

22. Harold Burson, "The Role of the Public Relations Professional," *Current Media* (Fall 1996).

Suggested Readings

Center, Allen H., and Patrick Jackson. *Public Relations Practices: Managerial Case Studies and Problems,* 5th ed. Upper Saddle River, NJ: Prentice Hall, 2000.

Cutlip, Scott M., Allen H. Center, and Glen M. Broom, *Effective Public Relations,* 8th ed. Upper Saddle River, NJ: Prentice Hall, 2000. (Without question, the first and still most comprehensive textbook in the field.)

Dilenschneider, Robert L., ed. *Dartnell Public Relations Handbook,* 4th ed. Chicago: Dartnell Corp., 1996.

Dozier, David M., Larissa A. Grunig, and James E. Grunig. *Manager's Guide to Excellence in Public Relations and Communication Management.* Hillsdale, NJ: Lawrence Erlbaum Associates, 1995.

Dwyer, Thomas. *Simply Public Relations: Public Relations Made Challenging, Complete and Concise.* Stillwater, OK: New Forums, 1992.

Gordon, Joye C. "Interpreting Definitions of Public Relations: Self Assessment and a Symbolic Interactionism-Based Alternative." *Public Relations Review* (Spring 1997): 57–66.

Hutton, James G. "The Definition, Dimensions and Domain of Public Relations," *Public Relations Review* (Summer 1999): 199–214.

Lesly, Philip, ed. *Lesly's Handbook of Public Relations and Communications,* 5th ed. Lincolnwood, IL: NTC Business Books, 1998.

Mickey, Thomas J. "A Postmodern View of Public Relations: Sign and Reality," *Public Relations Review* (Fall 1997): 271–284.

Rhody, Ron. *The CEO's Playbook: Managing the Outside Forces That Shape Success.* Sacramento, CA: Academy Publishing, 1999.

Selame, Elinor. "Public Relations' Role and Responsibility in Reflecting Changes in Companies' Culture, Structure, Products and Services," *Public Relations Quarterly* (Summer 1997): 12–17.

Wilcox, Dennis, ed. *Public Relations: Strategies and Tactics.* Reading, MA: Addison-Wesley, 1997.

History professor Stuart Ewen's history of the practice of public relations is not particularly flattering. The link between "truth" and "hype," according to the professor, is not altogether clear. More often than not, he writes, the history of public relations is a recounting of "virtual factuality," in which the construction of "reality" has become a fact of American life.

The book recounts tales of AT&T using advertising to sway previously uncooperative newspaper editors; Standard Oil of New Jersey launching a communications offensive to defuse revelations it colluded with the Nazis; and Ronald Reagan using public relations "techniques" to transform him from a B actor to President of the United States. Professor Ewen's conclusion, that public relations systematically has manipulated public opinion over the course of nine decades, may not be either right or fair—but it's worth reading, if only to find out how the adversaries think.

CASE STUDY

The Great Coke Contamination Controversy

Next to mom and apple pie, nothing says "America" like Coca Cola. For years, the Atlanta, Georgia-headquartered Coca-Cola Company has stood for honor and virtue among U.S. products.

With nearly 50 percent of the domestic soft drink market and growing worldwide domination, it seemed that the whole world was concluding that things do, indeed, "go better with Coke."

Then one day in June 1999, after a 14-year-old Belgian high school student contracted a stomachache from a can of Coke, the company's fortunes—and its reputation—took a sudden and seismic stumble.

STRANGE SMELLS

The boy complained of nausea and said the Coke he had drunk at school had "smelled funny." A classmate, who drank two Cokes, also felt nauseated. Two hours later, both boys were rushed to a local hospital, where a physician concluded they were suffering from "probable intoxication."

And thus began Coca-Cola's worst nightmare.

Forty children around the same Belgian town became ill after drinking Coca-Cola, and ultimately 200 people reported sickness due to drinking Coke. The company quickly recalled 2.5 million bottles around the area of Belgium where the cases occurred.

The nation of Belgium, which had earlier been rebuked for acting slowly on a meat and poultry contamination issue, this time seized the initiative and banned Coca-Cola sales in its country. Coca-Cola plants in Antwerp and Ghent were ordered closed, after the company detected defective CO_2 and less-than-ideal quality procedures in its Antwerp plant.

Health officials in France, the Netherlands, and Luxembourg, fearing similar outbreaks in their own countries, imposed bans on Coca-Cola sales.

Health officials in Switzerland asked the mortified soft drink company to publish information allowing consumers to identify where the company's products were made, for fear Swiss stores would carry the contaminated wares.

The health minister of the Central African Republic—far away from the contamination crisis—declared to his citizens that they should avoid Coke "until further notice" because of health questions.

Ultimately, Coke recalled 14 million cases of its product, the largest single recall in corporate history. It cost the company $60 million in special charges in one quarter alone and sent Coke's stock—which had been flying high—careening downward at breakneck speed.

On top of everything else, the company was crucified in the media for helping perpetrate a "public relations disaster."

IGNORED EARLY WARNING
One criticism was that Coke was slow to act.

Ironically, Coke's public relations problems might have been avoided had the company acted a month earlier, when the owner of a Belgian pub complained that four people at his bar had become sick after drinking "bad-smelling Coca-Cola."

The company claimed that it had "checked out" the earlier report but found no reason to be concerned. The soda in question was produced at the same plant that later caused the illnesses of the schoolchildren.

Although the bar patrons were examined at a local hospital, laboratory tests proved inconclusive.

FIGURE 1–3 **The culprit.**

So Coke, in effect, ignored the early warning.

Indeed, the company was roundly criticized for its deliberative pacing in terms of the crisis. The consumer affairs minister of France complained that it took Coke 48 hours to provide information on how to identify which soft drink cans might pose further risks. The delay triggered French reaction to remove Coke cans from store shelves.

ABSENT CHAIRMAN

Another criticism involved Coke CEO Douglas Ivester's late start on the crisis. It took Mr. Ivester a full week after the illness of the schoolchildren to apologize for the problem.

Because the company didn't explain or apologize for a week, the media vacuum was filled with rumor and innuendo about the contamination of Coca-Cola. When the company realized the extent of the publicity fallout, Mr. Ivester was dispatched to Belgium to make an appearance.

He defended his decision not to rush into it, saying that he was "monitoring the situation closely" and was asked to refrain by the Belgian health minister.

"He made it very clear he didn't want this tried in the PR arena, and in a case like this you want to follow the minister's guidance," Mr. Ivester reported.

The Belgian minister's reluctance to try the case in the media was understandable. The company had been roundly criticized for acting slowly on its recent contamination scares, and national elections were rapidly approaching. The last thing Belgium's politicians wanted was public criticism for their handling of the latest contamination case.

Thus Coke remained silent and took its lumps.

Eventually, Mr. Ivester made public amends to the Belgian people and agreed to pay medical expenses for those who had been rendered ill. The bans were lifted and Coke began again to sell its products.

CRITICAL AFTERMATH

The public relations fallout was bad enough. However, raising even more questions about Coke's handling of the issue, the supplier of the CO_2 in question denied that its product caused any problems. The company tested the CO_2 and concluded, "There is no problem on our part. It must be something else."

In light of this revelation, some crisis managers felt Coke acted too precipitously to recall its product and accept blame. Said one, "They should simply announce, 'There is no health hazard at all from our product. It is a figment of your imagination.'"

In any event, the Coca-Cola contamination experience proved the worst public relations crisis in Coke history, one from which it still hadn't recovered by the turn of the century. Indeed, as the old millennium came to a close, another group of Antwerp 12-year-olds reported feeling ill from drinking Coke-product Fanta. And once again, company officials had to quickly evaluate the products in question and just as rapidly reassure Europeans that Coca-Cola products were safe to drink.

In light of all the negative publicity, it was little wonder that Coke abruptly canceled a free drink promotion in Belgium in November 1999, after a court ruled the company had "abused its position as the country's largest maker of soft drinks." Although Coke vowed to appeal the decision, the damage to its reputation was done.

Said the Belgian teenager who started the initial controversy after sipping from a tainted bottle, "I'll never drink Coke again."

CEO POSTSCRIPT

The final straw of the great Coke contamination came in December 1999, when CEO Douglas Ivester, who had succeeded to the chairmanship only two years earlier, suddenly announced that he was resigning from the company. Such was the downside of negative public relations in the days of the new millennium.

Questions

1. Do you think Coke acted too slowly when first apprised of the "foul odor" problem? What should it have done?
2. What should have been the role of the CEO after word of the contamination spread? What about the concerns of the Belgian government officials?
3. What is your reaction to those who argue that Coke should have held the line and not capitulated to pressure by recalling its product?
4. Find out how Coca-Cola announced the return of its soft drinks to Belgium by reading the news release on the company's news page (www.thecoca-cola-company.com/news/index.html). Scroll down to the bottom of the page and continue to click on the "next" link until you find the press release dated July 1, 1999 ("Coca-Cola Set to Return to Belgian Marketplace This Weekend"). What publics are being addressed in this news release? How is the company using this news release to reassure consumers about the safety of its products?

For further information about the Coca-Cola contamination case, see Chris Cobb, "The Aftermath of Coke's Belgian Waffle," *Public Relations Tactics,* September 1999, 1–4; "Coke Promotion Is Halted," *New York Times,* November 30, 1999, C2; Alan Cowell, "The Coke Stomach Ache Heard Round the World," *New York Times,* June 25, 1999, C1–2; Cowell, "Coke Scare Was Preceded by a May Case," *New York Times,* June 29, 1999, C1–10; *Nikhil Deogun,* "Besieged CEO Jets to Brussels Amid PR Fiasco," *Wall Street Journal,* June 18, 1999, B1–4; William Echikson, "Things Aren't Going Better with Coke," *Business Week,* June 28, 1999, 49; James R. Hagerty and Amy Barrett, "France, Belgium Reject Pleas to Lift Ban," *Wall Street Journal,* June 18,1999, B1–4; James R. Hagerty and John Carreybou, "Safety of Coke Drinks Comes Up Again in Europe As Belgian Children Feel Ill," *Wall Street Journal,* October 25, 1999, A4; Betsy McKay, "Coke Reports 21% Decline in Earnings," *Wall Street Journal,* July 16, 1999, A3.

OVER THE TOP

An Interview with Ray Gaulke

Since 1993, Ray Gaulke has been the world's highest-ranking public relations association executive. As president and chief operating officer of the Public Relations Society of America, he oversees the policies and activities of the largest association of public relations professionals. In his career, Mr. Gaulke has held top posts in public relations, advertising, marketing, media sales, and magazine publishing. He was chief marketing officer of the Newspaper Association of America, president of Gannett Media Sales, and president and publisher of *USA Weekend* magazine.

What is the state of the practice of public relations in the new millennium?
We have entered the golden age of public relations, where senior management recognized that organizational success depends on building and sustaining mutually rewarding relationships. While public relations has always had a role as the external voice of the organization, today it must also be the "earpiece" that brings the concerns of stakeholders to the boardroom. Many believe that brands are built with public relations and advertising. And this, too, is

accelerating the practice of public relations as a vital management tool.

What are the greatest challenges confronting the profession?

There are two, and they both relate to people. First, we must attract the brightest and best into the profession. Public relations careers must be perceived to be as attractive as careers in management consulting or investment banking. Second, we must open the doors of the profession to more African Americans, Hispanics, Asians, and all minority groups. Since it interfaces with all aspects of society, public relations must reflect that society.

What is the status of women in the field?

The "glass ceiling" has been broken. Although women don't dominate the field in terms of leading the largest public relations firms, they have achieved top positions in corporate settings and excelled at opening and growing highly successful midsized public relations firms. The future for women in public relations, as practitioners, owners, and senior managers, is very bright indeed.

What is the status of minorities in the field?

Not enough minorities are aware of the opportunities in public relations. We must take on the responsibility of "marketing the profession" to minorities. That means practicing professionals must embrace the role of marketing public relations in their local communities. There is no more important mandate for our profession.

What are the opportunities for young people?

The opportunities are there. The challenge is to choose an opportunity where the organization you join is committed to training and where senior mentors are available to challenge, set high standards, and lead by example. Public relations is constantly responding to societal changes, and the young practitioner must find an environment where he or she can learn from others. So early choices are critical.

What is the best preparation for a career in public relations?

Some years ago, I spent a day with the late Edward Bernays, the great public relations pioneer. I asked him, "If we were to start the Bernays Academy of Public Relations, what should we teach?" Mr. Bernays responded, "Economics, psychology, mathematics, history, music, religion, art, and logic." He believed that practitioners should be well-rounded generalists with an interest in everything. Indeed, today's best practitioners are students of popular culture. They see movies and plays, read, write, and are activists in all aspects of society.

What is the future of public relations in this new century?

No profession holds as bright a future as public relations. Futurists have said that the next phase after the "technology society" will be the "dream society," in which the most highly valued skill will be "storytelling." This view suggests that without a "story," you cannot have a strategy. Many people believe that at its core, public relations is about storytelling. If the future is in fact about storytelling—getting truthful and believable messages out to our publics—then public relations people will be in the right place at the right time. I believe in this future.

Chapter 2

The Evolution of Public Relations

It may surprise some people, but the practice of public relations was not born as an outgrowth of the Internet.

Nonetheless, public relations is still a young field, which will celebrate its 100th birthday early in the 21st century. Consequently, public relations as a modern American phenomenon is much younger than other disciplines.

The relative youthfulness of the practice means that the field is still evolving, and its status is improving daily. Indeed, the professionals entering the practice today are by and large superior in intellect, training, and even experience to their counterparts decades ago.

The strength of the practice of public relations today is based on the enduring commitment of the public to participate in a free and open democratic society. At least five trends are related to the evolution of public relations:

1. the growth of big institutions
2. the increasing incidence of change, conflict, and confrontation in society
3. the heightened awareness and sophistication of people everywhere as a result of technological innovations in communications
4. the increased importance of public opinion in the 21st century for positive democratic means as well as a use by those who would repress other people (Figure 2-1) and
5. the extraordinary growth of the Internet and the World Wide Web which has made millions of people around the world instant consumers of unlimited communication.

◪ *The size of today's society has played a significant role in the development of public relations. The days of the mom and pop grocery store, the tiny community college, and the small local bank are rapidly disappearing. In their place have emerged Wal-Marts, Home Depots, and Citigroups, statewide community college systems with populous branches in several cities, and multistate banking networks that perform every conceivable financial function. As institutions have grown larger, the public relations profession has evolved to interpret these large institutions to the publics they serve.*

23

▨ *The increasing incidence of change, conflict, and confrontation in society is yet another reason for the evolution of public relations. Women's rights, senior citizens' rights, gay rights, animal rights, consumerism, environmental awareness, downsizings, layoffs, and resultant unhappiness with large institutions all have become part of day-to-day society. With the growth of the Web, activists have become increasingly more daring, visible, and effective.*

▨ *A third factor in the development of public relations has been the heightened awareness of people everywhere. First came the invention of the printing press. Later it was the pervasiveness of mass communications: the print media, radio, and television. Then it was the development of cable, satellite, videotape, videodisks, video typewriters, portable cameras, word processors, fax machines, cell phones, the World Wide Web, and all the other communications technologies that have helped fragment audiences and make McGill University Professor Marshall McLuhan's "global village" idea of the 1960s a 21st-century reality.*

 In a world in which the image of a people under siege in their homeland in the villages of Kosovo in Eastern Europe or the fields of East Timor in Southern Asia can be flashed around the world to be seen on the evening news; when a hostage standoff in Peru can be witnessed in real time by people in their living rooms in Bangor, Maine; when a dictator in the Persian Gulf can be interviewed live by a reporter in Washington, there can be no doubt that the communications revolution has arrived.

▨ *Fourth, the outbreak of democracy in Latin America, Eastern Europe, the former Soviet Union, and South Africa has heightened the power of public opinion in the world. Just as increasing numbers of Americans made their voices heard through the civil rights movements, various consumer movements, the women's rights movement, and political movements throughout the ages, so, too, have oppressed peoples around the world risen up and spoken out. Accordingly, the practice of public relations as a facilitator in understanding more clearly and managing more effectively in the midst of such democratic revolution has increased in prominence.*

▨ *Finally, the amazing growth of the Internet and World Wide Web have quickly brought public relations into the 21st century. With 100 million Americans and countless other millions around the world now on the Net, people are united throughout communications like never before. The change this continues to bring to society is monumental.*

FIGURE 2-1 **Communicating evil.** The communications revolution sweeping the world fueled evil forces as well as good. Terrorists, knowledgeable of the media's power to broadcast their message instantaneously around the world, used their acts of destruction to spread their beliefs. (Courtesy of ADL)

Ancient Beginnings

Although modern public relations is a 20th-century phenomenon, its roots are ancient. Leaders in virtually every great society throughout history understood the importance of influencing public opinion through persuasion. For example, archeologists found a farm bulletin in Iraq that told farmers of 1800 B.C. the latest techniques of harvesting, sowing, and irrigating.[1] The more food the farmers grew, the better the citizenry ate and the wealthier the country became—a good example of planned persuasion to reach a specific public for a particular purpose; in other words, public relations.

Later on, the Greeks put a high premium on communication skills. The best speakers, in fact, were generally elected to leadership positions. Occasionally, aspiring Greek politicians enlisted the aid of Sophists (individuals renowned for both their reasoning and their rhetoric) to help fight verbal battles. Sophists would gather in the amphitheaters of the day and extol the virtues of particular political candidates. Thus, the Sophists set the stage for today's lobbyists, who attempt to influence legislation through effective communications techniques. From the time of the Sophists, the practice of public relations has been a battleground for questions of ethics. Should a Sophist or a lobbyist or a public relations professional "sell" his or her talents to the highest bidder, regardless of personal beliefs, values, and ideologies? When modern-day public relations professionals agree to represent repressive governments in Serbia or Nazi sympathizers in Switzerland or when Republican communications operatives like Dick Morris switch sides to join staunch Democrats like Bill Clinton and then reveal confidential campaign secrets, these ethical questions remain very much a focus of modern public relations.[2]

The Romans, particularly Julius Caesar, were also masters of persuasive techniques. When faced with an upcoming battle, Caesar would rally public support through assorted publications and staged events. Similarly, during World War I, a special U.S. public information committee, the Creel Committee, was formed to channel the patriotic sentiments of Americans in support of the U.S. role in the war. Stealing a page from Caesar, the committee's massive verbal and written communications effort was successful in marshaling national pride behind the war effort. According to a young member of the Creel Committee, Edward L. Bernays (later considered by many to be the father of public relations), "This was the first time in our history that information was used as a weapon of war."[3]

Even the Catholic Church had a hand in the creation of public relations. In the 1600s, under the leadership of Pope Gregory XV, the church established a college of propaganda to "help propagate the faith." In those days, the term propaganda did not have a negative connotation; the church simply wanted to inform the public about the advantages of Catholicism. Indeed, the roots of public relations lie in the development of propaganda, defined neutrally.[4] Today, the pope and other religious leaders maintain communications staffs to assist relations with the public. Indeed, the chief communications official in the Vatican maintains the rank of Archbishop of the Church.

Early American Experience

The American public relations experience dates back to the founding of the Republic. Influencing public opinion, managing communications, and persuading individuals at the highest levels were at the core of the American Revolution. The colonists tried to persuade King George III that they should be accorded the same rights as Englishmen. "Taxation without representation is tyranny" became their public relations slogan to galvanize fellow countrymen.

When King George refused to accede to the colonists' demands, they combined the weaponry of sword and pen. Samuel Adams, for one, organized Committees of Correspondence as a kind of revolutionary Associated Press to disseminate speedily anti-British information throughout the colonies. He also staged events to build up revolutionary fervor, like the Boston Tea Party, in which colonists, masquerading as Indians, boarded British ships in Boston Harbor and pitched chests of imported tea overboard—as impressive a media event as has ever been recorded sans television. Indeed, Adams's precept, "Put the enemy in the wrong and keep him there," is as solid persuasive advice today as it was more than two centuries ago.[5]

Thomas Paine, another early practitioner of public relations, wrote periodic pamphlets and essays that urged the colonists to band together. In one essay contained in his Crisis papers, Paine wrote poetically: "These are the times that try men's souls. The summer soldier and the sunshine patriot will, in this crisis, shrink from the service of their country." The people listened, were persuaded, and took action—testifying to the power of early American communicators.

Later American Experience

The creation of the most important document in our nation's history, the Constitution, also owed much to public relations. Federalists, who supported the Constitution, fought tooth and nail with anti-Federalists, who opposed it. Their battle was waged in newspaper articles, pamphlets, and other organs of persuasion in an attempt to influence public opinion. To advocate ratification of the Constitution, political leaders like Alexander Hamilton, James Madison, and John Jay banded together, under the pseudonym Publius, to write letters to leading newspapers. Today those letters are bound in a document called *The Federalist Papers* and are still used in the interpretation of the Constitution.

After ratification, the constitutional debate continued, particularly over the document's apparent failure to protect individual liberties against government encroachment. Hailed as the Father of the Constitution, Madison framed the Bill of Rights in 1791, which ultimately became the first 10 amendments to the Constitution. Fittingly, the first of those amendments safeguarded, among other things, the practice of public relations: "Congress shall make no law respecting an establishment of religion, or prohibiting the free exercise thereof; or abridging the freedom of speech, or of the press, or the rights of the people peaceably to assemble, and to petition the government for a redress of grievances." In other words, people were given the right to speak up for what they believed in and the freedom to try to influence the opinions of others. Thus was the practice of public relations ratified.[6]

Into the 1800s

The practice of public relations continued to percolate in the 19th century. Among the more prominent, yet negative, antecedents of modern public relations that took hold in the 1800s was press agentry. Two of the better-known—some would say notorious—practitioners of this art were Amos Kendall and Phineas T. Barnum.

In 1829, President Andrew Jackson selected Kendall, a writer and editor living in Kentucky, to serve in his administration. Within weeks, Kendall became a member of Old Hickory's "kitchen cabinet" and eventually became one of Jackson's most influential assistants.

Kendall performed just about every White House public relations task. He wrote speeches, state papers, and messages and turned out press releases. He even conducted basic opinion polls and is considered one of the earliest users of the "news leak." Although Kendall is generally credited with being the first authentic presidential press secretary, his functions and role went far beyond that position.

Among Kendall's most successful ventures in Jackson's behalf was the development of the administration's own newspaper, the *Globe*. Although it was not uncommon for the governing administration to publish its own national house organ, Kendall's deft editorial touch refined the process to increase its effectiveness. Kendall would pen a Jackson news release, distribute it for publication to a local newspaper, and then reprint the press clipping in the *Globe* to underscore Jackson's nationwide popularity. Indeed, that popularity continued unabated throughout Jackson's years in office, with much of the credit going to the president's public relations adviser.*

Most public relations professionals would rather not talk about P. T. Barnum as an industry pioneer. Barnum, some say, was a huckster, whose motto might well have been, 'The Public Be Fooled.' More sanguine defenders suggest that while Barnum may have had his faults, he nonetheless was respected in his time as a user of written and verbal public relations techniques to further his museum and circus.

BACKGROUNDER

The Legacy of P.T. Barnum

P.T. Barnum's methods to achieve publicity for his museum attractions and circus acts pales in comparison with the efforts of today's entertainment publicists to promote new movies.

With studios investing tens of millions of dollars in movies, which must score at the box office immediately to return the hundreds of millions studios seek, the element of publicity is as important as any other in the movie marketing mix.

So today's movie publicists play hardball.

In one 1996 study, more than half of 61 entertainment writers and film critics said the major Hollywood film studios "put more pressure on them to play by their rules." Nearly one-third said they had been "blacklisted" for not playing by the studio's publicity rules.[7] One writer reported being blacklisted by Disney for trashing the movie, *Beauty and the Beast*. The negative review got the writer barred from future Disney screenings, interviews, and junkets.

The study also reported that entertainment publicists make journalists sign agreements as to where a story may run and which sensitive subjects may not be broached in celebrity interviews. The fact is that most magazines will compromise every time to get an interview with Harrison Ford or Bruce Willis or Mariah Carey or Ricky Martin or Madonna or Cher or whomever else is hot at the moment. And if Carmen Electra doesn't wish to discuss Dennis Rodman, or Tom Cruise cares not to chat about Nicole Kidman, or Pamela Anderson would rather not dis Tommy Lee—so be it. If a journalist raises the issue, he is outa there.

Such is the publicity clout that today's show biz-dominated culture commands. When a movie, like the 1999 thriller '*The Sixth Sense*,' can command upwards of $20 million in a weekend opening, favorable publicity becomes a pivotal profitability variable.

Indeed, modern-day press agents have become so powerful that some publications derisively label such public relations practitioners "flacks." Say what they will, in the 21st century, at least in the area of entertainment publicity, it is the public relations publicist—in the best tradition of P.T. Barnum—who holds all the cards.

*Kendall was decidedly not cut from the same cloth as today's neat, trim, buttoned-down press secretaries. On the contrary, Jackson's man was described as "a puny, sickly looking man with a weak voice, a wheezing cough, narrow and stooping shoulders, a sallow complexion, silvery hair in his prime, slovenly dress, and a seedy appearance." (Fred F. Endres, "Public Relations in the Jackson White House," *Public Relations Review* 2, no. 3 [Fall 1976]: 5–12.)

Like him or not, Barnum was a master publicist. In the 1800s, as owner of a major circus, Barnum generated article after article for his traveling show. He purposely gave his star performers short names—for instance, Tom Thumb, the midget, and Jenny Lind, the singer—so that they could easily fit into the headlines of narrow newspaper columns. Barnum also staged bizarre events, such as the legal marriage of the fat lady to the thin man, to drum up free newspaper exposure. And although today's practitioners scoff at Barnum's methods, some press agents still practice his techniques. Nonetheless, when today's public relations professionals bemoan the specter of shysters and hucksters that still overhangs their field, they inevitably place the blame squarely on the fertile mind and silver tongue of P. T. Barnum.

Emergence of the Robber Barons

The American Industrial Revolution ushered in many things at the turn of the century, not the least of which was the growth of public relations. The 20th century began with small mills and shops, which served as the hub of the frontier economy, giving way to massive factories. Country hamlets, which had been the centers of commerce and trade, were replaced by sprawling cities. Limited transportation and communications facilities became nationwide railroad lines and communications wires. Big business took over, and the businessman was king.

The men who ran America's industries seemed more concerned with making a profit than with improving the lot of their fellow citizens. Railroad owners such as William Vanderbilt, bankers such as J. P. Morgan, oil magnates such as John D. Rockefeller, and steel impresarios such as Henry Clay Frick ruled the fortunes of thousands of others. Typical of the reputation acquired by this group of industrialists was the famous—and perhaps apocryphal—response of Vanderbilt when questioned about the public's reaction to his closing of the New York Central Railroad: "The public be damned!"

Little wonder that Americans cursed Vanderbilt and his ilk as robber barons who cared little for the rest of society. Although most who depended on these industrialists for their livelihood felt powerless to rebel, the seeds of discontent were being sown liberally throughout the culture. It was just a matter of time before the robber barons got their comeuppance.

Enter the Muckrakers

When the ax fell on the robber barons, it came in the form of criticism from a feisty group of journalists dubbed "muckrakers." The "muck" that these reporters and editors "raked" was dredged from the scandalous operations of America's business enterprises. Upton Sinclair's novel *The Jungle* attacked the deplorable conditions of the meat-packing industry. Ida Tarbell's *History of the Standard Oil Company* stripped away the public facade of the nation's leading petroleum firm. Her accusations against Standard Oil Chairman Rockefeller, many of which were grossly untrue, nonetheless stirred up public attention.

Magazines such as *McClure's* struck out systematically at one industry after another. The captains of industry, used to getting their own way and having to answer to no one, were wrenched from their peaceful passivity and rolled out on the public carpet to answer for their sins. Journalistic shock stories soon led to a wave of sentiment for legislative reform.

As journalists and the public became more anxious, the government got more involved. Congress began passing laws telling business leaders what they could and couldn't do. Trust-busting then became the order of the day. Conflicts between employers and employees began to break out, and newly organized labor unions came to the fore. The Socialist and Communist movements began to take off. Ironically, it was "a period when free enterprise reached a peak in American history, and yet at that very climax, the tide of public opinion was swelling up against business freedom, primarily because of the breakdown in communications between the businessman and the public."[8]

For a time, these men of inordinate wealth and power found themselves limited in their ability to defend themselves and their activities against the tidal wave of public condemnation. They simply did not know how to get through to the public effectively. To tell their side of the story, the business barons first tried using the lure of advertising to silence journalistic critics; they tried to buy off critics by paying for ads in their papers. It didn't work. Next, they paid publicity people, or press agents, to present their companies' positions. Often, these hired guns painted over the real problems and presented their client's view in the best possible light. The public saw through this approach.

Clearly, another method had to be discovered to get the public to at least consider the business point of view. Business leaders were discovering that a corporation might have capital, labor, and natural resources, yet be doomed to fail if it lacked intelligent management, particularly in the area of influencing public opinion. The best way to influence public opinion, as it turned out, was through honesty and candor. This simple truth was the key to the accomplishments of American history's first successful public relations counselor, Ivy Lee.

Ivy Lee: The Real Father of Modern Public Relations

Ivy Ledbetter Lee was a former Wall Street reporter who plunged into publicity work in 1903. Lee believed in neither Barnum's Public-Be-Fooled approach nor Vanderbilt's Public-Be-Damned philosophy. For Lee, the key to business acceptance and understanding was that The Public Be Informed.

Lee firmly believed that the only way business could answer its critics convincingly was to present its side honestly, accurately, and forcefully.[9] Instead of merely appeasing the public, Lee thought a company should strive to earn public confidence and good will. Sometimes this task meant looking further for mutual solutions. At other times, it even meant admitting that the company was wrong. Hired by the anthracite coal industry in 1906, Lee set forth his beliefs in a Declaration of Principles to newspaper editors:

> This is not a secret press bureau. All our work is done in the open. We aim to supply news. This is not an advertising agency; if you think any of our matter ought properly to go to your business office, do not use it. Our matter is accurate. Further details on any subject treated will be supplied promptly, and any editor will be assisted most cheerfully in verifying any statement of fact. . . . In brief, our plan is frankly and openly, on behalf of business concerns and public institutions, to supply to the press and public of the United States prompt and accurate information concerning subjects which are of value and interest.

In 1914, John D. Rockefeller Jr., who headed one of the most maligned and misunderstood of America's wealthy families, hired Lee. As Lee's biographer Ray Eldon Hiebert has pointed out, Lee did less to change the Rockefellers' policies than to give them a public hearing.[10] For example, when the family was censured scathingly for its role in breaking up a strike at the Rockefeller-owned Colorado Fuel and Iron Company, the family hired a labor relations expert (at Lee's recommendation) to determine the causes of an incident that had led to several deaths. The result of this effort was the formation of a joint labor-management board to mediate all workers' grievances on wages, hours, and working conditions. Years later, Rockefeller admitted that the public relations outcome of the Colorado strike "was one of the most important things that ever happened to the Rockefeller family."[11]

In working for the Rockefellers, Lee tried to "humanize" them, to feature them in real-life situations such as playing golf, attending church, and celebrating birthdays. Simply, Lee's goal was to present the Rockefellers in terms that every individual could understand and appreciate. Years later, despite their critics, the family came to be known as the nation's finest example of philanthropy. Indeed, today's billionaires, from Bill Gates to Warren Buffet to Ted Turner, have attempted to emulate the Rockefellers in terms of generosity.

Ironically, even Ivy Lee could not escape the glare of public criticism. In the late 1920s, Lee was asked to serve as adviser to the parent company of the German Dye Trust, which, as it turned out, was an agent for the policies of Adolf Hitler. When Lee realized the nature of Hitler's intentions, he advised the Dye Trust cartel to work to alter Hitler's ill-conceived policies of restricting religious and press freedom. For his involvement with the Dye Trust, Lee was branded a traitor and dubbed "Poison Ivy" by members of Congress investigating un-American activities. The smears against him in the press rivaled the most vicious ones against the robber barons.[12]

Despite his unfortunate involvement with the Dye Trust, Ivy Lee is recognized as the individual who brought honesty and candor to public relations. Lee, more than anyone before him, transformed the field from a questionable pursuit (i.e., seeking positive publicity at any cost) into a professional discipline designed to win public confidence and trust through communications based on openness and truth.

The Growth of Modern Public Relations

Ivy Lee helped to open the gates. After he established the idea that high-powered companies and individuals have a responsibility to inform their publics, the practice began to grow in every sector of American society.

Government

During World War I, President Woodrow Wilson established the Creel Committee, under journalist George Creel. Creel's group, composed of the nation's leading journalists, scholars, press agents, and other assorted press celebrities, mounted an impressive effort to mobilize public opinion in support of the war effort and to stimulate the sale of war bonds through Liberty Loan publicity drives. Not only did the war effort get a boost, but so did the field of public relations. The nation was mightily impressed with the potential power of publicity as a weapon to encourage national sentiment and support.

During World War II, the public relations field received an even bigger boost. With the Creel Committee as its precursor, the Office of War Information (OWI) was established to convey the message of the United States at home and abroad. Under the directorship of Elmer Davis, a veteran journalist, the OWI laid the foundations for the U.S. Information Agency as America's voice around the world.

World War II also saw a flurry of activity to sell war bonds, boost the morale of those at home, spur production in the nation's factories and offices, and, in general, support America's war effort as intensively as possible. By virtually every measure, this full-court public relations offensive was an unquestioned success.

The proliferation of public relations officers in World War II led to a growth in the number of practitioners during the peace that followed. One reason companies saw the need to have public relations professionals to "speak up" for them was the more combative attitude of President Harry Truman toward many of the country's largest institutions. For example, in a memorable address over radio and television on April 8, 1952, President Truman announced that, as a result of a union wage dispute, "the government would take over the steel plants." The seizure of the steel mills touched off a series of historic events that reached into Congress and the Supreme Court and stimulated a massive public relations campaign, the likes of which had rarely been seen outside the government.

Counseling

The nation's first public relations firm, the Publicity Bureau, was founded in Boston in 1900 and specialized in general press agentry. The first Washington, D.C., agency was begun in 1902 by William Wolff Smith, a former correspondent for the *New York Sun* and the *Cincinnati Inquirer.* Two years later, Ivy Lee joined with George Parker to begin a public relations agency that was later dissolved. Lee reestablished the agency in New York in 1919 and brought in T. J. Ross as a partner.

John W. Hill entered public relations in 1927 after a dozen years as a journalist. Together with William Knowlton, Hill founded Hill & Knowlton, Inc., in Cleveland. Hill soon moved East, and Knowlton dropped out of the firm. However, the agency quickly became one of the largest public relations operations in the world, with 1,050 employees in 20 countries and 20 U.S. cities. Hill stayed active in the firm for half a century and mused about the field's beginnings:

> In 1927, public relations was just in its infancy. Think of the contrast of the present with fifty years ago. Less than a handful of counseling firms anywhere in the world and barely a handful of practitioners tucked away and lost in the offices of a very few large corporations—far removed from the executive suite.[13]

In addition to Hill, Creel Committee Associate Chairman Carl Byoir launched his own public relations counseling firm in 1930. Ironically, 56 years later, Byoir's firm, Carl Byoir & Associates, merged with Hill & Knowlton to become the largest public relations company in the world.

Besides Byoir and Hill, Earl Newsom and Pendleton Dudley also founded early firms. Newsom, who began Newsom & Company in 1935, generally limited his public relations practice to counseling companies like Ford, General Motors, and Jersey Standard. In his otherwise critical treatment of public relations, *The Image Merchants,* author Irwin Ross paid tribute to Newsom's success:

The goal of a good many public relations men is someday to attain the lonely eminence of Earl Newsom. His fees are high; his clients include some of the most august names in the corporate roster; and his work involves pure consultation.[14]

Another early counselor, Harold Burson, emphasized marketing-oriented public relations, "primarily concerned with helping clients sell their goods and services, maintain a favorable market for their stock, and foster harmonious relations with employees."[15] Today, Burson-Marsteller ranks as the world's largest public relations agency, and Harold Burson was named at the end of the past millennium as "the most influential PR person of the 20th century."[16]

In the 1990s, the counseling business saw the emergence of international super-agencies. Among them, Hill & Knowlton, Burson-Marsteller, Edelman and Shandwick boasted worldwide networks with thousands of employees linked to serve clients with communications services throughout the world. Many of these—Hill & Knowlton and Burson-Marsteller—were merged into advertising agencies.

Latest to join the ranks of successful public relations agencies are those that specialize in online public relations. Such Internet specialists as Middleberg & Associates, Waggener Edstrom, and Weber Group comprise the next generation of public relations lead agencies. Indeed, in the 21st century, specialty and regional public relations firms will continue to proliferate.

As one counseling pioneer put it:

"It has been quite remarkable to see the dramatic growth of public relations firms in recent years. I believe that will continue. Specialist firms in technology, investor relations, health, and government relations will continue to play an important role. 'And, of course there always will be a strong local and regional firms.[17]

Corporations

Problems in the perception of corporations and their leaders dissipated in the United States after World War II. Opinion polls of that period ranked business as high in public esteem. People were back at work, and business was back in style.

Smart companies—General Electric, General Motors, and American Telephone & Telegraph (AT&T), for example—worked hard to preserve their good names through both words and actions. Arthur W. Page became AT&T's first public relations vice president in 1927. Page was a pacesetter, helping to maintain AT&T's reputation as a prudent and proper corporate citizen. Indeed, Page's five principles of successful corporate public relations are as relevant now as they were in the 1930s:

1. To make sure management thoughtfully analyzes its overall relation to the public
2. To create a system for informing all employees about the firm's general policies and practices
3. To create a system giving contact employees (those having direct dealings with the public) the knowledge needed to be reasonable and polite to the public
4. To create a system drawing employee and public questions and criticism back up through the organization to management
5. To ensure frankness in telling the public about the company's actions.[18]

Paul Garrett was another person who felt the need to be responsive to the public's wishes. A former news reporter, he became the first director of public relations for mighty General Motors in 1931, working directly for GM's legendary CEO Alfred Sloan. Garrett once reportedly explained that the essence of his job was to convince the public that the powerful auto company deserved trust, that is, "to make a billion-dollar company seem small." Ironically, as good as Garrett was, he still suffered from the universal public relations complaint of "never feeling like an insider" within his organization. [19]

Today, public relations advice remains essential, as companies from Nike to Microsoft to America Online are held accountable to maintain the public trust in the face of enormous wealth and power.

Education

One public relations pioneer who began as a publicist in 1913 was Edward L. Bernays, nephew of Sigmund Freud and author of the landmark book *Crystallizing Public Opinion* (see interview at the end of this chapter). Bernays was a giant in the public relations field for nearly the entire century. In addition to contributing as much to the field as any other professional in its history, Bernays was a true public relations scholar. He taught the first course in public relations in 1923.

Bernays's seminal writings in the field were among the first to disassociate public relations from press agentry or publicity work. As Bernays wrote later:

> At first we called our activity "publicity direction." We intended to give advice to clients on how to direct their actions to get public visibility for them. But within a year we changed the service and its name to "counsel on public relations." We recognized that all actions of a client that impinged on the public needed counsel. Public visibility of a client for one action might be vitiated by another action not in the public interest. [20]

Historian Eric Goldman credited Bernays with "[moving] along with the most advanced trends in the public relations field, thinking with, around, and ahead of them."[21]

Bernays was also at least indirectly responsible for encouraging the development of another public relations phenomenon that would take on added impetus in the 1990s—the emergence of women in the field. Bernays's associate (and later, wife), Doris E. Fleischman, helped edit a leaflet, called *Contact,* that helped American leaders understand the underpinnings of the new profession Bernays represented. Fleischman's important assistance in spreading the Bernays doctrine was an early contribution to a field that in the 21st century showed women to dominate with upwards of 70 percent of public relations jobs.

Public Relations Comes of Age

As noted, public relations really came of age as a result of the confluence of four general factors in our society:

1. The growth of large institutions and their sense of responsibility to the public
2. The increased changes, conflicts, and confrontations among interest groups in society
3. The heightened awareness of people brought about by increasingly sophisticated communications technology everywhere

A QUESTION OF ETHICS

Watergate: A Black Eye for Public Relations

On August 8, 1974, President Richard M. Nixon resigned in disgrace and humiliation. His administration had been tarnished by illegal wiretapping, illegal surveillance, burglary, and unlawful use of the law. The president and his men were toppled by the most profound political scandal in the nation's history, which grew out of a series of break-ins at the Democratic national headquarters in a Washington, D.C., apartment building named Watergate.

Nixon and his advisers steadfastly refused, throughout the long and arduous and publicly televised Watergate crisis, to acknowledge any role in the break-in.

President Nixon's response, in particular, was bizarre in its obstinacy.

- He ordered preparation of an "Enemies List" of journalists who had written negatively about Watergate.
- He discussed lying about the reasons for the Watergate break-in and another break-in at the office of the psychiatrist Daniel Ellsberg, an administration enemy who had leaked secret Pentagon papers to the *New York Times*.
- He decided to fire Archibald Cox, the special prosecutor appointed to get to the bottom of Watergate (Figure 2-2).
- Attorney General Elliott Richardson refused to carry out Nixon's order to fire Cox, and he, himself, resigned. And Richardson's deputy, William Ruckelshaus, also refused to carry out the order, and Nixon fired him.
- Nixon's relationship with the media, never good, deteriorated to the point of no return. At one heated press conference, he responded pointedly to a question posed by CBS correspondent Dan Rather with, "I am not a crook."

Ultimately, as a nation painfully watched in horror, Nixon's aides appeared at a televised Senate hearing and finally admitted to their role in the break-ins and their subsequent efforts to "cover up."

Nixon's resignation was unprecedented in the nation's history. And many blamed his downfall on one thing: an overriding concern about public relations. Observers argued that the president and his

FIGURE 2-2 **Tragicomedy.** Watergate's dubious cast of characters inspired this takeoff on the promotional work done for the movie *That's Entertainment.*

advisers were so consumed with covering up the facts—with public relations—that they orchestrated their own downfall.

In point of fact, what Nixon and his henchmen wrought was the exact opposite of proper public relations. As we have noted, public relations is neither distortion nor obfuscation nor cover-up but, rather, the communication of truth.

Nonetheless, no event in recent history has given the practice of public relations a blacker eye than Watergate.

4. The spread of global democracy
5. The growth of the Internet and World Wide Web

Growth of Large Institutions

Ironically, the public relations profession received perhaps its most important thrust when business confidence suffered its most severe setback. The economic and social upheaval caused by the Great Depression of the 1930s provided the impetus for corporations to seek public support by telling their stories. Public relations departments sprang up in scores of major companies, among them Bendix, Borden, Eastman Kodak, Eli Lilly, Ford, General Motors, Standard Oil, and U.S. Steel. The role that public relations played in helping regain post-Depression public trust in big business helped project the field into the relatively strong position it enjoyed during World War II.

The Truman years marked a challenging period for public relations, with government questioning the integrity of large business corporations. The ebbing and flowing conflict between government and business is unique to America. In other nations— Japan and Germany most prominently—government and business work more in concert to achieve common goals. In the United States, many businesses, both large and small, complain that government overregulation frustrates their ability to prosper. Businesses of every size have recognized that aggressively communicating corporate products and positions can help win public receptivity and support and ward off government intrusion.

Change, Conflict, and Confrontation

Disenchantment with big institutions peaked in the 1960s. The conflicts during the early part of the decade between private economic institutions—especially large corporations—and various disenfranchised elements of society arose from long-standing grievances. As one commentator put it: "Their rebellion was born out of the desperation of those who had nothing to lose. Issues were seen as black or white, groups as villainous or virtuous, causes as holy or satanic, and leaders as saints or charlatans."[22]

The social and political upheavals of the 1960s dramatically affected many areas, including the practice of public relations. The Vietnam War fractured society. Ralph Nader began to look pointedly at the inadequacies of the automobile industry. Women, long denied equal rights in the workplace and elsewhere, began to mobilize into activist groups such as the National Organization of Women (NOW). Environmentalists, worried about threats to the land and water by business expansion, began to support groups such as the Sierra Club. Minorities, particularly blacks and Hispanics, began to petition and protest for their rights. Homosexuals, AIDS activists, senior citizens, birth control advocates, and social activists of every kind began to challenge the legitimacy of large institutions. Not since the days of the robber barons had large institutions so desperately needed professional communications help.

Heightened Public Awareness

The 1970s and 1980s brought a partial resolution of these problems. Many of the solutions came from the government in the form of affirmative action guidelines, senior citizen programs, consumer and environmental protection acts and agencies, aids to education, and myriad other laws and statutes.

Business began to contribute to charities. Managers began to consider community relations a first-line responsibility. The general policy of corporations confronting their adversaries was abandoned. In its place, most large companies adopted a policy of conciliation and compromise.

This new policy of social responsibility continued into the 1990s. Corporations came to realize that their reputations are a valuable asset to be protected, conserved, defended, nurtured, and enhanced at all times. In truth, institutions in the 1990s had little choice but to get along with their publics.

By the new century, the vast majority of American homes had television, with millions wired for cable and another 100 million online. As a result of all this communication, publics have become much more segmented, specialized, and sophisticated. Public relations professionals have had to discard many of the traditional methods used to reach and influence these publics. Today, organizations face the new reality of communicating with their key publics instantaneously, real time, all the time. Optimizing communications in this environment is a daunting public relations challenge.

Global Democracy in the 21st Century

In the 21st century, with a few glaring repressive exceptions, democracy is virtually everywhere. The Berlin Wall's destruction was transmitted live around the world. So was the dissolution of the Union of Soviet Socialist Republics. In 1993, two longtime archenemies, Nelson Mandela and Nicholas DeKlerck, stood together to share the Nobel Peace Prize as free elections were held in South Africa and a black former prisoner of the state became president. Three years later, two equally ardent enemies, Israeli leader Benjamin Netanyahu and Palestinian leader Yassir Arafat, also came together to hammer out a peace proposal for their perpetually warring lands.

Even in societies slower to pick up the cudgel of democracy, there is change. China celebrates its anniversary by inviting Western business leaders to tour its new economy. Fidel Castro, the Communist holdout who held on as leader of Cuba despite all odds, softens perceptibly to let in the new world. Today, with the world now truly "safe for democracy," the public relations challenge has grown in intensity.

Growth of the Internet and the World Wide Web

In the 21st century, true two-way communications has arrived. Not only have cable, satellite, mobile phones, pagers, faxes, bar code scanners, voice mail systems, videodisk technologies, and all the rest revolutionized the information transmission and receiving process, but the emergence of the Internet and the World Wide Web have radically intensified the spread of communications even further.

By the end of 1999, the Internet economy had grown nearly 70 percent in 12 months, far outpacing the growth of the overall U.S. economy. Jobs connected to the Internet increased nearly 50 percent in a year, to more than two million. The Internet economy already is larger than the airline and publishing industries and is on its way higher and higher.[23]

The impact of the Web on public relations practice has been phenomenal. E-mail dominates internal communications. Journalists now regard the Internet as their number two choice of organizational contact—just behind a human source. A new generation of Americans has been weaned and depends on the Internet as its primary source of communication. High-tech public relations firms, which didn't exist a decade ago, account for fee income in excess of $500 million a year.[24]

In sum, knowledge of and facility with the Internet is no longer an "option" for public relations practitioners. It is a necessity.

Public Relations Education

As the practice of public relations has developed, so too has the growth of public relations education. In 1951, 12 schools offered major programs in public relations. Today well in excess of 200 journalism or communication programs offer concentrated study in public relations, with nearly 300 others offering at least one course dealing with the profession.

In 1999, the Commission on Public Relations Education, chartered by the Public Relations Society of America, recommended a public relations curriculum imparting knowledge in such nontraditional but pivotal areas as relationship building, societal trends, and multicultural and global issues.[25]

Although few data are available on public relations programs in business schools, the number of programs is increasing, especially those related to marketing. As the debate continues about where public relations education should appropriately be housed—either in business or journalism schools—the best answer is that both should offer public relations courses.[26]

In business, the practice of public relations has become an integral part of the way companies operate. Therefore, business students should be exposed to the discipline's underpinnings and practical aspects before they enter the corporate world. In journalism, with upwards of 70 percent of daily newspaper copy emanating from public relations-generated releases, journalists, too, should know what public relations is all about before they graduate. Wherever it is housed, the profession's role as an academic pursuit has continued to gain strength. This educational dimension has, in turn, contributed to the new respect accorded public relations in modern society.

SUMMARY

Today public relations is big, worldwide business.

- ☑ The Public Relations Society of America, organized in 1947, boasts a growing membership of 18,500 in 107 chapters nationwide
- ☑ The Public Relations Student Society of America, formed in 1968 to facilitate communications between students interested in the field and public relations professionals, has 5,000 student members at 180 colleges and universities
- ☑ More than 5,400 U.S. companies have public relations departments
- ☑ Upwards of 6,000 public relations agencies exist in the United States, some billing hundreds of millions of dollars per year
- ☑ More than 500 trade associations have public relations departments
- ☑ Top communications executives at major companies and agencies draw six-figure salaries

The scope of modern public relations practice is vast. Press relations, Web relations, employee communications, public relations counseling and research, local community relations, audiovisual communications, contributions, interactive public relations, and numerous other diverse activities fall under the public relations umbrella. Because of this broad range of functions, many public relations practitioners today seem preoccupied with the proper title for their calling: public relations, external affairs, corporate communications, public affairs, corporate relations, ad infinitum. They argue that the range of activities involved offers no hope that people will understand what the pursuit involves, unless an umbrella term is used.[27]

Practitioners also worry that as public relations becomes more prominent, its function and those who purportedly practice it will be subject to increasingly intense public scrutiny. There are more ardent calls for licensing of practitioners, echoing the sentiment of the late public relations pioneer, Edward Bernays. Professionalism, argue the people who guard the reputation of the practice, is all important. Greater minority membership in the field, particularly with respect to African Americans, is a recurring objective.[28] Then, too, all the high-profile ethical scandals of former Speaker of the House Newt Gingrich, former presidential policy advisor Dick Morris, and even former President Bill Clinton have cast a pall over the profession—just as Watergate did two decades earlier.

Indeed, there is no more important characteristic for public relations people to emulate than high ethical character and standards. The field's finest ethical moment occurred when the Johnson & Johnson Company, in the wake of unspeakable tragedy brought about by its lead product Tylenol, didn't hesitate to choose the ethical course. J&J removed its product from circulation not once but twice, both times to preserve its reputation. As the "Case Study" at the conclusion of this chapter suggests, the handling of the Tylenol tragedy was public relations' most shining hour.

Despite these concerns, the practice of public relations in the 21st century stands as a potent, persuasive force in society. Clearly, the public relations field today—whatever it is called and by whomever it is practiced—is in the spotlight. Its senior-most officers serve as members of the management committees that set policy for our great organizations.[29] Its professionals command higher salaries. Its counselors command increased respect. Its practice is taught in increasing numbers, not only in American colleges and universities but around the world.

With 200,000 men and women in the United States alone practicing public relations in some form and thousands of practitioners overseas, the field has become solidly entrenched as an important, influential, and professional component of our society.

Discussion Starters

1. What societal factors have influenced the spread of public relations?
2. Why do public relations professionals think of P. T. Barnum as a mixed blessing?
3. What is the significance to the practice of public relations of American revolutionary hero Samuel Adams?
4. What did the robber barons and muckrakers have to do with the development of public relations?
5. Why are Ivy Lee and Edward Bernays considered two of the fathers of public relations?
6. What impact did the Creel Committee and the Office of War Information have on the development of public relations?
7. What was the significance of Arthur Page to the development of corporate public relations?

8. Identify and discuss the significance of some of the earliest public relations counselors.
9. What are some of the yardsticks that indicated that public relations had arrived in the latter stages of the 20th century?
10. What are some of the issues that confront public relations in the 21st century?

Notes

1. Scott M. Cutlip, Allen H. Center, and Glen M. Broom, *Effective Public Relations*, 8th ed., (Upper Saddle River, NJ: Prentice Hall, 2000): 102.
2. James D. Sodt, "Why Would I Represent the Serbs," *The Public Relations Strategist* (Spring 1995): 32.
3. Edward L. Bernays, speech at the University of Florida Public Relations Symposium, Gainesville, FL, February 1, 1984.
4. Paul Swift, "The Antecedents," *Public Relations Quarterly* (Summer 1996): 6.
5. Frank Winston Wylie, "Book Reviews," *Public Relations Review* (Fall 1996): 312.
6. Harold Burson, speech at Utica College of Syracuse University, Utica, NY, March 5, 1987.
7. "Film Writers Complain About PR Pressure," Jack O'Dwyer's Newsletter, (November 27, 1996): 3.
8. Ray Eldon Hiebert, *Courtier to the Crowd: The Story of Ivy L. Lee and the Development of Public Relations* (Ames: Iowa State University Press, 1966).
9. Rex Harlow, "A Public Relations Historian Recalls the First Days," *Public Relations Review* (Summer 1981): 39–40.
10. Cited in Sherman Morse, "An Awakening in Wall Street," *American Magazine* 62 (September 1906): 460.
11. Hiebert, *Courtier to the Crowd*.
12. Cited in Alvin Moscow, *The Rockefeller Inheritance* (Garden City, NY: Doubleday, 1977): 23.
13. John W. Hill, *The Making of a Public Relations Man* (New York: David McKay, 1963): 69.
14. Irwin Ross, *The Image Merchants* (Garden City, NY: Doubleday, 1959): 85.
15. Burson, speech at Utica College.
16. "Burson Hailed as PR's No. 1 Influential Figure," *PR Week*, (October 18, 1999): 1.
17. Address by Daniel J. Edelman, Arthur Page Society, New Orleans, LA, September 21, 1997.
18. Cited in Noel L. Griese, "The Employee Communications Philosophy of Arthur W. Page," *Public Relations Quarterly* (Winter 1977): 8–12.
19. "An Afternoon with Peter Drucker," *The Public Relations Strategist* (Fall 1998): 10.
20. Edward L. Bernays, "Bernays: 62 Years in Public Relations," *Public Relations Quarterly* (Fall 1981): 8.
21. David L. Luis, "The Outstanding PR Professionals," *Public Relations Journal* (October 1970): 84.
22. James E. Gringo, "Teaching Public Relations in the Future," *Public Relations Review* (Spring 1989): 16.
23. Sara Nathan, "Internet Economy Soars 68%," *USA Today* (October 27, 1999): 1.
24. "1999 Fee Income of High-Tech PR Firms," O'Dwyer's PR Services Report (November 1999): 50.

25. John L. Paluszek, "Public Relations Students: Today Good, Tomorrow Better," *The Public Relations Strategist* (Winter 2000): 27.

26. J. David Pincus, "Changing How Future Managers View Us," *The Public Relations Strategist* (Spring 1997).

27. "Diverse Titles Splinter Image of Field: Report of PRSA's Special Committee on Terminology," *Public Relations Reporter* (April 20, 1987): Tips & Tactics.

28. Marilyn Kern-Foxworth, "Status and Roles of Minority PR Practitioners," *Public Relations Review* (Fall 1989): 39.

29. Harold Burson, "Introduction: The Maturation of Public Relations," *Journal of Corporate Public Relations-Northwestern University* (1994–1995): 6.

Suggested Readings

Arnold, James E., and Consultants. *Issues and Trends in the 1990's*. PRSA Counselors Academy, 1992.

Baskin, Otto, et al. *The Profession and the Practice*. 4th ed. Madison, WI: Brown & Benchmark, 1997.

Bernays, Edward L. *Crystallizing Public Opinion*. New York: Liveright, 1961.

Bernays, Edward L. *The Later Years: Public Relations Insights, 1956-1986*. Rhinebeck, NY: H & M, 1987.

Burson, Harold. "A Decent Respect to the Opinion of Mankind." Speech delivered at the Raymond Simon Institute for Public Relations (Burson-Marsteller, 866 Third Ave., New York, NY 10022), March 5, 1987. This speech highlights public relations activities that have influenced the United States from colonial times to the present day.

Cutlip, Scott M. *Public Relations History from the 17th to the 20th Century*. Hillsdale, NJ: Lawrence Erlbaum Associates, Inc., 1995.

Cutlip, Scott M. *The Unseen Power—Public Relations, A History*. Hillsdale, NJ: Lawrence Erlbaum Associates, 1994.

Garcia, Helio Fred. "Really-Old-School Public Relations," *The Public Relations Strategist* (Summer 1998): 16ff.

Hill, George, and Robert Farrell. *Blacks and Public Relations: History and Bibliography*. Daystar Publishers, 1988.

Marchand, Roland. *Creating the Corporate Soul: The Rise of Public Relations and Corporate Imagery in American Big Business*. Berkeley and Los Angeles, CA: University of California Press, 1998.

Merk, Frederick. *Fruits of Propaganda in the Tyler Administration*. Cambridge, MA: Harvard University Press, 1971.

Mitroff, Ian. I, and Warren Bennis. *The Unreality Industry: The Deliberate Manufacturing of Falsehood and What It Is Doing to Our Lives*. Secaucus, NJ: Carol Publishing Group, 1989.

Nevins, Allan. "The Constitution Makers and the Public, 1785-1790." An address before the Conference of the Public Relations Society of America, Nov. 13, 1962. Reprinted as "At the Beginning. . . A Series of Lecture-Essays." Gainesville, FL: The Institute for Public Relations Research and Education, 1997.

Newsom, Doug, Alan Scott, and Judy Van Slyke Turk. *This Is PR: The Realities of Public Relations,* 5th ed. Belmont, CA: Wadsworth, 1993.

Pratte, Paul Alfred. *Gods Within the Machine*. Westport, CT: Praeger Publishers, 1995. Chronicles the history of the American Society of Newspaper Editors and its role in developing a free press.

top of the shelf

Larry Tye

The Father of Spin: Edward L. Bernays and the Birth of Public Relations.
New York: Crown Publishers, 1998.

The author's background as a Boston Globe journalist, rather than a public relations practitioner or professor, both limits the depth of this biography and offers the refreshing viewpoint of an "outsider."

Tye uses Bernays's life "as a prism to understand the evolution of the craft of public relations and how it came to play such a critical—and sometimes insidious—role in American life." Granted a Nieman Fellowship at Harvard University to write this book, Tye waded into 800 boxes of personal and professional papers Bernays left the Library of Congress, papers that detail cases he worked on and tactics and strategies he employed over a career that spanned eight decades.

Enjoyable, enlightening reading, bolstered by a seven-page bibliography.

Public Relations News (1201 Seven Locks Road, Potomac, MD 61130). Weekly.

Public Relations Quarterly (P.O. Box 311, Rhinebeck, NY 12572).

Public Relations Review (10606 Mantz Rd., Silver Spring, MD 20903).

PR Reporter (P.O. Box 600, Exeter, NH 03833-0600). Weekly.

Public Relations Strategist (PRSA, 33 Irving Place, New York, NY 10003). Quarterly.

Shea, Christopher. "How Corporations Won the Hearts and Minds of America: New Books Explore the Strategic Triumph of Public Relations," *The Chronicle of Higher Education* (Spring 1998): A16ff

St. John, Burton. "Public Relations as Community-Building: Then and Now," *Public Relations Quarterly* (Spring 1998): 34–40.

CASE STUDY

The Tylenol Murders

Arguably, the two most important cases in the history of the practice of public relations occurred within four years of each other to the same company and product.

For close to 100 years, Johnson & Johnson Company of New Brunswick, New Jersey, was the epitome of a well-managed, highly profitable, and tight-lipped consumer products manufacturer.

ROUND I

That image changed on the morning of September 30, 1982, when Johnson & Johnson faced as devastating a public relations problem as had confronted any company in history.

That morning, Johnson & Johnson's management learned that its premier product, extra-strength Tylenol, had been used as a murder weapon to kill three people. In the days that followed, another three people died from swallowing Tylenol capsules loaded with cyanide. Although all the cyanide deaths occurred in Chicago, reports from other parts of the country also implicated extra-strength Tylenol capsules in illnesses of various sorts. These latter reports were later proved to be unfounded, but Johnson & Johnson and its Tylenol-producing subsidiary, McNeil Consumer Products Company, found themselves at the center of a public relations trauma the likes of which few companies had ever experienced.

Tylenol had been an astoundingly profitable product for Johnson & Johnson. At the time of the Tylenol murders, the product held 35 percent of the $1 billion analgesic market. It contributed an estimated 7 percent to the company's worldwide sales and almost 20 percent to its profits. Throughout the years, Johnson & Johnson had not been—and hadn't needed to be—a particularly high-profile company. Its chairman, James E. Burke, who had been with the company for almost 30 years, had never appeared on television and had rarely participated in print interviews.

Johnson & Johnson's management, understandably, was caught totally by surprise when the news hit. Initially, they had no facts and, indeed, got much of their information from the media calls that inundated the firm from the beginning. The company recognized that it needed the media to get out as much information to the public as quickly as possible to prevent a panic. Therefore, almost immediately, Johnson & Johnson made a key decision: to open its doors to the media.

On the second day of the crisis, Johnson & Johnson discovered that an earlier statement that no cyanide was used on its premises was wrong. The company didn't hesitate. Its public relations department quickly announced that the earlier information had been false. Even though the reversal embarrassed the company briefly, Johnson & Johnson's openness was hailed and made up for any damage to its credibility.

Early on in the crisis, the company was largely convinced that the poisonings had not occurred at any of its plants. Nonetheless, Johnson & Johnson recalled an entire lot of 93,000 bottles of extra-strength Tylenol associated with the reported murders. In the process, it telegrammed warnings to doctors, hospitals, and distributors, at a cost of half a million dollars. McNeil also suspended all Tylenol advertising to reduce attention to the product.

By the second day, the company was convinced that the tampering had taken place during the product's Chicago distribution and not in the manufacturing process. Therefore, a total Tylenol recall did not seem obligatory. Chairman Burke himself leaned toward immediately recalling all extra-strength Tylenol capsules, but after consulting with the Federal Bureau of Investigation, he decided not to do so. The FBI was worried that a precipitous recall would encourage copycat poisoning attempts. Nonetheless, five days later, when a copycat strychnine poisoning occurred in California, Johnson & Johnson did recall all extra-strength Tylenol capsules—31 million bottles—at a cost of more than $100 million.

Although the company knew it had done nothing wrong, Johnson & Johnson resisted the temptation to disclaim any possible connection between its product and the murders. Rather, while moving quickly to trace the lot numbers of the poisoned packages, it also posted a $100,000 reward for the killer. Through advertisements promising to exchange capsules for tablets, through thousands of letters to the trade, and through statements to the media, the company hoped to put the incident into proper perspective.

At the same time, Johnson & Johnson commissioned a nationwide opinion survey to assess the consumer implications of the Tylenol poisonings. The good news was that 87 percent of Tylenol users surveyed said they realized that the maker of Tylenol was

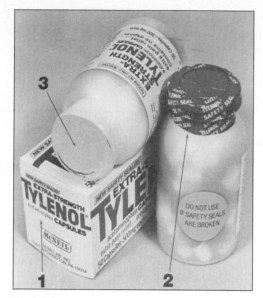

FIGURE 2-3 The triple-safety-sealed, tamper-resistant package for Tylenol capsules had (1) glued flaps on the outer box, (2) a tight plastic neck seal, and (3) a strong inner foil seal over the mouth of the bottle. A bright yellow label on the bottle was imprinted with a red warning: "Do not use if safety seals are broken." As it turned out, all these precautions didn't work.

not responsible for the deaths. The bad news was that 61 percent still said they were not likely to buy extra-strength Tylenol capsules in the future. In other words, even though most consumers knew the deaths weren't Tylenol's fault, they still feared using the product.

But Chairman Burke and Johnson & Johnson weren't about to knuckle under to the deranged saboteur or saboteurs who had poisoned their product. Despite predictions of the imminent demise of extra-strength Tylenol, Johnson & Johnson decided to relaunch the product in a new triple-safety-sealed, tamper-resistant package (Figure 2-3). Many on Wall Street and in the marketing community were stunned by Johnson & Johnson's bold decision.

So confident was Johnson & Johnson's management that it launched an all-out media blitz to make sure that people understood its commitment. Chairman Burke appeared on the widely watched Phil Donahue network television program and skillfully handled one hour of intense public questioning.

Johnson & Johnson invited the investigative news program *60 Minutes*—the scourge of corporate America—to film its executive strategy sessions to prepare for the new launch. When the program was aired, reporter Mike Wallace concluded that although Wall Street had been ready at first to write off the company, it was now "hedging its bets because of Johnson & Johnson's stunning campaign of facts, money, the media, and truth."

Finally, on November 11, 1982, less than two months after the murders, Johnson & Johnson's management held an elaborate video press conference in New York City, beamed to additional locations around the country, to introduce the new extra-strength Tylenol package. Said the chairman to the media:

> "It is our job at Johnson & Johnson to ensure the survival of Tylenol, and we are pledged to do this. While we consider this crime an assault on society, we are nevertheless ready to fulfill our responsibility, which includes paying the price of this heinous crime. But I urge you not to make Tylenol the scapegoat."

In the days and months that followed Burke's news conference, it became clear that Tylenol would not become a scapegoat. In fact, by the beginning of 1983, Tylenol had recaptured an astounding 95 percent of its prior market share. Morale at the company, according to its chairman, was "higher than in years" (Figure 2-4). The euphoria lasted until February of 1986, when, unbelievably, tragedy struck again.

ROUND II

Late in the evening of February 10, 1986, news reports began to circulate that a woman had died in Yonkers, New York, after taking poisoned capsules of extra-strength Tylenol.

The nightmare for Johnson & Johnson began anew.

Once again, the company sprang into action. Chairman Burke addressed reporters at a news conference a day after the incident. A phone survey found that the public didn't blame the company. However, with the discovery of other poisoned Tylenol

OUR CREDO

We believe our first responsibility is to the doctors, nurses and patients,
to mothers and fathers and all others who use our products and services.
In meeting their needs everything we do must be of high quality.
We must constantly strive to reduce our costs
in order to maintain reasonable prices.
Customers' orders must be serviced promptly and accurately.
Our suppliers and distributors must have an opportunity
to make a fair profit.

We are responsible to our employees,
the men and women who work with us throughout the world.
Everyone must be considered as an individual.
We must respect their dignity and recognize their merit.
They must have a sense of security in their jobs.
Compensation must be fair and adequate,
and working conditions clean, orderly and safe.
We must be mindful of ways to help our employees fulfill
their family responsibilities.
Employees must feel free to make suggestions and complaints.
There must be equal opportunity for employment, development
and advancement for those qualified.
We must provide competent management,
and their actions must be just and ethical.

We are responsible to the communities in which we live and work
and to the world community as well.
We must be good citizens — support good works and charities
and bear our fair share of taxes.
We must encourage civic improvements and better health and education.
We must maintain in good order
the property we are privileged to use,
protecting the environment and natural resources.

Our final responsibility is to our stockholders.
Business must make a sound profit.
We must experiment with new ideas.
Research must be carried on, innovative programs developed
and mistakes paid for.
New equipment must be purchased, new facilities provided
and new products launched.
Reserves must be created to provide for adverse times.
When we operate according to these principles,
the stockholders should realize a fair return.

Johnson & Johnson

FIGURE 2-4 **The Johnson & Johnson credo.**

capsules two days later, the nightmare intensified. The company recorded 15,000 toll-free calls at its Tylenol hotline. Once again, production of Tylenol capsules was halted. "I'm heartsick," Burke told the press. "We didn't believe it could happen again, and nobody else did either."

This time, although Tylenol earned some 13 percent of the company's net profits, the firm decided once and for all to cease production of its over-the-counter medications in capsule form. It offered to replace all unused Tylenol capsules with new Tylenol caplets, a solid form of medication that was less tamper-prone (Figure 2-5). This time the withdrawal of its capsules cost Johnson & Johnson upward of $150 million after taxes.

(Courtesy of Johnson & Johnson)

FIGURE 2-5 **A special message.**

Once again, in the face of tragedy, the company and its chairman received high marks. As President Reagan said at a White House reception two weeks after the crisis hit, "Jim Burke of Johnson & Johnson, you have our deepest appreciation for living up to the highest ideals of corporate responsibility and grace under pressure."

Questions

1. What might have been the consequences if Johnson & Johnson had decided to "tough out" the first reports of Tylenol-related deaths and not recall the product?
2. What other public relations options did Johnson & Johnson have in responding to the first round of Tylenol murders?
3. Do you think the company made a wise decision by reintroducing extra-strength Tylenol?
4. In light of the response of other companies not to move precipitously when faced with a crisis, do you think Johnson & Johnson should have acted so quickly to remove the Tylenol product when the second round of Tylenol murders occurred in 1986?
5. What specific lessons can be derived from the way in which Johnson & Johnson handled the public relations aspects of these tragedies?
6. See what information Johnson & Johnson offers for its customers on the Tylenol Web site (www.tylenol.com). Follow the links to the "Care Cards," "House Calls," and "FAQ" sections. How do these sections demonstrate Johnson & Johnson's concern for customers? How do you think Johnson & Johnson would use this Web site to communicate with the public if new health scares surfaced?

*For further information on the first round of Tylenol murders, see Jerry Knight, "Tylenol's Maker Shows How to Respond to Crisis," *Washington Post* (October 11, 1982): 1; Thomas Moore, "The Fight to Save Tylenol," *Fortune* (November 29, 1982): 48; Michael Waldholz, "Tylenol Regains Most of No. 1 Market Share, Amazing Doomsayers," *Wall Street Journal* (December 24, 1982): 1, 19; and *60 Minutes,* CBS-TV, December 19, 1982.

For further information on the second round of Tylenol murders, see Irvin Molotsky, "Tylenol Maker Hopeful on Solving Poisoning Case," *New York Times* (February 20, 1986); Steven Prokesch, "A Leader in a Crisis," *New York Times* (February 19, 1986): B4; Michael Waldholz, "For Tylenol's Manufacturer, the Dilemma Is to Be Aggressive—But Not Appear Pushy," *Wall Street Journal* (February 20, 1986): 27; and "Tylenol II: How a Company Responds to a Calamity," *U.S. News & World Report* (February 24, 1986): 49.

For an overall overview of Johnson & Johnson and Tylenol, see Lawrence G. Foster, *Robert Wood Johnson: The Gentleman Rebel,* State College, PA: Lillian Press, 1999.

An Interview with Edward L. Bernays

Edward L. Bernays, who died in 1995 at the age of 103, was a public relations patriarch. A nephew of Sigmund Freud, Bernays pioneered the application of the social sciences to public relations. In partnership with his late wife, he advised presidents of the United States, industrial leaders, and legendary figures from Enrico Caruso to Eleanor Roosevelt. This interview was conducted with the legendary counselor in his 98th year.

When you taught the first public relations class, did you ever envision the field growing to its present stature?

I gave the first course in public relations after *Crystallizing Public Opinion* was published in 1923. I decided that one way to give the term "counsel on public relations" status was to lecture at a university on the principles, practices, and ethics of the new vocation. New York University was willing to accept my offer to do so. But I never envisioned at that time that the vocation would spread throughout the United States and then throughout the free world.

What were the objectives of that first public relations course?

The objectives were to give status to the new vocation. Many people still believed the term "counsel on public relations" was a euphemism for publicity man, press agent, flack. Even H. L. Mencken, in his book on the American language, ranked it as such. But in his *Supplement to the American Language,* published some years later, he changed his viewpoint and used my definition of the term.

What are the most significant factors that have led to the rise in public relations practice?

The most significant factor is the rise in people power and its recognition by leaders. Theodore Roosevelt helped bring this about with his Square Deal. Woodrow Wilson helped with his New Freedom, and so did Franklin Delano Roosevelt with his New Deal. And this tradition was continued as time went on.

Do you have any gripes with the way public relations is practiced today?

I certainly do. The meanings of words in the United States have the stability of soap bubbles. Unless words are defined as to their meaning by law, as in the case of professions—for instance, law, medicine, architecture—they are in the public domain. Anyone can use them. Recently, I received a letter from a model agency offering to supply me with a "public relations representative" for my next trade fair at which we might exhibit our client's products. Today, any plumber or car salesman or unethical character can call himself or herself a public relations practitioner. Many who call themselves public relations practitioners have no education, training, or knowledge of what the field is. And the public equally has little understanding of the meaning of the two words. Until licensing and registration are introduced, this will continue to be the situation.

What pleases you most about current public relations practice?

What pleases me most is that there are, indeed, practitioners who regard their activity as a profession, an art applied to a science, in which the public interest, and not pecuniary motivation, is the primary consideration; and also that outstanding leaders in society are grasping the meaning and significance of the activity.

How would you compare the caliber of today's public relations practitioner with that of the practitioner of the past?

The practitioner today has more education in his subject. But, unfortunately, education for public relations varies with the institution where it is being conducted. This is due to the lack of a standard definition. Many institutions of higher learning think public relations activity consists of skillful writing of press releases and teach their students accordingly. This is, of course, not true. Public relations activity is applied social science to the social attitudes or actions of employers or clients.

Where do you think public relations will be 20 years from now?
It is difficult to appraise where public relations will be 20 years from now. I don't like the tendency of advertising agencies gobbling up large public relations organizations. That is like surgical instrument manufacturers gobbling up surgical medical colleges or law book publishers gobbling up law colleges. However, if licensing and registration take place, then the vocation is assured a long lifetime, as long as democracy's.

Validation Part II

Chapter 3

Public Opinion

Public opinion is an elusive and fragile commodity. At least one respected public relations practitioner didn't like what he saw of it as the 20th century wound down. Said Chester Burger, a man who started a greatly successful agency and counseled some of the most powerful corporations of his era:

> *"The best public relations campaign in the world can't build trust while reality is destroying it. Reality limits what public relations can accomplish. Today's events are severely damaging the president, the Congress, and the judiciary, but inescapably are damaging the fiber of trust and integrity that is essential to binding together a democratic nation.[1]*

Among the reasons for Mr. Burger's dismay were the following unfortunate public opinion lapses as the century turned.

- *Microsoft Corporation, the largest and arguably most powerful corporation in the world, was accused by the U.S. Justice Department of unfair competitive practices. Its antitrust trial was highlighted when Microsoft CEO Bill Gates (the wealthiest man in the world) seemed to get caught in a fib about the necessity of his Microsoft operating system being coupled to his Microsoft browser.*
- *The equally powerful Walt Disney Company, maker of family entertainment, also found itself in court, in a messy trial involving former Disney superstar Jeffrey Katzenberg. At one point in the proceedings, it was revealed that CEO Michael Eisner referred to his former trusted lieutenant as "that little midget."*
- *Basketball Hall of Famer Julius Erving, universally respected as the picture of an ethical and high-standing individual, denied that he had lied about the existence of an illegitimate daughter, after a newspaper prepared to publish that Erving secretly had fathered tennis phenomenon Alexandra Stevenson.[2]*
- *Baseball's umpires, in an attempt to seize on public opinion, threatened as the 1999 season wound down to resign en masse if they didn't*

receive more money. When baseball's commissioner Bud Selig took them up on their offer and announced new umpires to replace them, the umpires immediately changed their minds and begged for their old jobs back.

☑ *The National Rifle Association, already reeling from public opinion problems, decided shortly after two crazed high school students massacred their fellow students at Colorado's Columbine High School, to not let the rampage hold up the NRA convention in Denver several weeks later.[3]*

☑ *CNN, the world's most respected 24-hour news network, was found to have created out of whole cloth a story accusing the U.S. military of using nerve gas in the war in Cambodia. CNN's president apologized to the military and the nation, and those responsible for the bogus broadcast were fired or resigned shortly thereafter.*

☑ *The leader of the free world, President Bill Clinton, one of the most popular U.S. presidents in history according to public opinion polls, blatantly lied to the people who elected him about a liaison with an intern in the White House.*

And these sordid examples, as tennis star Andre Agassi once said, were but "scratching the iceberg."

So perhaps Mr. Burger has a point after all: that recent times have not been good ones for dealing with the delicate commodity of public opinion.

On the other hand, there is Michael Jordan. Mr. Jordan, the most widely recognized former athlete in the world, is perhaps as skillful at managing his public image as any individual on the planet. At the close of the century, Mr. Jordan had suffered the tragic murder of his father, an ill-fated attempt at playing professional baseball, and assorted accusations of gambling and selfishness. He subsequently retired from professional basketball at the start of the 1999 season, presumably to spend the rest of his life in obscurity. Yeah, right! The year he quit pro basketball, Michael Jordan's income totaled upwards of $50 million and his net worth soared to more than $320 million. In terms of public opinion, Michael Jordan continued to be seen in television ads and enjoyed a sky-high image (Figure 3-1).

Meanwhile, Jordan's former teammate, Dennis Rodman, ranked on the other side of the spectrum, as he ignominiously quit pro basketball, pierced and tattooed his body, and then married-divorced-reunited (and then who knows what) with former

FIGURE 3-1 **Public opinion hero.** No other individual in the 21st century came close to rivaling the popular appeal of former basketball star and marketing conglomerate Michael Jordan. Even though Jordan retired from basketball in 1999, he continued to ride high as corporate spokesman for a diverse array of products, from MCI WorldCom telecommunications to McDonald's hamburgers, from Nike shoes to Kellogg's Wheaties. People around the world still yearned to "be like Mike."

FIGURE 3-2 **Public opinion villain.** On the other hand, no other sports figure in the 21st century evoked more strident opinions—many not nice—as Jordan's former Chicago Bulls teammate Dennis Rodman. Whether dressing in women's clothes, starring in action movies, authoring tell-all books or marrying "Baywatch" vixen Carmen Electra (for about 30 minutes), the irrepressible Rodman was a public opinion lightning rod.

Baywatch lifeguard Carmen Electra. As diametrically opposite Jordan as Rodman was, the wayward rebounder nonetheless took in an annual income somewhere in the lower—but not too low—millions (Figure 3-2).

Such are the peculiarities of public opinion in a celebrity-dominated culture. Usually it's difficult to move people toward a strong opinion on anything. It's even harder to move them away from an opinion once they reach it. Recent research, in fact, indicates that mass media appeals may have little immediate effect on influencing public opinion.

Nonetheless, the heart of public relations work lies in attempting to affect the public opinion process. Most public relations programs are designed either to (1) persuade people to change their opinion on an issue, product, or organization; (2) crystallize uninformed or undeveloped opinions; or (3) reinforce existing opinions.

So public relations professionals must understand how public opinion is formed, how it evolves from people's attitudes, and how it is influenced by communication. This chapter discusses attitude formation and change, and public opinion creation and persuasion.

What Is Public Opinion?

Public opinion, like public relations, is not easily explained. Newspaper columnist Joseph Kraft called public opinion "the unknown god to which moderns burn incense." Edward Bernays called it "a term describing an ill-defined, mercurial, and changeable group of individual judgments."[4] Princeton professor Harwood Childs, after coming up with no fewer than 40 different yet viable definitions, concluded with a definition by Herman C. Boyle: "Public opinion is not the name of something, but the classification of a number of somethings."[5]

Splitting public opinion into its two components, public and opinion, is perhaps the best way to understand the concept. Simply defined, public signifies a group of people who share a common interest in a specific subject—stockholders, for example, or employees or community residents. Each group is concerned with a common issue: the price of the stock, the wages of the company, or the building of a new plant.

An opinion is the expression of an attitude on a particular topic. When attitudes become strong enough, they surface in the form of opinions. When opinions become strong enough, they lead to verbal or behavioral actions.

A forest products company executive and an environmentalist from the Sierra Club might differ dramatically in their attitudes toward the relative importance of pollution control and continued industrial production. Their respective opinions on a piece of environmental legislation might also differ radically. In turn, how their organizations respond to that legislation—by picketing, petitioning, or lobbying—might also differ.

Public opinion, then, is the aggregate of many individual opinions on a particular issue that affects a group of people. Stated another way, public opinion represents a consensus. That consensus, deriving as it does from many individual opinions, really begins with people's attitudes toward the issue in question. Trying to influence an individual's attitude—how he or she thinks on a given topic—is a primary focus of the practice of public relations.

What Are Attitudes?

If an opinion is an expression of an attitude on a particular topic, what then is an attitude? Unfortunately, that also is not an easy question to answer. It had been generally assumed that attitudes are predispositions to think in a certain way about a certain topic. But recent research has indicated that attitudes may more likely be evaluations people make about specific problems or issues. These conclusions are not necessarily connected to any broad attitude.[6] For example, an individual might favor a company's response to one issue but disagree vehemently with its response to another. Thus, that individual's attitude may differ from issue to issue.

Attitudes are based on a number of characteristics.

1. **Personal**—the physical and emotional ingredients of an individual, including size, age, and social status.

2. **Cultural**—the environment and lifestyle of a particular country or geographic area, such as Japan versus the United States or rural America versus urban America. National political candidates often tailor messages to appeal to the particular cultural complexions of specific regions of the country.
3. **Educational**—the level and quality of a person's education. To appeal to the increased number of college graduates in the United States today, public communication has become more sophisticated.
4. **Familial**—people's roots. Children acquire their parents' tastes, biases, political partisanships, and a host of other characteristics. Some pediatricians insist that children pick up most of their knowledge in the first seven years, and few would deny the family's strong role in helping to mold attitudes.
5. **Religious**—a system of beliefs about God or the supernatural. Religion is making a comeback. In the 1960s, many young people turned away from formal religion. At the turn of the century, even after several evangelical scandals, religious fervor has reemerged.
6. **Social class**—position within society. As people's social status changes, so do their attitudes. For example, college students, unconcerned with making a living, may dramatically change their attitudes about such concepts as big government, big business, wealth, and prosperity after entering the job market.
7. **Race**—ethnic origin, which today increasingly helps shape people's attitudes. The history of blacks and whites in America has been stormy, with peaceful coexistence often frustrated. Nonetheless, minorities in our society, as a group, continue to improve their standard of living. In so doing, African Americans, Latinos, Asians, and others have retained pride in and allegiance to their cultural heritage. These characteristics help influence the formation of attitudes. So, too, do other factors, such as experience, economic class, and political and organizational memberships. Again, recent research has indicated that attitudes and behaviors are situational—influenced by specific issues in specific situations. Nonetheless, when others with similar attitudes reach similar opinions, a consensus, or public opinion, is born.

How Are Attitudes Influenced?

Strictly speaking, attitudes are positive, negative, or nonexistent. A person is for something, against it, or neutral. Studies show that for any one issue, most people don't care much one way or the other. A small percentage expresses strong support, and another small percentage expresses strong opposition. The vast majority is smack in the middle: passive, neutral, indifferent. Former Vice President Spiro T. Agnew called them "the silent majority." In many instances—political campaigns being a prime example—this silent majority holds the key to success because they are the group most readily influenced by a communicator's message.

It's hard to change the mind of a person who is staunchly opposed to a particular issue or individual. Likewise, it's easy to reinforce the support of a person who is wholeheartedly in favor of an issue or individual. Social scientist Leon Festinger discussed this concept when he talked about cognitive dissonance. He believed that individuals tend to avoid information that is dissonant or opposed to their own points of view and tend to seek out information that is consonant with, or in support of, their own attitudes.[7] An organization might attempt to remove dissonance to reach its goals. For example, in the face of stinging government attacks against cigarette smoking in the late 1990s, Philip Morris and other leading tobacco companies have adopted ambitious anti-smoking programs (see "Over the Top," chapter 17). Nonetheless, states' attorneys general and the U.S. Justice Department have continued to go after Big Tobacco for punitive damages.

As Festinger's theory intimates, the people whose attitudes can be influenced most readily are those who have not yet made up their minds. In politics this group is often referred to as the swing vote. Many elections have been won or lost on last-minute appeals to these politically undecided voters. In addition, it is possible to introduce information that may cause dissonance in the mind of a receiver.

Understanding this theory and its potential for influencing the silent majority is extremely important for the public relations practitioner, whose objective is to win support through clear, thoughtful, and persuasive communication. Moving a person from a latent state of attitude formation to a more aware state and finally to an active one becomes a matter of motivation.

Motivating Attitude Change

People are motivated by different factors, and no two people respond in exactly the same way to the same set of circumstances. Each of us is motivated by different drives and needs.

The most famous delineator of what motivates people was Abraham Maslow. His hierarchy of needs helps define the origins of motivation, which, in turn, help explain attitude change. Maslow postulated a five-level hierarchy:

1. The lowest order is physiological needs: a person's biological demands—food and water, sleep, health, bodily needs, exercise and rest, and sex
2. The second level is safety needs: security, protection, comfort and peace, and orderly surroundings
3. The third level is love needs: acceptance, belonging, love and affection, and membership in a group
4. The fourth level is esteem: recognition and prestige, confidence and leadership opportunities, competence and strength, intelligence and success
5. The highest order is self-actualization, or simply becoming what one is capable of becoming; self-actualization involves self-fulfillment and achieving a goal for the purposes of challenge and accomplishment[8]

FIGURE 3-3 **Celebrity opinion leaders.** Husband and wife animal activists Kim Basinger and Alec Baldwin lent their showbiz appeal to People for the Ethical Treatment of Animals for this provocative ad designed to influence public opinion.

According to Maslow, the needs of all five levels compose the fundamental motivating factors for any individual or public.

In the 1990s, as people once again get involved in causes—from abortion to animal rights to environmentalism—motivating attitude change becomes more important (Figure 3-3). Many activist groups, in fact, borrow heavily from psychological research on political activism to accomplish attitude change. Six cardinal precepts of political activism are instructive in attempting to change attitudes:

1. **Don't use graphic images unless they are accompanied by specific actions people can execute.** Many movements—the gay rights campaign and the antiabortion movement, for example—began by relying heavily on graphic images of death and destruction. But such images run the risk of pushing people away rather than drawing them in. Disturbing presentations rarely lead to a sustained attitude change.

2. **Go to the public instead of asking the public to come to you.** Most people will never become directly involved in an activist campaign. They will shy away. But by recognizing the limits of public interest and involvement, you can develop realistic strategies to capitalize on public goodwill without demanding more than people are willing to give.

3. **Don't assume that attitude change is necessary for behavior change.** A large body of psychological research casts doubt on the proposition that the best way to change behavior is to begin by changing attitudes. Indeed, the relationship between attitudes and behavior is often quite weak. Therefore, informing smokers of the link between cigarettes and cancer is far easier than getting them to kick the habit.

4. **Use moral arguments as adjuncts, not as primary thrusts.** Moral views are difficult to change. It is much easier to gain support by stressing the practical advantages of your solution rather than the immorality of your opponent's. For example, it is easier to convert people to a meatless diet by discussing the health benefits of vegetables than by discussing whether the Bible gives people dominion over animals.

5. **Embrace the mainstream.** In any campaign, people from all walks of life are necessary to win widespread approval. No campaign can be won if it is dubbed radical or faddish. That is why the involvement of all people must be encouraged in seeking attitude change.

6. **Don't offend the people you seek to change.** Research on persuasion shows that influence is usually strongest when people like the persuader and see the persuader as similar to themselves. It is impossible to persuade someone whom you have alienated. Or, as my mother used to say, "You can attract more flies with honey than you can with vinegar." The same applies to people.[9]

Power of Persuasion

Perhaps the most essential element in influencing public opinion is the principle of persuasion. Persuading is the goal of the vast majority of public relations programs. Persuasion theory has myriad explanations and interpretations. Basically, persuasion means getting another person to do something through advice, reasoning, or just plain arm-twisting. Books have been written on the enormous power of advertising and public relations as persuasive tools.

Social scientists and communications scholars take issue with the view of many public relations practitioners that a story on network news or the front page of the *New York Times* has a tremendous persuasive effect. Scholars argue that the media has a limited effect on persuasion, doing more to reinforce existing attitudes than to persuade toward a new belief. There is little doubt, however, that the persuasiveness of a message can be increased when it arouses or is accompanied by a high level of personal involvement. In other words, an individual who cares about something and is in fundamental agreement with an organization's basic position will tend to be persuaded by a message supporting that view.

According to the persuasion theory of Michael Ray, called "the hierarchies of effects," there are at least three basic orderings of knowledge, attitude, and behavior relative to persuasion:

1. When personal involvement is low and little difference exists between behavioral alternatives, knowledge changes are likely to lead directly to behavioral changes
2. When personal involvement is high but behavioral alternatives are indistinguishable, behavioral change is likely to be followed by attitudinal change, similar to Festinger's cognitive dissonance approach
3. When personal involvement is high and clear differences exist among alternatives, people act in a more rational manner: First, they learn about the issue; second, they evaluate the alternatives; then they act in a manner consistent with their attitudes and knowledge[10]

To these complex theories of persuasion is added the simpler, yet no less profound, notion of former First Lady Hillary Clinton, whose "Listening Tour" of New York State in contemplation of a senate race in 1999 was built on the proposition that "one of the best ways to persuade others is to listen to them." No matter how one characterizes persuasion, the goal of most communications programs is, in fact, to influence a receiver to take a desired action.

How are people persuaded? Saul Alinsky, a legendary radical organizer, had a simple theory of persuasion: "People only understand things in terms of their own experience . . . If you try to get your ideas across to others without paying attention to what they have to say to you, you can forget about the whole thing."[11] In other words, if you wish to persuade people, you must cite evidence that coincides with their own beliefs, emotions, and expectations.

What Kinds of "Evidence" Persuade People?

1. **Facts.** Facts are indisputable. Although it is true, as they say, that "statistics sometimes lie," empirical data is a persuasive device in hammering home a point of view. This is why any good public relations program will always start with research—the facts.
2. **Emotions.** Maslow was right. People do respond to emotional appeals—love, peace, family, patriotism. Ronald Reagan was known as "the great communicator" largely as a result of his appeal to emotion. Even when the nation was outraged in 1983, when 200 American soldiers died in a terrorist attack in Lebanon, President Reagan reversed the skepticism by talking of one wounded U.S. marine lying in a Lebanese bed.

   > That Marine, and all those others like him, living and dead, have been faithful to their ideals, they've given willingly of themselves so that a nearly defenseless people in a region of great strategic importance to the free world will have a chance someday to live lives free of murder and mayhem and terrorism.[12]

In latter years, American presidents have been loath to risk the deaths of so many Americans, so that wars from Kuwait to Kosovo, from Mogadishu to East Timor, were entered with caution. But in an earlier day, President Reagan could win the support of his countrymen with simple appeals to their patriotism. Such is the persuasive power of emotional appeals.

3. **Personalizing.** People respond to personal experience.

   ◪ When poet Maya Angelou talks about poverty, people listen and respect a woman who emerged from the dirt-poor environs of the Deep South in a day of segregation.
   ◪ When Congresswoman Carolyn McCarthy crusades about gun control, people understand that her husband was killed and son seriously injured by a crazed gunman on the Long Island Railroad.
   ◪ When former baseball pitcher Jim Abbott talks about dealing with adversity, people marvel at a star athlete born with only one arm.

   Again, few can refute knowledge gained from personal experience.

4. **Appealing to "you."** The one word that people never tire of hearing is "you." "What is in this for me?" is the question that everyone asks. So one secret to persuading is to constantly think in terms of the audience and constantly refer to "you."

As simple as these four precepts are, they are difficult to grasp—particularly for business leaders, who frown on emotion or personalizing or even appealing to an audience. Some consider it "beneath them" to show human emotion. This, of course, is a mistake. The power to persuade—to influence public opinion—is the measure not only of a charismatic but an effective leader.[13]

Influencing Public Opinion

Public opinion is a lot easier to measure than it is to influence. However, a thoughtful public relations program can crystallize attitudes, reinforce beliefs, and occasionally change public opinion. First, the opinions to be changed or modified must be identified and understood. Second, target publics must be clear. Third, the public relations professional must have in sharp focus the "laws" that govern public opinion—as amorphous as they may be.

In that context, the 15 Laws of Public Opinion, developed many years ago by social psychologist Hadley Cantril, remain pertinent:

1. Opinion is highly sensitive to important events.
2. Events of unusual magnitude are likely to swing public opinion temporarily from one extreme to another. Opinion doesn't become stabilized until the implications of events are seen in some perspective.
3. Opinion is generally determined more by events than by words—unless those words are themselves interpreted as an event.
4. Verbal statements and outlines of courses of action have maximum importance when opinion is unstructured and people are suggestible and seek some interpretation from a reliable source.
5. By and large, public opinion doesn't anticipate emergencies—it only reacts to them.
6. Opinion is basically determined by self-interest. Events, words, or any other stimuli affect opinion only insofar as their relationship to self-interest is apparent.
7. Opinion doesn't remain aroused for a long period of time unless people feel that their self-interest is acutely involved or unless opinion—aroused by words—is sustained by events.
8. Once self-interest is involved, opinions aren't easily changed.

9. When self-interest is involved, public opinion in a democracy is likely to be ahead of official policy.

10. When an opinion is held by a slight majority or when opinion is not solidly structured, an accomplished fact tends to shift opinion in the direction of acceptance.

11. At critical times, people become more sensitive to the adequacy of their leadership. If they have confidence in it, they are willing to assign more than usual responsibility to it; if they lack confidence in it, they are less tolerant than usual.

12. People are less reluctant to have critical decisions made by their leaders if they feel that somehow they themselves are taking part in the decision.

13. People have more opinions and are able to form opinions more easily on goals than on methods to reach those goals.

14. Public opinion, like individual opinion, is colored by desire. And when opinion is based chiefly on desire, rather than on information, it is likely to shift with events.

15. By and large, if people in a democracy are provided with educational opportunities and ready access to information, public opinion reveals a hardheaded common sense. The more enlightened people are to the implications of events and proposals for their own self-interest, the more likely they are to agree with the more objective opinions of realistic experts.[14]

BACKGROUNDER

Rescuing a Red-Faced Disney

Few great organizations have gone through as much stress in recent years as the heralded Walt Disney Company.

While most entertainment companies were the darlings of Wall Street as the century turned, Disney was battered in a series of corporate missteps and ill fortunes, including:

- hiring and then firing incompetent executives (Michael Ovitz)
- losing and then suing competent ones (Jeffrey Katzenberg)
- being attacked by feminists for the "The Little Mermaid"
- being attacked by Civil War buffs objecting to the company's plans (later aborted) to build a theme park on the historic Manassas, Virginia, battleground
- being attacked by animal activists for the mysterious deaths of several exotic critters at its $800 million Animal Kingdom in Orlando.

The battered Disney public relations department thought it could breathe a sigh of relief when in early 1999 the firm released the video version of the top-selling animated movie in history, *The Rescuers*. The film takes grade schoolers through the magical adventures of costarring mice Bianca and Bernie as they tour the wonders of the world.

Regrettably, as freeze frames of the video subsequently revealed, that's not all they tour.

Unbeknownst to Disney when it shipped the blockbuster movie, embedded within two frames of the 110,000 frame film were images of a topless woman, the remnant of an apparent prank perpetrated when the film was first released in 1977. When embarrassed Disney officials froze the film to reveal Bianca and Bernie winging by the topless woman's window, they immediately recalled 3.4 million copies.

The recall, a first for Disney, was seized upon by religious fundamentalists, who have claimed for years that the company produces pornographic images. Indeed a spokesman for the Southern Baptist Convention's Ethics and Religious Liberty Commission praised Disney for doing the right thing and then added, "Such immoral high jinks from Disney are not surprising."*

Poor Disney couldn't win for losing.

Bruce Orwall, "Disney Recalls 'The Rescuers' Video Containing Image of a Topless Woman," The Wall Street Journal, January 9, 1999, B2.

Polishing the Corporate Image

Most organizations today and the people who manage them are extremely sensitive to the way they are perceived by their critical publics. This represents a dramatic change in corporate attitude from years past. In the 1960s, 1970s, and well into the 1980s, only the most enlightened companies dared to maintain anything but a low profile. Management, frankly, was reluctant to step out publicly, "to stand up for what it stood for."

In the 1990s, however, organizations—particularly large ones—had little choice but to go public. In the new millennium, organizations have learned that the intrusiveness and impersonality of the computer is yet another reason to stay in touch with their primary publics.

Consider the following corporate "learning experiences" from recent years:

- Bedrock American companies, heretofore the symbols of pristine and silent management decorum, were crucified for lackluster executives, inefficient organizations, and, ultimately, falling profits. In rapid succession, the chairmen of General Motors Corporation, American Express Company, AT&T, and IBM were beheaded in brutally public bloodlettings. So sensitive were big companies to public approval that some didn't wait to announce management problems. When Southwest Airlines Co. CEO Herb Kelleher contracted prostate cancer in 1999, he announced it immediately to analysts and the press and even "warned" subordinates that as a result of sticking around headquarters for treatments, "I'll probably be in the office more than usual."[15]

- Kelleher's frank but lighthearted reaction to his illness stood in sharp contrast to The Walt Disney Company's response to a related occurrence. When Disney CEO Michael Eisner underwent emergency quadruple bypass surgery in 1994, the company was typically tight-lipped about status and prognosis. "We're not discussing it," sniffed the firm's communications chief.[16] What compounded the issue was that Eisner had no successor in place.

- Two years later, in 1996, Disney again found itself in the succession soup, when touted superagent Michael Ovitz, whom Eisner had picked as his successor, was canned less than a year after joining the team. Ovitz was paid an outrageous $36 million in severance pay for the humiliation. Disney had noncommunicative egg on its face.

- In 1999, when Microsoft claimed at its Justice Department trial that it was impossible to de-link its browser from its operating system, the federal judge in the case brought in his laptop computer and proved that Microsoft's claim was false.

Most organizations today understand clearly that it takes a great deal of time to build a favorable image for a corporation but only one slip to create a negative public impression. In other words, the corporate image is a fragile commodity. Yet, most firms also believe that a positive corporate image is essential for continued long-term success.

In the 1970s, United Technologies Corporation ran a famous series of ads speaking to the importance of corporate reputation. As Ray D'Argenio, the former communications director of United Technologies, put it, "Corporate communications can't create a corporate character. A company already has a character, which communications can reinforce"[17] (Figure 3-4).

**Brighten
Your Corner**

Have you
noticed the
great difference
between the
people you
meet?
Some are as
sunshiny as
a handful of
forget-me-nots.
Others come on
like frozen mackerel.
A cheery, comforting
nurse can
help make a
hospital stay
bearable.
An upbeat secretary
makes visitors
glad they came
to see you.
Every corner of the
world has its clouds,
gripes, complainers,
and pains in the
neck—because many
people have
yet to
learn that
honey works better
than vinegar.
You're in control
of *your* small
corner of the
world.
Brighten it. . .
You *can*.

FIGURE 3-4 Although many companies attempted to construct a differentiable corporate image through advertising, few succeeded as well as United Technologies, which kept its messages succinct, savvy, and sparkling in a series of historic corporate image ads.

Beware the Traps of Public Opinion

Analyzing public opinion is not as easy as it looks. Once a company wins favorable public opinion for a product or an idea, the trick is to maintain it (Figure 3-5). The worst thing to do is sit back and bask in the glory of a positive public image; that's a quick route to image deterioration (Figure 3-6).

A QUESTION OF ETHICS

Bigger, Richer, Dumber

In the 21st century, there is no corporation more massive or powerful than mighty Microsoft. Run by the fabled computer genius Bill Gates, whose net worth through Microsoft stock alone has been valued in excess of $100 billion—thus distinguishing him as the wealthiest person in the world—Microsoft can call the shots in virtually any market around the world.

Pity it's such a public relations bozo.

Microsoft, despite its size and clout, developed a reputation through the 1990s of being aloof, arrogant, and heavy-handed in dealing with anyone who got in its way. This attitude culminated during its Justice Department trial in 1998, when it was shown to have lied to the court about its inability to include the opposing Netscape browser in its operating system.

Microsoft was mightily humiliated by this apparent ethical breach and sought to make amends.

Early in 1999, Microsoft and its CEO became the paragons of ethical propriety and corporate responsibility. The company and the Bill Gates Foundation agreed to donate millions of dollars worth of computers to public schools across the country. This was followed up by a pledge to donate $1 billion for public schools in minority areas.

Gates himself set out to dispel the image of arrogance. He sat down at home for a *20/20* interview with Barbara Walters. He penned a folksy column for his on-line publication, *Slate,* about how he preferred doughnuts and hamburgers to stretch limos and tuxedos. Why, the billion-dollar CEO even agreed to a tête-à-tête with *Live—Regis and Kathy Lee.*

And then, just when it looked like the image of a new, more ethical Microsoft would take hold, another shoe dropped. Late in 1999, the *New York Times* revealed that newspaper advertisements presented by a seemingly unbiased California institute that offered "independent views" supporting Microsoft's antitrust stance were secretly paid for by—any guesses?

The full-page ads, published in leading U.S. newspapers by the Independent Institute of Oakland, took the form of a letter signed by 240 academic experts, many of whom were mightily upset when they learned who really had foot the bill for their support.

Said one Temple University economist who signed the ad, "It's not right to use people as a vehicle for special interests."

Which begs the question, How can a company as smart as Microsoft be so dumb when it comes to managing public opinion?

Public opinion is changeable, and in assessing it, communicators are susceptible to a number of subtle yet lethal traps.

- ☑ *Cast in stone.* This fallacy assumes that just because public opinion is well established on a certain issue, it isn't likely to change. Not true. Consider an issue such as women's liberation. In the early 1960s, people laughed at the handful of women raising a ruckus about equal rights, equal pay, and equal treatment. By the early 1970s, women's liberation pervaded every sector of our culture. By the 1980s, trail-blazing women leaders, such as Golda Meir in Israel, had paved the way for the dominant world leadership of Margaret Thatcher in Great Britain. By the year 2000, women were taking leadership roles in the U.S. Congress, running for the U.S. presidency, and starring in collegiate and professional sports ranks. Nobody was laughing anymore.

- ☑ *Gut reaction.* This fallacy assumes that if management feels in its corporate gut that the public will lean strongly in a certain direction, then that must be the way to go. Be careful. Some managements are so cut off from the real world that their knee-jerk reactions to issues often turn out to be more jerk than

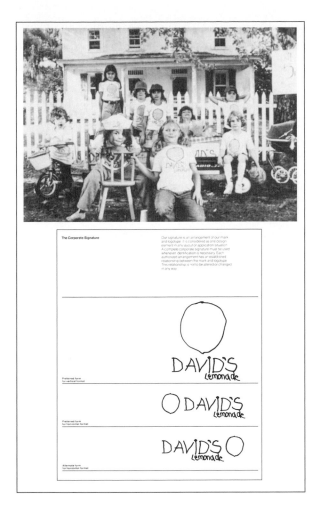

FIGURE 3-5 The key to a corporate image that gets through to people is a combination of simplicity, unity, and balance. These excerpts from the corporate identity manual of David's Lemonade, the creation of Fulton + Partners, Inc., are examples of a clear corporate image.

FIGURE 3-6 The Xerox Corporation has a unique name and logo problem. The Xerox name is so widely used that it must fight a continual battle to have the name treated as a proper adjective with a capital X, rather than a verb with a lowercase x—thus the frustration expressed in this ad. Complicating the issue, in the new millennium Xerox wants to be known not as the "copier company" but as the "document company."

anything else. One former auto company executive, perhaps overstating the case, described the problem this way: "There's no forward response to what the public wants today. It's gotten to be a total insulation from the realities of the world." Certainly, management's instincts in dealing with the public may be questionable at times. Generally, gut-reaction judgments should be avoided in assessing public opinion.

■ *General public.* There may well be a public at large, but there's no such thing as the general public. Even the smallest public can be subdivided. No two people are alike, and messages to influence public opinion should be as pointed as possible rather than scatter shot. Sometimes individuals may qualify as members of publics on both sides of an issue. In weighing the pros and cons of lower speed limits, for example, many people are both drivers and pedestrians. Categorizing them into one general group can be a mistake.

☑ *Words move mountains.* Perhaps they do sometimes, but public opinion is usually influenced more by events than by words. For example, the brutal 1998 slaying of a gay man, Matthew Shepard, because he was gay triggered nationwide concern about gay rights. Ironically, a year after Mr. Shepard's murder, there had been a record number of gay murders, causing some to fear a backlash.[18]

☑ *Brother's keeper.* It's true that most people will rise up indignantly if a fellow citizen has been wronged. But they'll get a lot more indignant if they feel they themselves have been wronged. In other words, self-interest often sparks public opinion. An organization wishing to influence public opinion might be well advised to ask initially, "What's in this for the people whose opinion we're trying to influence?"

BACKGROUNDER

Most Respected High-Tech Companies

Internet companies may indeed be taking over America, but they still haven't surpassed more tried and true companies when it comes to commanding the highest public opinion.

According to research at the end of the old millennium, America's most respected company at the end of the 20th century was none other than Johnson & Johnson, thanks primarily to the reputation it gained in handling the Tylenol murders.*

The top 10 most respected American companies rolled out thusly:

1. Johnson & Johnson
2. The Coca-Cola Company
3. Hewlett-Packard Company
4. Intel Corporation
5. Ben & Jerry's Homemade, Inc.
6. Wal-Mart Stores, Inc.
7. Xerox Corporation
8. The Home Depot, Inc.
9. Gateway, Inc.
10. The Walt Disney Company

The world's highest-valued company, Microsoft, came out 15th on the most respected list. In terms of the dot coms, the only two Internet-oriented corpora-

tions to penetrate the 20 most highly reputed high-tech companies were Red Hat and Yahoo! But with new Internet dynamos like Real Networks arriving on the scene at cyber-speed, the rankings were subject to rapid shift. Good thing for some. Of the 40 companies ranked, Amazon.com placed only 22nd, and America Online, the subject of service problems and consumer complaints, came in dead last.

Please check back 1,000 years from now to see how the list has changed during the current millennium.

*Based on research conducted by Harris Interactive Inc. and the Reputation Institute as reported in Ronald Alsop, "The Best Corporate Reputations in America," Wall Street Journal, September 23, 1999, C-1; and "Reputation Survey Names Digital 40," O'Dwyer's Newsletter, December 6, 1999, 6.

S U M M A R Y

Influencing public opinion remains at the heart of professional public relations work. Perhaps the key to realizing this objective is anticipating or keeping ahead of trends in our society. Anticipating trends is no easy task. But in the new millennium, trend watching has developed into a veritable cottage industry. One self-styled prognosticator riding the crest of trend analysis was John Naisbitt, whose book *Megatrends 2000* claimed to predict the new directions that would influence American lives in the 21st century. Among them are the following:

- Inflation and interest rates will be held in check
- There will be a shift from welfare to workfare
- There will be a shift from public housing to home ownership
- There will be a shift from sports to the arts as the primary leisure preference
- Consumers will demand more customized products
- The media will amplify bad economic news
- The rise of the Pacific Rim will be seen in terms of economic dominance
- Asia will add 80 million more people
- CEOs in a global economy will become more important and better known than political figures[19]

Some might argue that there is nothing revolutionary in these megatrends (and they might well be right). Nonetheless, such trends deserve to be scrutinized, analyzed, and evaluated by organizations in order to deal more effectively with the future. As the late public relations counselor Philip Lesly once pointed out, "The real problems faced by business today are in the outside world of intangibles and public attitudes."[20] To keep ahead of these intangibles, these public attitudes, and these kernels of future public opinion, managements will turn increasingly to professional public relations practitioners for guidance.

B A C K G R O U N D E R

The Longest Takeout

In the new millennium, with the competition for name recognition so intense, companies have had to resort to extreme measures to get noticed; few have been as far-reaching as Tricon Global Restaurants.

In 1999, the owners of Pizza Hut, Inc. announced plans to put the Pizza Hut logo on a Russian rocket carrying a piece of the International Space Station.

Plans called for a 30-foot advertisement to be placed on a 200-foot Proton rocket, carrying the station's living quarters. According to Pizza Hut CEO Mike Rawlings, the cost of the rocket sponsorship was about $1.2 million, roughly half the cost of a 30-second Super Bowl spot.

The rocket logo was a lot more viable than the company's initial preference. Pizza Hut communicators first considered putting the logo directly on the moon with lasers. But after consulting with astronomers and physicists, they found that the image would have to be as big as Texas to be seen from Earth and would have cost hundreds of millions of dollars.

Sounds like the rocket was a real bargain.

Discussion Starters

1. What is public opinion?
2. What are attitudes, and on what characteristics are they based?
3. How are attitudes influenced?
4. What is Maslow's hierarchy of needs?
5. Explain the law of cognitive dissonance.
6. How difficult is it to change a person's behavior?
7. What are Cantril's Laws of Public Opinion?
8. What kinds of "evidence" persuade people?
9. What were the elements of Disney's public opinion problem?
10. What are the traps of public opinion?

Notes

1. Chester Burger, Remarks to The Institute for Public Relations, Union League Club, New York, NY, December 2, 1998.
2. Selena Roberts, "Doctor J's Amazing Free Pass," *New York Times* (August 28, 1999): B15.
3. Matt Bai, "Clouds Over Gun Valley," *Newsweek* (August 23, 1999): 34.
4. Cited in Edward L. Bernays, *Crystallizing Public Opinion* (New York: Liveright, 1961): 61.
5. Cited in Harwood L. Childs, *Public Opinion: Nature, Formation, and Role* (Princeton, NJ: Van Nostrand, 1965): 15.
6. James E. Grunig and Todd Hunt, *Managing Public Relations* (New York: Holt, Rinehart & Winston, 1984): 130.
7. Leon A. Festinger, *A Theory of Cognitive Dissonance* (New York: Harper & Row, 1957): 163.
8. Abraham Maslow, *Motivation and Personality* (New York: Harper & Row, 1954).
9. S. Plous, "Toward More Effective Activism," *The Animal's Agenda* (December 1989): 24–26.
10. John V. Pavlik, *Public Relations: What Research Tells Us* (Newbury Park, CA: Sage, 1987): 74.
11. Saul D. Alinsky, *Rules for Radicals* (New York: Vintage Books, 1971): 81.
12. Ronald W. Reagan, Address by the President to the Nation, October 27, 1983.
13. Robert L. Dilenschneider, *Power and Influence* (New York: Prentice Hall, 1990): 5.
14. Hadley Cantril, *Gauging Public Opinion* (Princeton, NJ: Princeton University Press, 1972): 226–230.
15. "Southwest Airlines Chairman Begins Medical Treatment," Southwest Airlines news release, August 11, 1999.
16. Fraser P. Seitel, "Who's Runnin' the Company?" *Public Relations Tactics* (September 1994): 13.

17. Ray D'Argenio, speech at the Communications Executive of the Year Luncheon, sponsored by Corpcom Services, December 10, 1981.

18. Debbie Howlett and Patrick O'Driscoll, "Murder of Gays on the Rise," *USA Today* (October 11, 1999): 1.

19. John Naisbitt and Patricia Aburdene, *Megatrends 2000* (New York: Morrow, 1990).

20. Philip Lesly, "How the Future Will Shape Public Relations—and Vice Versa," *Public Relations Quarterly* (Winter 1981–82): 7.

Suggested Readings

Bleile, Paul. "PR & Propaganda . . . Where Do You Draw the Line?" *Communication World* (June–July 1998): 26ff

Creedon, Pamela J. *Women in Mass Communications: Challenging General Values.* Newbury Park, CA: Sage, 1989.

Crespi, Irving. *The Public Opinion Process: How the People Speak.* Mahwah, NJ: Lawrence Erlbaum Associates Inc., 1997.

Edelstein, Alex. S. *Total Propaganda: From Mass Culture to Popular Culture.* Mahwah, NJ: Lawrence Erlbaum Associates Inc., 1997.

Gilbert, Dennis A. *Compendium of American Public Opinion.* New York: Facts on File, 1988.

Glasser, Theodore L., and Charles T. Salmon. *Public Opinion and the Communication of Consent.* New York: Guiford Press, 1995. Anthology of articles spanning the history of the role of public opinion from ancient to contemporary times.

Kauffamn, James. "NASA in Crisis: The Space Agency's Public Relations Effort Regarding the Hubble Space Telescope," *Public Relations Review* (Spring 1997): 1–10.

Lipset, Seymour Martin, and William Schneider. *The Confidence Gap: Business, Labor and Government in the Public.* New York: Free Press, 1988.

McCombs, Maxwell, et al. *Contemporary Public Opinion: Issues and the News.* Hillsdale, NJ: Lawrence Erlbaum Associates, 1991.

Morley, Michael. *How to Manage Your Global Reputation: A Guide to the Dynamics of International Public Relations.* New York: New York University Press, 1998.

Pratt, Cornelius B. "The 40-Year Tobacco Wars: Giving Public Relations a Black Eye?" *Public Relations Quarterly* (Winter 1997–98): 5–10.

www.mediainfo.com. Editor & Publisher magazine's database offers access to more than 11,000 news Web sites.

www.prnewswire.com. Public Relations Newswire. Features corporate press releases and background, with a link to Expert Contacts.

www.publicagenda.org. Public Agenda Online. "The inside source for public opinion and policy analysis."

Young, Davis. *Building Your Company's Good Name: How to Create and Protect the Reputation Your Organization Wants and Deserves.* New York: AMACOM, 1996.

CASE STUDY

Pepsi Punctures the Great Syringe Soda Scare

PepsiCo's worst nightmare began inauspiciously enough on June 10, 1993, when an elderly Fircrest, Washington, couple claimed that they had discovered a syringe floating inside a can of Diet Pepsi.

For the next two weeks, the 50,000 people of PepsiCo—from CEO and corporate communications staff to independent bottlers—worked around the clock to mount a massive public relations offensive that effectively thwarted a potential business disaster for its 95-year-old trademark and a potential devastating blow to one of the world's foremost consumer reputations.

The Pepsi case is a tribute to sound communications thinking and rapid, decisive public relations action in the face of imminent corporate catastrophe. The day after the Fircrest complaint, a nearby Tacoma woman reported finding another hypodermic needle in a can of Diet Pepsi. The story of the two tampered cans—initially labeled "some sort of sabotage" by the local Pepsi bottler—ran on the Associated Press wire nationwide and sent shock waves throughout the country.

PepsiCo, while immediately forming a crisis management team headed by its president and CEO, Craig Weatherup, nonetheless chose to "hold its powder" publicly while first assessing all pertinent facts about the two incidents and devoting attention to the Seattle plant. Pepsi's perceived reluctance to confront the problem in a dramatic way—while it worked "behind the scenes"—drew initial fire from so-called crisis experts. One management communications professor warned, "They are underestimating the potential for rumors to feed off one another." Another crisis management counselor said, "This will be a terrible mistake if it turns out they should have acted in light of later events."

On June 13, the commissioner of the Food and Drug Administration (FDA), David A. Kessler, warned consumers in Washington, Oregon, Alaska, Hawaii, and Guam "to inspect closely cans of Diet Pepsi for signs of tampering and to pour the contents into a glass or cup before drinking."

In the face of criticism and with copycat tamperings accelerating, PepsiCo held its ground. Although critics urged the company to recall its products, the company continued to insist that its cans were virtually tamperproof. "We are 99 percent sure that you cannot open one and reseal it without its being obvious," the company assured its customers. Because there was "no health risk to either of the two consumers who filed the complaints or to the general public," PepsiCo urged its bottlers and general managers not to remove the product from shelves.

On June 14, PepsiCo issued an internal "consumer advisory" to its bottlers and general managers, reporting the results of its initial research on the reported claims:

- ☑ "The syringes that were found are those commonly used by diabetics for insulin. We do not have syringes of this type in any of our production facilities."
- ☑ "All cans used for Pepsi-Cola products are new packages. They are not reused or refilled at any time. There are two visual inspections during production: the first before cans are filled, the second while cans are on the filling line. The cans are then sealed."

PepsiCo's strong inference was that first, the speed and security of its bottling production process made it extremely unlikely that any foreign object could appear in an unopened Pepsi container, and second, what was being inserted wasn't being put into cans at the factory.

By June 14, the nation was awash in copycat Pepsi-Cola tamperings. PepsiCo was barraged with reports of syringes in its cans from Louisiana to New York, from Missouri to Wyoming, from Pennsylvania to Southern California. Adding to PepsiCo's nightmare was a media feeding frenzy the likes of which the company had never before encountered.

- ☑ "A 'Scared' Firm Fights to Save Its Good Name"—*New York Post*
- ☑ "FDA Warns Diet-Pepsi Drinkers"—Associated Press
- ☑ "Diet Pepsi Drinkers Warned of Debris"—*USA Today*
- ☑ "No Program for a Recall of Diet Pepsi"—*New York Times*

Pepsi tampering stories dominated the national media, leading the evening news and network morning programs for three days. Local crews throughout the nation positioned themselves at local Pepsi bottling plants. PepsiCo's president and six-person public relations staff put in 20-hour days in the company's Somers, New York, headquarters, each fielding 80 to 100 inquiries daily. The company was besieged by syringe-tampering mania.

Late on the evening of June 15, PepsiCo received its first break. A man in central Pennsylvania was arrested on the charge that he had fraudulently reported finding a syringe in a can of Pepsi.

With the first arrest made, PepsiCo seized the offensive.

MEDIA RELATIONS
PepsiCo's media strategy centered on one medium: television. Downplaying traditional print media—"the press conference is a dinosaur"—PepsiCo's communications

executives launched daily satellite feeds to the nation's electronic media to get out its side of the tampering allegations.

- An initial video news release (VNR) picturing the high-speed can-filling lines, (see figure 3-8) with voice-over narration by a plant manager, conveyed the message of a manufacturing process built on speed, safety, and integrity, in which tampering with products would be highly unlikely. The goal was to show that the canning process was safe. The initial VNR was seen by 187 million viewers (more than watched the 1993 Super Bowl) on 399 stations in 178 markets across the United States.
- A second VNR, picturing PepsiCo President Weatherup and additional production footage, reported the first arrest for a false claim of tampering. It made four critical points: (1) complaints of syringes reported to be found in Diet Pepsi cans in other cities are unrelated; (2) tampering appears to be happening after cans are opened; (3) the soft drink can is one of the safest packages for consumer food products; and (4) a recall is not warranted. This PepsiCo-produced VNR was seen by 70 million viewers on 238 stations in 136 markets.
- A third VNR, narrated by President Weatherup, presented a segment from a convenience store surveillance video (see figure 3-9) in which a woman was caught inserting a syringe into an open Diet Pepsi can. Weatherup thanked consumers for their support, reported additional arrests, and reaffirmed PepsiCo's decision not to recall its product. This surveillance video was broadcast to 95 million viewers on 325 stations in 159 markets and, in effect, "broke the back" of the Pepsi syringe scare.

FIGURE 3-8 Video news release. The subject of PepsiCo's first VNR to reassure the public about its processing speed and safety was this rapid glimpse of a Pepsi bottling plant.

☑ In addition to the VNRs, PepsiCo's media offensive included appearances by the company's president and a product safety expert on as many talk shows as could be fit into their schedules—each of the three major network evening newscasts, ABC's *Nightline,* CNN's *Larry King Live,* and so on.

PepsiCo's video media blitz was unparalleled in corporate public relations history.

GOVERNMENT RELATIONS

Meanwhile, PepsiCo cooperated fully with Commissioner Kessler and the FDA. While other consumer firms have adopted an adversarial position toward the watchdog agency, PepsiCo embraced the FDA's investigation.

It was the FDA's Office of Criminal Investigation (OCI), in fact, that reported the breakthrough in the arrest of the man in central Pennsylvania. In addition to the FDA's "consumer alert" in the Pacific Northwest, Commissioner Kessler issued a statement on the tampering and the possibility of copycats. Later, Mr. Kessler appeared with Weatherup on *Nightline* and took the unprecedented step of declaring that "calm is in order . . . a recall is not necessary."

On June 17, Commissioner Kessler held a press conference in Washington, D.C., unequivocally characterizing the controversy as a hoax—the product of "misguided

SCENES OF AN ALLEGED PRODUCT TAMPERING

FRAME: 08:32:15

An opened can of Diet Pepsi, held by a Colorado woman, appears to be lowered behind the counter of a convenience store, out of the clerk's line of sight.

FRAME: 08:32:27

The woman fumbles with her purse and pulls out what appears to be a syringe.

FRAME: 08:32:34

The woman appears to place the syringe in the opened can of Diet Pepsi while keeping it behind the counter.

FRAME: 08:32:39

The woman places the can back on the counter then asks the clerk for a cup into which she pours the Diet Pepsi and allegedly discovers the syringe.

FIGURE 3-9 Smoking gun. The evidence ending the Pepsi tampering hoax was this surveillance video of a woman caught stuffing a syringe into a Pepsi can.

individual acts, magnified and multiplied by the attendant glare of the media, and a predictable outbreak of copycat behavior."

On June 21, PepsiCo President Weatherup wrote to President Clinton, thanking him for the "excellent work" of Mr. Kessler and the FDA "in pursuing the recent product tampering hoax."

EMPLOYEE RELATIONS

In the area of employee relations—with its staff and bottlers—PepsiCo adopted a policy of full and immediate disclosure as soon as it had discerned the pertinent facts.

Consumer advisories were dispatched at least once a day, usually twice or three times on each day of the crisis, letting bottlers and general managers in PepsiCo's 400 field locations know what was going on, what had been reported, what the government was doing, and how the company was responding.

Managers were advised on how to "communicate with employees and customers" in the form of "Product Tampering Guidelines," as well as in procedures for reporting alleged tamperings.

President Weatherup also personally wrote to bottlers and general managers periodically during the crisis to keep them advised of breaking developments. When the surveillance video was found, Mr. Weatherup sent all Pepsi bottlers, by overnight mail, a videotape of Commissioner Kessler's news conference, along with the surveillance footage.

"Please share it with your customers," the president suggested.

By June 18, just one week—and what seemed like one millennium—after its product and reputation had been challenged, PepsiCo declared victory in national ads see figure 3-10:

Pepsi is pleased to announce . . . nothing.

What had begun as the worst kind of national nightmare, with critics and copycats threatening the company at every juncture, ended in a flurry of pervasive public praise. "Media-smart Pepsi" is how *Advertising Age* characterized the company's strategy. The *Milwaukee Sentinel,* in a rare journalistic admission of candor, labeled the media's leap to sensationalism on the Pepsi story "a mistake, a big mistake." *Business Week* credited the company for making "the right moves, Baby." The company was universally heralded for holding the line on a product recall and putting on the line its reputation and credibility.

Perhaps sweetest of all for PepsiCo, after the FDA/OCI's arrest of 55 suspected hoaxers, was the bottom-line aftermath: Not only had PepsiCo weathered the media storm and emerged with its credibility intact, but the impact on Pepsi's sales was negligible. President Weatherup reported that sales had fallen just 3 percent at the height of the crisis, approximately $30 million. By July and August, Pepsi sales were up 7 percent, the best summer in five years (Figure 3-11).

All in all, as one industry periodical put it, "Pepsi's response constituted nothing less than 'a textbook case' of how to come through a PR crisis."

Questions

1. Do you think PepsiCo erred by not immediately volunteering to recall its product?
2. How would you assess PepsiCo's overall public relations strategy?
3. How would you assess PepsiCo's government relations strategy?

Pepsi is pleased to announce...

...nothing.

As America now knows, those stories about Diet Pepsi were a hoax. Plain and simple, not true. Hundreds of investigators have found no evidence to support a single claim.

As for the many, many thousands of people who work at Pepsi-Cola, we feel great that it's over. And we're ready to get on with making and bringing you what we believe is the best-tasting diet cola in America.

There's not much more we can say. Except that most importantly, we won't let this hoax change our exciting plans for this summer.

We've set up special offers so you can enjoy our great quality products at prices that will save you money all summer long. It all starts on July 4th weekend and we hope you'll stock up with a little extra, just to make up for what you might have missed last week.

That's it. Just one last word of thanks to the millions of you who have stood with us.

Drink All The Diet Pepsi You Want.
Uh Huh.

DIET PEPSI and UH-HUH are registered trademarks of PepsiCo. Inc

FIGURE 3-10 Whew. With its crisis proven to be a hoax, PepsiCo triumphantly proclaimed its victory with this ad.

4. What were the pros and cons of ignoring print media and focusing instead on electronic media? Could this strategy backfire on PepsiCo?
5. What were the pros and cons of using PepsiCo's president as chief spokesperson?
6. What public relations lessons can be drawn from PepsiCo's experience for handling future product tampering cases?

FIGURE 3-11 **Case closed.** Uh huh!

7. To learn how PepsiCo is communicating with the public these days, visit its corporate Web site (www.pepsico.com). Follow the links to "Press Releases," then click on "Pepsi Releases." What topics do most of the recent Pepsi press releases focus on? If another syringe soda scare occurred, where on the Web site would you advise PepsiCo to post its position and actions?

For further information about the Pepsi syringe scare case, see Claudia Carpenter, "A 'Scared' Firm Fights to Save Its Good Name," *New York Post,* June 17, 1993, 25; Gerry Hinckley, " 'Big Mistake' Acknowledged on Syringe–Pepsi Story," *Milwaukee Sentinel,* June 21, 1993; Thomas K. Grose, "How PepsiCo Overcame Syringe Challenge," *TJFR Business News Reporter,* July 1993, 1; Michael Janofsky, "Under Siege, Pepsi Mounts a TV Counter Offensive," *New York Times,* June 17, 1993, D-1; Charles M. Madigan, "Recipe for National Scare: Pepsi, Media, Me-Too-Ism," *The Record,* June 21, 1993, D-1; Tom Mashberg, "Pepsi Puts Reputation on the Line," *Boston Globe,* June 17, 1993, A-1; "Media-Smart Pepsi," *Advertising Age,* June 28, 1993, 26; "Public Relations Victory Sweep for Pepsi-Cola Officials," *Washington Post News Service,* June 20, 1993; Gary Strauss, "Scare Fails to Flatten Pepsi Sales," *USA Today,* June 23, 1993, B-1; Laura Zinn, "The Right Moves, Baby," *Business Week,* July 5, 1993, 30.

O V E R   T H E   T O P

An Interview with Craig Weatherup

Craig Weatherup was chairman and chief executive officer of PepsiCo, one of the largest and most successful beverage businesses in the world, with annual sales in excess of $10 billion. Mr. Weatherup served as point man for the company's handling of the 1993 public relations crisis, when syringes were reportedly found in Diet Pepsi cans. He was in the catbird seat, making all of Pepsi's major decisions in the case.

What kind of advice do you seek from public relations professionals?
First, I look for either reaffirmation of my own gut instincts or if I've totally misread a situation. My initial concern is the core thought. Do we have it right in terms of what we're communicating? My public relations director is a great "calibrator" of getting things exactly right. Very secondarily, I look for counsel on the mechanics or the elements that can best be communicated. For me as a CEO, the real value is this constant calibration of what we are doing and ensuring that we are really in touch with our average consumer. I rely on the public relations director to be the primary source of this so that we absolutely have the right stake in the ground. If you have the right stake

in the ground, you deal with all the other stuff. If you don't, you're just going to be dangling in the wind, and you'll regret it.

What did you think when you heard that a syringe had been found in a can of Diet Pepsi?
I thought it was legitimate, at least from the standpoint of sabotage. Obviously, somebody had put it in the can. We announced we were doing the things we normally do in terms of checking the product, recalling any product that had specific codes, reexamining inventories, all those kinds of things.

What was your public relations strategy?
The core thing was we had this wonderful advantage: We knew it was a hoax. Every single can has a code on the bottom. As soon as we had the second can and realized these things were produced months apart in different plants, we knew it was fraudulent. And we had an idea to dispatch a crew to Philadelphia and film the can line and get it on the news.

What else did you decide to do?
The other decision we made—because this was the lead story three straight nights on the evening news and there was nothing else happening in the world, unfortunately—was that we would be very open and available. We had honest and credible information that we could share, and we knew we were right. So

we decided to take advantage of this media event by using the media. We did hundreds of interviews over those two days. Radio, television, print.

Didn't the *Wall Street Journal* suggest that you recall the product?
Yes, I got hacked up in the *Journal* one morning about how idiotic it was not to recall the product.

Did you consider recalling the product?
No. It would have been an absolute untruth.

What about your relationship with Commissioner Kessler of the FDA?
I think I was able to convince him that this was a hoax. After that, I must have talked to him a couple of times a day, including one very, very heated argument about bringing this to closure. We felt we'd been dangling out there for 72 hours, and another hour was too long. But I would give Kessler great marks. He could have been a lot heavier if he wanted to. Again, we were cooperating with his agency. We had the technical people talking, the lawyers talking, public relations people talking, and I was talking to Kessler.

How much did you spend on various public relations activities on the syringe problem?
We spent $250,000 on the video news releases, compared to $20 million on the coupon ad we ran immediately after the crisis.

What lessons did you take away from this public relations crisis?
First, stick with the truth. And I don't say that as a platitude either. We didn't have to guess at this. We knew what was happening. So we had to find a way to present these facts so that people would understand them. Second, be clear and totally accessible to the media.

Chapter 4

Ethics

Several years ago, sociologist Raymond Baumhart asked business people, "What does ethics mean to you?" Among their replies:

> *Ethics has to do with what my feelings tell me is right or wrong.*
> *Ethics has to do with my religious beliefs.*
> *Being ethical is doing what the law requires.*
> *Ethics consists of the standards of behavior our society accepts.*
> *I don't know what the word means.*

The meaning of ethics is hard to pin down, and the views many people have about ethics are uncertain. Nonetheless, ethical dilemmas are all around us. In many sectors of society today, institutions are sending out mixed signals about the value of moral conduct.

Consider the following:

■ *Two-term President Bill Clinton was, by virtue of performance and polls, a highly successful chief executive. Under his leadership, the country kept out of deadly wars, and the economy boomed as never before. But ethically, the Clinton administration constituted the country's lowest presidential ebb, with Clinton becoming only the nation's second president in history to suffer the ignominy of being impeached.*
—Scandals in the Clinton White House abounded. Whitewater, Travelgate, Koreagate, Interngate—all brought shame, embarrassment, and humiliation to the highest office in the free world.

Special Prosecutor Kenneth Starr spent $55 million of taxpayers' dollars and several years prosecuting Clinton associates and investigating all the tributaries flowing from President and Mrs. Clinton's questionable investment in the Whitewater real estate development in Arkansas.

The veteran travel office at the White House was summarily fired, supposedly by the First Lady, in order to make room for cronies.

President Clinton was accused of offering the Lincoln bedroom in the White House as a "reward" for significant campaign contributions, and a circle of well-connected Asian fundraisers was accused of soliciting White House favors for large contributions.

The culmination of the Clinton ethical collapse came when it was revealed that the president had lied about a continuing affair with a young White House intern, whose name would soon become known worldwide (See "Case Study" at the conclusion of this chapter).

Indeed, even after the Monica Lewinsky scandal left a permanent scar on the Clinton presidency, the president was accused at the end of his administration of pardoning a group of imprisoned Puerto Rican terrorists in order to help his wife's senatorial bid in New York, where Puerto Rican voters constituted an important New York City bloc.

◪ *The Clinton ethical legacy extended widely, to his friends and allies.*
—Clinton's chief media strategist Dick Morris was forced to resign when it was revealed he regularly hired a Washington prostitute who "listened in" on telephone strategy sessions with the president.

A slew of Clinton Cabinet secretaries and high-ranking executives—from Webster Hubbell to Henry Cisneros to the late Ron Brown—were brought up on federal charges and sued or worse. One old friend, Vincent Foster, entrusted with safeguarding the Whitewater records, committed suicide.

Not able to escape the ethical tarnish, Vice President Al Gore was accused of soliciting Democratic contributions from the White House, in violation of federal law and claimed he was "unaware" that a celebrated meeting in a Buddhist temple was really a campaign fund-raising meeting. Gore couldn't shake the stigma of steadfastly supporting Clinton, a loyalty that dogged his own presidential campaign.
—On the other side of the aisle, Republican Speaker of the House Newt Gingrich was reprimanded and heavily fined by a Congressional Ethics Committee for using an educational course as a "front" for raising campaign contributions. Eventually, Gingrich lost his speaker-ship and resigned his House seat.

The Republican candidate to succeed Clinton, Gov. George W. Bush of Texas, was "ethically challenged" when he refused to respond to allegations that he had taken cocaine while in college.

◪ *Journalism, too, was plagued by ethical transgressions.*
—ABC News commentator Barbara Walters did a glowing report on Sunset Boulevard *creator Andrew Lloyd Webber on her 20/20 program in late 1996. Ms. Walters made no mention of her investment of $100,000 in the very same Broadway production she lauded.[1]*
—Newsweek columnist Joe Klein was exposed as the author of a best-selling "fictional" work, which trashed President Clinton and others. Mr. Klein insistently denied he was the "Anonymous" author of Primary Colors, *until he was forced to admit the lie.[2]*
—CNN, the respected 24-hour news network was caught in an embarrassing ethical breach, when it was revealed that a program

inaugurating the network's affiliation with Time *magazine was bogus. The CNN report purported to prove that the U.S. military used deadly nerve gas during the Vietnam War. It was later revealed that reporters and producers had "skewed the evidence" and stretched credulity to "prove" their point. CNN apologized for the deception, and those responsible were fired.*

☑ *Profit-making and nonprofit-making organizations also could not escape ethical scandal.*

   The nation's leading cigarette manufacturers were hauled before Congress and the courts in the late 1990s, charged with knowing all along—but not admitting—that cigarette smoking was harmful and addictive (see "Case Study," chapter 19). Eventually, one major manufacturer, Liggett, admitted that it had known for years that smoking was addictive.[3] Finally, as the new millennium neared, even tobacco industry executives acknowledged, "We could have done a better job as an industry over the past 40 years."[4]

   —The Prudential Insurance Company, known as "the Rock" of financial integrity, was itself rocked by a scandal involving its salespeople in unscrupulous practices.

   —The American Express Company, among the world's largest and most prestigious corporations, contributed $8 million to settle a dispute with a former top executive, Edmund Safra, after acknowledging that it had tried to discredit Mr. Safra by linking him to illegal activities. Ironically, in 1999 Mr. Safra, died from smoke inhalation after a nurse set his Monaco apartment on fire.

   —Wal-Mart, for years a proponent of a "Buy America" program, was exposed as hiring underage workers to produce garments in Latin America and Asia. Even worse, tearful Wal-Mart partner Kathie Lee Gifford, a pristine TV personality, was accused of fronting for the slavish child laborers, who manufactured the garments bearing her name.[5]

   —United Way of America, the nation's largest nonprofit group, was humiliated when its chief executive was found to be spending the organization's funds on himself and hiring family members to work for him.

☑ *The World Wide Web, too, despite its relative youth, has not escaped its share of ethical skirmishes, particularly with respect to uncensored content. For example, the Web was cited for its free exposure of the kind of hate mongering that led to the horrible school killings in Littleton, Colorado and elsewhere at the decade's end. In 1999, one "gifted Web entrepreneur" even briefly advertised the sale of fertility eggs from gorgeous models—before public pressure forced him to withdraw the offensive offer.*

☑ *Even the public relations profession came under its share of ethical scrutiny.*

   —In 1996, public relations veteran John Scanlon was targeted by federal prosecutors for "obstructing justice," for dishing the dirt on a

former cigarette company executive who went public with charges against Scanlon client Brown & Williamson Tobacco Corp. Scanlon's dubious role in the drama was reprised in 1999, when Al Pacino starred in The Insider, *a film about the reluctance of* 60 Minutes *to blow the whistle on its cigarette industry sponsors.*
—In 1997, powerful New York public relations firm Kekst & Co., whose chief executive was a religious Jew, was chastised for agreeing to represent the banks of Switzerland, who were disclosed as having secretly sympathized with the Nazis during and after the Holocaust.

What's going on here?

Pollster Richard Wirthlin has discovered that, "For most organizations, image is determined not only by what goods and services are provided, but also by the persona of the corporation. The first imperative of leadership is 'honesty.' "[6]

So, what constitutes ethics for an organization? Sadly, there is no one answer. Ethical guidelines are just that—guidelines. They don't necessarily provide right answers, just educated guesses. Reasonable people can and do disagree about what is moral, ethical, and right in a given situation.

Nonetheless, when previously respected business, government, and religious leaders, as well as other members of society, are exposed as cheaters, con artists, and even crooks, those who would look up to and be influenced by such people are correctly appalled. Little wonder then that societal pressure in the area of ethics has never been more intense. In public relations, no issue is more critical than ethics—of both the practice and the practitioner.

The bigness of most institutions today—where megamergers are commonplace among business organizations, hospitals, media firms, public relations agencies, and other institutions—immediately makes them suspect. All have become concerned about their individual cultures—the values, ideals, principles, and aspirations that underlie their credibility and viability. As the internal conscience of many organizations, the public relations department has become a focal point for the institutionalization of ethical conduct. Increasingly, management has turned to public relations officers to lead the internal ethical charge, to be the keeper of the organizational ethic.

Ethics in Society

What exactly are ethics? The answer isn't an easy one.

In general, ethics refers to the values, that guide a person, organization, or society—the difference between right and wrong, fairness and unfairness, honesty and dishonesty. One's conduct is measured not only against his or her conscience but also against some norm of acceptability that has been societally, professionally, or organizationally determined.[7]

Roughly translated, an individual's or organization's ethics come down to the standards that are followed in relationships with others—the real integrity of the individual or organization. Obviously, a person's ethical construct and approach depends on numerous factors—cultural, religious, and educational, among others. Complicating the issue is that what might seem right to one person might not matter to another. No issue is solely black or white but rather a shade of gray—particularly in making public relations decisions.

That is not to say that classical ethical distinctions don't exist. They do. Utilitarianism, for example, suggests considering the greater good, rather than what may be best for you. Philosophers throughout the ages have debated the essence of ethics. To Aristotle, the golden mean of moral virtue could be found between two extreme points of view. Kant's categorical imperative recommended acting "on that maxim which you will to become a universal law." Mill's principle of utility recommended "seeking the greatest happiness for the greatest number." The traditional Judeo-Christian ethic prescribes "loving your neighbor as yourself." Indeed, this Golden Rule makes great good sense in the practice of public relations.

Because the practice of public relations is misunderstood by so many—even including some of those for whom public relations people work—public relations people, in particular, must be ethical. They can't assume that ethics are strictly personal choices without relevance or related methodology for resolving moral quandaries. Public relations people must adhere to a high standard of professional ethics, with truth as the key determinant of their conduct. Professional ethics, often referred to as "applied ethics," suggests a commonly accepted sense of professional conduct, translated into formal codes of ethics, monitored, assessed, and enforced through actions taken against those who deviate from the norm.[8] As the Code of Professional Standards of the Public Relations Society of America states (see appendix A), practitioners must be scrupulously honest and trustworthy, acting at all times in the public interest, which, by definition, also represents the best interests of individual organizations. Indeed, if the ultimate goal of the public relations professional is to enhance public trust of an organization, then only the highest ethical conduct is acceptable.

The essence of the Public Relations Society's code and that of the International Association of Business Communicators (Figure 4-1) is that honesty and fairness lie at the heart of public relations practice. In light of the field's public nature, these codes underscore the importance of members promoting and maintaining "high standards of public service and ethical conduct." Inherent in these standards of the profession is the understanding that ethics have changed and continue to change as society changes. Over time, views have changed on such issues as minority discrimination, double standards in the treatment of women, pollution of the environment, destruction of endangered species and natural resources, lack of concern for human rights, and on and on. Again, honesty and fairness are two critical components that will continue to determine the ethical behavior of public relations professionals.

The first question that public relations must pose in any management discussion is, "Are we doing the right thing?" Often the public relations professional will be the only member of management with the nerve to pose such a question. Sometimes this means saying "no" to what the boss wants to do. The bottom line for public relations professionals must always be what is in the best interests of the organization.

In the latter years of the last millennium, this was easier said than done.

◪ Hill & Knowlton, one of the world's largest public relations firms, was embarrassed by taking on certain clients, such as the antiabortion National

Conference of Catholic Bishops, the controversial Church of Scientology, and the scandalized Bank of Credit and Commerce International.

☑ One of the nation's best-known public relations counselors, Robert Dilenschneider, was slapped with a $50 million lawsuit for turning against a former client and seizing control of his business.[9]

☑ Kekst & Co., another of the nation's most successful public relations firms, was found to be representing both Paramount and Viacom in the latter's attempt to buy the former. What complicated the situation was that another hopeful acquirer, QVC, announced its willingness to pay the shareholders more for Paramount than Viacom—thus compromising the integrity of the Kekst initiative.[10]

☑ Political public relations counselors continually sacrificed truth for expediency—from James Carville, who constantly defended President Clinton against "bimbo attacks," only to be proven wrong most of the time; to Edward Rollins, who boasted to a media group that he had "bribed" black leaders in New Jersey to stay away from the polls so that his employer, Governor Christine Todd Whitman, could be re-elected; to Dick Morris, who wrote a tell-all book about his White House consultancy heroics in defiance of a Clinton edict to withhold such memoirs.

Examples like these point out the difficulty, in an increasingly competitive society, of maintaining high ethical standards in public relations practice specifically and in business in general.

IABC CODE OF ETHICS

The IABC Code of Ethics has been developed to provide IABC members and other communication professionals with guidelines of professional behavior and standards of ethical practice. The Code will be reviewed and revised as necessary by the Ethics Committee and the Executive Board.

Any IABC member who wishes advice and guidance regarding its interpretation and/or application may write or phone IABC headquarters. Questions will be routed to the Executive Board member responsible for the Code.

Communication and Information Dissemination

1. Communication professionals will uphold the credibility and dignity of their profession by encouraging the practice of honest, candid and timely communication.

The highest standards of professionalism will be upheld in all communication. Communicators should encourage frequent communication and messages that are honest in their content, candid, accurate and appropriate to the needs of the organization and its audiences.

2. Professional communicators will not use any information that has been generated or appropriately acquired by a business for another business without permission. Further, communicators should attempt to identify the source of information to be used.

When one is changing employers, information developed at the previous position will not be used without permission from that employer. Acts of plagiarism and copyright infringement are illegal acts; material in the public domain should have its source attributed, if possible. If an organization grants permission to use its information and requests public acknowledgment, it will be made in a place appropriate to the material used. The material will be used only for the purpose for which permission was granted.

Standards of Conduct

3. Communication professionals will abide by the spirit and letter of all laws and regulations governing their professional activities.

All international, national and local laws and regulations must be observed, with particular attention to those pertaining to communication, such as copyright law. Industry and organizational regulations will also be observed.

4. Communication professionals will not condone any illegal or unethical act related to their professional activity, their organization and its business or the public environment in which it operates.

It is the personal responsibility of professional communicators to act honestly, fairly and with integrity at all times in all professional activities. Looking the other way while others act illegally tacitly condones such acts whether or not the communicator has committed them. The communicator should speak with the individual involved, his or her supervisor or appropriate authorities – depending on the context of the situation and one's own ethical judgment.

Confidentiality/Disclosure

5. Communication professionals will respect the confidentiality and right-to-privacy of all individuals, employers, clients and customers.

Communicators must determine the ethical balance between right-to-privacy and need-to-know. Unless the situation involves illegal or grossly unethical acts, confidences should be maintained. If there is a conflict between right-to-privacy and need-to-know, a communicator should first talk with the source and negotiate the need for the information to be communicated.

6. Communication professionals will not use any confidential information gained as a result of professional activity for personal benefit or for that of others.

Confidential information can be used to give inside advantage to stock transactions, gain favors from outsiders, assist a competing company for whom one is going to work, assist companies in developing a marketing advantage, achieve a publishing advantage or otherwise act to the detriment of an organization. Such information must remain confidential during and after one's employment period.

Professionalism

7. Communication professionals should uphold IABC's standards for ethical conduct in all professional activity, and should use IABC and its designation of accreditation (ABC) only for purposes that are authorized and fairly represent the organization and its professional standards.

IABC recognizes the need for professional integrity within any organization, including the association. Members should acknowledge that their actions reflect on themselves, their organizations and their profession.

Printed with the assistance of the Mead Corporation and Brown & Kroger Printing, Dayton, OH

FIGURE 4-1 **IABC principles.** The International Association of Business Communicators adopted these seven tenets to guide the professional behavior of its members.

Ethics in Business

For many people today, regrettably, the term *business ethics* is an oxymoron. Its mere mention stimulates thoughts of disgraced financiers like Marvin Frankel and Martin Armstrong of the late 1990s, and Ivan Boesky and Michael Milken of the early 1990s—illegally raking in millions of dollars with insider stock tips and fraudulent schemes—or of tobacco companies being charged by congressional committees for withholding damaging data on the addictive properties of cigarettes.

Fraud, price gouging, discrimination, runaway pollution—all these allegations have made headlines in recent years. American business, perhaps the most ethical business system in the world, has been shocked—so much so that in 1987, the former Securities and Exchange Commission chairman, John Shad, donated $23 million to begin a program at Harvard Business School to make the study of ethics an integral part of the curriculum.*

In one significant study, a leading business group, the Business Roundtable, pointed out the "crucial role of the chief executive officer and top managers in establishing a strong commitment to ethical conduct and in providing constant leadership in tending and reviewing the values of the organization."[11] The Roundtable study debunked the myth that there is an inherent contradiction between ethics and profits. On the contrary, it emphasized that there is a strong relationship between acting ethically, maintaining a good reputation for fair and honest business, and making money.

Another study of key business leaders, conducted by the accounting firm Touche Ross, corroborated the notion that a majority of business leaders—63 percent—"believe that a business enterprise actually 'strengthens' its competitive position by maintaining high ethical standards." Only 14 percent said that a company with high ethical standards was a "weaker competitor."[12] The Touche Ross research on more than 1,000 business leaders also turned up other interesting findings about the current state of business ethics:

- Intense concentration on short-term earnings is a major threat to American business ethics today. Respondents ranked this threat almost equal to that posed by decay in cultural and social institutions.
- Respondents ranked the United States as having higher standards of business ethics than any other country—noting high standards also in the United Kingdom, Canada, Switzerland, and Germany.
- Among industries, respondents ranked commercial banking, utilities, and drugs, pharmaceuticals, and cosmetics as the three most ethical.
- Among all professions, respondents ranked the clergy, teachers, engineers, and accountants as the four most ethical.[13]

In the waning years of the 1990s, the outbreak of downsizings, mergers, and cutbacks helped create a serious "trust gap" between employers and workers.[14] In perhaps the most celebrated case of the decade, the CEO of AT&T Corp., Robert Allen, took an all-in compensation package of $18 million, while announcing that the company was laying off 40,000 workers. (Shortly thereafter, Mr. Allen was shown the door.) Where once workers trusted the ethics of their employers, in the 21st century, this is much less the case, as business struggles with increased computerization and concurrent declining employee loyalty.

---

*Ironically Mr. Shad himself was the subject of an embarrassing ethical dilemma. He was called in to head Drexel Burnham Lambert after the firm was fined and discredited for junk bond indiscretions led by Mr. Milken. Mr. Shad was duly mortified when Drexel Burnham went belly-up in 1989.

A QUESTION OF ETHICS

Virtual Morality: Tracking Ethics with Merlin and Qwizard

In recent years, the venerable Lockheed Martin Corporation has been no stranger to ethical dilemmas.

On the verge of its merger with Martin Marrietta Corporation in 1995, aerospace giant Lockheed Corporation agreed to pay a $24.8 million fine and plead guilty to conspiring to violate U.S. antibribery laws. Lockheed admitted that it illegally paid $1 million to an Egyptian lawmaker for helping sell its C-130 aircraft to that country. As a huge government contract recipient, Lockheed Martin has fired more than 200 people in the last five years of the century for ethical violations from conflicts of interest to misuse of assets.

To cut down on such occurrences, Lockheed Martin has turned to cyberspace to audit, record, and perfect the measurement of employee morals.

Using internal computer programs with names like Merlin and Qwizard, many of Lockheed Martin's 160,000 employees go on-line for step-by-step training on ethics. The system records each time an employee completes one of the sessions, which range from sexual harassment and insider trading to kickbacks and gratuities. Employees get credit for ethics sessions completed. Those who don't complete the sessions receive a reprimand.

Its electronics ethics program, which has won the company new respect among regulators and legislators, is complemented with an "Ethics Challenge Game," which every employee, up to and including the CEO, must play once a year. With cards and tokens, workers spend one-hour sessions debating ethical quandaries drawn from actual Lockheed experience. Among them:

1. A kickback may be in the form of:
   A. Cash
   B. Gifts to family members
   C. Donations to a charity at your request
   D. All of the above
      (Correct answer is D.)
2. Which is the best means of addressing harassment when it first occurs?
   A. Ignore the harasser
   B. Be direct and tell the harasser his or her behavior is unwelcome and offensive
   C. Report the harasser to your manager or Human Resources
      (Correct answer is B.)

While Lockheed Martin admits that computer-based ethics training will never replace face-to-face instruction, as one executive put it, having a system with mandatory clinics and quizzes will help "convince a prosecutor or regulator that the company is trying to prevent and detect problems."*

*For further information, see Michael J. McCarthy, "How One Firm Tracks Ethics Electronically," Wall Street Journal, October 21, 1999, B1–4.

Corporate Codes of Conduct

One manifestation of the increased attention to corporate ethics is the growth of internal codes of conduct. Codes of ethics, standards of conduct, and similar statements of corporate policies and values have proliferated in recent years. The reasons corporations have adopted such codes vary from company to company.

- **To increase public confidence.** The scandals concerning overseas bribery and domestic political campaign contributions during the 1970s led to a decline of public trust and confidence in business. Many firms responded with written codes of ethics.
- **To stem the tide of regulation.** As public confidence declined, government regulation of business increased. Some estimated the cost to society of compliance with regulations at $100 billion per year. Corporate codes of conduct, it was hoped, would serve as a self-regulation mechanism.

☑ **To improve internal operations.** As companies became larger and more decentralized, management needed consistent standards of conduct to ensure that employees were meeting the business objectives of the company in a legal and ethical manner.

☑ **To respond to transgressions.** Frequently when a company itself was caught in the web of unethical behavior, it responded with its own code of ethics. For example, Fiat, Italy's biggest private company, sought to extricate itself from a huge corruption scandal in the country by issuing the first Italian corporate code of ethical conduct for employees.[15]

Ralph Waldo Emerson once wrote, "An organization is the lengthened shadow of a man." Today, many corporate executives realize that just as an individual has certain responsibilities as a citizen, a corporate citizen has responsibilities to the society in which it is privileged to operate (Figure 4-2).

Corporate codes of conduct are not without their critics. Some ethics specialists say that what is contained in the codes doesn't really address ethics in general. A Washington State University study of ethical codes at 200 Fortune 500 companies found that while 75 percent failed to address the company's role in civic and community affairs, consumer relations, environmental safety, and product safety, more than 75 percent dealt with conflicts of interest—which can affect the bottom line.[16] Such skepticism notwithstanding, formal ethical codes, addressing such topics as confidentiality of corporate information, misappropriation of corporate assets, bribes and kickbacks, and political contributions, have become a corporate fact of life.

Corporate Social Responsibility

Closely related to the ethical conduct of an organization is its social responsibility, which has been defined as a social norm. This norm holds that any social institution, including the smallest family unit and the largest corporation, is responsible for the behavior of its members and may be held accountable for their misdeeds.

In the late 1960s, when this idea was just emerging, initial responses were of the knee-jerk variety. A firm that was threatened by increasing legal or activist pressures and harassment would ordinarily change its policies in a hurry. Today, however, organizations and their social responsibility programs are much more sophisticated. Social responsibility is treated just like any other management discipline: analyze the issues, evaluate performance, set priorities, allocate resources to those priorities, and implement programs that deal with issues within the constraints of the organization's resources. Many companies have created special committees to set the agenda and target the objectives.

Social responsibility touches practically every level of organizational activity, from marketing to hiring, from training to work standards. In 1996 when Texaco Inc., a worldwide company, discovered its executives were speaking disparagingly of African Americans—a violation of its social responsibility code—it had no alternative but to take prompt and forceful action. The company's CEO fired the executives involved and quickly settled a class-action bias suit against the company.[17] A partial list of social responsibility categories might include the following:

☑ **Product lines**—dangerous products, product performance and standards, packaging, and environmental impact

☑ **Marketing practices**—sales practices, consumer complaint policies, advertising content, and fair pricing

Code of Ethics and Business Conduct

LOCKHEED MARTIN
Setting the Standard

Dear Colleague:

Lockheed Martin aims to "set the standard" for ethical business conduct. We will achieve this through six virtues: Honesty, Integrity, Respect, Trust, Responsibility, and Citizenship.

Honesty: to be truthful in all our endeavors; to be honest and forthright with one another and with our customers, communities, suppliers, and shareholders.

Integrity: to say what we mean, to deliver what we promise, and to stand for what is right.

Respect: to treat one another with dignity and fairness, appreciating the diversity of our workforce and the uniqueness of each employee.

Trust: to build confidence through teamwork and open, candid communication.

Responsibility: to speak up – without fear of retribution – and report concerns in the work place, including violations of laws, regulations and company policies, and seek clarification and guidance whenever there is doubt.

Citizenship: to obey all the laws of the United States and the other countries in which we do business and to do our part to make the communities in which we live better.

You can count on us to do everything in our power to meet Lockheed Martin's standards. We are counting on you to do the same. We are confident that our trust in you is well placed and we are determined to be worthy of your trust.

DANIEL M. TELLEP   NORMAN R. AUGUSTINE   BERNARD L. SCHWARTZ

FIGURE 4-2 Lockheed code. The principles enumerated here represent the obligations that Lockheed Martin Corporation believes it has to its public in the wake of ethical tribulations in the 1990s.

- ☑ **Corporate philanthropy**—contribution performance, encouragement of employee participation in social projects, and community development activities
- ☑ **Environmental activities**—pollution-control projects, adherence to federal standards, and evaluation procedures for new packages and products
- ☑ **External relations**—support of minority enterprises, investment practices, and government relations
- ☑ **Employment diversity in retaining and promoting minorities and women**—current hiring policies, advancement policies, specialized career counseling, and opportunities for special minorities such as the physically handicapped
- ☑ **Employee safety and health**—work environment policies, accident safeguards, and food and medical facilities

More often than not, organizations have incorporated social responsibility into the mainstream of their practice. Most firms recognize that social responsibility, far from being an add-on program, must be a corporate way of life. Beyond this, some studies have indicated that those organizations that practice social responsibility over time rank among the most profitable and successful firms in society.

Ethics in Government

Politics has never enjoyed an unblemished reputation when it comes to ethics. In the final years of the 20th century, politics developed a particularly sleazy reputation.

As noted, the Clinton administration distinguished itself for being on the wrong end of ethical situations. The recurring campaign financing scandal was symptomatic of the ethical problems afflicting the administration in particular and politics in general. President Clinton handily turned back Republican challenger Bob Dole in the 1996 election campaign. Nonetheless, after the election, it was revealed that the Democrats used questionable judgment to entice huge contributions, particularly from representatives of nations like Indonesia, China, and Korea. Amidst calls for a new special prosecutor to coexist with the one already hired to investigate Whitewater, people couldn't help but question the ethics of a political process that depends on costly television advertising to get elected. Indeed, one Republican challenger for the presidency, Senator John McCain, in the primaries of 2000 ran on a platform of ending special interest contributions in politics. Although a decided underdog, McCain's message resonated well throughout the nation.

The sleaze factor in government, of course, is not confined to Democrats, nor is it a new phenomenon.

- ☑ In 1993, Oregon Republican Senator Robert Packwood was the subject of embarrassing publicity regarding unseemly sexual advances that Packwood had made to women over decades in politics. Packwood left politics shortly thereafter.
- ☑ On the other side of the political aisle, Illinois Congressman Mel Reynolds was hounded out of office for similar transgressions with an underage campaign worker.
- ☑ Still earlier, President George H. W. Bush was plagued by skepticism about his role in secret Iran–Nicaraguan Contra negotiations.
- ☑ Before that, President Ronald Reagan suffered an embarrassing scandal in his Housing and Urban Development Department and lobbying violations by several key assistants.

◪ In the winter of 1990, five U.S. senators were accused of serious ethical violations in support of Charles Keating, a savings and loan operator convicted of fraud. Four years later, four of the "Keating Five" senators were gone from the Senate. Ironically, the other, Senator McCain of Arizona, as noted, became a strong Republican contender for the presidency in the year 2000.

In the 21st century, the public is less willing to tolerate such ethical violations from their elected officials. It is likely that ethics in government will become an even more important issue as fed-up voters insist on representatives who are honest, trustworthy, and ethical.

BACKGROUNDER

Short, Sad Saga of the Political Sage

FIGURE 4-3 **Misguided sage.** From political guru to public relations casualty, former Clinton advisor-turned-talk-show-host Dick Morris.

No advisor symbolized better the "political ethics"—or lack thereof—of the late 1990s than Dick Morris (Figure 4-3).

As a strategist for national and local candidates, it apparently made no difference to Mr. Morris which side or inclination his candidates represented. Just as long as they "showed him the money," he was content, working for right-wingers, such as Senators Jesse Helms and Trent Lott, or left leaners, such as Senator Howard Metzenbaum and President Bill Clinton.

The latter, of course, was Mr. Morris' primary client. Indeed, when President Clinton's popularity sagged in the middle of his first term, he turned immediately to his old strategist to bail him out. Mr. Morris suggested that the president adopt a less liberal, more middle-of-the-

road platform. The president took the advice and made great progress.

Advisor Morris, however, let his access and power get the best of him. He flaunted his status, was nasty to others around him, and claimed credit for virtually anything that the administration did right. However, in a classic case of "what goes around comes around," in what should have been his finest hour, the advisor crashed and burned.

On the eve of President Clinton's party "coronation" in Chicago in the fall of 1996, it was revealed in rapid order that presidential confidante Morris had been less than highly ethical with his employer. To wit:

- He secretly signed a lucrative book contract, without telling the White House and in violation of administration ethical standards
- He regularly employed a D.C. prostitute and let her listen in on the extension as he counseled the Clintons on matters of national importance.
- He alienated most of the president's other associates, so that when it came time to "stick up for Dick," few allies rushed to defend their fallen comrade.

Poor Dick.

As he, himself, sadly lamented in his $2.5 million autobiography, "I began life weighing only two pounds, eleven ounces and spent my first three months in incubators, untouched by anyone, even my mother. Only after years of therapy did I begin to understand how this early deprivation affected my personality thereafter."

Poor, whiny Dick.

Ultimately, Mr. Morris was forced to resign from the president's employ. His wife announced she was leaving him. He started a political Web site, vote.com. In the most telling sign of how utterly impoverished his life had now become, Dick Morris became a radio talk show host and television political analyst. How low can one go!

Ethics in Journalism

The Society of Professional Journalists is quite explicit on the subject of ethics (Figure 4-4).

THE SOCIETY OF PROFESSIONAL JOURNALISTS, SIGMA DELTA CHI

THE SOCIETY of Professional Journalists, Sigma Delta Chi believes the duty of journalists is to serve the truth.

WE BELIEVE the agencies of mass communication are carriers of public discussion and information, acting on their Constitutional mandate and freedom to learn and report the facts.

WE BELIEVE in public enlightenment as the forerunner of justice, and in our Constitutional role to seek the truth as part of the public's right to know the truth.

WE BELIEVE those responsibilities carry obligations that require journalists to perform with intelligence, objectivity, accuracy and fairness.

To these ends, we declare acceptance of the standards of practice here set forth:

RESPONSIBILITY:

The public's right to know of events of public importance and interest is the overriding mission of the mass media. The purpose of distributing news and enlightened opinion is to serve the general welfare. Journalists who use their professional status as representatives of the public for selfish or other unworthy motives violate a high trust.

FREEDOM OF THE PRESS:

Freedom of the press is to be guarded as an inalienable right of people in a free society. It carries with it the freedom and the responsibility to discuss, question and challenge actions and utterances of our government and of our public and private institutions. Journalists uphold the right to speak unpopular opinions and the privilege to agree with the majority.

ETHICS:

Journalists must be free of obligation to any interest other than the public's right to know the truth.

1. Gifts, favors, free travel, special treatment or privileges can compromise the integrity of journalists and their employers. Nothing of value should be accepted.

2. Secondary employment, political involvement, holding public office and service in community organizations should be avoided if it compromises the integrity of journalists and their employers. Journalists and their employers should conduct their personal lives in a manner which protects them from conflict of interest, real or apparent. Their responsibilities to the public are paramount. That is the nature of their profession.

3. So-called news communications from private sources should not be published or broadcast without substantiation of their claims to news value.

4. Journalists will seek news that serves the public interest, despite the obstacles. They will make constant efforts to assure that the public's business is conducted in public and that public records are open to public inspection.

5. Journalists acknowledge the newsman's ethic of protecting confidential sources of information.

ACCURACY AND OBJECTIVITY:

Good faith with the public is the foundation of all worthy journalism.

1. Truth is our ultimate goal.

2. Objectivity in reporting the news is another goal, which serves as the mark of an experienced professional. It is a standard of performance toward which we strive. We honor those who achieve it.

3. There is no excuse for inaccuracies or lack of thoroughness.

4. Newspaper headlines should be fully warranted by the contents of the articles they accompany. Photographs and telecasts should give an accurate picture of an event and not highlight a minor incident out of context.

5. Sound practice makes clear distinction between news reports and expressions of opinion. News reports should be free of opinion or bias and represent all sides of an issue.

6. Partisanship in editorial comment which knowingly departs from the truth violates the spirit of American journalism.

7. Journalists recognize their responsibility for offering informed analysis, comment and editorial opinion on public events and issues. They accept the obligation to present such material by individuals whose competence, experience and judgment qualify them for it.

8. Special articles or presentations devoted to advocacy or the writer's own conclusions and interpretations should be labeled as such.

FAIR PLAY:

Journalists at all times will show respect for the dignity, privacy, rights and well-being of people encountered in the course of gathering and presenting the news.

1. The news media should not communicate unofficial charges affecting reputation or moral character without giving the accused a chance to reply.

2. The news media must guard against invading a person's right to privacy.

3. The media should not pander to morbid curiosity about details of vice and crime.

4. It is the duty of news media to make prompt and complete correction of their errors.

5. Journalists should be accountable to the public for their reports and the public should be encouraged to voice its grievances against the media. Open dialogue with our readers, viewers and listeners should be fostered.

PLEDGE:

Journalists should actively censure and try to prevent violations of these standards, and they should encourage their observance by all newspeople. Adherence to this code of ethics is intended to preserve the bond of mutual trust and respect between American journalists and the American people.

FIGURE 4-4 Journalists' code. The Society of Professional Journalists has elaborated in some detail on the ethical guidelines that should govern all journalists.

Journalists at all times will show respect for the dignity, privacy, rights, and well-being of people encountered in the course of gathering and presenting the news.

1. The news media should not communicate unofficial charges affecting reputation or moral character without giving the accused a chance to reply
2. The news media must guard against invading a person's right to privacy
3. The media should not pander to morbid curiosity about details of vice and crime

And so on.

Unfortunately, what is in the code often doesn't reflect what appears in print or on the air. More often than not, journalistic judgments run smack into ethical principles.

- In the new millennium, the proliferation of on-line media, publishing round-the-clock, as well as the exponential increase in TV news, cable stations, and programming on the Internet increased the pressure on news outlets to report as much as they could in as entertaining a manner as they could. Icon of a generation of Internet journalists was the intrepid, behatted Matt Drudge, who operated his tell-all Web site from the living room of his Los Angeles apartment. Absolute accuracy, intimated Drudge, was less critical than getting out the news. Other Internet reportorial vehicles were equally cavalier in their treatment of facts, thus introducing a new level of journalistic ethical problems.
- The end of the 1990s also saw an increase in the number of "tabloid television programs," from *A Current Affair* to *Inside Edition* to *Hard Copy,* and sleazy talk show hosts, from Jerry Springer to Ricki Lake to Jenny Jones. The most outrageous example of the depths to which television, in particular, had sunk, occurred in 1996 when a male guest on the *Jenny Jones* show later murdered another male guest who had revealed a "secret crush" on him during the show (Figure 4-5). At the trial against her program, Jones pleaded "ignorance" of any harmful effects the show might have caused.
- So-called more "legitimate" TV news programs also weren't immune from ethical scandal. The problems of NBC-TV News and, in particular, its *Dateline* program tarnished the reputation of television news in general. *Dateline*'s bogus presentation of exploding General Motors' trucks was but one example of the blurring of the distinction between news and entertainment. Not to be outdone, CNN's initial collaboration with *Time* magazine resulted in a bogus 1999 report about the U.S. Army's use of nerve gas and led to the inglorious exit of one of the medium's most respected reporters, Peter Arnett (see "A Question of Ethics," chapter 15).
- In print journalism, when a Steele County, Minnesota, woman's description of a bloody fight between two men was broadcast over the police radio band, she begged an *Owatonna People's Press* reporter not to use her name. She feared reprisal from either or both of the men. The next day's story reported her name, address, and an account of what she had seen. The following day, one of the men was found stabbed to death, and the other was arrested not far from the woman's home.
- As the century ended, high-profile media figures from *Boston Globe* columnist Mike Barnicle to wacky syndicated radio personality "the Greaseman" were unceremoniously dumped for ethical transgressions. The former was canned for publishing a column that borrowed heavily from, but did not attribute to, comedian George Carlin. This and other similar "editorial borrowing without

FIGURE 4-5 **Tabloid TV murder.** Television's ethical nadir came in 1996, when *Jenny Jones* show guest Jonathan Schmitz murdered a male neighbor who had revealed an amorous affection for him before a national TV audience.

attribution" was cause for dismissal in the eyes of the people at the *Globe*.[18] The latter was given the heave-ho after making questionable on-air racial comments. Despite profuse apologies, the Grease was no more.

The point is that a sense of ethics helps an individual make moral decisions, and journalists have to make their decisions with speed and certainty. They can't usually afford to say "maybe," and they can never say, "We'll have time to get back to this when the dust settles." Their decisions must meet a deadline. Usually, the principles, values, and ideals that get reported depend largely on the individual doing the reporting (Figure 4-6).

Ethics in Public Relations

In light of numerous misconceptions about what the practice of public relations is or isn't, it is imperative that practitioners emulate the highest standards of personal and professional ethics. Within an organization, public relations practitioners must be the standard bearers of corporate ethical initiatives. By the same token, public relations consultants must always counsel their clients in an ethical direction—toward accuracy and candor and away from lying and hiding the truth.

FIGURE 4-6 **Journalistic ethics.** The topic of journalistic ethics in the new millennium has become such an important one that magazines of journalistic criticism have begun to reemerge.

The Public Relations Society of America has been a leader in the effort to foster a strong sense of ethics among its membership. Its Code of Professional Standards is a model in the attempt to promulgate high standards of public service and ethical conduct. In recent years, this code has been tested on a variety of issues, ranging from noncompetition agreements with the employees of a public relations firm, to the protection of public relations campaign proposals to prospective clients, to paying employees and consultants finder's fees to obtain new accounts.

One study by the Foundation for Public Relations Research and Education revealed a strong adherence in the field to the ethical code originally adopted in 1950. During that period, 168 issues and complaints were registered and investigated. Articles of the code most frequently cited were these:

- ☑ A member shall deal fairly with clients or employers—past, present, and potential—with fellow practitioners, and with the general public
- ☑ A member shall adhere to truth and accuracy and to generally accepted standards of good taste
- ☑ A member shall conduct his or her professional life in accord with the public interest
- ☑ A member shall not intentionally communicate false or misleading information and is obligated to use care to avoid communication of false or misleading information
- ☑ A member shall not engage in any practice that tends to corrupt the channels of communication or the processes of government

The foundation concluded that the code, with its enforcement provisions, is a good one: "It has been, can be, and will be improved. It is a vibrant, living document that depends, as our future and that of public relations depends, on constant understanding and application by the society's members."[19]

Among the general public, the 1999 Public Relations Society of America study on credibility indicated that public relations people had suffered in terms of credibility; one presumes they suffered in terms of ethics as well. While Supreme Court justices and teachers ranked highest on the credibility index, public relations specialists ranked near the bottom.[20] Some suggested that in the wake of the Clinton scandals of the late 1990s, public relations became so associated with the evils of "spin" that the field was harshly tarnished. Combating this unethical mindset poses a great challenge for the field in the new millennium.

BACKGROUNDER

Test Your Workplace Ethics

So you want to enter the workplace? The question of ethics looms larger today than at any previous time, especially with the advent of technology and the potential abuses it brings.

To test how you might measure up as an ethical worker, answer the following questions. And don't cheat!

1. Is it wrong to use company e-mail for personal reasons?
2. Is it wrong to use office equipment to help your family and friends with homework?
3. Is it wrong to play computer games on office equipment during the workday?

4. Is it wrong to use office equipment to do Internet shopping?
5. Is it unethical to visit pornographic Web sites using office equipment?
6. What's the value at which a gift from a supplier or client becomes troubling?
7. Is a $50 gift to a boss unacceptable?
8. Is it okay to take a pair of $200 football tickets as a gift from a supplier?
9. Is it okay to take a $120 pair of theater tickets?
10. Is it okay to take a $100 holiday fruit basket?
11. Is it okay to take a $25 gift certificate?
12. Is it okay to accept a $75 prize won at a raffle at a supplier's conference?

Answers from a cross section of workers at nationwide companies were compiled by the Ethics Officer Association, Belmont, Massachusetts, and the Ethical Leadership Group, Wilmette, Illinois.

1. 34% said personal e-mail on company computers is wrong.
2. 37% said using office equipment for schoolwork is wrong.
3. 49% said playing computer games at work is wrong.
4. 54% said Internet shopping at work is wrong.
5. 87% said it is unethical to visit pornographic sites at work.
6. 33% said $25 is the amount at which a gift from a supplier or client becomes troubling. Another 33 percent said $50. Another 33 percent said $100.
7. 35% said a $50 gift to the boss is unacceptable.
8. 70% said it is unacceptable to take $200 football tickets.
9. 70% said it is unacceptable to take $120 theater tickets.
10. 35% said it is unacceptable to take a $100 fruit basket.
11. 45% said it is unacceptable to take a $25 gift certificate.
12. 40% said it is unacceptable to take the $75 raffle prize.

S U M M A R Y

The success of public relations in the 21st century and beyond will depend largely on how the field responds to the issue of ethical conduct. Public relations professionals must have credibility in order to practice. They must be respected by the various publics with whom they interact. To be credible and to achieve respect, public relations professionals must be ethical. It is that simple.

The final arbiter in assessing whether ethics is important is the public (Figure 4-7). Above all, the public is concerned with the credibility of an organization and of those who serve it. In light of this, the key job for public relations professionals is to "advise clients to adapt to changing conditions and societal expectations, rather than to try to manipulate the environment for the good of the organization."[21] For public relations practice in general and individual public relations professionals in particular, credibility in the next few years will depend on how scrupulously they observe and apply, in everything they do, the principles and practice of ethics.

Discussion Starters

1. How would you define ethics?
2. How would you describe the state of ethics in business, government, and journalism?
3. How important are ethics in the practice of public relations?

FIGURE 4-7 **Too graphic.** In 1987, a provocative and legendary series of three Associated Press photographs showed Pennsylvania treasurer R. Budd Dwyer motioning to reporters, putting a pistol in his mouth, and actually firing the shot that claimed his life. The photos were as graphic as any ever recorded. The first picture in the ethically challenging series is shown here; however, the other two are so graphic that ethical standards—not to mention good taste—precluded their presentation in this text.

4. What two concepts underscore ethical conduct in public relations?
5. Compare the ethical codes of the Society of Professional Journalists and the Public Relations Society of America.
6. What is corporate social responsibility?
7. What are corporate codes of conduct?
8. What was the ethical dilemma in the case of Dick Morris?
9. Is the public more or less tolerant of ethical violators today?
10. What is the significance, in terms of ethical practice, of Michael Armstrong and Ivan Boesky?

Notes

1. "ABC Admits Walters Had 'Sunset' Stake," *New York Times* (February 20, 1997): Metro 2.
2. Joe Klein, "A Brush with Anonymity," *Newsweek* (July 29, 1996): 76.
3. Warren E. Leary, "Cigarette Company Developed Tobacco with Stronger Nicotine," *New York Times* (June 22, 1994): A1–14.
4. "Joe Camel, the Marlboro Man and the Cynical Art of Denial," *New York Times* (October 21, 1999): E5.
5. Making the Fashion Industry Sweat," *Reputation Management* (September/October 1996): 33.
6. Dennis L. Wilcox, Phillip H. Ault, and Warren K. Agee. *PR Strategies and Tactics,* 5th ed. (New York, NY: Longman, 1998): 54.
7. Scott M. Cutlip, Allen H. Center, and Glen M. Broom. *Effective Public Relations* (Prentice-Hall, Inc.: Saddle River, NJ, 2000): 144.
8. Fraser P. Seitel, "Ethics and Decency," *United States Banker* (April 1993): 58.
9. Paul Tharp, " 'Double-crossing' PR Supremo Sued for $50 M," *New York Post* (September 22, 1993): 33.
10. James Cox, "Kekst Under Fire in Paramount Fight," *USA Today* (October 12, 1993): B2.
11. "An Overview of a Landmark Roundtable Study of Corporate Ethics," *Roundtable Report* (February 1988): 1.
12. "Ethics in American Business," *Touche Ross* (January 1988).
13. Ibid.
14. "The Dream in Danger," *The Public Relations Strategist* (Spring 1995): 43.
15. Alan Cowell, "Fiat, in Scandal, Adopts Ethics Code," *New York Times* (May 11, 1993).
16. Amanda Bennett, "Ethics Codes Spread Despite Skepticism," *Wall Street Journal* (July 15, 1988): 18, 19.
17. Robert A. Bennett, "Texaco's Bijur: Hero or Sellout," *The Public Relations Strategist* (Winter 1996): 18.
18. Howell Raines, "The High Price of Reprieving Mike Barnicle," *New York Times* (August 13, 1998): A22.
19. Public Relations Society of America, study of ethical files, 1950–85, Foundation for Public Relations Research and Education, April 17, 1987, New York.
20. Jennifer Harper, "Supreme Court Justices Rank Highest in Credibility, Index Says," *Washington Times,* (July 8, 1999): 20.
21. Kathie A. Leeper, "Public Relations Ethics and Communitarianism: A Preliminary Investigation," *Public Relations Review* (Summer 1996): 175.

top of the shelf

Gerald P. Koocher, ed.

Ethics in Cyberspace.
Mahwah, NJ: Lawrence Erlbaum Associates, 1996.

Ethics in Cyberspace is a special issue of the journal *Ethics & Behavior,* edited by Gerald P. Koocher of the Harvard Medical School. He writes:

The scope of topics addressed in this issue is as disparate as the range of interested authors. Electronic communication etiquette, electronic psychotherapy, radiation problems associated with computer use, consequences of providing and withdrawing Internet access to low-income research participants, and the impact of information technology on social systems are among the themes in the pages that follow.

Of particular interest to public relations professionals is "Ethical Dilemmas in the Use of Information Technology: An Aristotelian Perspective," in which the authors discuss privacy, information accuracy, access to information, and intellectual property rights.

Suggested Readings

Andron, Scott. "Food Lion Versus ABC," *Quill* (March 1997): 15–21.

Badaracco, Joseph. *Business Ethics: Roles and Responsibilities.* Burr Ridge, IL: Irwin Professional Publishing, 1995. Cases, readings and text aimed at the moral responsibilities of business executives.

Baker, Lee. *The Credibility Factor: Putting Ethics to Work in Public Relations.* Homewood, IL: Business One Irwin, 1992.

Beaucamp, Tom, and Norman E. Bowie, eds. *Ethical Theory and Business,* 3d ed. Upper Saddle River, NJ: Prentice Hall, 1988.

Beder, Sharon. *Global Spin: The Corporate Assault on Environmentalism.* White River Junction, VT: Chelsea Green Publishing, 1998.

Behrman, Jack N. *Essays on Ethics in Business and the Professions.* Upper Saddle River, NJ: Prentice Hall, 1988.

Blanchard, Kenneth and Norman Vincent Peale. *The Power of Ethical Management.* New York: Fawcett Crest, 1991.

Budd, John F., Jr. "For Rent—A Mission Statement: Need for Self-Inspection among Public Relations Practitioners," *Public Relations Quarterly* (Winter 1996): 46–47.

"Corporate Ethics: A Prime Business Asset." New York: Business Roundtable, February 1988. Members of TBR supplied information to develop this report on policy and practice in company conduct.

Day, Louis A. *Ethics in Media Communications: Cases and Controversies,* 2nd ed. Belmont, CA: Wadsworth, 1997.

Dilenschneider, Robert L. *Power and Influence: Mastering the Art of Persuasion.* New York: Prentice Hall, 1990.

"Ethics in American Business." New York: Deloitte & Touche, January 1988. This report on ethical behavior is based on a poll of key business leaders.

Ferre, James. *Public Relations Ethics: A Bibliography.* Boston: G. K. Hall, 1991.

Fink, Conrad C. *Media Ethics.* Needham, MA: Allyn and Bacon, 1995.

Henderson, Verne E. *What's Ethical in Business.* New York: McGraw-Hill, 1992.

Jensen, J. Vernon. *Ethical Issues in the Communications Process.* Mahwah, NJ: Lawrence Erlbaum Associates Inc., 1997.

Krukeberg, Dean. "Future Reconciliation of Multicultural Perspectives in Public Relations Ethics," *Public Relations Quarterly,* (Spring 1998): 45–48.

Martinson, David L. "Public Relations Practitioners Must Not Confuse Consideration of the Situation with Situational Ethics," *Public Relations Quarterly* (Winter 1997-98): 39–43.

McElreath, Mark P. *Managing Systematic and Ethical Public Relations.* Dubuque, IA: Wm. C. Brown, 1993.

McInerny, Paul M. "Ethics Throughout the Curriculum," *Public Relations Quarterly,* (Winter 1997-98): 44–47. Argues for teaching ethics in public relations education.

Pratt, Cornelius. "Food Lion Inc. v. ABC News Inc.: Invasive Deception for the Public Interest?" *Public Relations Quarterly* (Spring 1997): 18–20.

Schechter, William. "Food Lion's 'Victory'—But At What Price," *Public Relations Quarterly* (Spring 1997): 20–21.

Schick, Thomas A. "Technician Ethics in Public Relations." *Public Relations Quarterly* (Spring 1996): 30–35.

Schick, Thomas A., and Ida Critelli Schick. "The Ethics of Keeping Corporate Secrets," *Public Relations Strategist,* (Summer 1998): 29 ff.

Sevareid, Eric. "Ethics and the Media." New York: Conference Board, 1988: 12–13.

Smith, Ron F. *Groping for Ethics in Journalism.* Ames, IA: Iowa State University Press, 1999.

Stauber, John, and Sheldon Rampton. *Toxic Sludge Is Good for You: Lies, Damn Lies and the Public Relations Industry.* Monroe, ME: Common Courage Press, 1996.

Trevino, Linda K. and Katherine A. Nelson. *Managing Business Ethics: Straight Talk About How to Do it Right.* New York: John Wiley & Sons, 1995. Discusses not only what business ethics are, but also why business should care.

CASE STUDY

The President and the Intern

Of all the ethical transgressions that afflicted America in the final years of the 20th century, none was more public, more embarrassing, or more destructive to the institutions of politics and the American presidency than the case of Bill Clinton and Monica Lewinsky.

President Clinton, a competent and able Arkansas governor, campaigned for the presidency in 1992 under a cloud of extramarital rumors. During that campaign, in fact, the governor and wife Hillary had to appear on *60 Minutes* to put down spreading innuendo that Clinton had had a long-running affair with an Arkansas lounge singer named Gennifer Flowers. His contrition helped ease the situation, and Clinton became president of the United States.

In the White House, staff members were dispatched to shut down "bimbo eruptions," which might involve the boss. Despite recurring rumors about indiscretions with women in his past, President Clinton seemed to have acquitted himself professionally in the White House, and he sailed into another term.

But six years into his presidency, on January 21, 1998, the ethical wheels came off the Clinton juggernaut.

That was the day that stories first appeared on the Internet—courtesy of Matt Drudge's *Drudge Report*—and later in the mainstream media about certain scandalous goings-on in the White House between the president and a young, female intern. The intern, so the story went, was being hounded by Independent Prosecutor Kenneth Starr to turn state's evidence against Clinton. Starr had been hired to look into questionable Arkansas land transactions that the president and first lady had reportedly been involved in. Starr then expanded the investigation to encompass virtually any apparent Clinton indiscretion that he could get his hands on.

OBFUSCATION

On the evening of the first intern stories, the president was interviewed on the PBS program, *Newshour with Jim Lehrer*. Said Clinton in response to a question about the purported relationship and subsequent cover-up, "I did not ask anyone to tell anything other than the truth. There is no improper relationship."

Critics pointed out that the president purposely used the verb "is," because maybe there "was" once an improper relationship, but none at the present time. Indeed, NBC's Len Cannon suggested that the president seems to have "resistance to full body contact with the truth."

Meanwhile, the president's henchmen, among them longtime political advisors James Carville and Paul Begala, sought to discredit the subject of the reported presidential affections. The intern, according to reports from "sources close to the president," was described as a "stalker and unstable young woman, hopelessly in love with President Clinton." The broad implication of such "inside information" was that the woman involved was delusional and apparently the creator of a bizarre and unseemly fictional account of a relationship that likely might not even exist.

Later on in the brewing scandal, Hillary Clinton, after months of silence, appeared on the *Today Show* to denounce Starr and his cronies as being agents of a "vast right-wing conspiracy" against her and her husband.

All of these communications responses helped divert attention from the real subjects of the inquiry, the president and the intern.

STONEWALLING

In a matter of days after the initial revelations, the name of the intern was broadcast far and wide. Monica Lewinsky was described as a wealthy, 22-year-old Los Angeles-reared "valley girl," who had been pampered by her parents and who treated sexual matters cavalierly. A former college teacher even came forward to testify that he had had an affair with the undergraduate which almost ruined his marriage.

In the white-hot heat of the accusations, President Clinton came forward on January 26, with his wife at his side. He spoke with passion and conviction. His entire demeanor demonstrated determination, sincerity, and contained anger.

"I want you to listen to me," he said, jabbing his finger as he looked directly at his accusers, "I did not have sexual relations with that woman, Miss Lewinsky. . . . These allegations are false, and I need to go back to work for the American people."

And that was that.

As masterful a performance as the chief executive carried out, some still were left to wonder why he didn't go further in explaining away the rumors.

According to the *New York Times*, Clinton's political and public relations advisors had pushed for more candor, but the president listened to lawyers, who counseled him to say as little as possible.

The Clinton limited response was reminiscent of President Nixon's defense in the two-decades-earlier Watergate scandal, where Nixon's allies did all they could to stonewall the press and keep from answering embarrassing questions.

CREDIBILITY

While many chose to believe the president, his ethical problems rapidly worsened after his televised denial.

Details of the supposed relationship began to leak from every corner. Lewinsky's existence, it was reported, had come out as part of the Paula Jones case. Jones, a former Arkansas government worker, had accused Clinton of making an indecent proposition to her in a hotel room. (She was quickly denounced as "trailer park trash" by Carville, and her accusations were dismissed.) Clinton, it would be revealed later, first denied having an affair with Lewinsky during his Jones depositions.

Upon learning of Lewinsky, Starr and his prosecutorial bloodhounds set out to make her talk. They encouraged a Lewinsky friend, Linda Tripp, to turn over surreptiously tape-recorded telephone conversations with the intern. Tripp, herself a former White House worker who had been banished to work at the Pentagon, was later tried for violating a state law that prohibited secret telephone tapings. As payback for launching Lewinsky on the American public, the Pentagon public relations office released Tripp's confidential personnel file, which contained embarrassing personal details about her marital and financial background.

Tripp further revealed to a *Newsweek* reporter that Lewinsky wasn't the only White House staffer involved with Clinton. She mentioned another woman, Kathryn Willey, who Clinton had reportedly accosted. Willey later denied, then admitted, then recanted the Tripp version.

Meanwhile, it was reported that Clinton had asked good friend and powerful Washington attorney Vernon Jordan to find Lewinsky a job to get her out of Washington. Jordan acknowledged meeting with Lewinsky and introducing her to potential employers but denied any impropriety.

Finally, it was reported that Starr—diffident, circumspect, and standoffish to the media—had asked Lewinsky to secretly tape record her conversations with Jordan—i.e., wear a wire—in exchange for leniency for her and her mother. Lewinsky had first denied a Clinton relationship, as had her mother, even though, as the nation was soon to learn, a relationship between the president and the intern had in fact been going on for months.

These dizzying details about apparent ethical lapses on the part of all the various, sordid participants—Clinton, Lewinsky, Starr, Tripp, Willey, Carville, Jordan, and countless others—crushed the credibility of everyone involved (Figure 4-8).

TRUTH

By August 1998, Clinton's goose was cooked.

It seemed apparent that he had not only lied to a grand jury about the Lewinsky matter but also to the American public. He would soon be the subject of impeachment hearings in the Congress, and even his closest aides were crestfallen.

So on August 17, six months after the name Monica Lewinsky had burst onto the scene, the president made a televised address before the American public.

This performance may have been the least ethical of all.

Instead of apologizing for lying to the people who had voted for and trusted him, Clinton chose calculated lawyerly language and a flat delivery.

"I misled people. . . . I deeply regret that." While admitting that he "did have a relationship with Ms. Lewinsky that was not appropriate," the president spent much of his address attacking Starr and asserting his own right to privacy—both popular themes, according to opinion polls.

Clinton-Intern Roundup

Clinton	**Starr**	**Tripp**	**Jordan**	**Lewinsky**
Clinton	**Jones**	**Flowers**	**Willey**	

FIGURE 4-8 **THE PLAYERS.** The protagonists in the most ethically painful presidential drama in history.

It was a hollow, wholly unsatisfactory performance that made grudging reference to the truth.

In its wake, the *New York Times* editorialized, "Clinton went for the time-tested blend of minimal confession and contained tantrum that got him elected twice." The *Washington Post* wrote, "This speech wasn't a *mea culpa*. It was an everybody else culpa."

Understandably, after the speech, polls indicated that although 60 percent of Americans still approved Clinton's performance as president, a whopping 73 percent didn't believe he was honest or trustworthy.

Three days later, the president ordered assaults on suspected terrorist operations in Afghanistan and Sudan. In light of the half-truths and outright lies that had characterized the Lewinsky saga, some questioned whether Clinton had ordered the attacks simply to divert attention from his domestic ethical miseries.

AFTERMATH

In the aftermath of the startling and depressing Clinton-Lewinsky saga, the following came to pass:

- ◪ President Clinton, after an extended and acrimonious debate that split the Congress along party lines, became the second president in history to be impeached by the House of Representatives.
- ◪ Monica Lewinsky appeared on national television to confess her misdeeds, wrote a book that did well initially, and tried to figure out what to do with the rest of her life.

- Hillary Clinton, faithful spouse who stood by relatively silently after her "right-wing conspiracy" initiative, moved on to campaign for the Senate in New York state.
- Kenneth Starr, after successfully prosecuting several Clinton administration officials and spending $50 million of taxpayers' money in his pursuit, finally, thankfully, stepped down from his government post.
- Vice President Albert Gore, who announced at a White House pep rally after Clinton's impeachment vote that the president would go down in history as a great chief executive, was hounded by such comments during his own campaign for the presidency in 2000.
- Worst of all, the American public, both Democrats and Republicans, suffered yet another disappointing ethical lapse from yet another powerful politician, who had asked for and received the public's trust.

Questions

1. Had you been a Clinton White House advisor in January 1998, what would you have wanted to know from the president about the intern?
2. What would you have advised the president to do at the time?
3. If the president lied before the jury in the Paula Jones case and later before a grand jury in the Lewinsky matter, could he in fact tell the truth to the American public?
4. What's your view of the ethics displayed by President Clinton? Monica Lewinsky? Kenneth Starr? Linda Tripp? Vernon Jordan?
5. How do you respond to those who said at the time that the media had no right reporting about the president's private indiscretions and that they, not Bill Clinton, were most to blame for the scandal that ensued?
6. Visit the *Drudge Report* (www.drudgereport.com), the Web site of Matt Drudge, who first reported the story about President Clinton and Monica Lewinsky. Browse the headlines on the home page and then enter the site to read a story or two. Does the *Drudge Report* appear to follow the journalism code of ethics in Figure 4-4, based on what you see on the site?

For further information, see Aviva Diamond, "Lessons from a Troubled White House, *PR Tactics,* October 1998, 27–29; Albert R. Hunt, "Washington Events Fuel Disdain for Media, Politics," *Wall Street Journal,* September 17, 1998, A-12; Bill Sammon, "President's Pit Bull Goes on the Offensive," *Washington Times National Weekly,* June 22–28, 1998, 4; Sammon, "Starr Denies He Asked Lewinsky to Wear Wire," *Washington Times National Weekly,* June 22–28, 1998, 8; Fraser P. Seitel, "Blind Loyalty vs. Due Diligence," Ragan Report, March 30, 1998, 2; Seitel, "Top Public Relations Lessons of 1998," Ragan Report, January 4, 1999, 2; Merrie Spaeth, "The Top PR Stories of 1998," *PR Tactics,* January 1999, 15; and George Stephanopoulos, "What I Saw," *Newsweek,* March 15, 1999, 33.

An Interview with Harold Burson

Harold Burson is a legendary public relations practitioner. He is chairman of Burson-Marsteller, a worldwide public relations firm with 2,500 employees and 50 offices in 27 countries. He was CEO of Burson-Marsteller from its founding in 1953 until January 1988. Mr. Burson, widely cited as the standard bearer of public relations ethics, has received virtually every major honor awarded by the profession and in 1999 was named by *Inside PR* magazine as "the most distinguished public relations professional of the 20th century."

How do ethics apply to the public relations function?
In a single word, pervasively. Ethical behavior is at the root of what we do as public relations professionals. We approach our calling with a commitment to serve the public interest, knowing full well that the public interest lacks a universal definition and knowing that one person's view of the public interest differs markedly from that of another. We must therefore be consistent in our personal definition of the public interest and be prepared to speak up for those actions we take.

How has the business of public relations changed over time?
Public relations has, over time, become more relevant as a management function for all manner of institutions—public and private sector, profit and not-for-profit. CEOs increasingly recognize the need to communicate to achieve their organizational objectives. Similarly, they have come to recognize public relations as a necessary component in the decision-making process. This has enhanced the role of public relations both internally and for independent consultants.

What are the principal activities of a public relations firm?
The public relations function can be divided into two principal classes of activity: the strategic and the implementing. Public relations firms play a major role on behalf of clients in both areas. In the realm of the strategic, a public relations firm brings to a client an independent perspective based on broad organizational experience with a wide spectrum of clients and problems. The public relations firm is not encumbered with the many internal considerations that frequently enter into the corporate or institutional decision-making process. In implementing programs, the public relations firm has a broad range of resources, both functional and geographic, that can be brought to bear on a client's problem. Furthermore, the public relations firm can usually be held to more specific accountability—both in terms of results and costs.

What constitutes the ideal public relations man or woman?
Public relations today covers so broad a range of activity that it is difficult to establish a set of specifications for all the kinds of people wearing the public relations mantle. Generally, I feel four primary characteristics apply to just about every successful public relations person I know.

- They're smart—bright, intelligent people; quick studies. They ask the right questions. They have that unique ability to establish credibility almost on sight.
- They know how to get along with people. They work well with their bosses, their peers, their subordinates. They work well with their clients and with third parties like the press and suppliers. They are emotionally stable—even (especially) under pressure. They use the pronoun "we" more than "I."
- They are motivated, and part of that motivation involves an ability to develop creative solutions. No one needs to tell them what to do next; instinctively, they know. They don't fear starting with a blank sheet of paper. To them, the blank sheet of paper equates with challenge and opportunity. They can write; they can articulate their thoughts in a persuasive manner.

How do you assess the future of public relations?
More so than ever before, those responsible for large institutions whose existence depends on public acceptance and support recognize the need for sound public relations input. At all levels of society, public opinion has been brought to bear in the conduct of affairs both in the public and private sectors. Numerous CEOs of major corporations have been deposed following initiatives undertaken by the media, by public interest groups, by institutional stockholders—all representing failures that stemmed from a lack of sensitivity to public opinion. Accordingly, my view is that public relations is playing and will continue to play a more pivotal role in the decision-making process than ever before. The sources of public relations counsel may well become less structured and more diverse, simply because of the growing pervasive understanding that public tolerance has become so important in the achievement of any goals that have a recognizable impact on society.

Chapter 5

Research

In the winter of 1998, an e-mail message went forth across the land. It concerned the red-hot clothing magnate Tommy Hilfiger and read thusly:

I'm sure many of you watched the recent taping of the Oprah Winfrey Show where her guest was Tommy Hilfiger. On the show, she asked him if the statements about race he was accused of saying were true. Statements like if he'd known African-Americans, Hispanics and Asians would buy his clothes, he would not have made them so nice. He wished these people would not buy his clothes as they are made for upper class white people. His answer to Oprah was a simple, "yes." Whereafter she immediately asked him to leave her show.

There was one problem with this e-mail, distributed to hundreds of thousands of individuals across America. It was completely bogus.

The Hilfiger e-mail—one of the most notorious of so-called "urban legends" on the Internet—was the product of an Internet pretender. Designer Tommy Hilfiger, in fact, had never met Oprah Winfrey and had certainly never appeared on her television program. The e-mail was created out of whole cloth. But the impact on the Tommy Hilfiger company—in terms of embarrassment and even lost sales, from those who believed the bogus communication—was serious. The rumors eventually made it into USA Today. The Hilfiger public relations team vigorously denied the accusation on its own Web site and posted denials in news groups and other message boards. Oprah Winfrey even addressed the issue on her show.[1] But the damage was done.

Such was the impact of rumors spread through unregulated Internet chat rooms, news groups, and forums.

The advent of the World Wide Web, with its steady stream of comments—sometimes positive, often negative—about public companies, trade associations, political candidates, and many others has made it obligatory for public relations professionals to monitor what is being said. United Airlines better monitor what is being said at Untiedairlines.com and Microsoft at League of Microsoft Haters (L.O.M.H.) and Wal-Mart at www.walmartsucks.com

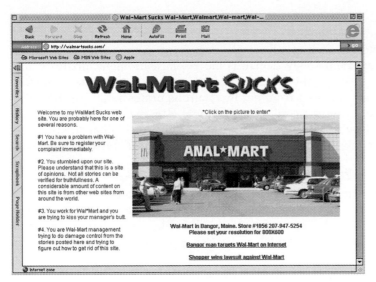

FIGURE 5-1 This rogue Web site, designed to embarrass the mighty Wal-Mart, was typical of anticorporate spaces on the Internet. Monitoring such destructive sites has become a research responsibility of the public relations department.

(Figure 5-1). Such sites and the news groups, forums, and chat rooms that spew out constant venom can be deadly, if a company is caught unawares of what is being said about it.[2]

Monitoring the Web has become a frontline responsibility of public relations departments. As an organization's eyes and ears to the public, it is obligatory that public relations professionals keep aware of what is being said that could impact their employer. This Internet monitoring function is an example of "research"—an aspect of public relations that has increased in importance as the Internet has grown, competition has intensified, and management has become more concerned about what it receives for the money it spends on public relations activities.

Essential First Step

Every public relations program or solution should begin with research. Most don't, which is a shame.

The four-step R-A-C-E and five-step R-O-S-I-E approaches to public relations problem solving, alluded to in chapter 1, both start with research. Because public relations is still a misunderstood and amorphous function to many, public relations recommendations must be grounded in hard data whenever possible. In other words, before recommending a course of action, public relations professionals must analyze audiences, assess alternatives, and generally do their homework. In other words, most clients are less interested in what their public relations advisors "think" than in what they "know." The only way to know what to do is by researching first. Indeed, research has become the essential first step in the practice of modern public relations.

Instinct, intuition, and gut feelings all remain important in the conduct of public relations work; but management today demands more—measurement, analysis, and evaluation at every stage of the public relations process. In an era of scarce resources, management wants facts and statistics from public relations professionals to show that their efforts contribute not only to overall organizational effectiveness but also to the bottom line. Why should we introduce a new intranet publication? What should it say and cost? How will we know it's working? Questions like these must be answered through research.

In a day when organizational resources are precious and companies don't want to spend money unless it enhances results, public relations programs must contribute to meeting business objectives.[3] That means that research must be applied to help segment market targets, analyze audience preferences and dislikes, and determine which messages might be most effective with which audiences. Research then becomes essential in helping realize management's goals.

Research should be applied in public relations work both at the initial stage, prior to planning a campaign, and at the final stage, to evaluate a program's effectiveness. Early research helps to determine the current situation, prevalent attitudes, and difficulties that the program faces. Later research examines the program's success, along with what else still needs to be done. Research at both points in the process is critical.

Even though research does not necessarily provide unequivocal proof of a program's effectiveness, it does allow public relations professionals to support their own intuition. It's little wonder, then, that the idea of measuring public relations work has steadily gained acceptance.[4]

What Is Research?

Research is the systematic collection and interpretation of information to increase understanding (Figure 5-2).[5] Most people associate public relations with conveying information; although that association is accurate, research must be the obligatory first step in any project. A firm must acquire enough accurate, relevant data about its publics, products, and programs to answer these questions:

- How can we identify and define our constituent groups?
- How does this knowledge relate to the design of our messages?
- How does it relate to the design of our programs?
- How does it relate to the media we use to convey our messages?
- How does it relate to the schedule we adopt in using our media?
- How does it relate to the ultimate implementation tactics of our program?

It is difficult to delve into the minds of others, whose backgrounds and points of view may be quite different from one's own, with the purpose of understanding why they think as they do. Research skills are partly intuitive, partly an outgrowth of individual temperament, and partly a function of acquired knowledge. There is nothing mystifying about them. Although we tend to think of research in terms of impersonal test scores, interviews, or questionnaires, they are only a small part of the process. The real challenge lies in using research—knowing when to do what, with whom, and for what purpose.

FIGURE 5-2 **Early research.** An early research effort, albeit a futile one, was the return of the biblical scouts sent by Moses to reconnoiter the land of Canaan. They disagreed in their reports, and the Israelites believed the gloomier versions. This failure to interpret the data correctly caused them to wander another 40 years in the wilderness. (An even earlier research effort was Noah's sending the dove to search for dry ground.)

Principles of Public Relations Research

For years, public relations professionals have debated the standards of measuring public relations' effectiveness. In 1997, the Institute for Public Relations Research and Education offered seven guiding principles in setting standards for public relations research.

- Establishing clear program objectives and desired outcomes, tied directly to business goals.
- Differentiating between measuring public relations "outputs," generally short-term and surface (e.g. amount of press coverage received or exposure of a particular message), and measuring public relations "outcomes," usually farther-reaching and carrying greater impact (e.g. changing awareness, attitudes, and even behavior).
- Measuring media content as a first step in the public relations evaluation process. Such a measure is limited, in that it can't discern whether a target audience actually saw a message or responded to it.
- Understanding that no one technique can expect to evaluate public relations effectiveness. Rather, this requires a combination of techniques, from media analysis to cyberspace analysis, from focus groups to polls and surveys.
- Being wary of attempts to compare public relations effectiveness with advertising effectiveness. One particularly important consideration is that while

advertising placement and messages can be controlled, their equivalent on the public relations side cannot be.

☑ The most trustworthy measurement of public relations effectiveness is that which stems from an organization with clearly identified key messages, target audiences and desired channels of communication. The converse of this is that the more confused an organization is about its targets, the less reliable its public relations measurement will be.

☑ Public relations evaluation cannot be accomplished in isolation. It must be linked to overall business goals, strategies, and tactics.[6]

Types of Public Relations Research

In general, research is conducted to do three things: (1) describe a process, situation, or phenomenon; (2) explain why something is happening, what its causes are, and what effect it will have; and (3) predict what probably will happen if we do or don't take action. Most research in public relations is either theoretical or applied. Applied research solves practical problems; theoretical research aids understanding of a public relations process.

Applied Research

In public relations work, applied research can be either strategic or evaluative. Both applications are designed to answer specific practical questions.

☑ **Strategic research** is used primarily in program development to determine program objectives, develop message strategies, or establish benchmarks. It often examines the tools and techniques of public relations. For example, a firm that wants to know how employees rate its candor in internal publications would first conduct strategic research to find out where it stands.

☑ **Evaluative research,** sometimes called summative research, is conducted primarily to determine whether a public relations program has accomplished its goals and objectives. For example, if changes are made in the internal communications program to increase candor, evaluative research can determine whether the goals have been met. A variant of evaluation can be applied during a program to monitor progress and indicate where modifications might make sense.

Theoretical Research

Theoretical research is more abstract and conceptual than applied research. It helps build theories in public relations work about why people communicate, how public opinion is formed, and how a public is created.

Knowledge of theoretical research is important as a framework for persuasion and as a base for understanding why people do what they do.

Some knowledge of theoretical research in public relations and mass communications is essential for enabling practitioners to understand the limitations of communication as a persuasive tool. Attitude and behavior change have been the traditional goals in public relations programs, yet theoretical research indicates that such goals may be difficult or impossible to achieve through persuasive efforts. According to such research, other factors are always getting in the way.

Researchers have found that communication is most persuasive when it comes from multiple sources of high credibility. Credibility itself is a multidimensional concept that includes trustworthiness, expertise, and power. Others have found that a message generally is more effective when it is simple, because it is easier to understand, localize, and make personally relevant. According to still other research, the persuasiveness of a message can be increased when it arouses or is accompanied by a high level of personal involvement in the issue at hand.

The point here is that knowledge of theoretical research can help practitioners not only understand the basis of applied research findings, but also temper management's expectations of attitude and behavioral change resulting from public relations programs.

Methods of Public Relations Research

Observation is the foundation of modern social science. Scientists, social psychologists, and anthropologists make observations, develop theories, and, hopefully, increase understanding of human behavior. Public relations research, too, is founded on observation. Three primary forms of public relations research dominate the field.

- ◪ Surveys are designed to reveal attitudes and opinions—what people think about certain subjects.
- ◪ Communication audits often reveal disparities between real and perceived communications between management and target audiences. Management may make certain assumptions about its methods, media, materials, and messages, whereas its targets may confirm or refute those assumptions.
- ◪ Unobtrusive measures—such as fact finding, content analysis, and readability studies—enable the study of a subject or object without involving the researcher or the research as an intruder.

Each method of public relations research offers specific benefits and should be understood and used by the modern practitioner.

Surveys

Survey research is one of the most frequently used research methods in public relations. Surveys can be applied to broad societal issues, such as determining public opinion about a political candidate, or to the most minute organizational problem, such as whether shareholders like the quarterly report. Surveys come in two types.

1. **Descriptive surveys** offer a snapshot of a current situation or condition. They are the research equivalent of a balance sheet, capturing reality at a specific point in time. A typical public opinion poll is a prime example.
2. **Explanatory surveys** are concerned with cause and effect. Their purpose is to help explain why a current situation or condition exists and to offer explanations for opinions and attitudes. Frequently, such explanatory or analytical surveys are designed to answer the question "Why?" Why are our philanthropic dollars not being appreciated in the community? Why don't employees believe management's messages? Why is our credibility being questioned?

Surveys generally consist of four elements: (1) the sample, (2) the questionnaire, (3) the interview, and (4) the analysis of results. (Direct mail surveys, of course, eliminate the interview step.) Because survey research is so critical in public relations, we will examine each survey element in some detail.

The sample. The sample, or selected target group, must be representative of the total public whose views are sought. Once a survey population has been determined, a researcher must select the appropriate sample or group of respondents from whom to collect information. Sampling is tricky. A researcher must be aware of the hidden pitfalls in choosing a representative sample, not the least of which is the perishable nature of most data. Survey findings are rapidly outdated because of population mobility and changes in the political and socioeconomic environment. Consequently, sampling should be completed quickly.

Two cross-sectional approaches are used in obtaining a sample: random sampling and nonrandom sampling. The former is more scientific, the latter more informal.

Random sampling. In random sampling, two properties are essential—equality and independence in selection. Equality means that no element has any greater or lesser chance of being selected. Independence means that selecting any one element in no way influences the selection of any other element. Random sampling is based on a mathematical criterion that allows generalizations from the sample to be made to the total population. There are four types of random or probability samples.

1. **Simple random sampling** gives all members of the population an equal chance of being selected. First, all members of the population are identified, and then as many subjects as are needed are randomly selected—usually with the help of a computer. Election polling uses a random approach; although millions of Americans vote, only a few thousand are ever polled on their election preferences. The Nielsen national television sample, for example, consists of 4,000 homes. The Census Bureau uses a sample of 72,000 out of 93 million households to obtain estimates of employment and other population characteristics.

How large should a random sample be? The answer depends on a number of factors, one of which is the size of the population. In addition, the more similar the population elements are in regard to the characteristics being studied, the smaller the sample required. In most random samples, the following population-to-sample ratios apply, with a 5 percent margin of error:

Population	Sample
1,000	278
2,000	322
3,000	341
5,000	355
10,000	370
50,000	381
100,000	383
500,000	383
Infinity	384

Random sampling owes its accuracy to the laws of probability, which are best explained by the example of a barrel filled with 10,000 marbles—5,000 green ones and 5,000 red ones. If a blindfolded person selects a certain number of marbles from the barrel—say, 400—the laws of probability suggest that the most frequently drawn combination will be 200 red and 200 green. These laws further suggest that with certain margins of error, a very few marbles can represent the whole barrel, which can correspond to any size—for example, that of city, state, or nation.

2. **Systematic random sampling** is closely related to simple random sampling, but it uses a random starting point in the sample list. From then on, the researcher selects every nth person in the list. As long as every person has an equal and independent chance to be selected on the first draw, then the sample qualifies as "random" and is equally reliable to simple random sampling. Random telephone dialing, for example, which solves the problem of failing to consider unlisted numbers, may use this technique.

3. **Stratified random sampling** is a procedure used to survey different segments or strata of the population. For example, if an organization wants to determine the relationship between years of service and attitudes toward the company, it may stratify the sample to ensure that the breakdown of respondents accurately reflects the makeup of the population. In other words, if more than half of the employees have been with the company more than 10 years, more than half of those polled should also reflect that level of service. By stratifying the sample, the organization's objective can be achieved.

4. **Cluster sampling** involves first breaking the population down into small heterogeneous subsets, or clusters, and then selecting the potential sample from the individual clusters or groups. A cluster may often be defined as a geographic area, such as an election district.

Nonrandom sampling.   Nonrandom samples come in three types: convenience, quota, and volunteer.

1. **Convenience samples,** also known as accidental, chunk, or opportunity samples, are relatively unstructured, rather unsystematic, and designed to elicit ideas and points of view. Journalists use convenience samples when they conduct person-on-the-street interviews. The most common type of convenience sample in public relations research is the focus group. Focus groups generally consist of eight to 12 people, with a moderator encouraging in-depth discussion of a specific topic. Focus groups generate concepts and ideas rather than validate hypotheses.

2. **Quota samples** permit a researcher to choose subjects on the basis of certain characteristics. For example, the attitudes of a certain number of women, men, blacks, whites, rich, or poor may need to be known. Quotas are imposed in proportion to each group's percentage of the population. The advantage of quota sampling is that it increases the homogeneity of a sample population, thus enhancing the validity of a study. However, it is hard to classify interviewees by one or two discrete demographic characteristics. For example, a particular interviewee may be black, Catholic, female, under 25, and a member of a labor union all at the same time, making the lines of demographic demarcation pretty blurry. (A derivative of quota sampling is called purposive sampling.)

3. **Volunteer samples** use willing participants who agree voluntarily to respond to concepts and hypotheses for research purposes.[7]

BACKGROUNDER

Creatively Measuring Press Coverage

Through the decades, the most tried and true public relations measurement technique was to measure press clipping inches to justify to employers the success of a particular publicity program. In recent years, the techniques surrounding press coverage measurement have become more sophisticated.

The Rowland Company, a New York-based public relations agency, has introduced the Rowland Publicity Index, which applies numerical values to such components as physical characteristics, message, context, and objectives. Measures are applied against such criteria as:

1. Length
   How long is the article?
   Is it a brief mention or an extensive story?
   What portion of the article is relevant to the topic?
2. Position
   Where does the story appear in the publication? On the page?
   Is it a main story, for example, page one?
   Is there a "teaser" on the front page for the story?
3. Graphics
   How big is the headline? One line or two?
   Is there a complementary photo?
   What is the size and quality of the photo?
   Is there a sidebar or similar element?
4. Key message
   Were the promotion's key messages included in the article?
   Were they up front or buried in the back?

Was a spokesperson quoted?
Were the messages present in the headline or cutline?

5. Context
   Does the story mention a product? In a positive or negative way?
   Does the story offer a substitution for a product?
   Is the story critical of the organization or industry?
   Does the article have a positive or negative tone?
6. Achieved objectives
   Did the article accomplish what we set out to achieve?
   Was it covered as a stand-alone or included in a wrap-up mention with other ideas?
   What was the overall impact of the article?

Another agency, Kaiser Associates of Vienna, Virginia, has introduced other media measurement criteria such as:

- Relative costs, such as media relations as a percentage of total revenues or media relations costs as a percentage of total costs.
- Processes, such as cycle times for the creation of news releases and media events.
- Benchmarking media clips against competitors.
- Rating media clips as positive, negative, or neutral in assessing "impact" on targeted publics.

For further information, see "PR Execs Measure the Worth of Traditional Measurements," PR News, February 10, 1997, 7; and Carter Griffin and Aimee P. Martin, "Creatively Measuring Media Relations," Public Relations Strategist, 36–40.

The questionnaire.   Before creating a questionnaire, a researcher must consider his or her objective in doing the study. What you seek to find out should influence the specific publics you ask, the questions you raise, and the research method you choose. After determining what you're after, consider the particular questionnaire design. Specifically, researchers should observe the following in designing their questionnaire:

1. **Keep it short.** Make a concerted attempt to limit questions. It's terrific if the questionnaire can be answered in five minutes.

2. **Use structured, not open-ended, questions.** People would rather check a box or circle a number than write an essay. But leave room at the bottom for general comments or "Other." Also, start with simple, nonthreatening questions before getting to the more difficult, sensitive ones. This approach will build respondent trust as well as commitment to finishing the questionnaire.

3. **Measure intensity of feelings.** Let respondents check "very satisfied," "satisfied," "dissatisfied," or "very dissatisfied" rather than "yes" or "no." One popular approach is the semantic differential technique shown in Figure 5-3.

Guest Satisfaction Survey

Our records indicate that you recently had reservations at the hotel shown above on the date indicated.

MARKING INSTRUCTIONS

• Do not use red ink.

• Do not use a marker that will bleed through the page.

• You may use pencil or pen to complete this survey.

Please be sure to fill the response oval completely.

CORRECT MARK   INCORRECT MARKS

Please take a moment and answer the following questions.
If a question is not applicable to your stay, please skip to the next question.

How would you rate our hotel on:

1. QUALITY OF ACCOMMODATIONS...

EXCELLENT ... POOR

Cleanliness of your guest room upon entering
Cleanliness and servicing of your room during stay
Overall cleanliness of bathroom
Cleanliness of tub and tile
Overall cleanliness of bedroom
Condition of bedspread
Overall guest room quality

Overall maintenance and upkeep
Condition of the grounds
Condition of the lobby area
Condition of the restaurants and lounges
Functionality of guest room
Condition of pool and pool area

Everything in your room in working order? ◯ Yes ◯ No

What was your room number? _____

Please share any comments you may have about the quality of our rooms, lobby, and outside areas.

2. QUALITY OF HOTEL STAFF AND SERVICES...

Did you make your room reservation through the hotel? ◯ Yes ◯ No

When you arrived at the hotel, was the information the hotel had concerning your reservation correct? ◯ Yes ◯ No

FIGURE 5-3 **Client satisfaction research.** In questionnaires, one common device to measure intensity of feelings is the semantic differential technique, which gives respondents a scale of choices from the worst to the best. Marriott Hotels used this technique in evaluating its facilities, service levels, and people.

4. **Don't use fancy words or words that have more than one meaning.** If you must use big words, make the context clear.

5. **Don't ask loaded questions.** "Is management doing all it can to communicate with you?" is a terrible question. The answer is always no.

6. **Don't ask double-barreled questions.** "Would you like management meetings once a month, or are bimonthly meetings enough?" is another terrible question.

7. **Pretest.** Send your questionnaire to a few colleagues and listen to their suggestions.

8. **Attach a letter explaining how important the respondents' answers are, and let recipients know that they will remain anonymous.** Respondents will feel better if they think the study is significant and their identities are protected. Also, specify how and where the data will be used.

9. **Hand-stamp the envelopes, preferably with unique commemorative stamps.** Metering an envelope indicates assembly-line research, and researchers have found that the more expensive the postage, the higher the response rate. People like to feel special.

10. **Follow up your first mailing.** Send a reminder postcard three days after the original questionnaire. Then wait a few weeks and send a second questionnaire, just in case recipients have lost the first.

11. **Send out more questionnaires than you think necessary.** The major weakness of most mail surveys is the unmeasurable error introduced by nonresponders. You're shooting for a 50 percent response rate; anything less tends to be suspect.

12. **Enclose a reward.** There's nothing like a token gift of merchandise or money—a $2 bill works beautifully—to make a recipient feel guilty for not returning a questionnaire.[8]

Appendix B gives an example of a survey questionnaire.

Interviews

Interviews can provide a more personal, firsthand feel for public opinion. Interview panels can range from focus groups of randomly selected average people to Delphi panels of so-called opinion leaders. Interviews can be conducted in a number of ways, including face to face, telephone, mail, and through the Internet.

Focus groups. This approach is used with increasing frequency in public relations today. Such interviews can be conducted one-on-one or through survey panels. These panels can be used, for example, to measure buying habits or the impact of public relations programs on a community or organizational group. They can also be used to assess general attitudes toward certain subjects, such as new products or advertising.

With the focus group technique, a well-drilled moderator leads a group through a discussion of opinions on a particular product, organization, or idea. Participants represent the socioeconomic level desired by the research sponsor—from college students to office workers to millionaires. Almost always, focus group participants are paid for their efforts. Sessions are frequently videotaped and then analyzed, often in preparation for more formal and specific research questionnaires.

Focus groups should be organized with the following guidelines in mind:

1. **Define your objectives and audience.** The more tightly you define your goals and your target audience, the more likely you are to gather relevant information. In other words, don't conduct a focus group with friends and

family members, hoping to get a quick and inexpensive read. Nothing of value will result.

2. **Recruit your groups.** Recruiting participants takes several weeks, depending on the difficulty of contacting the target audience. Contact is usually made by phone, with a series of questions to weed out employees of competitors, members of the news media (to keep the focus group from becoming a news story), and those who don't fit target group specifications. Persons who have participated in a group in the past year should also be screened out; they may be more interested in the money than in helping you find what you're looking for.

3. **Choose the right moderator.** Staff people who may be excellent conversationalists are not necessarily the best focus group moderators. The gift of gab is not enough. Professional moderators know how to establish rapport quickly, how and when to probe beyond the obvious, how to draw comments from reluctant participants, how to keep a group on task, and how to interpret results validly.

4. **Conduct enough focus groups.** One or two focus groups usually are not enough. Four to six are better to uncover the full range of relevant ideas and opinions. Regardless of the number of groups, however, you must resist the temptation to add up responses. That practice gives the focus group more analytical worth than it deserves.

5. **Use a discussion guide.** This is a basic outline of what you want to investigate. It will lead the moderator through the discussion and keep the group on track.

6. **Choose proper facilities.** The discussion room should be comfortable, with participants sitting around a table that gives them a good view of each other. Observers can use closed-circuit TV and one-way mirrors, but participants should always be told when they are being observed.

7. **Keep a tight rein on observers.** Observers should rarely be in the same room with participants; the two groups ordinarily should be separated. Observers should view the proceedings seriously; this is not "dinner and a show."

8. **Consider using outside help.** Setting up focus groups can be time-consuming and complicated. Often the best advice is to hire a firm recommended by the American Marketing Association or the Marketing Research Association so that the process, the moderator, and the evaluation are as professional as possible.[9]

Telephone interviews.   In contrast to personal interviews, telephone interviews suffer from a high refusal rate. Many people just don't want to be bothered. Such interviews may also introduce an upper-income bias because lower-income earners may lack telephones. However, the increasing use of unlisted numbers by upper-income people may serve to mitigate this bias. Telephone interviews must be carefully scripted so that interviewers know precisely what to ask, regardless of a respondent's answer. Calls should be made at less busy times of the day, such as early morning or late afternoon.

With both telephone and face-to-face interviews, it is important to establish rapport with the interview subject. It may make sense to begin the interview with nonthreatening questions, saving the tougher, more controversial ones—on income level or race, for example—until last. Another approach is to depersonalize the research by explaining that others have devised the survey and that the interviewer's job is simply to ask the questions.

Mail interviews.   This is the least expensive approach, but it often suffers from a low response rate. You are aiming for a 50 percent response rate. Frequently, people who return mail questionnaires are those with strong biases either in favor of or (more commonly) in opposition to the subject at hand. As noted, one way to generate a higher response from mail interviews is through the use of self-addressed, stamped envelopes or enclosed incentives such as dollar bills or free gifts.

Drop-off interviews.   This approach combines face-to-face and mail interview techniques. An interviewer personally drops off a questionnaire at a household, usually after conducting a face-to-face interview. Because the interviewer has already established some rapport with the interviewee, the rate of return with this technique is considerably higher than it is for straight mail interviews.

Delphi panels.   The Delphi technique is a more qualitative research tool that uses opinion leaders—local influential persons as well as national experts—often to help tailor the design of a general public research survey. Designed by the Rand Corporation in the 1950s, the Delphi technique is a consensus-building approach that relies on repeated waves of questionnaires sent to the same select panel of experts. Delphi findings generate a wide range of responses and help set the agenda for more meaningful future research. Stated another way, Delphi panels offer a "research reality check."[10]

Internet interviews.   The latest technique of interviewing constituent publics is via the Internet. This is a particularly effective technique in gathering rapid support for a political position. In 1999, disgraced former Clinton advisor Dick Morris created Vote.com to measure voters' attitudes on a variety of arbitrary issues selected by Morris. Since "polling" merely required Internet access, Morris received voluminous responses to his questionnaires and flooded the Clinton White House with e-mail polling results. The White House responded by blocking such e-mail so as not to be overrun by it.

Results analysis.   After selecting the sample, drawing up the questionnaire, and interviewing the respondents, the researcher must analyze the findings. Often a great deal of analysis is required to produce meaningful recommendations.

The objective of every sample is to come up with results that are valid and reliable. A margin of error explains how far off the prediction may be. A sample may be large enough to represent fairly the larger universe; yet, depending on the margin of sampling error, the results of the research may not be statistically significant. That is, the differences or distinctions detected by the survey may not be sizable enough to offset the margin of error. Thus, the margin of error must always be determined.

This concept is particularly critical in political polling, where pollsters are quick to acknowledge that their results may accurately represent the larger universe, but normally with a 3 percent margin of error. Thus, the results could be 3 percent more or less for a certain candidate. Consequently, a pollster who says a candidate will win with 51 percent of the vote really means that the candidate could win with as much as 54 percent or lose with as little as 48 percent of the vote.

Political polls are fraught with problems. They cannot predict outcomes scientifically. Rather, they provide a snapshot, freezing attitudes at a certain point in time—like a balance sheet for a corporation. Obviously, people's attitudes change with the passage of time, and pollsters, despite what they claim, can't categorically predict the outcome of an election. Perhaps the most notorious example of this was the political poll sponsored by the *Literary Digest* in 1936, which used a telephone polling technique to predict that Alf Landon would be the nation's next president. Landon thereupon suffered one of the worst drubbings in American electoral history at the hands of Franklin Roosevelt. It was probably of little solace to the *Literary Digest* that most of its telephone respondents, many of whom were Republicans wealthy enough to afford phones, did vote for Landon.

The point is that in analyzing results, problems of validity, reliability, and levels of statistical significance associated with margins of error must be considered before concrete recommendations based on survey data are offered.

A QUESTION OF ETHICS

Assessing an "Unbiased" Testing Agency

For six decades, there was no more trusted research source of information about products and their strengths and weaknesses than *Consumer Reports*. The independent, self-proclaimed bastion of "independent testing and research" was looked upon as one of the most unbiased sources of pertinent product information in the United States.

By the end of the century, however, questions emerged as to just how "unbiased" the vaunted research agency was.

What triggered the questions was a *Consumer Reports* attack on Isuzu Motors Limited, maker of the successful Trooper, a popular sport utility vehicle.

The drama started one August morning in 1996 when executives of Isuzu Motors in California were notified by *Consumer Reports* that "an Isuzu product would be discussed at a news conference in 30 minutes." Isuzu had no clue as to which product would be discussed and what would be said about it. Their suspicion was that whatever was said, it wouldn't be very good.

Boy were they right.

At the news conference, *Consumer Reports* played a videotape that showed an out-of-control Isuzu Trooper, unable to negotiate a turn with its right wheels more than two feet off the ground, headed for immediate disaster. The conference concluded with a warning from *Consumer Reports'* technical director that, "Consumers shouldn't buy the Isuzu Trooper, and owners of the vehicle should drive it only when necessary."

Five minutes after the news conference, Isuzu received its first call from the media. By day's end, it had received more than 100 press calls, and that night, the incriminating report was prominently featured on CBS and CNN; the next day, it was in all of the nation's most prestigious newspapers. It mattered little that the company adamantly claimed that the Trooper had never experienced any problems. The damage was done.

In the 12 months following the news conference, sales of the Isuzu Trooper declined from 23,000 to 13,000—the dramatic, but not wholly unexpected, impact from a negative piece in a magazine rated as "the most believable and objective source of information about products and services."

Deeply stung, Isuzu fired back. It sued the magazine and questioned its testing methods, claiming that *Consumer Reports* is beholden to its funders, including foundations with specific antibusiness agendas. Specifically, Isuzu charged that *Consumer Reports* and its parent company, Consumers Union, nurtured a long-standing bias against SUVs.

The company alleged that *Consumer Reports'* charges were trumped up as ammunition in its parent company's battle with the federal government over regulation of SUVs. Indeed, prior to the Isuzu offensive, the magazine had run three stories in a year and a half asking, "How safe are SUVs?" Consumers Union even petitioned the National Highway Traffic Safety Administration to tighten standards for SUVs.

In its suit, Isuzu alleged that the Consumers Union test driver purposely tipped the vehicle and also that the driver chose to negotiate around an object in his path, rather than hitting the brakes. In other words, Isuzu claimed that *Consumer Reports* rigged the test to increase sales of its magazine.

Consumer Reports denied all charges, and the case went to court in December 1999. The president of *Consumer Reports* suggested that discovery documents indicated Isuzu considered the lawsuit a "PR tool" and expected Consumers Union to "shut up" when attacked.

Regardless of the verdict, it was curious that the testing agency gave Isuzu only a brief warning before its press conference. In addition, Isuzu claimed it could learn nothing about how the test was conducted until after the damage had been done. This, too, is curious, especially for a revered consumer research testing service that claims to be "unbiased."

For further information, see Jennifer Greenstein, "Testing Consumer Reports," Brill's Content, September 1999, 70–77; and Rhonda H. Kapartkin, "When Attacked CU Will Probably Shut Up," Consumer Reports, December 1999.

Communication Audits

When the gigantic Exxon Corporation merged with the equally gigantic Mobil Corporation in December 1999, it turned to an increasingly important method of research in public relations work: the communications audit. Such audits are used frequently by corporations, schools, hospitals, and other organizations to determine whether a communications group is running effectively and also how the institution is perceived by its core constituents. Communications audits help public relations professionals understand more clearly the relationships between management actions and objectives, on the one hand, and communications methods to promote those objectives, on the other.

Communication audits are typically used to analyze the standing of a company with its employees or community neighbors; to assess the readership of routine communication vehicles, such as annual reports and news releases; or to examine an organization's performance as a corporate citizen. Communication audits often provide benchmarks against which future public relations programs can be applied and measured.

Communication audits typically are used to provide information on how to solve the following problems:

- Bottlenecked information flows
- Uneven communication workloads
- Employees working at cross-purposes
- Hidden information within an organization that is not being used, to the detriment of the institution
- Conflicting or nonexisting notions about what the organization is and does.[11]

The most effective communication audits start with a researcher who (1) is familiar with the public to be studied, (2) generally understands the attitudes of the target public toward the organization, (3) recognizes the issues of concern to the target public, and (4) understands the relative power of the target public vis-à-vis other publics.

Unobtrusive Methods

Of the various unobtrusive methods of data collection available to public relations researchers, probably the most widely used is simple fact finding. Facts are the bricks and mortar of public relations work; no action can be taken unless the facts are known, and the fact-finding process is continuous.

Each organization must keep a fact file of the most essential data with which it is involved. For example, such items as key organization statistics, publications, management biographies and photos, press clippings, media lists, competitive literature, pending legislation, organizational charters and bylaws should be kept on file and updated. Even better, computerized listings of such facts offer easier access when research is called for in these areas.

Another unobtrusive method is content analysis, the primary purpose of which is to describe a message or set of messages. For example, an organization with news releases that are used frequently by local newspapers can't be certain, without research, whether the image conveyed by its releases is what the organization seeks. By analyzing the news coverage, the firm can get a much clearer idea of the effectiveness of its communications. Such content analysis might be organized according to the following specific criteria:

- **Frequency of coverage.** How many releases were used?
- **Placement within the paper.** Did releases appear more frequently on page 1 or 71?

- ◪ **People reached.** What was the circulation of the publications in which the releases appeared?
- ◪ **Messages conveyed.** Did the releases used express the goals of the organization, or were they simply informational in content?
- ◪ **Editing of releases.** How much did the newspaper edit the copy submitted? Were desired meanings materially changed?
- ◪ **Attitude conveyed.** Was the reference to the organization positive, negative, or neutral?

Another unobtrusive method, the readability study, helps a communicator determine whether messages are written at the right educational level for the audience. Typical measures include the Flesch Formula, the FOG Index, and the SMOG Index—all based on the concept that the greater the number of syllables in a passage, the more difficult and less readable the text.[12]

Clearly, there is nothing particularly mysterious or difficult about unobtrusive methods of research. Such methods are relatively simple to apply, yet they are essential for arriving at appropriate modifications for an ongoing public relations program.

Evaluation

No matter what type of public relations research is used, results of the research and the research project itself should always be evaluated. Evaluation is designed to determine what happened and why, measuring results against established objectives.

Evaluation of public relations programs depends on several things:

- ◪ **Setting measurable public relations program objectives.** Goals should specify who the target publics are, what impact the program seeks to have on those publics, and when the results are expected.
- ◪ **Securing management commitment.** Public relations people and management should always agree in advance on the program's objectives, so that the results can be clearly evaluated. Without management "buy in" that the program is objective and well targeted, management may not believe the results.
- ◪ **Selecting the most appropriate outcomes.** At one end of outcome evaluation is a measurement of the press clippings a program received, that is, the number of column inches or airtime devoted to the program. At the other end of the evaluative spectrum is a "content analysis" of the messages conveyed as a result of the program. This is a more sophisticated evaluation of program effectiveness.
- ◪ **Determining the best way to gather data.** Again, raw program records and observation are a rudimentary but acceptable method of evaluative measurement. Better would be attitude pre-and post-testing to determine if a particular program helped facilitate a shift in attitudes toward a program, company, or issue. Surveys may or may not be called for.
- ◪ **Reporting back to management.** Evaluation findings should be shared with management. This reinforces the notion that public relations is contributing to management goals for the organization.

In any event, in evaluating after the fact, researchers can learn how to improve future efforts. Were the target audiences surveyed the right ones? Were the research assumptions applied to those audiences correct? Were questions from research tools left unanswered?

Again, research results can be evaluated in a number of ways. Perhaps the most common (alas) in public relations is a "seat-of-the-pants" evaluation, in which anecdotal observation and practitioner judgment are used to estimate the effectiveness of the public relations program. Such evaluation might be based on feedback from members of a key public, personal media contacts, or colleagues, but the practitioner alone evaluates the success of the program with subjective observation.

More scientific evaluation results from public relations opinion polls and surveys and fact-finding research, such as content analysis, in which the numerical tabulation of results is evaluated and often combined with seat-of-the-pants observation. One of the most effective evaluative techniques to determine the success of a program is to pretest target audiences before the public relations program is implemented and then post-test after the program is completed.

Comparing the results of the two tests enables a more scientific assessment of the program's success.

An ongoing system for monitoring public relations activities is yet another way to evaluate programs. Monitoring a public relations campaign, for example, may indicate necessary changes in direction, reallocation of resources, or redefinition of priorities. Another way to evaluate is to dissect public programs after the fact. Such postmortem evaluation can provide objective analysis when a program is still fresh in one's mind. This can be extremely helpful in modifying the program for future use.

In the fiercely competitive, resource-dear 21st century, the practice of public relations will increasingly be called on to justify its activities and evaluate the results of its programs.

Research and the Web

The Internet is in its infancy, and that means that research techniques in evaluating the effectiveness of programs and products on the Web are also in their infancy.

In assessing the impact of the Web, the two most frequent research terms discussed are "hits" and "eyeballs." The former refers to the number of times a Web site is visited by an individual. The latter refers to the orbital lobes affixed to that "hit." Obviously, these are but the most rudimentary of measurement tools, in that they don't assess the visitors' interest in the product or service or information conveyed, the duration of their stay at the site or whether they had the inclination to take the next step—buy the product, subscribe to the service, or vote for the candidate. Indeed, the first 5,000 hits to a new Web site may mean nothing more than the firm's employees checking out the latest communications tool.

Again, the Web is a new phenomenon. Over time, research sophistication in evaluating its content and services will develop. Most likely, just like everything else associated with the Internet, measurement techniques will develop rapidly. Consider the additional contributions Web research offers:

- **Intimacy.** Site-based research can bring organizations closer to their constituents.
- **Precision.** Web-based research can provide more detailed answers about consumers than traditional research methods.
- **Timeliness.** Web-based research is eminently more timely than traditional methods.
- **Cost.** Web-based research will reduce costs considerably, compared to traditional surveying methods.[13]

Figures and Faces—Lie

If you don't believe the old maxim that "figures lie and liars figure," consider the following: In often-repeated research, randomly selected participants are shown the following two faces and asked, "Which woman is lovelier?" Invariably, the answer is split 50-50.

However, when each woman is named, one "Jennifer" and the other "Gertrude," respondents overwhelmingly—upwards of 80 percent—vote for Jennifer as the more beautiful woman.

Why? "Jennifer" is more hip, more happening, more, uh, "phat." (Sorry all you Gertrudes out there!)

The point is that people can't help but introduce their own biases, including in presumably "objective" research experiments. So this factor always should be taken into account in evaluating public relations research.

So the value of Web-oriented research is indisputable. In preparing for such Internet evaluation, however, an organization should take several factors into consideration first:

1. **Establish objectives.** Again, implicit in any meaningful measurement is beginning with objective setting. Why are we on the Web? What is our site designed to do? What are we attempting to communicate?
2. **Determine criteria.** Define success with tangible data; for example, percentage of people likely to purchase from the site and positive interactive publication mentions that the site will receive.

3. **Determine benchmarks.** Project the "hits" the site will receive. Base this on competitive data, to see how this site stacks up against the competition or other forms of communication.

4. **Select the right measurement tool.** Numerous software packages exist and are being developed to track site traffic. Maybe using a survey on the site is a more meaningful measurement; or, maybe more than one tool is called for.

5. **Compare results to objectives.** Success of on-line marketing and communications cannot be concluded in a vacuum. Numbers of visitors, hits, and eyeballs must be correlated with original objectives. If the objective is to strengthen investor relations, then determine how many visitors made their way to the annual report and how long they stayed reading it. Combine that information with the cost to print the annual report, and this will help determine how much money the Web might save the company.

6. **Draw actionable conclusions.** Research indicates you've received 100,000 visitors to the site. So what? Interpret the significance of the numbers and do something with the data to make progress.[14]

Finally, in terms of researching the Web, there is the aspect of "monitoring" what is being said about the organization. With the proliferation of rogue sites, anti-business chat rooms and news groups, and chain letter e-mail campaigns, monitoring the Web has become a frontline public relations responsibility. The Internet has been called the "great equalizer," which means that all individuals can have their say—mean, nasty, belligerent—and organizations must constantly keep track of what is being said about them.[15]

Using Outside Research Help

Despite its occasional rough spots, public relations research has made substantial gains in quantifying the results of public relations activities. Counseling firms have organized separate departments to conduct attitude and opinion surveys as well as other types of research projects.

Ketchum Public Relations, for example, has devised a computer-based measurement system that evaluates public relations results on both a quantitative and qualitative basis. The Ketchum system focuses on the differences in placement of publicity, that is, where in a periodical publicity has a better chance of being noticed. Although the Ketchum system cannot predict attitudinal or behavioral change, it is a step forward in providing practitioners with a mechanism to assess the extent to which their publicity has been seen.

Interactive public relations specialists have emerged to help monitor organizational references on the Web. Some outside agencies even volunteer to launch "whisper" campaigns in chat rooms to neutralize negative or inaccurate messages about clients.

It often makes sense to use outside counsel for research assistance. Once a firm is hired, public relations professionals should avoid the temptation of writing the questions or influencing the methodology. The best contribution a public relations practitioner can make to an outside-directed research endeavor is to state the objectives of the project clearly and then stand back and let the pros do the job.[16]

Often, before turning to outside consultants, the best first step is to determine whether research has already been done on your topic. Because research assistance is expensive, it makes little sense to reinvent the wheel. It is much wiser to piggyback on existing research.

S U M M A R Y

Research is a means of both defining problems and evaluating solutions. Even though intuitive judgment remains a coveted and important skill, management must see measurable results.

Nonetheless, informed managements recognize that public relations may never reach a point at which its results can be fully quantified. Management confidence is still a prerequisite for active and unencumbered programs. Indeed, the best "measurement" of public relations value is a strong and unequivocal endorsement from management that it supports the public relations effort. However, such confidence can only be enhanced as practitioners become more adept in using research.

Frankly, practitioners don't have a choice. With efficiency driving today's bottom line and with communications about organizations percolating at a 24/7 clip around the world through a variety of media, organizations must always know where they stand. It is the job of public relations to keep track, record, and research changing attitudes and opinions about the organizations for which they work. Therefore, it will become increasingly incumbent on public relations people to reinforce the value of what they do and what they stand for through constantly measuring their contribution to their organization's goals.[17]

Discussion Starters

1. Why is research important in public relations work?
2. What are several methods of public relations research?
3. What are the four elements of a survey?
4. What is the difference between random and stratified sampling?
5. What are the keys to designing an effective questionnaire?
6. What are the several rules of thumb in organizing focus groups?
7. What is a communication audit?
8. What is the most widely used unobtrusive method of public relations research?
9. Why is evaluation important in public relations research?
10. What values will Internet research hold for organizations?

Notes

1. Erik Battenberg, "Dealing with Cyberspace Attacks," *PR Tactics* (November 1999): 14.
2. David Grady and Judith Gimple, "Virtual Barbarians at the Gate," *Public Relations Strategist* (Fall 1998): 23.
3. Jennifer Nedeff, "The Bottom Line Beckons: Quantifying Measurement in Public Relations," *Journal of Corporate Public Relations* Northwestern University (1996–1997): 34.
4. Lisa Richter and Steve Drake, "Apply Measurement Mindset to Programs," *Public Relations Journal* (January 1993): 32.
5. John V. Pavlik, *Public Relations: What Research Tells Us* (Newbury Park, CA: Sage, 1987): 16.

6. Walter K. Lindenmann, "Setting Minimum Standards for Measuring Public Relations Effectiveness," *Public Relations Review* (Winter 1997): 394–395.

7. Lindenmann, "Opinion Research: How It Works; How to Use It," *Public Relations Journal* (January 1977): 13.

8. Lindenmann, *Attitude and Opinion Research: Why You Need It, How to Do It,* 3rd ed. (Washington, D.C.: Council for Advancement and Support of Education, 1983): 35–38.

9. David L. Nasser, "How to Run a Focus Group," *Public Relations Journal* (March 1988): 33–34.

10. "The Delphi: A Forecasting Methodology You Can Use to Generate Expert Opinion on Any Subject," *PR Reporter* (June 29, 1992): 3.

11. Seymour Hamilton, "Selling the CEO on a Communication Audit," *IABC Communication World* (May 1988): 33.

12. Pavlik, op. cit, 39.

13. Michael Krauss, "Research and the Web: Eyeballs or Smiles?" *Marketing News* (December 7, 1998): 18.

14. Katherine D. Paine and Beth Roed, "The Basics of Internet Measurement," *Ragan's Interactive PR* (March 1999): 7.

15. Don Middleberg, "The Dark Side of the Net," *Reputation Management* (October 1997): 70–72.

16. Andrea L. Simpson, "Ten Rules of Research," *Public Relations Quarterly* (Summer 1992): 27–28.

17. Nedeff, "The Bottom Line Beckons."

top of the shelf

Internet Search Engines

The Internet and the continuous proliferation of Web sites have revolutionized every aspect of research, including the typical research tasks faced by public relations practitioners. Businesses and organization can even keep tabs on their competitors and opponents. Enormous databases—including those of hundreds of government agencies—are easily accessible, often for free. Most standard directories are also available on-line, and for obvious reasons they are more up-to-date than their print versions.

A selection of some of the Web sites commonly used by public relations researchers is included in "Suggested Readings." Most of them also provide numerous links to related Web sites.

Search engines are the researcher's Holy Grail. Search engines allow you to search the contents of the World Wide Web, usenet groups, and other Internet data. Once you keyboard in a search term, you receive a list of items that match your query. Here are the leading search engines:

- AltaVista. www.altavista.digital.com. (Digital Equipment Corp.)
- HotBot. www.hotbot.com. The favorite search engine of Shel Holtz, author of *Public Relations on the Net* (see Chapter 10).
- InfoSeek. www.infoseek.com. A combination index and engine.
- Lycos. www.lycos.com. A combination index and engine.
- Search.Com. www.search.com. An index of search engines and indexes.
- Yahoo! www.yahoo.com. Considered by many the best of the search indexes, including other elements such as news, weather, and maps.

Suggested Readings

Barzun, Jacques, and Henry F. Graff. *The Modern Researcher,* 5th ed. Ft. Worth, TX: HBJ College Publications, 1992.

Bell, Quentin. "Beware of Sailing into the Shallow Sea of Research," *Marketing* (Feb. 19, 1998): 7. Discusses the superficiality behind surveys and public relations research.

Berger, Arthur Asa. *Media Research Techniques,* 2nd ed. Thousand Oaks, CA: Sage Publications, 1998.

Blakenship, A. B., and George Breen. *State of the Art Marketing Research.* Lincolnwood, IL: NTC Business, 1992.

Boyatis, Richard E. *Transforming Qualitative Information.* Thousand Oaks, CA: Sage Publications, 1998.

Broom, Glen M., and David M. Dozier. *Using Research in Public Relations: Applications to Program Management.* Upper Saddle River, NJ: Prentice Hall, 1990.

www.businesswire.com. Business Wire, "The International Media Relations Wire Service," offers news releases on major U.S. corporations, including a majority of Fortune 500 and NASDAQ companies.

Crispell, Diane. *The Insider's Guide to Demographic Know-How.* Chicago: Probus, 1992.

Davis, Mitchell P. *Yearbook of Experts, Authorities & Spokespersons.* Washington, D.C.: Broadcast Interview Source. Annual. www.YearbookNews.com.

Fink, Arlene, and Jacqueline Kosecoff. *How to Conduct Surveys: A Step-by-Step Guide,* 2nd ed. Thousand Oaks, CA: Sage Publications, 1998.

Fowler, Floyd J., Jr. *Survey Research Methods,* 2nd ed. Newbury Park, CA: Sage Publications, 1993.

Hoover's Handbooks of: American Business, Major U.S. Companies, World Business, Emerging Companies, and Private Companies. Austin, TX: Hoover's Inc. www.hoovers.com features Hoover's Online: The Business Network. Profiles of more than 12,000 public and private companies.

www.infopls.com. Updated daily, the venerable *Information Please Almanac's* Web site also includes data from *Information Please Sports Almanac, Entertainment Almanac, Columbia Encyclopedia,* and *Infoplease Dictionary.* It also offers hyperlinks to key subject areas.

Lehman, Carol M., William Himstreet, and Wayne Baty. *Business Communications,* 11th ed. Cincinnati, OH: South-Western College Publishing, 1996.

Lindolf, Thomas R. *Qualitative Communication Research Methods.* Thousand Oaks, CA: Sage Publications, 1995. Updated review of research methods in communication.

Marcoulides, George A., ed. *Modern Methods for Business Research.* Mahwah, NJ: Lawrence Erlbaum Associates Inc., 1998.

www.marketingsource.com/associations. The Marketing Resource Center's Associations Database provides a directory of business-related associations around the world.

The Markets Directory. Dobbs Ferry, NY: Dobbs Directories, 1993 www.mediainfo.com. Editor & Publisher magazine makes it easy to find on-line news pages anywhere in the world, and its database offers access to more than 11,000 Web sites.

www.odwyerpr.com. *Jack O'Dwyer's Newsletter* offers online logos, agency statements and complete listings of 550 PR firms. There is no cost for accessing any part of the Web site, including news from the newsletter and other publications, hyperlinks to articles on PR, job listings, and more than 1,000 PR services in 58 categories.

Nasser, David L. "How to Run a Focus Group." *Public Relations Journal* (March 1988): 33, 34.

Pavlik, John V. *Public Relations: What Research Tells Us.* Newbury Park, CA: Sage, 1987. Old but a classic in the field.

Payne, Katherine Delahaye. "Escape from Measure-Not Land," *Public Relations Tactics,* (July 1997): 30–31. Makes the case for measuring public relations and marketing efforts.

Rea, Louis M., et al. *Designing and Conducting Survey Research: A Comprehensive Guide.* San Francisco: Jossey-Bass Publishers 1997.

Rossi, Peter H., and Howard E. Freeman. *Evaluation: A Systematic Approach,* 5th ed. Newbury Park, CA: Sage Publications, 1999.

Rubenstein, Sondra Miller. *Surveying Public Opinion.* Belmont, CA: Wadsworth Publishing, 1995.

Schwab, Donald P. *Research Methods for Organizational Studies.* Mahwah, NJ: Lawrence Erlbaum Associates, 1998.

Sudman, Seymour. *Thinking About Answers: The Application of Cognitive Process to Survey Methodology.* San Francisco: Jossey-Bass, 1995.

www.world-chambers.com. The World Network of Chambers of Commerce and Industry features a global index of chambers of commerce and chambers for international business development.

CASE STUDY

Researching a Position for Alan Louis General

The administrator at Alan Louis General Hospital confronted a problem that he hoped research could help solve. Alan Louis General, although a good hospital, was smaller and less well known than most other hospitals in Bangor, Maine. In its area alone, it competed with 20 other medical facilities. Alan Louis needed a "position" that it could call unique to attract patients to fill its beds.

For a long time, the Alan Louis administrator, Sven Rapcorn, had believed in the principle that truth will win out. Build a better mousetrap, and the world will beat a path to your door. Erect a better hospital, and your beds will always be 98 percent filled. Unfortunately, Rapcorn learned, the real world seldom recognizes truth at first blush.

In the real world, more often than not, perception will triumph. Because people act on perceptions, those perceptions become reality. Successful positioning, Rapcorn learned, is based on recognizing and dealing with people's perceptions. And so, Rapcorn set out with research to build on existing perceptions about Alan Louis General.

As a first step, Rapcorn talked to his own doctors and trustees to gather data about their perceptions, not only of Alan Louis General, but also of other hospitals in the community. From this effort, pictures of each major competitor began to emerge. For example, the University Health Center had something for everybody—exotic care, specialized care, and basic bread-and-butter care. Bangor General was a huge, well-respected hospital whose reputation was so good that only a major tragedy could shake its standing in the community. Mercy Hospital was known for its trauma center. And so on.

As for Alan Louis itself, doctors and trustees said that it was a great place to work, that excellent care was provided, and that the nursing staff was particularly friendly and good. The one problem, everyone agreed, was that "nobody knows about us."

The second step in Rapcorn's research project was to test attributes important in health care. Respondents were asked to rank eight factors in order of importance and to tell Rapcorn and his staff how each of the surveyed hospitals rated on those factors. The research instrument used a semantic differential scale of 1 to 10, with 1 the worst and 10 the best possible score. Questionnaires were sent to two groups: 1,000 area residents and 500 former Alan Louis patients.

The third step in the research was to tabulate the results. Among area residents who responded, the eight attributes were ranked accordingly:

1. Surgical care—9.23
2. Medical equipment—9.20
3. Cardiac care—9.16
4. Emergency services—8.96
5. Range of medical services—8.63
6. Friendly nurses—8.62
7. Moderate costs—8.59
8. Location—7.94

After the attributes were ranked, the hospitals in the survey were ranked for each attribute. On advanced surgical care, the most important feature to area residents, Bangor General ranked first, with University Health Center a close second. Alan Louis was far down on the list. The same was true of virtually every other attribute. Indeed, on nursing care, an area in which its staff thought Alan Louis excelled, the hospital came in last in the minds of area residents. Rapcorn was not surprised. The largest hospitals in town scored well on most attributes; Alan Louis trailed the pack.

However, the ranking of hospital scores according to former Alan Louis patients revealed an entirely different story. On surgical care, for example, although Bangor General still ranked first, Alan Louis came in a close second. Its scores improved similarly on all other attributes. In fact, in nursing care, where Alan Louis came in last on the survey of area residents, among former patients its score was higher than that of any other hospital. It also ranked first in terms of convenient location and second in terms of costs, range of services, and emergency care.

The fourth step in Rapcorn's research project was to draw some conclusions. He reached three conclusions:

1. Bangor General was still number one in terms of area hospitals.
2. Alan Louis ranked at or near the top on most attributes, according to those who actually experienced care there.
3. Former Alan Louis patients rated the hospital significantly better than the general public did.

In other words, thought Rapcorn, most of those who try Alan Louis like it. The great need was to convince more people to try the hospital.

But how could this be accomplished with a hospital? Other marketers generate trial by sending free samples in the mail, offering cents-off coupons, holding free demonstrations, and the like. Hospitals are more limited in this area. Rapcorn's challenge was to launch a communications campaign to convince prospects to see other area hospitals in a different, less favorable light or to give people a specific reason to think about trying Alan Louis. In other words, he needed to come up with a communications strategy that clearly differentiated Alan Louis—admittedly, among the smallest of area hospitals—from the bigger, less personal hospitals. Rapcorn was confident that the data he had gathered from the research project were all he needed to come up with a winning idea.

Questions

1. What kind of communications program would you launch to accomplish Rapcorn's objectives?
2. What would be the cornerstone—the theme—of your communications program?
3. What would be the specific elements of your program?
4. In launching the program, what specific steps would you follow—both inside and outside the hospital—to build support?
5. How could you use the Internet to conduct more research about area hospitals and residents' perceptions of the care at these hospitals? How could you use the Internet to research the effectiveness of the communications program you implement?

OVER THE TOP

An Interview with Nick Trivisonno

Nick Trivisonno is chief executive officer of ACNielsen, the global leader in market research, information and analysis—dissecting consumer attitudes, preferences, and behavior patterns for more than 9,000 corporate customers in 90 countries. ACNielsen became an independent company in 1996, when it was spun off from Dun & Bradstreet.

How do you build a new company?
We had four constituents—employees, a brand-spanking-new board of directors, investors, and our clients—who needed to know what ACNielsen was about, what our financial situation was, what our operating philosophy was, and how we were going to turn the company around from a loss of $65 million.

What were the communications steps you followed?
It became very, very obvious that we needed a communication plan to cover the whole gamut. So we put together a road show to tell our story to the investment community. And we realized that there could only be one story for ACNielsen that had to be shared with all of the interested parties.

How was research involved?
We continued an employee satisfaction survey each year. We have surveyed 18,000 people on the Internet and received 16,500 responses. That is a world-class response rate for any survey. Our score was 55 percent, up from 40 percent. We also link 25 percent of our annual executive incentive bonus to employee satisfaction. The point is our people are charged up and interested.

What about the external ACNielsen profile?
Extremely important. It's not good enough to think you're the best. You want to be recognized as the best. We need to get the message out around the world, taking advantage of every type of communication technique we can use. Those country managing directors and regional managers are key to spreading the word. We are very visible.

How important is it to have a "corporate brand?"
There is no question about building a brand. We want to be recognized as one company worldwide. We want our clients to know that no matter where they go, it's one touch, one feel, and that we do things the ACNielsen way. That is a major effort right now of not only branding but also getting us to do things the same way around the world.

How essential is the communications function? Some companies subordinate communications to the legal department.

No, no, no, no. It can't be. It has to be right there on the leading edge. The communications group has got to control the message. They are the keeper, to a large degree, of all of our messages.

What do you look for in a communications director?

Somebody who can work 30 hours a day, run faster than anybody else, and get out there and have the energy to draw the communications group together; that is an integral part of drawing the rest of the corporation together.

Chapter 6

The Law

Public relations and the law begins with the First Amendment to the Constitution that guarantees freedom of speech in our free society. But in the 21st century, ensuring "freedom of speech" is not as easy as it sounds. The question is, Where does one's freedom start and another's end? Nowhere is this question more pertinent than regarding the Internet.

Consider the case of Ivan Wong, the California high school student sued in 1999 by venerable investment banking company Morgan Stanley Dean Witter & Company for creating a Web site that infringed on the firm's trademarks.

Mr. Wong's Web site, www.msdwonline.com was named, he said, after Mud Sweat & Gears, the shop that sold him his mountain bikes. What could be wrong with that? Plenty, said Morgan Stanley et al., which noted in court that Mr. Wong's father had registered dozens of domain names, many derived from the names of investment banks—among them, goldmansachsdirect.com and jpmorganonline.com. Young Mr. Wong, argued Morgan Stanley, was clearly guilty of "cybersquatting," the dubious practice of registering Internet addresses, at $70 each, expressly to resell them to companies for exorbitant prices.[1]

This was just the tip of the legal iceberg confronting Internet law and freedom of speech. Legal complications with the Internet were typical of the growing interrelationship between public relations and the law in the new millennium.

Publicity and the Law

In today's America, the higher profile the legal case, the more likely attorneys will resort to the tactics of publicity and public relations to influence the outcome.

- In 1999, when several high school students were thrown out of school for starting a riot at a football game, their legal advisors called for the high-profile Reverend Jesse Jackson to help influence public support. A year earlier, when a New York police officer brutally beat a Haitian immigrant outside a bar, the man's lawyers welcomed the equally high-profile Reverend Al Sharpton to increase the public heat.

- Two years earlier, when Air Force bomber pilot Lieutenant Kelly Flinn was charged with adultery, violating a direct order, and lying to her superiors, she and her advisors seized an unprecedented strategy on the way to her court-martial: They went public. After tearful appearances with her family on *60 Minutes* and interviews with all the major media, Lieutenant Flinn convinced Air Force Secretary Sheila Widnall to grant her a general discharge, thus staving off a tidal wave of negative publicity for the military (see "Over the Top," chapter 12).[2]

- When the Supreme Court ruled against President Clinton in his attempt to delay the Paula Jones sexual harassment suit against him, the president's lead attorney, Robert Bennett, told interviewer Ted Koppel that if the case proceeded, he would have no choice but to disclose Jones's past sexual history. Later, after backing down from this threat, the president's and Jones's lawyers appeared on competing Sunday morning television talk shows, each launching "trial balloons" to seek an out-of-court settlement.

- One of the most celebrated legal cases of the last century involved sports icon O. J. Simpson, who was charged with the brutal killings of his ex-wife and her friend. The Heisman Trophy winner's high-priced lawyers studiously worked the media and, despite overwhelming evidence against their client, managed to evoke a "not guilty" verdict from a Los Angeles jury.

Today, publicity and public relations have become so important, particularly in high-profile legal cases, that many times such activities become more critical than events in the courtroom—in the rare instances when such cases actually reached the courtroom.

Despite increasing use by lawyers of public relations strategies and methods, the job of a lawyer differs markedly from that of a public relations counselor. A lawyer, the old saw goes, tells you what you *must* do. A public relations professional, on the other hand, tells you what you *should* do. Therein lies the difference and the tension between the two functions.

A lawyer, correctly, must counsel the client on how best to perform in a court of law. A public relations professional must counsel a client on how to perform most effectively in another court—the court of public opinion.

There is a huge difference.

"Conclusions to be reached in a case will be induced only by evidence and argument in open court and not by outside influence, whether private talk or public print," proclaimed U.S. Supreme Court Justice Oliver Wendell Holmes in 1907. The esteemed justice obviously had no idea that approximately 90 years later, advances in technology would allow potential jurors throughout the community, as well as worldwide, to view an incident on video dozens of times and to listen to hundreds of commentators offer their opinions on a case before ever being invited to enter a courtroom.[3]

In recent years, defendants ranging from sports stars Darryl Strawberry and Mike Tyson to broadcaster Marv Albert to President Bill Clinton have found themselves judged guilty before ever entering a courtroom. So pervasive and powerful is communication in our society that public relations professionals have come to play an increasingly pivotal role in influencing public opinion, winning contested settlements, and, in general, affecting the outcome of legal issues.

Public Relations and the Law: An Uneasy Alliance

The legal and public relations professions have historically shared an uneasy alliance. Public relations practitioners must always understand the legal implications of any issue with which they become involved, and a firm's legal position must always be the first consideration.

From a legal point of view, normally the less an organization says prior to its day in court, the better. That way, the opposition can't gain any new ammunition that will become part of the public record. A lawyer, the saying goes, tells you to say two things: "Say nothing, and say it slowly!" From a public relations standpoint, though, it may often make sense to go public early on, especially if the organization's integrity or credibility is being called into public question. In the summer of 1997, for example, when respected broadcaster Marv Albert was charged with abusing a woman friend, Albert immediately held a press conference denying the charges, and his advisors followed with questions about the woman's veracity. (Later, he pleaded guilty to a lesser charge.)

The point is that legal advice and public relations advice may indeed be different. In an organization, a smart manager will carefully weigh both legal and public relations counsel before making a decision.

It also should be noted that law and ethics are interrelated. The Public Relations Society of America's Code of Professional Standards (see appendix A) notes that many activities that are unethical are also illegal. However, there are instances where something is perfectly legal but unethical, and other instances in which things might be illegal but otherwise ethical. Thus, when a public relations professional reflects on what course to take in a particular situation, he or she must analyze not only the legal ramifications but also the ethical considerations.[4]

This chapter will examine the relationship between the law and public relations and the more prominent role the law plays in public relations practice and vice versa. The discussion will not be all-encompassing. Rather, it will introduce the legal concerns of public relations professionals today: First Amendment considerations, insider trading, disclosure law, ethics law, privacy law, copyright law, and the laws concerning censorship of the Internet—concerns that have become primary for public relations in the 21st century.

Public Relations and the First Amendment

Any discussion of law and public relations should start with the First Amendment, which states: "Congress shall make no law . . . abridging the freedom of speech or the press." The First Amendment is the cornerstone of free speech in our society: This is what distinguishes America from many other nations.

The latter years of the 20th century saw a blizzard of First Amendment challenges.

- In the fall of 1999, New York Mayor Rudolph Giuliani threatened to cut off city funding for an art exhibition at the Brooklyn Museum, which featured one painting depicting the Madonna speckled with elephant dung (Figure 6-1). Giuliani termed the painting "blasphemous." The American Civil Liberties Union defended the work as "freedom of expression." The court ultimately agreed.

- Mayor Giuliani did better when his administration challenged the right of the Ku Klux Klan to hold a hooded rally in Manhattan in 1999. A federal appellate panel upheld New York's right to block the "white pride" rally. The *New York Times* bemoaned the decision as a "low moment for the First Amendment."[5]

- Earlier in the year, a campaign led by Former Education Secretary Republican William Bennett and Democratic Senator Joseph Lieberman decried the lack of standards in music, movies, video games, the Internet, and on television that were influencing children to commit violent, antisocial acts.

- In the summer of 1996, Reebok International was chastised for reaching a tentative agreement with the University of Wisconsin on a sports product contract that included a clause that prohibited the university from criticizing the company. The resulting free speech furor caused Reebok to drop the clause.

FIGURE 6-1 Art or obscenity? This work, depicting one artist's conception of the Madonna, decorated with elephant dung, touched off a legal battle in New York City in 1999.

- In the spring of 1997, the publisher of the *Wall Street Journal,* Dow Jones & Company, Inc., was stunned when a Texas court awarded a brokerage firm $222.7 million in damages for an article that the company claimed put it out of business.[6]

- In the summer of 1997, a Delaware judge dismissed a lawyer for a teenager charged with murdering her newborn son, because the girl's attorney made comments about the impending case on ABC's *20/20,* including an assertion that his client was innocent. The judge claimed the lawyer's statements had a "substantial likelihood of materially prejudicing" potential jurors.[7]

- In 1993, the Federal Communications Commission decided to delay deals totaling $170 million by the Infiniti Broadcasting Corporation because it employed foul-mouthed radio personality Howard Stern. As a result of Stern's scatological humor, Infiniti was fined well over $1 million by the FCC.[8]

- That same year, the Supreme Court reaffirmed its view that advertising is a form of speech protected by the First Amendment. The Court ruled that a city may not automatically exclude advertising brochures from the newspaper vending machines that it licenses for use on public property. The Court's ruling reaffirmed the First Amendment protection of commercial speech.[9] Such a privilege was established in a landmark 1978 case, *First National Bank of Boston v. Belloti,* in which the Supreme Court struck down a Massachusetts law that permitted a business corporation to speak only on those issues "that materially affect its business, property, or assets."[10]

As these skirmishes suggest, interpreting the First Amendment is no simple matter. One person's definition of obscenity may be someone else's definition of art. Interestingly, the verdict in the Dow Jones case was later reduced, and, as noted, New York's attempt to stifle the Brooklyn Art Museum's controversial show was itself stifled. Despite continuing challenges to the First Amendment, Americans continue to enjoy broad freedom of speech and expression. Because the First Amendment lies at the heart of the communications business, defending it is a front-line responsibility of the public relations profession.

BACKGROUNDER

Promoting O. J.

Perhaps never has a legal trial gripped the entire nation so pervasively as the murder charges against Orenthal J. Simpson in the killings of Nicole Brown Simpson and Ron Goldman in 1994. O. J. Simpson was a revered football player, broadcaster, and actor who seemed to be leading a charmed life, until one summer evening he stunned the nation by leading it—via national TV—on a low-speed car chase through the highways and byways of Brentwood, California (Figure 6-2).

The Simpson trial shocked the nation, but the real drama lay in how Simpson's high-powered attorney team of Johnnie Cochran, F. Lee Bailey, and Robert Shapiro used publicity to forward their cause and wallop the hapless Los Angeles District Attorney's Office.

Here's how Mr. Shapiro described the winning public relations approach.

■ **Lawyer as public relations person** "When we are retained for those high-profile cases, we are instantly thrust into the role of a public relations person—a role for which the majority of us have no education, experience, or training. The lawyer's role as spokesperson may be [as] equally important to the outcome of a case as the skills of an advocate in the courtroom."

■ **Power of the media** "The importance and power of the media cannot be overemphasized. The first impression the public gets is usually the one that is most important."

■ **"No comment"** "'No comment' is the least appropriate and least productive response.

FIGURE 6-2 **Fallen—but not convicted—hero, O. J. Simpson.**

Coming at the end of a lengthy story, it adds absolutely nothing and leaves the public with a negative impression."

- **Lying to the media** "It is never a good idea to lie to the press. To simply make up facts in the hope that they will later prove correct is too big a risk."
- **Media relationships** "Initial relationships with legitimate members of the press are very important. Many times a lawyer will feel it is an intrusion to be constantly beset by seemingly meaningless questions that take up a tremendous amount of time. But the initial headlines of the arrest often make the sacred presumption of innocence a myth. In reality, we have the presumption of guilt. This is why dealing with the media is so important."
- **Responding to the press** "The wire services depend on immediate updates. Therefore, all calls should be returned as quickly as possible. Wire service reporters can also provide a valuable source of information to you."
- **Framing answers** "Just as you would do in trial, anticipate the questions a reporter will pose. Think out your answers carefully. My personal preference is to initially talk to a reporter off the record and get an idea what questions the reporter is interested in and where the story is going. I then respond to the questions that are appropriate. Use great care in choosing your words. Keep your statements simple and concise. Pick and choose the questions you want to answer. You do not have to be concerned with whether the answer precisely addresses the question, since only the answer will be aired."
- **The tabloids** "My experience is that cooperating with tabloid reporters only gives them a legitimate source of information which can be misquoted or taken out of context and does little good for your client. My personal approach is not to cooperate with tabloid reporters."
- **Dealing with TV hordes** "The television media, either consciously or unconsciously, create an atmosphere of chaos. Immediately upon arriving at the courthouse, you are surrounded by television crews. We have all seen people coming to court and trying to rush through the press with their heads down or covering them with newspapers or coats. Nothing looks worse. I always instruct my clients upon arrival at the courthouse to get out in a normal manner, to walk next to me in a slow and deliberate way, to have a look of confidence and acknowledge with a nod those who are familiar and supportive."*

Excerpted from Robert Shapiro, "Secrets of a Celebrity Lawyer," Columbia Journalism Review, September/October 1994, 25–29.

Public Relations and Insider Trading

Every public relations professional should know the laws that govern an organization. A practitioner in a hospital should have an understanding of managed care and its ramifications. A practitioner working for a nonprofit organization should understand the laws that govern donors and recipients. A practitioner who works in a particular industry—chemicals, computers, sports—should understand the laws germane to that particular area.

With 70 million Americans direct participants in the securities markets, nowhere in public relations practice is an understanding of the law more important than in the area of financial disclosure. Every public company has an obligation to deal frankly, comprehensively, and immediately with any information that is considered material in a decision to buy, sell, or even hold the organization's securities. The Securities and Exchange Commission (SEC)—through a series of court cases, consent decrees, complaints, and comments over the years—has painted a general portrait of disclosure requirements for practitioners (see appendix F), with which all practitioners in public companies should be familiar. The SEC's mandate stems from the Securities Act of 1933 and the Securities Exchange Act of 1934, which attempted to protect the public from abuses in the issuance and sale of securities.

The SEC's overriding concern is that all investors have an opportunity to learn about material information as promptly as possible. Basically, a company is expected to release news that may affect its stock market price as quickly as possible.[11] Through its general antifraud statute, Rule 10b-5 of the Securities and Exchange Act, the SEC strictly prohibits the dissemination of false or misleading information to investors. It also prohibits insider trading of securities on the basis of material information not disclosed to the public.

The final decade of the 20th century started and ended with front page insider trading scandals. In the early part of the 1990s, the public was shocked by a series of celebrated cases involving the use of insider information to amass illegal securities gains. The two most celebrated insider trading cases were those of Ivan Boesky and Michael Milken, Wall Street legends who were both slapped with nine-figure fines and jail terms. Many of their associates, equally guilty of insider trading violations, also were dispatched to the slammer.

Nor did journalists escape the ignominy of insider trading convictions. The most famous case involved a *Wall Street Journal* reporter, R. Foster Winans Jr., who was convicted in the summer of 1985 of illegally using his newspaper column in a get-rich-quick stock-trading scheme.

Basically, Winans gave favorable opinions about companies in which a couple of his stockbroker friends had already invested heavily. The stocks then generally went up, and the brokers and their clients profited handsomely; Winans eventually was sentenced to prison. In 1996, *Money* magazine columnist and CNN financial commentator Dan Dorfman was similarly accused of reporting stock tips, from which his sources profited. He was not renewed and wound up as an Internet financial columnist.

In the final days of the 1990s, Wall Street was once again rocked by allegations that a respected brokerage company CEO, James J. McDermott, Jr., had given inside information on pending bank mergers to one Kathryn Gannon, aka Marilyn Star, pornographic actress and Web site proprietress, with whom he allegedly had an "intimate relationship." The SEC came down hard on Mr. McDermott and Ms. Gannon, intending as trial commenced in 2000 to send a message to all of those participating in the hyperinflated stock market that insider trading would continue to be dealt with harshly.

Public Relations and Disclosure Law

Besides cracking down on insider trading, the SEC has challenged corporations and public relations firms on the accuracy of information they disseminate for clients. The SEC's "Adoption of Integrated Disclosure System" attempts to bring some order to the chaotic SEC requirements by making the instructions governing corporate disclosure of information more uniform. Today, in an environment of mergers, takeovers, consolidations, and the incessant rumors that circulate around them, a knowledge of disclosure law, a sensitivity to disclosure requirements, and a bias toward disclosing rather than withholding material information is an important attribute of public relations officials.

In the new millennium, with securities trading extending beyond the traditional 9:30 A.M.–4 P.M. stock market trading day and with instantaneous on-line trading a reality, the responsibilities on public relations people for full and fair disclosure have become intensified. The SEC, in turn, has increased its focus on private meetings between companies and analysts, which are closed to the media. Such private gatherings may provide large institutional investors with unfair advantage over individual investors who rely on the media for financial information.[12]

BACKGROUNDER

Victim of Voice Mail

Communications technology in the 21st century may save time, but it also must be approached with caution—especially where disclosure law is concerned.

In the latter months of 1999, a securities analyst received a voice mail message from the director of investor relations at Abercrombie & Fitch, a hot department store chain. The cryptic message, in response to the analyst's own voice mail inquiry, suggested that the firm's sales growth had become sluggish. The analyst immediately notified his clients, and the stock plummeted.

The problem was that the public had not been informed. By the time the disclosure was more widely dispersed, the damage to the Abercrombie & Fitch stock was done. Class-action lawsuits, charging selective disclosure in violations of the SEC Act of 1934, commenced.

While the disposition of the suits would take time to resolve, two responses from the inadvertent voice mail leak were immediate. First, the SEC proposed new rules that would bar companies from selectively disclosing information to Wall Street analysts and others before making it public. Second, the director of investor relations of Abercrombie & Fitch was given a leave of absence and relieved of his duties.

The lesson for all of us: In these days of instant communications and dire consequences for premature disclosure, never take voice mail for granted.*

*"A&F Sued for Leaking Information," Jack O'Dwyer's Newsletter, November 24, 1999, 1; and Marcy Gordon, "SEC Proposes Ban on Leaks to Analysts," The Record, December 16, 1999, B1.

As the Dow Jones Index ascended steadily in the runaway bull market that roared into the new millennium, the practice of investor relations has emerged as an important element of public relations that focuses on proper disclosure to investors.

Public Relations and Ethics Law

The laws on ethical misconduct in society have gotten quite a workout in recent years.

- ☑ In 1996, when Swiss banks were accused of making it difficult for the heirs of Jewish Holocaust victims to recover the assets of relatives, the Swiss Bank Association hired Kekst & Co., a New York firm long associated with Jewish causes, to defend the banks. Critics accused the firm of an ethical breach, allowing its clients to exploit it.
- ☑ In a celebrated case, translated into the 1999 movie *The Insider,* public relations counselor John Scanlon faced a grand jury subpoena, stemming from his efforts to discredit Jeffrey Wigand, an internal critic of cigarette client Brown & Williamson.[13]
- ☑ In the political public relations arena, Lyn Nofziger, former White House political director and communications counselor, was sentenced to 90 days in prison and fined $30,000 for violating the Federal Ethics in Government Act, which forbids lobbying former contacts within one year of leaving the government. A related fate was meted out to former White House Deputy Chief of Staff Michael K. Deaver, another well-known public relations professional, who was found guilty of perjury over his lobbying activities. He also faced a lengthy jail sentence and a serious fine.

A QUESTION OF ETHICS

Out of the Legal Loop

In the annals of political ethical violations, few incidents have more morally outraged the nation than President Clinton's transgressions with a White House intern in 1998. (See case study, chapter four.)

After the walls came closing in on him, Clinton relied on his lawyers to choreograph his every word. Although the president was eventually fined for contempt of court in a related case in Arkansas, Clinton—a lawyer himself—deftly provided answers throughout the conflict that were generally evasive but not untruthful.

Meanwhile, most of the president's aides—longtime associates such as James Carville and Paul Begala and newer White House believers such as Rahm Emanuel and Ann Lewis—kept up a steady public drumbeat defending Clinton against the doubters. All lost their own credibility in the process.

One Clinton ally, however, maintained his integrity, even though his was among the most difficult and public assignments in the White House. Presidential Press Secretary Mike McCurry, whose job was to meet the press every day to explain the president's actions, drew the line at lying and, as a result, maintained his credibility while all those around him were losing theirs (Figure 6-3).

McCurry realized that while a lawyer tells a client what he "must" do to defend himself in a court of law, public relations advice tells you what you "should" do to represent yourself in the court of public opinion. There is often a great ethical difference.

McCurry refused to succumb to the notion—accepted by most of those around the president—that Clinton was "innocent" simply because he claimed to

FIGURE 6-3 Maintaining credibility. Presidential Press Secretary Mike McCurry.

be. When McCurry was asked at White House press briefings if the president "had a relationship with the intern," McCurry's recurring answer was, "The president said he 'didn't.'" When McCurry was asked if he, himself, thought the president had had a relationship with the intern, McCurry claimed to be "out of the loop."

Although McCurry argued with Clinton's lawyers to allow the president to make a public confession of what he had done, the attorneys rejected his arguments.

Only once during the controversy did McCurry let down his guard. In an interview with the *Chicago Tribune*, McCurry said he thought the real story of Clinton and the intern "would probably turn out to be a lot more complicated than any of us now know."

He was right, of course, and when the truth came out, many of those who had relied exclusively on the lawyers for guidance were embarrassed and ashamed for defending their boss.

Public relations professional McCurry was not among them. He had nothing to be ashamed about.

For further information, consult Daniel Klaidman and Mark Hosenball, "Are the Walls Closing In?" Newsweek, September 14, 1998, 28; Fraser P. Seitel, "Presidential Public Relations Endgame," Ragan Report, August 10, 1999, 2; and Roger Simon, "Spinners vs. Lawyers," AOL Newstalk, August 4, 1998, 1.

The activities of lobbyists, in particular, have been closely watched by Congress since the imposition of the Lobbying Act of 1947. In recent years, however, the practice of lobbying has expanded greatly.

Complicating the lobbyist issue still further, foreign governments are particularly eager to retain savvy Washington insiders to guide them through the bureaucratic and congressional maze and to polish their images in the United States. In 1998, the Clinton administration drew public fire for accepting political contributions from influential representatives of Indonesia and China. This was the problem late Commerce Secretary Ron Brown confronted when he reportedly was approached by Asian business operatives. Indeed, in 1997, after Brown's death in a plane crash, a former business partner said Brown had taken money from foreign business executives.

Public relations counselors are strictly mandated by law to register the foreign entities they represent. However, in recent years, a number of representatives of foreign clients have, themselves, been the subject of scandals and legal investigations.

The increasing number of government officials who resign to become play-for-pay lobbyists may indicate that those who govern and those who attempt to influence them will in the future be scrutinized more closely for how ethically they do business and how scrupulously they follow the law.

Public Relations and Privacy Law

The laws that govern a person's privacy also have implications for the public relations profession. Privacy laws, particularly those that touch on libel and slander by the media, are curious indeed. When such alleged defamation involves a public figure, the laws get even more curious. Generally, the privacy of an ordinary citizen is protected under the law. A citizen in the limelight, however, has a more difficult problem, especially in proving defamation of character.

To prove such a charge, a public figure must show that the media acted with actual malice in its reporting. "Actual malice" in a public figure slander case means that statements have been published with the knowledge that they were false or with reckless disregard for whether the statements were false. In a landmark case in 1964, *New York Times v. Sullivan,* the Supreme Court nullified a libel award of $500,000 to an Alabama police official, holding that no damages could be awarded "in actions brought by public officials against critics of their official conduct" unless there was proof of "actual malice." And proving actual malice is difficult.

Several historic libel cases have helped pave the case law precedent.

- In 1992, the *Wall Street Journal* and its award-winning reporter Bryan Burrough were served with a $50 million libel suit by Harry L. Freeman, former executive vice president of American Express. The suit stemmed from the way Freeman was characterized in Burrough's book, *Vendetta: America Express and the Smearing of Edmund Safra.*[14]
- In 1993, writer Janet Malcolm was sued by Dr. Jeffrey M. Masson over charges that Malcolm fabricated quotations in her *New Yorker* magazine article, which defamed Dr. Masson. Jurors agreed that in several instances Malcolm acted with "reckless disregard" for the accuracy of the quotations and that Masson had indeed been damaged. This clarified an important legal principle that "placing statements materially altered to change their meaning between quotation marks and attributing them to a plaintiff is not an editorial prerogative and can be evidence of actual malice."[15]
- A decade earlier, in a landmark case, the *Washington Post* initially lost a $2 million suit after a federal jury decided that the newspaper had libeled William P. Tavoularas when it alleged that he had used his position as president of Mobil Oil to further his son's career in a shipping business. The next year, a federal judge overturned the verdict against the *Post* because the article in question didn't contain "knowing lies or statements made in reckless disregard of the truth."

Later, a federal appeals court reinstated the $2 million libel verdict against the *Post*. But later that year, the U.S. Court of Appeals of the District of Columbia agreed to reconsider the reinstatement. Finally, almost six years after the initial verdict, the

Supreme Court ruled in favor of the *Post* by throwing out the Tavoulareas suit for lack of merit. A contrary ruling would have restricted the limits of investigative journalism and broadened the interpretation of defamation of character. Reporters breathed a sigh of relief at the decision.

- In another celebrated case, Israeli General Ariel Sharon brought a $50 million libel suit against *Time* magazine. It, too, ended without a libel verdict. However, once again, the jury criticized *Time* for negligent journalism in reporting Sharon's role in a massacre in a Palestinian refugee camp.
- In 1988, the Supreme Court threw out a suit brought by conservative televangelist-preacher Jerry Falwell against *Hustler* magazine and publisher Larry Flynt, accusing the sex-oriented periodical with defaming his character in a fictitious liquor advertisement about his mother. Despite the grossness of the ad, the Supreme Court ruled that what was written was clearly a spoof of a public figure and that Falwell, therefore, didn't have a case. In 1996, film-maker Oliver Stone and actor Woody Harrelson glorified the smarmy publisher and his court saga in *The People vs. Larry Flynt.*
- In 1996, Atlanta security guard Richard A. Jewell sued both *NBC News* and the *Atlanta Journal-Constitution* for reporting that he was the lead suspect in the Atlanta Olympic bombing, which led to two deaths. The reports caused a media feeding frenzy, which disrupted Jewell's life and tarnished his name. Late in the year, Jewell was cleared of any involvement in the bombing and reached a settlement with his media accusers, averting a libel lawsuit and presumably compensating him handsomely for the undeserved humiliation.[16]
- In 1997, the *Wall Street Journal* lost a $227 million libel verdict in Texas when it was found to have inaccurately reported on the troubles of MMAR Group, a mortgage-backed securities firm in Houston, which ultimately went out of business after the *Journal* story.[17] Later that year, hedge fund manager Julian Robertson commenced an action against *Business Week* magazine for $1 billion, after a critical cover story on his firm.
- In 1999, the U.S. Court of Appeals reversed a lower court verdict in the case of *Food Lion v. ABC,* finding that Food Lion did not prove ABC's negative report on its food services practices was done with actual malice. Rather than suing for libel, Food Lion had sued ABC for the duplicitous ways its reporters had gone about gathering their "facts."[18]

What all these cases illustrate is a growing trend in society to challenge the media over its invasion of personal privacy. Although cases like these tend to confirm the rights of the media to report on public figures, in other cases—particularly those involving gossip-oriented tabloids—the courts have recently been more inclined to award settlements to celebrities who have been wronged.

Public Relations and Copyright Law

One body of law that is particularly relevant to public relations professionals is copyright law and the protections it offers writers. Copyright law provides basic, automatic protection for writers, whether a manuscript is registered with the Copyright Office or even published. Under the Copyright Act of 1976, an "original work of authorship" has copyright protection from the moment the work is in fixed form. As soon as an article, short story, or book is put on paper or a computer disk or is spoken into a tape recorder, it is protected by copyright law. You created it, and you own it. What you sell to an editor isn't the article itself but the right to use the material.

Copyright protection exists for broad categories of works: literary works; musical works, including any accompanying words; dramatic works, including any accompanying music; pantomimes and choreographic works; pictorial, graphic, and sculptural works; motion pictures and other audiovisual works; and sound recordings. Copyright law gives the owner of the copyright the exclusive right to reproduce and authorize others to reproduce the work, prepare derivative works based on the copyrighted material, and perform and/or display the work publicly. That's why Michael Jackson had to pay $47.5 million for the rights to the Beatles' compositions to the duly sworn representatives and heirs of John, Paul, George, and Ringo.

What courts have stated again and again is that for the purposes of criticism, news reporting, teaching, scholarship, or research, use of copyrighted material is not an infringement but rather constitutes "fair use." Although precise definitions of "fair use"—like everything else in the law—is subject to interpretation, such factors as "the effect on the future market" of the copyrighted work in question or the "volume of quotation used" or even whether the "heart" of the material was ripped off are often considered.[19]

In 1989, the Supreme Court strengthened the copyright status of freelance artists and writers when it ruled that such professionals retain the right to copyright what they create "as long as they were not in a conventional employment relationship with the organization that commissioned their work." The Court's revision of the copyright law set the stage for a wholesale reassessment of the ownership of billions of dollars in reproduction rights for computer programs, fiction and nonfiction writing, advertising copy, drawings, photographs, and so on. As a result of the modification, public relations professionals must carefully document the authorization that has been secured for using freelance material. In other words, when engaging a freelance professional, public relations people must know the law.

Several categories of material are not eligible for copyright protection, such as titles and short slogans; works consisting entirely of information from common sources and public documents, such as calendars, lists, and tables; and speeches and performances that have not been fixed on paper or recorded. Work in the public domain—material that was never covered by copyright or for which the copyright has lapsed, material that lacks sufficient originality, and basic themes and plots—can't be protected by copyright.

Ideas cannot be protected either. This means that an old idea newly packaged is absolutely permissible, legal, and even recommended. Indeed, there are few truly new ideas in the world, only old ideas put together in new and different ways. So a public relations practitioner shouldn't be overly concerned with violating copyright laws when devising a campaign, program, or manuscript in support of a client's activity.

Public Relations and Internet Law

The Internet has introduced a new dimension to the law affecting free speech.

The premise in American law is that "not all speech is created equal."[20] Rather there is a hierarchy of speech, under Supreme Court precedents dating back many decades that calibrate the degree of First Amendment protection with the particular medium of expression. For example, speech that would be perfectly acceptable if uttered in a public park could constitutionally be banned when broadcast from a sound truck.

As the 21st century approached, dealing with the Internet introduced new ramifications to this legal principal.

In 1996, Congress passed the Communications Decency Act (CDA) as an amendment to a far-reaching telecommunications bill. The CDA introduced criminal penalties, including fines of as much as $250,000 and prison terms up to two years for making "indecent" speech available to "a person under 18 years of age." A Philadelphia court a few months later struck down the law, contending that such censorship would chill all discourse on the Internet.[21]

Then, in the summer of 1997, the Supreme Court, in a sweeping endorsement of free speech, declared the CDA unconstitutional. The decision, unanimous in most respects, marked the highest court's first effort to extend the principles of the First Amendment into cyberspace and to confront the nature and the law of this new, powerful medium. In summarizing the court's finding, Justice John Paul Stevens said the court considered the "goal of protecting children from indecent material as legitimate and important," but concluded that "the wholly unprecedented breadth of the law threatened to suppress far too much speech "among adults and even between parents and children."[22] The issue, like all free speech law, is extraordinarily complex.

So, too, is the issue of cybersquatting. In 1999, hamburger giant Wendy's International, Inc. filed a lawsuit against Beswick Adams Corp. for allegedly registering a number of Internet domain names, such as www.wendysrestaurants.com, all closely related to the Wendy's trademark. Earlier, the Kmart Corporation successfully mounted a legal challenge to fight a rogue Web site, Kmartsucks.com. Ultimately, the site was forced to change its name to Themartsucks.com. Current trademark law prohibits a company from registering a name that exactly duplicates a registered trademark, but cybersquatters frequently register names that differ only slightly. They know that Web surfers will type in a variation of a company's name when searching for its site. They then either attempt to sell the names or use the sites to disrupt the company's commerce.[23]

The World Wide Web is fraught with such legal issues. Web sites even have been sued for not living up to their legal obligation to accommodate the disabled. In virtually every case, corporations have settled out-of-court when confronted with such

BACKGROUNDER

Apreemptivestrategy.com

One 21st-century antidote to beating back cybersquatters and avoiding expensive lawsuits is to preempt the infiltrators at their own game.

Specifically, smart companies have adopted the practice registering both positive and negative names themselves, for a meager $70 a pop, in order to preempt cybersquatters and critics from holding them up later on.

For example, in the eagerly anticipated New York State Senate race pitting Mayor Rudy Giuliani against former First Lady Hillary Clinton, the Giuliani camp registered more than a dozen domain names, including NoGiuliani.com, RudyNo.or, HillaryNo.com and even HillaryYes.com. (Eventually, the mayor decided not to run.) Similarly, companies today regularly register such domain names to keep their critics and others at bay.

While it is obviously impossible to preempt every close or nasty domain name—if you register McDonaldssucks.com, someone might counter with McDonaldsReallysucks.com—nonetheless going after obvious hits, such as NorthworstAirlines.com or UntiedAirlines.com makes real.common sense.

challenges. In 1999, the National Federation of the Blind filed a lawsuit against America Online, Inc., alleging that the service violated the Americans with Disabilities Act by remaining inaccessible to blind users. The suit could mark a precedent in terms of Internet accessibility to blind users. Smart organizations, therefore, will design Web sites for screen reader accessibility. The readers, which blind users install on their Internet browsers, dictate text on computer screens.

Beyond the matter of sight, of course, is the matter of speech. On the one hand are those who argue that the Internet is the most democratic of democratic institutions, allowing all access to all manner of speech. As such, this argument goes, adults should have every right to exercise their constitutional right to free speech. On the other side are those who contend that the Internet threatens to give children a "free pass into an adult bookstore."[24] Further complicating the issue, of course, is the fact that the Internet is changing every day. A law that applies today may be irrelevant or outdated tomorrow.

This, in essence, is the conundrum that confronts lawmakers as they attempt to construct laws to govern the Internet.

Public Relations and the Legal Profession

What has always been an uneasy alliance between lawyers and public relations professionals has today evolved into a relationship of grudging mutual respect. Lawyers, in fact, are making more use of public relations strategies than ever before.

In the decade of the 1990s, it was estimated that 75 percent of all major law firms used public relations consultants.[25] Lawyers and legal consultants attributed the increased use of public relations firms to heightened competition within the top tier of the legal profession. Many law firms have grown rapidly in the last decade and have to fight harder for clients and for top law school graduates. As a result, public relations has emerged as an important tool to get these firms' names circulated among clients, potential clients, and possible hires.

In 1984, the Supreme Court eased the ban on self-advertisement by lawyers. Although some lawyers are still reluctant to trumpet their capabilities, others are not. The leader of this ilk is Jacoby & Meyers, which, because of its pervasive national advertising, was derided by some as a "fast-food law firm."[26] But there was nothing funny about Jacoby & Meyers's client roster of 175,000 people and its $42 million business in 1989. For Jacoby & Meyers, advertising and publicity have paid off very well indeed.

Other law firms, like Searcy Denney Scarola Barnhart & Shipley of West Palm Beach, use community relations techniques to enhance their image in the local area. Searcy Denney, for example, contributes significantly to community causes, provides volunteers for community events, and sponsors public service announcements to promote the good works of particular local charities. The firm's slogan in such endeavors is, "Taking Time to Care."

For their part, public relations counselors have become more open to lawyers and have relaxed the tensions that have existed between the two professions. One public relations practitioner offers this advice for working with lawyers:

1. **Become an equal partner with legal counsel.** At all times, maintain an overview of the legal cases that are before your organization or industry. Take the initiative with legal counsel to discuss those that you believe may have major public relations implications.

2. **Combat the legal "no comment" syndrome.** Research cases in which an organization has publicly discussed issues without damage.

3. **Take the initiative in making announcements.** This will help manage the public perception of the issue. If an indictment is pending, consult the legal staff on the advisability of making statements—before you become a target.

4. **Research the background of the jury.** Past lists of jurors in a particular jurisdiction indicate occupations and other important demographic information.

5. **Winning may not be everything.** Outside law firms, trained in an adversarial mode and charging fees that depend on the size of the award, always want to "win." For legal counsel the stakes may also include a winning reputation, which helps to secure future cases. Public relations must bring a long-term perspective to strategic decisions.

6. **Beware of leaving a paper trail.** Any piece of paper that you create may end up in court. That includes desk calendars and notes to yourself. So be careful.[27]

Litigation Public Relations

The most critical use of public relations strategies and techniques for lawyers arrives prior to, during, or after litigation. In the 21st century, court cases at every level involving every manner of defendant—from celebrities like O. J. Simpson, Marv Albert, and Bill Clinton to lesser-known individuals on the local level—have used public relations assistance to complement legal litigation techniques.

Although court proceedings have certain rules and protocol, dealing in the public arena with a matter of litigation has no such strictures. Lawyers often are unprepared for the spontaneity and unpredictability of dealing with the media. That's why public relations counsel is so important in a public legal battle.

According to one counselor who works exclusively with litigation, there are seven keys to litigation visibility.

1. **Learn the process.** All involved should be aware of the road map for the case and the milestones ahead, which may lend themselves to publicity.

2. **Develop a message strategy.** Think about what should be said at each stage of a trial to keep the press and public focused on the key messages of the client.

3. **Settle fast.** Settlement is probably the most potent litigation visibility management tool. The faster the settlement, the less litigation visibility there is likely to be. This is often a positive development.

4. **Anticipate high-profile variables.** Often in public cases, everybody gets into the act—judges, commentators, jury selection experts, psychologists. Always anticipate all that could be said, conjectured, and argued about the case. Always try to be prepared for every inevitability.

5. **Keep the focus positive.** Ultimately, it's a positive, productive attitude that leads to effective negotiations with the other side. So the less combative you can be—especially near settlement—the better.

6. **Try settling again.** Again, this ought to be the primary litigation visibility strategy—to end the agony and get it out of the papers.

7. **Fight nicely.** Wars are messy, expensive, and prone to produce casualties. It is much better to be positive. This will give both sides a greater chance of eventually settling.[28]

BACKGROUNDER

Ladiieeeees and Gentlemen, Let's Get Ready to Sue

America in the 21st century is the world's most litigious society. Nowhere is this more true than in the world of celebritydom, where stars of every description have taken to the courts to protect their identity, their looks, their acts, their mannerisms, their voice, and, in one case, their five-word signature slogan.

The latter distinction belonged to one Michael Buffer, former model and journeyman announcer, who all of a sudden struck it rich with a call to arms, developed for the World Wrestling Federation: "Let's get ready to rumbllllllle!"

Buffer parlayed his clarion call into high-paid appearances in championship fights, NFL football broadcasts, NBA playoff games, movies, concerts, and even on the supreme honorary platform—an appearance as himself on *The Simpsons*.

No wonder Buffer sued Sony's Columbia Pictures for appropriating his "rumble" call in promotional ads for the epic movie *Booty Call*. When the Walt Disney Company wanted to use the call in its 1997 release *Hercules,* Buffer was paid a license fee. Buffer made it clear to one and all—including Guardian Angel-turned-radio-talk-show-host Curtis Sliwa, who used the call without permission as his theme song—that he would sue to protect his trademark. Sliwa got the last word, however, when he dropped the Buffer theme and replaced it instead with a soundalike announcer bellowing, "Let's kick some butt."

SUMMARY

As our society becomes more contentious, fractious, and litigious, public relations must become more concerned with the law. Indeed, public relations has already become involved with the law in many areas of communications beyond those already cited in this chapter.

- ☑ The Federal Communications Commission (FCC) ruled in 1987 that the Fairness Doctrine, the subject of years of debate among broadcasters and others, unconstitutionally restricted the First Amendment rights of broadcasters. The FCC said that broadcasters were no longer obligated to provide equal time for dissenting views. Congressional efforts to turn the doctrine into law were vetoed by President Reagan, but the debate may not be finished.

- ☑ The right of publicity has been challenged by the estates of deceased celebrities like Charlie Chaplin, W. C. Fields, Mae West, and the Marx brothers, whose likenesses have been portrayed in product advertisements without the permission of their heirs.

- ☑ In 1993, the Supreme Court ruled that the rap group 2 Live Crew could release a vulgar rewrite of the old Roy Orbison hit "Pretty Woman," even though those who copyrighted the original material had refused permission. The Court ruled that the raunchy rappers were entitled to "fair use" of the material for the purpose of parody. But in 1997, Texas became the first state in the nation to prohibit its agencies from investing in companies that produce or distribute music with lyrics that are sexually explicit or extol violence, aka "gangsta rap."[29]

- ☑ Also in 1997, in a landmark agreement with a group of state attorneys general, the tobacco industry agreed to a $368 billion agreement that ultimately would over time impose strict limits on tobacco marketing and advertising, including a ban on vending machines, outdoor billboards, and even Joe Camel.[30]

In addition to all of these legal areas, the public relations business itself increasingly is based on legal contracts: between agencies and clients, between employers and employees, between purchasers and vendors. All contracts—both written and oral—must be binding and enforceable.

In recent years, controversy in the field has erupted over "noncompete clauses," in which former employees are prohibited, within certain time parameters, from working for a competitor or pitching a former account. Likewise, legal challenges have been made relative to the markup of expenses that public relations agencies charge clients. Legal issues also have arisen over the postal laws that govern public relations people who disseminate materials through the mail. Add to these the blurring of the lines between public relations advice on the one hand and legal advice on the other, and it becomes clear that the connection between public relations and the law will intensify dramatically in the 21st century.

Discussion Starters

1. What is the difference between a public relations professional's responsibility and a lawyer's responsibility?
2. What have been recent challenges to the First Amendment?
3. What is meant by the term "insider trading"?
4. What was the essence of the 1999 case of *New York City v. the Brooklyn Museum*?
5. What kinds of information must public companies disclose immediately?
6. What is meant by the legal term "actual malice" with respect to privacy law?
7. Whom does copyright law protect?
8. What are the issues in legislating the Internet?
9. What is the attitude of law firms toward public relations counsel?
10. What general advice should a public relations professional consider in working with lawyers?

Notes

1. Patrick McGeehan and Matt Richtel, "What's in a Web Address? Maybe a Lawsuit," *New York Times* (October 22, 1999): 1.
2. Steven Komarow and Patrick O'Driscoll, "Case Forces the Military to Take a Look at Itself," *USA Today* (May 21, 1997): 1.
3. "Guilty Until Proven Innocent?" *Inside PR* (August 1993): 41.
4. Gerhart L. Klein, *Public Relations Law: The Basics* (Mt. Laurel, NJ: Anne Klein and Associates, Inc., 1990): 1–2.
5. "The Klan Loses," *New York Times* (October 25, 1999): A26.
6. Iver Peterson, "Firm Awarded $222.7 Million in a Libel Suit vs. Dow Jones," *New York Times* (March 21, 1997): D1.
7. Robert Hanley, "Judge Ousts Lawyer for Teenager Charged in Baby's Death," *New York Times* (July 4, 1997): B4.
8. Edmund L. Andrews, "F.C.C. Delays Radio Deals by Howard Stern's Employer," *New York Times* (December 31, 1993): A1, D2.
9. Linda Greenhouse, "Rights of Commercial Speech Affirmed," *New York Times* (March 25, 1993): A7.
10. Stephen Wermiel, "U.S. State Officials Win Wider Leeway to Restrict Free Speech of Corporations," *Wall Street Journal* (June 30, 1989): B6.

11. "SEC Set to Tighten Disclosure Rules," *O'Dwyer's PR Services Report* (June 1999): 22.

12. "SEC Set to Tighten Disclosure Rules."

13. Alix M. Freedman and Suein L. Hwang, "Brown & Williamson Faces Inquiry," *Wall Street Journal* (February 6, 1996): A1.

14. Thomas K. Grose, "$50 Million Lawsuit Against WSJ and Burrough May Make Some Authors-to-Be Think Twice," *TFJR Report* (April 1992): 3.

15. John J. Walsh, "Dealing with Misbehavior by News Media," Presentation before Annual Meeting of the Arthur W. Page Society, September 1997.

16. "Media Briefs," *Jack O'Dwyer's Newsletter* (December 18, 1996): 3.

17. Larry Reibstein, "One Heck of a Whupping," *Newsweek* (March 31, 1997): 54.

18. "The Press Wins," *New York Times* (October 25, 1999): A26.

19. Harold W. Suckenik, "PR Pros Should Know the Four Rules of 'Fair Use,'" *O'Dwyer's PR Services Report* (September 1990): 2.

20. Linda Greenhouse, "What Level of Protection for Internet Speech?" *New York Times* (March 24, 1997): D5.

21. Steven Levy, "U.S. v. the Internet," *Newsweek* (March 31, 1997): 77.

22. Linda Greenhouse, "Decency Act Fails," *New York Times* (June 27, 1997): 1.

23. "In Pursuit of Cybersquatters," *CFO Magazine* (November 1999): 16.

24. Levy, "U.S. v. the Internet."

25. Ellen Joan Pollock, "Lawyers Are Cautiously Embracing PR Firms," *Wall Street Journal* (March 14, 1990): B1.

26. Robyn Kelley, "Legal Beagles," *Spy* (August 1990): 74.

27. Lloyd Newman, "Litigation Public Relations: How to Work with Lawyers," *PR Reporter Tips and Tactics* (November 23, 1987): 2.

28. James E. Lukaszewski, "Managing Litigation Visibility: How To Avoid Lousy Trial Publicity," *Public Relations Quarterly* (Spring 1995): 18–24.

29. "Elsewhere," *San Jose Mercury News* (June 21, 1997): A11.

30. John M. Broder, "Cigarette Makers in a $368 Billion Accord to Curb Lawsuits and Curtail Marketing," *New York Times* (June 21, 1997): A1.

Suggested Readings

"Bridging the Gap Between PR Pros and Lawyers." *Public Relations Tactics* (June 1998): 30.

Corbin, Jeffrey. "Lawyers and Us—A Synergistic Relationship." *Public Relations Quarterly* (Winter 1997–98): 15–17.

Dennis, Everette E., ed. "Covering the Courts." *Media Studies Journal* (Winter 1998). Article authors include Fred Graham, J. Anthony Lukas, Johnnie Cochran, Jeffrey Toobin, Bruce Sanford, Linda Fairstein, Barry Scheck, and Judge Judith Kaye.

Geithnes, Edgar E. "Dealing with Client Indemnity Clauses." *Public Relations Tactics* (May 1998): 16–17.

Gibson, Dirk C. "Litigation Public Relations: Fundamental Assumptions." *Public Relations Quarterly* (Spring 1998): 19ff.

Klein, Gerhart L. *Public Relations Law: The Basics.* Mt. Laurel, NJ: Anne Klein and Associates, Inc., 1990. Presents the legal issues practitioners need to check before performing their duties, including the First Amendment, restrictions on free speech, copyright and trademark law, and financial disclosure.

Lukaszewski, James. "The Other Prosecutors." *Public Relations Quarterly* (Spring 1997): 23–29. Public relations tips for organizations in litigation.

top of the shelf

David Johnston

Cyberlaw: What You Need to Know About Doing Business Online.
Don Mills, OH: Stoddart Publishing Co. Ltd., 1997.

Your client has just been featured in a major article in the *New York Times,* and it's even highlighted as a hyperlink on the *Times'* home page. Is it legal for you to download the article and distribute it electronically to the two dozen financial analysts in your Rolodex? If you don't know the answer, *Cyberlaw* is for you. It steers the non-lawyers among us through the changing atmosphere of new information technology and its effects on business practice and possible legal consequences of doing business on the Internet.

Cyberlaw reviews existing laws that apply to the Internet and on-line transactions. Examples include contract law, torts, intellectual property law (where you'll find the answer to the above question), privacy, conflict of laws, and security in electronic commerce. It's packed with useful information for the layperson interested in cyberlaw, starting with a discussion of digital technology and businesses in transition.

Moore, Roy L., Ronald T. Farrar, and Erik L. Collins. *Advertising and Public Relations Law.* Mahwah, NJ: Lawrence Erlbaum Associates, 1997.

Rosenoer, Jonathan. *Cyberlaw: The Law of the Internet.* New York: Springer-Verlag, 1996

Roschwalb, Susanne A., and Richard A. Stack. *Litigation Public Relations: Courting Public Opinion.* Littleton, CO: Fred B. Rothman & Co., 1995. This is as good a treatise on legal public relations as currently exists. The authors explore the importance of communications in helping prevail in court.

The SEC, the Securities Market and Your Financial Communications. New York: Hill & Knowlton, 1991.

Trademark Basics. New York: International Trademark Association, 1995. Defines trademarks, how they differ from patents and copyrights, and spells out the rights and protection of trademark owners.

CASE STUDY

Burned by the Media: General Motors Extinguishes NBC

It is difficult now to believe that a proposal to send a camera crew to Indiana to tape two old Citation cars being driven into two pickup trucks fitted with igniters would be taken seriously.

> Report of Inquiry into Crash Demonstrations Broadcast on *Dateline NBC* November 17, 1992, NBC Internal Report, issued March 21, 1993

The estimated 17 million viewers of the November 17, 1992, *Dateline NBC* program couldn't help but be horrified as they observed a General Motors full-size pickup truck burst into flames after being hit broadside by a remote control-operated Citation.

The clear conclusion for any viewer watching the debacle was that GM trucks were dangerous and ought to be taken off the road—immediately!

There was only one slight problem.

The NBC crash demonstration was a sham. The test was rigged. The segment was flawed from start to finish. And the reporting of *NBC News* was flatly fraudulent, it would soon be learned.

NBC News would have gotten away with its trickery had not GM struck back with a public relations vengeance unprecedented in American corporate history.

Immediately after the damaging NBC broadcast, GM embarked on a painstaking mission to research the facts of the NBC demonstration and expose the network's falsified report. That effort would never have been seen had it not been for a lucky break— a call from a newsman who had discovered witnesses to the rigged demonstration on a rural road near Indianapolis.

Pete Pesterre, editor of *Popular Hot Rodding Magazine,* wrote an editorial criticizing the *Dateline NBC* story. Soon afterward, a reader of the magazine turned up a firefighter who had witnessed the filming of the crash and had filmed his own video of the incident.

GM obtained the firefighter's video, which proved to be the turning point in GM's efforts. The video clearly showed that the test was rigged. GM investigators found the two trucks used in the staged crash at a salvage yard in Indiana and purchased them. In one of the pickups, a used model rocket engine was found.

Between the time the show aired in November 1992 and January 1993, four letters were sent to NBC by GM. They received no adequate response. GM then threatened suit. NBC continued to state that the story, according to *NBC News* President Michael Gartner, "was entirely accurate." In February 1993, GM filed a lawsuit against the National Broadcasting Company, charging that *Dateline NBC* had rigged the crash. GM also immediately went into crisis mode.

GM's crisis communications program was managed by two members of its recently reorganized communications staff—William J. O'Neill, then director of communications for GM's North American Operations (NAO), and Edward S. Lechtzin, director of legal and safety issues for the NAO communications staff. O'Neill, in fact, had agreed that GM would participate in the original *Dateline NBC* program but hadn't been told during the interview session about NBC's taped test. O'Neill and Lechtzin spearheaded a unique public relations team that also included three GM attorneys and two engineers.

The public relations professionals, attorneys, and engineers together provided a nucleus that could make key decisions quickly and authoritatively.

Lechtzin's boss, GM General Counsel Harry J. Pearce, was selected to face off with the media. At the center of the group's public relations offensive would be a press conference, conducted by Pearce, to lay bare the NBC deception. Further, the GM crisis communications team made a conscious decision to target television as the key medium to deliver GM's strongest message that it had been wronged and wasn't going to take it.

Going to War with NBC

Given the old adage, "Don't pick a fight with the guy who buys ink by the barrel," a large number of "crisis communications consultants" wondered aloud during the days before the Pearce press conference if GM was doing the right thing.

At GM, there was never any doubt that the NBC deception should be publicized— as widely as possible. Briefed during an inaugural event for President Clinton, GM President Jack Smith told his public relations executives, "Don't overplay it, but do what's right."

During the three-week period before the press conference, the group pulling together the case against NBC was asked only two questions: (1) Do we have enough information? and (2) Are we doing the right thing? No presentations. No briefing books. No background meetings. No groups of 15 to 20 people in a room trying to decide what was right. It was left to the small crisis task force to select the right strategy.

Harry Pearce was scheduled to take the stage in the GM showroom at 1 P.M. on February 8, 1993. Only one question remained: How would the media react?

THE PEARCE PRESS CONFERENCE

From the moment Harry Pearce strode onstage until the time he concluded more than two hours later, the assembled media personnel—numbering nearly 150 journalists and 25 camera crews—were mesmerized.

"What I'm about to share with you should shock the conscience of every member of your profession and mine, and I believe the American people as well," Pearce began, speaking to an uncommonly quiet media audience. "I will not allow the good men and women of General Motors and the thousands of independent businesses who sell our products and whose livelihood depends upon our products to suffer the consequences of NBC's irresponsible conduct transmitted via the airwaves throughout this great nation in the November *Dateline* program. GM has been irreparably damaged and we are going to defend ourselves."[1]

For the next two hours, speaking without notes, Pearce systematically shredded any vestiges of defense that NBC might have had. The media audience was transfixed. There was no rushing to phones to call in the story, no shuffling of papers or sighs of boredom. The only sound that interrupted Pearce's devastating dissection of NBC was the intermittent click of camera shutters. Pearce was a skilled trial lawyer weaving a two-hour summation.

The GM attorney concluded by reading a brief statement issued earlier in the day by NBC in which the network said, "We feel that our use of those demonstrations was accurate and responsible." His reply was a challenge of the kind that a good lawyer gives to a jury—in this case, the assembled reporters and thousands of others watching the broadcast. "Well, you decide that one," Pearce said. "And that's going to prove your mettle within your own profession. It's sometimes most difficult to police abuse in one's own profession."

THE CRASH DEMONSTRATION

At the heart of the Pearce press conference was a repeat of NBC's 55-second crash demonstration within a 16-minute broadcast segment. Using videotape, Pearce demonstrated that the segment was flawed from start to finish. It loaded the evidence to prove that GM's 19?? full-size C/K pickup trucks, equipped with so-called side-saddle fuel tanks, had a fatal flaw that in a high-speed side impact collision caused them to rupture and spew burning gasoline. The clear implication was that the trucks were unsafe. This view was corroborated by the grieving parents of crash victims.

However, no source—not even the internal report generated by NBC after the affair—fully explained what the crashes of two aged Citations being pushed into the sides of two Chevy pickups were supposed to prove. They certainly didn't prove the trucks were dangerous. If anything, the performance of the two old trucks—hit at speeds of 39 and 48 miles per hour, respectively—was superb. The only fire generated,

---

[1] General Motors press conference transcript, Detroit, February 8, 1993.

as Pearce showed the reporters, was a 15-second grass fire caused by gasoline spewing from an overfilled filler tube after an ill-fitting gas cap came off on impact.

Careful editing from three views left the impression of a conflagration. As NBC's own investigative report indicated:

> We believe that the combined effect of the shot from the bullet car and the slow motion film creates an impression that the flames are about to consume the cabin of the truck. These images in the edited tape convey an impression quite different from what people saw at the scene. The fire was small, it did not consume the cabin of the truck, and it did not last long.[2]

Although the subsequent filmed truck crash resulted in no holocaust, the program, coupled with a well-orchestrated campaign by the plaintiff's attorneys, helped build public pressure that led the National Highway Traffic Safety Administration (NHTSA) to open an investigation into the safety of GM's trucks just one month after the broadcast.

THE NBC RETRACTION

GM's historic news conference literally brought *NBC News* to its knees.

On the day following Pearce's performance, NBC initiated a negotiating session with the company that lasted for 12 hours. GM would accept nothing less from NBC than a full public retraction of its prior broadcast.

On February 9, 1993, a day after the news conference, that is precisely what NBC did. *Dateline NBC* co-anchors Jane Pauley and Stone Phillips read a four-minute, on-air retraction that put the blame for the bogus broadcast squarely at NBC's door and apologized to GM.

In the aftermath, three *Dateline* producers were fired, the on-air reporter was demoted and reassigned, and ultimately, *NBC News* President Gartner resigned in humiliation. NBC agreed to reimburse GM the roughly $2 million it had spent in a three-week period investigating the false report. In exchange, GM agreed to drop the defamation suit it had filed against NBC.

For its part, GM was spared years of costly litigation over its suit. The company also was quickly able to put to rest what could have been a nightmarish visual every time GM trucks were mentioned on the evening news.

The cloak-and-dagger story on how GM put its case together remains tantalizingly vague. Nonetheless, what is clear was that in a single day, with a single press conference, GM successfully transformed the pickup truck story from a sensationalized and slanted media feeding frenzy into a serious question of journalistic ethics and integrity.

GM Communications Director O'Neill was blunt in his assessment: "I quite honestly wanted this to happen and I was glad it did happen, because I think these people purposely lied and misrepresented the facts and knew they were doing it. I do not think there is any room for that in this business."[3]

THE AFTERMATH

After NBC's stunning mea culpa, GM increased its public relations offensive to counter concerns about the safety of its trucks.

---

2. "NBC Internal Report of Inquiry into Crash Demonstrations Broadcast on *Dateline NBC,* November 17, 1992," issued March 21, 1993.
3. Catherine Gates, "NBC Learns a Lesson," *Public Relations Quarterly* (Winter 1993–1994): 42.

It sought to show that the plaintiff's bar—the trial lawyers—had a vested financial interest in nurturing the idea that the trucks were dangerous. So did another group, the so-called safety experts, cited by NBC and others, who either were financed by the plaintiff's attorneys or served as expert witnesses in mounting legal action against the company. In the same scrupulous way it had dissected NBC's case, GM systematically discredited the credentials and objectivity of the so-called safety experts.

Apparently galvanized by the publicity, the NHTSA demanded—even before it had completed its own investigation—that GM voluntarily recall its pickup trucks. The company refused. In April 1993, GM sponsored two two-hour shirtsleeve briefings by Pearce with key members of the media, explaining why the company wouldn't recall its trucks and why NHTSA's conclusions were flawed. Interestingly, television representatives were not invited to these sessions because it was felt that the medium could only "enflame the situation further."

In subsequent months, the GM-*NBC News* controversy received lengthy coverage in newspapers and magazines. In most, NBC fared poorly. Summarized one journalist:

> An investigation of past network auto-safety coverage reveals that both CBS and ABC have run the same sorts of material facts about the tests and relied on the same dubious experts with the same ties to plaintiff's bar.[4]

The Executive Summary of NBC's internal report concluded, "The story of this ill-fated crash demonstration and its aftermath is rather a story of lapsed judgment—serious lapses—by persons generally well-intentioned and well-qualified. And it is a story of a breakdown in the system for correction and compliance that every organization, including a news organization and network, needs."[5]

Questions

One could add that it is also a story that may never have been told had it not been for a gutsy, unyielding public relations initiative by an organization that refused to be dealt with unfairly.

1. What other options did GM have in addition to going public in the wake of the *Dateline NBC* report?
2. What was the downside risk for GM of being so public in its response?
3. Do you agree with GM's strategy on sending its general counsel to confront the media?
4. Do you agree with GM's decision not to invite television to its media briefings after the initial Pearce press conference?
5. In terms of reputation and credibility, what do you think its response to the *Dateline NBC* broadcast meant to GM?
6. General Motors, like other auto manufacturers, faces numerous public relations challenges. Scan the list of news releases on the General Motors Web site (www.generalmotors.com/cgi-bin/pr_index.pl) and follow the links to read one or two news releases about product recalls. What publics are being targeted with these news releases? What are the legal implications of such recall announcements?

4. "It Didn't Start with *Dateline NBC*," *National Review* (June 21, 1993): 41.
5. "NBC Internal Report": 8.

OVER THE TOP

An Interview with Harry J. Pearce

Harry Pearce, an executive vice president in charge of all corporate staffs at General Motors, was the automaker's general counsel at the time of the *Dateline NBC* affair in 1992 and 1993. Pearce served as GM's chief spokesman in the *Dateline NBC* crisis.

What were the relative contributions of public relations and law to GM's handling of the *Dateline NBC* issue?

GM's handling of the *Dateline NBC* issue was unique because the traditional distinctions between the purely legal and public relations lines got blurred. Dedicating key disciplines to a single team allowed each member the ability to focus on the same goal, and the individual contributions of the members became irrelevant.

Because of the litigation aspect of the pickup truck issue, there were some technical issues that only an attorney could address. However, in the larger challenge presented by NBC and the likely media coverage of the dispute, the common goal eliminated a lot of the traditional boundaries between lawyers, engineers, and public relations experts.

What was your objective in going after NBC?

The common goal was at once simple and critical. GM needed to create an environment where facts—not shrill and rhetorical sound bites or sensational video footage—would prevail. In simple terms, we had to neutralize the rhetoric with hard facts, and we needed to shock the media so that it would listen to our message. We knew that we had solid evidence that the *Dateline NBC* segment had crossed the ethical boundaries. And we knew that we had the right facts about the safety of our pickup trucks. We needed to create a climate where that became more, rather than less, important.

Once the facts about NBC's irresponsible conduct were clear to us, the question was really quite easy to answer. The lawsuit was necessary to preserve our legal rights. We then had to ask: "How do we best commu-nicate the truth about the inaccuracies and deception NBC perpetrated against GM and the American people?" It would have been wrong to let the *Dateline NBC* segment go unchallenged. It was obviously a high-stakes decision to go as public as we did, but when you operate on the principle that you are going to do what's right, it really isn't difficult to understand what needs to be done once you have the facts.

How would you characterize the journalistic ethics in the *Dateline* case?

In retrospect, NBC was probably shell-shocked because, as gross as we revealed the segment to be, I'd bet there are dozens of other examples of TV news programs that exhibited a similar bias. The difference in this case was that we were able to obtain the hard physical evidence of the deception—and it was one that we felt the American public would understand. Frankly, the work their so-called experts did was so sloppy and the technical advice they got was so incompetent, that it made our job easy once we knew where to look.

The "ethics" of what *Dateline* did, and failed to do, are manifest throughout the 16-minute segment itself. Though some at the network once would have liked to hide behind a facade that the show was fair except for the "rigged rocket" segment, the fact is that it was biased from start to finish. It was evident that *Dateline* had already decided the trucks were unsafe before even starting to film the segment and relied heavily on plaintiff attorneys and a family ready to go to trial for much of its input. There was never an attempt to present an objective look at the issue—just to provide sensational footage and grieving parents to gain rating points.

How important is the practice of public relations for a company like GM?

Public relations is a critical function, but we need to be clear how we at GM view this role. These folks aren't just mouthpieces. We will ultimately succeed or fail in any endeavor based on the quality of our products and services. That's as it should be. The role for PR at GM is to help communicate the facts effectively on any given situation. It sounds simple, but when you commit yourself as a company to being straight-forward with employees, the public, and the media, you eliminate a lot of unnecessary complication.

What should be the relationship between public relations and law?

We live in an age when instant communications and sound bites are a way of life, so the link between the law and public relations is both obvious and unavoidable. However, corporations don't often try to win their cases in the media, as do plaintiff attorneys and industry critics. We simply try to neutralize the bombastic rhetoric and distortions to create an environment where the facts can become the focus of the discussion. That's all we ever wanted, and we believe GM was able to achieve that environment in the truck issue.

However, given the media's love of sensationalism and the willingness of members of the legal profession to exploit it, there is a temptation on the part of some on our side of the fence to engage in the same tactics. It's a temptation that both the public relations and legal staffs have to resist.

How would you compare the ethical principles of a lawyer to those of a public relations professional?

In general, the legal duties of a lawyer to a client and to the profession are much higher than the legal or ethical duty of a public relations person. Although there is no Code of Professional Responsibility, with the associated legal consequences, for a member of the public relations profession who fails to follow specific ethical guidelines, PR professionals do have a Code of Ethics administered by the Public Relations Society of America. It is strict and brings with it consequences for inappropriate actions.

In practical terms, all GM PR professionals must conduct themselves by the highest ethical standards. We will not compromise integrity at GM, and our PR staff is the public face of credibility.

How would you characterize the shift in GM's public relations strategy in recent years?

It's probably a fair criticism of GM that we've tended to hold back and avoid taking very aggressive public positions when we were unfairly attacked in the press. Maybe it's a function of our history of being the biggest target for such abuse.

However, it makes no sense to us to let false reports and inaccurate statements about our products go unchallenged. We don't seek an unfair advantage with the media, but we fervently believe that GM is entitled to fair treatment. If that means we must be aggressive to get the facts out, so be it.

Part III Activation

Chapter 7

Communication

In the 21st century, words can kill you. Doubt it? Consider the following:

☑ *In the winter of 1999, the Republican front-runner for the presidential nomination, George W. Bush, was being questioned on foreign policy by a Boston television interviewer, obviously intent on making a name for himself.*

Reporter:	*Can you name the president of Chechnya?*
Bush:	*No, can you?*
Reporter:	*Can you name the general who is now in charge of Pakistan?*
Bush:	*Yes, General.*
Reporter:	*What is his name, sir?*
Bush:	*The general is General. I don't know his last name.*
Reporter:	*And the prime minister of India?*
Bush:	*The new prime minister of India is. . . . Can you name the foreign minister of Mexico?*
Reporter:	*No sir, but I would say to that, I'm not running for president.*

Were the reporter's questions unfair? Irrelevant? Even below-the-belt? Of course they were. But the point is that the candidate came across as arrogant, pretentious, even a bully.[1] In the 21st century, like it or not, words carry consequences and perception is reality.

☑ *President Clinton confronted this reality earlier that year when he compared combatants in the Northern Ireland conflict to "a couple of drunks walking out of the bar for the last time." The comment sparked immediate anger among some in Northern Ireland. "This is an insult!" bellowed Protestant preacher-politician Ian Paisley, himself a confirmed teetotaler. Always sensitive to the power of communication, Clinton backtracked almost instantly. "Earlier today, I used a metaphor that was inappropriate. I want to express my regret for any offense my remark caused," he said.[2]*

> ◪ *If those both on the right and on the left put their feet in their mouths occasionally, those in the "middle" did it with even more alarming frequency. The best—or worst—example was independent Governor Jesse Ventura of Minnesota, whose interview in* Playboy *magazine in the winter of 1999 caused his approval ratings in his state to plummet. Among other comments, the wrestling governor called religion "a sham." After the backlash, the governor, himself, seemed to "get religion." "I'm not going to offer my personal opinions on anything. It's sad . . . but in light of my family and self-preservation, I know that I have to change."*[3]

The lesson here is obvious: In the 21st century, communications must be handled with great care.

The public relations practitioner is a professional communicator. More than anyone else in an organization, the practitioner must know how to communicate. This knowledge sets the public relations professional apart from other employees.

Fundamentally, communication is a process of exchanging information, imparting ideas, and making oneself understood by others. Importantly, it also includes understanding others in return. Indeed, understanding is critical to the communications process. If one person sends a message to another, who disregards or misunderstands it, then communication hasn't taken place. But if the idea received is the one intended, then communication has occurred. Thus, a boss who sends subordinates dozens of memos isn't necessarily communicating with them. If the idea received is not the one intended, then the sender has done little more than convert personal thoughts to words—and there they lie.

Although all of us are endowed with some capacity for communicating, the public relations practitioner must be better at it than most. Indeed, the effectiveness of public relations professionals is determined by their own ability to communicate and to counsel others on how to communicate. Before public relations practitioners can earn the respect of management and become trusted advisors, they must demonstrate a mastery of many communications skills—writing, speaking, listening, promoting, and counseling. Just as the controller is expected to be an adept accountant, and the legal counsel is expected to be an accomplished lawyer, the public relations professional must be the best communicator in the organization. Period.

Communications Theory

Books have been written on the subject of communications theory. Consequently, we won't attempt to provide an all-encompassing discussion on how people ensure that their messages get through to others. But in its most basic sense, communication commences with a source, who sends a message through a medium to reach a receiver, who, we hope, responds.

One early theory of communication, the two-step flow theory, stated that an organization would beam a message first to the mass media, which would then deliver that message to the great mass of readers, listeners, and viewers for their response. This theory may have given the mass media too much credit. People today are influenced by a variety of factors, of which the media may be one but not necessarily the dominant one. Another theory, the concentric-circle theory, developed by pollster Elmo Roper, assumed that ideas evolve gradually to the public at large, moving in concentric circles from great thinkers to great disciples to great disseminators to lesser disseminators to the politically active to the politically inert. This theory suggests that people pick up and accept ideas from leaders, whose impact on public opinion may be greater than that of the mass media. The overall study of how communication is used for direction and control is called *cybernetics.*

One key element in communication—and particularly in public relations—is feedback. In cybernetic theory, feedback is communication that helps a source control a receiver's behavior. However, just as a thermostat gives indications as to how to adjust temperature, so, too, feedback doesn't necessarily imply "active communication" from a receiver. By contrast, in a theoretical communications approach called the *two-way symmetric model,* dialogue is key—from both senders and receivers. In this model of public relations communication, both senders and receivers have an equal chance of persuading and being persuaded.[4]

Although there are numerous models of communication, one of the most fundamental is the S-M-R approach. This model suggests that the communication process begins with the source (S), who issues a message (M) to a receiver (R), who then decides what action to take, if any, relative to the communication. This element of receiver action, or feedback, underscores that good communication always involves dialogue between two or more parties. The S-M-R model has been modified to include additional elements: (1) an encoding stage, in which the source's original message is translated and conveyed to the receiver, and (2) a decoding stage, in which the receiver interprets the encoded message and takes action. This evolution from the traditional model has resulted in the S-E-M-D-R method, which illustrates graphically the role of the public relations function in modern communications; both the encoding (E) and the decoding (D) stages are of critical importance in communicating any public relations message.

The Source

The source of a message is the central person or organization doing the communicating. The source could be a politician giving a campaign speech, a school announcing curriculum changes, or even, as one superior court judge in Seattle ruled, a topless go-go dancer in the midst of gyrating.

Although the source usually knows how it wants the message to be received, there is no guarantee that it will be understood that way by the receiver. In many cases—a public speech, for example—the speaker is relatively limited in ability to influence the interpretation of the message. Gestures, voice tone, and volume can be used to add special importance to certain remarks, but whether the audience understands what is intended may ultimately depend on other factors, particularly the encoder.

The Encoder

What the source wants to relate must be translated from an idea in the mind to a communication. In the case of a campaign speech, a politician's original message may be subject to translation or reinterpretation by at least three independent encoders.

1. The politician may consult a speech writer to help put ideas into words on paper. Speech writers become encoders in first attempting to understand the politician's message clearly and then in translating that message effectively into language that an audience will understand and, hopefully, accept.
2. Once the speech is written, it may be further encoded into a news release. In this situation, the encoder—perhaps a different individual from the speech writer—selects what seem to be the most salient points of the speech and provides them to media editors in a fairly brief format.
3. A news editor may take the news release and retranslate it before reporting it to the voters, the ultimate audience for the politician's message. Thus, the original message in the mind of the politician has been massaged three separate times before it ever reaches the intended receivers. Each time, in all likelihood, the particular encoder has added new subjective shadings to the politician's original message. The very act of encoding depends largely on the encoder's personal experience.

Words/semantics.   Words are among our most personal and potent weapons. Words can soothe us, bother us, or infuriate us. They can bring us together or drive us apart. They can even cause us to kill or be killed. Words mean different things to different people, depending on their backgrounds, occupations, education, or geographic locations. What one word means to you might be dramatically different from what that same word means to your neighbor. The study of what words really mean is called *semantics,* and the science of semantics is a peculiar one indeed.

Words are perpetually changing in our language. What's in today is out tomorrow. What a word denotes according to the dictionary may be thoroughly dissimilar to what it connotes in its more emotional or visceral sense. Even the simplest words—liberal, conservative, profits, consumer activists—can spark semantic skyrockets. Many times, without knowledge of the territory, the semantics of words may make no sense. Take the word *fat.* In our American culture and vernacular, a person who is fat is generally not associated with the apex of attractiveness. A person who is "thin," on the other hand, may indeed be considered highly attractive. But along came hip-hop, and pretty soon *phat*—albeit with a new spelling—became the baddest of the bad, the coolest of the cool, the height of fetching pulchritudinousness. (if you get my drift).

Words used in the encoding stage have a significant influence on the message conveyed to the ultimate receiver. Just consider the impact on society of advertising slogans (Figure 7-1). Thus, the source must depend greatly on the ability of the encoder to accurately understand and effectively translate the true message—with all its semantic complications—to the receiver.

1. "All the News That's Fit to Print."
2. "How Do You Spell Relief?"
3. "The Un-cola."
4. "Takes a Licking and Keeps on Ticking."
5. "Because It's Your Stuff."
6. "Just Do It."
7. "A Different Kind of Company. A Different Kind of Car."
8. "The Pause That Refreshes."
9. "You Deserve a Break Today."
10. "Let Your Fingers Do the Walking."
11. "We're Number Two. We Try Harder."
12. "Come Fly the Friendly Skies."
13. "Have It Your Way."
14. "Don't Leave Home Without It."
15. "We'll Leave the Light on for You."

16. "Be All That You Can Be."
17. "Think Different."
18. "The World on Time."
19. "We Bring Good Things to Life."
20. "Because I'm Worth It."
21. "Please Don't Squeeze the Charmin."
22. "Tell 'Em Charlie Sent You."
23. "A Little Dab'll Do Ya."
24. "Does She or Doesn't She?"
25. "Melts in Your Mouth, Not in Your Hand."
26. "Plop, Plop, Fizz, Fizz."
27. "M'm, M'm, Good."
28. "Get a Piece of the the Rock."
29. "Good to the Last Drop."
30. "They're Gr-r-r-reat!"

Answers: 1. The *New York Times,* 2. Rolaids, 3. 7-Up, 4. Timex, 5. Iomega, 6. Nike, 7. Saturn, 8. Coca-Cola, 9. McDonald's, 10. Bell System Yellow Pages, 11. Avis, 12. United Airlines, 13. Burger King, 14. American Express, 15. Motel 6, 16. U.S. Army, 17. Apple Computer, 18. FedEx, 19. General Electric, 20. L'Oreal, 21. Charmin, 22. StarKist, 23. Brylcreem, 24. Miss Clairol, 25 M&Ms, 26. Alka-Seltzer, 27. Campbell soup, 28. Prudential Insurance, 29. Maxwell House coffee, 30. Kellogg's Frosted Flakes.

FIGURE 7-1 **What's in a slogan?** How many of these advertising slogans can you attach to the appropriate products? (Don't peek!)

BACKGROUNDER

When in Rome . . .

It's hard enough to understand English words if you speak the language, but if English isn't your first language, it's even more confounding to understand why when words are apparently put together in the proper construction—they don't exactly mean what they should.

Here are a few overseas examples.

- In a Paris hotel elevator: "Please leave your values at the front desk."
- Outside a Hong Kong tailor shop: "Ladies may have a fit upstairs."
- In a Zurich hotel: "Because of the impropriety of entertaining guests of the opposite sex in the bedroom, it is suggested that the lobby be used for this purpose."

- In a Bangkok dry cleaners: "Drop your trousers here for best results."
- In a Bucharest hotel: "The lift is being fixed for the next day. During that time, we regret that you will be unbearable."
- In a Rome laundry: "Ladies, leave your clothing here and spend the afternoon having a good time."
- Advertisement for donkey rides in Thailand: "Would you like to ride on your own ass?"
- In an Acapulco hotel: "The manager has personally passed all the water served here."
- In a Copenhagen airport: "We take your bags and send them in all directions."
- In a Budapest zoo: "Please do not feed the animals. If you have any suitable food, give it to the guard on duty."

The Message

Once an encoder has taken in the source's ideas and translated them into terms a receiver can understand, the ideas are then transmitted in the form of a message. The message may be carried in a variety of communications media: speeches, newspapers, news releases, press conferences, broadcast reports, and face-to-face meetings. Communications theorists differ on what exactly constitutes the message, but here are three of the more popular explanations.

1. **The content is the message.** According to this theory, which is far and away the most popular, the content of a communication—what it says—constitutes its message. According to this view, the real importance of a communication—the message—lies in the meaning of an article or in the intent of a speech. Neither the medium through which the message is being communicated nor the individual doing the communicating is as important as the content.

2. **The medium is the message.** Other communications theorists—the late Canadian professor Marshall McLuhan being the best known—argue that the content of a communication is not the message at all. According to McLuhan, the content is less important than the vehicle of communication.

   McLuhan's argument stemmed largely from the fact that many people today are addicted to television. He said that television is a "cool" medium—that is, someone can derive meaning from a TV message without working too hard. On the other hand, reading involves hard work to grasp an idea fully; thus, newspapers, magazines, and books are "hot" media. Furthermore, McLuhan argued, a television viewer can easily become part of that which is being viewed. This has particular implications as television—and streaming Internet video for that matter—becomes more and more interactive.

   One direct outgrowth of this medium-is-the-message theory was the development of the friendly team style of local television news reporting. Often called the *eyewitness approach,* this format encouraged interaction among TV newscasters in order to involve viewers as part of the news team family.

   The medium of television has become particularly important to U.S. presidents. Commencing with the cool, polished television demeanor of John F. Kennedy and proceeding through modern-day presidents, television has become the great differentiator in terms of presidential popularity. Ronald Reagan, a former movie actor and media spokesman for General Electric, was a magnificent master of the TelePrompTer. Reagan's televised speeches were studies in proper use of the medium. George Bush, not as good as his predecessor, nonetheless had his moments. Bill Clinton, while not as polished as Reagan with prepared speeches, was greatly skilled in using the medium to suggest a committed, concerned, and undeniably human commander-in-chief.

3. **The person is the message.** Still other theorists argue that it is neither the content nor the medium that is the message, but rather the speaker. For example, Hitler was a master of persuasion. His minister of propaganda, Josef Goebbels, used to say, "Any man who thinks he can persuade, can persuade." Hitler practiced this self-fulfilling communications prophecy to the hilt. Feeding on the perceived desires of the German people, Hitler was concerned much less with the content of his remarks than with their delivery. His maniacal rantings and frantic gestures seized public sentiment and sent friendly crowds into a frenzy. In every way, Hitler himself was the primary message of his communications.

B A C K G R O U N D E R

Are You Sure You Saw What You Thought You Saw?

First read the sentence that follows:

FINISHED FILES ARE THE RESULT OF YEARS OF SCIENTIFIC STUDY COMBINED WITH THE EXPERIENCE OF MANY YEARS.

Now, count the Fs in the sentence. Count them only once, and do not go back and count them again.

Question
How many *F*s are there?

Answer
There are six *F*s. However, because the *F* in OF sounds like a *V*, it seems to disappear. Most people perceive only three *F*s in the sentence. Our conditioned, habitual patterns (mental blocks) restrict us from being as alert as we should be. Frequently, we fail to perceive things as they really are.

Today, in a similar vein, we often refer to a leader's charisma. Frequently, the charismatic appeal of a political leader may be more important than what that individual says. President Clinton, for example, could move an audience by the very inflection of his words. Likewise, Jesse Jackson on the Democratic side and Alan Keyes on the Republican side can bring an audience to its feet merely by shaking a fist, picking up the pace, or raising the pitch of their voices. Accomplished speakers, from retired military leaders like Colin Powell and Norman Schwarzkopf, to business consultants like Tom Peters and Stew Leonard, to sports coaches like Pat Riley and Bill Parcells, can also rally listeners with their personal charismatic demeanor.

Often people cannot distinguish between the words and the person who speaks them. The words, the face, the body, the eyes, the attitude, the timing, the wit, the presence—all form a composite that, as a whole, influences the listener. As political consultant-turned-television-executive Roger Ailes has put it, it comes down to the "like" factor in communication. Ailes points out that some candidates get votes just because people like them. "They forget that you're short, or you're fat, or you're bald . . . they say 'I like that guy.' "[5] In such cases, the source of the communication becomes every bit as important as the message itself.

The Decoder

After a message has been transmitted, it must be decoded by a receiver before action can be taken. This stage is like the encoding stage in that the receiver takes in the message and translates it into his or her own common terms. Obviously, language again plays a critical role. The decoder must fully understand the message before acting on it; if the message is unclear or the decoder is unsure of its intent, there's probably little chance that the action taken by the receiver will be the action desired by the source. Messages must be understood in common terms.

How a receiver decodes a message depends greatly on that person's own perception. How an individual looks at and comprehends a message is a key to effective communications (Figure 7-2). Remember that everyone is biased; no two people perceive a message identically. Personal biases are nurtured by many factors, including stereotypes, symbols, semantics, peer group pressures, and—especially in today's culture—the media.

What do you see: Fish or fowl?

FIGURE 7-2 **Fish or fowl?** Often what we see may not be what others see. (Hint: There are both white fish and black fowl.)

Stereotypes. Everyone lives in a world of stereotypical figures. Yuppies, Midwesterners, feminists, bankers, blue-collar workers, PR types, and thousands of other characterizations cause people to think of certain specific images. Public figures, for example, are typecast regularly. The dumb blond, the bigoted right-winger, the computer geek, and the shifty used-car salesman are the kinds of stereotypes our society—particularly television—perpetuate.

Like it or not, most of us are victims of such stereotypes. For example, research indicates that a lecture delivered by a person wearing glasses will be perceived as significantly more believable than the same lecture delivered before the same audience by the same lecturer without glasses. The stereotyped impression of people with glasses is that they are more trustworthy and more believable.

Symbols. The clenched-fist salute, the swastika, and the thumbs-up sign all leave distinct impressions on most people. Marshaled properly, symbols can be used as effective persuasive elements (Figure 7-3). The Statue of Liberty, the Red Cross, the Star of David, and many other symbols have been used traditionally for positive persuasion. On the other hand, when unrelated Middle Eastern terrorists selected American targets to sabotage in the 1990s, they chose to bomb the World Trade Center early in the decade and shoot up the Empire State Building later in the decade. No doubt, these locations were chosen because of their symbolic value as American icons.

Semantics. Public relations professionals make their living largely by knowing how to use words effectively to communicate desired meanings. Occasionally, this is tricky because the same words may hold contrasting meanings for different people. In the 21st century, the contentious abortion debate is couched in the confusing semantic terms *pro-life*—those against abortion—and *pro-choice*—those in favor of allowing abortions. Especially vulnerable are politically sensitive phrases such as *capital punishment, law and order, liberal politician, right-winger,* and on and on, until you reach the point where the Oakridge Mall in San Jose, California, demanded that the gourmet hamburger restaurant on its premises, with a logo depicting a smiling hamburger with a monocle and top hat, either change its "suggestive name" or leave the mall. The restaurant's name? Elegant Buns.

Controversy also surrounds the semantics associated with certain forms of rap music. To critics, some rap music artists preach a philosophy of violence and hate. But gangster rappers claim that they are "telling it like it is" or "reporting what we see in the streets." When reporters and record company executives give credence to such misguided rhetoric, they become just as guilty for the often unfortunate consequences that result— for example, the killings in the late 1990s of enemy rap artists, Tupac Shakur and Notorious B.I.G.[6]

Because language and the meanings of words change constantly, semantics must be handled with extreme care. Good communicators always consider the consequences of the words they plan to use before using them.

FIGURE 7-3 **What's in a symbol?** Located on Mount Lee in Griffith Park, the Hollywood sign is the most famous sign in the world. Originally built in 1923 for $21,000 as an advertising gimmick to promote home sales, the 45-foot high, 450-foot long, 480,000 pound sign was restored in 1978—Tinseltown's most enduring and instantly identifiable symbol. (Courtesy of Global Icons)

Peer groups. In one famous study, students were asked to point out, in progression, the shortest of three lines.

A   _____

B   _____

C   _____

Although line B is obviously the shortest, each student in the class except one was told in advance to answer that line C was the shortest. The object of the test was to see whether the one student would agree with his peers. Results generally indicated that, to a statistically significant degree, all students, including the uncoached one, chose C. Peer pressure prevails.

Media. The power of the media—particularly as an agenda setter or reinforcement mechanism—is also substantial. A common complaint among lawyers is that their clients cannot receive fair trials because of pretrial publicity leading to preconceived verdicts from potential jurors who read newspapers and watch television. Such was the case in 2000, when the murder trial of four white New York City police officers, who shot and killed an unarmed black man, was moved to upstate Albany and out of the politically volatile atmosphere of the Bronx, where the murder was committed.

It is clear that people often base perceptions on what they read or hear, without bothering to dig further to elicit the facts. Although appearances are sometimes revealing, they are often deceiving.

What's in a Dot.com Name?

Answer? $$$$$$$$$$. Lots of them.

In the early years of the 21st century, words on the Internet came at a sky-high premium—particularly generic words.

In 1999, a Texas entrepreneur sold the address Business.com to a California company for a cool $7.5 million. The Texan bought the name from someone else in 1997 for $150,000.

Such was the frenzy to seize prosaic names for spiffy Internet sites. Both Wine.com and Autos.com sold for $3 million. Wallstreet.com went for more than $1 million, and Drugs.com fetched a relatively meager $823,000.

No wonder there were more than 10,000 trademarked domain names by 2000. The rush to register generic domain addresses on the Web became so intense that legislation to control the practice became a real possibility.

Nonetheless, the feeding frenzy to register more and more generic names continued unabated into the new millennium. Indeed, a Washington, D.C., public relations professional who paid $40 to register the name Publicrelations.com had high hopes of auctioning off his cherished namesake for a cool $3 million.

Good.com luck!

The Receiver

You really aren't communicating unless someone is at the other end to hear and understand what you're saying. This situation is analogous to the old mystery of the falling tree in the forest: Does it make a noise when it hits the ground if there's no one there to hear it? Regardless of the answer, communication doesn't take place if a message doesn't reach the intended receivers and exert the desired effect on those receivers.

Even if a communication is understood clearly, there is no guarantee that the motivated action will be the desired one. In fact, a message may trigger several different effects.

1. **It may change attitudes.** This result, however, is very difficult to achieve and rarely happens.
2. **It may crystallize attitudes.** This outcome is much more common. Often a message will influence receivers to take actions they might already have been thinking about taking but needed an extra push to accomplish. For example, a receiver might want to contribute to a certain charity, but seeing a child's photo on a contribution canister might crystallize his or her attitude sufficiently to trigger action.
3. **It might create a wedge of doubt.** Communication can sometimes force receivers to modify their points of view. A persuasive message can cause receivers to question their original thinking on an issue.
4. **It may do nothing.** Often communication results in no action at all. When the American Cancer Society waged an all-out campaign to cut into cigarette sales, the net impact of the communication campaign was hardly significant.

Feedback is critical to the process of communication. A communicator must get feedback from a receiver to know what messages are or are not getting through and how to structure future communications. Occasionally, feedback is ignored by professional communicators, but this is always a mistake.

A QUESTION OF ETHICS

The Insensitive Racial Slur Firing

New Washington, D.C., Mayor Anthony A. Williams wanted to get off to a good start in 1999 to erase the memory of his predecessor, the infamous Marion Berry, most well known for smoking crack on an FBI videotape.

Alas for Mayor Williams, his was not a fluid start. Early in the Williams administration, it was reported that a white aide, David Howard, the mayor's ombudsman and first openly gay employee, used a "racially offensive" word in a budget discussion with two black coworkers. Mr. Howard said, "I will have to be 'niggardly' with this fund because it's not going to be a lot of money."

The others at the meeting immediately objected to what they perceived to be a racial slur. Mr. Howard apologized, offered his resignation to the mayor, and Mayor Williams unhesitatingly accepted it.

But wait a minute. According to *Webster's Dictionary,* the word *niggardly* means "miserly" and is of Scandinavian origin. It has no racial overtones whatsoever and no relationship at all with the racial slur to which it was linked.

That's exactly what activist homosexual groups told the mayor, when they vehemently objected to Mr. Howard's undeserved firing. For his part, the mayor said he would "review" the situation and quickly ducked for cover.

Defended his spokeswoman, "It may have been poor judgment for someone in his position to use that word, and based on that, the mayor accepted his resignation."

Rebutted one gay activist, "David Howard is the one owed an apology. The mayor has been making incredibly lame statements defending the fact that he accepted his resignation without even looking into it first."

Ultimately, Mr. Howard was allowed to remain in the administration, albeit in a less sensitive post.

Said the fired/reinstated nonracist linguist about his ordeal, "I used bad judgment in using the world 'niggardly.' I learned it for my SAT test as a junior in high school. It's an arcane word that's unfamiliar to a lot of people, and I can see how someone not familiar with the word could perceive it differently."

Melinda Henneberger, "Race Mix-up Raises Havoc for Capital," New York Times, January 29, 1999, A8.

BACKGROUNDER

Whaaat?

Extra credit for anyone who can decode the following sentence:

We respectfully petition, request, and entreat that due and adequate provision be made, this day and the date herein after subscribed, for the satisfying of this petitioner's nutritional requirements and for the organizing of such methods as may be deemed necessary and proper to assure the reception by and for said petitioner of such quantities of baked products as shall, in the judgment of the aforesaid petitioner, constitute a sufficient supply thereof.*

Whaaat?

*Give us this day our daily bread.

Ohhh. Perhaps this one is easier to decode.
1. The Lord is my external-internal integrative mechanism.
2. I shall not be deprived of gratifications for my visogeneric hungers or my need dispositions.
3. He motivates me to orient myself toward a nonsocial object with affective significance.
4. He positions me in a nondecisional situation.
5. He maximizes my adjustment.*
*1. The Lord is my shepherd.
 2. I shall not want.
 3. He leadeth me beside the still waters.
 4. He maketh me to lie down in green pastures.
 5. He restoreth my soul.

Whether the objectives of a communication have been met can often be assessed by such things as the amount of sales, number of letters, or number of votes obtained. If individuals take no action after receiving a communication, feedback must still be sought. In certain cases, although receivers have taken no discernible action, they may have understood and even passed on the message to other individuals. This person-to-person relay of received messages creates a two-step flow of communications: (1) vertically from a particular source and (2) horizontally from interpersonal contact. The targeting of opinion leaders as primary receivers is based on the hope that they will distribute received messages horizontally within their own communities.

S U M M A R Y

Some communications consultants believe the future of 21st-century communication may be a "step back in time." The advent of the World Wide Web, narrowcasting, and communicating to more targeted, smaller audiences will mean a return to more direct communication between people. By combining the new technology—cable, Internet telemarketing, floppy disks, CD-ROM, and all the rest—people will need the help of public relations professionals to communicate effectively.[7]

There is no trick to effective communication. In addition to some facility with techniques, it is knowledge, hard work, and common sense that are the basic guiding principles. Naturally, communication must follow performance; organizations must back up what they say with action. Slick brochures, engaging speeches, intelligent articles, and a good press may capture the public's attention, but in the final analysis, the only way to obtain continued public support is through proper performance.

Discussion Starters

1. Above all else, the public relations practitioner is a professional what?
2. Describe the process of communication.
3. Why do words like *liberal, conservative, profits,* and *consumer activist* spark semantic skyrockets?
4. What communications vehicle did President Reagan and President Clinton use to maximum effectiveness?
5. What is meant by the "symmetric model" of communication?
6. Describe the S-E-M-D-R approach to communication.
7. How does perception influence a person's decoding?
8. Why is feedback critical to the communications process?
9. What common mistakes do people make when they communicate?
10. Why do some communications consultants believe that the future of communications may be a "step back in time"?

Notes

1. Fraser Seitel, "Forgetting His M.A.P.s: George Junior Loses His Way," *Ragan Report* (November 22, 1999): 2.

2. "Clinton's Comment Gets Reaction," *Jakarta Post* (October 10, 1999): 2.
3. Matt Bai, "The Taming of Jesse," *Newsweek* (October 25, 1999): 38.
4. Louis Uchitelle, "The New Buzz: Growth is Good," *New York Times* (June 18, 1996): B1.
5. "The 'Like Factor' in Communications," *Executive Communications* (February 1988): 1.
6. Brent Staples, "The Politics of Gangster Rap," *New York Times* (August 27, 1993).
7. "Communication May Step Back in Time '90s," *IABC Communication World* (February 1990): 9.

Suggested Readings

Bell, Arthur H. *Tools for Technical and Professional Communication*. Lincolnwood, IL: NTC Publishing Group, 1995.

Bovee, Courtland L., and John V. Thill. *Business Communication Today,* 5th ed. New York: McGraw-Hill, 1998.

Communications Booknotes Quarterly. Mahwah, NJ: Lawrence Erlbaum Associates Inc. A review service for books, reports, documents, and electronic publications on all aspects of mass communication.

Corman, Steven R., et al. *Foundations of Organizational Communication: A Reader*. White Plains, NY: Longman, 1994.

Edelstein, Alex S. *Total Propaganda: From Mass Culture to Popular Culture*. Mahwah, NJ: Lawrence Erlbaum Associates Inc., 1997.

Grunig, James E., ed. *Excellence in Public Relations and Communications Management*. Hillsdale, NJ: Lawrence Erlbaum Associates, 1992.

Hewes, Dean E., ed. *The Cognitive Bases of Interpersonal Communication*. Hillsdale, NJ: Lawrence Erlbaum Associates, 1995.

International Encyclopedia of Communication, vol. 4. New York: Oxford University Press, 1989.

Kanzler, Ford. "The Positioning Statement: Have One Before You Start Communicating." *Public Relations Quarterly* (Winter 1997–98): 18–22.

Leeds-Hurwitz, Wendy. *Social Approaches to Communication*. New York: Guilford Press, 1995.

Lutz, William. *The New Doublespeak: Why No One Knows What Anyone's Saying Anymore*. New York: HarperCollins Publishers, 1996.

Mickey, Thomas J. *Sociodrama: An Interpretative Theory for the Practice of Public Relations*. Lanham, MD: University Press of America, 1997.

Perloff, Richard M. *Political Communication: Politics, Press, and Public in America*. Mahwah, NJ: Lawrence Erlbaum Associates Inc., 1997.

Ragan Report. Chicago: Ragan Communications. Weekly. Pointed commentary on current communications issues; particularly pointed columnists.

Sigman, Stuart J., ed. *The Consequentiality of Communication*. Hillsdale, NJ: Lawrence Erlbaum Associates, 1995. Goes beyond the "effects" of communication, exploring the procedures, dynamics, and structures.

Thill, John V., and Courtland L. Bovee. *Excellence in Business Communication,* 3rd ed. New York: McGraw-Hill, 1996.

Weiner, Richard. *Webster's New World Dictionary of Media and Communications*. New York: Macmillan, 1996.

CASE STUDY

Exxon Corporation's Bad Good Friday

In the history of public relations practice, few communications issues have been handled as questionably, received as much global notoriety, and had such far-reaching implications on the profession as those involving the Exxon Corporation in 1989.

At 8:30 A.M. on March 24, 1989—Good Friday, no less—Lawrence G. Rawl, chairman and chief executive of the Exxon Corporation, one of the world's largest companies, was in his kitchen sipping coffee when the phone rang.

"What happened? Did it lose an engine? Break a rudder?" Rawl asked the caller.

"What happened" was that an Exxon tanker had run aground and was dumping gummy crude oil into the frigid waters of Prince William Sound, just outside the harbor of Valdez, Alaska.

What was about to happen to Mr. Rawl and his company —and to the environment—was arguably the worst environmental disaster in the history of the United States.

The facts, painfully portrayed in media across the country, were these: The *Exxon Valdez,* a 987-foot tanker, piloted by a captain who was later revealed to have been legally drunk, ran aground on a reef 25 miles southwest of the port of Valdez. The resulting rupture caused a spill of 260,000 barrels, the largest spill ever in North America, affecting 1,300 square miles of water, damaging some 600 miles of coastline, and killing as many as 4,000 Alaskan sea otters. The disaster also enshrined the name Exxon in the all-time Public Relations Hall of Shame.

Exxon's communications dilemma broke down roughly into five general categories.

TO GO OR NOT TO GO

The first problem that confronted Exxon and its top management after news of the Good Friday spill had broken was whether Chairman Rawl should fly to Prince William Sound to demonstrate the company's concern. This was what Union Carbide Chairman Warren Anderson did when his company suffered a devastating industrial explosion in Bhopal, India. It was also what Ashland Oil's Chairman John R. Hall did when his company suffered an oil spill earlier in 1989.

If Rawl went to Alaska, the reasoning went, he might have been able to reassure the public that the people who run Exxon acknowledged their misdeed and would make amends. What could be a better show of concern than the chairman flying to the local scene of the tragedy?

On the other hand, a consensus of executives around Rawl argued that he should remain in New York. "What are you going to do?" they asked. "We've already said 'we've done it, we're going to pay for it, and we're responsible for it.'" Rawl's more effective role, said these advisers, was right there at Exxon headquarters in Manhattan.

In the end, the latter view triumphed. Rawl did not go to Alaska. He left the cleanup in "capable hands" and sent a succession of lower-ranking executives to Alaska to deal with the spill. As he summarized in an interview one year after the Prince William Sound nightmare, "We had concluded that there was simply too much for me to coordinate from New York. It wouldn't have made any difference if I showed up and made a speech in the town forum. I wasn't going to spend the summer there; I had other things to do."

Rawl's failure to fly immediately to Valdez struck some as shortsighted. Said one media consultant about Rawl's communications decision, "The chairman should have been up there walking in the oil and picking up dead birds."

WHERE TO ESTABLISH MEDIA CENTRAL

The second dilemma that confronted Exxon was where to establish its media center.

This decision started, correctly enough, with Exxon senior managers concluding that the impact of the spill was so great that news organizations should be kept informed as events unfolded. Exxon, correctly, wanted to take charge of the news flow and give the public, through the news media, a credible, concerned, and wholly committed corporate response.

It decided that the best place to do this would be in Valdez, Alaska, itself. "Just about every news organization worth its salt had representatives in Valdez," said Exxon's publicity chief. "But in retrospect, we should have sent live broadcasts of news conferences to several points around the country." The problem was that Valdez was a remote Alaskan town with limited communications operations. This complicated the ability of Exxon to disseminate information quickly. As *Oil & Gas Journal* stated later: "Exxon did not update its media relations people elsewhere in the world. It told reporters it was Valdez or nothing."

Additionally, there was a four-hour time difference between Valdez and New York. Consequently, "Exxon statements were erratic and contradictory," said the publisher of another oil bulletin. The phone lines to Valdez quickly became jammed, and even Rawl couldn't find a knowledgeable official to brief him. That left news organizations responsible for keeping the public informed cut off from Exxon information during the early part of the crisis. Because news conferences took place at unsuitable viewing hours for television networks and too late for many morning newspapers, predictable accusations of an Exxon "cover-up" resulted. Said one Exxon official about the decision to put the communications center in Valdez, "It didn't work."

RAPIDITY OF RESPONSE

A cardinal rule in any crisis is: Keep ahead of the information flow—try not to let events get ahead of you. Here Exxon had serious problems.

First, it took Chairman Rawl a full week to make any public comment on the spill. When he did, it was to blame others: The U.S. Coast Guard and Alaskan officials were "holding up" his company's efforts to clean up the spill. But Rawl's words were too little, too late. The impression persisted that, in light of the delay in admitting responsibility, Exxon was not responding vigorously enough.

A full 10 days after the crisis, Exxon placed an apologetic advertisement in 166 newspapers. To some readers, the ad seemed self-serving and failed to address the many pointed questions raised about Exxon's conduct.

"It seems the company was a bit too relaxed in its capabilities," offered the president of the Public Relations Society of America. Meanwhile, one group that wasn't relaxed was the Alaska state legislature, which enacted a tax increase on oil from the North Slope fields within weeks of the Exxon spill. Congressional committees in Washington moved just as quickly to increase liability limits and potential compensation for oil-spill damage and to increase the money available through the industry-financed Offshore Oil Pollution Compensation Fund. When Exxon hesitated, its opponents seized the initiative. Concluded another public relations executive, "They lost the battle in the first 48 hours."

HOW HIGH THE PROFILE

Exxon's communications response in the face of this most challenging crisis in its history was, to put it mildly, muted.

From an operations and logistics viewpoint, Exxon did a good job. The company immediately set up animal rescue projects, launched a major cleanup effort, and agreed to pick up a substantial percentage of the cost. But it made the mistake of downplaying the crisis in public.

Exxon's public statements sometimes contradicted information from other sources. At one point, an Exxon spokesman said that damage from the oil spill would be minimal. Others watching the industry said the damage was likely to be substantial.

Chairman Rawl, an otherwise blunt and outspoken CEO, seemed defensive and argumentative in his public comments. In one particularly disastrous personal appearance on *CBS Morning News,* Rawl glared at interviewer Kathleen Sullivan and snapped: "I can't give you details of our cleanup plan. It's thick and complicated. And I haven't had a chance to read it yet. The CEO of a major company doesn't have time to read every plan."

Exxon's attempts to calm the public also were criticized. Its ad drew fire for not expressing enough concern. It hired an outside firm to do a series of video news releases to show how the company was cleaning up the spill. At an estimated cost of more than $3 million, a 13-minute tape was shown at the corporation's annual meeting. The video, called *Progress in Alaska,* attracted intense criticism from those attending the conference, as well as from the press. The film implied, argued *Boston Globe* reporter Robert Lenzner, that "the brutal scenes of damage to Alaskan waters seen nightly on television news programs were false." *USA Today* called the tape "Exxon's worst move of the day." When the consultant who devised the video wrote an op-ed article in the *New York Times* defending Exxon's approach in Alaska, the Alaskan representative to the National Wildlife Federation responded with a blistering letter to the editor, noting that the consultant omitted in his article that the spill had resulted in the death of more than 15,000 sea birds and numerous otters and eagles.

Exxon then added an environmental expert to its board of directors, but only after pension funds, which control a large chunk of its stock, demanded such a response.

DEALING WITH THE AFTERMATH

Finally, Exxon was forced to deal with all the implications of what its tanker had wrought in Valdez.

The company became embroiled in controversy when it sent a $30,000 contribution to the Alaska Public Radio Network, which covered the crisis on a daily basis. The network, sniffing "conflict of interest," flatly turned down Exxon's attempted largesse. Subsequently, a special appropriations bill was introduced in the Alaskan legislature to forward an identical amount to Alaska Public Radio.

The accident and the company's reaction to it also had consequences for the oil industry. Plans to expand drilling into the Alaskan National Wildlife Refuge were shelved by Congress, and members called for new laws increasing federal involvement in oil spills.

The company's employees, too, felt confused, embarrassed, and betrayed. Summarizing the prevailing mood at the company, one Exxon worker said, "Whenever I travel now, I feel like I have a target painted on my chest."

In 1994, more than five years after the tanker ran aground, Exxon went to court in Anchorage to defend itself against $15 million in civil claims. Early in 1996, the company still battled its past demons, as the company and its new chairman, Lee R. Raymond, were accused of making "side deals" with plaintiffs in the case — even though they denied, under oath, that they had done so.

In November 1996, seven years after the *Exxon Valdez* ran aground, a weary Exxon announced to the world that it was closing the books on its unforgettable disaster. Total cost to Exxon: $2.5 billion.

But that wasn't all. In 1999, a full decade after the *Exxon Valdez* dumped 11 million gallons of oil into Prince William Sound, the Exxon Corporation—rechristened Exxon Mobil—went to court in Alaska to get the courts to overturn an unusual federal restriction. The unique law barred one ship, the *Exxon Valdez,* from ever again sailing into Prince William Sound. Exxon alleged that the ship, renamed the *SeaRiver Mediterranean,* was being unfairly singled out among dozens of tankers that freely sail into Alaska waters. "Nonsense," said a spokeswoman for Alaska Senator Ted Stevens, the law didn't single out any ship by name. Rather, she said, the language of the provision bars "vessels that have spilled more than 1 million gallons of oil into the marine environment after March 22, 1989" from entering Prince William Sound. Coincidentally, only one sailing vessel fit that description. Yup.

THE LESSONS

The lessons of the *Exxon Valdez's* Good Friday oil spill would not soon be forgotten by corporate managers. The episode, predicted one, "will become a textbook example of what not to do when an unexpected crisis thrusts a company into the limelight." Said another, "Exxon's response is fast becoming the stuff of PR legend."

Questions

1. What would you have recommended Chairman Rawl do upon learning of the Prince William Sound oil spill?
2. How would you have handled the media in this case?

3. What would have been your timing in terms of public relations responses in this case?
4. What would be your overall public relations strategy—aggressive, low-key, etc.—if you were Exxon's public relations director?
5. Do you think this case will ever qualify as a "textbook example" of what not to do in a crisis?
6. Now that Exxon has merged with Mobil, what is the corporation doing about environmental issues? Visit the news release home page (www.exxon.com/em_newsrelease/index.html) and follow the link to browse the oil giant's recent news releases. What is ExxonMobil doing about environmental issues? Why would the company continue to issue news releases about environmental activities so many years after the *Exxon Valdez* incident?

For further information about the *Exxon Valdez* case, see Richard Behar, "Exxon Strikes Back," *Time* (March 26, 1990): 62–63; Claudia H. Deutsch, "The Giant with a Black Eye," *New York Times* (April 2, 1989): B1–4; E. Bruce Harrison, with Tom Prugh, "Assessing the Damage," *Public Relations Journal* (October 1989): 40–45; John Holusha, "Exxon's Public-Relations Problem," *New York Times*, (April 21, 1989): D1–4; Peter Nulty, "Exxon's Problem: Not What You Think," *Fortune* (April 23, 1990): 202–204; James Lukaszewski, "How Vulnerable Are You? The Lessons from Valdez," *Public Relations Quarterly* (Fall 1989): 5–6; Phillip M. Perry, "Exxon Falters in PR Effort Following Alaskan Oil Spill," *O'Dwyer's PR Services Report* (July 1989): 1, 16–22; Bill Richards, "Exxon Is Battling a Ban on an Infamous Tanker," *Wall Street Journal* (July 29, 1998): C1; Allanna Sullivan, "Rawl Wishes He'd Visited Valdez Sooner," *Wall Street Journal* (June 30, 1989): B7; Joseph B. Treaster, "With Insurers' Payment, Exxon Says Valdez Case is Ended," *New York Times* (November 1, 1996): B2; and Paul Wiseman, "Firm Finds Valdez Oil Fowls Image," *USA Today* (April 26, 1990): B1.

O V E R T H E T O P

An Interview with Maggie Hughes

As far as Maggie Hughes is concerned, there's nothing unusual about her rise from public relations consultant to president and chief operating officer of a $5.5 billion insurance holding company. As president of Life USA Holding, Inc. of Minneapolis, Minnesota, she is one of the highest-ranking female executives in the nation and certainly the highest-ranking female to emanate from the practice of public relations.

Did you study communications in college?
Yes, I have a degree in journalism. It was the late '60s, early '70s. I worked on the college newspaper. I was fairly radical and an activist, so journalism was a must, a way of expressing the emotions of the times.

Do you consider yourself a writer?
I'm a writer, absolutely. That's the easiest form of communication for me. Actually learning to speak in a comprehensive fashion has come over the years, as I became a consultant to business.

Did you like the communications consulting business?
What was interesting to me was finding out what people's business objectives were and then figuring out how to communicate them. In the process of having to put together professional communications that communicated people's projects or services, I began to get a lot of information on business strategy. That led me to believe that I could offer value in terms of helping companies achieve all kinds of objectives, everything from employee relations to crisis management.

What kind of public relations consultant were you?
Well, what I've been told by my board of directors is that I have a knack at getting at the truth of things. Truth, I have come to understand, is a subjective thing. But, I'm a digger and maybe that's my journal-istic background. And so I would dig for solutions. I'd also dig for what the issues really were. When you're a public relations consultant, often when management from a company comes to you, they come to you with symptoms of an issue that they would like you to resolve. What I thought I had a special knack for was when people came to me with an issue or problem, I had the ability to get at all the facts behind that symptom, to really define the issue, so we could more effectively put together the strategy to help resolve the situation.

What do you find lacking in public relations consultants?
The problem that I've seen now from the other side of the table is that a public relations specialist can come in with a methodology but won't dig far enough. Oftentimes they don't have a deep enough business understanding of the environment, the issues, the constituency, to bring real value to what are often fast-moving opportunities. Nothing is more frustrating that to get a canned approach to something that you could plug any company into, but it is not germane to the nuances of my specific industry.

Could you see others in communications areas following your route to top management?
Absolutely, because you learn to operate in a dynamic environment. I mean you never know what's coming at you, be it a crisis or opportunity when you're a public relations consultant. You can make decisions quickly. You can garner different resources to come together with the right answer. The training is very good training for management.

Let's say someone reading this wants to follow your lead. How do they begin?
Okay, two answers. First, silly answer, follow your bliss. But it's not too silly. Second, decide what industry interests you, and then do your research and look for companies who look like they could use a strength you could bring to the table. Don't look for ads in newspapers. Choose. Don't be chosen. Choose. Go after it.

Chapter 8

Management

It has been said that the only difference between the public relations director and the CEO is that the latter gets paid more.

In many ways, that's quite true. The CEO, after all, is the firm's top manager, responsible for, in addition to setting strategy and framing policy, serving as the organization's chief spokesperson, corporate booster, and reputation defender—not at all unlike the responsibilities assigned the public relations professional. In the rare instance when a company is dominated by a visible CEO—Bill Gates at Microsoft, Steve Case at America Online, Jeff Bezos at Amazon.com, Michael Armstrong at AT&T, etc.—the corporation takes on the identity of its chief (Figure 8-1). But in an age when business is dominated by mainly faceless corporations, many of them e-commerce firms reached directly via computer, the practice of public relations—of presenting a human face to the public—becomes a core critical management function.

That noted, it is also true in the new millennium that like most other organizational pursuits in an era of rising costs, shrinking resources, and increased competition, public relations must compete for its survival. In the 21st century, top management will insist that public relations be run as a management process.

Like other management processes, professional public relations work emanates from clear strategies and bottom-line objectives that flow into specific tactics, each with its own budget, timetable, and allocation of resources. Stated another way, public relations today is much more a planned, persuasive social-managerial science than a knee-jerk, damage-control reaction to sudden flare-ups.

On the organizational level, as public relations has enhanced its overall stature, it has been brought increasingly into the general management structure of institutions. Indeed, the public relations function works most effectively when it reports directly to top management.

On the individual level, public relations practitioners are increasingly expected to have mastered a wide variety of technical communications skills, such as writing, editing, placement of articles, production of printed materials,

FIGURE 8-1 **Master CEO.** In an age dominated by faceless Internet managers, at least one CEO stood above most others in setting the tone for his corporation. Southwest Airlines CEO Herb Kelleher, regularly ranked highly among top executives, prescribed a corporate formula based largely on having fun.

and video programming, both off- and on-line. At the same time, by virtue of their relatively recent integration into the general management process, public relations professionals are expected to be fluent in management theory and technique. In other words, public relations practitioners themselves must be, in every sense of the word, managers.

Reporting to Top Management

The public relations function, by definition, must report to top management.

Nowhere has this proven more true today than in high-tech companies. In the business of dotcoms, where "early buzz" translates not only to recognition but venture capital financing, the public relations function is as key as any other management discipline.[1] High-tech companies, in fact, have trouble differentiating themselves from their myriad competitors unless they have demonstrated savvy public relations management. This is why one area where public relations professionals are in high demand is Silicon Valley, the high-tech hotbed outside of San Francisco, and its equivalent geographies elsewhere in the United States.

In non-high-tech organizations, alas, public relations is often subordinated to advertising, marketing, or legal or human resources. This is a shame because, as noted in chapter 1, public relations must be the interpreter of the organization—its philosophy, policy, and programs. These emanate from top management. Therefore, public relations must report to those who run the organization.

Increasingly, the public relations director reports directly to the CEO. While marketing and advertising promote the product, public relations promotes the entire organization. So if the public relations chief were to report to the director of marketing or advertising, the job would become one of promoting specific products. There's a big difference. Thus, if public relations is made subordinate to any other discipline—marketing, advertising, legal, administration, whatever—then its independence, credibility, and, ultimately, value as an objective, honest broker to management will be jeopardized.

Whereas the marketing and advertising groups must, by definition, be defenders of their specific products, the public relations department has no such mandated allegiance. Public relations, rightfully, should be the corporate conscience. An organization's public relations professionals should enjoy enough autonomy to deal openly and honestly with management. If an idea doesn't make sense, if a product is flawed, if the general institutional wisdom is wrong, it is the duty of the public relations professional to challenge the consensus. As the legendary CEO of the Berkshire Hathaway

BACKGROUNDER

Chainsawed for Lack of Public Relations

FIGURE 8-2

Rusted chainsaw.
When Sunbeam profits went south, the board directed CEO "Chainsaw Al" Dunlap to follow them.

Among the most feared of 20th-century corporate managers was "Chainsaw" Al Dunlap, the man famous for joining companies in the 1990s as CEO and then obliterating thousands of jobs and firing managers (Figure 8-2).

CEO Dunlap earned a faithful following on Wall Street for his take-no-prisoners ways. Among those Dunlap particularly delighted in firing were public relations staff members. As he noted in his 1998 autobiography, *Mean Business,* public relations departments are of limited value, especially when they work for a CEO as public as the author.

True to his history, when Chainsaw Al took the helm at the Sunbeam Corporation in 1997, he began by slashing 12,000 jobs and getting rid of, among others, the internal public relations department. He then proceeded to go on a one-man investor relations campaign, assuring his loyal followers on Wall Street that he was once again about to turn around a lagging company. The analysts lapped up the CEO's predictions, and Sunbeam's stock soared.

Contrary to the chairman's statements, financial results began to get worse. Mr. Dunlap continued to provide thumping assurances that he would work his magic. But while he courted the financial community, the CEO virtually ignored Sunbeam's employees and customers. Morale sagged and sales soured.

So in June 1998, approximately one year after Chainsaw Al had ridden to the rescue, he, himself, was beheaded after an emergency board meeting. Predictably, the media skewered his failure, bringing the humbled, fired CEO to tears.

It was an inglorious end for a man who gloated in his disdain for the practice of public relations.*

*For further information, see Martha Branigan and James R. Hagerty, "Sunbeam, Its Prospects Looking Ever Worse, Fires CEO Dunlap," Wall Street Journal, June 15, 1998, A1–14; and "Sunbeam: Lack of PR Hurts Image in Wake of Financial Crisis," PR News, July 13, 1998, 1–6.

company, Warren Buffet, has put it, "We can afford to lose money—even a lot of money. But we cannot afford to lose reputation—even a shred of reputation."[2]

This is not to say that advertising, marketing, and all other disciplines shouldn't enjoy a close partnership with public relations. Clearly, they must. All disciplines must work to maintain their own independence while building long-term, mutually beneficial relationships for the good of the organization. However, public relations should never shirk its overriding responsibility to enhance the organization's credibility by ensuring that corporate actions are in the public interest.

Management Theory of Public Relations

By the end of its first century as a management function, public relations had developed its own theoretical framework as a management system. The work of communications professors James Grunig and Todd Hunt, while not the only relevant management theory, nonetheless has done much to advance this development.[3] Grunig and Hunt suggest that public relations managers perform what organizational theorists call a boundary role; they function at the edge of an organization as a liaison between the organization and its external and internal publics. In other words, public relations managers have one foot inside the organization and one outside. Often, this unique position is not only lonely, but also precarious.

As boundary managers, public relations people support their colleagues by helping them communicate across organizational lines both within and outside the organization. In this way, public relations professionals also become systems managers, knowledgeable about and able to deal with the complex relationships inherent in the organization.

- They must consider the relationship of the organization to its environment—the ties that unite business managers and operations support staff, for example, and the conflicts that separate them.
- They must work within organizational confines to develop innovative solutions to organizational problems. By definition, public relations managers deal in a different environment from that of their organizational colleagues. Public relations people deal with perceptions, attitudes, and public opinion. Other business managers deal in a more empirical, quantitative, concrete domain. Public relations managers, therefore, must be innovative, not only in proposing communications solutions, but also in making them understandable and acceptable to colleagues.
- They must think strategically. Public relations managers must demonstrate their knowledge of the organization's mission, objectives, and strategies. Their solutions must answer the real needs of the organization. They must reflect the big picture. Business managers will care little that the company's name was mentioned in the morning paper unless they can recognize the strategic rationale for the reference.
- Public relations managers also must be willing to measure their results. They must state clearly what they want to accomplish, systematically set out to accomplish it, and measure their success. This means using such accepted business school techniques as management by objectives (MBO), management by objectives and results (MOR), and program evaluation and research technique (PERT).

☑ Finally, as Grunig and Hunt point out, in managing an organization's public relations system, practitioners must demonstrate comfort with the various elements of the organization itself: (1) functions, the real jobs of organizational components; (2) structure, the organizational hierarchy of individuals and positions; (3) processes, the formal decision-making rules and procedures the organization follows; and (4) feedback, the formal and informal evaluative mechanisms of the organization.[4]

Such a theoretical overview is important to consider in properly situating the practice of public relations as a management system within an organization.

Planning for Public Relations

Like research, planning for public relations is essential not only to know where a particular campaign is headed but also to win the support of top management. Indeed, one of the most frequent complaints about public relations is that it is too much a seat-of-the-pants activity, impossible to plan and difficult to measure. Clearly, planning in public relations must be given greater shrift. With proper planning, public relations professionals can indeed defend and account for their actions.

Before organizing for public relations work, practitioners must consider objectives and strategies, planning and budgets, and research and evaluation. The broad environment in which the organization operates must dictate overall business objectives. These, in turn, dictate specific public relations objectives and strategies. Once these have been defined, the task of organizing for a public relations program should flow naturally.

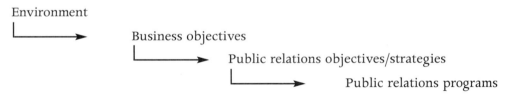

Environment → Business objectives → Public relations objectives/strategies → Public relations programs

Setting objectives, formulating strategies, and planning are essential if the public relations function is to be considered equal in stature to other management processes. Traditionally, the public relations management process involves four steps, echoing the R-A-C-E definition discussed in chapter 1:

1. **Defining the problem or opportunity.** This requires researching current attitudes and opinions about the issue or product or candidate or company in question and determining the essence of the problem.
2. **Programming.** This is the formal planning stage, which addresses key constituent publics, strategies, tactics, and goals.
3. **Action.** This is the communications phase, where the program is implemented.
4. **Evaluation.** The final step in the process is the assessment of what worked, what didn't, and how we might improve in the future.[5]

Each of these four process steps is important. Most essential is starting with a firm base of research and a solid foundation of planning.

All planning requires thinking. Planning a short-term public relations program to promote a new service may require less thought and time than planning a longer-term campaign to win support for a public policy issue. However, in each case, the public relations plan must include clear-cut objectives to achieve organizational goals, strategies to reach those objectives, tactics to implement the strategies, and measurement to determine whether the tactics worked.

Among the most important aspects of public relations practice is setting clear goals, objectives, and targets for the tactics applied. Public relations activities are meaningless unless designed to accomplish certain measurable goals.

For example, consider the following elementary public relations plan:

I. *Environment*
We need to increase product sales in the local market. Currently we are number 3 in the market, running close behind the second-place supplier but far behind the market leader.

II. *Business objectives*
Our goal is to build market share for our product in the local area. We seek to surpass the number 2 provider and edge closer to number 1.

III. *Public relations objectives*
   - Confirm our company's solid commitment to local customers
   - Convince potential customers that our company offers the staff, expertise, products, and responsiveness that match their needs
   - Position our company as formidable competition to the two market leaders

IV. *Public relations strategies*
Position our company as the expert in the market through company-sponsored surveys and research directed at local decision makers; media placement of company-related articles; speaking platforms of company executives; and company-sponsored seminars to demonstrate our expertise.

V. *Public relations programs/tactics*
   - Seek media placements and bylined articles discussing company products for local media.
   - Solicit profile features and interviews with company officials on an exclusive basis with leading trade publications.
   - Sponsor a quarterly survey of local companies. Mail the survey to local decision makers, focus on a current topic of concern, and offer information and comment from the customer's view.
   - Sponsor four seminars a year for emerging product-using companies in the local area. Tailor each seminar to particular audiences—women, minorities, small businesses, specific industries, not-for-profit groups. Seminars should feature company experts and well-known outside speakers. Thus, they should reinforce our commitment to the local market and also stimulate publicity.
   - Launch a company speakers bureau wherein company speakers address important groups throughout the area.

After the adoption of such public relations programs, the success or failure of the campaign must be evaluated. In devising the public relations plan along these lines, an organization is assured that their public relations programs will reinforce and complement their overall business goals.

Managing by Public Relations Objectives

An organization's goals must define what its public relations goals will be, and the only good goals are ones that can be measured. Public relations objectives and the strategies that flow from them, like those in other business areas, must be results-oriented. As the baseball pitcher Johnny Sain used to say, "Nobody wants to hear about the labor pains, but everyone wants to see the baby."

So, too, must public relations people think strategically. Strategies are the most crucial decisions of a public relations campaign. They answer the general question, "How will we manage our resources to achieve our goals?" The specific answers then become the public relations tactics used to implement the strategies. Ideally, strategies and tactics should profit from pretesting.

As for objectives, good ones stand up to the following questions:

- ☑ Do they clearly describe the end result expected?
- ☑ Are they understandable to everyone in the organization?
- ☑ Do they list a firm completion date?
- ☑ Are they realistic, attainable, and measurable?
- ☑ Are they consistent with management's objectives?

Increasingly, public relations professionals are managing by objectives, adopting MBO and MOR techniques to help quantify the value of public relations in an organization. The two questions most frequently asked by general managers of public relations practitioners are, "How can we measure public relations results?" and "How do we know whether the public relations program is making progress?" MBO can provide public relations professionals with a powerful source of feedback. MBO and MOR tie public relations results to management's predetermined objectives. Even though procedures for implementing MBO programs differ, most programs share four points:

1. Specification of the organization's goals, with objective measures of the organization's performance
2. Conferences between the superior and the subordinate to agree on achievable goals
3. Agreement between the superior and the subordinate on objectives consistent with the organization's goals
4. Periodic reviews by the superior and the subordinate to assess progress toward achieving the goals

Again, the key is to tie public relations goals to the goals of the organization and then to manage progress toward achieving those goals. The goals themselves should be clearly defined and specific, practical and attainable, and measurable.

The key to using MBO effectively in public relations work can be broken down into seven critical steps:

1. Defining the nature and mission of the work
2. Determining key result areas in terms of time, effort, and personnel
3. Identifying measurable factors on which objectives can be set
4. Setting objectives or determining results to be achieved
5. Preparing tactical plans to achieve specific objectives, including:
   - ☑ Programming to establish a sequence of actions to follow
   - ☑ Scheduling to set time requirements for each step
   - ☑ Budgeting to assign the resources required to reach the goals

A QUESTION OF ETHICS

Ready, Fire, Aim at the NRA

That public relations must be considered a management function was never more obvious than in spring 1999, when the National Rifle Association was anticipating its annual convention. It was planned for Denver, Colorado.

Just 12 days before the convention was to get underway, the nation suffered its most horrible school massacre when, on April 20, two heavily armed Littleton, Colorado, students opened fire on their Columbine High School classmates. When the carnage had ceased, 15 had died, including the shooters. The cry for stricter new federal gun control escalated across the country.

The ethical question the association now confronted was, Should the meeting go on as scheduled or should it be canceled, in deference to those grieving from the tragedy committed just miles away?

The stakes for the decision were high.

The NRA had three options: (1) hold the annual meeting as scheduled, (2) cancel it, or (3) hold a scaled-back meeting.

Denver Mayor Wellington Webb repeatedly asked the group to cancel its three-day meeting. But NRA President Charlton Heston (Figure 8-3) was defiant in opposition to the mayor's request. "What saddens me most," said the Oscar-winning actor, "is how that suggests complicity. It implies that 80 million honest gun owners are somehow to blame . . . that you and I should not be as shocked and horrified as everyone else."

In that spirit, the NRA scaled back its Denver meeting from three days to one and canceled all exhibits. Many delegates wore blue and silver Columbine memorial ribbons, fastened with NRA buttons.

Despite the NRA's protestations, 8,000 antigun demonstrators marched in protest outside the convention headquarters. "Maybe somebody needs to tell Charlton Heston this is not a movie," said one of the organizers. The crowd was bolstered by the father of a student killed at Columbine. The man carried a sign that read, "My son, Daniel, died at Columbine. He'd expect me to be here today." A color picture of a blond-haired Daniel smiled out at the crowd. Other teenagers carried signs that read, "I don't want to die."

FIGURE 8-3 **Charlton the defiant.** The National Rifle Association and its president, actor Charlton Heston, were criticized in 1999 for holding their annual meeting in Denver, shortly after the Columbine High School massacre.

Predictably, the protesters and the NRA appeared prominently on newscasts and in newspapers across America. One homemade sign that made most of the papers was one that read simply, "Charlton Heston. Bad actor. Bad wig. Bad ideas. Bad timing."*

For further information, see Matt Bai, "Clouds Over Gun Valley," Newsweek, August 23, 1999; Paul M. Barrett, "Evolution of a Cause: Why the Gun Debate Has Finally Taken Off," Wall Street Journal, October 21, 1999, A1–19; and Gwen Florio and Diane Mastrull, "8,000 Protest at NRA Convention," Sunday Record, May 2, 1999,

- ☑ Fixing individual accountability for the accomplishment of the objectives
- ☑ Reviewing and reconciling through a testing procedure to track progress
6. Establishing rules and regulations to follow
7. Establishing procedures to handle the work.[6]

Budgeting for Public Relations

Forecasting expected activities has always been one of the most uncertain tasks in public relations. Many argue that "measurement" in a practice like public relations is, by definition, an imperfect art. As a consequence, many public relations operations almost routinely overrun planned budget targets.[7]

Nonetheless, like any other business activity, public relations programs must be based on sound budgeting. After identifying objectives and strategies, the public relations professional must detail the particular tactics that will help achieve those objectives. No organization can spend indiscriminately. Without a realistic budget, no organization can succeed. Likewise, public relations activities must be disciplined by budgetary realities.

The key to budgeting may lie in performing two steps: (1) estimating the extent of the resources—both personnel and purchases—needed to accomplish each activity, and (2) estimating the cost and availability of those resources. With this information in hand, the development of a budget and monthly cash flow for a public relations program becomes easier. Such data also provide the milestones necessary to audit program costs on a routine basis and to make adjustments well in advance of budget crises.

In recent years, public relations budgets have increased. In perhaps the largest public relations budget ever awarded, the American Legacy Foundation—established as a result of the Master Settlement Agreement between 46 states and the tobacco industry in 1999—named Arnold Communications of Boston and its partnering agencies to lead an antismoking public education campaign. The fee? The contract was valued at 50 percent to 85 percent to the $300 million received annually by the foundation.[8]

Whew!

Notwithstanding the huge public relations anti-tobacco effort, most public relations programs still operate on limited budgets. Therefore, whenever possible, adaptable programs—which can be readily recycled and redesigned to meet changing needs—should be considered. For example, television, magazine, newspaper, and even Internet advertising generally are too expensive for most public relations budgets. On the other hand, special events, personalized literature, direct mail, personal contacts, and promotional displays are the kinds of relatively less expensive communications vehicles that can be easily duplicated.

One way to ensure that budgets are adhered to is to practice the process of open bidding for public relations materials and suppliers. An open bidding process allows several vendors to demonstrate how they would fulfill the specifications enumerated for the job. These specifications should take into account programmatic considerations in terms of both quality and quantity. Public relations budgets should be reasonable—ordinarily, a fraction (10 percent or so)—of advertising budgets and flexible enough to withstand midcourse corrections and unexpected cost overruns.

Most public relations agencies treat client costs in a manner similar to that used by legal, accounting, and management consulting firms: The client pays only for services rendered, either on a monthly or yearly retainer basis or on minimum charges based on

BACKGROUNDER

A La Carte Public Relations

While hourly rates and retainers are standard in the public relations business, at least one Washington, D.C., agency doesn't mess around with such details. It gets paid *only* when it gets publicity for clients. No publicity—no pay!

Levick Strategic Consulting bills its clients, mostly law firms, by the number of media "opportunities" per month in a program called "Success Billing." Clients identify what they consider "success" in terms of media placement. If a reporter calls for an interview or a story mentions the client, that's an "opportunity."

Clients pay extra for media training, ghost writing, expert coaching, or strategy development. The a la carte cost schedule includes the following:

$10,000 per month: six to eight opportunities
$12,000 per month: nine to 12 opportunities
$15,000 per month: 13 to 20 opportunities
Ghost writing: $175/hour
Media training: $3,700 to $10,000 per day

Because the Levick "pay for play" system takes great courage—consider the downside—it is safe to say that most public relations agencies will not soon adopt a similar budgeting strategy.

---

staff time. Time records are kept by every employee—from chairperson to mail clerk— on a daily basis to be sure that agency clients know exactly what they are paying for. Hourly charges for public relations agency employees can range from low double figures per hour to upwards of $350 to $500 an hour for agency superstars.

Because agency relationships are based on trust, it is important that clients understand the derivation of costs. In recent years, debate has raged over markups on expenses paid in behalf of clients by public relations firms. Out-of-pocket expenses— for meals, hotels, transportation, and the like—are generally charged back to clients at cost. But when an agency pays in advance for larger expense items—printing, photography, graphics, design—it is standard industry practice to mark up such expenses by a factor approximating 17.65 percent. This figure, which the vast majority of agencies adhere to, was borrowed from the advertising profession and represented the multiplicative inverse of the standard 15 percent commission that ad agencies collected on advertising placement.

The guiding rule in agency budgeting is to ensure that the client is aware of how charges are being applied, so that nasty surprises might be avoided when bills are received.

Preparing the Public Relations Plan

The public relations campaign puts all of the aspects of public relations planning— objectives, strategies, research, budgeting, tactics, and evaluation—into one cohesive framework. The plan specifies a series of "what's" to be done and "how's" to get them done—whatever is necessary to reach the objectives.

Again, the public relations plan must track the strategies and objectives of the organization. Accordingly, the blueprint for the public relations campaign should be the R-A-C-E or R-O-S-I-E approaches to public relations, defined in chapter 1. Time should be taken in advance to determine what public relations approaches and activities are most likely to reach organizational goals. Every aspect of the public relations plan should be designed to be meaningful and valuable to the organization. The skeleton of a typical public relations campaign plan resembles the following:

1. **Backgrounding the problem.** This is the so-called situation analysis, background, or case statement that specifies the major aims of the campaign. It can be a general statement that refers to audiences, known research, the organization's positions, history, and the obstacles faced in reaching the desired goal. A public relations planner should divide the overriding goal into several subordinate objectives, which are the "what's" to be accomplished.

2. **Preparing a proposal.** The second stage of the campaign plan sketches broad approaches to solve the problem at hand. It outlines the strategies—the "how's" and the public relations tools to be used to fulfill the objectives. The elements of the public relations proposal may vary, depending on subject matter, but generally include the following:

   ☑ Situational analysis—description of the challenge as it currently exists, including background on how the situation reached its present state
   ☑ Scope of assignment—description of the nature of the assignment: what the public relations program will attempt to do
   ☑ Target audiences—specific targets identified and divided into manageable groups
   ☑ Research methods—specific research approach to be used
   ☑ Key messages—specific selected appeals: What do we want to tell our audiences? How do we want them to feel about us? What do we want them to do?
   ☑ Communications vehicles—tactical communications devices to be used
   ☑ Project team—key players who will participate in the program
   ☑ Timing and fees—a timetable with proposed costs identified

The specific elements of any proposal depend on the unique nature of the program itself. When an outside supplier submits a proposal, additional elements—such as cancellation clauses, confidentiality of work, and references—should also be included.

3. **Activating the plan.** The third stage of a campaign plan details operating tactics. It may also contain a time chart specifying when each action will take place. Specific activities are defined, people are assigned to them, and deadlines are established. This stage forms the guts of the campaign plan.

4. **Evaluating the campaign.** To find out whether the plan worked, evaluation methods should be spelled out here.
   ☑ Did we implement the activities we proposed?
   ☑ Did we receive appropriate public recognition for our efforts?
   ☑ Did attitudes change—among the community, customers, management—as a result of our programs?

Pre- and post-testing of audience attitudes, quantitative analysis of event attendance, content analysis of media success, surveys, sales figures, staff reports, letters to management, and feedback from others—the specific method of evaluative testing is up to the practitioner. But the inclusion of a mechanism for evaluation is imperative.[9]

A public relations campaign plan should always be spelled out—in writing—so that planners can keep track of progress and management can assess results. Although planning in public relations is important and should be taken more seriously than it presently is by public relations professionals, the caveat of management gurus Thomas Peters and Robert Waterman must always be considered: "The problem is that the planning becomes an end in itself."[10] In public relations this cannot be allowed. No matter how important planning may be, public relations is assessed principally in terms of its action, performance, and practice.

Implementing Public Relations Programs

The duties and responsibilities of public relations practitioners are as diverse as the publics with whom different institutions deal. Basically, public relations tasks can be divided into four broad categories:

1. **Advice**—provided to management on organizational decisions and policies, to ensure that they are consistent with the public interest
2. **Communications service**—including the outward communication of information to various external publics and the inward communication of corporate philosophy, policies, and programs to the employees
3. **Public issues research and analysis**—identifying, evaluating, and communicating to management, the external information that may be most relevant to organizational policies and programs
4. **Public relations action programs**—designed to generate goodwill through comprehensive programs focused on a particular issue or audience[11]

Specific public relations tasks are as varied as the organizations served. Here is a partial list of public relations duties:

- ☑ Reaching the employees through a variety of internal means, including Intranet, newsletters, television, and meetings. Traditionally, this role has emphasized news-oriented communications rather than benefits-oriented ones, which are usually the province of personnel departments.
- ☑ Coordinating relationships with the on-line, print, and electronic media, which includes arranging and monitoring press interviews, writing news releases and related press materials, organizing press conferences, and answering media inquiries and requests. A good deal of media relations work consists of attempting to gain favorable news coverage for the firm.
- ☑ Coordinating activities with legislators on local, state, and federal levels. This includes legislative research activities and public policy formation.
- ☑ Orchestrating interaction with the community, perhaps including open houses, tours, and employee volunteer efforts designed to reflect the supportive nature of the organization to the community.
- ☑ Managing relations with the investment community, including the firm's present and potential stockholders. This task emphasizes personal contact with securities analysts, institutional investors, and private investors.
- ☑ Supporting activities with customers and potential customers, with activities ranging from hard-sell product promotion activities to "soft" consumer advisory services.
- ☑ Coordinating the institution's printed voice with its public through reprints of speeches, annual reports, quarterly statements, and product and company brochures.
- ☑ Coordinating relationships with outside specialty groups, such as suppliers, educators, students, nonprofit organizations, and competitors.

- ☑ Managing the institutional—or nonproduct—advertising image as well as being called on increasingly to assist in the management of more traditional product advertising.
- ☑ Coordinating the graphic and photographic services of the organization. To do this task well requires knowledge of typography, layout, and art.
- ☑ Coordinating the organization's on-line "face," including Web site design and ongoing counsel, updating and even management of the site.
- ☑ Conducting opinion research, which involves assisting in the public policy formation process through the coordination and interpretation of attitudinal studies of key publics.
- ☑ Managing the gift-giving apparatus, which ordinarily consists of screening and evaluating philanthropic proposals and allocating the organization's available resources.
- ☑ Coordinating special events, including travel for company management, corporate celebrations and exhibits, dinners, groundbreakings, and grand openings.
- ☑ Management counseling, which involves advising administrators on alternative options and recommended choices in light of public responsibilities.

Organizing the Public Relations Department

Once an organization has analyzed its environment, established its objectives, set up measurement standards, and thought about appropriate programs and budgets, it is ready to organize a public relations department. Departments range from one-person operations to far-flung networks of hundreds of people, such as General Motors or Exxon Mobil, with staff around the world, responsible for relations with the press, investors, civic groups, employees, and many different governments.

Today, many corporate public relations departments typically have suffered the impact of 1990s downsizing and decentralization. The former has led to the shrinkage of once-large operations; the latter has led to the formation of decentralized, line-oriented departments to complement smaller central units. The two together have led many corporate public relations people to fear for the security of positions they once took for granted.[12] What's the best way to organize for public relations in an organization? There is no one answer. However, again, the strongest public relations department is one led by a communications executive who reports directly to the CEO. This is eminently preferable to reporting to a legal or financial or administrative executive, who may tend to "filter" top management messages.[13]

In government, public relations professionals typically report directly to department heads. In universities, the public relations function is frequently coupled with fund-raising and development activities. In hospitals, public relations is typically tied to the marketing function.

As for the names of the departments in which public relations is housed, organizations use a wide variety of names for the function. Ironically, the trend today seems to be away from use of the traditional term *public relations* and toward *corporate communications.* In one comprehensive analysis, about 30 percent of the organizations surveyed still use *public relations,* whereas *corporate communications* or just plain *communications* is used by nearly 20 percent. About 8 percent use *public affairs,* and another 8 percent use *advertising/public relations.* Among the other titles in use are *corporate relations* and *public information.*

Organizing the Public Relations Agency

The biggest difference between an external agency and an internal department is perspective. The former is outside looking in; the latter is inside looking out (often literally for itself). Sometimes the use of an agency is necessary to escape the tunnel-vision syndrome that afflicts some firms, in which a detached viewpoint is desperately needed. An agency unfettered by internal corporate politics might be better trusted to present management with an objective reading of the concerns of its publics.

An agency has the added advantage of not being taken for granted by a firm's management. Unfortunately, management sometimes has a greater regard for an outside specialist than for an inside one. This attitude frequently defies logic but is nonetheless often true. Generally, if management is paying (sometimes quite handsomely) for outside counsel, it tends to listen carefully to the advice.

Agencies generally organize according to industry and account teams. Larger agencies are divided into such areas as health care, sports, fashion, technology, finance, and so on. Account teams are assigned specific clients. Team members bill clients on an hourly basis, with most firms, as noted, intending to retain two-thirds of each individual's hourly billing rate as income. In other words, if an account executive bills at a rate of $300 per hour—and many senior counselors do—the firm expects to retain $200 of that rate toward its profit. In recent years, as clients have begun to manage resources more rigorously, agencies have gotten much more "systematic" in measuring success and in keeping customers from "migrating" to a competitor. Indeed, if not actively and directly addressed on an ongoing basis, customer satisfaction will, inevitably decline.[14]

Public relations agencies today, as noted, are huge businesses. Most of the top firms have been subsumed by advertising agencies. Burson-Marsteller, the largest agency in the world, is owned by Young & Rubicam, but CEO of the parent company is Burson public relations alumnus Tom Bell. Hill and Knowlton, the second-largest agency, is owned by J. Walter Thompson. The top eight agencies earn net fees in excess of $100 million per year, and both Burson and Hill and Knowlton—which were both subsumed by WPP, Inc. in 2000—earn more than $240 million in net fees per year (Table 8-1).

Public relations counsel is, by definition, a highly personalized service. A counselor's prescription for a client depends primarily on what the counselor thinks a client needs and how that assessment fits the client's own perception of those needs. Often an outsider's fresh point of view is helpful in focusing a client on particular problems and opportunities and on how best to conquer or capitalize on them.

On the other hand, because outside agencies are just that—outside—they are often unfamiliar about details affecting the situation of particular companies and with the idiosyncrasies of company management. The good external counselor must constantly work to overcome this barrier. The best client–agency relationships are those with free-flowing communications between internal and external public relations groups so that both resources are kept informed about corporate policies, strategies, and tactics. A well-oiled, complementary department–agency relationship can result in a more positive communications approach for an organization.

TABLE 8-1

1999 PR FEE Income of 50 Firms Supplying Documentation to O'Dwyer's Directory of Public Relations Firms

Firm (advertising agency parent in parentheses)	1999 Net Fees	Employees	% Change from 1998
1. Burson-Marsteller* (Young & Rubicam)	$274,631,000	2,000	+6.3
2. Hill & Knowlton* (WPP Group)	243,300,000	1,570	+18.1
3. Shandwick International (Interpublic)	240,203,000	2,054	+41.1
4. Porter Novelli* (Omnicom)	214,895,000	2,483	+17.4
5. Fleishman-Hillard (Omnicom)	213,445,000	1,563	+32.8
6. Edelman PR Worldwide	186,036,804	1,692	+17.9
7. Ketchum* (Omnicom)	149,769,000	1,204	+19.6
8. BSMG Worldwide (True North)	144,683,078	858	+21.6
9. Ogilvy PR* (WPP Group)	125,004,700	1,100	+58.8
10. GCI Group/APCO Assocs.* (Grey)	112,731,019	900	+41.5
11. Weber PR Worldwide (Interpublic)	101,446,537	556	+30.0
12. Manning Salvage & Lee* (MacManus)	95,404,720	520	+25.5
13. Brodeur Worldwide* (Omnicom)	70,100,000	700	+106.1
14. Golin/Harris International* (Interpublic)	59,479,000	427	+12.3
15. Ruder Finn	59,400,000	418	+16.0
16. Waggener Edstrom	50,550,000	415	+23.6
17. Rowland Worldwide* (Saatchi plc)	49,735,000	277	+53.5
18. Cohn & Wolfe (Young & Rubicam)	47,287,000	359	+16.7
19. Text 100	36,816,868	500	+47.6
20. MWW Group	27,002,400	200	+56.8
21. Morgen-Walke (Lighthouse group of IR & graphics cos.)	26,242,884	201	+12.8
22. Publicis Dialog* (Publicis)	23,505,716	200	+106.1
23. Cunningham Communication	23,379,560	140	+14.0
24. Schwartz Communications	21,043,233	193	+40.1
25. Lois Paul & Partners (Omnicom)	16,243,872	150	+20.5
26. FitzGerald Communications	13,400,000	121	+50.5
27. Gibbs & Soell	12,793,000	104	+9.4
28. Chandler Chicco Agency	11,675,981	52	+26.0
29. Middleberg + Assocs.	11,390,018	114	+119.0
30. Earle Palmer Brown PR (E. P. Brown Cos.)	10,860,000	89	+23.5
31. Dan Klores Assocs.	10,800,000	95	+3.9
32. Access Communications* (Interpublic)	10,500,000	70	+54.4
33. Cone (Omnicom)	9,590,066	70	+51.9
34. Kamber Group	9,225,600	58	−25.5
35. Cramer-Krasselt PR (Cramer-Krasselt Adv.)	9,074,000	66	+11.2
36. DeVries PR	8,829,439	37	+74.2
37. Hoffman Agency	8,700,000	65	+24.1
38. The Hawthorn Group	8,674,982	41	+16.9
39. Stoorza, Ziegaus & Metzger	8,660,866	83	+0.9
40. KCSA PR Worldwide	8,550,080	71	+1.0
41. Neale-May & Partners	8,252,006	44	+102.6
42. Makovsky & Co.	8,201,000	65	+15.5
43. Applied Communications	8,199,000	59	+100.3
44. Rogers & Associates*	8,193,894	73	+15.3
45. Padilla Speer Beardsley	8,112,045	83	+10.6
46. Wilson McHenry Co.	7,800,200	61	+21.4
47. Kratz & Jensen	7,696,822	70	+24.3
48. Morgan & Myers*	7,559,850	92	+34.3
49. Kemper Lesnik Communications	7,406,973	45	+4.2
50. Vollmer PR*	7,140,670	77	+104.2
Totals	$2,843,621,883	22,485	

*Figures supplied by the Council of PR Firms. The O'Dwyer Co. has not received CPA agreed-upon statements for these income and employee totals.

Source: © Copyright 2000, J. R. O'Dwyer Co. Inc.

Big Business. *Public relations agencies have become significant, multimillion dollar enterprises as society's communications demand has increased.*

Where Are the Jobs?

In the 21st century, public relations jobs are plentiful and public relations practitioners in high demand.

◪ The high-tech industry, in particular, needs skilled communicators to help differentiate organizations and persuade consumers, investors, and potential employees of relative value and attractiveness. As the competition for start-up venture capital and subsequent stockholder capital increases, emerging Internet and related firms will be in great need of public relations professionals. Already, in headquarters of high-tech markets—Northern California's Silicon Valley, Seattle, Salt Lake City, Chicago, Boston, New York—Internet CEOs have voiced concern of a paucity of qualified public relations people. As one successful Internet CEO put it: "With a start-up technology company, it's all about building momentum. Smart public relations can help you create a brand within the industry. So the challenge for a public relations professional is to take the entrepreneur's vision and communicate it so that the word gets spread."[15]

◪ More traditional corporations, too, are in the market for qualified communicators. Many CEOs are willing to pay more for such assistance in the new millennium, but they also demand additional skills, beyond the traditional ones. Such new competencies include matrix management, which involves team building and teamwork; virtual management, where one operates at a distance using e-mail, video-conferencing, and other new age tools; business literacy, knowing how a company and industry make money; and working effectively with consultants as more and more tasks get outsourced to conserve internal resources.[16]

◪ In a related sense, public relations agencies will continue to expand in the new century. The last three years of the 20th century brought new prominence and success to many in the agency field. Just as a plethora of high-tech public relations agencies emerged in the latter years of the last century, so, too, is it likely that the move toward public relations specialization among agencies will continue in 2000 and beyond.

◪ In the nonprofit realm, public relations positions in hospitals, in particular, are likely to grow, as managed care becomes the reality and health care organizations become more competitive in attracting patients and winning community approval. Other nonprofits—schools, museums, associations—will also require increased public relations help as the competition for development and membership funds increases as well.

◪ In terms of the functions of public relations, employee communications is one that will rank high on the agenda of CEOs. Employees in the 21st century, cognizant of the massive corporate reengineering of the 1990s, require active and strategic communications to maintain corporate loyalty and job productivity.[17] Other areas of the field—investor relations, government relations, media relations for on-line and off-line journalists, and strategic counseling—all will be in great demand.

What's It Pay?

Without question the communications function has increased in importance and clout in the new century. Top communications professionals in many large corporations today draw compensation packages well into six figures. Entry-level jobs for writers and editors generally fall into the $20,000-$30,000 range. Managers of public relations units, press relations, consumer relations, and financial communications may earn anywhere from $40,000 to beyond $100,000. Agency account executives fall into a similar territory. Public relations directors may range in salary from $40,000 to upwards of $500,000.

A fortunate few corporate practitioners, able to profit from corporate stock options, may earn in excess of $1 million annually. Agency executives, who either own their firms outright or have significant stock in parent holding companies, also may reach seven-figure earnings. Not bad for public relations work.

The median public relations salary, according to a landmark study by the Public Relations Society of America, is slightly more than $49,000 a year (Table 8-2).[18] Men and women, however, at the moment seem to be paid differently, with men's salaries higher but with women closing the gap.

Among other findings, the study determined:

- Public relations salaries are markedly higher in the Northeast and the West than in the Midwest or South.
- Investor relations is the highest-paying public relations specialty, with a median salary of more than $72,000.
- The lowest-paying public relations jobs are found in government, health care, and nonprofit organizations, with the median salaries approximately $43,000 for each (Table 8-3).
- There is little difference between median salaries in public relations agencies and corporations.

TABLE 8-2

Overall Public Relations Salaries

	Total Respondents %	PRSA Members			Non-Members %
		Total %	APR %	Non-APR %	
Total Respondents	100	100	100	100	100
Less than $45,000	42	40	23	46	43
Less than $15,000	3	1	2	*	4
$15,000 - $24,999	8	4	2	5	10
$25,000 - $34,999	14	17	6	21	13
$35,000 - $44,999	17	18	13	19	17
$45,000 - $74,999	33	34	42	31	3
$45,000 - $54,999	15	16	20	15	14
$55,000 - $64,999	11	11	14	11	11
$65,000 - $74,999	8	7	9	6	
$75,000 or more	21	22	31	19	20
$75,000 - $99,999	11	11	16	10	10
$100,000 - $149,999	8	7	10	7	8
$150,000 or more	3	3	4	3	3
No answer	4	5	5	4	4
Median	**$49,070**	**$49,830**	**$58,840**	**$46,370**	**$48,660**

*Less than 0.5%

TABLE 8-3

Public Relations Salaries by Organization Type			
	P.R. Firms %	Corporations %	Government Health Care/Nonprofit %
Total Respondents	100	100	100
Less than $45,000	39	39	53
Less than $15,000	2	3	1
$15,000 - $24,999	9	9	5
$25,000 - $34,999	12	13	22
$35,000 - $44,999	16	15	25
$45,000 - $74,999	24	36	32
$45,000 - $54,999	11	15	16
$55,000 - $64,999	6	12	9
$65,000 - $74,999	6	8	7
$75,000 or more	29	21	12
$75,000 - $99,999	11	11	8
$100,000 - $149,999	11	8	5
$150,000 or more	7	2	*
No answer	8	4	2
Median	**$51,430**	**$50,770**	**$43,260**

*Less than 0.5%

- ◪ Members of the Public Relations Society of America have higher salaries than nonmembers.
- ◪ The larger the number of public relations professionals employed at a specific business location, the higher the median salary.
- ◪ Entry-level salaries are basically the same from industry to industry, generally in the $20,000 range (Table 8-4). Since getting in the door is often the toughest part of employment in the public relations profession, a lower entry-level salary may be sufficient relative to the potential earnings power later on.

TABLE 8-4

Entry-level Public Relations Salaries by Type of Organization			
	P.R. Firms %	Corporations %	Government/ Health Care/Nonprofit %
Total Respondents	100	100	100
Less than $15,000	7	6	3
$15,000 - $19,999	27	19	19
$20,000 - $24,999	37	29	39
$25,000 - $29,999	7	20	19
$30,000 or more	6	17	14
No answer	16	9	5
Median	**$21,110**	**$23,550**	**$23,210**

*Less than 0.5%

What Manner of Man/Woman?

What kind of individual does it take to become a competent public relations professional?

The Report of the Commission on Public Relations Education in 1999 listed an even dozen areas of competence that emerging public relations students must have to succeed in the new century:

1. Communication and persuasion concepts and strategies
2. Communication and public relations theories
3. Relationships and relationship building
4. Societal trends
5. Ethical issues
6. Legal requirements and issues
7. Marketing and finance
8. Public relations history
9. Uses of research and forecasting
10. Multicultural and global issues
11. Organizational change and development
12. Management concepts and theories[19]

Beyond these academic areas, in order to make it, a public relations professional ought to possess a set of specific technical skills as well as an appreciation of the proper attitudinal approach to the job. On the technical side, these seven skills are important:

1. **Knowledge of the field**—the underpinnings of public relations, culture and history, philosophy, and social psychology.
2. **Communications knowledge**—the media and the ways in which they work, communications research, and, most important, the writing process.
3. **Technological knowledge**—the computer, the Net, the World Wide Web, cyberspace, all are imperative in the new century.
4. **Knowledge of what's going on around you**—current events and factors that influence society: literature, language, politics, economics, and all the rest—from Herzegovina to Hebron, from a unified Germany to a divided Zaire; from Dr. Kevorkian to Dr. Dre; from Kobe Bryant to Bryant Gumbel; from Jay Z to Jamiroquai to the Squirrel Nut Zippers. A public relations professional must be, in the truest sense, a Renaissance man or woman.
5. **Business knowledge**—how business works, a bottom-line orientation, and a knowledge of one's company and industry.
6. **Knowledge of bureaucracy**—how to get things done in a bureaucratic organization, how to use and gain power for the best advantage, and how to maneuver in a politically charged environment.
7. **Management knowledge**—how public policy is shaped and what pressures and responsibilities fall on senior managers.

In terms of attitude, public relations professionals ought to possess the following four characteristics:

1. **Communications orientation**—a bias toward disclosing rather than withholding information. Public relations professionals should want to communicate with the public. They should practice the belief that the public has a right to know.

2. **Advocacy**—a desire to be advocates for their employers. Public relations people must stand up for what their employers represent. Although they should never distort, lie, or hide facts, occasionally it may be in an organization's best interest to avoid comment on certain issues. If practitioners don't believe in the integrity and credibility of their employers, their most honorable course is to quit.

3. **Counseling orientation**—a compelling desire to advise senior managers. As noted, top executives are used to dealing in tangibles, such as balance sheets, costs per thousand, and cash flows. Public relations practitioners understand the intangibles, such as public opinion, media influence, and communications messages. Practitioners must be willing to support their beliefs—often in opposition to lawyers or personnel executives. They must even be willing to disagree with management at times. Far from being compliant, public relations practitioners must have the gumption to say "no."

4. **Personal confidence**—a strong sense of honesty and ethics, a willingness to take risks, and, not unimportant, a sense of humor. Public relations professionals must have the courage of their convictions and the personal confidence to represent proudly a curious—yet critical—role in any organization.

In recent years many more women have joined the public relations ranks. Women now account for upwards of 70 percent of all practitioners and, according to the research, are gaining on men in terms of earnings power in the field.

The issue of increased feminization, as noted, is a particularly thorny one for the practice of public relations. University public relations programs across the country report a preponderance of female students, outnumbering males by as much as 80 percent. However, the ranks of women executives in public relations, as opposed to their male counterparts, are still relatively thin. Hence the picture of, on the one hand, public relations becoming a "velvet ghetto" of women workers and, on the other hand, a profession in which women have not achieved upper-management status. This is a paramount concern to the profession.[20]

In addition to gender gap problems, there is the issue of minority public relations professionals. According to the Bureau of Labor Statistics, only 7 percent of public relations professionals are minorities—one-third less than the national average for minorities in professional fields. To help more minorities enter the field, the Public Relations Society of America has launched a program of scholarships and internships at public relations agencies for minority professionals. In 1997, the society named educator Debbie Miller as its first African-American president.

SUMMARY

In the 21st century, the practice of public relations is firmly accepted as part of the marketing mix and part of the management process of any well-run organization.

Public relations objectives and goals, strategies, and tactics must flow directly from the organization's overall goals. Public relations strategies must reflect organizational strategies, and tactics must be designed to realize the organization's business objectives.

So, despite its stereotypes and demographic idiosyncrasies, public relations requires neither a false smile nor a glad hand. Rather, it demands a solid grounding in all aspects of professional communications, human relations, and judgmental and learning skills. Most of all, it takes hard work.

Discussion Starters

1. Describe the elements of a public relations plan.
2. How does MBO relate to public relations?
3. How are public relations objectives derived?
4. What elements go into framing a public relations budget?
5. What are the four general steps in preparing a public relations campaign plan?
6. What activities constitute the four broad categories of public relations practice?
7. What is the ideal reporting relationship for a director of public relations?
8. What are the technical skills that a public relations professional should possess?
9. What kinds of attitudinal characteristics should a public relations professional possess?
10. What is meant by the term *velvet ghetto*?

Notes

1. "An Interview with Ron Higgins," *The Public Relations Strategist* (Spring 1999): 9.
2. Internal Berkshire Hathaway memo from Warren Buffet, August 12, 1998, as quoted in *Business Week* (July 5, 1999): 62.
3. James E. Grunig and Todd Hunt, *Managing Public Relations* (New York: Holt, Rinehart, and Winston, 1984): 89–97.
4. Grunig and Hunt, *Managing Public Relations*: 89–97.
5. Scott Cutlip, Allen Center, and Douglas Broom, *Effective Public Relations* vol. 8 (Saddle Brook, NJ: Prentice-Hall, Inc., 2000): 340.
6. George L. Morrisey, *Management by Objectives and Results for Business and Industry,* 2nd ed. (Reading, MA: Addison-Wesley, 1977): 9.
7. H. Lawrence Smith, "Accountability in PR: Budgets and Benchmarks," *Public Relations Quarterly* (Spring 1996): 15.
8. "American Legacy Foundation Board Names Arnold Communications for Multi-Million Dollar Anti-Tobacco Account," American Legacy Foundation news release, September 15, 1999.
9. Anthony Fulginiti, "How to Prepare a Public Relations Plan," *Communication Briefings* (May 1985): 8a, b.
10. Thomas J. Peters and Robert H. Waterman, Jr., *In Search of Excellence* (New York: Harper & Row, 1982): 40.
11. Charles H. Prout, "Organization and Function of the Corporate Public Relations Department," in *Lesly's Handbook of Public Relations and Communications* (Chicago: Probus Publishing Company, 1991): 228–729.
12. "PR Opinion Items," *Jack O'Dwyers Newsletter* (March 19, 1997): 8.

13. Prout, "Organization and Function": 6.
14. Kenneth D. Makovsky, "Seven Strategies to Ensure Quality Control," *Public Relations Strategist* (Summer 1996): 19.
15. "An Interview with Ron Higgins," *The Public Relations Strategist* (Spring 1999): 9.
16. William C. Heyman, "Moving On Up in the Year 2000," *The Public Relations Strategist* (Summer 1999): 22.
17. Heyman, "Moving On Up."
18. *Salary Survey of Public Relations Professionals,* New York: The Public Relations Society of America, 1996.
19. "A Port of Entry: The Report of the Commission on Public Relations Education," *Institute for Public Relations* (October 1999): 3.
20. James G. Hutton, "Exploding the Myth of the Public Relations Gender Gap," *The Public Relations Strategist* (Fall 1996): 49.

Suggested Readings

Campbell, Andrew. "What's Wrong With Strategy?" *Harvard Business Review* (November–December 1997):42–51. Explains why strategy often fails.

Center, Allen H., and Patrick Jackson. *Public Relations Practices, Managerial Case Studies and Problems,* 5th ed. Upper Saddle River, NJ: Prentice Hall, 1995.

Champy, John. *Reengineering Management: The Mandate for New Leadership.* New York: Harper Business, 1995. Best-seller that focuses on the need for new leadership from the top down.

Christ, William G. *Leadership in Times of Change.* Mahwah, NJ: Lawrence Erlbaum Associates, 1998.

top of the shelf

Elaine Biech. *The Business of Consulting: The Basics and Beyond. San Francisco: Jossey-Bass/Pfeiffer, 1999.*

Geoffrey M. Bellman. *The Consultant's Calling: Bringing Who You Are to What You Do. San Francisco: Jossey-Bass/Pfeiffer, 1998.*

For PR practitioners who can cock their heads back and see themselves in the bigger picture of consulting, these two books from Jossey-Bass offer a combination of perspectives vital to success: the practical and the philosophical.

Elaine Biech's *The Business of Consulting* provides an introduction and overview of the profession as practical as a business form (in fact, the book comes with a diskette containing numerous ready-made forms). Geoffrey Bellman's *The Consultant's Calling* is as philosophical as you can get while still getting paid.

Biech focuses on the business side of consulting: how to develop a business plan, how to market your firm, how to charge for your services, how to build a client relationship, how to develop the business, how to ensure your continued professional growth, and how to make money.

Bellman, on the other hand, is a bit touchy-feely, citing Abraham Maslow, for instance, and his self-actualization needs and self-esteem and belonging needs. As his subtitle implies, he tells you how to bring "who you are to what you do."

D'Aprix, Roger. *Communication for Change: Connecting the Workplace with the Marketplace*. San Francisco: Jossey-Bass/Pfeiffer Publishers, 1996.

Fleisher, Craig S., and Darren Mahaffy. "A Balanced Scorecard Approach to Public Relations Management Assessment." *Public Relations Review* (Summer 1997): 117–142.

Galbraith, Jay R. *Designing Organizations*. San Francisco: Jossey-Bass/Pfeiffer, 1995.

Godin, Seth. *Wisdom Inc*. New York: Harper Business, 1995. Names 30 business virtues to turn ordinary people into extraordinary leaders.

Grunig, James E. *Excellence in Public Relations and Communications Management*. Hillsdale, NJ: Lawrence Erlbaum Associates, 1992.

Hammer, Michael. *Beyond Reengineering*. New York: Harper Business, 1995. Another best-seller that explains what needs to be done after an organization reengineers itself.

Hardy, G. *Successfully Managing Change*. Hauppauge, NY: Barron's Educational Series Inc., 1997. A pocket guide for managers undergoing organizational change.

Heath, Robert L. *Management of Corporate Communication: From Interpersonal Contacts to External Affairs*. Mahwah, NJ: Lawrence Erlbaum Associates, 1994.

Heath, Robert L. *Strategic Issues Management: Organizations and Public Policy Challenges*. Thousand Oaks, CA: Sage Publications, 1997.

Harris, Thomas L. *Choosing and Working with Your Public Relations Firm*. Lincolnwood, IL: NTC Business, 1992.

Hon, Linda Childers. "What Have You Done for Me Lately? Exploring Effectiveness in Public Relations." *Journal of Public Relations Research* 9, no. 1 (1997): 1–30.

Hendrix, Jerry A. *Public Relations Cases,* 2nd ed. Belmont, CA: Wadsworth, 1997.

Joyce, William F. *Megachange*. Burr Ridge, IL: Irwin Professional Publishing, 1995. Explores the new logic for radically transforming organizations.

Kotter, John P. *The New Roles*. New York: The Free Press, 1995. Rewrites rules for success in management.

Ries, Al. *Focus*. New York: Harper Business, 1995. The future of American business depends on "focus," according to this marketing guru.

Simon, Raymond. *Cases in Public Relations Management*. Lincolnwood, IL: NTC Publishing Group, 1994.

Spicer, Christopher. *Organizational Public Relations: A Political Perspective*. Mahwah, NJ: Lawrence Erlbaum Associates, 1997.

Toffler, Alvin, and Heidi Toffler. *Creating a New Civilization*. Atlanta: Turner Publishing Inc., 1995. Creates a blueprint for managing change that transcends one single organization.

Trout, Jack, and Steve Rivkin. *Differentiate or Die*. New York: John Wiley, 2000. The future of organizations depends on their ability to separate themselves from the pack—or else, *sayonara*.

Trout, Jack, and Steve Rivkin. *The New Positioning*. New York: McGraw-Hill, 1996.

C A S E   S T U D Y

Dow Corning in the Crucible

The sprawling Dow Corning Corporation campus sits peacefully amidst the rolling fields of Midland, Michigan. Thousands of employees, most of them Dow Corning veterans, arrive early, work diligently, and devote themselves happily to a company they consider almost family.

But the pastoral tranquillity of the campus and the friendly devotion of the workers belie a turbulent and uncertain reality. Dow Corning and its management are involved in a public war of claims and counterclaims, accusations and denials, and public relations judgments that may mean billions of dollars in losses and ultimately, the viability of the company itself.

With $5 billion in assets, 50,000 customers, 9,600 products, 8,700 employees and operations on four continents—Dow Corning is in Chapter 11 bankruptcy, its future by no means clear.

The company is being sued for billions of dollars by attorneys representing thousands of women, who claim that silicone gel-filled breast implants, manufactured by Dow Corning and others, have caused, among other ailments, autoimmune disease. Stated simply, Dow Corning and the others are charged with manufacturing dangerous devices, foisted on unsuspecting women.

CBS HATCHET JOB

Dow Corning's precarious situation, was the ultimate public relations management crisis.

Breast implants first came on the market in the early 1960s, and the Food and Drug Administration began approving the devices in 1976. Given the long track record of breast implants, the FDA presumed that they were reasonably safe. In 1988, however, the FDA announced that breast-implant manufacturers would henceforth have to submit evidence of safety.

Two years later, on December 10, 1990, Dow Corning was thrust into a spotlight from which it has still not recovered. On her CBS television show, *Face to Face with Connie Chung,* the moderator trotted out a parade of women, seemingly terrified and victimized, who claimed that their silicone breast implants had given them autoimmune disease. Although several supportive breast implant users and doctors were interviewed for the Chung show, none made it on air. Connie Chung never called Dow Corning for comment or participation on the program (Figure 8-4).

FIGURE 8-4 **The hammer.** Connie Chung "lowered the boom" on Dow Corning with a vicious report in 1990.

After the national television broadcast, Dow Corning said nothing publicly but quickly put together a 30-second commercial, with women who could speak positively about their experience with breast implants. The company planned to air the spots around the country to follow the rebroadcast of the Chung show and bought time on CBS-owned and operated stations.

A few hours before the program was scheduled to be broadcast, however, the CBS stations notified Dow Corning that the spot would not run, because it would open them up to "equal time considerations" they couldn't honor.

THE ROOF CAVES IN

After the Chung rebroadcast, the roof caved in for Dow Corning. Congress held public hearings. Ralph Nader's Public Citizen group pressed the issue in the media and the courts. A San Francisco jury awarded more than $7 million to a woman who claimed that her Dow Corning breast implants had caused her to have mixed connective tissue disease. And in April 1992, FDA Commissioner David Kessler banned the sale of silicone gel–filled breast implants, except for use in clinical trials of breast reconstruction after cancer surgery.

The ban, Dr. Kessler took pains to point out, was not because breast implants had been found dangerous—indeed Dow Corning insisted that the implants were safe. He banned the sale, because the manufacturers had not "proved scientifically that the products were safe."

This fine distinction—that there was no evidence of danger—was lost on the million or so women who already had implants. Why would the FDA ban a product if it wasn't dangerous? Predictably, women panicked. Large numbers came forward complaining of various illnesses caused by their breast implants. Media-seeking doctors and scientists popped up with evidenceless theories explaining how breast implants affected the immune system. The media, in response, jumped on the story with a vengeance. Plaintiff's attorneys, capitalizing on the budding crop of "expert witnesses" and media attention, successfully converted the trickle of breast implant lawsuits into a flood.

LOW-KEY RESPONSE

Through the trauma, there was an eerie silence from the people in Midland, Michigan.

Dow Corning management insisted that their product was fundamentally safe. But they wanted to reconfirm that fact with undisputed scientific evidence. Dow Corning committed to spend tens of millions of dollars—upwards of $30 million through 1997—to sponsor independent university research to do the necessary epidemiology studies that would answer the safety questions.

While the company proceeded with the painstaking and prolonged task of scientific research, the media had a field day, in effect, issuing a constant drumbeat of "corporate guilt."

Dow Corning stuck to its guns with a reasoned, low-key public relations response that built up gradually:

- ☑ In 1991, it released to the general public more than 10,000 pages of proprietary information on silicone breast implants.
- ☑ In 1992, it made available complete sets of its FDA breast implant application to medical schools.
- ☑ That same year, it distributed 90 documents—nearly 1,400 pages of internal company memos and scientific studies about the safety aspects of its breast implant product.

▨ Later, it began to hold news conferences to rebut false allegations, and its new chairman, Richard Hazelton, began to make himself available to the media, including one stormy session facing angry breast implant users on *The Oprah Winfrey Show*.

TOO LITTLE, TOO LATE

Dow Corning's actions couldn't stem the onrushing tide.

In 1993, Dow Corning exited the breast implant business.

In 1994, breast implant manufacturers, desperate to limit their losses, agreed to the largest class-action settlement in history, with $4.25 billion to be set aside for all women with breast implants. The lawyers' take would be $1 billion. Nearly half of all women with breast implants registered for the settlement, with half of the claimants claiming to be suffering from implant-related illnesses.

With so many women opting out of the settlement and deciding to continue with their lawsuits and their attorneys' exorbitant demands, Dow Corning filed for Chapter 11 bankruptcy protection in May 1995. The settlement collapsed shortly thereafter.

In December 1996, Dow Corning filed a proposed $3 billion bankruptcy reorganization plan, $2 billion of which could potentially be set aside to cover breast implant claims. The Dow Corning plan was met by derision among plaintiffs' attorneys, who argued that the settlement fell far short of what was needed.

By 1997, Dow Corning's fate once again rested with the courts. CEO Hazelton, reflecting on the controversy and the decisions that management made throughout, said, "I feel like all of us have done the best we could under the circumstances. Obviously, there are a lot of lessons that everybody has learned that I hope we all take to heart to prevent something like this from ever happening again."

Questions

1. What's your opinion of how *Face to Face with Connie Chung* handled the breast implant story?
2. What options did Dow Corning have in responding to the story?
3. How would you characterize Dow Corning's public relations strategy?
4. What other strategic public relations options did Dow Corning management have in answering the silicone breast implant charges?
5. What should the company's public relations strategy be going forward?
6. What has happened to Dow Corning and its breast implant business? See the latest announcements on the company's special Web site (http://www.implantclaims.com/). Why would the company maintain this special site? Do you agree with the way Dow Corning is using the Internet to communicate with some of its publics?

An Interview with Richard Hazelton

Richard Hazelton, a lifetime employee of Dow Corning, was named chairman and CEO in 1993, well after the company's breast implant problems began. Mr. Hazelton was at the company's helm when it declared bankruptcy and eventually settled with those who sued over the silicone implants.

Prior to the escalation of the silicone breast implant publicity, how would you describe Dow Corning's approach to communications?

I would describe the company as "reserved" in the sense that our product line and customers are largely other businesses. So we had neither a history nor a tradition of needing to be highly visible, of taking a highly proactive approach to communications.

Did Connie Chung approach you about her program?

We were never approached about the program or asked to participate.

How did you respond to the accusations raised on the Chung show?

We quickly put together a 30-second spot, with people who could speak very positively about the breast implant. And we bought time on CBS-owned and operated stations around the country, to follow the scheduled rebroadcast of the Chung program. But the commercials never aired. Just a few hours before the program was scheduled to be broadcast, we were notified by the CBS stations that they couldn't run the spots, because it would open them up to "equal time considerations" they couldn't honor.

What was your response after the coverage increased?

In late 1991 and 1992, the whole thing exploded on us. We were unprepared and surprised by how quickly and how intense the whole media storm became. In terms of getting our message out, compared with the message that was hung out by our adversaries, we were pretty much overwhelmed.

What was your "side of the story"? Did you believe the product caused autoimmune problems?

No. Nor do we today. Nor does 99 percent of the scientific community.

So what strategy did you adopt?

The strategy was to put the scientific process in place that would develop our research that would confirm our position. That was the key. We committed to spend tens of millions of dollars—and today we're past $30 million and still counting—to sponsor independent research to do the necessary epidemiology studies that would answer the questions.

Were you concerned in spending millions of dollars to see if the product was safe that this would be interpreted as an admission of guilt?

No. First, it was the right thing to do. Wherever the science would lead, whatever the answers are, we'll deal with the consequences. But, second, we were quite confident in the safety of the product.

What was your communications strategy?

To continue to cooperate as much as possible with the regulatory agencies. To be open and responsive to the media. To keep our business healthy, because this product never constituted more than 1 percent of our sales.

What did this situation teach you about the media?

I don't believe the people in the media are deliberately trying to shade a story to make it more sensational or get more air time or more column inches, but I do fault the media for developing a herd instinct that quickly forms a conventional wisdom, that builds up such momentum that it's extremely difficult and slow to recover from.

Chapter 9

Crisis Management

Crisis, which counselor James Lukaszewski once described as "unplanned visibility," can strike at any time to anyone.[1] To wit:

☑ *Among the highest fliers of the end-of-the-century stock market boom was telecommunications giant Lucent Technologies. For years, its stock price rocketed upward seemingly without limit. Then crisis struck.*

On January 6, 2000, Lucent announced after the market closed that its first-quarter profit would fall short of analyst expectations for the first time in its brief history. The next day, Lucent stock lost almost one-third of its value, falling by $20.

A week later, Lucent stock was hit hard once again, amid speculation the Securities and Exchange Commission was investigating its accounting methods. Said a Lucent spokesman, "We're not aware of any such inquiry."[2]

☑ *On the same day Lucent was taking its lumps, a grand jury was indicting Grammy-winning entrepreneur Sean "Puffy" Combs on weapons charges after a stolen handgun was found in his car. The Puffster, who was taken into custody along with his girlfriend singer-actress Jennifer Lopez, insisted he was innocent.*

But after his indictment, Mr. Combs left it to Ms. Lopez and his new attorney, O. J. Simpson savior Johnnie Cochran, to defend him. "I am surprised and saddened to learn of the indictment against Sean Combs. I support him wholeheartedly throughout this difficult time," said Ms. Lopez.[3]

The Puffmeister and Lucent Technologies both found themselves engaged in what has become a typical public relations pastime in the 21st century: crisis damage control.

Indeed, in the new century, the most well regarded and highest-paid people in public relations have achieved this status through their efforts in attempting to "manage" crises.

In a world of instantaneous communications, tabloid news journalism, and exploding communications challenges, the number and depth of crises affecting business, government, labor, nonprofits, and even private individuals have expanded exponentially.

◪ *Millennial celebrations are called off in Seattle after terrorists are found at the Canadian border. The federal building in Oklahoma City, Oklahoma, is bombed by right-wing extremists and hundreds perish. The World Trade Center in New York City is also bombed, and the Empire State Building is the scene of a fanatic intruder.*

◪ *A six-year-old beauty queen is found brutally murdered in Boulder, Colorado, and, after years of controversial investigating, her parents and immediate family are apparently exonerated as the chief suspects.*

◪ *The International Olympic Committee was mightily embarrassed in 1999 over revelations of bribes to officials from cities eager to host the games. Imperious IOC Chief Executive Juan Manuel Samaranch fumbled an appearance before the U.S. Congress, and the image of the Olympics suffered.*

◪ *The Walt Disney Company is sued by former Disney executive Jeffrey Katzenberg, who, it is revealed during the bitter trial, was described by Disney CEO Michael Eisner as "that little midget." Katzenberg collects plenty from his former employer.*

◪ *Mitsubishi Motor Manufacturing of America Inc. is rocked by a major class-action suit by the Equal Employment Opportunity Commission for sexual harassment of 29 women.[4] Similar allegations are charged at W. R. Grace, CNA Insurance, Salomon Smith Barney, and a host of other firms.*

◪ *Political crises—from President Clinton's sexcapades to Vice President Al Gore's Buddhist campaign contributions to Republican challenger George W. Bush's rumored dalliances with illegal substances— are weekly occurrences.*

These are but the tip of the iceberg—a very few of the hundreds of small and large crises that afflict elements of society today in ever-expanding magnitude (Figure 9-1).

No wonder when public relations professionals are asked what subject they want covered in midcareer seminars, "crisis communications" invariably heads the list. Helping to manage crisis is the ultimate assignment for a public relations professional. Smart managements value public relations advice in developing an organization's response not only to crises but to public issues in general. Companies have created executive posts for "issues managers," whose task is to help the organization define and deal with the political, economic, and social issues that affect it.

The list of such issues—and of the crises they often evoke—is unending. In the 21st century, society is flooded with front-burner issues that affect individuals and organizations. From poverty to abortion to AIDS, from discrimination to downsizing, from environmentalism to energy conservation, the domain of issues management has become increasingly important for public relations professionals.

If you can't do a thing about the way you look, call us.

Beauty is only skin deep. But if you're a battered woman, your bruises go straight to the heart. And you can make up, but it never lasts. You're not alone. One out of every two women in America will be abused by a man who says he loves her. You deserve our help. So do your kids. Call Rose Brooks' 24-hour crisis line at **861-6100**. Because you can't keep turning the other cheek.

Rose Brooks
For Battered Women and Their Children

FIGURE 9-1 **Societal issues.** In a day of managed care and more competitive hospitals, health care institutions have accelerated communications appeals to the public to deal with individual crises.

Death of a Tiny Beauty Queen

The horrible killing of JonBenet Ramsey (Figure 9-2), six-year-old daughter of a wealthy Boulder, Colorado, couple, on Christmas Day 1996, stunned the nation.

Boulder police reported no signs of forced entry and concluded that the murderer was either someone known to the family or perhaps even a family member.

Almost immediately, JonBenet's image was flashed nonstop across the country on TV news and tabloid programs. The Ramseys had encouraged JonBenet to become a child beauty queen, complete with makeup,

FIGURE 9-2 Tragedy. The late JonBenet Ramsey.

teased hair, and fashion model clothing. The media jumped on this bizarre aspect of the case with a vengeance. Predictably, the girl's parents and brother became prime suspects in her murder.

The Ramseys' immediate response to the national outcry was equally bizarre. They embarked on an elaborate public relations campaign to proclaim their innocence.

- First, they hired two teams of high-powered criminal attorneys—one for Mr. Ramsey, the other for his wife, to assist in the investigation.
- Second, they secured a Washington, D.C., crisis management firm, led by a former Ronald Reagan public relations professional, to handle the hundreds of reporters covering the story.
- Third, both parents appeared on national TV a week after the killing to deny they had killed their little girl. "We are a Christian, God-fearing family," a teary Patsy Ramsey told CNN.
- JonBenet's parents began their own Web site to explain their innocence in vivid detail.
- In 1999, the family sued *The National Star* for libeling their young son, Burke, by calling him the primary murder suspect.
- In 2000, the Ramseys published a book about their daughter and toured the TV talk shows to profess their innocence.

Despite their efforts at public relations, the Ramseys, who moved from Colorado to Atlanta, remained the focus of nonstop tabloid stories and nasty rumors. They cooperated minimally with investigators. In the winter of 1999, the Boulder district attorney announced that a grand jury investigation had been inconclusive, with no primary suspects found in the murder of JonBenet Ramsey. The Boulder DA publicly hinted that "no murderer might ever be found."

Many in the public, however, had their own views on who might be responsible.

Issues Management

The term *issues management* was coined in 1976 by public relations counselor W. Howard Chase, who defined it this way:

> Issues management is the capacity to understand, mobilize, coordinate, and direct all strategic and policy planning functions, and all public affairs/public relations skills, toward achievement of one objective: meaningful participation in creation of public policy that affects personal and institutional destiny.[5]

Issues management is a five-step process that:

1. Identifies issues with which the organization must be concerned
2. Analyzes and delimits each issue with respect to its impact on constituent publics
3. Displays the various strategic options available to the organization
4. Implements an action program to communicate the organization's views and to influence perception on the issue
5. Evaluates its program in terms of reaching organizational goals.

Many suggest that the term *issues management* is another way of saying that the most important public relations skill is "counseling management." Others suggest that issues management is another way of saying "reputation management"—orchestrating the process whose goal is to help preserve markets, reduce risk, create opportunities, and manage image as an organizational asset for the benefit of both an organization and its primary shareholders.[6]

In specific terms, issues management encompasses the following elements:

- **Anticipate emerging issues.** Normally, the issues management process anticipates issues 18 months to 3 years away. Therefore, it is neither crisis planning nor postcrisis planning, but rather pre-crisis planning. In other words, issues management deals with an issue that will hit the organization a year later, thus distinguishing the practice from the normal crisis planning aspects of public relations.
- **Identify issues selectively.** An organization can influence only a few issues at a time. Therefore, a good issues management process will select several— perhaps 5 to 10—specific priority issues with which to deal. In this way, issues management can focus on the most important issues affecting the organization.
- **Deal with opportunities and vulnerabilities.** Most issues, anticipated well in advance, offer both opportunities and vulnerabilities for organizations. For example, in assessing promised federal budget cuts, an insurance company might anticipate that less money will mean fewer people driving and therefore fewer accident claims. This would mark an opportunity. On the other hand, those cuts might mean that more people are unable to pay their premiums. This, clearly, is a vulnerability that a sharp company should anticipate well in advance.
- **Plan from the outside in.** The external environment—not internal strategies—dictates the selection of priority issues. This differs from the normal strategic planning approach, which, to a large degree, is driven by internal strengths and objectives. Issues management is very much driven by external factors.

- ◪ **Profit-line orientation.** Although many people tend to look at issues management as anticipating crises, its real purpose should be to defend the organization in light of external factors as well as to enhance the firm's business by seizing imminent opportunities.
- ◪ **Action timetable.** Just as the issues management process must identify emerging issues and set them in order, it must propose policy, programs, and an implementation timetable to deal with those issues. Action is the key to an effective issues management process.
- ◪ **Dealing from the top.** Just as a public relations department is powerless without the confidence and respect of top management, the issues management process must operate with the support of the chief executive. The chief executive's personal sanction is critical to the acceptance and conduct of issues management within a firm.

Implementing Issues Management

In a typical organization, the tactical implementation of issues management tends to consist of four specific job tasks:

1. **Identifying issues and trends.** Issue identification can be accomplished through traditional research techniques as well as through more informal methods. Organizations are most concerned about issues that affect their own residential area.

   One way to keep informed about what is being said about a company, industry, or issue is to subscribe to issues-oriented publications of every political persuasion—from *Mother Jones* and *The Village Voice* on the far left to the *Liberty Lobby's Spotlight* on the far right and everything else in between.

2. **Evaluating issue impact and setting priorities.** Evaluation and analysis may be handled by issues committees within an organization. Committees can set priorities for issues management action. At the Pharmacia & Upjohn Company, for example, a senior policy committee—composed of managers in each of the firm's major divisions, as well as public affairs and legal staff members—meets quarterly to set issues priorities.

3. **Establishing a company position.** Establishing a position can be a formal process. After the Upjohn senior policy committee has met and decided on issues, Upjohn's public affairs staff prepares policy statements on each topic. At PPG Industries, individual issues managers prepare position papers for executive review on topics of direct concern.

4. **Designing company action and response to achieve results.** The best-organized companies for issues management orchestrate integrated responses to achieve results. Typically, organizations may coordinate those responses with their Washington offices, state lobbying operations, management speeches, advertising messages, and employee communications (Figure 9-3).

In Defense of a Little Virginity

a message from Focus on the Family

FIGURE 9-3
Controversial issue.
As a compliment to its national religious broadcasts, the group Focus on the Family sponsored this ad in response to such developments as the public school distribution of condoms. This ad was placed in more than 1,300 newspapers across the country and was translated into six languages in eight foreign countries.

A QUESTION OF ETHICS

Off His Rocker

In January of 2000, a baseball pitcher, with the most appropriate name of John Rocker—as in "rock head"—learned first-hand what "crisis management" is all about.

Rocker (Figure 9-4), the star relief pitcher for the Atlanta Braves, had experienced a rough reception during the 1999 baseball season, first at Shea Stadium in New York during the National League play-offs and then at Yankee Stadium in New York during the World Series. The newspapers, talk shows, and

FIGURE 9-4 **Pilloried pitcher.** Atlanta Braves pitcher John Rocker got his "knickers caught in a twist," as the British might say, for dumb and bigoted remarks after the 1999 World Series.

fans were less than hospitable to the outspoken Rocker. In fact, they were downright nasty.

After the Series, Rocker disappeared into the southern woodwork, only to reemerge with a vengeance in the pages of *Sports Illustrated* magazine. Escorted by a reporter as he drove through Atlanta, the volatile pitcher proceeded to malign immigrants, AIDS patients, young mothers, and people with purple hair—all in response to a question about what he "thought of New Yorkers." In the same interview, Rocker called a teammate "a fat monkey." And that was just for starters!

The response, not only in New York but around the nation, was immediate and unforgiving. Many called for Rocker's expulsion from baseball. Major League Baseball ordered the harebrained reliever to undergo a psychological examination. This touched off another national firestorm, with many claiming that as obnoxious as the pitcher's remarks were, this still is a free country.

Three weeks after the pitcher put his foot in his mouth, after the full brunt of public opinion had fallen on his poor, pointed head, Rocker appeared on ESPN to apologize for his offensive remarks and ask forgiveness. "All I can do is apologize and offer my deepest regrets," said the embattled hurler. "I saw that as a forum to try to retaliate at all the wrong and injustice that had been done toward me and my teammates, and it went a little too far," he said.

How far the Braves were willing to go with Rocker remained a mystery. The pitcher was too good to give up on, but the crisis into which he had dug his team was major league all the way. The Braves were on the horns of an ethical dilemma with their wayward pitcher. It would be a long while, if ever, before John Rocker's life returned to normal.*

Jack Curry, "Rocker Lands Off Base in His ESPN Interview," New York Times (January 14, 2000), D3.

Growth of Risk Communication

The 1990s saw the emergence of "risk communication" as an outgrowth of issues management. Risk communication is basically the process of taking scientific data related to health and environmental hazards and presenting them to a lay audience in a manner that is both understandable and meaningful.[7]

Models of risk communication have been developed based on the position that "perception is reality"—a concept that has been part of public relations for years. Indeed, the disciplines of risk communication and public relations have much in common. Risk communication deals with a high level of emotion. Fear, confusion, frustration, and anger are common feelings in dealing with environmental issues. For example, when two student gunmen opened fire on helpless classmates and teachers at Colorado's Columbine High School (Figure 9-5), the national outcry against handguns was unyielding (Figure 9-6).

Occasionally—even often—intense emotion flows from a lack of knowledge and understanding about the science that underlies societal risk. Therefore, frequent and forceful communication is necessary to inform, educate, and even dampen emotion. The first rule in responding to a perceived public risk is to take the matter seriously.

FIGURE 9-5 National crisis. Unspeakable horror at Columbine High School in Littleton, Colorado, fueled . . .

FIGURE 9-6 . . . National outrage. This ad, signed by opinion leaders throughout America, helped focus the national spotlight on the National Rifle Association and gun control laws, in the wake of Columbine.

After this, according to risk management expert William Adams, seven steps are helpful in planning a risk communication program:

1. Recognize risk communication as part of a larger risk management program and understand that the whole program is based on politics, power, and controversial issues.
2. Encourage management to join the "communications loop" and help train them to deal effectively with the news media.
3. Develop credible outside experts to act as news sources for journalists.
4. Become an in-house expert, in your own area of risk to enhance your credibility with journalists.
5. Approach the news media with solid facts and figures before they approach you. Verify the veracity of your data.
6. Research perceptions of your organization by the media and other publics to gauge credibility and help determine if your messages will be believable.
7. Understand your target audiences and how the news media can help you communicate effectively.[8]

Like any other area of public relations, risk communication depends basically on an organization's actions. In the long run, deeds, not words, are what count in communicating risk.

Managing in a Crisis

The most significant test for any organization comes when it is hit by a major accident or disaster. How it handles itself in the midst of a crisis may influence how it is perceived for years to come. Poor handling of events with the magnitude of Coca-Cola's European contamination problem, PepsiCo's syringe scare, Dow Corning's silicone breast implant controversy, NASA's shuttle disaster or Tylenol's capsule poisoning not only can cripple an organization's reputation but also can cause it enormous monetary loss. In some cases, such as ValuJet's Everglades airline crash cited in the "case study" at the end of this chapter, it can cause the demise of an organization. It is essential, therefore, that such emergencies be managed intelligently and forthrightly with the news media, employees, and the community at large.

As any organization unfortunate enough to experience a crisis recognizes, when the crisis strikes, seven instant warning signs invariably appear:

1. **Surprise.** When a crisis breaks out, it's usually unexpected. Often, it's a natural disaster—a tornado or hurricane. Sometimes, it's a human-made disaster—robbery, embezzlement, or large loss. Frequently, the first a public relations professional learns of such an event is when the media calls and demands to know what immediate action will be taken.
2. **Insufficient information.** Many things happen at once. Rumors fly. Chat rooms come alive with wild stories. Wire services want to know why the company's stock is falling. It's difficult to get a grip on everything that's happening.
3. **Escalating events.** The crisis expands. The Stock Exchange wants to know what's going on. Will the organization issue a statement? Are the rumors true? While rumors run rampant, truthful information is difficult

to obtain. You want to respond in an orderly manner, but events are unfolding too quickly.

4. **Loss of control.** The unfortunate natural outgrowth of escalating events is that too many things are happening simultaneously. Erroneous stories hit the wires, then the newsstands, and then the airwaves. As in the case of the mouse in the Coors can, rampant rumors can't easily be controlled.

5. **Increased outside scrutiny.** The media, stockbrokers, talk-show hosts, and the public in general feed on rumors. "Helpful" politicians and observers of all stripes comment on what's going on. The media wants responses. Investors demand answers. Customers must know what's going on.

6. **Siege mentality.** The organization, understandably, feels surrounded. Lawyers counsel, "Anything we say will be held against us." The easiest thing to do is to say nothing. But does that make sense?

7. **Panic.** With the walls caving in and with leaks too numerous to plug, a sense of panic pervades. In such an environment, it is difficult to convince management to take immediate action and to communicate what's going on.[9]

Planning in a Crisis

One irrefutable key in crisis management is being prepared. If there is one certainty in dealing with crisis, it is that all manner of accidents or disruptions make for spectacular headlines and sensational reporting. Reporters, as noted, march to a different drummer. They consider themselves the "guardians of the public trust" and therefore may be quick to point fingers and ascribe blame in a crisis.

Thus, heightened preparedness is always in order.

In terms of dealing with the media, four planning issues are paramount.

- ☑ **First, for each potentially impacted audience, define the risk.** "The poison in the pill will make you sick." "The plant shutdown will keep you out of work." "The recall will cost the stockholders $100 million." The risk must be understood—or at least contemplated—before framing crisis communications.

- ☑ **Second, for each risk defined describe the actions that mitigate the risk.** "Don't take the pill." "We are recalling the product." "We are studying the possibility of closing the plant." If you do a credible job in defining the risk, the public will more closely believe in your solutions.

- ☑ **Third, identify the cause of the risk.** If the public believes you know what went wrong, they are more likely to accept that you will quickly remedy the problem. That's why people get back on airplanes after crashes. Moreover, if the organization helps identify the cause of the problem, the coverage of the crisis is likely to be more balanced.

- ☑ **Fourth, demonstrate responsible management action.**[10] Essential to the planning phase is to appear to be in control of the situation. Certainly early on in a crisis, control is lost. The best firms are those that seize command early and don't acquiesce it to outside so-called experts. Letting people know that the organization has a plan and is implementing it helps convince them that you are in control. Defining the issues means both having a clear sense internally of what the focus of communications should be and effectively moving that focus out into the marketplace to reach key constituents.[11]

Simple but appropriate watchwords for any crisis plan are the following:

- ◪ Be prepared
- ◪ Be available
- ◪ Be credible

All of this implies that you must be willing to communicate in a crisis.

Communicating in a Crisis

The key communications principle in dealing with a crisis is not to clam up when disaster strikes. Lawyers invariably advise clients to (1) say nothing, (2) say as little as possible and release it as quietly as possible, (3) say as little as possible, citing privacy laws, company policy, or sensitivity, (4) deny guilt and/or act indignant that such charges could possibly have been made, or (5) shift, or, if necessary, share the blame with others.

Public relations advice, by contrast, takes a different tack. The most effective crisis communicators are those who provide prompt, frank, and full information to the media in the eye of the storm. Invariably, the first inclination of executives is to say, "Let's wait until all the facts are in." But as President Carter's press secretary, Jody Powell, used to say, "Bad news is a lot like fish. It doesn't get better with age." In saying nothing, an organization is perceived as already having made a decision. Indeed, research sponsored by public relations agency Porter Novelli suggests that when most

BACKGROUNDER

De-Fanging an Internet Crisis

In the 21st century, the Internet, besides all its wonderful properties, is also a prime source of corporate crisis.

In 1999, a rogue Web site started a rumor—completely untrue—that Procter & Gamble's (P&G) new household cleaner, Febreze, would poison your pet. The rumor stimulated a chain letter that generated more than 1,500 calls and e-mails per day to P&G headquarters, demanding to know the truth of the rumor.

From the beginning, P&G took the Internet crisis seriously and immediately devised a retaliatory attack.

It launched a targeted letter campaign to more than 60,000 pet breeders and veterinarians, to communicate that Febreze was safe for pets.

It created a Web site campaign, soliciting statements from third-party organizations that refuted the rumor.

It launched an aggressive TV and print ad campaign to assure consumers that the product was safe for pets.

In every case, P&G's response was straightforward and hard hitting. It answered all the questions that the Internet rumor had raised. The company sought out testimonials from such groups as the American Society for the Prevention of Cruelty to Animals, the Humane Society and the American Veterinary Medical Association.

Finally, the company contacted the managers of so-called Urban Legend Web sites—sites that follow vicious, unfounded rumors—to request that they notify P&G the next time such slanderous accusations are discovered.

P&G's retaliatory campaign cost the company $100,000. As to finding the originator of the rumor and taking legal action against them—forget it. It's almost impossible. The best, and often only, response to Internet rumors, as P&G demonstrated, is to take them very seriously.

people—upwards of 65%—hear the words "no comment," they perceive the no-commenter as "guilty." Silence angers the media and compounds the problem. On the other hand, inexperienced spokespersons, speculating nervously or using emotionally charged language, are even worse.

Most public relations professionals consider the cardinal rule for communications during a crisis to be: TELL IT ALL AND TELL IT FAST!

As a general rule, when information gets out quickly, rumors are stopped and nerves are calmed. There is nothing complicated about the goals of crisis management. They are (1) terminate the crisis quickly, (2) limit the damage, and (3) restore credibility.[12] When crisis hits, the organization must assess its communications—particularly in evaluating media requests—by answering the following questions:

1. **What do we gain by participating?** If you have absolutely nothing to gain from an interview, then don't give one. Period.
2. **What are the risks?** The answer is based on your level of comfort with the medium, who the interviewer is, the amount of preparation time available to you, legal liability, and how much the organization loses if the story is told without the interview.
3. **Can we get our message across?** Will this particular medium allow us to deliver our message clearly to the public?
4. **Is this audience worth it?** Often, a particular television program or newspaper may not be germane to the specific audience the organization needs to reach.
5. **How will management react?** An important variable in assessing whether to appear is the potential reaction of top management. In the final analysis, you have to explain your recommendation or action to them.
6. **Does your legal liability outweigh the public interest?** This is seldom the case, although company lawyers often disagree.
7. **Is there a better way?** This is a key question. If an uncontrolled media interview can be avoided, do so. However, reaching pertinent publics through the press is often the best way to communicate in a crisis.[13]

A shorthand approach to communicating in crisis would include the following 10 general principles:

1. Speak first and often
2. Don't speculate
3. Go off the record at your own peril
4. Stay with the facts
5. Be open, concerned, not defensive
6. Make your point and repeat it
7. Don't war with the media
8. Establish yourself as the most authoritative source
9. Stay calm, be truthful and cooperative
10. Never lie

In the final analysis, communicating in a crisis depends on a rigorous analysis of the risks versus the benefits of going public. Communicating effectively also depends on the judgment and experience of the public relations professional. Every call is a close one, and there is no guarantee that the organization will benefit, no matter what course is chosen. One thing is clear: Helping to navigate the organization through the shoals of a crisis is the ultimate test of a public relations professional.

BACKGROUNDER

The Lessons of Valdez

Remember the *Exxon Valdez* case discussed in chapter 7? Because you've probably already dissected it thoroughly, it won't matter if we divulge here, courtesy of crisis expert Tim Wallace, how Exxon should have handled the situation.

1. **Develop a clear, straightforward position.** In a crisis, you can't appear to waffle. You must remain flexible enough to respond to changing developments, but you must also stick to your underlying position. Exxon's seemed to waver.
2. **Involve top management.** Management must not only be involved, it must also appear to be involved. In Exxon's case, from all reports, Chairman Lawrence Rawl was involved with the Gulf of Valdez solutions every step of the way. But that's not how it appeared in public. Rather, he was perceived as distant from the crisis. And Exxon suffered.
3. **Activate third-party support.** This support may come from Wall Street analysts, independent engineers, technology experts, or legal authorities. Any objective party with credentials can help your case.
4. **Establish an on-site presence.** The chairman of Union Carbide flew to Bhopal, India, in 1984, when a Carbide plant explosion killed thousands. His trip at least showed corporate concern. When Chairman Rawl explained that he "had better things to do" than fly to Valdez, Exxon effectively lost the public relations battle.
5. **Centralize communications.** In any crisis, a communications point person should be appointed and a support team established. It is the point person's job—and his or hers alone—to state the organization's position.

6. **Cooperate with the media.** In a crisis, journalists are repugnant; they're obnoxious; they'll stoop to any level to get the story. But don't take it personally. Treat the media as friendly adversaries and explain your side of the crisis. Making them enemies will only exacerbate tensions.
7. **Don't ignore employees.** Keeping employees informed helps ensure that the organization's business proceeds as normally as possible. Employees are your greatest ally. Don't keep them in the dark.
8. **Keep the crisis in perspective.** Often management underreacts at the start of a crisis and overreacts when it builds. The prevailing wisdom seems to be, "Just because we're paranoid doesn't mean they're not out to get us!" Avoid hunkering down. Exxon made this mistake, and it cost them dearly.
9. **Begin positioning the organization for the time when the crisis is over.** Concentrate on communicating the steps that the organization will take to deal with the crisis. Admit blame if it's due. Then quickly focus on what you are doing now rather than on what went wrong.
10. **Continuously monitor and evaluate the process.** Survey, survey, survey. Take the pulse of your employees, customers, suppliers, distributors, investors, and, if appropriate, the general public. Determine whether your messages are getting through. Constantly check to see which aspects of the program are working and which are not. Adjust accordingly.*

Tim Wallace, "Crisis Management: Practical Tips on Restoring Trust," The Journal of Private Sector Policy (November 1991): 14.

BACKGROUNDER

The "Gates" of Scandal

Government crisis has dogged every recent American administration. Most of the time, the crisis is conveniently dubbed "gate" of one form or another. Here, alphabetically listed, are some of the most well-known presidential "gates."

- Billygate—President Carter's brother represented business interests of terrorist nation Libya
- Bimbogate—Collective reference to charges that President Clinton has a roving eye
- Coffeegate—President Clinton hosted White House "coffees" to raise funds for Democrats
- Filegate—Low-level operatives in the Clinton administration obtained hundreds of classified FBI files
- Irangate (aka Olliegate or Contragate)—Operatives in President Reagan's administration traded arms for U.S. hostages and used the cash to finance Nicaraguan rebels
- Iraqgate—President Bush's administration encouraged massive shipments of arms to Saddam Hussein in his fight against Iran

- Lancegate—President Carter's budget director Bert Lance entangled himself in dubious banking deals
- Lippogate—President Clinton was accused of currying favor with the Lippo group of Indonesia that gave massive campaign contributions
- Nannygate—President Clinton's attorney general appointees were defeated because of federal tax infractions regarding their child-care workers
- Passportgate—President Bush's State Department searched for rival Clinton's passport records to prove he dodged the draft
- Travelgate—President Clinton's White House travel staff was dismissed for apparent political motives
- Watergate—President Nixon's undoing that started it all

With a new century and new president in the White House, it remains to be seen what new "gates" await us all.

SUMMARY

Although prevention remains the best insurance for any organization, crisis management has become one of the most revered skills in the practice of public relations. Organizations of every variety are faced, sooner or later, with a crisis. The issues that confront society—from energy and the environment, to health and nutrition, to corporate social responsibility and minority rights—will not soon abate.

All of this suggests that experienced and knowledgeable crisis managers who can skillfully navigate and effectively communicate, turning crisis into opportunity, will be valuable resources for organizations in the 21st century. In the years ahead, few challenges will be more significant for public relations professionals than helping to manage crisis.

Discussion Starters

1. What is meant by the term *issues management?*
2. How can an organization influence the development of an issue in society?
3. What are the general steps in implementing an issues management program?
4. What are the usual stages that an organization experiences in a crisis?
5. What are the principles in planning for crisis?

```
        top of the shelf
```

Joe Marconi

Crisis Marketing: When Bad Things Happen to Good Companies, 2nd ed.
Lincolnwood, IL: NTC Business Books, 1997.

"It can't happen to us." Don't be so sure. The possibilities of a crisis are endless: natural disasters, equipment breakdown, sabotage on the Internet, workplace violence, a product recall, litigation—you name it. Rise above complacency. Be a good public relations professional. Be a good scout. Be prepared.

Joe Marconi, a prolific, award-winning author (*The Complete Guide to Publicity, Image Marketing*), is also a seasoned pro in crisis marketing and management.

In this book, he draws on that experience in providing guidelines for identifying what can go wrong, showing how to position your organization before a crisis occurs, explaining why you should expect and be ready for a crisis, and telling you what to do first in the face of a crisis and what to do next.

Crisis Marketing helps you develop a framework for managing when public or business sentiment seems likely to turn against your company.

6. What is the cardinal rule for communicating in a crisis?
7. What are the keys to successful crisis communication?
8. What is the meaning of the term *reputation management?*
9. Why were people suspicious of the parents of JonBenet Ramsey?
10. What are likely to be the flashpoint crisis issues in the new century?

Notes

1. Helio Fred Garcia, *Crisis Communications* vol. 1 (New York: American Association of Advertising Agencies, 1999): 9.
2. "Lucent Falls Amid Speculation It's Under SEC Probe," *Bloomberg News Service* (January 14, 2000).
3. Samuel Maull, "Grand Jury Indicts Rap Artist 'Puffy' on Weapons Charges," *The Record* (January 14, 2000): A–4.
4. Rochelle Sharpe, "Mitsubishi U.S. Unit Hasn't Contacted Government of Sexual Harassment Cases," *Wall Street Journal* (April 26, 1996): B2.
5. "Issues Management Conference—A Special Report," *Corporate Public Issues* 7, no. 23 (December 1, 1982): 1–2.
6. Kerry Tucker and Glen Broom, "Managing Issues Acts as Bridge to Strategic Planning," *Public Relations Journal* (November 1993): 38.
7. Jeffrey P. Julin, "Is 'PR' a Risk to Effective Risk Communication?" *IABC Communication World* (October 1993): 14–15.
8. William C. Adams, "Strategic Advice in Handling Risk," presented during the Business, Environmental Issues, and Risk Conference, Washington, D.C., November 12, 1992.
9. Fraser P. Seitel, "Crisis Communications: The Strategy Is to Have a Strategy," *401(k) Alert* (April 1998):1, 3.
10. Sam Ostrow, "Managing Terrorist Acts in the Age of Sound Byte Journalism," *Reputation Management* (November–December 1996): 75–76.

11. Garcia, *Crisis Communications:* 42.

12. Kathy R. Fitzpatrick and Maureen Shubow Rubin, "Public Relations vs. Legal Strategies in Organizational Crisis Decisions," *Public Relations Review* (Spring 1995): 22.

13. Martin Arnold, "Crisis Communication: My View," *IABC Communication World* (June 1989): 44.

Suggested Readings

Antin, Angel. "Dealing with Deadly Bacteria." *Public Relations Tactics* (March 1998): 1–3.

Budd, John F., Jr. "The Downside of Crisis Management." *Public Relations Strategist* (Fall 1998): 36.

Bugliarello, George. "Telecommunities: The Next Civilization." *The Futurist* (September–October 1997): 23–26. Without loyalties to country, region, etc., telecommunities will change society economically, politically, and culturally.

Center, Allen H., and Patrick Jackson. *Public Relations Practices: Managerial Case Studies and Problems,* 6th ed. Upper Saddle River, NJ: Prentice Hall, 2000.

Coombs, Timothy W. "An Analytic Framework for Crisis Situations: Better Responses from a Better Understanding of the Situation." *Journal of Public Relations Research* 10, no. 3 (1998): 177.

Cooper, Martin M. "Working with Senior Management in a Crisis." *Public Relations Tactics* (March 1997): 2.

Coulter, Patrick. "A Merger Is Nothing but a Planned Crisis." *Communication World* (December 1996–January 1997): 22–24,

Davidson, D. Kirk. *Selling Sin: The Marketing of Socially Unacceptable Products.* Westport, CT: Quorum Books, 1996. Discusses the way crisis-oriented products, such as cigarettes, alcohol, gambling, and firearms are marketed and the problems they present.

Dosier, Dow. "Employee Communications at Kerr-McGee in the Aftermath of the Oklahoma City Bombing." *Public Relations Quarterly* (Summer 1998): 13.

Fallows, James. *Breaking the News: How the Media Undermine American Democracy.* New York: Pantheon, 1996. *U.S. News and World Report*'s editor-in-chief goes at the journalistic jugular vein, exposing the media as a collection of pompous pretenders who delight in creating crisis out of any insignificant issue. (And that's the good part!)

Fearn-Banks, Kathleen. *Crisis Communications: A Casebook Approach.* Mahwah, NJ: Lawrence Erlbaum Associates, 1996. Recommends a plan for preventing and dealing with crises based on communication theories.

Ferguson, Mary Ann, Joann M. Valenti, and G. Melwani. "Communicating with Risk Takers: A Public Relations Perspective." *Public Relations Research Annual,* vol. 3. Hillsdale, NJ: Lawrence Erlbaum Associates, 1993.

Frazier, Douglas. "Crisis Planning for Digital Disasters." *Public Relations Tactics* (July 1998): 16.

Gantz, Stanton A., John Slade, Lisa A. Bero, Peter Hanauer, and Deborah E. Barnes. *The Cigarette Papers.* Berkeley: University of California Press, 1996. The authors analyze some 10,000 pages of documents from Brown and Williamson Tobacco Corporation on the company's research into the addictive aspects of cigarettes and smoking. A fascinating dissection.

Gjelten, Tom. *Sarajevo Daily: A City and Its Newspaper Under Siege.* New York: HarperCollins Publishers, 1995. A story from the heart of the Bosnian crisis, written by the National Public Radio correspondent in the region during the vicious Bosnian war.

Gonzalez, Hernando, and William C. Adams. "A Life-Saving Public-Private Partnership: Amoco and Florida International University's Hurricane Preparedness Program." *Public Relations Quarterly* (Winter 1997–98):28.

Hendrix, Jerry A. *Public Relations Cases,* 3rd ed. Belmont, CA: Wadsworth, 1997.

Howard, Elizabeth. "Swooshed! What Activists Are Teaching Nike." *Public Relations Strategist* (Fall 1998): 38.

Lerbinger, Otto. *The Crisis Manager.* Mahwah, NJ: Lawrence Erlbaum Associates, 1997. Focuses on organizations that have no choice but to accept crises as the price of doing business.

Logan, Dever. "Swissair Flight 111 Crash Tests PR Crisis Plans." *Public Relations Tactics* (December 1998): 4.

Mitroff, Ian I., et al. *The Essential Guide to Managing Corporate Crises: A Step-by-Step Handbook for Surviving Major Catastrophes.* New York: Oxford University Press, 1996.

O'Dwyer, Jack, ed. *Jack O'Dwyer's Newsletter.* Weekly newsletter. (271 Madison Ave., New York, NY 10016).

Pocket Guide to Preventing Sexual Harassment. Madison, CT: Business & Legal Reports, Inc., 1996. Thorough analysis of what constitutes sexual harassment and what to do about it.

Poe, Randall. "Where to Turn When Your Reputation Is at Stake." *Across the Board* (February 1998): 16.

PR Reporter. Weekly newsletter. (Box 600, Exeter, NH 03833).

Public Relations Review. Quarterly. (Available from the Foundation for Public Relations Research and Education, University of Maryland College of Journalism, College Park, MD 20742.)

Shrader-Frechette, K. S. *Risk and Rationality: Philosophical Foundations for Populist Reforms.* Berkeley: University of California Press, 1991.

Simon, Raymond, and Frank W. Wylie. *Cases in Public Relations Management.* Lincolnwood, IL: NTC Publishing Group, 1994. Two eminent professionals discuss some of the most famous crisis management cases, including Hill & Knowlton, Kuwait, and Procter & Gamble, and news leaks.

Smith, Billy Layne. "Southern Cross: Jasper, Texas, Officials Diffuse a Potential Racial Powder Keg." *Public Relations Tactics* (September 1998): 2.

St. John, Burton. "Recovery Communications: Helping Your Employees Heal after Workplace Violence." *Public Relations Tactics* (May 1997): 1, 14, 27.

Suskind, Lawrence E. *Dealing with an Angry Public.* New York: The Free Press, 1996. Recommends strategies for dealing with crises, issues, and major public policies.

Tedeschi, Richard G., Crystal L. Park, and Lawrence G. Calhoun. *Posttraumatic Growth: Positive Growth in the Aftermath of Crisis.* Mahwah, NJ: Lawrence Erlbaum Associates, 1997.

Tucker, Kerry, Doris Derelian, and Donna Rouner. *Public Relations Writing: An Issue-Driven Behavioral Approach.* Upper Saddle River, NJ: Prentice Hall, 1997.

Vanderford, Marsha L., and David H. Smith. *The Silicone Breast Implant Story: Communication and Uncertainty.* Mahwah, NJ: Lawrence Erlbaum Associates, 1996.

Wenger, Ty. "When the Sports Hits the Fan: Crisis PR in the Age of Athlete Scandals." *Public Relations Tactics* (March 1997): 14–15.

Young, Davis. *Building Your Company's Good Name: How to Create the Reputation Your Organization Wants and Deserves.* New York: AMACOM, 1996. A how-to-book on reputation for business managers in organizations of all types.

C A S E   S T U D Y

Rebounding from the Ultimate Crisis

The worst tragedy that can befall any company is to see people die as a result of using your product.

When people died after contracting botulism from Bon Vivant soup, the company couldn't contain the media onslaught and quickly went out of business. By contrast, in history's greatest example of an effective public relations response, when individuals lost their lives after ingesting tainted Tylenol capsules, Johnson & Johnson and its clear-thinking CEO James Burke immediately stripped the product from store shelves—not once, but twice—to preserve the company's reputation and integrity.

On Saturday, May 11, 1996, after a ValuJet flight (Figure 9-7) went down in the alligator-infested waters of Florida's Everglades, the company added its name to the growing number of organizations opting for candor and honesty and human concern in the face of unspeakable horror, in this case the deaths of all 110 on board.

THE CRASH

When CEO Lewis Jordan got the call, he was heading a group of ValuJet employees who were building a Habitat for Humanity home that ValuJet Airlines was donating to a needy family. The program called for construction to start on May 11, with May 12 off, and then six days of work after that, with a dedication the following Saturday. This was the first day.

The communications director's pager registered "911," which signified an emergency. Jordan knew instinctively that the news wasn't good.

He jumped in his car and drove quickly to ValuJet's headquarters, near the Atlanta airport. When he reached the building and met with operational staff members, he knew the worst had happened. ValuJet had lost an airplane with 110 passengers and a crew of five—including a captain Jordan had personally hired.

THE PRESS CONFERENCE

Although he didn't have a great deal of information, approximately two hours later, Jordan removed his work shirt, put on a blue ValuJet pullover shirt, and proceeded to lead a hastily organized press conference. He decided immediately to communicate whatever information he had as quickly as possible.

Jordan understood the pitfalls that were possible in going public early, talking openly to the press, and in dealing with the toughest questions. He decided not to screen out any questions, refuse to take any questions, or cut anybody short. "To the contrary, I decided to take more time and if it meant answering the same question 10 times to do so. I've been in the airline industry long enough that I certainly had an appreciation that legal liability is a concern. I had an appreciation that there were financial implications and insurance issues and all kinds of issues. But I can tell you that beyond any of those thoughts—far and above any of the other concerns—the human side of this issue was the most important. And it was my honest belief that in setting the tone for what kind of a company ValuJet Airlines is in the face of a crisis—it was a certainty to me to put human compassion above everything else."

CRISIS PRIORITIES

Jordan also decided not to fly to the Everglades crash scene immediately. Rather, he decided to prioritize those things that needed to be done, that would have the most realistic and genuine probability of effectively handling the situation. At 2 a.m. Sunday he was on a flight to Miami for a morning media briefing, and to attend a family meeting.

The number 1 concern was for the family members who lost loved ones on the airplane. The ValuJet president said, "I also had a responsibility for leadership to the people of ValuJet Airlines. I had a responsibility to the community where this airline is based to answer any questions. As the news began to unfold, we still had another 50 airplanes out there in operation and part of my responsibility was to stand up and talk openly to the public about everything we knew and the things that we didn't know. I considered it not particularly wise in light of all this to depart Atlanta until later after first conducting a press briefing."

Jordan also chose not to subordinate the role of chief spokesperson to the press. "I really never thought that was an option," he said. He felt that with 30-plus years in the airline business, his background as an aerospace engineer, and experience in running maintenance and operations dictated that he was the one best suited to stand up there.

Added Jordan, "We knew there was speculation about whether the age of the airplane was a problem, and we didn't think that that was something that would be appropriate for others to be faced with answering. That was not a public relations issue. This was a real issue for our company, our customers, our employees, our shareholders."

THE COVERAGE

Immediately after the crash, Lewis Jordan went on a one-man offensive to save his company. Although the government suspended ValuJet in the aftermath of the crash, the company's president continued to publicly assert that ValuJet would survive and "be back stronger than ever."

What Jordan particularly resented about the coverage was what he called the "rush to judgment." He urged the press to withhold their thoughts on what might have caused the accident. Nonetheless, in the first 48 hours, reports aired all over the United States speculating on what may have caused the accident. Some reported, "These are 26-year-old airplanes; this must be an aging aircraft issue." Others said, "Everybody knows that ValuJet requires its pilots to pay for their own training." Some questioned the Pratt & Whitney engine, which had had failures in other airplanes. Jordan viewed all of this as "unfair, especially to family members who deserved to have facts." In the end, mismarked flammable containers placed in the cargo hold were found to have caused the tragedy.

Despite problems with coverage, ValuJet and Jordan maintained a totally open posture with the media. Assessing the coverage, Jordan said that he "found some really class people who showed a tremendous amount of dignity and poise and compassion. They understood what we were going through, and many would come up after the interview and shake hands and say, 'We're pulling for you and hang in there and you're doing a great job.' But we had others trying to win some sort of 'jerk of the year award.' Frankly, there were some isolated cases of people who just seemed to want to be nasty and provoke me. We were on a battlefield, where we were going to take hits. And we began to understand that certain publications and certain producers weren't going to tell our side in the world of sound bites and quick quotes; they would get something negative and put it out there."

The Employees, the Critics, the Aftermath

Through the crisis, ValuJet "embraced" its employees as surrogates in the company's fight for survival. The company began to immediately share all the information that it had with key managers. ValuJet put out internal bulletins, internal faxes, and regular updates through its voice mail system. At least once a week, Jordan would conduct a systemwide voice mail update for all employees.

Critics, like former government aviation watchdog Mary Schiavo, and various similarly disposed reporters, took ValuJet to task for inferior operations. The airline took the criticism stoically, choosing not to respond frontally but rather to point out how speculative the allegations were.

Although the airline faced difficult odds, it made a commitment not to give up. Jordan pointed to the support of his 4,000 employees that kept the organization going. By the summer of 1997, ValuJet was back up to about half the size of the airline when the crash occurred, with about 2,000 employees operating 31 airplanes and serving 24 cities. Even the harshest industry critics commended ValuJet and Jordan for facing up without hesitation to the enormity of the situation and the barrage of questions and accusations that could have spelled the demise of ValuJet itself.

Through it all, ValuJet's Jordan continually expressed a sincere concern for the families touched by the tragedy and a steadfast resolve that ValuJet, as an airline, would overcome its awful adversity. Despite significant odds against it, ValuJet returned to the skies and slowly but steadily increased its routes and regained customer confidence. In 1997, the airline merged with AirTran Airways and—probably wisely—changed its name to AirTran. For a time, reporters added their own tag line, "the airline formerly known as ValuJet."

Bonus Case: The Fall of TWA

Two months after the ValuJet crash, tragedy struck the airline industry again. Shortly after taking off from Long Island's Kennedy Airport on July 12, 1996, TWA Flight 800 blew up in a ghastly fireball over Long Island.

As opposed to the generally positive reviews that ValuJet received in its handling of its crash, TWA was assessed much more harshly.

Within hours of the initial reports of the crash, a frazzled TWA vice president of airport operations reluctantly faced the cameras and microphones. He was jacketless, his TWA employee badge draped around his neck, and way over his head. As the questions poured in—"Was it terrorism?" "Are there survivors?" "Was it a new crew?"—it became obvious that the TWA spokesman had few answers. Mercifully, after 15 minutes of non-answers, the operations manager excused himself and went home to sleep.

Meanwhile, TWA CEO Jeffrey Erickson was stranded in London, desperately trying to get to the Long Island crash. TWA's public relations spokespersons were stuck in corporate headquarters in St. Louis, also desperately trying to get to New York.

Alas, they arrived barely in time to pick up the pieces.

By the day after the crash, New York City Mayor Rudy Giuliani, other government officials, and even the families of those who died on board all blamed TWA management for "callousness and indifference." By the end of the tumultuous first week of the crash, President Clinton promised to "look into TWA's handling of the tragedy."

Later, TWA became more focused on its public relations response, and CEO Erickson appeared on network TV—most of the time in tandem with the head of the TWA flight attendants union. In fairness, TWA was hampered by an FBI and National Transportation Safety Board investigation that suspected terrorism and probably didn't want to say too much too soon. How much this hampered the TWA response is unclear. What is clear is that the airline's credibility was severely damaged by its non-response response to its most devastating crash.

Three months later, in October, Erickson, widely credited with reviving the financial fortunes of the airline, abruptly resigned as president of TWA. By the winter of 1997, the cause of what brought down Flight 800 was still not proven.

Postscript

In 1998 when a Swissair jet went down over the coast of Newfoundland, the CEO of Swissair—having learned from the experiences of both ValuJet and TWA—first flew to New York City for a press conference and turned around the next day for another session with the press in Newfoundland. Although once again, all aboard perished, Swissair's prompt and sensitive public response spared it the criticism that greeted TWA.

Questions

1. How would you characterize ValuJet's response to its crisis?
2. How would you describe Lewis Jordan's approach to public relations?
3. Was it wise for ValuJet not to delegate the role of chief spokesperson?
4. How would you contrast ValuJet's response to that of TWA in its crash?
5. How would you contrast the image of ValuJet's Jordan to TWA's Erickson?
6. Assuming the FBI limited TWA's response in its crash, what could the airline have done or said to bolster its credibility?
7. How is TWA announcing news about crises and potential problems? Visit its news release page (www.twa.com/pressrelease/) and read one or two news releases dealing with problems such as unscheduled landings and crash landings. Why would TWA issue press releases about problems in which no one was hurt and no property was damaged?

For further information about the ValuJet and TWA cases, see John Elsasser, "TWA's Long, Hot Summer," *Public Relations Tactics* (September 1996): 1; Chris Francescani and Kyle Smith, "Horror in the Sky: Downs 747 Off L.I.," *New York Post* (July 18, 1996): 3; Kenneth N. Gilpin, "TWA Chief Quits After Report of Loss," *New York Times* (October 25, 1996): D1; Michael J. Major, "After the Crash: Will ValuJet Fly High Again?" *Public Relations Tactics* (August 1996): 1; "Nothing Can Prepare You for This," *Reputation Management* (September–October 1996): 69; Carl Quintanilla, "TWA's Response to Crash is Viewed as Lesson in How Not to Handle Crisis," *Wall Street Journal* (July 19, 1996): Fraser Seitel, "TWA: Tragically Wrong Approach," *Ragan Report* (July 29, 1996): 2; "ValuJet Rebounding from Tragedy," *The Public Relations Strategist* (Summer 1997): 6.

An Interview with Lewis Jordan

Lewis H. Jordan was president of ValuJet Airlines when one of its airplanes went down in the alligator-infested waters of Florida's Everglades. The company responded by opting for candor and honesty and human concern in the face of unspeakable horror—the deaths of all 110 on board. Ultimately, the company was renamed AirTran, and Mr. Jordan succeeded in keeping it alive long enough to emerge with a new identity.

When you first got word of the crash, did you suspect the worst?
I knew that this was something very serious. You hope that a number of people survived and, even if there's been an accident, that maybe many people survived and it's all on a very serious but relative scale. I think human nature is such that you remain hopeful as long as you can.

What was going through your mind?
Extreme emotions of just the horror of losing the airplane with 110 people and a crew of five. We were recognizing names of people that we had known, like Captain Kubick, a woman I had personally participated in hiring.

Did you have a crisis plan?
Yes. There are responsibilities that go to each officer within the airline who is in touch with the National Transportation Safety Board. There is a "Go Team" that is immediately activated. An 800 number is set up for family members. And, of course, when we arrived at our office, the media were already sitting in the parking lot trying to get into the building. We knew we had to communicate whatever information we had as quickly as possible.

Were you concerned about saying something at the press conference that could cause legal problems?
I thought about many of the pitfalls that were possible in going public early and talking openly to the press, in dealing with the toughest questions. I decided not to screen out any questions, not to refuse to take any questions, and not to cut anybody short. I've been in the airline business long enough that I certainly had an appreciation that legal liability is a concern, that there were financial implications and insurance issues. But I can tell you that beyond any of those thoughts—far and above any of the other concerns—the human side of this issue was the most important. And it was my honest belief that in setting the tone for what kind of a company ValuJet Airlines is in the face of a crisis, it was a certainty to me to put human compassion above everything else.

How would you characterize the coverage the crash received and the treatment ValuJet was accorded?
The single, biggest factor that continues to stand out was what I call the "rush to judgment." I don't know how many times I urged the press to withhold their thoughts about what might have caused the accident. In the first 48 hours, reports aired all over the United States speculating what may have caused the accident—without any foundation. "These are 26-year-old airplanes; this must be an aging aircraft issue." People began to question the Pratt & Whitney engine, which had features in other airplanes. All of this was unfair, especially to family members who deserved to have the facts.

Did you feel it was your personal responsibility to interact with the families who lost people on the plane?
I knew it would be the toughest thing I had ever done in my life to walk into a large room full of families who had just lost loved ones on our airplane—recognizing that I would be allowing myself to be the most identifiable human being associated with ValuJet Airlines in a leadership role. But I remained very much involved with the families.

What was your overriding objective in managing the crisis?
We made a commitment not to give up. We had a company of 4,000 wonderful people who stood up and said they were proud of their company. I never had a doubt that we would make it back, because of the dedication of our people.

Chapter 10

Integrated Marketing Communications

In the 21st century, when Internet start-up companies think "public relations," they reach for the stars.

Hollywood stars, that is.

In order to break through the clutter and forge an identity through media publicity, new Internet companies are hitching their identity to that of well-known sports and entertainment personalities.

William Shatner, Captain Kirk of Star Trek *fame, became priceline.com's lead spokesman. Instead of cash, the actor took 100,000 stock options. Actress Whoopi Goldberg signed up with Flooz.com., a Web discount coupon site. Supermodel Cindy Crawford teamed up with eStyle, a women's retail outlet. Even "no respect" comic Rodney Dangerfield and 7-foot-tall drag queen RuPaul got into the act, with the former representing BargainBid.com and the latter WebEx, a provider of interactive Web meeting services.[1]*

Charities, too, recognized the impact of star power. Actor Michael J. Fox became a national spokesman for Parkinson's disease, with which he had been diagnosed. Talk show host Rosie O'Donnell authored a book on breast cancer, donated its proceeds to the cause, and became its spokesperson. Singer Patti LaBelle was recruited to warn minorities of the dangers of diabetes.[2]

Pop culture is so important as a publicity tool that corporations compete with each other to land plum properties. American Eagle Outfitters ousted J. Crew Group as the official provider of cargo pants, surfing shirts, and halter tops to the highly rated teen television drama "Dawson's Creek." American Eagle, in fact, not only sponsored the show but also agreed to feature the actors wearing its clothes in catalogs, store ads, and at its Web site.[3]

What all these tie-ins represent, according to at least one observer, is the death of "the practices of marketing, advertising, and public relations, as we have known them."[4]

What this perhaps overzealous observer referred to was the irrepressible intertwining of the heretofore separate disciplines of advertising, marketing, sales promotion, and public relations into a sometimes "unholy alliance" to win consumer support. The symbiosis of these different disciplines was dubbed integrated marketing communications.

As integrated marketing becomes more and more the rule in agencies and companies, the need for communications cross-training—to learn the different skills of marketing, advertising, sales promotion, and public relations becomes a requirement for all communicators.

Integrated marketing means approaching communications issues from the customer's perspective. Consumers don't separate promotional material or newspaper advertising or community responsiveness into separate compartments. They lump everything together to make judgments about services and organizations.

Integrated marketing expert Mitch Kozikowski lists six maxims that can guide public relations professionals through the communications cross-training process:

1. *Integrated marketing communication is not about ads, direct mail pieces, or public relations projects. It is about understanding the consumer and what the consumer actually responds to. In other words, behavioral change is the communicator's mission. If the customer doesn't act, the communicator—and the communication—have failed.*

2. *Organizations can't succeed without good relationships with their publics. Organizations need relationships with their customers that go beyond the pure selling of a product or service. They need to build relationships. As the world becomes more competitive in everything from health care to auto repair, from selling insurance to selling cereal, relationship building becomes more critical.*

3. *Integrated marketing communications requires collaboration on strategy, not just on execution. This means that the entire communications function must be part of the launch of a product, service, campaign, or issue from its inception. In other words, communicators must participate in the planning of a campaign, not just in the implementation of communications vehicles.*

4. *Strategic plans must be clear on the role that each discipline is to play in solving the problem. The roles of advertising, marketing, and public relations are different, none of them can do everything by itself. Therefore, although advertising might control the message, and marketing and product promotion might provide support, it is public relations that should provide credibility for the product and, even more important, for the organization.*

5. *Public relations is about relationships. Public relations professionals can become proprietors of integrated marketing communications. Because the essence of public relations is building relationships between an institution and its publics, public relations professionals, perhaps more than any other, should lead the integrated marketing initiative. Public relations professionals have long understood the importance of the two-way communication that builds strong relationships with customers and others. Such an understanding is pivotal to the successful rendering of integrated marketing communications.*

6. *To be players in integrated marketing communications, public relations professionals need to practice more than the craft of public relations. Simply stated, public relations people must expand their horizons, increase their knowledge of other disciplines, and willingly seek out and participate in interdisciplinary skills building. In other words, public relations professionals must approach their task, in the broadest terms, to enhance customer relationships through a strategy of total communications.*[5]

Elements of public relations—among them product publicity, special events, spokesmanship, and similar activities—can enhance a marketing effort. A new discipline—marketing communications—has emerged that uses many of the techniques of public relations. Although some may labor over the relative differences and merits of public relations versus advertising versus marketing versus sales promotion, the fact remains that a smart communicator must be knowledgeable about all of them.

Public Relations Versus Marketing

Marketing, literally defined, is the selling of a service or product through pricing, distribution, and promotion. Public relations, liberally defined, is the marketing of an organization. Most organizations now realize that public relations can play an expanded role in marketing. In some organizations, particularly service companies, hospitals, and nonprofit institutions, the selling of both individual products and the organization itself are inextricably intertwined.

Stated another way, although the practice of marketing creates and maintains a market for products and services and the practice of public relations creates and maintains a hospitable environment in which the organization may operate, marketing success can be nullified by the social and political forces public relations is designed to confront—and thus the interrelationship of the two disciplines.[6]

In the past, marketers treated public relations as an ancillary part of the marketing mix. They were concerned primarily with making sure that their products met the needs and desires of customers and were priced competitively, distributed widely, and promoted heavily through advertising and merchandising. Gradually, however, these traditional notions among marketers began to change for several reasons.

- ◪ Consumer protests about both product value and safety and government scrutiny of the truth behind product claims began to shake historical views of marketing
- ◪ Product recalls—from automobiles to tuna fish—generated recurring headlines
- ◪ Ingredient scares began to occur regularly
- ◪ Advertisers were asked how their products answered social needs and civic responsibilities

◪ Rumors about particular companies—from fast-food firms to pop-rock manufacturers—spread in brushfire manner

◪ General image problems of certain companies and industries—from oil to banking—were fanned by a continuous blaze of media criticism

The net impact of all this was that even though a company's products were still important, customers began to consider a firm's policies and practices on everything from air and water pollution to minority hiring.

Beyond these social concerns, the effectiveness of advertising itself began to be questioned. The increased number of advertisements in newspapers and on the airwaves caused clutter and placed a significant burden on advertisers who were trying to make the public aware of their products. In the 1980s, the trend toward shorter TV advertising spots contributed to three times as many products being advertised on TV as there were in the 1970s. In the 1990s, the spread of cable TV added yet another multichanneled outlet for product advertising. In the 2000s, the proliferation of Internet advertising—$1.5 billion in the last quarter of 1999 alone—intensified the "noise" and "clutter." Against this backdrop, the potential of public relations as an added ingredient in the marketing mix has become increasingly credible.

Indeed, marketing guru Philip Kotler has suggested that to the traditional four Ps of marketing—product, price, place, and promotion—a fifth P, public relations, should be added. Kotler argues that a firm's success depends increasingly on carrying out effective marketing thinking in its relationships with 10 critical players: suppliers, distributors, end users, employees, financial firms, government, media, allies, competitors, and the general public. In other words, public relations.[7]

Product Publicity

In light of how difficult it now is to raise advertising awareness above the noise of so many competitive messages, marketers are turning increasingly to product publicity as an important adjunct to advertising. Although the public is generally unaware of it, a great deal of what it knows and believes about a wide variety of products comes through press coverage.

In certain circumstances, product publicity can be the most effective element in the marketing mix. For example:

◪ Creating an identity for an Internet company that can't afford to blast out expensive advertising but must be "heard" above the din of thousands of competitors.

◪ Introducing a revolutionary new product. Product publicity can start introductory sales at a much higher level of demand by creating more awareness of the product.

◪ Eliminating distribution problems with retail outlets. Often, the way to get shelf space is to have consumers demand the product. Product publicity can be extremely effective in creating consumer demand.

◪ Small budgets and strong competition. Advertising is expensive. Product publicity is cheap. Often, publicity is the best way to tell the story. Sam Adams Boston Lager beer, for example, became a household word almost solely through publicity opportunities.

◪ Explaining a complicated product. The use and benefits of many products are difficult to explain to mass audiences in a brief ad. Product publicity, through extended news columns, can be invaluable.

FIGURE 10-1 **Ringing the bell.** Ernie Keebler rings the opening bell, marking the first day of public trading for the stock of Keebler Foods Company on the New York Stock Exchange.

- Generating new consumer excitement for an old product. Repackaging an old product for the media can serve as a primary marketing impetus.
- Tying the product to a unique representative. "Morris the Cat" was one answer to consumer uninterest in cat food. Ronald McDonald attended the Academy Awards ceremonies. On April Fool's Day, 1996, Taco Bell "bought" the Liberty Bell before announcing the ruse.[8] Figure 10-1 illustrates yet another unique and memorable representative.

Third-Party Endorsement

Perhaps more than anything else, the lure of third-party endorsement is the primary reason smart organizations value product publicity as much as they do advertising. Third-party endorsement refers to the tacit support given a product by a newspaper, magazine, or broadcaster who mentions the product as news. Advertising often is perceived as self-serving. People know that the advertiser not only created the message but also paid for it. Publicity, on the other hand, which appears in news columns, carries no such stigma. Editors, after all, are considered objective, impartial, indifferent, neutral. Therefore, publicity appears to be "news" and is therefore more trustworthy than advertising, paid for by a clearly nonobjective sponsor.

Editors have become sensitive to mentioning product names in print. Some, in fact, have a policy of deleting brand or company identifications in news columns. Public relations counselors argue that such a policy does a disservice to readers, many of whom are influenced by what they read and may desire the particular products

FIGURE 10-2 **Sticky subject.** But also publicizable. When the Peanut Advisory Board wished to publicize its favorite product, it helped students at a high school in Peanut, Pennsylvania, create the world's largest peanut butter and jelly sandwich, measuring nearly 40 feet long.

discussed. Counselors further argue that journalists who accept and print public relations material for its intrinsic value and then remove the source of the information give the reader or viewer the false impression that the journalist generated the facts, ideas, or photography.

Equally reprehensible are the public relations practitioners who try to place sponsored features without disclosing promotional origins. In other words, some companies will distribute cartoons or stories—either directly or through mail-order services—without identifying the sponsor of the material. Obviously, such a practice raises ethical questions. Understandably, editors do not soon forgive firms that sponsor such anonymous articles. One solution to achieve product recognition through the "endorsement" of objective editors is to create events that are certain to attract publicity (Figure 10-2).

Building a Brand on the Web

The "watchword" in business today is *branding,* creating a differentiable identity for a company or product.

In more traditional times, it took years for brands like Pepsi, Coke, McDonald's, and Wal-Mart to establish themselves. Today, with the advent of the World Wide Web, Internet companies like Yahoo!, Amazon.com, eBay, and E*TRADE have become household words in a historical nanosecond. Using integrated marketing communications to establish a unique brand on the Web requires adherence to the following principles.[9]

- **Be early.** Web history—and product history as well—indicates it is better to be first than to be best. This results from the "law of primacy," which posits that people are more likely to remember you if you were the first in their minds in a particular category. Whether yours is really the "first" Web brand is less important than establishing primacy in the minds of consumers.

A QUESTION OF ETHICS

Meanie Beanies

FIGURE 10-3 **The end of an era? Not exactly.**

"Good-bye Beanie Babies".

Alas, that was the plaintive cry of youngsters around the world after beanie maker Ty Inc. of Oak Brook, Illinois, made the following startling announcement on its Web site in September 1999:

> "VERY IMPORTANT NOTICE: On December 31, 1999, 11:59 P.M. (CST) all Beanies will be retired."

Worldwide reaction among Beanie Baby consumers was a combination of shock and sadness.

- "Beanie Babies May be Going Bye Bye," headlined *USA Today*. "Beanie Baby Blues," headlined the *New Jersey Record*.
- The *New York Times* reported one Las Vegas mother trying to figure out what to tell her 10-year old. "I think it will be sad for the kids," she said.

For its part, the company was about as forthcoming as a politician caught in a sex scandal.

Customer service representatives, reached at headquarters, suggested that the staff had been told of the "retirement" only the day before and had no further information. Ty public relations managers told the media, "We have no comment; we have nothing to say." As far as interviews with the firm's reclusive CEO, Ty Warner, as his spokesmen put it, "It's not going to happen."

Some observers thought the whole thing was a giant marketing hoax, designed to prop up interest in a rapidly flagging product.

- *USA Today* quoted the editor of an industry newsletter who noted that Beanie Babies were waning as the toy of choice among children and that "word of new releases or retirement always gets the hype back up."
- Likewise, a dubious New Jersey toy store proprietor concluded, "They're trying to start a rush on the stores by saying, 'This is the end of it forever.' "

Others wondered how a company that depends, after all, on the faith and trust and goodwill of children could possibly be so capricious with such a tender commodity.

The first part of the answer arrived in the last week of the old millennium.

On December 24, 1999, just as suddenly as the "Beanie Baby retirement" announcement had appeared, www.ty.com posted the following:

> "I have received hundred of letters from children, educators, hospitals, clinics, charities, and collectors around the world asking me to reconsider my decision and create new Beanies.
>
> "After much thought, I am willing to put the fate of Beanie Babies in your hands."
>
> Ty Warner

The public, he said, would call an 800 number to "vote" on whether Beanie Babies would continue to be produced in the millennium. If the public voted, "yes," than Mr. Warner, in an unprecedented act of kindness and generosity, would accede to the children's wishes.

Not surprisingly, on January 3 of the new millennium, Ty Inc. announced that the public had voted to continue producing Beanie Babies, and the public would be served.

Some observers hailed Mr. Warner as a marketing genius in the best traditions of P. T. Barnum—able to resurrect a commodity heading south with a burst of unbridled showmanship. Others—perhaps recalling how benign and lovable an earlier generation's darlings, the Cabbage Patch Kids (Figure 10-4), were—felt it was unfair, even unethical, to so transparently play on the emotions of children, not to mention a gullible public. Mr. Warner couldn't be reached for comment.

FIGURE 10-4 **Cabbage Patch Kids in happier times.**

☑ **Be memorable.** Equally important is to fight through the clutter with your URL, by creating a memorable brand. There is no more competitive area in business today than the Internet. Hundreds of thousands of companies are fighting for recognition. Dotcoms, in particular, need to generate awareness and attention to introduce themselves to the public and get noticed by Wall Street.[10] The 2000 Super Bowl, for example, drew nearly 20 Internet advertisers, from Angeltips.com to Oxygen Media, that paid an estimated average of $2 million for each 30-second commercial.

☑ **Be aggressive.** A successful Web brand also requires a constant drumbeat of publicity to keep the company's name before the public. Potential customers need to become familiar with the brand. Potential investors need to become confident that the brand is an active one. Indeed, more and more, marketers, Web-based and others, are "taking to the streets" to spread their message (Figure 10-5). So while traditional jewelry companies might be more refined and understated, Web jeweler Mondera.com was eager to announce in January 2000 that it had completed the "largest confirmed on-line diamond sale."[11] An Internet economy leaves little room for demure integrated marketing communications.

☑ **Choose a proper partner.** Most successful Web brands have built their franchise by teaming up with others. A most significant partnership was the marriage in 2000 of venerable Time Warner and upstart America Online. Affiliating with a prominent partner helps, through a positive association, to improve and expand the image of the organization.

☑ **Create a personality.** It is probably more important for an Internet company to create a "personality" for its brand than it is for a more traditional firm. That personality should be reflected on-line and in all communications materials the organization produces. A celebrity front person can greatly enhance such an organization's image. Iconoclastic rocker David Bowie, for example, lent his name in 2000 to on-line financial services provider USABancShares.com. Earlier, the aging rock star offered security bonds backed by sales of his record titles and created an on-line fan club, BowieNet that attracted 15,000 members at $5.95 a pop to join.

FIGURE 10-5 **Taking it to the streets.** Transportation displays to promote brands, such as this traveling Hershey's Kissmobile created by mobile marketing expert Marketing Werks, have become popular marketing devices for Web-based and non-Web companies alike.

◪ **Promote the IPO.** In the 21st century, when an Internet company sells its shares to the public, it is big news. Such Initial Public Offerings (IPOs) should be promoted aggressively, again to lift a brand above the Web clutter. This was the approach in introducing the Dr.koop.com IPO in the late 1990s, which attached its name to the fame of its founder, former surgeon general C. Everett Koop. The early effort proved valuable, not only in promoting the stock to great heights but also in ensuring that Dr.koop.com was among the top health sites on the Internet, attracting 2.5 million visitors monthly.[12]

As more and more companies each year attempt to bust through the Internet clutter by resorting to such marketing devices as banner ads, proprietary Web sites, free classified advertising, e-zines and e-mail marketing, the challenge to create a differentiable Web brand becomes that much more difficult.

Public Relations Marketing Activities

Beyond integrated marketing on the Web, a number of more traditional public relations activities are regularly used to help market products. These activities include article reprints, trade show participation, the use of spokespersons, and cause-related marketing.

Article Reprints

Once an organization has received product publicity in a newspaper or magazine, it should market the publicity further to achieve maximum sales punch. Marketing can be done through article reprints aimed at that part of a target audience—wholesalers, retailers, or consumers—that might not have seen the original article. Reprints also help reinforce the reactions of those who read the original article.

As in any other public relations activity, use of reprints should be approached systematically, with the following ground rules in mind:

1. **Plan ahead, especially if an article has major significance to the organization.** Ideally, reprints should be ordered before the periodical goes to press so that customers can receive them shortly after the article hits the newsstands.
2. **Select target publics and address the recipients by name and title.** This strategy will ensure that the reprint reaches the most important audience.
3. **Pinpoint the reprint's significance.** Accomplish this either by underlining pertinent information in the article, making marginal notes, or attaching a cover letter. In this way, the target audience will readily understand.
4. **Integrate the reprint with other similar articles and information on the same or related subjects.** Often, several reprints can be combined into a single mailing piece. Also, reprints can be integrated into press kits and displays.

Trade Show Participation

Trade show participation enables an organization to display its products before important target audiences. The decision to participate should be considered with the following factors in mind:

1. **Analyze the show carefully.** Make sure the audience is one that can't be reached effectively through other promotional materials, such as article reprints or local publicity. Also, be sure the audience is essential to the sale of the product. For example, how responsible are the attendees for the actual purchase?
2. **Select a common theme.** Integrate public relations, publicity, advertising, and sales promotion. Unify all elements for the trade show and avoid, at all costs, any hint of interdepartmental rivalries.
3. **Make sure the products displayed are the right ones.** Decide well in advance exactly which products are the ones to be shown.
4. **Consider the trade books.** Often, trade magazines run special features in conjunction with trade shows, and editors need photos and publicity material. Always know what special editions are coming up as well as their deadline schedules.
5. **Emphasize what's new.** Talk about the new model that's being displayed. Discuss the additional features, new uses, or recent performance data of the products displayed. Trade show exhibitions should reveal innovation, breakthrough, and newness.
6. **Consider local promotional efforts.** While in town during a trade show, an organization can enhance both the recognition of its product and the traffic at its booth by doing local promotions. This strategy involves visiting trade

magazine editors and local media people to stir up publicity for the product during the show.[13]

7. **Evaluate the worth.** Always evaluate whether the whole exercise was worth it. This involves counting, qualifying, and following up on leads generated as well as looking at other intangibles to see if marketing objectives were met.[14]

Use of Spokespersons

In recent years, the use of spokespersons to promote products has increased. Spokespersons shouldn't disguise the fact that they are advocates for a particular product. Their purpose is to air their sponsor's viewpoint, which often means going to bat for a controversial product.

Spokespersons must be articulate, fast on their feet, and thoroughly knowledgeable about the subject. When these criteria are met, the use of spokespersons as an integrated marketing tool can be most effective.

Lately, the use of spokespersons to promote products has become so crazed that in his rookie year, professional basketball player Allen Iverson not only signed a $50 million multiyear contract for Reebok sportswear, but got stock on top of it. Then along came another rookie basketball phenom, Vince Carter, who walked away from a 10-year, $800,000 annual endorsement contract from Puma, because the shoe company didn't quickly introduce a shoe line in the star's name.[15]

Then there is the case of Tiger Woods who, in 1997, after winning the Masters Golf Tournament, announced that he would "limit" his sponsorships, so he "dipped his toe in the water" by signing a $40 million deal with Nike for athletic shoes and apparel, a $20 million deal with Titleist for golf clubs and balls, and a $7 million deal with Official All Star Cafe, the celebrity restaurant chain, whose co-owners included fellow sports stars Andre Agassi, Wayne Gretzky, Shaquille O'Neal, and Ken Griffey Jr.[16] Not a bad "dip."

Spokespersons come in a variety of sizes, shapes, and occupations. They range from corporate chairmen like Wendy's CEO Dave Thomas, who regularly hawks his hamburgers, to comedian Jay Leno for Doritos brand corn chips to former news anchor David Brinkley for Archer Daniels Midland food products.

Beyond question, however, the most lucrative spokesmanship contract in history belongs to former boxing champ George Foreman, who in 1999 sold his name and image to Salton, the maker of George Foreman's Lean Mean Fat-Reducing Grilling Machine. The price to Salton and payday for Mr. Foreman? $137.5 million.[17] Who says boxers are punchy?

Cause-Related Marketing

Special public relations events also help to market products. Grand-opening celebrations, for example, are a staple in the public relations arsenal. They present publicity opportunities and offer businesses a chance to meet customers face-to-face. With the cost of print and broadcast advertising going up each year, companies increasingly are turning to sponsorship of the arts, education, music, festivals, anniversaries, sports, and charitable causes for promotional and public relations purposes.

Such cause-related marketing is popular. Cause-related marketing brings together the fund-raising needs of nonprofit groups with the business objectives of sponsoring companies. The latest trend is Web-based cause-related marketing, where e-retailers donate part of their on-line sales to charitable institutions.

Such cause-related marketing will continue to grow in the 21st century. Baby boomers are now middle-aged and more concerned about issues that affect their lives, like protecting the environment and aiding the less fortunate. This change in itself will drive the creation of events and decision making by corporate sponsors.

In planning special events and cause-related marketing activities, public relations people should first determine what area will best suit their organization's particular marketing objectives—culture, sports, community sponsorship, entertainment, and so on. Once objectives are decided, cause-related marketing can significantly enhance the reception and overall sales of a product or institution.

Public Relations Advertising

Traditionally, organizations used advertising to sell products. In 1936, though, a company named Warner & Swasey initiated an ad campaign that stressed the power of America as a nation and the importance of American business in the nation's future. Warner & Swasey continued its ads after World War II and thus was born a unique type of advertising—the marketing of an image rather than a product. This technique became known variously as *institutional advertising, image advertising, public service advertising,* and ultimately *public relations advertising.*

In the 1970s, opponents of American business began to flex their muscles, with advertisements critical of big business and its practices. Corporations responded with ads of their own that talked about social responsibility, equal employment hiring, minority assistance, and so on. This practice was labeled image advertising. In the 1980s, the logical extension of image advertising was issues advertising, which advocated positions from the sponsor's viewpoint. Often these concerned matters of some controversy. Organizations, led by the outspoken Mobil Corporation, continued the practice of issue ads into the 1990s. Indeed, Mobil's practice of placing an issues ad on the Op-Ed page of the *New York Times* and other leading newspapers each Thursday continued into its fourth decade and is still going strong in the new century. In the 2000s, public interest groups have once again seized upon the most pressing issues of the day and are running ads to characterize their questions of business practices (Figure 10-6).

Purposes of Public Relations Advertising

Traditional public relations, or nonproduct, advertising—as opposed to image or issue positioning—is still widely used. Such advertising can be appropriate for a number of activities:

1. **Mergers and diversifications.** When one company merges with another, the public needs to be told about the new business lines and divisions. Advertising provides a quick and effective way to convey this message.
2. **Personnel changes.** A firm's greatest asset is usually its managers, its salespeople, and its employees. Presenting staff members in advertising not only impresses a reader with the firm's pride in its workers, but also helps build confidence among employees themselves.
3. **Organizational resources.** A firm's investment in research and development implies that the organization is concerned about meeting the future intelligently, an asset that should be advertised. The scope of a company's services also says something positive about the organization.

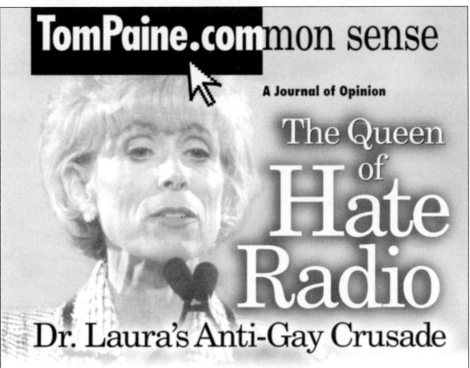

TomPaine.common sense

A Journal of Opinion

The Queen
of
Hate
Radio

Dr. Laura's Anti-Gay Crusade

Sometimes bigotry earns its just reward . . . sometimes not.

Atlanta Braves pitcher John Rocker . . . suspended. The same for *60 Minutes'* Andy Rooney. Ex-NFL star Reggie White and CBS commentator Jimmy The Greek . . . both fired.

All were penalized for making bigoted comments in public about minorities—gay people, Native Americans, African Americans.

Then there's Dr. Laura Schlessinger.

Twenty million listeners make her talk radio's top-rated host.

Her mean and arrogant advice has made her wealthy. It's proof that cheap thrills sell. If that's what people want to hear, no problem.

But Dr. Laura also uses her electronic pulpit to broadcast bigotry and misinformation about homosexuals.

She says homosexuality is a "biological error." She calls gays and lesbians "deviants" who "undermine civilization." She associates homosexuality with pedophilia. She claims gay parents are bad parents, and that homosexuality can be cured.

Scientific research soundly refutes her, yet Dr. Laura's profitable fear-mongering continues.

Now prominent religious leaders, mental health experts, human rights and civil rights groups,

almost 200 organizations and individuals in all, have called on Dr. Laura to end her gay baiting.

They don't want to censor her. They just want her to stop and think.

"This is an appeal for Dr. Laura to consider the consequences of the anti-gay prejudice she is regularly spouting," says Peter Teague of the Horizons Foundation, which is leading the call (www.horizonsfoundation.org). "She needs to recognize the connection between words and violence against gay people."

Ironically, now Dr. Laura is teaming up with Paramount Studios to launch a TV show.

Paramount grants benefits to the same-sex partners of its employees. It seems Dr. Laura doesn't mind doing business with "deviants" who "undermine civilization" . . . if there's money to be made.

So much for her convictions.

Sometimes bigotry does NOT earn its just reward.

***This week at TomPaine.com: The Queen of Hate Radio—Dr. Laura's Anti-Gay Crusade.** Featuring An Open Letter to Dr. Laura . . . A profile by Bill Berkowitz, Alternet.org . . . Ellen Ratner on Leaving Well Enough Alone . . . and our Unofficial Sources links.*

■ **TomPaine.com.** *Money and Politics. Environment. Media Criticism. History.*

© 2000 The Florence Fund, 1636 Connecticut Avenue NW, Washington, DC 20009

FIGURE 10-6 **Issues advertising.** In the best tradition of pioneer public relations pamphleteer Thomas Paine, tompaine.com and the Florence Fund sponsored hard-hitting ads, such as this about a popular radio cum TV talk show host.

4. **Manufacturing and service capabilities.** The ability to deliver quality goods on time is something customers cherish. A firm that can deliver should advertise this capability. Likewise, a firm with a qualified and attentive servicing capability should let clients and potential clients know about it.

5. **Growth history.** A growing firm, one that has developed steadily over time and has taken advantage of its environment, is the kind of company with which people want to deal. It is also the kind of firm for which people will want to work. Growth history, therefore, is a worthwhile subject for non-product advertising.

6. **Financial strength and stability.** A picture of economic strength and stability is one that all companies like to project. Advertisements that highlight the company's financial position earn confidence and attract customers and investors.

7. **Company customers.** Customers can serve as a marketing tool, too. Well-known personalities who use a certain product may be enough to win additional customers. This strategy may be especially viable in advertising for higher priced products such as expensive automobiles or sports equipment.

8. **Organization name change.** With firms in industries from banking to consumer products to communications now either merging with each other or streamlining their operations, company names change—from AOL, Time and Warner Brothers to AOLTime Warner, from Federal Express to FedEx, from Kentucky Fried Chicken to KFC. To burnish the new name in people's minds, a name change must be well promoted and well advertised. Only through constant repetition will people become familiar with the new identity.

9. **Trademark protection.** Companies such as Xerox and Coca-Cola, whose products are household names, are legitimately concerned about the improper generic use of their trademarks in the public domain. Such companies run periodic ads to remind people of the proper status of their marks. In one such ad, a perplexed secretary reminds the boss, "If you had ordered 40 photocopies instead of 40 Xeroxes, we wouldn't have been stuck with all these machines!" (Figure 10-7).

10. **Corporate emergencies.** Occasionally, an emergency situation erupts—a labor strike, plant disaster, or service interruption. One quick way to explain the firm's position and procedures without fear of distortion or misinterpretation by editors or reporters is to buy advertising space. This tactic permits a full explanation of the reasons behind the problem and the steps the company plans to take to resolve the dilemma.

Integrated Marketing for the 21st Century

Beyond advertising, marketing, and public relations techniques, integrated marketing, too, must keep pace with the ever-changing world of promotional innovations to help sell products and services. Selling products on the Internet, as noted, introduces a new spectrum of possibilities for public relations support. Communications professionals also must be familiar with such increasingly popular vehicles as infomercials, 900 numbers, and movie product placements.

You can't Xerox a Xerox on a Xerox.

But we don't mind at all if you copy a copy on a Xerox copier.

In fact, we prefer it. Because the Xerox trademark should only identify products made by us. Like Xerox copiers and Xerox printing systems.

As a trademark, the term Xerox should always be used as an adjective, followed by a noun. And it's never used as a verb.

XEROX® is a trademark of XEROX Corporation.

Of course, helping us protect our trademark also helps you. Because you'll continue to get what you're actually asking for.

And not an inferior copy.

XEROX
The Document Company

FIGURE 10-7 Too "household" a name. Xerox is one company with the rare problem of a brand name that is so well known, it has become generic.

Infomercials

Infomercials were greeted with universal catcalls in the 1980s when they were introduced as program-length commercials, shamelessly hawking products. Even today, the infomercial remains the Rodney Dangerfield of marketing, shunned and doubted for many reasons—state and federal investigations of infomercial producers, complaints about product performance, and, most important, the belief, still, that a lengthy commercial disguised as a conventional program—like a talk show, complete with theme song and studio audience—unfairly masks what is nothing more than a failed spiel.[18]

Nonetheless, infomercials are growing in popularity for one reason: They work. Indeed, George Foreman's success with his grills is just one example. Between $1 billion and $2 billion worth of merchandise is sold each year as a result of infomercials. Today even the most well-established organizations run infomercials. Celebrities from Cher to Martin Sheen to Suzanne Somers to Dionne Warwick have joined the growing parade of infomercial pitchmen.

900 Numbers

Establishing a 900 telephone number is another way of publishing and selling information. Such numbers charge callers for the privilege of tuning in to current business news headlines, stock quotes, or sports information. Just as infomercials were laughed at, 900 numbers were once associated more with parties and steamy adult sex than with mainstream marketing. In the 1990s, though, that situation has changed. At the same time as the government has cracked down on 900 phone services with increased regulations, Fortune 500 corporations, publishers, TV and movie companies, consumer products manufacturers, law firms, counseling services, nonprofit organizations, and even government agencies have joined the 900 marketing cavalcade, and revenues from 900 numbers total upwards of $900 million a year.

FIGURE 10-8 The pioneer. This lovable alien professed his predilection for Reese's Pieces, and a new integrated marketing discipline was born.

TV-Movie Product Placements

Product placements in films and TV shows also are proliferating at a rapid rate. The turning point in product plugs occurred three decades ago when M&M/Mars turned down filmmaker Steven Spielberg, when he offered to link M&Ms to the hero of his new movie, E. T. Reese's Pieces, however, took up the movie producer's offer, and the rest is history (Figure 10-8). AOL, Coca-Cola, McDonald's, and Microsoft all pay huge sums for the privilege of having their product's name mentioned by Sylvester Stallone or Wesley Snipes or Arnold Schwartzenegger. Such product placements in films have become another merchandising resource that communicators should consider as part of their integrated marketing communications strategy.

BACKGROUNDER

Of Clammy Sosa and Shark McGwire: IMC for the New Century

There is no question that, with the Internet, more rapid and pervasive communications, and shorter attention spans among consumers, communicators must pull out all the creative and innovative stops in the new century to stimulate, interest, entertain, and persuade.

In the 2000s, messages must be delivered with a verve and imaginativeness that cuts through the noise and dislodges the clutter attendant in 24/7 communications around the globe.

Introducing. . . . ZOOperstars!, an integrated marketing creation for the new century.

The brainchild of three Louisville, Kentucky, promotionally savvy sports enthusiasts, ZOOperstars! entertains at baseball diamonds, hockey arenas, and basketball courts throughout the land. Through its combination of sports heroes and "animal magnetism," ZOOperstars! provides a fresh approach to using celebrities as drawing cards.

The height of integrated marketing communications for the 21st century.

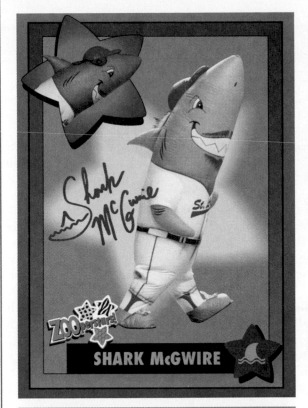

SHARK McGWIRE

CLAMMY SOSA

DENNIS FROGMAN

HARRY CANARY

FIGURE 10-9 **ZOOperstars!** The latest approach to celebrity "spokespersons"?

S U M M A R Y

Marketing expert Al Ries, who cut his teeth in the advertising industry, has changed his tune. "In the past, it may have been true that a beefy advertising budget was the key ingredient in the brand-building process. . . . Today brands are born, not made. A new brand must be capable of generating favorable publicity in the media or it won't have a chance in the marketplace."[19] In other words, says Ries, it is public relations and its attendant communications form not advertising alone that differentiates an organization, product, or issue.

In other words, what is needed now is an integrated approach to communications, combining the best of marketing, advertising, sales promotion, and public relations. Some public relations people feel threatened by such talk. The thought of working closely with marketing, advertising, direct mail, sales promotion, and database marketing specialists worries them.[20] They fear the subjugation of the practice of public relations to these other disciplines.

Nonetheless, relationship building for organizations of every stripe now holds the key to a successful enterprise. Building lasting relationships—including, importantly, over the Internet—must be the objective for any intelligent organization.

This implies the need for a communications professional knowledgeable about all aspects of the communications mix. Integrated marketing communications then becomes paramount in preparing public relations professionals for the challenges of the 21st century.

Discussion Starters

1. What is meant by integrated marketing communications?
2. Describe the differences among advertising, marketing, and public relations.
3. What is meant by third-party endorsement?
4. Discuss the phenomenon of the integrated marketing on the Web.
5. Describe the pros and cons of using someone well-known as a spokesperson.
6. What is cause-related marketing?
7. What is image advertising? Issues advertising?
8. What are the purposes of public relations advertising?
9. What stimulated the reemergence of public relations advertising in the 1990s?
10. What are infomercials? 900 phone numbers?

Notes

1. Stephanie Arnout, "Big Names Striking Big Deals on the Net," *USA Today* (December 28, 1999): 1, 2.
2. Helen Bond, "Cause Celeb," *Dallas Morning News* (November 8, 1999): C1, 2.
3. Rebecca Quick, "Fashion Coup at Dawson's Creek," *Wall Street Journal* (June 22, 1999): B1, 6.
4. Fraser P. Seitel, "Communications Cross-Training," *U.S. Banker* (June 1993): 53.

5. Mitchell Kozikowski, "The Role of Public Relations in Integrated Marketing Public Relations," address presented to the National Conference of the Public Relations Society of America, November 15, 1993, Orlando, FL.

6. "Colloquium of Marketing and PR Spokespersons Agrees Organizations Suffer When Turf Wars Occur," *Public Relations Reporter* (February 13, 1989): 1.

7. Tom Harris, "Kotler's Total Marketing Embraces MPR," *MPR Update* (December 1992): 4.

8. Judann Pollack, "New Marketing Spin: The PR 'Experience,' " *Advertising Age* (August 5, 1996): 33.

9. Julie McHenry, "Building Brands on the Web," *Tactics* (November 1999): 15, 16.

10. Stuart Elliott, "The Super Bowl is Attracting a Crowd of New Competitors," *New York Times* (November 29, 1999): C22.

11. "Jewel of the Bile," *The Industry Standard* (January 24, 2000): 39.

12. "RX For Success," *The Industry Standard* (January 24, 2000): 284.

13. Susan Friedman, "Tips for Internal and External Trade Show Visitors," *Business Marketing* (June 1995).

14. Kathy Burnham, "Trade Shows: Make Them Worth the Investment," *Tactics* (September 1999): 11.

15. Sam Walker, "NBA Star Cries Foul, Walks Away from Puma Shoe Deal," *Wall Street Journal* (December 1, 1999): B2.

16. Kerry Capell, "Tiger, Inc.," *Business Week* (April 28, 1997): 32.

17. Richard Sandomir, "A Pitchman with Punch," *New York Times* (January 21, 2000): C1, 4.

18. Stuart Elliot, "Some Big Marketers Join Audience for Infomercials," *New York Times* (June 5, 1992): D9.

19. Al Ries and Laura Ries, "The Power of Publicity," *The Public Relations Strategist* (Winter 1998): 19.

20. "Integrated Marketing: Is It PR's Nemesis or Salvation?" *O'Dwyer's PR Services Report* (January 1995): 1.

top of the shelf

Al Ries and Laura Ries

The 22 Immutable Laws of Branding: How to Build a Product or Service into a World-Class Brand. New York: HarperBusiness, 1998.

"Branding" was probably public relations and marketing's last buzzword of the last millennium, but it is bound to be with us for sometime to come. In this little (182 pages) book, two world-renowned marketing experts distill the complex principles and theories espoused in other long-winded, high-priced books. They offer 22 quick and easy-to-read vignettes using such well-known companies as Starbucks, Miller Brewing, Honda, and Heineken to illustrate, both in the practice and in the breach, the authors' "22 Immutable Laws."

Note Law number 3: The Law of Publicity: "The birth of a brand is achieved with publicity, not advertising."

Suggested Readings

Aaker, David A. *Building Strong Brands.* New York: The Free Press, 1995. Predicts over the next three decades there will be an unmitigated "battle of the brands."

Albrecht, Karl. *The Only Thing That Matters: Bring the Power of the Customers into the Center of Your Business.* New York: Harper Business, 1993.

Beard, Christel K. "Web Site Worthiness: How Some Organizations Reap Rewards." *Public Relations Tactics* (Nov. 1998): 28.

Caywood, Clarke L., ed. *The Handbook of Strategic Public Relations and Integrated Communications.* New York: McGraw-Hill, 1997.

"Changing World of Marketing: Conference Summary Report No. 92-112." Cambridge, MA: Marketing Science Institute, 1992.

Corporate Advertising Practices. New York: Association of National Advertisers, 1991.

Fowles, Jib. *Advertising and Popular Culture.* Thousand Oaks, CA: Sage, 1995.

Frank, Robert H., and Philip J. Cook. *The Winner Take All Society.* New York: The Free Press, 1996. A critical look at a marketing society that encourages economic waste, growing economic inequality, and senseless consumption.

Gregory, James R., and Jack G. Wiechmann. *Marketing Corporate Image.* New York: NTC Business Books, 1998.

Harris, Thomas L. *The Marketer's Guide to Public Relations.* New York: John Wiley & Sons, 1993.

Harris, Thomas L. *Value-Added Public Relations: The Secret Weapon of Integrated Marketing.* Lincolnwood, IL: NTC Business Books, 1998.

Hartman, Jason. *Become the Brand of Choice: How to Earn Millions Through Relationship Marketing.* Greensboro, NC: Lifestyles Press, 1999.

Howard, Carole M. "Marketing Communications: Teamwork and Sophisticated Sequencing Will Maximize Results." *Public Relations Quarterly* (Winter 1997–98): 23ff.

Hutton, James G. "Integrated Marketing Communications and the Evolution of Marketing Thought." *Journal of Business Research* 37, 1998, 155–62. Distinguishes among "integrated marketing communications," "integrated marketing," and "integrated communications."

Janal, Daniel S. *Online Marketing Handbook.* New York: Von Nostrand Reinhold, 1995. How to sell, advertise, publicize, and promote products on the Internet.

Janal, Daniel S. *The Online Marketing Handbook: How to Promote, Advertise and Sell Your Products and Services on the Internet.* New York: John Wiley & Sons, 1996.

Marconi, Joe. *Image Marketing.* New York: NTC Business Books, 1996.

Mingo, Jack. *How the Cadillac Got Its Fins.* New York: Harper Business, 1995. Case histories behind the invention and marketing of famous products.

Ogilvy, David. *Confessions of an Advertising Man.* New York: Macmillan, 1963.

Parmerlee, David. *Preparing the Marketing Plan.* New York: NTC Business Books, 1996.

Percy, Larry. *Strategies for Implementing Integrated Marketing Communications.* Lincolnwood, IL: NTC Business Books, 1997.

Ritchie, Karen. *Marketing to Generation X.* New York: Lexington Books, 1995. Foreshadowing the interactive, integrated marketing communications in the 21st century.

Schmitt, Bernd, and Alex Simpson. *Marketing Aesthetics: The Strategic Management of Brands, Identity and Image.* New York: The Free Press, 1997.

Schultz, Don E., Stanley I. Tannenbaum, and Robert F. Lauterborn. *Integrated Marketing Communications: Putting It Together and Making It Work.* Lincolnwood, IL: NTC Business Books, 1998.

Spataro, Mike. "Net Relations: A Fusion of Direct Marketing and Public Relations." *Direct Marketing* (August 1998): 16ff. Companies must use the Internet as an essential part of their marketing mix.

CASE STUDY

Gloriously Promoting a Dead President

On Saturday, December 18, 1999, exactly 200 years to the day after the funeral of George Washington, the president's memorial homestead of Mount Vernon faithfully re-created the event. The reenactment brought to a close a full year of activities commemorating the bicentennial of Washington's death.

It also closed the curtain on one of the most successful integrated marketing efforts of all times.

The planning and implementation by Mount Vernon Executive Director James Rees and Public Relations Manager Sally McDonough of The George Washington Bicentennial is testimony to the impact of public relations on an integrated marketing program.

Here, in step-by-step progression, is what the Mount Vernon officials pulled off and how they accomplished it.

THE BACKGROUND

George Washington is the most familiar face in American history (Figure 10-10). If we're lucky, we see him every day when we open our wallets.

President George is a public relations professional's dream: a client with instant, universal name recognition. But getting people to focus on and appreciate Washington's importance is quite another matter.

Fifty years ago, George Washington's portrait hung in virtually every classroom in the nation. Thirty years ago, George Washington's birthday was an important national holiday, complete with a day off and commemorative parades. Today, alas, this is no longer the case. Indeed, some locales—New Orleans is a prominent one—have even taken to removing Washington's name from schools, because he was a slave owner.

As the century ended, the problem of our first president's fading recognition was a particularly urgent one for the people responsible for managing and staffing historic Mount Vernon, Washington's Virginia homestead (Figure 10-11). Faced with shrinking attendance, due in part to an overall decline in America's interest in history museums, Mount Vernon officials contemplated steadily dwindling revenues from entrance fees.

FIGURE 10-10 The big guy.

FIGURE 10-11 **The homestead.**

FIGURE 10-12 **The logo.**

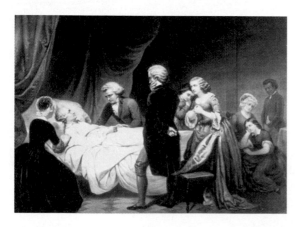

FIGURE 10-13 **The death.**

Educational surveys provided the early warning signs:

- Half of America's children couldn't name the purpose of the Declaration of Independence
- Only 7 percent of fourth graders could identify "an important event" that took place in Philadelphia in 1776
- Only six of 10 children knew why the Pilgrims came to America
- Seven of 10 fourth-grade students believed that Illinois, California, or Texas were among the 13 original colonies

Clearly, Mount Vernon had a problem.

THE CHALLENGE

The "Big Guy" had lost his importance in the minds of many Americans. The task of winning back those hearts and minds fell to the Mount Vernon staff. To change perceptions about Mount Vernon and George Washington required the full panoply of communications tools: partners, programs, publications, exhibitions, special events, and lots of media attention. That, in essence, was the challenge.

THE HOOK

With society moving at warp speed, people needed a reason to slow down and learn more about George Washington. They needed a "hook." The hook became the 200th anniversary of Washington's death, December 14, 1999. Critics, upon hearing of the hook, warned that celebrating someone's death was not only morbid and depressing but, frankly, wouldn't work.

THE LOOK

An early decision was to create a special logo for the bicentennial anniversary (Figure 10-12). This approach was so innovative that it attracted a front-page story in the *New York Times*, "Calling Up the P.R. Troops for the Father of His Country." The story talked about how $3 million would be spent on the public relations facelift. Mount Vernon's celebration was off and running.

THE PARTNERS

Part of Mount Vernon's strategy was to enlist respected partners to help share the burden of mounting a major bicentennial celebration (Figure 10-13). (Mount Vernon officials learned early not to "celebrate" Washington's death but rather to celebrate his life and "commemorate" his death.) Other patriotic groups were recruited to participate, and the Ford Motor Company, which had been a long-standing supporter of Mount Vernon, agreed to become a major partner.

THE PROGRAM

Armed with a hook, a look, money, and committed partners, Mount Vernon officials now needed "substance"—a program to celebrate, uh, commemorate. They began, fittingly, with research, polling historians, surveying their publics and relying on historical facts. They met with numerous experts to ensure historical accuracy of the programs contemplated. They discussed the delicate balancing act between morbid and educational, even including a facsimile of the room where Washington was bled four times with crude instruments and ultimately died (Figure 10-14). Most of all, they set out to design events that would overcome the "George Washington boring" image and the Mount Vernon "been there, done that" syndrome.

FIGURE 10-14 The death scene.

THE PREPARATION

To mount a national exhibition, historic Mount Vernon had to literally be transformed. Buildings were painted, rooms restored, and acquisitions made. Enthusiasm among staff members was contagious.

THE PROMISE

Visitors were promised that if they came to Mount Vernon during 1999, they would view an all-new property, including 100 different, original objects in Washington's home. To do this, Mount Vernon had to borrow most of the valuable artifacts from sister institutions. In the process, the Mount Vernon board had to install a state-of-the art climate control, which angered some who believed authenticity would be ruined with such a system.

With the system in place, however, the museum was able to borrow and display rare items, such as Washington's last will and testament and his presidential desk (Figure 10-15).

THE PLAN

The first-ever traveling exhibition, "Treasures from Mount Vernon," was launched. It pictured Washington as a friend, father, and statesman. Pulling out all the stops, the exhibition even included George Washington's famous false teeth, made of wood as it turned out. Smaller exhibitions also were staged, and objects were loaned to other institutions. A 16-page bicentennial community celebration planner was mailed to 50,000 communities to help them stage their own celebrations. Nearly 1,000 did just that.

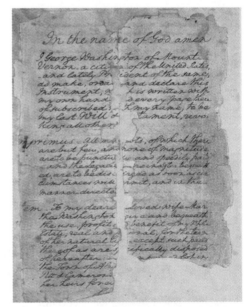

FIGURE 10-15 The will.

The U.S. Postal Service designed a special stamp and postcard. The U.S. Mint designed a commemorative coin. The governors of 38 states sponsored special Washington bicentennial proclamations. Three pieces of original music and nine new Washington statues were commissioned around the celebration.

THE RESULTS

Mount Vernon closed the year 1999 with more than 1 million visitors, its highest attendance in two decades. Mount Vernon was featured in 10 articles in the *New York Times,* 25 in the *Washington Post,* five in *USA Today,* two in the *Wall Street Journal*

FIGURE 10-16 **The tomb.**

and at least one in the top 10 newspapers in the nation. Major features were run on *CBS Sunday Morning,* ABC's *Good Morning America, The CBS Evening News,* CNN and C-Span. Major articles appeared in magazines such as *New Yorker, Modern Maturity, Colonial Homes,* and *Virginia Cavalcade,* which devoted an entire issue to the "Father of Our Country."

When the celebration ended with the reenactment of Washington's funeral (Figure 10-16), attended by the president's descendants and relatives of the original pallbearers—all dressed in 18th-century mourning attire—the words of one of Washington's greatest admirers were recalled. Abraham Lincoln once said:

"Washington is the mightiest name of earth. . . To add brightness to the sun or glory to the name of Washington is alike impossible. Let none attempt it. In solemn awe pronounce the name, and in its naked deathless splendor leave it shining on."

Questions

1. What was the public relations "downside" of launching such a massive integrated marketing program for Mount Vernon?
2. What other integrated marketing communications elements might the organizers have considered to reinforce the bicentennial?
3. How important was publicity in the program to restore Washington's image?
4. What follow-up programs to continue the bicentennial momentum might Mount Vernon consider?
5. Why did the Pilgrims come to America?
6. Mount Vernon is using the Internet as part of its integrated marketing communications strategy (www.mountvernon.org.) What special events are being prominently promoted on the home page? What is the purpose of the guest book on this site?

OVER THE TOP

An Interview with Marvin Runyon

A veteran Ford Motor Company executive and head of the Tennessee Valley Authority, Marvin Runyon served as U.S. Postmaster General from 1992 to 1998. He quickly made a name for himself by transforming the bloated, lethargic, 800,000-employee operation, which was hemorrhaging $2 billion a year, into a leaner marketing machine, focused on one idea: "meeting customer needs." In addition to instituting service improvements across the board, Mr. Runyon adopted an aggressive integrated marketing program—including delivering the mail himself!—to shake up the post office's stodgy image.

What were among your first actions when you arrived at this gigantic, money-losing bureaucracy?
Two weeks after I got there, I sat down with all my officers. For two hours we talked about reducing over-

head. And so at the end of two hours we had a break, and I opened the discussion by explaining we needed to reduce overhead by 40 percent. Big silence. Finally, the first question somebody asked was, "What is overhead?" Good question. I said, "You know what, I hadn't thought about that." I'm new in the postal service, and I didn't know how you define overhead. So I defined it as anybody who doesn't touch the mail. And then we went to work in earnest. And in a couple of months, we had 46,000 people who retired.

Weren't you concerned about morale?
We were concerned, but I felt we should do it at once and be done with it. If you're going to do something, do it, and let the people know the parameters in which you're going to operate. We were very candid with everybody. We told them what was going on. We were going to operate like a business.

What about changing the culture?
The culture has to change. That's a very hard thing to work at. You do it by example. The first thing you had to change in the philosophy of the organization was to make people realize we were in business to serve our customers. You have to be credible. Credibility is something you really have to work on.

How can you enforce "credibility"?
You have to put some accountability into the organization. I started to talk to people about having to be accountable, credible. We finally got the organization to the point where they understood they could do good quality work more effectively and cheaper than bad work.

How did you assess the communications function in all this?
The communications department is not really capable of communicating with the entire organization. Rather, the job is to help people do the communication they need to do with their key publics. We've got a lot of publics. And as I see it, it's up to the communications organization to help come up with the messages that we need to be putting out and to make sure the message gets told. I see them as counselors, as opposed to being communicators. They're advisors and counselors to me.

How important is the communications function in an organization?
To me, communications is the most important thing you do in business. I have been saying that an awfully long time. If you can't communicate with your employees, your customers, your suppliers, then you're not going to do a good job.

What about visiting employees directly?
I'd interact with 1,000 people at a plant. Or I'd walk into a post office and interact with 15. We had a tremendous grapevine in the post office that is one of the best communications tools. I could walk into a post office with 10 employees and make a statement and be assured that every post office would hear it.

What are you proudest of in terms of your tenure at the post office?
I'm most proud of the postal service employees, who are being recognized for dealing with their customers in a very positive way, doing an outstanding job on service and on cost. We've got a lot of things that we've changed. The culture of the post service is different than it was. That's the thing that I'm most proud of.

FIGURE 10-18 **Marvin delivers the mail.**

Execution Part IV

Chapter 11

Public Relations Writing

Even in the age of the computer, writing remains the key to public relations.

The practice of public relations distinguishes professional communicators from amateurs. All of us know how to write and speak. But public relations professionals should write and speak better than their colleagues. Communication—that is, effective writing and speaking—is the essence of the practice of public relations.

What this means is that the ability to write easily, coherently, and quickly distinguishes the public relations professional from others in an organization. It's not that the skills of counseling and judgment aren't just as important; some experts argue that these skills are far more important than knowing how to write. Maybe. But not knowing how to write—how to express ideas on paper— may reduce the opportunities to ascend the public relations success ladder.

Senior managers usually have finance, legal, engineering, or sales back-grounds, where writing is not stressed. But when they reach the top, they are expected to write e-mails, articles, speeches, memos, and testimony. They then need advisers, who are often their trusted public relations professionals. That's why it's imperative that public relations students know how to write—even before they apply public relations techniques to cyberspace. Beginning public relations professionals are expected to have mastery over the written word. Chapters 11 and 12, properly preceding a discussion of "Public Relations and the Internet," focus on what public relations writing is all about.

What does it take to be a public relations writer? For one thing, it takes a good knowledge of the basics. Although practitioners probably write for a wider range of purposes and use a greater number of communications methods than do other writers, the principles remain the same, whether writing for the Internet, an annual report or a case history, an employee newsletter, or a pub-lic speech. This chapter and the next will explore the fundamentals of writing: (1) discussing public relations writing in general and news releases in particu-lar, (2) reviewing writing for reading, and (3) discussing writing for listening.

Writing for the Eye and the Ear

Writing for a reader differs dramatically from writing for a listener. A reader has certain luxuries a listener does not have. For example, a reader can scan material, study printed words, dart ahead, and then review certain passages for better understanding. A reader can check up on a writer; if the facts are wrong, for instance, a reader can find out pretty easily. To be effective, writing for the eye must be able to withstand the most rigorous scrutiny.

On the other hand, a listener gets only one opportunity to hear and comprehend a message. If the message is missed the first time, there's usually no second chance.

This situation poses a special challenge for the writer—to grab the listener quickly. A listener who tunes out early in a speech or a broadcast is difficult to draw back into the listening fold.

Public relations practitioners—and public relations students—should understand the differences between writing for the eye and the ear. Although it's unlikely that any beginning public relations professional would start by writing speeches, it's important to understand what constitutes a speech and how it's prepared and then be ready for the assignment when opportunity strikes. Because writing lies at the heart of the public relations equation, the more beginners know about writing, the better they will do. Any practitioner who doesn't know the basics of writing and doesn't know how to write—even in the age of the Internet—is vulnerable and expendable.

Fundamentals of Writing

Few people are born writers. Like any other discipline, writing takes patience and hard work. The more you write, the better you should become, provided you have mastered the basics. Writing fundamentals do not change significantly from one form to another.

What are the basics? Here is a foolproof, three-part formula for writers, from the novice to the novelist:

1. **The idea must precede the expression.** Think before writing. Few people can observe an event, immediately grasp its meaning, and sit down to compose several pages of sharp, incisive prose. Writing requires ideas, and ideas require thought. Ideas must satisfy four criteria:

   ☑ They must relate to the reader.
   ☑ They must engage the reader's attention.
   ☑ They must concern the reader.
   ☑ They must be in the reader's interest.

   Sometimes ideas come quickly. Other times, they don't come at all. But each new writing situation doesn't require a new idea. The trick in coming up with clever ideas lies more in borrowing old ones than in creating new ones. What's that, you say? Is your author encouraging "theft"? You bet! The old cliche, "Don't reinvent the wheel," is absolutely true when it comes to good writing. Never underestimate the importance of maintaining good files.[1]

2. **Don't be afraid of the draft.** After deciding on an idea and establishing the purpose of a communication, the writer should prepare a rough draft. This is a necessary and foolproof method for avoiding a mediocre, half-baked product. Writing, no matter how good, can usually be improved with a second look. The draft helps you organize ideas and plot their development before you commit them to a written test. Writing clarity is often enhanced if you know where you will stop before you start. Organization should be logical; it should lead a reader in a systematic way through the body of the text. Sometimes, especially on longer pieces, an outline should precede the draft.

3. **Simplify, clarify, aim.** In writing, the simpler the better. Today, with more and more consumers reading from computer screens, simplicity is imperative. The more people who understand what you're trying to say, the better your chances for stimulating action. Shop talk, jargon, and "in" words should be avoided. Clear, normal English is all that's required to get an idea across. In practically every case, what makes sense is the simple rather than the complex, the familiar rather than the unconventional, and the concrete rather than the abstract. Clarity is another essential in writing. The key to clarity is tightness; that is, each word, each passage, each paragraph must belong. If a word is unnecessary, a passage redundant, a paragraph vague—get rid of it. Writing requires judicious editing; copy must always be reviewed with an eye toward cutting.

4. **Finally, writing must be aimed at a particular audience.** The writer must have the target group in mind and tailor the message to reach them. To win the minds and deeds of a specific audience, one must be willing to sacrifice the understanding of certain others. Writers, like companies, can't expect to be all things to all people. Television journalist Bill Moyers offers this advice for good writing:

> Strike in the active voice. Aim straight for the enemy: imprecision, ambiguity, and those high words that bear semblance of worth, not substance. Offer no quarter to the tired phrase or overworn idiom. Empty your knapsack of all adjectives, adverbs, and clauses that slow your stride and weaken your pace. Travel light. Remember the most memorable sentences in the English language are also the shortest: "The King is dead" and "Jesus wept."[2]

Flesch Readability Formula

Through a variety of writings, the late Rudolf Flesch staged a one-man battle against pomposity and murkiness in writing.* According to Flesch, anyone can become a writer. He suggested that people who write the way they talk will be able to write better. In other words, if people were less inclined to obfuscate their writing with 25-cent words and more inclined to substitute simple words, then not only would communicators communicate better, but receivers would receive more clearly.

In responding to a letter, Flesch's approach in action would work as follows: "Thanks for your suggestion, Tom. I'll mull it over and get back to you as soon as I can." The opposite of the Flesch approach would read like this: "Your suggestion has been received; and after careful consideration, we shall report our findings to you."

---

*Among the more significant of Flesch's books are *Say What You Mean, The Art of Plain Talk, The Art of Readable Writing,* and *How to Be Brief: An Index to Simple Writing.*

B A C K G R O U N D E R

Speaking Like the Suits

Worried about fitting in a corporate environment? Concerned that the suits speak and write a different language than do you—more convoluted, hyperextended, and obtuse?

Relax. Thanks to a former corporate communicator at a Virginia bank, you can rely on the following "Jargon Master Matrix," a chart consisting of three columns of jargon words that can be mixed and matched for any occasion.*

Just select any three words from the three columns, such as "value-based process model" or "overarching support centralization" and you will fit right in.

1. overarching	visionary	objectives
2. strategic	support	alternatives
3. special	customer-oriented	expectations
4. specific	stretch	mechanisms
5. core	planning	assessment
6. long term	marketing	update
7. defined	service	model
8. technology-based	process	product
9. formal	fundamental	centralization
10. exceptional	sales	incentive
11. value-based	budget	initiatives
12. executive	operating	feedback
13. immediate	discretionary	infrastructure
14. interactive	tracking	proposition

Eileen Kinsella, "After All, What's a News Article but a Formalized Update Process?" Wall Street Journal, August 1, 1996, C1.

See the difference? In writing for the Internet, such straightforward writing is the only approach.

There are countless examples of how Flesch's simple dictum works.

☑ Few would remember William Shakespeare if he had written sentences like "Should I act upon the urgings that I feel or remain passive and thus cease to exist?" Shakespeare's writing has stood the test of centuries because of sentences such as "To be or not to be?"

☑ A scientist, prone to scientific jargon, might be tempted to write, "The biota exhibited a 100 percent mortality response." But, oh, how much easier and infinitely more understandable to write, "All the fish died."

☑ One of President Franklin D. Roosevelt's speechwriters once wrote, "We are endeavoring to construct a more inclusive society." FDR changed it to "We're going to make a country in which no one is left out."

☑ Even the most famous book of all, the Bible, opens with a simple sentence that could have been written by a twelve-year-old: "In the beginning, God created the heaven and the earth."

Flesch gave seven suggestions for making writing more readable.

1. Use contractions like "it's" or "doesn't."
2. Leave out the word "that" whenever possible.

3. Use pronouns like "I," "we," "they," and "you."

4. When referring back to a noun, repeat the noun or use a pronoun. Don't create eloquent substitutions.

5. Use brief, clear sentences.

6. Cover only one item per paragraph.

7. Use language the reader understands.

To Flesch, the key to all good writing was getting to the point. Stated another way, public relations writers, in writing for the Internet or any other medium, should remember their A's and B's:

- ☑ Avoid big words.
- ☑ Avoid extra words.
- ☑ Avoid cliches.
- ☑ Avoid Latin.
- ☑ Be specific.
- ☑ Be active.
- ☑ Be simple.
- ☑ Be short.
- ☑ Be organized.
- ☑ Be convincing.
- ☑ Be understandable.[3]

In addition to Flesch, a number of other communications specialists have concentrated on how to make writing more readable. Many have developed their own instruments to measure readability. The most prominent, the Gunning Fog Index, designed by Robert Gunning, measures reading ease in terms of the number of words and their difficulty, the number of complete thoughts, and the average sentence length in a piece of copy. Good writing can't be confusing or unclear. It must be understandable.

BACKGROUNDER

Nonreadability

Although Rudolf Flesch stressed the "readability" of writing, everyday we see numerous examples of writing that seeks to be anything but readable. To wit, the following, "Accident Report."

The party of the first part hereinafter known as Jack and the party of the second part hereinafter known as Jill ascended or caused to be ascended elevation of undetermined height and degree of slope, hereinafter referred as "hill." Whose purpose it was to obtain, attain, procure, secure, or otherwise, gain acquisition to, by any and/or all means available to them a receptacle or container, hereinafter known as "pail," suitable for the transport of a liquid whose chemical properties shall be limited to hydrogen and oxygen, the proportions of which shall not be less than or exceed two parts for the first men-tioned element and one part for the latter. Such a combination will hereinafter be called "water."

On the occasion stated above, it has been established beyond a reasonable doubt that Jack did plunge, tumble, topple, or otherwise be caused to lose his footing in a manner that caused his body to be thrust in a downward direction. As a direct result of these combined circumstances, Jack suffered fractures and contusions of his cranial regions. Jill, whether due to Jack's misfortune or not, was known to also tumble in a similar fashion after Jack. (Whether the term, "after," shall be interpreted in a spatial or time passage sense, has not been determined.)

The Beauty of the Inverted Pyramid

Newspaper writing is the Flesch formula in action. Reporters learn that words are precious and are not to be wasted. In their stories every word counts. If readers lose interest early, they're not likely to be around at the end of the story. That's where the inverted pyramid comes in. Newspaper story form is the opposite of that for a novel or short story. Whereas the climax of a novel comes at the end, the climax of a newspaper story comes at the beginning. A novel's important facts are rolled out as the plot thickens, but the critical facts in a newspaper story appear at the start. In this way, if readers decide to leave a news article early, they have already gained the basic ideas.

Generally, the first tier, or lead, of the inverted pyramid is the first one or two paragraphs, which include the most important facts. From there, paragraphs are written in descending order of importance, with progressively less important facts presented as the article continues—thus, the term inverted pyramid.

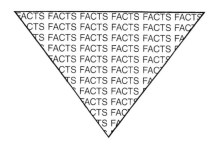

The lead is the most critical element, usually answering the questions concerning who, what, why, when, where, and occasionally how. For example, the following lead effectively answers most of the initial questions a reader might have about the subject of the news story.

> The Washington Bullets announced today that basketball legend Michael Jordan has become a part owner and will become president of basketball operations.

That sentence tells it all; it answers the critical questions and highlights the pertinent facts. It gets to the point quickly without a lot of extra words. In only 22 words it captures and communicates the essence of what the reader needs to know.

After the lead, the writer must select the next most important facts and array them in descending order, most important facts higher in the story. In this way, the inverted pyramid style is more the "selection and organization" of facts than it is an exercise in creative "writing."

This same style of straightforward writing forms the basis for the most fundamental and ubiquitous of all public relations tools: the news release (Figure 11-1).

The News Release

A valuable but much-maligned device, the news release is the granddaddy of public relations writing vehicles. Most public relations professionals swear by it. Some newspaper editors swear about it. Indeed, PR Newswire, a paid wire service used by public relations people to distribute releases, issues about 1,500 news releases every day.[4] The reason is that everyone uses the release as the basic interpretive mechanism to let people know what an organization is doing. There is no better, clearer, more

PEANUT BUTTER & JELLY CUPS

Contact: Felicia Roff
Vorhaus & Company Inc.
212.554.7438 – telephone
888.639.9857 – pager
froff@vorhaus.com

Don't You Wish You Could Be A Kid Again? Now You Can...

Russell Stover Introduces Peanut Butter and Jelly Cups
"Gushing With Flavor™"

Kansas City, MO, September 7, 1999 – Russell Stover introduces *Russell Stover Peanut Butter and Jelly Cups*, combining three of America's childhood favorites - peanut butter, jelly and chocolate. The new candy bar will be made with Welch's® Jelly, available in two flavors – grape and red raspberry, and promises to bring out the kid in all of us. The candy bar will be available in stores nationwide by July of 1999.

The concept for the new candy came from the company's co-president, Tom Ward, who cites his home life as the brainchild behind this new idea.

"Raising children renewed my love of peanut butter and jelly, and I realized we could combine these great tastes with chocolate and create something truly delicious," he said with a big smile. "*Peanut Butter and Jelly Cups* from Russell Stover are just plain good tasting fun."

To launch its new product, Russell Stover has embarked on one of the largest marketing campaigns in the candy industry, aiming at a nationwide audience. The campaign includes television and magazine advertising and a promotional newspaper coupon campaign.

- more -

Gushing with Flavor™

Russell Stover Candies, 4900 Oak Street, Kansas City, Missouri, 64112-2702, 1-800-777-4004

FIGURE 11-1 All the facts. Inverted pyramid writing style immediately answers everything you need to know about the newest candy bar creation.

persuasive way to announce news about an organization, its products and their applications than by issuing a news release.[5] That's why the news release deserves special attention as a public relations writing vehicle.

A news release may be written as the document of record to state an organization's official position—for example, in a court case or in announcing a price or rate increase. More frequently, however, releases have one overriding purpose: to influence a publication to write favorably about the material discussed. Each day, in fact, professionals send releases to editors in the hope of stimulating favorable stories about their organizations.

Most news releases are not used verbatim. Rather, they may stimulate editors to consider covering a story. In other words, the release becomes the point of departure for a newspaper, magazine, radio, or television story. Why, then, do some editors and others describe news releases as "worthless drivel"?[6] The answer, says researcher Linda Morton of the University of Oklahoma's Herbert School of Journalism, is threefold:

1. **Releases are poorly written.** Professor Morton found that most news releases are written in a more complicated and difficult-to-read style than most newspaper stories. "This could be the result of pressure from administrators as they review and critique press releases," she reasoned.

2. **Releases are rarely localized.** Newspapers focus largely on hometown or regional developments. The more localized a news release, the greater the chance it has of being used. However, according to Professor Morton, "Practitioners may not want to do the additional work that localization requires." This is a bad decision because research indicates that a news release is 10 times more likely to be used if it is localized.

3. **Releases are not newsworthy.** This is the grand dilemma. An editor will use a public relations release only if he or she considers it news. If it's not newsworthy, it won't be used. What determines whether something is news? Professor Morton suggests five requisites:

   ◪ Impact: a major announcement that affects an organization, its community, or even society

   ◪ Oddity: an unusual occurrence or milestone, such as the one millionth customer being signed on (Figure 11-2).

   ◪ Conflict: a significant dispute or controversy, such as a labor disagreement or rejection of a popular proposal

   ◪ Known principal: the greater the title of the individual making the announcement—president versus vice president—the greater the chance of the release being used

   ◪ Proximity: how localized the release is or how timely it is, relative to the news of the day.[7]

Beyond these characteristics, human interest stories, which touch on an emotional experience, are regularly considered newsworthy.[8] Research, however, indicates that the vast majority of public relations releases don't contain any of these elements, limiting their chances of "seeing the light of print."[9]

With these findings as backdrop, it is not surprising that research also indicates that less than 10 percent of all news releases are published.[10] Nonetheless, each day's *Wall Street Journal, New York Times, USA Today,* Thestreet.com, Marketwatch.com, and other daily publications and Internet services around the nation, are filled with stories generated by public relations professionals.

UNITED STATES POSTAL SERVICE

POSTAL NEWS

USPS Contact: Sue Brennan
(202) 268-6353
Pager: (800) SKY-PAGE PIN 573-1647
E-Mail: sbrennan@email.usps.gov
USPS Web Site: http://www.usps.gov
Release Number 97-053

FOR IMMEDIATE RELEASE
July 7, 1997

DOLLED UP POSTAGE STAMPS
COMMEMORATE PRECIOUS COLLECTIBLES

WASHINGTON - Providing comfort and delight to millions of children of all ages for the past century, dolls not only continue to be favorite childhood playthings today, but the hobby of doll collecting has become an international pastime, surpassed only by stamp and coin collecting in this country and abroad.

The U.S. Postal Service will pay tribute to this collectible with the issuance of the Classic American Dolls stamps, featuring 15 special dolls that reflect the tradition, heritage, culture and artistic style from various geographical regions of this country.

Postal Service Governor LeGree Daniels and the president of the United Federation of Doll Clubs (UFDC), Patricia Gosh, will officially dedicate the stamps on Monday, July 28, at a 7 p.m. ceremony held at the Anaheim Hilton and Towers Hotel in Anaheim, California. This ceremony will be held in conjunction with the annual membership meeting of the UFDC and subsequent week long convention.

"These delightful, charming stamps illustrate the joys of collecting, appreciating and cherishing classic dolls," said Daniels. "I believe these images will recall memories of many sweet, tender moments of our youth."

The dolls featured on the stamps are identified by either the doll's maker, designer, trade name or common name and include:

"Alabama Baby" and Martha Chase. Ella Smith designed the cloth Alabama Baby doll with molded and painted features. These dolls were originally named "The Alabama Indestructible Doll" and were made from 1900-1925. The second doll was created by Martha Chase and is an all-cloth doll made between 1890-1925.

- more -

FIGURE 11-2 **Oddity sells.** The U.S. Postal Service announcement of Classic American Dolls stamps is an example of a unique newsworthy event.

FIGURE 11-2 **Continued.**

So the fact is that the news release—despite the harsh reviews of some—remains the single most important public relations vehicle.

Internet News Releases

The Internet has revolutionized news releases and news release writing. Before the Internet, public companies would issue news releases only when they had newsworthy announcements to make. Today, companies regularly issue releases merely to be included on on-line databases. Why? This indicates to the consumers and investors who access the Web directly that the company is progressing. In addition, the numerous on-line-only news sources—including e-zines, Internet radio programs, bulletin boards, Web-based discussion groups, newsgroups, on-line services, and mailing lists—make targeting the Internet with news releases an obligatory assignment for public relations writers.

A QUESTION OF ETHICS

Phony Internet Release is April Fool

Three on-line message board users claimed their 1999 April Fool's gag was all in fun, but Business Wire wasn't laughing.

The paid wire service sued three regular users of the Silicon Investor on-line discussion forum, alleging that the three used Business Wire to distribute a bogus news release. The release touted Webnode, a fake company that they said planned to sell pieces of the Internet to investors.

The prank centered on the notion that people could buy pieces of the Next Generation Internet, which was an actual project. Webnode claimed it had a contract with the U.S. Energy Department that permitted it to sell segments of the new Internet.

The three impostors created a fake Web site and invited prospective investors to fill out a form indicating their interest in the venture. The form provided names and e-mail addresses, but the pranksters claimed they did that only to make the site appear more realistic and didn't ask for money.

Perhaps. But Business Wire failed to see the humor.

Said Business Wire's executive vice president, "A joke is one thing, but they've gone beyond the boundaries of what is a joke. They think they're very funny. We don't."

Rebutted one of the three alleged perpetrators, "This whole thing is ridiculous. They're trying to leave the impression that we're trying to scam people."

Undaunted by the lawsuit, the three defendants said they would continue to pursue similar April Fool's pranks in the future but, "We probably won't use Business Wire again."

In terms of writing for the Internet, brevity and succinctness are paramount. Reading from a computer screen is more difficult and tedious than extracting from paper. Therefore, Internet writing must appeal to the eye. Short paragraphs. Short sentences. Frequent lists. Use of bullets, dashes, numbers. According to Business Wire, another paid news release service used by public relations people, the average news release is 500 words in length.[11] Releases tailored to the Internet, particularly if they are delivered as e-mails, must be even shorter—confined to one or two screens, no more.

As to Internet releases themselves, they must, like print releases, interest the recipient early in the news value of the subject matter. That means making sure the release's headline and lead explain, up front and without hyperbole, what is new and different. Ideally, Internet releases should tailor messages to the individual recipient's needs or interests. Also, keywords in the release should be linked to a glossary defining industry terms and other jargon.

News Value

The key challenge for public relations writers is to ensure that their news releases reflect news (Figure 11-3). What is "news"? That's an age-old question in journalism. Traditionally, journalists said that when "a dog bites a man, it's not news," but when "a man bites a dog, that's news." The best way to learn what constitutes "news value" is to scrutinize the daily press and broadcast news reports and see what they call news. In a general sense, news releases ought to include the following elements:

- Have a well-defined reason for sending the release
- Focus on one central subject in each release
- Make certain the subject is newsworthy in the context of the organization, industry, and community
- Include facts about the product, service, or issue being discussed

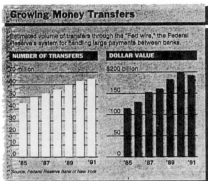

FIGURE 11-3 **On the news.** A news release is only valuable if it gets published. The key to getting published is to ensure that the release is newsworthy, such as this announcement of a new payments system.

The New York Times

FRIDAY, NOVEMBER 27, 1992

A Fund-Shifting System That's Open All Night

By MICHAEL QUINT

The Global Settlement Fund may sound like a common money market fund, but behind that bland title is a novel 24-hour money transfer system that might some day be used by all kinds of businesses for sending payments to one another.

While securities and currencies are traded 24 hours a day in London, New York and Tokyo, there has not been any way for traders to send or receive payments outside of business hours in their local market.

The Bankers Trust Company, creator and manager of the new fund, began offering it earlier this month to members of the Chicago Mercantile Exchange. The exchange, whose 87 members include most of the nation's leading banks and securities firms, recently changed its rules so members can satisfy daily margin calls by sending the fund's shares to the exchange rather than cash or Treasury bills.

A 24-Hour Cash Exchange

Shares in the fund are the equivalent of money that can be transferred instantly to another shareholder, 24 hours a day, without a transaction fee.

The fund invests only in Treasury securities. Shares may only be bought by corporations and institutions that have the required computer connections with the fund's control room in New York. The minimum purchase is $100,000.

The rapidity of payment and round-the-clock access was important to the Chicago Merc, which started night-time trading of futures contracts in

Eileen Bedell, Bankers Trust director of global settlement services, expects the new fund to appeal to corporations that are tired of paying bank fees.

June. The exchange had been seeking a way to collect margin during hours that the banking system and Federal Reserve were closed.

"Right now, there are a lot of people on the sidelines waiting to see it work," said Robin B. Perlin, vice president of cash management at the Chicago Research and Trading Group, a Chicago Merc member firm that has decided to buy shares in the fund. "Hopefully, all the exchanges are going to approve the fund, which will give us a lot more flexibility to move funds between our accounts."

Designs Beyond Traders

Bankers Trust, which spent five years developing Global Settlement and obtaining the necessary approvals from banking and securities regulators, has grander visions for the

(over)

- Provide the facts "factually"—with no puff, no bluff, no hyperbole
- Rid the release of unnecessary jargon
- Include appropriate quotes from principals, but avoid inflated superlatives that do little more than boost management egos
- Include product specifications, shipping dates, availability, and price, and all pertinent information for telling the story
- Include a brief description of the company (aka "boilerplate") at the end of the release, what it is, and what it does
- Write clearly, concisely, forcefully[12]

Format

The format of a news release is important, whether print or on-line. Because the release is designed to be used in print, it must be structured for easy use by an editor. Certain mechanical rules of thumb should be followed.

- **Spacing.** News releases should always be typed and double-spaced on 8½-by-11-inch paper. No editor wants to go rummaging through a handwritten

FIGURE 11-3 **Continued.**

GL❂BESETNews

T H E   G L O B A L   S E T T L E M E N T   F U N D.   I N C.

FOR IMMEDIATE RELEASE   Contact: Doff Meyer
                                                  212-222-3436

GLOBESET℠, WORLD'S FIRST ROUND-THE-CLOCK,
MULTI-CURRENCY PAYMENT SYSTEM, BEGINS OPERATION

The Global Settlement Fund, Inc. (GlobeSet℠), the world's
first 24-hour-a-day, multi-currency payment system, has begun
operation as a new form of margin collateral for futures
trades. A mutual fund as well as a payment system, GlobeSet
seeks to earn income for its shareholders.

Unlike traditional collateral management and payment systems,
GlobeSet is the world's first system to offer the following
features:

    · Payments using GlobeSet shares are instantaneous and
      final.

    · Payments using GlobeSet shares can be made 24 hours a
      day, every business day, 7 a.m. Monday, Tokyo time,
      through 8 p.m. Friday, New York time.

    · GlobeSet is designed to accept payments in multiple
      currencies — initially United States Dollars,
      Japanese Yen and British Pound Sterling.

--- more ---

release or a single-spaced, oversized piece of paper. Although most releases are typed on only one side, in these days of environmental concern, releases typed on both sides of a page are acceptable.

- ☑ **Paper.** Inexpensive paper stock should be used. Reporters win Pulitzer Prizes with stories written on plain copy paper. Nothing irritates an editor more than seeing an expensively embossed news release while watching newspapers die due to soaring newsprint costs.

- ☑ **Identification.** The name, address, and telephone number of the release writer should appear in the upper part of the release in case an editor wants further information. It's a good idea to list two names, with office and home telephone numbers. For on-line releases, printing contact information at both the top and bottom of the release reduces the need for scrolling.

- ☑ **Release date.** Releases should always be dated, either for immediate use or to be held until a certain later date, often referred to as an embargoed date. In this day of on-line communication, however, publications frown on embargoes. Only in the most extreme cases—for example, proprietary or confidential medical or government data—will they be honored. Therefore, the best policy is to plan on immediate release.

◪ **Margins.** Margins should be wide enough for editors to write in, usually about 1 to 1½ inches.

◪ **Length.** A news release is not a book. It should be edited tightly so that it is no more than two to two-and-a-half pages long, or, as noted, two on-line screens. Words and sentences should be kept short.

◪ **Paragraphs.** Paragraphs should also be short, no more than six lines. A single sentence can suffice as a paragraph. Because typographical composers may type exactly what they see, words should not be broken at the end of a line. Likewise, paragraphs should be completed before a new page is begun to ensure that a lost page in the news or composing room will not disrupt a particular thought in the release.

◪ **Slug lines.** Journalistic shorthand, or slug lines, should appear on a release—such things as "more" at the bottom of a page when the release continues to another page and "30" or "###" to denote the end of the release. Page numbers and one-word descriptions of the topic of the release should appear on each page for quick editorial recognition.

◪ **Headlines.** Headlines are a good idea and help presell a print or on-line editor on the news release that follows. Releases should be folded with the headline showing.

◪ **Proofreading.** Grammar, spelling, and typing must be perfect. Misspellings, grammatical errors, or typos are the quickest route to the editorial wastebasket.

◪ **Timing.** News release writers must be sensitive to editorial deadlines. Newspapers, magazines, and broadcast stations work under constant deadline pressure. Because stale news is no news, a release arriving even a little late may just as well never have been mailed. This is particularly the case today, where faxes and e-mail deliver documents immediately.

◪ **Internet prudence.** Increasingly, journalists use technology for news collection. However, many journalists have two sets of e-mail: one for correspondence they seek, the other for extraneous material, normally discarded. So it is important for a public relations writer to recognize that e-mailing releases, stating the lead over voice mail, or messengering a disk won't guarantee that a reporter will even see a release. The best advice is to check a particular reporter's preferred way of receiving news releases before dispatching them.

Style

The style of writing, particularly news release writing, is almost as critical as content. Alas, many in the public relations profession overlook the importance of proper writing style. Sloppy style can break the back of any release and ruin its chances for publication. Style must also be flexible and evolve as language changes.

Most public relations operations follow the style practiced by major newspapers and magazines rather than that of book publishers. This news style is detailed in various guides published by such authorities as the Associated Press and the *New York Times*.

Because the press must constantly update its style to conform to changing societal concepts, news release style is subjective and ever-changing. However, a particular firm's style must be consistent from one release to the next. The following are examples of typical style rules:

◪ **Capitalization.** Most leading publications use capital letters sparingly; so should you. Editors call this a down style because only the most important words begin with capital letters.

BACKGROUNDER

Just the Facts

Writing in news release style is easy. It is less a matter of formal writing than it is of selecting, organizing, and arraying facts in descending sequence.

Here are 10 facts:

Fact 1: Attorney General Janet Reno will speak in Lansing, Michigan, tomorrow.

Fact 2: She will be keynote speaker at the annual convention of the American Bar Association.

Fact 3: She will speak at 8 p.m. in the Michigan State University Field House.

Fact 4: Her speech will be a major one.

Fact 5: Her topic will be capital punishment.

Fact 6: She will also address university law classes while she is in Lansing.

Fact 7: She will meet with the university's chancellor while she is in Lansing.

Fact 8: She is serving her second term as attorney general under President Clinton.

Fact 9: She is a former Florida prosecutor.

Fact 10: She has, in the past, steadfastly avoided addressing the subject of capital punishment.

Organize these facts into an American Bar Association news release for tomorrow morning's Lansing newspaper. One right answer appears later in this chapter. Just don't peek.

☑ **Abbreviations.** Abbreviations present a many-faceted problem. For example, months, when used with dates, should be abbreviated, such as Sept. 2, 1999. But when the day of the month is not used, the month should be spelled out, such as September 1999. Days of the week, on the other hand, should never be abbreviated. In addition, first mention of organizations and agencies should be spelled out, with the abbreviation in parentheses after the name, such as Securities and Exchange Commission (SEC).

☑ **Numbers.** There are many guidelines for the spelling out of numbers, but a general rule is to spell out numbers through nine and use figures for 10 and up. Yet figures are perfectly acceptable for such things as election returns, speeds and distances, percentages, temperatures, heights, ages, ratios, and sports scores.

☑ **Punctuation.** The primary purpose of punctuation is to clarify the writer's thoughts, ensure exact interpretation, and make reading and understanding quicker and easier. Less punctuation rather than more should be the goal. The following are just some of the punctuation marks a public relations practitioner must use appropriately.

1. The colon introduces listings, tabulations, and statements and takes the place of an implied "for instance."
2. The comma is used in a variety of circumstances, including before connecting words, between two words or figures that might otherwise be misunderstood, and before and after nonrestrictive clauses.
3. In general, exclamation points should be resisted in releases. They tend to be overkill!
4. The hyphen is often abused and should be used carefully. A single hyphen can change the meaning of a sentence completely. For example, "The six-foot man eating tuna was killed" means the man was eating tuna; it should probably be punctuated "The six-foot, man-eating tuna was killed."

BACKGROUNDER

In Style with the Internet

The Internet, of course, has a writing style all its own.

In chat rooms, a correctly spelled word may be a sign of the inarticulate. Consider, for example, this conversation:

Wuzup?

n2m

well g/g c ya

Literal translation by anyone who spends 8 to 10 hours a day in chat rooms: Not too much is up with the respondent, and so the writer has got to go and will see his friend later.

Indeed, in terms of e-mail vocabulary, the following shortened vernacular can be adjudged as "chat ready":

✓	pls	please
✓	flfre	feel free
✓	btw	by the way
✓	brb	be right back
✓	irl	in real life
✓	IMHO	in my humble opinion
✓	lol	laughing out loud
✓	rotfl	rolling on the floor laughing
✓	u r	you are
✓	info	information
✓	doc	document
✓	convo	conversation
✓	latr	later

Latr.

5. Quoted matter is enclosed in double or single quotation marks. The double marks enclose the original quotation, whereas the single marks enclose a quotation within a quotation.

✓ **Spelling.** Many words, from adviser to zucchini, are commonly misspelled. The best way to avoid misspellings is to have a dictionary always within reach. When two spellings are given in a dictionary, the first spelling is always preferred.

These are just a few of the stylistic stumbling blocks that writers must consider. In the news release, style should never be taken lightly. The style, as much as any other part of the release, lets an editor know the kind of organization that issued the release and the competence of the professional who wrote it.[13]

Content

Again, the cardinal rule in release content is that the end product be newsworthy. The release must be of interest to an editor and readers. Issuing a release that has little chance of being used by a publication serves only to crush the credibility of the writer.

When a release is newsworthy and of potential interest to an editor, it must be written clearly and concisely, in proper newspaper style. It must get to the facts early and answer the six key questions. From there it must follow inverted pyramid structure to its conclusion. For example, consider the following lead for the Janet Reno news release posed earlier in this chapter.

LANSING, MICHIGAN—Attorney General Janet Reno will deliver a major address on capital punishment at 8 p.m. tomorrow in the Michigan State University Field House before the annual convention of the American Bar Association.

This lead answers all the pertinent questions: who (Attorney General Janet Reno), what (a major address on capital punishment), where (Michigan State University Field House), when (tomorrow at 8 p.m.), and why (American Bar Association is holding a convention). In this case, how is less important. Whether or not the reader chooses to delve further into the release, the gist of the story has been successfully communicated in the lead.

To be newsworthy, news releases must be objective. All comments and editorial remarks must be attributed to organization officials. The news release can't be used as the private soapbox of the release writer. Rather, it must appear as a fair and accurate representation of the news that the organization wishes to be conveyed.

News releases can be written about almost anything. Three frequent subjects are product and institutional announcements, management changes, and management speeches.

The Announcement

Frequently, practitioners want to announce a new product or institutional development, such as earnings, mergers, acquisitions, or company celebrations. The announcement release should have a catchy yet significant lead to stimulate an editor to capitalize on the practitioner's creative idea.

> "Tennis whites," the traditional male court uniform, will yield to bright colors and fashion styling this spring as Jockey spearheads a new wave in tennis fashion with the introduction of a full line of tennis wear for men.

Typically, in an announcement release, after the lead identifies the significant aspects of the product or development, a spokesperson is quoted for additional product information. Editors appreciate the quotes because they then do not have to interview a company official.

> The new, lightweight plastic bottle for Coca-Cola began its national rollout today in Spartanburg, S.C. This two-liter package is the nation's first metric plastic bottle for soft drinks. "We are very excited about this new package," said John H. Ogden, president, Coca-Cola U.S.A. "Our two-liter plastic bottle represents an important advancement. Its light weight, toughness, and environmental advantages offer a new standard of consumer benefits in soft drink packaging."

The subtle product "plug" included in this release is typical of such announcements. Clearly, the organization gains if the product's benefits are described in a news story. But editors are sensitive to product puffery, and the line between legitimate information and puffery is thin. One must always be sensitive to the needs and concerns of editors. A professional avoids letting the thin line of product information become a short plank of puffery.

The Management Change

Newspapers are often interested in management changes, but editors frequently reject releases that have no local angle. For example, the editor of the Valdosta, Georgia, *Citizen* has little reason to use this announcement:

NEW YORK, NY, SEPT. 5, 2000—Ronald O. Schram has been named manager of the hosiery department at Bloomingdale's Paramus, NJ, store.

On the other hand, the same release, amended for local appeal, would almost certainly be used by the *Citizen*.

NEW YORK, NY, SEPT. 5, 2000—Ronald O. Schram, son of Mr. and Mrs. Siegfried Schram of 221 Starting Lane, Valdosta, has been named manager of the hosiery department at Bloomingdale's Paramus, NJ, store.

Sometimes one must dig for the local angle. For example, suppose Mr. Schram was born in Valdosta but went to school in Americus, Georgia. With this knowledge, the writer might prepare the following release, which would have appeal in the newspapers of both Georgia cities.

NEW YORK, NY, SEPT. 5, 2000—Ronald O. Schram, son of Mr. and Mrs. Siegfried Schram of 221 Starting Lane, Valdosta, and a 1976 graduate of Americus High School, was named manager of the hosiery department of Bloomingdale's Paramus, NJ, store.

Penetrating local publications with the management change release is relatively easy once the local angle has been identified, but achieving publication in a national newspaper or magazine is much harder. The *Wall Street Journal,* for example, will not use a management change announcement unless the individual has attained a certain level of responsibility, usually corporate vice president or higher, in a major firm. In other words, if a release involves someone who has not attained senior executive status at a listed company, forget it, at least as far as the *Wall Street Journal* is concerned.

For national consumption it is the importance or uniqueness of the individual or company that should be emphasized. For example, an editor might not realize that the following management change is unique:

WASHINGTON, D.C., JUNE 6, 2000—Howie Barmad of Jersey City, NJ, today was promoted to the rank of admiral in the United States Navy.

However, the same release stands out clearly for its news value when the unique angle is played up.

WASHINGTON, D.C., JUNE 6, 2000—Howie Barmad, born in Yugoslavia, today was named the first naturalized admiral in the history of the United States Navy.

One can never go wrong by being straightforward in a news release, but a local or unique angle to help sell the story to an editor should always be investigated.

The Management Speech

Management speeches are another recurring source of news releases. The key to a speech news release is selecting the most significant portion of the talk for the lead. A good speech generally has a clear thesis, from which a lead naturally flows. Once the thesis is identified, the remainder of the release simply embellishes it.

BOONEVILLE, MO, OCT. 18, 2000—Booneville Mining Company is "on the verge of having several very profitable years," Booneville Mining President J. Kenneth Krafchik said today.

Addressing the Booneville Chamber of Commerce, the Missouri mining company executive cited two reasons for the positive projections: The company's orders are at an all-time high, and its overseas facilities have "turned the corner" on profitability in the current year.

Normally, if the speechmaker is not a famous person, the release should not begin with the speaker's name but rather with the substance of the remarks. If the speaker is a well-known individual, leading with the name is perfectly legitimate.

Federal Reserve Chairman Alan Greenspan called today for a "new attitude toward business investment and capital formation."

The body copy of a speech release should follow directly from the lead. Often, the major points of the speech must be paraphrased and consolidated to conform to a two-page release. In any event, it is frequently a significant challenge to convert the essence of a management speech to news-release form.

The Importance of Editing

Editing is the all-important final touch for the public relations writer. In a news release, a careful self-edit can save the deadliest prose. An editor must be judicious. Each word, phrase, sentence, and paragraph should be weighed carefully. Good editing will "punch up" dull passages and make them sparkle. For instance, "The satellite flies across the sky" is dead; but, "The satellite roars across the sky" is alive.

In the same context, good editing will get rid of passive verbs. Invariably, this will produce shorter sentences. For example, "George Washington chopped down the cherry tree" is shorter and better than "The cherry tree was chopped down by George Washington."

A good editor must also be gutsy enough to use bold strokes—to chop, slice, and cut through verbiage, bad grammar, misspellings, incorrect punctuation, poorly constructed sentences, misused words, mixed metaphors, non sequiturs, cliches, redundancies, circumlocutions, and jargon. Sentences like, "She is the widow of the late Marco Picardo" and "The present incumbent is running for reelection" are intolerable to a good editor.

A good unabridged dictionary and a thesaurus provide the practitioner with significant writing and editing support. To these might be added *Bartlett's Familiar Quotations,* the *World Almanac,* and an encyclopedia. Editing should also concentrate on organizing copy. One release paragraph should flow naturally into the next. Transitions in writing are most important. Sometimes it takes only a single word to unite two adjoining paragraphs. Such is the case in the following example, which uses the word "size" as the transitional element.

The machine works on a controlled mechanism, directed by a series of pulleys. It is much smaller than the normal motor, requiring less than half of a normal motor's components. Not only does the device differ in size from other motors, but it also differs in capacity.

Writing, like fine wine, should flow smoothly and stand up under the toughest scrutiny. Careful editing is a must.

B A C K G R O U N D E R

Deobfuscating Obfuscatory Proverbs

Test your editing skills by tightening up these annoyingly verbose proverbs.

1. Avian entities of identical plummage inevitably congregate.
2. Pulchritude possesses profundity of a merely cutaneous nature.
3. It is fruitless to become lachrymose over precipitately departed lacteal fluid.
4. It is inefficacious to indoctrinate a superannuated canine with innovative maneuvers.
5. Eschew the implement of correction and vitiate the scion.
6. Visible vapors that issue from ignited carbonaceous materials are a harbinger of simultaneous or imminent conflagration.
7. Lack of propinquity causes an effulgence of partiality in the cardiac area.
8. A revolving mass of lithic conglomerate does not accumulate a congery of small green bryophitic plants.
9. Presenter of the ultimate cachinnation thereby obtains the optimal cachinnation.
10. Ligneous or petrous projectiles may have the potential to fracture my osseous structure, but perjorative appellations remain eternally innocuous.

Answers

1. Birds of a feather flock together.
2. Beauty is only skin deep.
3. There's no use crying over spilt milk.
4. You can't teach an old dog new tricks.
5. Spare the rod and spoil the child.
6. Where there's smoke, there's fire.
7. Absence makes the heart grow fonder.
8. A rolling stone gathers no moss.
9. He who laughs last laughs best.
10. Sticks and stones may break my bones, but names can never hurt me.

S U M M A R Y

Writing is the essence of public relations practice, whether involved with print or on-line work. The public relations professional, if not the best writer in his or her organization, must at least be one of the best. Writing is the communications skill that sets public relations professionals apart from others.

Some writers are born. But writing can be learned by understanding the fundamentals of what makes interesting writing; by practicing different written forms; and by working constantly to improve, edit, and refine the written product. When an executive needs something written well, one organizational resource should pop immediately into his or her mind: public relations.

Discussion Starters

1. What is the difference between writing for the ear and for the eye?
2. What are several of the writing fundamentals one must consider?
3. What is the essence of the Flesch method of writing?
4. What is the inverted pyramid and why does it work?

5. What is the essential written communications vehicle used by public relations professionals?
6. Why is the format of a news release important to a public relations professional and the organization?
7. What are common purposes of news releases?
8. Should a news release writer try to work his or her own editorial opinion into the release?
9. What are the keys in writing releases for the Internet?
10. What is the purpose of editing?

Notes

1. Fraser P. Seitel, "Steal!" *United States Banker* (1992): 44.
2. Bill Moyers, "Watch Your Language," *The Professional Communicator* (August–September, 1985): 6.
3. Fraser P. Seitel, "Getting It Write," *United States Banker* (December 1991): 54.
4. "PRN Averages 1,500 News Releases a Day," *Jack O'Dwyer's Newsletter* (September 15, 1999): 4.
5. G. A. Marken, "Press Releases: When Nothing Else Will Do, Do It Right," *Public Relations Quarterly* (Fall 1994): 9.
6. "J-Prof Says PR Releases Are 'Worthless,' " *Jack O'Dwyer's Newsletter* (July 14, 1993): 4.
7. "How to Get Editors to Use Press Releases," *Jack O'Dwyer's Newsletter* (May 26, 1993): 3.
8. "What Makes a Story Newsworthy," *Communicator* (September 1997): 1.
9. "Researcher Finds Complaints Against Press Releases Are Justified," *Editor and Publisher* (May 8, 1993): 42, 52.
10. Linda P. Morton, "Producing Publishable Press Releases," *Public Relations Quarterly* (Winter 1992–1993): 9–11.
11. "In 36 Years, Releases Are Longer and the Competition Is All but Gone," *Business Week Newsletter* (March 1998): 1.
12. Marken, "Press Releases: When Nothing Else Will Do, Do It Right," 10.
13. "Tired Words to Ban from Press Releases," *Ragan's Media Relations Report* (March 17, 1997): 3–5.

Suggested Readings

Aronson, Merry, and Donald E. Spetner. *The Public Relations Writer's Handbook*. New York: Lexington Books, 1993.

Bivins, Thomas. *The Handbook for Public Relations Writing: The Essentials of Style and Format*. Lincolnwood, IL: NTC Business Books, 1999.

Bivins, Thomas, and William E. Ryan. *How to Produce Creative Publications: Traditional Techniques and Computer Applications*. Lincolnwood, IL: NTC Publishing Group, 1992.

Block, Mervin. *Writing Broadcast News—Shorter, Sharper, Stronger, Revised and Expanded*. Chicago: Bonus Books, 1997.

Braden, Marie, with Richard Ross. *Getting the Message Across: Writing for the Mass Media*. Boston: Houghton Mifflin Company, 1997. Includes in-depth treatment of persuasive writing.

Cormier, Robin A. *Error-Free Writing: A Lifetime Guide to Flawless Business Writing.* Alexandria, VA: EEI Press, 1995.

Crystal, David. *The Cambridge Encyclopedia of the English Language.* Cambridge, England: Cambridge University Press, 1995.

Fensch, Thomas. *Sports Writing Handbook,* 2nd ed. Hillsdale, NJ: Lawrence Erlbaum Associates, 1995. Updates a special type of writing for sports information.

Fink, Conrad C. *Writing Opinion for Impact.* Ames, IA: Iowa State University Press, 1999.

Hudson, Howard Penn. *Publishing Newsletters,* 3rd ed. Rhinebeck, NY: H&M Publishers, 1997.

King, Janice. *Writing High-Tech Copy That Sells.* New York: John Wiley & Sons, 1995. A guide to preparing persuasive promotional materials for high technology products and services.

Marsh, Charles. *A Quick and Not Dirty Guide to Business Writing.* Scottsdale, AZ: Gorsuch Scarisbrick Publishers, 1997. Guide to writing and formatting 25 of the most common business and public relations documents.

Simon, Raymond, and Joseph Zappala. *Public Relations Workbook: Writing and Techniques.* Lincolnwood, IL: NTC Publishing Group, 1996.

Smith, Peggy. *Letter Perfect: A Guide to Practical Proofreading.* Alexandria, VA: EEI Press, 1995.

Strunk, W., and E. B. White. *Elements of Style.* New York: Allyn & Bacon, 1999.

Success in Newsletter Publishing. Newsletter Association (1341 G. St., NW, Washington, D.C. 20007). Biweekly.

Tucker, Kerry, Doris Derelian, and Donna Rouner. *Public Relations Writing: An Issue-Driven Behavioral Approach.* Upper Saddle River, NJ: Prentice Hall, 1997.

Wilcox, Dennis L., and Lawrence W. Nolte. *Public Relations Writing and Media Techniques.* New York: Harper College Press, 1996.

Writing That Works: The Business Communications Report. Springfield, VA: Communications Concepts Inc. Monthly newsletter.

Yale, David R. *The Publicity Handbook: How to Maximize Publicity for Products, Services and Organizations.* Lincolnwood, IL: NTC Publishing Group, 1991.

top of the shelf

Doug Newsom and Bob Carrell

Public Relations Writing, 5th ed.
Belmont, CA: Wadsworth Publishing Company, 1997.

One feature of the fifth edition of this classic that will appeal to practitioners is an expanded section of the effects of computer-related technology, including Web pages, electronic research, e-mail campaigns, and CD-ROMs.

Public Relations Writing also contains recent social and economic trends and effects on public relations. The book combines the practical aspects of all kinds of public relations writing with the principles and theories of public relations interwoven, "so students write with understanding and purpose."

Part One sets the scene for the kinds of writing public relations people do and the context in which they do it. Part Two concentrates on the work of writing. Part Three focuses on writing for small audiences. Part Four describes writing for the mass media. Part Five focuses on special audiences.

CASE STUDY

The Raina News Release

Background: The Raina, Inc., Carborundum plant in Blackrock, Iowa, has been under pressure in recent months to remedy its pollution problem. Raina's plant is the largest in Blackrock, and even though the company has spent $1.3 million on improving its pollution-control equipment, black smoke still spews from the plant's smokestacks, and waste products are still allowed to filter into neighboring streams. Lately, the pressure on Raina has been intense.

- On September 7, J. J. Kelinson, a private citizen, called to complain about the "noxious smoke" fouling the environment.
- On September 8, Mrs. Janet Greenberg of the Blackrock Garden Club called to protest the "smoke problem" that was destroying the zinnias and other flowers in the area.
- On September 9, Clarence "Smoky" Salmon, president of the Blackrock Rod and Gun Club, called to report that 700 people had signed a petition against the Raina plant's pollution of Zeus Creek.
- On September 10, WERS Radio editorialized that "the time has come to force area plants to act on solving pollution problems."
- On September 11, the Blackrock City Council announced plans to enact an air and water pollution ordinance for the city. The council invited as its first witness before the public hearing Leslie Sludge, manager of the Raina Carborundum Blackrock plant.

NEWS RELEASE DATA

1. Leslie Sludge, manager of Raina's Carborundum Blackrock plant, appeared at the Blackrock City Council hearing on September 11.
2. Sludge said Raina had already spent $1.3 million on a program to clean up pollution at its Blackrock plant.
3. Raina received 500 complaint calls in the past three months protesting its pollution conditions.
4. Sludge said Raina was "concerned about environmental problems, but profits are still what keeps our company running."
5. Sludge announced that the company had decided to commit another $2 million for pollution-abatement facilities over the next three months.
6. Raina is the oldest plant in Blackrock and was built in 1900.
7. Raina's Blackrock plant employs 10,000 people, the largest single employer in Blackrock.
8. Raina originally planned to delay its pollution-abatement program but speeded it up because of public pressure in recent months.
9. Sludge said that the new pollution-abatement program would begin in October and that the company projected "real progress in terms of clean water and clean air" as early as two years from today.
10. Five years ago, Raina, Inc., received a Presidential Award from the Environmental Protection Agency for its "concern for pollution abatement."
11. An internal Raina study indicated that Blackrock was the "most pollutant laden" of all Raina's plants nationwide.

12. Sludge formerly served as manager of Raina's Fetid Reservoir plant in Fetid Reservoir, New Hampshire. In two years as manager of Fetid Reservoir, Sludge was able to convert it from one of the most pollutant-laden plants in the system to the cleanest, as judged by the Environmental Protection Agency.

13. Sludge has been manager of Blackrock for two months.

14. Raina's new program will cost the company $2 million.

15. Raina will hire 100 extra workers especially for the pollution-abatement program.

16. Sludge, 35, is married to the former Polly Usion of Wheeling, West Virginia.

17. Sludge is author of the book *Fly Fishing Made Easy*.

18. The bulk of the money budgeted for the new pollution-abatement program will be spent on two globe refractors, which purify waste destined to be deposited in surrounding waterways, and four hyperventilation systems, which remove noxious particles dispersed into the air from smokestacks.

19. Sludge said, "Raina, Inc., has decided to move ahead with this program at this time because of its long-standing responsibility for keeping the Blackrock environment clean and in response to growing community concern over achieving the objective."

20. Former Blackrock plant manager Fowler Aire was fired by the company in July for his "flagrant disregard for the environment."

21. Aire also was found to be diverting Raina funds from company projects to his own pockets. In all, Aire took close to $10,000, for which the company was not reimbursed. At least part of the money was to be used for pollution control.

22. Aire, whose whereabouts are presently not known, is the brother of J. Derry Aire, Raina's vice president for finance.

23. Raina's Blackrock plant has also recently installed ramps and other special apparatus to assist handicapped employees. Presently, 100 handicapped workers are employed in the Raina Blackrock plant.

24. Raina's Blackrock plant started as a converted garage, manufacturing plate glass. Only 13 people worked in the plant at that time.

25. Today the Blackrock plant employs 10,000, covers 14 acres of land, and is the largest supplier of plate glass and commercial panes in the country.

26. The Blackrock plant was slated to be the subject of a critical report from the Private Environmental Stabilization Taskforce (PEST), a private environmental group. PEST's report, "The Foulers," was to discuss "the 10 largest manufacturing polluters in the nation."

27. Raina management has been aware of the PEST report for several months.

Questions

1. If you were assigned to draft a news release to accompany Sludge to the Blackrock City Council meeting on September 11, which items would you use in your lead (i.e., who, what, why, where, when, how)?

2. Which items would you avoid using in the news release?

3. If a reporter from the *Blackrock Bugle* called and wanted to know what happened to former Blackrock manager Fowler Aire, what would you tell him?

4. How could Raina use the Internet to research public opinion of the pollution problem? How could the company use the Internet to communicate its position in advance of the Blackrock city council meeting?

An Interview With Bill Adams

William C. Adams is an associate professor in the School of Journalism and Mass Communication at Florida International University. Prior to joining FIU in 1990, Professor Adams spent 25 years in corporate public relations, including management positions with Amoco Corporation, Phillips Petroleum Company, and ICI Americas. He has written and lectured extensively in the field and is affectionately known as "The Professor," a regular columnist in *Public Relations Tactics* magazine.

How important is writing in public relations?

Good writing is the essence of public relations. It's the lifeblood of our profession and is often what sets us apart from others in the organizations we serve. It's also a balancing act. By "good," I'm referring to well-thought-out, grammatically correct, targeted, purposeful, and effective writing. Writing to communicate effectively both inside and outside the organization is the most critical thing a student can learn when studying the many elements of public relations.

By "balancing act," I mean that public relations writers are both translators and interpreters of concepts and ideas, while also being the organization's advocates/persuaders. It's skillfully achieving that fine balance between news and advocacy that gets your writing looked at and read by internal and external audiences alike.

What's the quality of public relations writing?

Unfortunately, much of it is not very good. And what is good—or even passable—is often mundane and perfunctory, devoid of even a whiff of humor or cleverness. News releases, for example, too often miss their target audiences, are loaded with jargon and legalese, aren't newsy and interesting, or offer nothing but hype. Many simply are not well written. (Ask any journalist.)

The same goes for other public relations communications tools, such as newsletters, brochures, memos, and even letters. I see too much sloppiness in sentence construction, a lack of smooth-flowing transition between paragraphs and thoughts, and an overall carelessness in editing and proofing (and don't blame Spell-Check!).

Are news releases still worthwhile?

It depends upon whom you ask. Some reporters and editors claim never to use news releases, while others find them indispensable for covering their beats. The trick, much like targeting audiences you wish to reach with your communications program, is to find out who prefers what. For example, one writer on a specific beat may prefer "fact sheets" or even a phone call, while another wants news releases.

Research has shown that the reasons most releases don't get used is because they have poor-quality writing, are full of hype, or are not newsy enough. A well-prepared, professional-appearing, and targeted release has an excellent chance of being used—or at least getting the reporter's or editor's attention. A daily newspaper columnist once told one of my public relations writing classes not to "bother him" with "junk mail" (news releases) when they went out into the "real world." They were stunned until a reporter from that same newspaper followed by saying, "Don't believe him . . . he couldn't write his column without help from public relations people and their news releases."

What's the key to writing a good news release?

You and the reporters and editors should ask basically the same questions: "Is it news?" "Is it timely?" "Is it localized?" The newsperson asks a critical fourth question: "Is it important to my readers/listeners/viewers?" If the answer to all four of the questions is "yes," there's an excellent chance that your release will be used, or at least provide a basis from which a reporter will call you for further information.

Also important as a "use factor" is a well-crafted informational lead and the overall quality of the release itself, which includes grammar, punctuation, sentence structure, and style—free from jargon and hype.

What's the secret to effective public relations writing?

Clarity and conciseness are the keys to successful public relations writing (correct grammar goes without saying). You also must be able to grab a journalist's attention with a newsy and interesting opening statement (it is a "pitch," after all), followed with a reason that reporter should be interested in your story idea.

Does writing remain important throughout one's career?

The answer is a solid "yes." Even at the managerial level, writing remains a crucial part of the public relations profile.

First of all, to get to that level of success, public relations managers generally move through the "technician" stage, wherein they hone their communication skills, increasing their value to the organization.

Writing well is an art, however, and often scares young people just entering the profession. For example, once after speaking to a group of students, I was approached by a potential public relations major who asked, timidly, "If I go into PR, do I have to do all that writing stuff?" The answer remains "yes."

Chapter 12

Writing for the Eye and Ear

In the early days of the 21st century, the most powerful man in America was a mild-mannered, bespectacled economist named Alan Greenspan.

As chairman of the Federal Reserve Board, which controlled the U.S. money supply, interest rates, and inflation, Mr. Greenspan's words—primarily enunciated through speeches before Congress and business groups—moved markets in the United States and around the world. Consequently, Mr. Greenspan's speeches were meticulously crafted to leave subtle impressions as to where markets might be headed. When Alan Greenspan talked, people listened.

Writing for reading and speaking is a hallmark of the practice of public relations.

Writing for reading emphasizes the written word. Writing for listening emphasizes the spoken word. The two differ significantly. Writing for the eye traditionally has ranked among the strongest areas for public relations professionals. Years ago, most practitioners entered public relations through print journalism. Accordingly, they were schooled in the techniques of writing for the eye, not the ear. Today, of course, a background in print journalism is not necessarily a prerequisite for public relations work. Just as important today is writing for the ear—writing for listening. The key to such writing is to write as if you are speaking. Use simple, short sentences, active verbs, contractions, and one- and two-syllable words. In brief, be brief.

This chapter will focus on two things: First, the most frequently used communication vehicles designed for the eye, beyond the news release; and second, the most widely used methods for communicating through the ear, particularly speeches and presentations. Communicating via the Internet will be the focus of chapter 13.

Today's public relations professional must be conversant in writing for both the eye and the ear.

The Media Kit

Beyond the news release, the most ubiquitous print vehicle in public relations work is the media or press kit. Press kits—in print or on-line format—incorporate several communications vehicles for potential use by newspapers and magazines. A bare-bones media kit consists of a news release, backgrounder, biography, photo, perhaps a CD-ROM and any other item that will help a reporter understand and tell a story. The kit is designed to answer all of the most likely questions that the media might ask about the organization's announcement.

Media kits may also require fact sheets or Q&A (question-and-answer) sheets. The public relations professional must weigh carefully how much information is required in the media kit. Journalists don't appreciate being overwhelmed by too much copy and too many photos.

In preparing a media kit, public relations professionals must keep the following points in mind:

- Be sure the information is accurate and thorough and will answer a journalist's most fundamental questions.
- Provide sufficient background information material to allow the editor to select a story angle.
- Don't be too commercial. Offer balanced, objective information.
- Confine opinions and value judgments to quotes from credible sources.
- Never lie. That's tantamount to editorial suicide.
- Visually arresting graphics may mean the difference between finding the item in the next day's paper or in the same day's wastebasket.

The Biography

Next to the news release, the most popular tool is the biography, often called the biographical summary or just plain bio. The bio recounts pertinent facts about a particular individual. Most organizations keep a file of bios covering all top officers. Major newspapers and wire services prepare standby bios on well-known people for immediate use on breaking news, such as sudden deaths.

Straight Bios

The straight bio lists factual information in a straightforward fashion in descending order of importance, with company-oriented facts preceding more personal details. For example, the straight biography of Madison Square Garden CEO David W. Checketts might begin this way:

> David W. Checketts was named president and chief executive officer of Madison Square Garden on September 20, 1994. He began his career at the Garden as president of the New York Knicks in March 1991. In his four full seasons, the team twice finished in first place, made it to the Eastern Conference Finals twice, and emerged as Eastern Conference Champions in 1994.
>
> Mr. Checketts came to the Knicks from the National Basketball Association headquarters, where he served as vice president and general manager of NBA International, since September 1980.
>
> Mr. Checketts spent six years with the Utah Jazz, beginning in 1983 and during that time, brought the team into prominence as one of the NBA's most successful organizations. At 28, he was the youngest chief executive in the NBA.

This biography is written straightforwardly, a chronology of the subject's work history and accomplishments, with little editorializing.

Narrative Bios

The narrative bio, on the other hand, is written in a breezier, more informal way. This style gives spark and vitality to the biography to make the individual come alive.

In the case of the CEO of Madison Square Garden, the narrative bio, rather than being a straight chronological recitation, talks about special achievements in moving the Garden forward. The narrative bio, in addition to bringing the individual to life, doubles as a speech of introduction when that individual serves as a featured speaker. In effect, the narrative bio becomes a speech.

The Backgrounder

Background pieces, or backgrounders, provide additional information generally to complement the news release. (Thus the use of the term *Backgrounder* to signify complementary material in this book.) Backgrounders can embellish the announcement, or they can discuss the institution making the announcement, the system behind the announcement, or any other appropriate topic that will assist a journalist in writing the story.

Backgrounders are longer and more general in content than the news release. For example, a two-page release announcing the merger of two organizations may not permit much description of the companies involved. A four- or five-page backgrounder provides editors with more depth on the makeup, activities, and history of the merging firms. Backgrounders are usually not used in their entirety by the media but are excerpted.

Subject matter dictates backgrounder style. Some backgrounders are written like a news release, in a snappy and factual manner. Others take a more descriptive and narrative form.

Example One: News Release Style

BACKGROUNDER—SWENSEN'S ICE CREAM COMPANY

The original Swensen's Ice Cream Shoppe was established in 1948 by Earle Swensen at the corner of Union and Hyde in San Francisco.

In 1963 Mr. Swensen licensed the company's predecessor, See Us-Freeze, Inc., later known as United Outlets, Inc., to use Swensen's trade names, trade secrets, recipes, and methods of operation as the basis for Swensen's franchise system. The license agreement was modified in June 1975 and permits the company to use the licensed property and franchise Swensen's shops in all areas of the world except the city and county of San Francisco.

Example Two: Descriptive, Narrative Style

BACKGROUNDER—SICKLE CELL DISEASE

The man was a West Indian black, a 20-year-old student in a professional school in Illinois. One day in 1904, he came to James B. Herrick, an eminent Chicago cardiologist, with symptoms Herrick had never seen before and could not find in the literature. The patient had shortness of breath, a disinclination for exercise, palpitation, jaundice, cough, dizziness, headache, leg ulcers, scars from old leg ulcers, many palpable lymph nodes, pale mucous membranes, muscular rheumatism, severe upper abdominal pain, dark urine, and anemia. Blood smears showed many odd-shaped cells, but what arrested the eye was the presence of numerous sickle-shaped cells.

Herrick kept the patient under observation for many years. He did not suspect that he was looking at a disease that afflicted millions of people, including thousands of blacks in America.

In devising a backgrounder, a writer enjoys unlimited latitude. As long as the piece catches the interest of the reader/editor, any style is permissible.

Fact Sheets, Q&As, Photos, Etc.

Beyond bios and backgrounders, media kits may contain any other information that will help a journalist tell a story. Increasingly today, journalists are accessing organizational media kits on-line. They want information in a hurry, without being delayed by voice mail or foot-dragging. Therefore, the following make great sense to include in media kits.

- ◪ **Fact sheets,** which compile the most relevant facts concerning the product, issue, organization, or candidate discussed in quick and easily accessible fashion.
- ◪ **Q&As,** which present the most probable questions posed about the subject matter at hand and then the answers to those questions. Again, this preempts a reporter's questions to a live—and often unavailable—public relations person.
- ◪ **Photos,** which illustrate the subject. The popularity of *USA Today,* a national full-color newspaper, stimulated virtually every competitor to move to full-color printing. With 80 percent of photo editors now downloading from the Web, on-line color media kit photos are a necessity.

  Although a detailed discussion of photographic terms and techniques is beyond the scope of this book, public relations practitioners should be relatively conversant with photographic terminology and able to recognize the attributes of good photos:

  1. Photos should be taken "live," in real environments with believable people, instead of in studios with stilted models.
  2. They should focus clearly on the issue, product, image, or person that the organization wishes to emphasize, without irrelevant, visually distracting clutter in the foreground or background.
  3. They should be eye-catching, using angles creatively—overhead, below, to the side—to suggest movement.
  4. They must express a viewpoint—an underlying message.
  5. Most of all, photos must make a visual impact. The best photos are those that remain in a person's mind long after written appeals to action have faded. These are the photos that are "worth 10,000 words."[1]

- ◪ **Etc, etc., etc.** What other material should be included in media kits? Additional pertinent photos, advertising schedules and slicks, CD-ROMs, speeches—there is no hard and fast rule. However, as noted, journalists have little patience for being overwhelmed with extraneous material. Therefore, as with news releases, in media kits, less is more (Figure 12-1).

Contact: Felicia Roff
Vorhaus & Company Inc.
212.554.7438 – telephone
888.639.9857 – pager
froff@vorhaus.com

**Peanut Butter and Jelly
Fun Facts**

Everybody Loves Peanut Butter and Jelly

- **Jack Nicholson** told *Marie Claire Magazine* that peanut butter and ⌷ he needs in the bedroom.*
- During the Senate Impeachment hearings, **Senator Mike DeWine** (⌷ brown bag containing a peanut butter and jelly sandwich.
- While on the campaign trail for re-election, **Governor George Bush** ⌷ butter and jelly sandwich.

A Longtime Favorite

- Peanut butter and jelly sandwiches are the 3rd most frequently eaten
- Peanut butter and jelly sandwiches ranked 5th out of 100 favorite Am⌷
- In a six month period, it is estimated that 131 million adults will eat ⌷

Restaurants Are Catching On…

- A restaurant in New York City, called Peanut Butter and Company, ⌷ dishes only made with peanut butter, including the favorite peanut b⌷
- East of Chicago Pizza Company boasts a popular pizza topped with ⌷

A Nutritional Choice

- A peanut butter and jelly sandwich provides 18 percent of the daily ⌷ useful in the prevention of birth defects.***

* * *

* *Marie Claire Magazine*, February 1999
** *March of Dimes and Southeastern Peanut Farmers Brochure*
*** NET, 52 weeks ending 11/22/97

'Gushing with Flav⌷

Russell Stover Candies, 4900 Oak Street, Kansas City, Misso⌷

Contact: Felicia Roff
Vorhaus & Company Inc.
212.554.7438 – telephone
888.639.9857 – pager
froff@vorhaus.com

What Do Bill Clinton and Marilyn Monroe Have In Common?

New York, September 7, 1999 – According to a nationwide survey, Americans most want to eat peanut butter and jelly with President Clinton and Marilyn Monroe. The nationwide survey was conducted by Yankelovich Partners[1] for Russell Stover Candies to announce their new candy, *Peanut Butter and Jelly Cups*. Other favorites include Jimi Hendrix, Sophia Loren and Albert Einstein.

Some highlights of the Peanut Butter and Jelly Survey include:

What television show reminds you of peanut butter and jelly?

- Americans are torn between the 50's classic, *Leave it to Beaver* and the 70's favorite, *The Brady Bunch*.

Baby Boomers want to hold onto their youth…with food:

- Three in four adults believe that the world would be a better place if everyone took time out of their day to remember their childhood.
- Seven out of ten Americans say peanut butter and jelly was among their favorite foods as a child.
- 75% of Americans ate their first peanut butter and jelly sandwich before age 7 and two out of three Americans still savor peanut butter and jelly today.

Peanut butter and jelly is…

- 46% said "an American tradition"
- 36% said "fun"
- 26% said "nostalgic"
- 7% said "sexy" (including Jack Nicholson)

In addition to being the nation's largest manufacturer of boxed chocolates, Russell Stover produces America's favorite candy bars including The Pecan Delight Bar and The Mint Dream Bar with plans to introduce more candy bars and other exciting products in the coming months. The third largest chocolate manufacturer in the country, Russell Stover has been producing **only the finest** candy for over 75 years. The company is headquartered in Kansas City, Missouri and remains a family owned business, run by co-presidents, Scott and Tom Ward.

ity, Missouri, 64112-2702, 1-800-777-4004

FIGURE 12-1 **Filling in the blanks.** When Russell Stover announced its Peanut Butter & Jelly Cups, it offered this fact sheet and survey report to complement media kit information.

The Case History

Beyond the news release and the media kit, another popular and foolproof public relations writing vehicle to attract publicity is the case history.

The case history is frequently used to tell about a customer's favorable use of a company's product or service. Generally, the case history writer works for the company whose product or service is involved. Magazines, particularly trade journals, often welcome case histories, contending that one person's experience may be instructive to another.

Case history articles generally follow a five-part formula:

1. They present a problem experienced by one company but applicable to many other firms.
2. They indicate how the dimensions of the problem were defined by the company using the product.
3. They indicate the solution adopted.
4. They explain the advantages of the adopted solution.
5. They detail the user company's experience after adopting the solution.

Trade book editors, in particular, are often willing to share a case that can be generalized—and is therefore relevant—to the broader readership. Done skillfully, such a case history is soft sell at its best: beneficial to the company and interesting and informative to the editor and readers.

The Byliner

The bylined article, or byliner, is a story signed and ostensibly authored by an officer of a particular firm. Often, however, the byliner is ghostwritten by a public relations professional. In addition to carrying considerable prestige in certain publications, byliners allow corporate spokespeople to express their views without being subject to major reinterpretation by the publication.

Perhaps the major advantage of a byliner is that it positions executives as experts. The fact that an organization's officer has authored an informed article on a subject means that not only are the officer and the organization credible sources, but also, by inference, they are perhaps more highly regarded on the issues at hand than their competitors. The ultimate audience exposed to a byliner may greatly exceed the circulation of the periodical in which the article appears, because organizations regularly use byliner reprints as direct mail pieces to enhance their image with key constituent groups.

The Op-Ed

Similar to the byliner, the op-ed article is an editorial written by an organizational executive and then submitted for publication to a leading newspaper or magazine. Most leading newspapers include a page opposite their editorial pages for outside opinions, thus "op-ed."

Being included on a publication's op-ed page is a prestigious publicity forum, and op-ed submissions are therefore plentiful. Op-ed pieces then must be written in a style that attracts attention. According to writing counselor Jeffrey D. Porro, the good ones contain the following elements:

Grabber, which starts off the piece and "grabs" attention
Point, which hammers home the thesis of the article
Chain of evidence, which gives the facts that support the argument
Summation, which summarizes the argument
Good-bye zinger, which leaves the reader with something to think about[2]

The Round-Up Article

Reporters get rewarded for two things in particular: scoops and trends. The former refers to breaking a story before anyone else. The latter concerns breaking a story that speaks of an emerging trend afoot or relevant to an industry. Although many publications discourage publicity about a single company, they encourage articles that summarize, or "round up," the experiences of several companies within an industry. These trend articles may be initiated by the publications themselves or at the suggestions of public relations people. Weaker or smaller companies, in particular, can benefit from being included in a roundup story with stronger, larger adversaries. Thoroughly researching and drafting roundup articles is a good way to secure stories that mention the practitioner's firm in favorable association with top competitors. The *Wall Street Journal,* the *New York Times, USA Today,* CNN—all regularly use roundups.

The Pitch Letter

The pitch letter is a sales letter, pure and simple. Its purpose is to interest an editor or reporter in a possible story, interview, or event. Figure 12-2 offers an example of two excellent pitch letters for the same product. Although letter styles run the gamut, the best are direct and to the point, while being catchy and evocative.

Pitch letters, like sales letters, may contain elements that seek to entice a reader's active participation in attending an event or covering a story. Among approaches that work are the following:

- **Challenge.** "Are you prepared to unravel the mysteries of. . . ."
- **Question.** "Will you do your readers a favor?"
- **News.** "An important announcement for all those concerned. . . ."
- **Invitation.** " We are pleased to inform you that you have been . . . ."
- **Urgency.** "We have now decided to hold an emergency session. . . ."
- **Narrative.** "You don't have to suffer it firsthand to know the. . . ."
- **Action.** "If you can be with us, we need to reserve your place immediately so. . . ."[3]

Pitch letters that sell generally contain several key elements. First, they open with a grabber, an interesting statement that impels the reader to continue reading. Next, they explain why the editor and/or publication should be interested in the pitch, or invitation, and why it is relevant to their readership. That means it must allude to the scope and importance of the story. Finally, they are personally written to specific people, rather than being addressed to "editor" (which is the journalistic equivalent of "occupant").

National Lampoon

This Is Your Last Chance . . .

Say good-bye, sweetheart. This is it! You can kiss the $7.95 one-year subscription to the *National Lampoon* good-bye just as you've said *au revoir* and *harry verderchi* to the fifty-cent gallon of gas, the ten-cent cigar, and the twenty-cent bus ride.

The price is going up and we're giving you fair warning. We're not saying exactly how much we're going to charge for the new one-year subscription but — it's less than the gross national product of Yugoslavia and more than a rubdown in a midget massage parlor.

The reasons for the increase in price are numerous in addition to greed:

1. The cost of paper has skyrocketed. All right, let's examine that. What does it mean to a magazine operation? Well, our editors drink a lot of coffee and this means an increase in the price of coffee cups. They throw paper airplanes around the room while trying to think of funny things to say. Up your cost of paper airplanes by 50 percent.
2. The cost of typewriters has increased. This doesn't affect us since no one on our staff knows how to type.
3. The cost of manufacturing has increased. This means that our editor in chief will be paying more for his Mercedes-Benz this year, and that means more for you to kick in. Would you ask the editor in chief of the world's most widely read adult humor magazine to drive around in last year's Mercedes-Benz?
4. The price of grain is spiraling. (We don't know what that means, but it is an exact quote from the *Wall Street Journal* so it must be important.)

O.K., put this all together and it means — raise the subscription prices. No more $7.95. So, this is it. This is your last chance. From here on in, it's clipsville. You pay more.

If you really want to save, take out a two- or three-year subscription. The savings are so big that we actually lose money every time you or anyone else subscribes for two or three years. We do it only because our subscription manager is insecure and he wants to know that he'll have at least a handful of people around for a long time.

No more message. If you want the latest in yocks, mirth, and lovable satire, subscribe today and subscribe at these pre-inflation prices.

Sincerely,

Herbert Hoover
Subscription Manager

IF YOU EVER WANT TO SEE THE LITTLE NATIONAL LAMPOON ALIVE AGAIN IN YOUR CRUMMY MAILBOX, YOU KNOW WHAT YOU HAVE TO DO!!!!

YOU'VE BEEN WARNED.
DON'T PLAY CUTE.

FIGURE 12-2 Catching the pitch. This letter from the subscription department of the National Lampoon magazine may not be a "public relations pitch letter" per se, but it is exactly the kind of enticing, catchy, and evocative letter necessary to capture the interest of a prospect.

A QUESTION OF ETHICS

Congratulations. You're a Big Winner! (NOT)

"YOU'VE JUST BEEN POSITIVELY IDENTIFIED AS OUR $1,000,000 MYSTERY MILLIONAIRE FROM FLORIDA."

Junk mail from a sweepstakes promoter seems to address you personally and often makes it sound as if you will soon receive money in your bank account. Most of the time, you won't.

In recent years, sweepstakes companies, such as Publishers Clearing House, American Family Publishers, and Reader's Digest, have been called to task for composing pitch letters that sound too good to be true and usually are.

Most of the letters clearly indicate that "No Purchase Is Necessary," but thousands of people still believe that a purchase helps win all that cash. In 1999, as a result of class-action suits filed against the biggest sweepstakes companies, some questionable practices are being altered.

For example, it was always fair game for your sweepstakes letter to list your past orders and indicate that you are either "meeting the criteria for winning" or imply that "you're not ordering enough." Nonbuyers might have to use a reply envelope that says, "No Reward Entitled."

Older people make up a disproportionate number of players, and sweepstakes companies regularly use such trusted figures as Ed McMahon and Dick Clark to hawk their contests. In recent years, states attorneys general have received increasing complaints from families whose gullible, elderly relatives are squandering their limited incomes reaching for the sweepstakes brass ring.

In response to growing litigation and government scrutiny, companies like Publishers Clearing House have developed education and assistance programs to protect consumers and taken out ads to explain their philosophy. Clearly, no company should profit from people who can't understand what they are reading.

Related to the pitch letter is the "media alert" to grab the attention of editors and news directors. This format eschews the use of long paragraphs in favor of short, bulleted items highlighting the "5Ws" used by journalists: who, what, when, where, and why. The premise of the media alert is that it "talks to the media in a language it has been trained to accept."[4]

Internal Writing Tools

The E-mail Memorandum

Humorist Art Buchwald tells of the child who visited his father's office. When asked what his dad did, the son replied, "He sends pieces of paper to other people, and other people send pieces of paper to him." Most people who work know a great deal about memoranda, which these days is most likely to be distributed via e-mail. E-mail today is by far the number one internal communications vehicle and may just be the number one communications vehicle externally as well.

E-mail memos are written for a multitude of purposes and take numerous forms. Even though almost everyone gets into the memo-writing act, writing memos correctly takes practice and hard work.

The keys to writing good e-mail memos are clear thinking and brevity. Many memos reflect unclear thinking and are plagued by verbosity and fuzzy language. Inverted pyramid style is often a good way to compose a memo. More often, rewriting turns out to be the key.

Public relations people are expected to write good e-mail and print memos. This is no easy feat. The key is to keep in mind the six primary elements of a meaningful memo:

1. **State the issue.** Don't dilly dally. Memos don't require preambles. Get right to the issue at hand.
2. **Back it up with data.** Put the issue into a clear, snappy context so that the recipient understands your thought processes.
3. **Present alternatives.** List all the possibilities that must be considered before rendering a decision. Again, brevity is a virtue.
4. **Offer your solution or recommendation.** Be decisive. Stick your neck out. Suggest a clear course of action.
5. **Back it up with detail.** Explain, again briefly, why you believe the action you've recommended is justifiable.
6. **Call for the question.** Always end with a question that demands action.

Don't leave things up in the air. Memos, particularly e-mails, can't end by drifting into space. Avoid this. Make the recipient get back to you by asking a question to which he or she must respond, such as "Do you agree with this?" or "Can we move on this?"[5]

The Position Paper

Public relations people are frequently called on to write the "position paper," also called the "white paper." Written primarily for internal background purposes, position papers are long and rigorously document the facts and assumptions that lead to a particular "position" that the organization is suggested to take. Such documents form the basis of review and discussion and ultimately serve as the nucleus for a corporate position. After such a position is ratified by management, a "sanitized" position paper may be made available for distribution to opinion leaders and the general public.

The Standby Statement

Organizations sometimes take actions or make announcements they know will lead to media inquiries or even public protests. In such cases, firms prepare concise statements to clarify their positions, should they be called to explain. Such standby statements generally are defensive—and certainly not meant to be volunteered.

They should be brief and unambiguous so as not to raise more questions than they answer. Such events as executive firings, layoffs, price increases, and extraordinary losses are all subject to subsequent scrutiny by the media and are therefore proper candidates for standby statements. At any one time, a public relations professional, doing his or her job right, will have several standby statements at the ready should the dreaded call come in.

The Speech

Speechwriting has become one of the most coveted public relations skills. Increasingly, speechwriters have used their access to management to move up the organizational ladder. The prominence they enjoy is due largely to the importance government and business executives place on making speeches. Today's executives are called on to defend

BACKGROUNDER

Don't—Repeat—Don't Use "Do Not"

In writing standby statements, public relations practitioners should keep in mind that publications sometimes mistakenly drop words in print. Invariably, the most important words are the ones dropped.

For example, the public relations officer of the labor union who issues the statement "We do not intend to strike" may have his quote appear in the next day's paper as "We do intend to strike"—the "not" having been inadvertently dropped by the paper. A slight yet significant change.

The remedy: Use contractions. It's pretty hard to drop a significant word or distort the intended meaning when the statement is "We don't intend to strike."

their policies, justify their prices, and explain their practices to a much greater degree than ever before. In this environment, a good speechwriter becomes a valuable—and often highly paid—asset.

A speech possesses five main characteristics:

1. **It is designed to be heard, not read.** The mistake of writing for the eye instead of the ear is the most common trap of bad speeches. Speeches needn't be literary gems, but they ought to sound good.
2. **It uses concrete language.** The ear dislikes generalities. It responds to clear images. Ideas must be expressed sharply for the audience to get the point.
3. **It demands a positive response.** Every word, every passage, every phrase should evoke a response from the audience. The speech should possess special vitality—and so, for that matter, should the speaker.
4. **It must have clear-cut objectives.** The speech and the speaker must have a point—a thesis. If there's no point, then it's not worth the speaker's or the audience's time to be there.
5. **It must be tailored to a specific audience.** An audience needs to feel that it is hearing something special. The most frequent complaint about organizational speeches is that they all seem interchangeable—they lack uniqueness. That's why speeches must be targeted to fit the needs of a specific audience. Beyond adhering to these five principles and before putting words on paper, a speechwriter must have a clear idea of the process—the route—to follow in developing the speech.

The Speechwriting Process

The speechwriting process breaks down into four components: (1) preparing, (2) interviewing, (3) researching, and (4) organizing and writing.

Preparing

One easy way to prepare for a speech is to follow a 4W checklist: Answer the questions who, what, where, and when.

- ☑ **Who.** The "who" represents two critical elements: the speaker and the audience. A writer should know all about the speaker—manner of speech, use of humor, reaction to an audience, background, and personality. It's almost impossible to write a speech for someone you don't know.

The writer should also know something about the audience. What does this audience think about this subject? What are its predispositions toward the subject and the speaker? What are the major points with which it might agree? The more familiar the writer is with the "who" of a speech, the easier the writing will be.

- ◪ **What.** The "what" is the topic. The assigned subject must be clearly known and well-defined by the writer before formal research is begun. If the writer fails to delineate the subject in advance, much of the research will be pointless.

- ◪ **Where.** The "where" is the setting. A large hall requires a more formal talk than a roundtable forum. Often, the location of the speech—the city, state, or even a particular hall—bears historic or symbolic significance that can enhance a message.

- ◪ **When.** The "when" is the time of the speech. People are more awake in the morning and get sleepier as the day progresses, so a dinner speech should be kept short. The "when" also refers to the time of year. A speech can always be linked to an upcoming holiday or special celebration.

Interviewing

Interviewing speakers in advance is essential. Without that chance, the results can be dismal. A good interview with a speaker often means the difference between a strong speech and a poor one. Stated another way, the speechwriter is only as good as his or her access to the speaker.

In the interview, the speechwriter gets some time—from as little as 15 minutes to more than an hour—to observe the speaker firsthand and probe for the keys to the speech. The interview must accomplish at least three specific goals for the speechwriter:

1. **Determine the object of the talk.** The object is different from the subject. The subject is the topic, but the object is the purpose of the speech—that is, what exactly the speaker wants the audience to do after he or she is finished speaking. Does the speaker want them to storm City Hall? To love big business? To write their congressional representatives? The interviewer's essential question must be "What do you want to leave the audience with at the conclusion of your speech?" Once the speaker answers this question, the rest of the speech should fall into place.

2. **Determine the speaker's main points.** Normally, an audience can grasp only a few points during a speech. These points, which should flow directly from the object, become touchstones around which the rest of the speech is woven. Again, the writer must determine the three or four main points during the interview.

3. **Capture the speaker's characteristics.** Most of all, during the interview, the writer must observe the speaker. How comfortable is the speaker with humor? How informal or deliberate is he or she with words? What are the speaker's pet phrases and expressions? The writer must file these observations away, recall them during the writing process, and factor them into the speech.

Researching

Like any writer, a speechwriter sometimes develops writer's block, the inability to come up with anything on paper. One way around writer's block is to adopt a formalized research procedure.

1. **Dig into all literature, books, pamphlets, articles, speeches, and other writings on the speech subject.** Prior speeches by the speaker are also important documents to research. A stocked file cabinet is often the speechwriter's best friend.
2. **Think about the subject.** Bring personal thoughts to bear on the topic. Presumably, the speaker has already discussed the topic with the writer, so the writer can amplify the speaker's thoughts with his or her own.
3. **Seek out the opinions of others on the topic.** Perhaps the speaker isn't the most knowledgeable source within the organization about this specific subject. Economists, lawyers, accountants, doctors, and other technical experts may shed additional light on the topic. Outside sources, particularly politicians and business leaders, are often willing to share their ideas when requested.

Organizing and Writing

Once preparation, interviewing, and research have been completed, the fun part begins. Writing a speech becomes easier if, again, the speech is organized into its four essential elements: introduction, thesis, body, and conclusion.

Introduction. Writing a speech introduction is a lot like handling a bar of soap in the shower: The first thing to do is get control. An introduction must grab the audience and hold its interest. An audience is alert at the beginning of a talk and is with the speaker. The writer's job is to make sure the audience stays there.

The speechwriter must take full advantage of the early good nature of the audience by making the introduction snappy. Audience members need time to settle in their seats, and the speaker needs time to get his or her bearings on the podium. Often, the best way to win early trust and rapport with the audience is to ease into the speech with humor.

Thesis. The thesis is the object of the speech—its purpose or central idea. A good thesis statement lets an audience know in a simple sentence where a speech is going and how it will get there. For example, its purpose can be to persuade:

The federal government must regulate content on the Internet.

Another thesis statement might be to reinforce or crystallize a belief:

Free and accessible Internet content underscores the most essential of Constitutional freedoms.

The purpose of yet another thesis statement might merely be to entertain:

The extent of Internet content is wondrous to behold. Let's take a tour of the Internet.

In each case, the thesis statement lets the audience know early what the point of the speech will be and leads listeners to the desired conclusion.

Body. The speech body is just that—the general body of evidence that supports the three or four main points. Although facts, statistics, and figures are important elements, writers should always attempt to use comparisons or contrasts for easier audience understanding. For example:

In a single week, 272 million customers passed through the checkout counters of American supermarkets. That's equal to the combined populations of Spain, Mexico, Argentina, France, West Germany, Italy, Sweden, Switzerland, and Belgium.

Such comparisons dramatically hammer points home to a lazy audience.

Conclusion. The best advice on wrapping up a speech is to do it quickly. As the old Texas bromide goes, "If you haven't struck oil in the first 20 minutes, stop boring." Put another way, the conclusion must be blunt, short, and to the point. It may be a good idea to review orally the major points and thesis one last time and then stop.

The Spoken Word

Speeches are meant to be heard, so the writer should take advantage of tools—figures of speech—that emphasize the special qualities of the spoken word. Used skillfully, these devices can elevate a mediocre speech into a memorable one:

- **Alliteration,** the repetition of initial sounds in words
- **Antithesis,** using sharply opposed or contrasting ideas in the same passage
- **Metonymy,** substituting one term for another closely associated one to give a passage more figurative life
- **Metaphor and simile,** which figuratively connect concepts that have little literal connection
- **Personification,** which gives life to animals, inanimate objects, or ideas
- **Repetition,** using the same words or phrases over and over again
- **Humor** that is relevant, fresh, and in good taste

The best public speakers of all time—Franklin Roosevelt, Martin Luther King, John F. Kennedy, Ronald Reagan, Jesse Jackson, Mario Cuomo—all used these kinds of devices.

A derivative of speechwriting is constructing "talking points"—highlights of a speech that a manager can allude to in speaking more extemporaneously. The key to speechwriting, as with any other kind of writing, is experience. As speechwriting has become a more competitive, highly paid, and sought-after pursuit in public relations, it has become increasingly difficult for an interested novice to break in. Don't be dismayed. Most political candidates or nonprofit community organizations are more than willing to allow beginners to try their hand at drafting speeches. Although the pay for such endeavors may be limited—or nonexistent—such voluntary efforts are a good way to learn the ropes of speechwriting.

Few other activities in public relations offer as much fulfillment—in both psychological and monetary rewards—as speechwriting.

The Four Most Eloquent Words in History

At the end of the century, a group of 137 communications professors from across the nation ranked the top speeches of the century.

Their list of the top 100 is a diverse mixture of race, gender, and philosophy, from women's suffragist Carrie Chapman Catt to Professor Anita Hill, from trial lawyer Clarence Darrow to novelist William Faulkner.

Three of the top 10 speeches were delivered by black Americans, reflecting the civil rights movement and also the rich oral tradition of black culture. Seven speeches on the list were delivered in the 1990s, five by women. Topping the 1990s list at number 35 was Hillary Clinton's address to the United Nations on "Women's Rights" in 1995.

Predictably, most speeches on the list are from politicians. A precious few are from business leaders. The Top 10:

1. "I Have a Dream," Martin Luther King, August 28, 1963
2. "Inaugural Address," John F. Kennedy, January 20, 1961
3. "Inaugural Address," Franklin D. Roosevelt, March 4, 1933
4. "War Message," Franklin D. Roosevelt, December 8, 1941
5. "Democratic National Convention Keynote," Barbara Jordan, July 12, 1976
6. "Checkers Speech," Richard M. Nixon, September 23, 1952
7. "The Ballot or the Bullet," Malcolm X, April 3, 1964
8. "The Challenger Address," Ronald Reagan, January 28, 1986
9. "Greater Houston Ministerial Association Speech," John F. Kennedy, September 12, 1960
10. "Voting Rights Speech," Lyndon B. Johnson, March 15, 1965

And the four most eloquent words in history? "I have a dream." *

*Dru Sefton, "I Have a Dream," USA Today, December 30, 1999, 8D.

Making an Effective Presentation

A business presentation is different from a speech. A presentation generally is designed to sell a product, service, or idea. Everyone, somewhere along the line, must deliver a presentation. Like any other speaking device, an effective presentation depends on following established guidelines. Here are 10 points worth pursuing prior to presenting:

1. **Get organized.** Before considering your presentation, consider the 4Ws of speechwriting. Who are you addressing? What are you trying to say? Where and when should something happen?
2. **Get to the point.** Know your thesis. What are you trying to prove? What is the central purpose of your presentation?
3. **Be logical.** Organize the presentation with some logic in mind. Don't skip randomly from one thought to another. Lead from your objective to your strategies to the tactics you will use to achieve your goal.
4. **Write it out.** Don't wing it. If Jay Leno and David Letterman write out their ad-libs, so should you. Always have the words right in front of you.
5. **Anticipate the negatives.** Keep carping critics at bay. Anticipate their objections and defuse them by examining and dismissing vulnerabilities in the presentation.

6. **Speak, don't read.** Sound as if you know the information. Practice before the performance. Make the presentation part of you. Reading suggests uncertainty. Speaking asserts assurance.

7. **Be understandable.** Speak with clarity and concreteness so that people understand you. If you want to make the sale, you must be clear.

8. **Use graphics wisely.** Audiovisual supports should do just that—support the presentation. Graphics should be used more to tease than to provide full information. They shouldn't be crammed with too much information. This will detract from the overall impact of the presentation. Because many audiovisual channels are available to a presenter (see Appendix D), it may be wise to seek professional help in devising compelling graphics for a presentation.

9. **Be convincing.** If you aren't enthusiastic about your presentation, no one else will be. Be animated. Be interesting. Be enthusiastic. Sound convinced that what you're presenting is an absolute necessity for the organization.

10. **STOP!** A short, buttoned-up presentation is much more effective than one that goes on and on. At his inaugural, U.S. President William Henry Harrison delivered a two-hour, 6,000-word address into a biting wind on Pennsylvania Avenue. A month later, he died of pneumonia. The lesson: When you've said it all, shut up!

BACKGROUNDER

Every Picture Tells a Story

As executive speechmaking has become more important, a plethora of counseling firms have sprung up to advise executive speakers on how to create and deliver winning speeches. Communispond, Inc., developed one of the most novel concepts.

Because most executives are neither comfortable at a podium nor confident in their ability to perform before a large audience, Communispond came up with the concept of drawing pictures to replace formal written speeches. Essentially, after gathering all available evidence and support material and outlining in words what they want to cover, Communispond-trained executives are encouraged to draw pictures, called ideographs, to reflect accurately the subject at hand. For example, a corporate speaker who wants to express the notion that the ship of American capitalism is still being fired on by entrenched socialist salvos around the world might sketch an ideograph similar to the one here.

In this way, Communispond-trained speakers are taught to use their nervousness to convey natural, human conviction. Not constrained by lifeless written copy, an executive is free, as Communispond puts it, "to speak as well as you think."

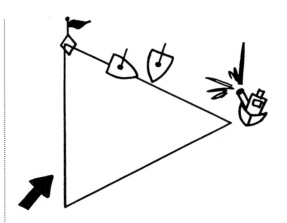

Although not right for everyone, Communispond's unique approach, when mastered, allows for a much more extemporaneous and lively discourse than the average prepared text. Fortunately, however (at least as far as corporate speechwriters are concerned), most executives still insist on the security blanket of a full written text.

Is learning how to make an effective presentation really worth it? Are you kidding? When General Norman Schwarzkopf retired after the Gulf War, he marched into the speaking world at $80,000 per speech.[6] That was $20,000 less than former President George Bush began charging when he ventured into the speech market in 1994. And the speaking fee numbers for outgoing President Bill Clinton, a folksy and effective communicator, will likely exceed his predecessor's numbers.

S U M M A R Y

Skillful writing lies at the heart of public relations practice. Basically, public relations professionals are professional communicators. Ergo, each person engaged in public relations work must be adept at writing.

In today's overcommunicated society, everyone from newspaper editors to corporate presidents complains about getting too much paper. So, before a professional even thinks of putting thoughts on paper, he or she must answer the following questions:

1. Will writing serve a practical purpose? If you can't come up with a purpose, don't write.
2. Is writing the most effective way to communicate? Face-to-face or telephone communication may be better and more direct than writing.
3. What is the risk? Writing is always risky; just ask a lawyer. Once it's down in black and white, it's difficult or impossible to retract. And the risks have increased with the immediacy and pervasiveness of the Internet. So, think before you write.
4. Are the timing and the person doing the writing right? Timing is extremely important in writing. A message, like a joke, can fall flat if the timing is off. The individual doing the writing must also be considered. A writer should always ask whether he or she is the most appropriate person to write.

The pen—or, more likely, the PC or laptop—is a powerful weapon. Like any other weapon, writing must be used prudently and properly to achieve the desired result.

Discussion Starters

1. What are the essential elements of a media kit?
2. What is the difference between a straight biography and a narrative biography?
3. What is a backgrounder?
4. What are the benefits of a roundup story?
5. When might an organization require a standby statement?
6. What are the essential characteristics of a speech?
7. What questions does one ask to begin the speechwriting process?
8. What are the elements that constitute an effective presentation?
9. What is the purpose of using "figures of speech" in a presentation and what types are useful?
10. What are possible pitfalls that must be considered before writing anything?

top of the shelf

Roger C. Parker

Roger C. Parker's Guide to Web Content and Design: Eight Steps to Web Site Success. New York: MIS Press, 1997.

In the introduction to this lively, informed, and informative book, Jay Conrad Levinson (author of *Guerilla Marketing*) says, "One billion? Two billion? Five billion? I'm trying to figure how many dollars have been wasted by web site owners who lacked the information in this book."

Roger Parker, author of the all-time best-selling desktop publishing book, *Looking Good in Print,* is a natural-born teacher. His style is engaging. As Levinson says,

"What I personally like best about the book is that it asks you questions and when you have answered them, you have a roadmap to your own personal success."

For PR professionals increasingly involved in—even responsible for—company and client Web sites, *Guide to Web Content and Design* should be a welcome partner. Parker encourages readers to "let me know how things work out for you. Contact me through my web site located at www.rcparker.com."

Notes

1. G. A. Marken, "Public Relations Photos . . . Beyond the Written Word," *Public Relations Quarterly* (Summer 1993): 7–12.
2. Jeffrey D. Porro, Porro Associates, 1120 Connecticut Ave., Suite 270, Washington, D.C. 20036.
3. "Writing Irresistible Teaser Copy," *Communicator* (July 1998): 6.
4. "Farewell to the Pitch Letter," *Public Relations Journal* (July 1990): 13.
5. Fraser P. Seitel, "Meaningful Memos," *United States Banker* (November 1993): 77.
6. Randall Poe, "Talk Isn't Cheap," *Across the Board* (September 1992): 19–24.

Suggested Readings

Bakshian, Aaron, Jr. *The American Speaker.* Washington, D.C.: Georgetown Publishing House, 1995. Written by a former Ronald Reagan speechwriter, this book receives more ingenious self-promotion than probably any work in the history of the world. But it does have its qualities, among them excellent anecdotes from a number of excellent public speakers.

Decker, Bert. *You've Got to Be Believed to Be Heard.* New York: St. Martin's Press, 1992. One of America's foremost speech coaches shares his secrets.

Detz, Joan. *How to Write and Give a Speech.* New York: St. Martin's Press, 1992.

Erlich, Henry. *Writing Effective Speeches.* New York: Paragon House, 1992.

Goldstein, Norm, ed. *The Associated Press Stylebook and Libel Manual.* New York: The Associated Press. 1998. Appendices include "Copyright Guidelines," "Freedom of Information Act," "Photo Captions," and "Filing the Wire."

Filson, Brent. *Executive Speeches.* Williamstown, MA: Williamstown Publishing Company, 1991.

Hanson, Garth A. *Say It Right: A Guide to Effective Oral Business Presentations.* Burr Ridge, IL: Irwin Professional Publishing, 1995.

The New York Public Library Writer's Guide to Style and Usage. Alexandria, VA: New York: HarperCollins Publishers, 1994.

O'Shaughnessy, William. *Airwaves: A Collection of Radio Editorials from the Golden Apple.* New York: Fordham University Press, 1999. Poignant, vividly portrayed, and emotion-laden stories written for the radio.

Ross, Marilyn, ed. *National Directory of Newspaper Op-Ed Pages.* Buena Vista, CO: Communication Creativity. 1999. Description, contact information, and comments.

Smith, Terry C. *Making Successful Presentations,* 2nd ed. New York: John Wiley & Sons, 1991.

Speechwriter's Newsletter (Available from Ragan Communications, 407 S. Dearborn, Chicago, IL 60605).

Torricelli, Robert, and Andrew Carroll. *In Our Own Words, Extraordinary Speeches of the American Century.* New York: Kodansha International, 1999. A U.S. senator and his co-editor choose 150 seminal speeches of our time, from Al Capone to Billy Sunday, from Jane Fonda to Richard Nixon.

United Press International. *Broadcast Stylebook* (220 E. 42nd Street, New York, NY 10017). This is not a rule book, but it suggests methods and treatment for properly preparing news copy, with examples of wire copy and brief comments on correct and incorrect methods of news wire copy preparation. It's designed to help people write the kind of copy used by an announcer.

Variety (Available from 475 Park Ave. South, New York, NY 10016; published weekly on Wednesday). This paper publishes news, features, and commentary each week on every aspect of show business, with extensive reviews of productions around the world.

CASE STUDY

Illinois Power's Reply

For three decades, no network news program has rivaled the incredible impact of CBS-TV's *60 Minutes*. Watched each Sunday night by more than 20 million Americans, *60 Minutes* still ranks as one of the most popular programs in the nation and the show most feared by public relations professionals. When *60 Minutes* comes calling, scandal, or at least significant problems, can't be far behind.

Such was the thinking at Illinois Power Company (IP) in Decatur in the fall of 1979, when *60 Minutes* sent reporter Harry Reasoner to find out why the company's Clinton nuclear reactor project was behind schedule and over budget.

What followed—the exchange between Reasoner and IP—still ranks as history's most classic confrontation between television and corporate public relations professionals. Because IP suspected that *60 Minutes* wanted to do a hatchet job, the company agreed to be interviewed only if it, too, videotaped the *60 Minutes* filming on its premises. In other words, IP would videotape the videotapers; it would report on the reporters; it would meet *60 Minutes* on its own terms. Reasoner and his producer reluctantly agreed to the arrangement.

So in early October, IP's executive vice president sat for an hour-and-a-half interview before the *60 Minutes*—and the IP—cameras. He answered Reasoner's questions straightforwardly and comprehensively. And he and his company prepared for the worst.

Which is precisely what they received.

On November 25, *60 Minutes* broadcast a 16-minute segment on the Clinton plant, charging IP with mismanagement, missed deadlines, and costly overruns that would be passed on to consumers. Viewers saw three former IP employees accuse the utility of making no effort to control costs, allowing slipshod internal reporting, and fabricating estimates of construction completion timetables. One of the accusers was shown in silhouette with a distorted voice because, as reporter Reasoner intoned, "He fears retribution." To add salt to the IP wound, the 90-minute interview with the company's executive vice president merited less than 2 minutes of edited, misleading air time.

Worst of all, 24 million Americans viewed the crucifixion in their living rooms.

The day after the CBS story, IP's stock fell a full point on the New York Stock Exchange in the busiest trading day in the company's history. Rather than responding as most companies do—with bruised feelings, a scorched reputation, and feeble cries of "foul" to its stockholders—IP lashed back with barrels blazing. Within days of the broadcast, IP produced *60 Minutes/Our Reply,* a 44-minute film incorporating the entire *60 Minutes* segment, punctuated by insertions and narrative presenting the company's rebuttal.

The rebuttal included videotape of CBS film footage not included in the program, much of which raised serious questions about the integrity of the material CBS used. The rebuttal also documented the backgrounds and possible motives of the three former employees CBS quoted, all of whom had been fired for questionable performance. One of the former employees, in fact, was the leader of the local antinuclear group opposing IP.

Initially, the reply tape was aired to a relatively small audience: the company's employees, customers, shareholders, and investors. But word traveled quickly that IP had produced a riveting, broadcast-quality production, so true to the *60 Minutes* format—ticking stopwatch and all—that it could easily be mistaken for the original. Within a year, close to 2,500 copies of the devastating rebuttal had been distributed to legislators, corporate executives, journalists, and others. Excerpts were broadcast on television stations throughout the nation, and the IP production became legendary. As the *Wall Street Journal* put it, "The program focuses new attention on news accuracy. . . . Although even a telling, polished, counter-program like Illinois Power's can't reach the masses of a national broadcast, the reply tape has proven effective in reaching a significant 'thinking' audience."

Even CBS was impressed. The producer of the original *60 Minutes* segment called the rebuttal highly sophisticated, especially for a company that had first seemed to him to be a "down-home cracker barrel" outfit. The IP tape soon spawned imitators. Companies such as Chevron, Union Carbide, Commonwealth Edison, and many others began experimenting with defensive videotaping in dealing with television journalists.

Although *60 Minutes* admitted to some sloppiness in its reporting and to two minor factual inaccuracies, it essentially stood by its account. Complained CBS executive producer Don Hewitt, "We went in as a disinterested party and did a news report. They made a propaganda film for their side, using our reporting for their own purposes."

Perhaps. But one irrefutable result of the dramatic confrontation between the huge national network and the tiny local utility was that IP—by turning the television tables on the dreaded *60 Minutes*—had earned its place in public relations history.*

Questions

1. Do you agree with IP's original decision to let *60 Minutes* in despite the suspicion that the program would be a hatchet job? What might have happened if IP turned down the *60 Minutes* request?

2. If *60 Minutes* had turned down IP's request to videotape the Reasoner interviews, would you have still allowed the filming?

3. Presume that IP didn't tape the *60 Minutes* filming on its premises. What other communications options might the company have pursued to rebut the *60 Minutes* accusations?

4. Do you think IP did better by allowing *60 Minutes* in to film or would they have been better off keeping CBS out?

5. How would IP communicate with the press in the event of a nuclear emergency at its Clinton plant? Find out by reading the company's on-line news release on this subject (www.illnoispower.com/pa.nsf/Web/JPIC). What tools would IP's public relations professionals use in such a situation? How often would IP hold a news conference during this kind of emergency?

*Sandy Graham, "Illinois Utility Sparks Widespread Interest with Its Videotape," the *Wall Street Journal* (April 12, 1980): 23. For further information on the IP case, see Punch, Counterpunch: *"60 Minutes"* vs. Illinois Power Company (Washington, D.C.: Media Institute, 1981), and, "Turning the Tables on '60 Minutes,' " *Columbia Journalism Review* (May–June 1980): 7–9.

OVER THE TOP

An Interview with Shirley Carter

Shirley Staples Carter is professor and chairperson of the Department of Mass Communications and Journalism at Norfolk State University, Norfolk, Virginia. Prior to that, she was associate professor/director and former inaugural chairperson of the Department of Communications and Visual Arts at the University of North Florida. Carter directs the university's efforts to plan and develop new communications technologies, such as instructional television fixed-services delivery systems, other broadcast initiatives, and cable and community education. Carter's experience spans two decades in higher education administration and teaching. She is the first African-American female to serve as a department chairperson in journalism/mass communications at a mainstream university.

What does it take to become an effective print writer?

We need to return to the basics, which include reading, listening, and observing skills. As our society prepares for the explosion of the information superhighway, the effective print writer should incorporate visual elements into the writing task as well.

What does it take to become an effective writer for the spoken word?

The same, basically. We must be literate in terms of the environment, our society, political systems, and evolution. The broadcast writer must be able to stir the imagination of the listener if the medium is audio or evoke the desired response or emotion in the viewer if the medium is video.

How important is it for a public relations student to hone his or her writing skills?

It is extremely important. The most important tool for the public relations professional is writing. And perhaps one of the great challenges of the new information society is that writers must be versatile and knowledgeable about how to communicate with multicultural audiences or markets.

What is the caliber of public relations students today?

They are a diverse lot. Some are more mature, more focused, and tend to be highly specialized in their career aspirations, for example, international relations, government relations, public affairs, sports marketing, political communications. They expect a tremendous technological impact on the industry and society in general, and they are beginning to understand, thanks to the global reach of CNN and other factors, that our world is getting smaller. Some have a great deal of potential, even if their notions about what public relations is (an easy job) and what public relations requires (a pretty smile) are erroneous. These qualities in our students make public relations education especially challenging and exciting.

What is the status of minorities in public relations?

There are still too few, as in other communications and related fields. Minorities account for less than 5 percent of midlevel jobs in midmanagement; they are virtually invisible in senior management. We can do more at the grass-roots level to attract minorities to the public relations industry. University programs might focus as much on retention efforts as on recruitment and encourage minority student participation in organizations such as Public Relations Student Society of America and mainstream public relations internships. Professionals can take this one step further by mentoring and nurturing minorities interested in public relations careers. Now is the best time to prepare for the changes already taking shape in the workplace, the shifting demographics, the increasing black and Latino consumer markets, and expanding global opportunities.

What is the future for minorities in public relations?

I think the future is quite bright. The opportunities will definitely be there, but we need students who are fully prepared to take advantage of them. Education and awareness will be the key determinants. The responsibility of minority students is to develop essential skills such as writing, mastery of a foreign language, and appreciation of foreign cultures, and to attain a strong liberal arts background and computer literacy. Minority students should also seek exposure to public relations career opportunities and be keenly aware of the possibilities open to them as a result of ethnic, global, and technological changes in our society.

Chapter 13

Public Relations and the Internet

"If you're not online, you don't exist"

—British Futurist Peter Cochrane

In 1998, Mr. Cochrane could have rightfully been accused of being "all wet." But by the 21st century, he is "right as rain"—cyber rain, that is. Or, more specifically, cyber "reign." Make no mistake: In the 21st century, the Internet rules. That goes for the practice of public relations as well as every other sector of society.

What is the Internet? It's a cooperatively run, globally distributed collection of computer networks that exchange information via a common set of rules. It started around 1980, as a government-funded project that would allow communications in the event of a nuclear attack.

The World Wide Web, the most exciting and revolutionary part of the Internet, was developed in 1989 by physicist Tim Berners-Lee to enlarge the Internet for multiple uses. The Web is a collection of millions of computers on the Internet that contain information in a single format: HTML or hypertext markup language. By combining multimedia—sound, graphics, video, animation, and more—the Web has become the most powerful tool in cyberspace.

Without question, the Internet and the World Wide Web are playing an increasingly significant role in our everyday lives. They are transforming the way people work, the way we buy things, the way we entertain ourselves, the way business is conducted, and, most important to public relations professionals, the way we communicate with each other. The Internet phenomenon, pure and simple, is a revolution.

In 1999, the Internet economy grew by 68 percent, topping one-half trillion dollars and far outpacing the growth of the overall U.S. economy.[1] Illustrative of how the Internet economy was replacing traditional economic names and values were the names of the new companies added that year to the Dow Jones Industrial average: Microsoft, Intel, and SBC Communications. Who were the old-timers they replaced? Chevron, Goodyear, Sears Roebuck, and Union Carbide.

As phenomenal as the Internet's growth has been, the fact is, we have barely begun, as tennis star Andre Agassi once put it, "to scratch the iceberg." By the start of the new century, only between one-third and one-half of America was on-line, much of that on slow phone connections. Nonetheless, by 2000, Americans were spending nearly eight hours a week on-line, sending three times as much e-mail as regular mail, and spending $20 billion on on-line retail purchases. Internet traffic doubles every 95 days. Americans alone add two million pages to the World Wide Web daily.[2]

So the Internet is just getting started as a communications tool. As to the future, consider a few likely outcomes.

- *U.S. business trade over the Internet will more than double to $251 billion.*
- *The U.S. on-line populations will reach nearly 140 million, up from just under 100 million in 1999.*
- *11 million U.S. households will make their first on-line purchase.*
- *On-line prescription drug purchases will reach $450 million.*
- *Nearly four million households will invest on-line, a 25 percent increase over 1999.*
- *More than 32 million adults will go on-line for game-related content.*
- *35 million U.S. surfers will hunt for music content on-line, spending $700 million on CDs and cassettes.[3]*

In the public relations business, as in other lines of work, the Internet has taken hold with a ferocity. Every organization, from the largest corporation to the smallest nonprofit, today has a Web site. Often, it is the Web site that serves as that organization's "first face" to the public. Public relations departments now have interactive specialists and groups. Public relations agencies now boast on-line departments. Agencies that specialize in new media and on-line communications are flourishing.

Journalists meanwhile—still the primary responsibility for most in public relations—are also moving to the Internet for research and reporting. By the turn of the new century, more than half of the nation's journalists were on-line and using Web sites as a primary source of organizational research. Photo editors were downloading 80 percent of their photos. The growth of on-line newspapers and e-zines was skyrocketing.[4]

Increasingly, companies are marketing their products, their stocks, and themselves on the Internet. The lure of "communicating direct" to customers, investors, suppliers, neighbors, even the media is an enticing one. If anyone doubts the future of Internet commerce, all one has to do is consider the following projections to 2003:

- *Retail shopping on the Internet will surpass $100 billion*
- *Banking and investing will produce $80 billion in on-line sales*
- *Travel-related services will post almost $70 billion in e-commerce sales*

◪ *Meanwhile, global exposure on the Internet will only be about 10 to 15 percent in terms of e-commerce—with 85 percent of the world to go![5]*

As a consequence of the tremendous boom in Internet communications, no area of public relations work is "hotter" today than the development of Web sites, intranet operations, and the general harnessing of the Web to communicate with target publics. Although the wonders of the Web are still only evolving, attention to the computer and what it can provide the public relations practitioner are the topics that dominate discussion in the public relations industry.

Growing WWW Use and Concern

The nation was taken aback in the winter of 1999 when a controversial study reported the growth of the nation's on-line audience had slowed dramatically. According to the research, only 3.9 million adults went on-line for the first time during the first six months of the year, versus 12 million in the same period a year earlier.[6] Only 3.9 million new users in six months! Man the lifeboats!

Such hiccups notwithstanding, the growth of the Internet and World Wide Web is unstoppable. One in four Americans—69 million American adults—used the Internet by the end of the last century. Over the next few years, that number will rise to more than 100 million—nearly half of all adults—and nearly 200 million including children.

In the United States today, more than half log on from home, and about 30 percent are in the 25- to 34-year-old population, the fastest-growing segment of the on-line population. Males are heavier Internet users than women by three to one, but the latter comprise the fastest-growing segment of users. Nearly half of all users in this early

---

stage of Web development rate their overall on-line satisfaction as "very good" or "excellent."[7] Internet users, predictably are generally smart and affluent. Nearly 50 percent have completed college. Mean annual income of Internet users is $62,000.[8]

Beyond the United States, of the 128 million people around the world with on-line access, about 40 percent are non-English speaking. This group will become an increasingly larger part of the on-line population.

The burgeoning growth of the World Wide Web is not without its downside.

Although the Internet increases in popularity every day, it is too often bogged down—gridlocked—by too many users contributing a continuous and unrestrained stream of communication, much labeled "shovelware" or, literally translated, unadulterated garbage.[9] The number of pages on the Web has mushroomed from a few thousand in 1992 to 50 million and climbing today. In terms of how clogged it is, government scientists have warned that the Internet is in a "dangerous state," particularly when comparing the volume of information available to that which is useful.

The glut of Internet startup companies, some with little more than an "optimistic concept," has also introduced wariness on the Web. In the early years of the 21st century, investors have fallen all over themselves to "bid up" Internet stocks. Many Web startups have seen their initial public offering (IPO) stock price skyrocket from opening levels. The stock market has created scores of instant millionaires among Internet entrepreneurs. This, in turn, has led to a resurgence in the economy and new opportunities for employees, suppliers, consultants, and many others—all good.

The problem, of course, is that few of these companies make any money.[10] Although traffic on the world's computer network is booming and more people are accessing the Web than ever before, most Internet firms—with few exceptions, such as AOL and Yahoo!—are not yet profitable. The "hope"—and thus far, that's all it is— for the future is that as Web usage continues to grow, higher volume will bring increased profitability.[11] Even Amazon.com, whose CEO Jeff Bezos was *Time* magazine's 1999 "Man of the Year" and whose company is perhaps the number-one Web retailer, still hadn't earned a profit into the new century.

As the tidal wave of money-losing Internet IPOs coming to market continues to surge and as more and more people invest their savings in these companies, some fear a shakeout among Internet firms. For example, they ask, can folks really be expected to distinguish between 10 on-line drugstores? The question then becomes one of "differentiation," separating my "brand" from all others on the Web. That's where public relations comes in.

Public Relations as Web Differentiator

As noted in chapter 10 ("Building a Brand on the Web") creating a differentiable identity for a company or product is crucial in the 21st century, not only to become profitable but to stay alive.

Differentiating oneself from all others isn't easy, and most organizations have trouble separating themselves from their competitors. For example, being a "solutions provider" may sound good, but it doesn't explain how a company is different or better. Then, too, a brand promise must make sense and be credible, truthful. A brand, after all, is neither a sign nor a label, but a commitment to perform.[12]

One traditional approach by organizations to differentiate was to purchase advertising to blast out its message. The Internet economy has tried this with limited success. Super Bowl XXXIV in January 2000 was dubbed the "dotcom bowl" because

32 EAST 57TH ST./ 7TH FLOOR   NEW YORK NY 10022
212.292.5367   212.888.8650   info@eyada.com

www.eYada.com

Contact: Michael Kaminer, michael@mkpr.com
Patrick Kowalczyk, patrick@mkpr.com
Michael Kaminer Public Relations, 212/627.8098

eYada.com: WEB'S FIRST ALL-STAR, ALL-TALK NETWORK DEBUTS

*Richard Johnson, Rush & Molloy, Bob Berkowitz, Lionel
Join Star-Studded Roster of On-Air Talent*

http://www.eYada.com

New York (**September 13, 1999**) – Move over Imus and Oprah.

eYada.com http://www.eyada.com is bringing a star-studded lineup of on-air
personalities to the Internet, including **Richard Johnson**, the editor of the *New York
Post*'s "Page Six," **George Rush and Joanna Molloy**, the *Daily News*' husband and wife
gossip duo, **Bob Berkowitz**, the former host of CNBC's sex advice program "Real
Personal," and **Lionel**, one of talk radio's top ten hosts.

Providing both a kick-in-the-pants to talk – the world's most popular broadcast format –
and a much-needed dose of celebrity to the Web, *eYada.com* will Webcast live, original,
and provocative programming throughout the day from its Manhattan studios.

Boasting a talent roster that would be the envy of any TV or radio programmer,
eYada.com's lineup also includes: **Julie Gordon**, founder of *The Velvet Rope*
www.velvetrope.com, the exclusive online community for music industry insiders;
Michael Lewittes, gossip guru for E! Entertainment Channel; **Lori Kramer,** Boston's
award-winning and top-rated talk radio host; **Chaunce Hayden**, *Steppin' Out*'s celebrity
journalist extraordinaire; and **Tim Reid**, former celebrity interviewer and movie reviewer
for MTV Radio Network.

eYada.com is the brainchild of CEO and president **Bob Meyrowitz**, the TV and radio
innovator behind the *King Biscuit Flower Hour*, the groundbreaking syndicated rock
radio show, and many of cable's most successful pay-per-view events.

"By combining real star power with the best technology available, *eYada.com* will
reinvent the talk format and bring millions of new fans to the Web," said Meyrowitz.
"It's fun, informative and one notch beyond anything you've ever heard or seen on radio
and television."

(more)

FIGURE 13-1 **Day of the release.** The news release has been reborn thanks to the Internet.
Companies like eYada.com use releases and access to the press to help them rise above the
"noise" of so many advertisers.

more than a dozen Internet companies, some in existence less than a year, plunked down $2 million for a 30-second chance to expose millions of viewers to Autotrader.com or Britannica.com or Pets.com.[13] But with all the competing advertising—called "noise" in the industry—clamoring for attention (not to mention all those Super Bowl parties with the sound off!), many Internet companies have gone another direction to differentiate themselves: public relations.

Today, public relations is reshaping the Internet, and the Internet, in turn, is redefining the practice of public relations.[14] At least, that's what many Web entrepreneurs and the venture capitalists who finance them would say. Publicity and public perception are often as important in differentiating a Web startup as its product engineering. For example, when eBay Inc., the Web auction site, went public, it was hailed by the media as "a new leap forward." eBay's IPO price of $18 a share immediately climbed to $234 per share on the favorable publicity. Quite a "leap" indeed!

With so many dotcom firms muscling to get recognized and with budgets limited to venture capital allocations, new Internet companies depend on public relations—more specifically, publicity—to help get them to market. They want a continuous stream of news releases to keep them before the public and, importantly, the venture capitalists who financed them. The end result has been a resurgence in that most maligned of public relations products: the news release (Figure 13-1). Indeed, the old investor axiom was: "Buy on the rumor, sell on the news." Today, with positive releases causing stocks to boom, the new axiom is: "Buy on the press release, sell on the news."[15]

While such prominence in assisting Web companies has proved a decided boon to the practice of public relations, the phenomenon is not without its problems: unnecessary and even erroneous releases, faulty claims on Web sites, even spurious research reports touting a company's products.[16] The ethical issues confronting public relations as a result of Web activity is but one outgrowth of the increasing role of public relations in the development of the Internet.

BACKGROUNDER

Kosher Web Wars

The publicity surrounding Jewishnet, a London, England Web site featuring a cyber rabbi and virtual synagogue, was enough to propel it and its 17-year-old founder, Benjamin Cohen, to instant Internet stardom.

Jewishnet, started from young Master Cohen's bedroom, featured a Jewish dating service and a Yellow Pages of Jewish businesses, enough to attract more than two million visitors annually and no shortage of venture capitalists wishing to take the company public.

But success breeds imitation, and sure enough, the battle was joined in late 1999 when a group of competing British entrepreneurs announced plans to launch Kosherline, dubbed "the definitive on-line guide to everything Jewish." Kosherline, launched by "old-timer" Steven Burns, 31, planned a Jewish business-to-business advertising section, a "Bagel Date" dating service, and a chat room. In addition, Kosherline planned to allocate 20 percent of the company's shares to Jewish and Israeli charities.

As the two combatants warily eyed each other, the world wondered which Web site would emerge supreme. The media lapped it up.

Internet Challenge to Public Relations

Use of the Internet by public relations practitioners inevitably will grow in the future, for three reasons in particular.

- **The demand to be educated versus being sold.** Today's consumers are smarter, better educated, and more media savvy. They know when they are being hustled by self-promoters and con artists. So communications programs must be grounded in education-based information, rather than blatant promotion. The Internet is perhaps the world's greatest potential repository of such information.
- **The need for real-time performance.** The world is moving quickly. Everything happens instantaneously, in real-time. As media visionary Marshall McLuhan predicted four decades ago, in the twenty-first century the world has become a "global village," wired for immediate communications. Public relations professionals can use this to their advantage to structure their information to respond instantly to emerging issues and market changes.
- **The need for customization.** There used to be three primary television networks. Today, there are more than 500 television channels. Today's consumers expect more focused, targeted, one-on-one communications relationships. More and more, organizations must broadcast their thoughts to narrower and narrower population segments. The Internet offers such narrowcasting to reporters, analysts, opinion leaders, and consumers.[17]

Such is the promise of the Internet to the practice of public relations. Beyond its role as an integral component in the Internet marketing mix, public relations has become prominent in several other cyber areas:

- **E-mail.** E-mail has become the most pervasive internal communications vehicle. In a growing number of organizations, e-mail, delivered on-line and immediately, has replaced traditional print publications and fax technology as a rapid delivery information vehicle. An outgrowth of e-mail—intranets or internal Web sites—are another growing phenomenon.
- **Web sites.** Another rapidly expanding use of the Internet by public relations professionals is the creation and maintenance of Web sites to profile companies, promote products, or position issues. A Web site gives an individual or institution the flexibility and freedom of getting "news out" without having it filtered by an intermediary. But there are more than one million Web sites sitting there, waiting for visitors. Public relations agencies have been born that specialize in creating winning Web sites.
- **On-line media relations.** Beyond the creation of Web sites, public relations practitioners are using the Internet to communicate to the media. An increasing number of journalists use the Web as a primary source of organizational information. More journalists, too, are communicating with public relations sources via e-mail. This is especially true in the high-tech reporting area. Finally, the growing number of on-line spinoffs of major print publications and the development of a growing number of e-zines present a new, enlarged field of potential publicity play for public relations practitioners.
- **On-line monitoring.** The Web's easy accessibility has also ushered in a whole, new challenge to public relations professionals to monitor on-line for negative comments and even threats against their organizations. The preponderance of "rogue Web sites" that condemn organizations makes it a necessity

that public relations professionals regularly monitor such Web sites, chat rooms and discussion groups.

◪ **Product promotion.** The ability to reach customers and potential customers directly is another benefit created by the Web. In this area, public relations supports integrated marketing efforts on the Web.

◪ **Investor relations.** Speaking directly to investors and potential investors is yet another new challenge to public relations people. The Web allows investors to check the activities of their holdings on a daily basis, enabling companies to increase their communications efforts relative to their shareholders.

In a general sense, what television and cable TV were to the advertising industry, the Internet is for public relations. For the first time in communications history, organizations are able to build reputations directly with the public, investors, consumers, and the media. Unlike in the past, they face no "obstruction" from their message being filtered by some third-party intermediary. This is the true challenge of the Internet to public relations.

Dominance of E-mail

E-mail has become far and away the most pervasive organizational communications vehicle. In most organizations, e-mail is already the internal medium of choice for newsletters, bulletins, and internal announcements.

While many managers are reluctant to confront employees face-to-face, e-mail tends to produce more honest and immediate feedback than traditionally had been the case. Since e-mail is quick and almost effortless, a manager can deliver praise or concern without leaving the office. Thus, e-mail has by and large improved organizational communications.

It has also unseated the traditional employee print newsletter. At Tandem Computers, for example, five on-line newsletters have replaced traditional internal print products. Such vehicles are both more immediate and more interactive than print counterparts. Employees can "feed back" to what they've read or heard instantaneously. The organization, in turn, can apprise itself quickly of relevant employee attitudes and opinions. Such on-line vehicles also lend an element of timeliness that print magazines and newspapers often have a hard time offering.

E-mail newsletters for external use—to customers, investors, or the media—are equally popular and valuable. These differ from their print brethren in several important areas:

1. **No more than one page.** People won't read lengthy newsletters on the computer. So e-mail newsletter writers must write short.
2. **Link content.** Copy should be peppered with links to other material, such as teasers to full-length articles and product offers.
3. **Regular dissemination.** It is also important to send e-mail newsletters at regular intervals, so that recipients expect them.
4. **Encourage feedback.** Web site visitors should be required to provide full name, e-mail address, company name, and format preference (HTML or plain text).[18]

E-mail newsletters and notices can be used to sell products and services. Advertising giant J. Walter Thompson marketed the Ford Taurus automobile with a comprehensive e-mail campaign, including on-line brochures, flyers, and chat room for prearranged cyber conferences. The latter was set up much as a call-in radio show, with designers answering consumer questions about the new car.

Creating a Winning Web Site

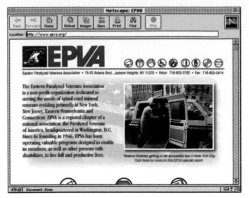

FIGURE 13-2 **First line of communication.** The organizational Web site, such as this one of the Eastern Paralyzed Veterans Association, arguably serves as the most visible—and often most important—source of communication for the agency.

No self-respecting company, trade association, nonprofit agency, political candidate, or entrepreneur today can afford to be without his or her or its own Web site (Figure 13-2).

As organizational Web sites have improved in terms of content, a debate has developed over who should control the site: operations, systems, marketing, or public relations. In many firms, public relations groups fight to extend the site beyond a mere product or service orientation. In a growing number of companies, extranets, designed to serve as "corporate newsrooms" exclusively for the use of the media, have developed.

How should one create a winning Web site? By first asking and answering several strategic questions.

1. **What is our goal?** To extend the business? Sell more products? Make more money? Win support for our position? Turn around public opinion? Introduce our company? Without the answers to these fundamental questions, the "what" and "how" of a Web site are inconsequential. Just as in any other pursuit in public relations, the overriding goal must be established first.

2. **What content will we include?** The reason some Web sites are tedious and boring—and they are!—is that little forethought has gone into determining the content of a site. Simply cramming chronological news releases onto a Web site won't advance an organization's standing with its publics. Rather, content must be carefully considered, in substance and organization, before proceeding with a site.

3. **How often will we edit?** Often, the answer to this question is, Not often enough. Stale news and the lack of updating are common Web site problems. Sites must regularly be updated. Another problem is overwriting. People seem to feel that because the Web is "free," they can write endlessly. Of course, they can. But no one will read it. So an editorial process to cull information down to its most essential parts is a necessity for a good Web site.

4. **How will we enhance design?** Like it or not, the "style" of the site is most important. If an organization's home page isn't attractive, it won't attract many "hits." Good design makes complicated things understandable, and this is essential in a Web site. The Web is a largely "visual" medium, so great care should be taken to professionally design a site.

5. **How interactive will it be?** Traditional communications is unidirectional, one way. You read or view it, and that's where the process stops. The great attraction of the Web, on the other hand, is that it can be bi-directional. Communication can be translated into an interactive vehicle, a game, an application, or an e-mail chat vehicle. This is what distinguishes good sites from mediocre ones.

6. **How will we track use?** As in any other communications project, the use of a Web site must be measured. The most basic form of cyberspace measurement is the very rough yardstick of "hits" to the site. But like measuring press clippings, this doesn't tell you whether your information is being appreciated, acted on, or even read. It is the site itself that allows direct "con-

versations" with customers and potential customers to find out what they really think. Measuring site performance, therefore, should be a multifaceted exercise that includes such analysis as volume during specific times of day, kind of access, specific locations on the site to which visitors are clicking first, and the sequencing through the site that visitors are following.

7. **Who will be responsible?** Managing a Web site, if it is done correctly, must be someone's full-time job. Companies may subordinate the responsibility to someone—occasionally in the public relations department—who has many other "more important" responsibilities. Wrong. Or, as noted, the function may be a shared one. Also, wrong.

   Much better is to treat the Web site as a first line of communication to the public, which requires full-time attention.[19]

Managing the Web Site

An organization's Web site is often the first and most visible communications vehicle accessed by someone interested in learning about that entity. In that sense, it can be argued that in the 21st century, an organization's most important communications vehicle is its Web site. Therefore, to ensure that the site is managed professionally, public relations practitioners should observe "Web site six" rules:

1. **No dead links.** All links should work. Little is more annoying than to go to a site, click on a link and—nothing. It's like reading a newspaper article that is supposed to continue on another page but doesn't. Links must do just that: link.

2. **Contact information.** If the viewer needs more information, he or she should be told how to get it. Then, the request must be answered. If not, the site and the company are stamped "unprofessional" in the mind of the prospect.

3. **Placement of information.** Since we read from left to right, more important information should be placed on the left side of the screen to ensure the viewer reads it first.

4. **Use of color.** Color schemes are important because they affect load time as well as represent the company. It is always best to use standard colors, which are handled best by most computers and browsers. Some exotic color combinations are difficult to read on the screen.

5. **Ease of use.** Information also must be readily available and placed in logical order. Hyperlinks need to be accurate and clearly marked. Each level within the site should allow the user to get back to the previous level and go forward to the next. Also, the viewer must always be able to return to the home page. Viewers are rightfully frustrated when they can't return to the home page and start again.

6. **Purpose.** The purpose of a Web site determines the quantity and type of information included. Web sites generally fall into three categories:

   - Presence model: designed to establish a presence on the Web, used primarily as a promotional tool
   - Informational model: heavy with material, including press information, designed to provide a comprehensive organizational portrait
   - E-commerce model: designed to create and establish sales.[20]

Media Relations on the Internet

The growth of reporters using the Web as a primary source of their daily activity has been astronomical in recent years. Likewise, the growth of newspaper Web sites, e-zines and on-line news services has been equally nonstop. Consider the research:

- 62 percent of U.S. reporters are on-line, compared to 45 percent in 1997 and 16 percent in 1994
- 65 percent of U.S. reporters use the Web for research
- 80 percent of the nation's photo editors use digital photos
- U.S. newspaper Web sites are being established at a rate of 50 a month
- In terms of handling known sources, e-mail contact ranked first both in magazines and newspapers[21]

Overall, corporate Web sites constitute the number two source of journalistic information, right behind personal contact with sources, such as public relations people.

For reporters in the high-tech area, the numbers are even more profound. One study found that 96 percent of high-tech journalists publish news stories that appear in both print and on-line versions, and 76 percent run news stories that can only be found on-line. Additionally, high-tech reporters regularly use information-gathering sites such as CNET and ZDNet.[22]

The downside of the new technology is reminiscent of the downside of media relations generally. Specifically, many reporters complain that their e-mail has become as crowded as their voice mail, which became as crowded as the little pink telephone reminder slips on their desk.

The basics of on-line media relations include the following:

- **Web site newsroom.** The best organizations create extranets, devoted exclusively to serving the media, as derivatives of their Web sites. These corporate newsrooms include all the traditional press materials that the media require.

   News releases: Every Web site begins with news releases, most organized chronologically. However, journalists complain that they don't know precisely when an organization raised its prices or announced its earnings or promoted its president. Therefore, the best Web newsrooms organize releases both chronologically and by subject, with a search engine capable of pointing readers toward specific subjects.

   Executive speeches: All major speeches delivered by management should be included at the corporate newsroom site. The best sites offer an interactive speech feature, through which speeches are automatically e-mailed to journalists or others who request them.

   Annual/quarterly reports: Every public company is obligated to report earnings to shareholders four times a year and typically issue three quarterly reports and one annual. Quarterlies and annuals, too, should appear on the corporate newsroom site.

   Annual meetings: Companies in remote locations, in particular, have begun to videocast their annual gathering of shareholders over the Internet, so that those unable to attend in person may do so electronically.

   Interviews: On-line press conferences and interviews have also become standard fare, with a company notifying journalists of the time and pass-

20/20 Foresight on the Internet

Ask most public relations people what you can do when you're caught in the cross hairs of a network television expose, and they'll answer, "Not much."

Ask California public relations counselor Michael Sitrick, and he'll say, "Hit the Internet."

That's precisely what Mr. Sitrick and his client, vitamin maker Metabolife, did when they felt victimized by a 1999 interview on ABC's *20/20*. When the company's CEO didn't like the trend of the questions he was asked and worried about how the interview might be edited for air, Metabolife and its public relations agency took a bold step.

They preempted the ABC broadcast by offering an uncut videotape of the *20/20* interview on the Metabolife Web site, the first time the Internet had been used to issue an advance rebuttal to an upcoming broadcast. By displaying the entire interview, Metabolife hoped to blunt the impact of what, in its view, could have been a biased TV report.

To point people to the Web site—to "see the complete unedited footage"—Metabolife spent $2 million on an advertising campaign, including full-page ads in the *New York Times* and *New York Post* and nationwide radio commercials.

Communications professionals were sharply divided over the ethics of Metabolife's bold move.

- One Internet author liked the idea. "Your comments can be taken out of context, or you can be misquoted. Through the Internet and cheap computing, you have the ability to set the record straight," he said.
- A journalism professor, on the other hand, disagreed. "In essence, it's an effort at intimidation. It's borderline prepublication censorship. I think it has a very chilling effect on journalism."

Metabolife wasn't phased by the criticism. In fact, the company was so confident, it purchased a 15-second ad that aired during the *20/20* broadcast itself, asking viewers to visit the site and vote on whether the Metabolife segment was balanced or not. Par for the course, the vote was relatively inconclusive.*

*"Firm Uses Internet as Potent PR Tool," O'Dwyer's PR Services Report (November 1999): 20.

word necessary to access a particular executive presiding as an on-line interviewee.

Photographs, profiles, ad copy, etc.: On-line executive photos and other relevant photographs are standard at corporate newsroom sites. So, too, are executive biographical profiles. Other corporate newsrooms might even offer video versions of corporate advertising.

Digital press kits: All the material included in a corporate press kit—releases, photos, backgrounders—are duplicated on the Internet for downloading purposes to journalists.

◢ **News release via newswires.** It has become essential for public companies to issue news releases over news wires. Why? Newswire copy gets picked up by on-line data bases, such as AOL, Yahoo!, and Lexis Nexis. If a company wants its shareholders and potential investors to know of its activities, in order to notify them on-line, its releases must be included on newswires. Newswires are of three types:

1. *General wires:* The Associated Press (AP) is the granddaddy of all general wire services, reporting on general news of interest to the broad society. United Press International (UPI), which used to compete directly with AP, has fallen into financial ill health in recent years and dissipated as a news factor.

2. *Financial wires:* Dow Jones, the wire service of the *Wall Street Journal,* the nation's business newspaper, is perhaps the most well-known financial wire. Reuters is known as the international financial wire. Bloomberg, the creation of a former Wall Street broker, has emerged as another powerful financial wire service force. Bridge News is yet another financial wire.

3. *Paid wires:* As opposed to general and financial wires, other wire services— the most prominent being PR Newswire and Business Wire—are paid services that reproduce organizational news announcements verbatim, for a fee.

All of these wire services report on-line, which is why organizations should release via wire.

☑ **Online publicity.** As noted, the proliferation of on-line versions of major periodicals, from the *Chicago Tribune* and the *New York Times* to *Business Week* and *US News and World Report,* have opened new publicity channels to public relations professionals. Most such on-line variations of established publications are staffed by journalists dedicated exclusively to the on-line version.

Beyond established publications on the Web, the number of e-zines, such as *Salon* and *Slate,* and on-line news services, such as TheStreet.com and CBSMarket Watch.com, have also opened new outlets for publicity.

Finally, the Web offers the ability to deliver publicity directly to targeted segments—women's news to iVillage, senior citizens news to SeniorNet, African American news to NetNoir, etc. The plethora of bulletin boards, discussion groups, newsgroups, on-line services, and mailing lists presents vast new vistas for publicity. For the first time, public relations people, through the Internet, have the ability to reach potential investors, customers, or supporters without having to depend on the cooperation of a journalistic intermediary.

BACKGROUNDER

Bad Net News for AP, Worse News for Bob Hope

The Internet has allowed journalists to speed up news delivery. Sometimes, it's absolutely too speedy.

In mid-1998, an Associated Press article, being prepared in the event of the death of entertainment legend Bob Hope, was inadvertently displayed on its Web site.

The Web piece said:

Bob Hope Dead

LOS ANGELES (AP)—Bob Hope, the master of the one-liner and tireless morale-booster for servicemen from World War II to the Gulf War, xxxxxxxxx He was xx. (born May 29, 1903).

Although the Web story only mentioned in its headline that Hope was "dead," House Majority Leader Dick Armey saw a copy of the AP Internet story and immediately asked a colleague to announce the comedian's death on the House floor. The House announcement then triggered wire service stories across the country.

When it was determined a few minutes later that the 95-year-old Hope was alive and, at that moment, having breakfast with his family in Palm Springs, an embarrassed Armey apologized to the Hope family. The Associated Press, no doubt infinitely smarter about the power—and danger—of the Internet, removed the Hope item from its Web site.

On-Line Monitoring

Whether an organization uses the Internet for publicity, uses e-mail extensively, or even has a Web site, the one necessity for any organization today is to monitor the Internet.

The World Wide Web is riddled with unhappy consumers spilling their guts, disgruntled stockholders badmouthing management, and rogue Web sites condemning this or that organization.

◢ **Discussion groups and chat rooms** are hotbeds for discontented shareholders and consumers. The Yahoo! finance boards, for example, are the source of continuing commentary about public companies from anonymous commentators, all using mysterious pseudonyms. One will start with a cryptic message. Then another will add to it. And a third will chime in. This continuous commentary—called, "the thread" on Wall Street—is the bane of many a company.

The thread has become such a source of corporate discontent that monitoring firms have emerged to keep track of what is being said about companies in chat rooms. One such firm, NewGate Internet, Inc., organizes "whisper campaigns." To wit:

> Using our proprietary database as a starting point, we constantly monitor the public access areas of the Internet (newsgroups, listservs, and forums). Wherever we find such mentions, we use an extremely subtle approach to incorporate positive information about your business into the discussion. We never denigrate or criticize the competition; instead we add to the discussion by "whispering" useful reminders about your company or product.[23]

Small companies, in particular, must be constantly vigilant of what is being said about them in on-line forums. That means monitoring newsgroups as a regular public relations function.

◢ **Rogue web sites** must also be monitored by the organizations they attack. For example, search for United Airlines on the Web and, chances are, you'll come across www.untied.com, which bills itself as "The Web site that offers frustrated former United Airlines passengers a chance to speak out." The site includes letters from United customers with attention-getting headlines, such as "Paid for first class? Sorry, you fly coach" and "Bomb Threat Ignored."

Many other companies wrestle with similar rogue sites. McDonalds, Nike, Wal-Mart, Ford, and many others all have battled these negative sites. Among the most "popular" such sites is aolsucks.com, which lambastes the world's most successful and largest on-line access provider (Figure 13-3).

A corporation's knee-jerk reaction—to call in the lawyers—hasn't resulted in great victory in battling the rogues. In perhaps the most celebrated case, Kmart sued www.kmartsucks.com, a Web site hosted by a disgruntled employee. The copyright infringement suit did succeed in forcing the site to change its name—to www.martsucks.com—but the considerable national media attention the suit received helped put the rogue Web site on the map.[24]

So with lawsuits having minimal impact on the masters of rogue sites, the best response is to keep such sites under close scrutiny, again, as a regular public relations monitoring function.

FIGURE 13-3 Freedom of speech. That's what the World Wide Web is all about, and that's why rogue Web sites such as this one are regularly monitored by companies like AOL.

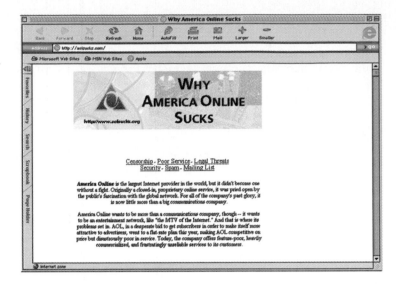

■ **Urban legends** are yet another requisite for on-line monitoring. These are the growing body of corporate horror stories that have emerged from bogus Internet rumors. Most are spread by e-mail at lightning speed across the country and the world. For example:

Upscale retailer Nordstroms was accused by an anonymous e-mailer of charging a $200 fee for its special cookie recipe. "Outrageous," cried the thousands who received the e-mail. Also, completely untrue. Nordstroms doesn't have a cookie recipe.

Mrs. Fields also outraged the populace, when an e-mail dispatch reported that she had sent a batch of her famous cookies to O.J. Simpson after he won his infamous murder trial. Also, totally false.

In perhaps the most pervasive and pernicious urban legend of all, retailer Tommy Hilfiger was, according to the official-sounding e-mail, evicted from *The Oprah Winfrey Show* by the lady herself, when the clothes manufacturer admitted his garments weren't made for "African Americans, Hispanics, and Asians" (Figure 13-4). The reality was that Tommy Hilfiger never met Oprah Winfrey, was never on her show, and certainly didn't design his clothing solely for white people. The lesson: Public relations professionals must monitor the Web.

FIGURE 13-4 Stuff of legends. Urban legends like this e-mail, discussing a bogus appearance by Tommy Hilfiger on *The Oprah Winfrey Show*, have become increasingly frequent as more people, some with questionable motives, access the Internet.

Subject: Tommy Hilfiger

MESSAGE:

I'm sure many of you watched the recent taping of the Oprah Winfrey Show where her guest was Tommy Hilfiger. On the show she asked him if the statements about race he was accused of saying were true. Statements like if he'd known African-Americans, Hispanics and Asians would buy his clothes he would not have made them so nice. He wished these people would *not* buy his clothes, as they are made for upper class white people. His answer to Oprah was a simple "yes". Where after she immediately asked him to leave her show.

Product Promotion on the Internet

The Internet provides a virtual laboratory to mesh public relations, advertising, and marketing techniques to promote products. The shift from a "bricks" to a "clicks" economy is the most profound commercial force in our society (Figure 13-5).

Northern Light Technology Incorporated
222 Third Street • Suite 1320
Cambridge, MA 02142
Tel: 617-577-0239 • Fax: 617-621-3459

NorthernLight.com

AN OPEN INVITATION TO ALL ALTAVISTA USERS

FROM: David Seuss, CEO, Northern Light Technology

I am sure most of you noticed AltaVista's transformation from its original focus on great searching to something quite different: a "megaportal" with a shopping opportunity at every turn, a rock concert-broadcasting channel, an ISP, a little of this, and a little of that. Just think, it was only four years ago when AltaVista introduced the first powerful and fast Web search engine. Those qualities were probably the reasons you started using it in the first place.

What happened to the importance of great searching?

At Northern Light we are convinced that there remains a vital need for a company that concentrates *all* of its energy, talent, and technology on great searching. As one such company, we believe we have succeeded in building the most comprehensive, effective, and organized Web search engine on the planet. But don't take our word for it, look at the list of accolades that Northern Light has won from some pretty tough critics:

"Editors' Choice," PC Magazine, October 1999
Most comprehensive Web search engine database, Nature, July 1999
"Top 100 Web Site," PC Magazine, July 1999
"Best of 1998," PC Magazine, January 1999
"Editors' Choice," PC Magazine, December 1998
"Best 50 Web Site," CIO magazine, July 1998
"Editors' Choice," Database magazine, March 1998

On behalf of the employees of Northern Light, I would like to invite all AltaVista users to try our award-winning search engine. The next time you need to find some information on the Web, try the same search on both AltaVista and Northern Light, and then compare the two.

When you see how effective Northern Light is, you may suddenly feel like you are coming home again.

Cordially,

David Seuss
Chief Executive Officer
Northern Light Technology, Inc.

www.northernlight.com

AltaVista is a registered trademark of AltaVista Company. Northern Light is a registered trademark of Northern Light Technology, Inc.

FIGURE 13-5 **From bricks to clicks.** Without question, the Internet economy has taken over. Not only are Internet companies battling with traditional bricks-and-mortar firms, they are, as this ad suggests, competing ferociously with their Internet brethren as well.

On the positive side, buyers and potential buyers can access your information directly. On the negative side, you are competing with hundreds of thousands of other information providers for a visitor's attention. So promotional messages must be evocative, eye-catching, and brief.

One popular product promotion device is the "adlink." The adlink is a small display advertisement that promotes another site or page. The adlink may be less than a square inch or may stretch across the screen in a rectangular block. Usually, the adlink promotes another site with a tantalizing line of copy and bit of art. In addition, the adlink will automatically hyperlink, or connect you to the site referenced. Adlink "hits" are easily measured to determine their effectiveness. They can serve as excellent entry points for production promotional messages.

On-line discussion groups provide another potential source of product promotion. As noted, the Internet is flooded with news groups. Smart organizations research news groups to see if their company's name, product's name, or specialty area is being mentioned. If it is, they respond by e-mailing participants with product information, thus increasing awareness and, hopefully, sales.

Web-based integrated marketing can create a new "relationship" with customers. Not only do good sites sell products, but they also offer "information" and "education" about those products. This is where public relations support comes in. At www.cdnow.com, for example, a potential record buyer can develop his or her taste in music. The site's "Album Advisor" recommends tune selections. By downloading an audio player, such as RealPlayer Plus, customers can play tracks from the albums they're interested in before they buy. Through another CDNow service, customers can create customized CDs, featuring only the tracks of the artists they want.[25]

All these product promotion opportunities introduced by a medium that communicates directly with the customer represent great potential for the practice of public relations.

Investor Relations on the Internet

The same is true with respect to investor relations, the public relations activity that deals with a company's stockholders and the communities—brokers and analysts—serving them.

Public companies increasingly use the Internet as a more controlled communications mechanism to reach potential investors. For the small investor, who has seen the flow of corporate information increasingly directed towards analysts, brokers, or larger institutions, the Internet is an informational blessing. Investors can keep track of their investments and the market's "real time," without depending on intermediaries to inform them.

The government that "watches over" securities markets is less convinced that the Internet is such a blessing for investors. For one thing, securities regulators are worried about the anonymous nature of on-line information and the ability of short sellers and other people "whose interests stray far from fairness and transparency to misinform and corrupt the market for information."[26] For another, they cringe at the inadvertent Web-based mistakes that can send volatile markets into fits of apoplexy. In September 1999, the National Association of Purchasing Management prematurely released economic data on its Web site, sending the stock market on an unnecessary and unplanned one-day roller coaster ride. More such Web-related incidents are what the SEC fears.

Despite government concerns, the Internet has opened enormous new avenues of investor contact for public relations people.

Accordingly, companies have invested more heavily in the investor relations Internet space. One study indicated that the majority of annual report producers are thinking of adapting traditional publications to Internet use. Although the printed document remains the most prominent communications vehicle for most companies, on-line annual reports are becoming more important for several reasons:

☑ Electronic versions are more easily integrated with other communications. Analysts can "pull out" financial data and spreadsheets in electronic reports, which don't depend on stapled pages. The electronic medium can "reshape" the report at the touch of a key, making analysis and study much easier.

☑ Electronic reports are less static than print reports. Electronic reports can help companies "come to life" before a stockholder or prospect. Graphics can be enhanced, and sound and motion added. Not only might this provide a clearer portrait of a company but also might help "sell" it to the viewer.

☑ Electronic versions are longer lasting. No longer will investors be forced to keep dog-eared copies of the printed annual report in their files. Access to last year's report can be attained through the push of a button. Indeed, it is not too far-fetched to assume that in the 21st century, print annual reports will be subordinated to electronic versions.

In its purest form, using the Internet for investor relations can assure all stock-holders, and not just large ones, an equal opportunity for access to corporate news and information.

Intranets, Extranets, and CD-ROMs

Among the growing selection of additional cyberspace communications vehicles, three—intranets, extranets, and CD-ROMs—deserve special reference.

☑ **Intranets** are another rapidly expanding phenomenon among U.S. companies. The vast majority of U.S. businesses either have deployed or will deploy an intranet. What is an intranet?

Generally defined, an intranet is an internal vehicle, which integrates communication with workflow, process management, infrastructure, and all other aspects of completing a job. Intranets allow communicators, management, and employees to exchange information quickly and effectively, much more quickly and effectively than any similar vehicle. Intranets, in other words, are Internets for specific organizations, designed to provide the necessary proprietary information to improve productivity.[27]

By communicating through their intranets, organizations try to create an "ownership culture," in which all members share in comprehensive knowledge about the firm. With an intranet, every employee can learn about company finances, update project schedules, exchange messages on computer bulletin boards, consult more frequently, and engage in live "chat sessions" for brainstorming and work teams.

☑ **Extranets,** on the other hand, allow a company to use the Internet to communicate information to targeted external groups, such as the media, investors, vendors, key customers, Hispanic rap artists, left-handed female CNN producers,

BACKGROUNDER

Geekspeak

As a public service to any graduate wishing to cash in his sheepskin for an instant billion-dollar IPO, here is all you need to know about the interactive vocabulary that Wall Street laps up.

- **Value proposition:** the New Economy way of saying, "the point"
- **Internet space:** euphemism for the word "business"
- **Dirt world:** I-world's description of bricks-and-mortar businesses
- **Offline:** used to mean when a computer wasn't hooked up; then it referred to an interruptive conversation during a meeting; but now it

means people who "don't get it," i.e. the Luddites
- **Viral marketing:** the crux of every e-business plan, to get happy customers to spread the word about your service by "word of mouth"
- **Monetize:** the stage in the business plan where the company goes public, and the creators cash out and move to Maui
- **Internet time:** what everyone says you must do everything in—or else
- **Extensible:** no one knows what this means, but you better say it, or you won't get the cash*

Joan O'C. Hamilton, "How to Talk the Talk," Business Week, September 27, 1999, 92–93.

college freshmen with eye rings, whatever. In segmenting the information in such a focused fashion—and protecting its dissemination through a complex series of firewalls—the targeted audience is assured that the data will remain confidential to it alone. Only approved individuals can access the information by using an assigned ID and password, restricted to extranet users exclusively.

☑ **CD-ROMs** have become an important tool in public relations work. CD-ROM stands for Compact Disc Read Only Memory, which means you can read information from it but can't change that information.

CD-ROMs boast great storage capacity, capable of holding 650 megabytes of information—the equivalent of 451 floppy discs. CD-ROMs can supply 72 minutes of sound and 20 minutes of video, not to mention text and graphics, to tell a full and rich story about a product, company, candidate, or issue. Public relations professionals have begun to dispatch CD-ROMs in place of print handouts and videotapes. Indeed, while the VCR created the industry of bringing movies home and allowed greater access to information, the CD-ROM does the same thing but introduces one exciting extra element: interaction.

SUMMARY

A few years ago, when this tome was last updated, the Internet, frankly, was more wish than reality in terms of the practice of public relations. Today, it has clearly arrived and is here to stay.

When venerable financial news producer Reuters announces it has a new Internet strategy, and its stock immediately soars 23 percent, there is no question that in today's society, the Internet rules.[28] The number of people over 16 years old who use the

Internet has climbed to 92 million, and the number of individuals making purchases on-line continues to rise dramatically.[29] Accordingly, American industry's 21st-century dash into cyberspace has sarcastically been compared to the gold rush of the 19th century, when prospectors panned for the elusive commodity that would make them rich.[30]

While not all the digital miners will find their fortune, enough will so that the public relations profession must adapt accordingly. That means that knowing the new technology and becoming comfortable and competent with it is a frontline necessity for public relations practitioners.

Those who can blend the traditional skills of writing and media and communications knowledge with the new on-line skills of the Internet will find a rewarding calling in the practice of public relations in this new century.

Discussion Starters

1. What is the status of the Internet and World Wide Web in public relations today?
2. How has the Internet impacted journalism? Commerce? Internal communications?
3. What are the characteristics that make up a good Web site?
4. What elements might be included in a corporate newsroom site?
5. What is an e-zine, and why is it important to public relations people?
6. What is the impact of the "thread" on public companies?
7. What are the benefits of product promotion on the Web?
8. What is the most pervasive computer-oriented communications vehicle?
9. What is the difference between intranet and extranet?
10. How essential is a knowledge of the Internet to public relations people?

Notes

1. Sara Nathan, "Internet Economy Soars 68%," *USA Today* (October 27, 1999): 1.
2. Frank Rich, "The Future Will Resume in 15 Days," *New York Times* (December 18, 1999): A23.
3. "Forecasts for the Year 2000," *The Industry Standard* (January 24, 2000): 252–53.
4. Jerry Walker, "Middleberg/Ross Study Shows Internet Trends," *O'Dwyer's PR Services Report* (April 1999): 64.
5. Bryan Perry and Mark Burkhardt, *It Came from the Web,* Potomac, MD: Phillips Publishing, Inc., 2000, 6.
6. Paul Davidson, "Report: Growth of New Web Users Sinks," *USA Today* (December 3, 1999): 1.
7. Mike Snider, "Growing On-Line Population Making Internet 'Mass Media,'" *USA Today* (February 19, 1997): A1.
8. "Who is Using the Internet," *Ragan's Interactive Public Relations* (June 21, 1996): 8.
9. Bart Ziegler, "Slow Crawl on the Internet," *Wall Street Journal* (August 23, 1996): B1.
10. Brad Stone, "Stop and Go Start-Ups," *Newsweek* (September 6, 1999): 61.
11. Bart Ziegler, "Net is Rarely Pipeline to Profit," *Wall Street Journal* (August 23, 1996): B1.

12. Claude Singer, "The Problem with Being a 'Solutions' Company," *The Public Relations Strategist* (Winter 2000): 16.

13. Stuart Elliott, "Advertising," *New York Times* (January 18, 2000): C8.

14. Michael Krauss, "Good PR Critical to Growth on the Net," *Marketing News* (January 18, 1999): 8.

15. Susan Pulliam, "Stop the Press (Releases)! Internet Firms Love to Churn Them Out; Investors Gobble Them Up," *Wall Street Journal* (November 11, 1999): C1.

16. Susan Antilla, "Internet 'Research Reports': Ads Created by Hired Guns," *New York Observer* (June 29–July 6, 1998): 26.

17. Lawrence Weber, "Internet Rewrites Rules of Public Relations Game," *PR Tactics* (November 1996): 20.

18. "10 Tips to Improve Response to Your Email Newsletters," *Interactive Public Relations* (September 1999): 1, 2.

19. Phaedra Hise, "Seven Common Mistakes in Developing Web Sites," @ Issue (Fall 1996): 26–31.

20. Louis K. Falk, "Creating a Winning Web Site," *The Public Relations Strategist* (Winter 2000): 39, 40.

21. Walker, "Middleberg/Ross Study Shows Internet Trends."

22. "Web Continues to Change the Information Flow for High-Tech Reporters," Tsantes & Associates, Campbell, CA, May 3, 1999.

23. newgate.com, NewGate Internet Web site, September 12, 1999.

24. "Control the Rogue," *Interactive Public Relations* (April 1998): 5.

25. Michael Krauss, "How the Web is Changing the Customers," *Marketing News* (August 31, 1998): 10.

26. Bill Barnhart, "Nothing but Net: A Commentary on the Impact of the Internet on Investor Relations," *Journal of Corporate Public Relations-Northwestern University* (1996–1997): 16.

27. "What Do Intranets Look Like?" *Technology Workshop for Editors* (January 1997): 1.

28. Andrew Ross Sorkin, "Reuters' Shares Soar on Internet Strategy," *New York Times* (February 9, 2000) : C4.

29. "Surprise! Internet Use Increasing," *PR Tactics* (August 1999): 7.

30. Seth Schiesel, "Payoff Still Elusive in Internet Gold Rush," *New York Times* (January 2, 1997): C17.

Suggested Readings

Alexander, James M. "Setting up a Web Site Surveillance System." *Public Relations Tactics* (November 1996): 6.

Cohen, Ephraim. "Conducting an Online Public Affairs Campaign." *Public Relations Tactics* (November 1997): 13ff.

Coombs, Timothy W. "The Internet As Potential Equalizer: New Leverage for Confronting Social Responsibility." *Public Relations Review* (Fall 1998): 289ff.

Conner-Sax, Kierston, and Ed Krol. *The Whole Internet: The Next Generation.* Sebastopol, CA: O'Reilly & Associates, 1999. See "Top of the Shelf," chapter 7.

Eddings, Joshua. *How the Internet Works.* New York: Ziff-Davis, 1994.

Eder, Peter F. "The Emerging Interactive Society." *The Futurist,* (May–June 1997): 43–46.

top of the shelf

Shel Holtz

Public Relations on the Net. New York: AMACOM, 1999.

This book's subtitle is about as direct, succinct, and thorough as public relations on the Internet should be: "Winning Strategies to Inform and Influence the Media, the Investment Community, the Government, the Public, and More!"

A five-time winner of the Gold Quill Award from the International Association of Business Communicators, Shel Holtz is not only a master of both subjects of his book—public relations and the Internet— but also the synergistic relationship between the two. At 322 pages, *Public Relations on the Net* is a verita-

ble handbook, covering in detail such subjects as: "The Principles of Influencing Audiences Online," "Monitoring Your Company or Client Online," "Media Relations," "Investor Relations," "Activism on the Internet," "Crisis Communication," "Going Directly to the Public," and "Measuring the Effectiveness of Your Online Efforts."

Appendices include "Working with IT Staff ("Who are these guys?")," "Writing for the Computer Screen," "Online Resources," and a seven-page "Recommended Reading."

Ellsworth, Jill M., and Matthew V. Ellsworth. *Marketing on the Internet*. New York: John Wiley & Sons, 1998.

Fidler, Roger. *Mediamorphosis: Understanding New Media*. Thousand Oaks, CA: Pine Forge Press, 1997.

Gates, Bill, Nathan Myhrvold, and Peter Rinearson. *The Road Ahead*. New York: Viking Press, 1996.

Gralla, Preston. *How the Internet Works, Millennium Edition*. Indianapolis, IN: Que Corp., 1999.

Interactive Public Relations, biweekly published by Ragan Communications, 212 West Superior St., Chicago, IL 60610. Updates on public relations progress on the Internet.

Janal, Daniel S. *The Online Marketing Handbook: How to Promote, Advertise and Sell Your Products and Services on the Internet*. New York: John Wiley & Sons, 1996.

Janal, Daniel S. *Risky Business*. New York: John Wiley & Sons, 1998. An eye-opening look at the numerous on-line threats that can wreak havoc with a business and about which public relations people should be aware.

Levinson, Jay Conrad, and Charles Rubin. *Guerilla Marketing Online*. Boston: Houghton Mifflin Co., 1996.

Marken, G.A. "The Internet and the Web: The Two-Way Public Relations Highway." *Public Relations Quarterly* (Spring 1998): 31–33.

Marlow, Eugene. *Electronic Public Relations*. Belmont, CA: Waworth, 1996.

M. Booth & Associates. *Promoting Issues & Ideas: A Guide to Public Relations for Nonprofit Organizations*. New York: The Foundation Center, 1996. Excellent explanation of advantages of and requirements for designing a Web site for nonprofit organizations.

Negroponte, Nicholas. *Being Digital."* New York: Alfred A. Knopf, 1995.

O'Keefe, Steve. *Publicity on the Internet: Creating Successful Publicity Campaigns on the Internet and the Commercial Online Services.* New York: John Wiley & Sons, 1996.

Pavlick, John V. *New Media Technology: Cultural and Commercial Perspectives.* Boston: Allyn & Bacon, 1995.

Pitter, Keiko, and Robert Minato. *Every Student's Guide to the World Wide Web.* New York: McGraw-Hill, 1996.

Selnow, Gary W. *Electronic Whistle-Stops: The Impact of the Internet on American Politics.* Westport, CT: Praeger Publishers, 1998.

Solberg, Ron. "How to Locate PR Listservs and Newsgroups." *Public Relations Tactics* (January 1997): 19.

Spataro, Mike. "Net Relations: A Fusion of Direct Marketing and Public Relations." *Direct Marketing* (August 1998): 16ff. Companies must use the Internet as an essential part of their marketing mix.

SpinWARE. Miami, FL: SpinWARE Software Publishing, Inc., 1996. A computer software designed for public, media, and investor relations professionals. Assists in tracking media lists, distributing press releases and other messages by mail and fax, analyzing press clippings, and organizing schedules.

Thornburg, David D. *Putting the Web to Work.* San Carlos, CA: Starstrong Publications, 1996.

Vivian, John. *The Media of Mass Communications,* 4th ed. Boston: Allyn & Bacon, 1997.

C A S E   S T U D Y

Reinventing Movie Promotion with "Witchcraft"

Here's the story line:

A couple of enterprising filmmakers shoot a clever horror flick for $35,000. It starts with a title card announcing that three film students disappeared in the Maryland woods in 1994, while trying to document local tales of a malevolent spirit called the Blair Witch. The footage they shot with crude handheld cameras was found, the card claims, and edited into the film that follows.

Thus was born *The Blair Witch Project* (Figure 13-6), one of 1999's most successful films and a movie that, in effect, introduced the Internet to Hollywood.

STRONG TO THE INTERNET

Three weeks after its summer debut, the little movie had grossed $35 million, headed for $50 million before summer's end. All without the benefit of the heretofore irreplaceable element of movie marketing: television advertising.

How did *Blair Witch* do it?

By going on-line.

The film's producers sought to find a niche audience not served by major studios. Industry analysts reported that young cinephiles, hooked on the Internet, were difficult to reach with mainstream releases. So they turned to this audience in the only medium they apparently consulted.

Enter the *Blair Witch* Web site: www.blairwitch.com.

In June 1998, a year before the film's release, the filmmakers launched a thoroughly realistic-looking Web site and continued to add information to it over time. To build anticipation, the site reported on these "events" surrounding the students' disappearance:

- ☑ Journal entries from one of the student filmmakers
- ☑ Police reports on this and other local crimes
- ☑ Newspaper clippings about the mysterious phenomenon
- ☑ A history of the Blair Witch

WORD-OF-MOUTH MARKETING

Aficionados of the site began to discuss the Blair Witch in chat rooms. A small core audience was forming. Fans set up hypertext links between the various chat sites, as well as to other film or occult sites, funneling thousands of people a day through the Blair Witch experience.

The Blair Witch cult was born.

After the film's appearance at the Sundance Film Festival, its production company kept placing new information on the Web site. They added outtakes from the "discovered" film reels and "interviews" with the parents of the missing filmmakers that suggested a police coverup.

The updated Web site was tied in with a blitzkrieg of promotions, from books and TV specials to special college campus events. Eventually, the filmmakers produced a soundtrack CD, which itself was unusual, since the film had no music.

LAUGHING ALL THE WAY

The film itself, grainy with no plot and less action, was roundly panned by most critics, who thought the whole thing a gigantic ruse. Huffed the grownup *Wall Street Journal* reviewer, "After seeing what a trifle the movie is, one may be tempted to believe that the American population really does cleave cleanly between two kin of people: idiot kids who can't tell fiction from fact, and rational grownups who've got better ways of wasting their time."

Hmph.

The filmmakers, now rich beyond their wildest expectations, could have cared less about the post-Witch carping. As the president of the company that purchased the project for a paltry $1.1 million put it, "This is the first time that the Web has been the most basic and important tool in getting to a movie's audience."

Clearly, it won't be the last.

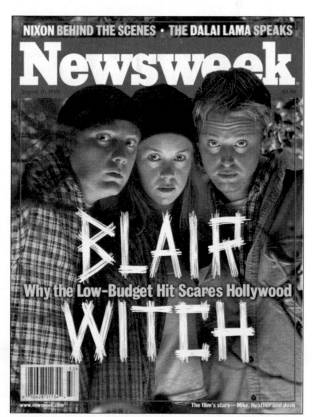

FIGURE 13-6 **Scary success.** *The Blair Witch Project.*

Questions

1. What options did *Blair Witch* filmmakers have in marketing their movie?
2. What else might the filmmakers have done to increase interest in their Web site?
3. What other integrated marketing vehicles might they have incorporated with the Web site?
4. Do you think the Internet will continue to be used for movie promotion? (Duh)
5. How is the Blair Witch Web site currently being used? Visit the site (www.blairwitch.com), examine the home page, and check out some of the links. What are the filmmakers promoting on the site at this time? How are they continuing to harness word-of-mouth marketing via the Web site?

OVER THE TOP

An Interview with Ron Higgins

Ron Higgins admits he is "a serial entrepreneur." He likes to begin companies that emulate a "vision," serve a purpose, employ numerous people, and earn millions of dollars. In 1995, he created Digital Island, a global corporate Internet transport service. He started with three others, initially with his wife and a global networks advisor, and a short time later with a director of public relations. In 1999, Digital Island went public, and the stock soared to six times its opening price. Mr. Higgins gives much of the credit to public relations.

What inspired you to start Digital Island?
Just because the Internet is wired worldwide, there is an underlying assumption—false as it turns out—that it is global. The Internet actually was designed by the military, basically as a backup data network in the event of nuclear war. It was not designed to sell products and particularly not as an international medium. In other words, if you're overseas, you can't just plug into the Internet and expect to be connected globally.

Where does public relations fit into your scheme of things?
Public relations is critical, particularly for a high-tech start-up. You've got to have a professional help you communicate your vision. The typical user is a sophisticated person, who is skeptical of advertising. They believe much more in word of mouth. And that means public relations.

Do you see the practice of public relations as more important for a high-tech firm than other companies?
I do. Because of the velocity of change in this industry, public relations is enormously important. Unlike other forms of communications, public relations can turn on a dime. That's important in an industry moving as fast as this one. Public relations is not only helping invent the language of this industry, it's helping invent the industry itself.

How did you generally define the public relations challenge upon starting Digital Island?
With a start-up technology company, it's all about building momentum. Smart public relations can help you create a brand within the industry. So the challenge for a public relations professional is to take the entrepreneur's vision and communicate it so that the word gets spread.

And what specifically was the goal of the company's public relations activity?

The goal was to create an illusion of momentum: to make Digital Island seem bigger than it was, to give us the aura of a Fortune 500 company. That fact is, we believed in our vision and no question but that it would work. We believed in ourselves, and our investors believed in us. But, the reality is that when you start a business, you have nothing. So your success is tied enormously to how you are perceived.

And what does that perception depend on?

There's a saying in technology that "Every positive article is worth $1 million in valuation." In fact, without third-party endorsement, I doubt if you can be successful in this industry.

What's the business impact of all this publicity?

We leverage it all through our marketing and sales materials. It has helped us grow the business to 80 multinational customers. We've got 140 employees today and will double the staff soon. Our results have been terrific.

What does that say about the future of public relations in high tech?

Our industry is outstripping the growth of any other industry. Because of that, I have no question that you'll continue to see a shortage of good public relations people in high tech.

The Publics Part V

Chapter 14

Print Media

To most business people, the term public relations *is synonymous with two things: "dealing with the press" and "getting publicity."*

Indeed, 20th-century public relations practice got its start as an adjunct to journalism, with former press people, such as Ivy Lee, hired to refine the image of well-to-do clients. In the old days (pre-1990), most of the professionals who entered the practice of public relations were former journalists.

Today, of course, with public relations professionals emanating from many different fields of study and directly from the university, the field is no longer dominated by former journalists. Nonetheless, the importance of the media to the practice of public relations cannot be denied.

Put simply, if you're in public relations, you must know how to deal with the press.

Therein lies the problem, because in the 21st century, the "press" has changed, often for the worst. Consider the following:

◼ *In 1996, the identity of the "Anonymous" author of the nation's number-one best-selling book,* Primary Colors, *was kept secret so the author,* Newsweek *columnist Joe Klein, could keep his day job. Klein even lied to his own colleagues about his authorship, until he was forced to admit the charade, when handwriting analysis of manuscript pages revealed his identity (Figure 14-1).*

◼ *In one of the most celebrated journalistic causes célèbres of the late-1990s,* Boston Globe *award-winning columnist Mike Barnacle was fired, after he admitted "borrowing" material from a book written by comedian George Carlin and attributing it to someone else.*

◼ *In the summer of 1999, the* Chicago Tribune *apologized for a travel story in which the author recounted her harrowing experience on an Air Zimbabwe flight, when the pilot put the plane on autopilot once it reached cruising altitude, left the cockpit to use the bathroom, while propping the cockpit door open with a rubber band. Harrowing indeed. But also completely untrue.[1]*

FIGURE 14-1 **Liar, liar pants on fire.** An embarrassed *Newsweek* columnist Joe Klein (left) aka Anonymous, admits he authored the best-seller he denied writing.

☑ *In the fall of 1999, the editor of the* Journal of the American Medical Association *was replaced, after he ran a survey of college students' sexual attitudes that supported President Clinton during Clinton's impeachment trial. The editor, a Clinton loyalist, was dismissed.*[2]

☑ *In the winter of 2000, Steven T. Brill, editor of a magazine that served as a "media watchdog," announced formation of a publication sales Web site in partnership with several of the very organizations he was supposed to be monitoring. The Brill deal with NBC, CBS, and Primedia, among others, raised eyebrows throughout journalism.*[3]

☑ *Even "journalists" themselves have become highly suspect— especially when one considers that such latter-day luminaries as disgraced presidential advisor Dick Morris, humbled former House Speaker Newt Gingrich, bumbling O. J. Simpson district attorneys Marcia Clark and Christopher Darden, and the less-than-objective but eminently objectionable Geraldo Rivera are all billed as "impartial reporters."*

What all this means is that dealing with the press has never been more challenging. When one adds the growing impact of Internet journalism, where 70 percent accuracy is looked upon as acceptable, dealing with the media has become a high-risk business.

> *This is the business of the public relations professional, who serves as the first line of defense and explanation with respect to the media. It is the public relations practitioner who meets the reporter head-on. In the 21st century, this is not a job for the squeamish.*

Number One Medium

Despite the growth of the Internet and electronic media, print still stands as the number-one medium among public relations professionals.[4]

Why?

The answer probably lies in the fact that many departments at newspapers and magazines use news releases and other publicity vehicles, compared to limited opportunities on network TV. Since on-line data bases, as noted in chapter 13, use wire service material destined for print usage, the Internet often serves as a residual target compared to print.

It is no secret that as the Internet and MTV generations have become the dominant members of society, newspaper readership has slipped in the United States and around the world. According to research of The World Association of Newspapers, only one-third of 54 countries surveyed did not drop in newspaper circulation during the five years through 1997. "Lowlights" of the research showed the following:

- ✓ The world's two biggest economies, the United States and Japan, both experienced declines in readership
- ✓ In the European Union, newspaper sales slowed nearly 4 percent over the five years
- ✓ In Russia, which used to boast the largest newspaper circulation in the world, circulation fell an alarming 54 percent.[5]

The better news, particularly in the industrialized world, is that circulation declines seem to be narrowing. Indeed, according to 1999 figures, five of the nation's six top newspapers, led by the *Wall Street Journal,* have begun to gain in circulation (Table 14-1). Moreover, according to the Roper Center for Public Opinion Research, most Americans use a variety of news sources at least several times a week. And the importance Americans assign to news is great and becoming greater. The vast majority (70 percent) feel that news is either very or somewhat helpful to them in making practical decisions.[6]

Similar heartening signs are beginning to be seen around the world, such as in Singapore, where newspaper readership is increasing.[7]

In the United States today, 1,489 daily newspapers are published, a little more than half in the afternoon or evenings, with a total circulation of 10.5 million. In terms of readership, according to the Newspaper Association of America, total daily readership is more than 125 million and total Sunday readership is more than 136 million.[8]

Also in the United States, there are 10,857 magazines published. The magazine field, too, after a rough patch in the mid-1990s is being reborn, with specialty publications leading the way.

TABLE 14-1

Top 100 Daily Newspapers in the U.S. by Circulation

Rank	Newspaper	Daily	Sunday	Rank	Newspaper	Daily	Sunday
1	Wall Street Journal	1,792,452	None	51	(Oklahoma City) Daily Oklahoman	222,876	304,553
2	USA Today	1,739,294	2,133,467	52	Omaha World-Herald	219,433	269,882
3	New York Times	1,120,555	1,687,959	53	Almeda Newspaper Group (CA)	216,109	175,100
4	Los Angeles Times	1,081,747	1,385,787	54	Hartford Courant	211,866	298,143
5	Washington Post	799,594	1,095,520	55	Cincinnati Enquirer	205,890	328,432
6	(New York) Daily News	705,734	835,429	56	(Norfolk) Virginian-Pilot	203,584	236,453
7	Chicago Tribune	631,531	1,029,241	57	St. Paul Pioneer Press	199,121	263,086
8	Newsday	553,889	660,104	58	(Nashville) Tennessean	197,064	272,152
9	Houston Chronicle	541,782	736,212	59	(Los Angeles) Daily News	196,002	211,622
10	Dallas Morning News	513,544	775,493	60	Richmond Times-Dispatch	195,457	226,339
11	(Phoenix) Arizona Republic	488,905	614,422	61	Seattle Post-Intelligencer	190,204	500,426
12	San Francisco Chronicle	468,669	592,492	62	Austin American-Statesman	187,593	244,293
13	Boston Globe	465,095	730,420	63	Contra Costa (CA) Times	187,119	197,620
14	Chicago Sun-Times	450,418	407,240	64	Palm Beach (FL) Post	185,169	235,536
15	New York Post	419,372	351,970	65	Rochester Democrat & Chronicle	180,373	242,052
16	Detroit Free Press	406,108	783,864	66	Arkansas Democrat-Gazette (Little Rock)	179,810	280,851
17	(Newark) Star-Ledger	396,865	605,308	67	(Memphis) Commercial Appeal	178,056	245,985
18	Philadelphia Inquirer	395,637	802,492	68	Jacksonville Times-Union	177,490	241,401
19	(Cleveland) Plain Dealer	394,740	504,411	69	Atlanta Journal	176,569	695,765
20	San Diego Union-Tribune	381,256	453,666	70	Riverside (CA) Press-Enterprise	166,418	172,798
21	(Minneapolis) Star Tribune	370,532	674,066	71	Raleigh News & Observer	165,040	208,676
22	Denver Post	370,423	523,324	72	Providence Journal	164,626	237,786
23	Orange County (CA) Register	367,003	424,439	73	Las Vegas Review-Journal	163,776	221,281
24	Atlanta Constitution	364,378	695,765	74	Dayton Daily News	162,608	207,048
25	St. Petersburg Times	359,214	452,723	75	Tulsa World	160,160	219,153
26	Denver Rocky Mountain News	359,068	461,103	76	Fresno Bee	159,665	195,470
27	Miami Herald	355,824	462,606	77	Des Moines Register	159,090	258,881
28	(Portland) Oregonian	353,010	436,061	78	Birmingham News	158,580	190,177
29	Baltimore Sun	327,511	474,385	79	Asbury Park Press	157,213	222,332
30	St. Louis Post-Dispatch	311,556	517,474	80	Journal-News (White Plains, NY)	150,532	179,313
31	Detroit News	296,304	783,864	81	(Bergen County, NJ) Record	148,392	201,402
32	San Jose Mercury News	293,761	338,516	82	Toledo Blade	146,000	200,501
33	Sacramento Bee	293,737	352,855	83	Philadelphia Daily News	145,600	None
34	Kansas City Star	288,037	401,562	84	(Chicago suburban) Daily Herald	145,234	142,135
35	Milwaukee Sentinel	284,175	459,757	85	Akron Beacon Journal	144,121	205,544
36	Fort Lauderdale Sun-Sentinel	274,373	391,996	86.	Grand Rapids Press	142,714	192,488
37	Buffalo News	270,886	360,853	87	Salt Lake City Tribune	133,561	161,857
38	Orlando Sentinel	267,445	390,851	88	Allentown Call	129,952	174,442
39	New Orleans Times-Picayune	263,066	298,463	89	Tacoma News Tribune	129,922	148,137
40	Boston Herald	252,762	169,184	90	Wilmington News Journal	125,997	147,996
41	Columbus Dispatch	252,491	386,218	91	Knoxville News-Sentinel	124,905	166,270
42	Investor's Business Daily	251,867	None	92	Lexington Herald-Leader	123,936	159,512
43	Fort Worth Star-Telegram	247,434	344,005	93	Columbia (SC) State	121,950	159,497
44	Charlotte Observer	247,360	301,484	94	Tribune (Phoenix area)	120,295	101,301
45	Pittsburgh Post-Gazette	243,483	436,765	95	Sarasota Herald-Tribune	118,112	146,465
46	Tampa Tribune	238,889	332,329	96	(Spokane) Spokesman-Review	117,206	140,407
47	San Antonio Express-News	236,713	369,094	97	Albuquerque Journal	113,219	162,137
48	Indianapolis Star	235,790	385,869	98	Charleston (SC) Post & Courier	108,927	120,620
49	Louisville Courier-Journal	230,503	303,389	99	Copley Chicago Newspapers	107,457	121,547
50	Seattle Times	228,429	500,426	100	Worcester Telegram & Gazette	107,405	134,067

Source: Copyright 1999 Luce Press Clippings, Inc.

The four leading circulation newspapers in the United States all boast readerships of more than one million daily.

While purists may be disheartened at the falloff in newspaper readership even as the world's population increases dramatically, one extenuating factor may be the Internet.

According to the Pew Research Center for the People and the Press, the number of Americans getting their news from the Internet has increased at an astonishing rate. Specifically, Pew found that 20 percent of U.S. adults, or 36 million people now get news from the Internet at least once a week. This was triple the number just two years earlier. Part of this increase no doubt comes from people reading their favorite newspapers on-line. Looked at from this perspective, print readership statistics don't look nearly as dismal.

In any event, with all these print outlets—newspapers, magazines, and on-line publications—the waterfront for public relations publicity is broad and deep.

Power of Publicity

Whether the mass media has lost relative influence to other proliferating alternative communications vehicles or not, the fact remains that securing positive publicity through the media still lies at the heart of public relations practice.

This chapter focuses on how to coexist with the print media, with whom public relations professionals deal the most. Chapter 15 addresses the electronic media. We explore here what it takes to work with the media to convey the most effective impression for an organization: that is, attracting positive publicity.

Why attract publicity?

The answer, as we will see, is that publicity is regarded as "more credible" than advertising. To attract positive publicity requires establishing a good working relationship with the media. This is easier said than done. In the 21st century, faced with intense competition from on-air and on-line journalists, print reporters are, by and large, more aggressive, some would argue more hostile. As former professional basketball coach Doug Collins once put it to a reporter:

> I know what this business is all about. Let's find something we can stir up. A good story isn't fun. How many good stories do you read? How many times do you pick up something and say, "Boy, wasn't that nice," where there wasn't a slant to it? How many good stories do you read anymore?"[9]

Ironically, Collins became an outstanding broadcast journalist when he stopped coaching! Nonetheless, there is truth in his words.

When the media takes aim at a particular individual or institution, the results can be devastating. Indeed, in 1997, it took nothing less than a $1 billion lawsuit from legendary Wall Street investor Julian Robertson to get *Business Week* magazine to acknowledge in print the inaccuracy of its hatchet job about the stock picker, sympathetically titled, "The Fall of the Wizard of Wall Street."[10] Other companies, similarly singed, have also resorted to taking legal action against news organizations.

On the other hand, when the media go to bat for an organization or individual, the rewards can be substantial. Former boxer Rubin Carter, for example, the subject of a 2000 movie, *The Hurricane,* was freed from prison after a wave of publicity called into question his murder conviction. Republican Senator John McCain, for another, caught positive fire in the press during the 2000 presidential primary race, and his popularity soared.

A primary responsibility of a public relations professional vis-à-vis the media, then, is to help promote the organization when times are good and help defend the organization in time of attack. This requires a ready working knowledge of what drives the press.

Objectivity in the Media

The presumed objective of a journalist is objectivity—fairness, the intention of remaining neutral in reporting a story. But total objectivity is impossible. All of us have biases and preconceived notions about most things. Likewise, in reporting, pure objectivity is unattainable; it would require complete neutrality and near-total detachment in reporting a story. Reporting, then, despite what some journalists might suggest, is subjective. Nevertheless, scholars of journalism believe that reporters and editors should strive for maximum objectivity (Figure 14-2).

THE JOURNALIST'S Creed

I believe IN THE PROFESSION OF JOURNALISM.

I BELIEVE THAT THE PUBLIC JOURNAL IS A PUBLIC TRUST; THAT ALL CONNECTED WITH IT ARE, TO THE FULL MEASURE OF THEIR RESPONSIBILITY, TRUSTEES FOR THE PUBLIC; THAT ACCEPTANCE OF A LESSER SERVICE THAN THE PUBLIC SERVICE IS BETRAYAL OF THIS TRUST.

I BELIEVE THAT CLEAR THINKING AND CLEAR STATEMENT, ACCURACY, AND FAIRNESS ARE FUNDAMENTAL TO GOOD JOURNALISM.

I BELIEVE THAT A JOURNALIST SHOULD WRITE ONLY WHAT HE HOLDS IN HIS HEART TO BE TRUE.

I BELIEVE THAT SUPPRESSION OF THE NEWS, FOR ANY CONSIDERATION OTHER THAN THE WELFARE OF SOCIETY, IS INDEFENSIBLE.

I BELIEVE THAT NO ONE SHOULD WRITE AS A JOURNALIST WHAT HE WOULD NOT SAY AS A GENTLEMAN; THAT BRIBERY BY ONE'S OWN POCKETBOOK IS AS MUCH TO BE AVOIDED AS BRIBERY BY THE POCKETBOOK OF ANOTHER; THAT INDIVIDUAL RESPONSIBILITY MAY NOT BE ESCAPED BY PLEADING ANOTHER'S INSTRUCTIONS OR ANOTHER'S DIVIDENDS.

I BELIEVE THAT ADVERTISING, NEWS AND EDITORIAL COLUMNS SHOULD ALIKE SERVE THE BEST INTERESTS OF READERS; THAT A SINGLE STANDARD OF HELPFUL TRUTH AND CLEANNESS SHOULD PREVAIL FOR ALL; THAT THE SUPREME TEST OF GOOD JOURNALISM IS THE MEASURE OF ITS PUBLIC SERVICE.

I BELIEVE THAT THE JOURNALISM WHICH SUCCEEDS BEST—AND BEST DESERVES SUCCESS—FEARS GOD AND HONORS MAN; IS STOUTLY INDEPENDENT, UNMOVED BY PRIDE OF OPINION OR GREED OF POWER, CONSTRUCTIVE, TOLERANT BUT NEVER CARELESS, SELF-CONTROLLED, PATIENT, ALWAYS RESPECTFUL OF ITS READERS BUT ALWAYS UNAFRAID, IS QUICKLY INDIGNANT AT INJUSTICE; IS UNSWAYED BY THE APPEAL OF PRIVILEGE OR THE CLAMOR OF THE MOB; SEEKS TO GIVE EVERY MAN A CHANCE, AND, AS FAR AS LAW AND HONEST WAGE AND RECOGNITION OF HUMAN BROTHERHOOD CAN MAKE IT SO, AN EQUAL CHANCE; IS PROFOUNDLY PATRIOTIC WHILE SINCERELY PROMOTING INTERNATIONAL GOOD WILL AND CEMENTING WORLD-COMRADESHIP; IS A JOURNALISM OF HUMANITY, OF AND FOR TODAY'S WORLD.

Walter Williams

DEAN SCHOOL OF JOURNALISM, UNIVERSITY OF MISSOURI, 1908-1935

FIGURE 14-2 **Code of objectivity.** "The Journalist's Creed" was written after World War I by Dr. Walter Williams, dean of the School of Journalism at the University of Missouri.

By virtue of their role, the media views officials, particularly business and government spokespersons, with a degree of skepticism. Reporters shouldn't be expected to accept on faith the party line. By the same token, once a business or government official effectively substantiates the official view and demonstrates its merit, the media should be willing to report this accurately, without editorial distortion.

Stated another way, the relationship between the media and the establishment—that is, public relations people—should be one of "friendly adversaries" rather than of bitter enemies. Unfortunately, this is not always the case. According to one *Washington Post* columnist, the fault may lie with the American public:

> We are only incidentally bringing truth to the world—although don't get me wrong, from time to time we manage to do just that. But most journalists most of the time are just trying to give the public what it wants—and much of the time, the public wants trash."[11]

That is not to say that the vast majority of journalists don't try to be fair. They do. Most want to get the facts from all sides, and they acknowledge and respect the public relations practitioner's role in the process. If they are dealt with fairly, most will reciprocate in kind. However, some executives fail to understand the essential difference between the media and their own organizations. The reporter wants the "story" whether bad or good. Organizations, on the other hand, want things to be presented in the best light. Because of this difference, some executives consider journalists to be the enemy, and they fear and distrust the media.

The Internet Factor

Further complicating the relationship between journalists and those they cover is the Internet.

To some, the Internet has ushered in a new age of journalistic reporting: immediate, freewheeling, unbridled. To others, the Internet is responsible for the collapse of journalistic standards and the ascendancy of rumor-mongering.

The credit—or blame—for the rise in Internet reporting may lie with a particular journalistic creation of the latter part of the 1990s: Matt Drudge (Figure 14-3).

Mr. Drudge, a fedora-wearing, tough-talking "new-age journalist," reported both fact and fiction parading as fact on his Web site, which at its height, ranked near the top 200 sites in Web traffic each day. Occasionally, Mr. Drudge broke some big stories; for example, he was the first to report that Monica Lewinsky had retained an incriminating blue dress from her liaisons with President Clinton. The story was quickly picked up throughout the nation and turned out to be the "smoking gun" leading to President Clinton's impeachment trial. But just as often, Mr. Drudge got it wrong, such as accusing Clinton aide Sidney Blumenthal of beating his wife. (Mr. Blumenthal sued the pseudo reporter for millions.)

In the end, Mr. Drudge, himself, was dumped from a Fox News program he hosted, when the network refused to air a photo of an unborn fetus that he wanted to display. But the door he helped open and the challenge he introduced to public relations people and the organizations they work for will not soon go away. As he put it:

> "We have entered an era vibrating with the din of small voices. I envision a future where there'll be some 300 million reporters, where anyone from anywhere can report for any reason."[12]

FIGURE 14-3 **Drudge as in sludge.** Be he journalistic curse or blessing, Matt Drudge had a profound influence on how the Internet impacted journalistic coverage.

What this suggests is that the media and the organizations they cover will likely remain on different philosophical wavelengths for some time to come. The challenge for public relations professionals is to foster a closer relationship between their organizations and those who present the news. The key, once again, is fairness, with each side accepting—and respecting—the other's role and responsibility.

Dealing with the Media

It falls on public relations professionals to orchestrate the relationship between their organizations and the media. To be sure, the media can't ordinarily be manipulated in our society. They can, however, be confronted in an honest and interactive way to convey the organization's point of view in a manner that may merit being reported. First, an organization must establish a formal media relations policy (Figure 14-4). Second, an organization must establish a philosophy for dealing with the media, keeping in mind the following dozen principles:

1. **A reporter is a reporter is a reporter.** A reporter is never "off duty." So, anything you say to a journalist is fair game to be reported. Remember that and never let down your guard, no matter how friendly you are.

Organization and Policy Guide

**Unit with Primary
Responsibility for Review** Corporate Communications

It is frequently in Chase's best interest to take advantage of interest from the media to further the reputation and services of the bank. In dealing with the media, Chase officers must be careful to protect the best interests of the bank, particularly with regard to the area of customer confidence.

The following policies will serve as a guideline for media relationships. Specific questions regarding the media should be addressed to the Public Relations Division.

Inquiries from the Media

Most journalists call the Public Relations Division when they need information about the bank or wish to arrange an interview with a bank officer. Many times, public relations officers are able to handle inquiries directly. Occasionally, however, more complex questions require input from appropriate bank officers. In these cases, inasmuch as journalists are often under deadline pressures, it is important that bank officers cooperate as fully and respond as promptly as possible. Such cooperation enhances Chase's reputation for integrity with the news media.

Less frequently, reporter inquiries will go directly to line officers. In this case, either one of two responses may be appropriate:

1. If a journalist seeks simple, factual information such as Chase's current rate on a particular savings instrument or the factual details of a new bank service, officers may provide it directly.

2. If a reporter seeks Chase policy or official opinion on such subjects as trends in interest rates, legislation, etc., responses should be reviewed with the Public Relations Division. If an officer is unfamiliar with a particular policy or requires clarification of it, he or she should always check first with the Public Relations Division before committing the bank in print.

In talking with a reporter, it is normally assumed that whatever a bank officer says may be quoted and attributed directly to him or her by name as a spokesperson for the bank. An officer not wishing to be quoted must specify that desire to the journalist.

FIGURE 14-4 Media relations policy. Every organization should have a formal policy like this to guide its activities with the press. Public relations should have the primary responsibility as liaison with the media.

2. **You are the organization.** In the old days, reporters disdained talking to public relations representatives, who they derisively labeled "flacks" (as in "catching flak" or bad news). Public relations people therefore were rarely quoted. Today the opposite is true. The public relations person represents the policy of an organization, so every word out of the public relations professional's mouth must be carefully weighed in advance.

Most reporters with whom the bank deals will respect an officer's wishes to maintain anonymity. Most journalists recognize that it is as important for them to honor the wishes of their sources at the bank as it is for the bank to disseminate its comments and information to the public through the news media. Chase's policy toward the media should be one of mutual trust, understanding and benefit.

Interviews With the Media

In order to monitor the bank's relationships with journalists, all requests for interviews with bank officers by journalists must be routed through the Public Relations Division.

As a rule, public relations officers check the credentials of the journalist and determine the specific areas of inquiry to be examined. The public relations officer will then decide whether the interview is appropriate for the bank. When the decision is affirmative, the public relations officer will discuss subject matter with the recommended interviewee and together they will decide on a course of action and Chase objectives for the interview.

A member of the public relations staff is normally present during any face-to-face interview with an officer of the bank. The purpose of the public relations staffer's attendance is to provide assistance in handling the interview situation as well as to aid the reporter with follow-up material.

When a reporter calls an officer directly to request an interview, the officer should check with the Public Relations Division before making a commitment.

Authorized Spokespersons

Vice presidents and above are normally authorized to speak for the bank on matters in their own area of responsibility.

Normally, officers below the level of vice president are not authorized to speak for attribution on behalf of the bank except where they are specialists in a particular field, such as technical directors, economists, etc.

Exceptions may be made in special situations and in concert with the Public Relations Division.

Written Material for the Media

Chase articles bylined by officers may either be written by the officer approached or by a member of the public relations staff. If an officer decided to author his or her own article, the public relations division must be consulted for editing, photographic support and policy proofing.

Occasionally, customers or suppliers may wish to include Chase in an article or advertisement they are preparing. This material too must be routed through the Public Relations Division for review.

FIGURE 14-4 **Continued.**

3. **There is no standard issue reporter.** The fact is that most business managers want nothing to do with the press. They believe them villains. But that isn't necessarily true. As noted, most are simply trying to do their jobs, like anyone else. So each should be treated as an individual, unless known to be unworthy of trust.

4. **Treat journalists professionally.** As long as they understand that your job is different than theirs and treat you with deference, you should do likewise. A journalist's job is to get a story, whether good or bad. A public relations person's job is to present the organization in the best light. That difference understood, the relationship should be a professional one.

5. **Don't sweat the skepticism.** Journalists aren't paid to ask nice questions. They are paid to be skeptical. Some interviewees resent this. Smart interviewees realize it comes with the territory.

6. **Don't "buy" a journalist.** Never try to threaten or coerce a journalist with advertising. The line between news and advertising should be a clear one. No self-respecting journalist will tolerate someone trying to, in effect, "bribe" him for a positive story.

7. **Become a trusted source.** Journalists can't be "bought" but they can be persuaded by becoming a source of information for them. A reporter's job is to report on what's going on. By definition, a public relations person knows more about the company and the industry than does a reporter. So become a source, and a positive relationship will follow.

8. **Talk when not "selling."** Becoming a source means sharing information with journalists, even when it has nothing to do with your company. Reporters need leads and story ideas. If you supply them, once again a positive relationship will follow.

9. **Don't expect "news" agreement.** A reporter's view of "news" and an organization's view of "news" will differ. If so, the journalist wins. (It's his paper after all!) Don't complain if a story doesn't make print. Sometimes, there is no logical reason. So never promise an executive that a story will "definitely make the paper."

10. **Don't 'cop a 'tude.** Meaning, don't have an "attitude" with reporters. They need the information that you possess. If you're coy or standoffish or reluctant to share, they will pay you back. Reporters vary in look and type, but they all share one trait: They remember.

11. **Never lie.** This is the cardinal rule. As one *Wall Street Journal* reporter put it, "Never lie to a reporter or that reporter will never trust you again."[13]

12. **Read the paper.** The number-one criticism of public relations people by journalists is that they often don't have any idea what the journalist writes about. This is infuriating, especially when a journalist is approached on a story pitch. Lesson: Read the paper.

Reporters, while some may deny it, are human beings. So there is no guarantee that even if these principles are followed, they will be fair or objective. Most of the time, following these dozen rules of the road will lead to a better relationship between the journalist and the public relations professional.

Attracting Publicity

Publicity, through news releases and other methods, is eminently more powerful than advertising.

Publicity is most often gained by dealing directly with the media, either by initiating the communication or by reacting to inquiries. While most people—especially CEOs!—confuse the two, publicity differs dramatically from advertising.

First and most important, advertising costs money—upwards of $140,000 for a full-page ad in newspapers like the *New York Times* and *Wall Street Journal*. Since you pay for your ad, advertising allows you to control the following:

- ☑ **Content:** what is said and how it is portrayed and illustrated
- ☑ **Size:** how large a space is devoted to the organization

Bazooka Backfire at the LA Times

The line between advertising and editorial has always been sacred in newspaper journalism. Sacred, that is, until cereal executive Mark Willes took over as chairman of the *Los Angeles Times* in 1997.

Willes vowed to use a "bazooka" to blow up the wall separating the ad department from the newsroom.

He followed through on this promise in October 1999, when the paper devoted an entire issue of its Sunday magazine to the city's new basketball and hockey arena, the Staples Center. While the special edition didn't raise eyebrows when it was printed, it did when the financial arrangement behind it was revealed.

Specifically, the *Times* entered into an agreement with the subject of the edition, the Staples Center, to share the advertising profit received from the maga-zine. While executives at the paper insisted that the editorial department had full freedom to write anything it wanted, the arrangement was unprecedented, and the line had been crossed.

And *LA Times* editors and reporters blew a gut.

In short order, a special internal investigation was launched of the *Times* senior management itself. A month after the controversial magazine was printed, an even more controversial 14-page section appeared in the *Times* blasting its own management for "a tangled tale of ignorance and arrogance."

Mr. Willes and his fellow managers had learned the hard way just how seriously journalists considered the dividing line between editorial freedom and paid advertising.

- **Location:** where in the paper the ad will appear
- **Reach:** the audience exposed to the ad, i.e. how many papers the ad is in
- **Frequency:** how many times the ad is run

This latter characteristic is extremely important. Today, with 500 television channels, thousands of newspapers and magazines, and thousands more Internet sites, people often skip over or surf by the ads or commercials. The only way to get through is to repeat the ad over and over again. In that manner, the largest advertisers—McDonald's, General Motors, IBM—blast their way into public consciousness.

Publicity, on the other hand, offers no such controls. Typically, publicity is subject to review by news editors, who may decide to use all of a story, some of it, or none of it. Many news releases, in fact, never see the light of print.

When the story will run, who will see it, and how often it will be used are all subject to the whims of a news editor. However, even though publicity is by no means a sure thing, it does offer two overriding benefits that enhance its appeal far beyond that of advertising:

- First, although not free, publicity costs only the time and effort expended by public relations personnel and management in conceiving, creating, and attempting to place the publicity effort in the media. Therefore, relatively speaking, its cost is minimal compared to advertising; rough rule of thumb is 10 percent of equivalent advertising expenditures.
- Second and more important, publicity, which appears in news rather than in advertising columns, carries the implicit—third-party—endorsement of the news source that reports it. In other words, publicity is perceived not as the sponsoring organization's self-serving view but as the view of the objective, neutral, impartial news source. For years, for example, when surveys asked people to

name their "most trusted American," they invariably answered not the president or first lady but rather Walter Cronkite, the former news reader at CBS.

That is the credibility that a news reporter or publication enjoys. So when publicity is reported by such a source, it becomes more credible, believable, and therefore valuable "news."

That, in essence, is the true benefit of publicity over advertising.

Value of Publicity

For any organization, then, publicity makes great sense in the following areas:

- **Announcing a new product or service.** Because publicity can be regarded as news, it should be used before advertising commences. A new product or service is news only once. Once advertising appears, the product is no longer news. Therefore, one inflexible rule—that most organizations, alas, break—is that publicity should precede advertising.

- **Reenergizing an old product.** When a product has been around for a while, it's difficult to make people pay attention to advertising. Therefore, publicity techniques—staged events, sponsorships, and so on—may pay off to rejuvenate a mature product.

- **Explaining a complicated product.** Often there isn't enough room in an advertisement to explain a complex product or service. Insurance companies, banks, and mutual funds, which offer products that demand thoughtful explanation, may find advertising space too limiting. Publicity, on the other hand, allows enough room to tell the story.

- **Little or no budget.** Often, organizations don't have the budget to accommodate advertising. To make an impact, advertising requires frequency—the constant repetition of ads so that readers eventually see them and acknowledge the product. In the case of Samuel Adams Lager Beer, for example, the company lacked an advertising budget to promote its unique brew. So it used public relations techniques to spread the word about this different-tasting beer. Over time, primarily through publicity about its victories at beer-tasting competitions, Samuel Adams grew in popularity. Today, its advertising budget is robust. But the company's faith in publicity endures.

- **Enhancing the organization's reputation.** Advertising is, at its base, self-serving. When a company gives to charity or does a good deed in the community, taking out an ad is the wrong way to communicate its efforts. It is much better for the recipient organization to commend its benefactor in the daily news columns.

- **Crisis response.** In a crisis, publicity techniques are the fastest and most credible means of response. In 1996, when Texaco was charged with racism, the company took to the public airwaves to dispel the criticism. Earlier, when PepsiCo suffered its tampering scare (see "Case Study," chapter 3), the company launched an immediate publicity response. Only when the crisis was resolved and Pepsi had won did the company authorize ads thanking its employees and customers for their loyalty amid the turmoil.

These are just a few of the advantages of publicity over advertising. A smart organization, therefore, will always consider publicity a vital component in its overall marketing plan.

Pitching Publicity

The activity of trying to place positive publicity in a periodical—of converting publicity to news—is called "pitching." After getting the release written, the following hints may help achieve placement:

1. **Know deadlines.** Time governs every newspaper. Even with the rapidity of the Internet, newspapers have different deadlines for different sections of the paper. For example, the *New York Times* business section essentially closes down between 6:00 and 7:00 P.M. News events should be scheduled, whenever possible, to accommodate deadlines. An old and despised practice (at least by journalists) is to announce bad news close to deadline time on Friday afternoon, the premise being that newspaper journalists won't have time to follow up on the story and that few people will read Saturday's paper anyway. Although this technique may work on occasion, it leaves reporters and editors hostile.

2. **Generally write, don't call.** Reporters are barraged with deadlines. They are busiest close to deadline time, which is late afternoon for morning newspapers and morning for afternoon papers. Thus, it's preferable to mail or send news releases by messenger rather than try to explain them over the telephone. Follow-up calls to reporters to "make sure you got our release" also should be avoided. If reporters are unclear on a certain point, they'll call to check.

3. **Direct the release to a specific person or editor.** Newspapers are divided into departments: business, sports, style, entertainment, and the like. The release directed to a specific person or editor has a greater chance of being read than one addressed simply to "Editor." At smaller papers, one person may handle all financial news. At larger papers, the financial news section may have different editors for banking, chemicals, oil, electronics, and many other specialties. Public relations people should know who covers their beat and target releases accordingly.

4. **Determine how the reporter wants to be contacted.** E-mail, mail, fax, paper, whatever. The reporter is the "client." How he or she prefers to get the news should guide how you deliver it.

5. **Don't badger.** Newspapers are generally fiercely independent about the copy they use. Even a major advertiser will usually fail to get a piece of puffery published. Badgering an editor about a certain story is bad form, as is complaining excessively about the treatment given a certain story. Worst of all, little is achieved by acting outraged when a newspaper chooses not to run a story.

6. **Use exclusives, but be careful.** Reporters get credited for getting "scoops" and citing "trends." So public relations people might promise exclusive stories to particular newspapers. The exclusive promises one publication or other news source a scoop over its competitors. For example, practitioners frequently arrange to have a visiting executive interviewed by only one local newspaper. Although the chances of securing a story are heightened by the promise of an exclusive, the risk of alienating the other papers exists. Thus, the exclusive should be used sparingly.

7. **When you call, do your own calling.** Reporters and editors generally don't have assistants. Most do not like to be kept waiting by a secretary calling for

the boss. Public relations professionals should make their own initial and follow-up calls. Letting a secretary handle a journalist can alienate a good news contact. Above all, be pleasant and courteous.

8. **Don't send clips of other stories about your client.** This will just suggest to the journalist that others have been there before him and make the story potential less attractive.

9. **Develop a relationship.** Relationships are the name of the game. The closer you know a reporter, the more understanding and accommodating to your organization he will be.

10. **Never lie.** The cardinal rule.

Although cynics continue to predict "the end of reading as we know it," newspapers and magazines continue to endure. Although some predicted a decline in the magazine business in the 1990s, today almost 11,000 magazines are published in the United States. They range from the mainstream *Time* and *Newsweek,* to the hot Internet leaders *Industry Standard* and *Red Herring,* from the gossipy *People* and *Vanity Fair,* to publications further afield, such as *OUT,* catering to the upscale gay and lesbian market, and *Chile Pepper,* the bimonthly that covers peppers of all types.

The fact remains that dealing with the print media is among the most essential technical skills of the public relations professional. Anyone who practices public relations must know how to deal with the print press.

Pitching On-Line

With online outlets increasing in numbers and use, it is important to consider nuances in terms of pitching publicity on-line.

- In pitching on-line, the place to start is with a techno-savvy media database. Such firms as Newstips, Global Internet News Agency and the Internet News Bureau all offer services that deliver releases to cyberspace audiences.

- Don't assume that just because a reporter has an e-mail address that he or she wants to get spammed (receive unsolicited e-mail). It's best to first send a brief e-mail message, identifying yourself and inquiring whether e-mail is the preferred route to send news announcements.

- Ideally, the more you can target to a particular reporter, the better the chance the story will be used. The Internet, after all, is a more personalized medium. So the more personal the pitch, the better.

- E-mail newsletters in publicity efforts. Such services as AnchorDesk, Netsurfer Digest, TechWeb, InfoBeat, and IDG all deliver e-mail announcements to target publics.

- Don't ignore Web-based news sites, such as ZDNet, Mecler, and CMPNet. The on-line news outlets may or may not duplicate standard wire services like Dow Jones or Reuters.

- By the way, Reuters shouldn't be ignored either. Many Web sites use Reuters as a principal news feed.

- Also, don't forget discussion forums, where individuals discuss products and companies. Increasingly, discussion forums create the "buzz" for a product. Hollywood, for example, is often accused of "salting" chat rooms and discussion groups with "ringers," who will recommend a particular film.[14]

BACKGROUNDER

One-Minute Media Relations

How well would you do if you were asked to go toe-to-toe with a reporter? Take this yes-or-no quiz, and find out. Answers are given below.

1. When addressing a print reporter or electronic medium moderator, should you use his or her first name?
2. Should you ever challenge a reporter in a verbal duel?
3. Are reporters correct in thinking that they can ask embarrassing questions of anyone in public office?
4. Should you answer a hypothetical question?
5. Should you ever say "No comment"?
6. When a reporter calls on the telephone, should you assume that the conversation is being taped?
7. Do audiences remember most of the content of a TV interview 30 minutes after it is broadcast?
8. Should you ever admit you had professional training to handle the media?
9. If you don't know the correct answer to a reporter's question, should you try to answer it anyway?

Bonus question:
What did Henry Kissinger say at the start of his press briefings as secretary of state?

Answers
1. Yes. In most cases, using first names is the best strategy. It makes the discussion much more conversational and less formal than using "Mr." or "Ms."

2. No. Most people should try to gain goodwill in an interview. This is rarely achieved by getting into an acrimonious debate.
3. Yes. Journalists must be suspicious of any claim by a public person that he or she is telling not only the truth, but the whole truth. Anyone in public office must be prepared to respond to such questions.
4. No. Avoid hypothetical questions. Rarely can you win by dealing with them.
5. No. It is tantamount to taking the Fifth Amendment against self-incrimination. You appear to be hiding something.
6. Yes. Many state laws no longer require the "beep" that signals a taped call. Always assume that everything you say is being recorded and will be used.
7. No. Studies have found that audiences remember only 60 percent of the content after 30 minutes. They remember 40 percent at the end of the day and 10 percent by the end of the week.
8. Yes. By all means. You should point out that good communication with the public is a hallmark of your organization and that you're proud it has such a high priority.
9. No. Don't be afraid to say, "I don't know." Offer to find the answer and get back to the interviewer. Don't dig yourself into a hole you can't get out of.

Bonus answer: "Does anyone have any questions . . . for my answers?"

☑ Finally, consider the cyber-media tour, another wrinkle in on-line publicity. Traditional media tours link a spokesman in a studio with TV stations around the nation. The cyber-media tour, links the spokesman with television, radio, Web site, and print journalists via satellite, the Web, and telephone simultaneously. Thus the cyber-media tour takes advantage of streaming video and audio, both gaining exponentially in Web usage.

While establishing a relationship with on-line reporters may not be as easy as with print journalists, because of the physical remoteness, the principle still holds: The closer you are to reporters, the more fairly they will treat you.

Dealing with the Wires

An additional word is in order about the wire services, particularly the paid wires.

As noted in chapter 13, the Associated Press, with more than 15,000 clients world-wide, is the most traditional of wire services. It and the three primary financial wires—Dow Jones, Reuters, and Bloomberg—actively report news of the largest companies around-the-clock.

The onslaught of 21st-century competition to make news is so ferocious that organizations of even moderate size should consider using one of the paid wire services to make their voices heard. While PR Newswire and Business Wire are the two primary paid wires, U.S. Newswire is another paid wire that specializes in government and nonprofit clients and transmits news essentially about public policy. All charge a flat fee for a release—normally $200 to $800, depending on distribution—with an additional fee for more words.

In preparing copy for paid wires, public relations professionals must consider the following:

- **Always include headlines.** This is essential. Most editors receive this wire service copy over their computers, and all they initially see is the headline. So it must be eye-catching and provocative.
- **The "lead" is critical.** The lead or first paragraph will generally indicate whether the release will be used. Include the dateline of the release, so the editor knows the place and date of release.
- **Identify the stock symbol.** One purpose of the release is to get it into as many on-line databases as possible. Therefore, public companies must list right after the first mention of their name the stock symbol of the release originator and the symbol of any other public entity mentioned, for example (Nasdaq MSFT) for Microsoft. This is the key to database entry.
- **Include contact names and numbers at the end.** Reporters must know who to call for accuracy and follow-up.
- **Specify timing.** The busiest times of day are 8:00 to 10:00 A.M. and 4:00 to 5:00 P.M. So if you can, avoid these busy periods, and announce news via the wires in off hours to encourage pickup.
- **Specify targets.** The list of targeted recipients is up to you. Part of a paid wire's service is to feed the release to any media outlet you indicate.
- **Check for accuracy.** Wires make mistakes. In the final analysis, the wire copy is your responsibility.

In terms of on-line distribution, there are numerous other services, besides www.prnewswire.com and www.businesswire.com, that will distribute releases. Among them are Newstips (www.newstips.com), Techwire (www.ezwire.com) and Press Flash (www.pressflash.com).

Beyond the wire services, feature syndicates, such as the Washington Post Syndicate, North American Newspaper Alliance, and King Features, are another source of editorial material for newspapers and magazines. They provide subscribing newspapers with a broad spectrum of material, ranging from business commentaries to comic strips to gossip columns. Some of their writers—such as Art Buchwald, Dave Barry, and Jane Bryant Quinn—have built national reputations. Many such columnists depend heavily on source material provided by public relations personnel.

Homemade Headlines

Headlines are critical in influencing editors to use publicity releases. But sometimes even the editors get confused when it comes to constructing a clear and coherent headline.

Consider this confusing cross section gleaned from the daily paper.

- "Include Your Children When Baking Cookies"
- "Something Went Wrong in Jet Crash, Experts Say"
- "Police Begin Campaign to Run Down Jaywalkers"

- "Iraqi Head Seeks Arms"
- "Prostitutes Appeal to Pope"
- "Panda Mating Fails; Veterinarian Takes Over"
- "Teacher Strikes Idle Kids"
- "Clinton Wins Budget; More Lies Ahead"
- "Miners Refuse to Work after Death"
- "Stolen Painting Found by Tree"
- "Man Struck by Lightning Faces Battery Charge"
- "New Study for Obesity Looks for Larger Test Group"
- "Astronaut Takes Blame for Gas in Space"

Media Directories

Another publicity support is the media directory, which describes in detail the various media.

1. *Gale's Directory of Publications* lists about 20,000 publications, including daily and weekly newspapers, as well as general circulation, trade, and special interest magazines. *Gale's* also includes the names, addresses, and phone numbers of publication editors.
2. *Bacon's Publicity Checker* provides data on almost 5,000 U.S. and Canadian trade and business publications that are organized in some 100 categories—from accounting and advertising to woolens and yachting. *Bacon's* includes editors' names, addresses, and phone numbers.
3. *Broadcasting Yearbook* contains information on radio and TV stations in the United States, Canada, and Latin America. It also lists key personnel, along with their addresses and telephones.
4. *Editor & Publisher Yearbook* lists newspapers across the United States (daily, weekly, national, black, college and university, foreign language) and their personnel.
5. *Working Press of the Nation* is a five-volume publication. It lists locations and editorial staff for newspapers, magazines, radio, television, feature syndicates, and house magazines.
6. Specialized directories—from *Hudson's Washington News Media Directory* and *Congressional Staff Guide* to the *Anglo-Jewish Media List*—and various state media directories, published by state press or broadcasters' associations, are also excellent resources for publicity purposes.

Measuring Publicity

After an organization has distributed its press materials, it needs an effective way to measure the results of its publicity. A variety of outside print and on-line services can help.

Press Monitoring Bureaus

Press clipping bureaus monitor company mentions in the press, supplying newspaper and magazine clippings on any subject and about any company. The two largest, Burrelle's and Luce, each receive hundreds of newspapers and magazines daily. Both services dispatch nearly 50,000 clippings to their clients each day. Burrelle's, for example, employs about 800 people and subscribes to about 1,700 daily newspapers, 8,300 weeklies, 6,300 consumer and trade magazines, and various other publications.

These bureaus may also be hired in certain regions to monitor local news or for certain projects that require special scrutiny. Most charge monthly fees that are around $200 in addition to clipping charges per article.

Both Luce and Burrelle's also offer on-line monitoring, delivering clippings to e-mail boxes. While print clips take a week to get to their destination, e-mail clips are delivered real time and arrive in a matter of minutes. Other Web-only monitoring services include eWatch (www.ewatch.com) and Deja News (www.dejanews.com). Both track Web hits for customer names across the World Wide Web.

For a practitioner who must keep management informed of press reports on the firm, the expense of a monitoring service—particularly on the Internet—is a necessity.

Broadcast Transcription Services

Specialized transcription services have been created to monitor broadcast stories. A handful of such broadcast transcription services exist in the country, with Radio-TV Reports and the Video Monitoring Service the largest, with offices in several cities. These firms monitor major radio and TV stations around the clock, checking for messages on client companies. After a client orders a particular segment of a broadcast program, Radio-TV Reports either prepares a typed transcript or secures an audiotape. Costs for transcripts are relatively high.

Media Distribution Services

Public relations people often resort to outside agencies to assist in distributing releases and other press materials. Media Distribution Services offers the largest public relations printing, mailing, fax and e-mail service. Its Mediamatic database contains more than 250,000 editorial contacts by name and "beat" covered. It also offers a Windows-based media management system for the computer. PR Newswire offers a related service, Profnet, an on-line service that notifies subscribers several times daily with "leads" about journalists working on specific topics.

Content Analysis Services

A more sophisticated analysis of media results is supplied by firms that evaluate the content of media mentions on clients. Firms such as Ketchum Public Relations, Delahaye Associates, and PR Data use computer analysis to find positive and negative mentions about organizations. Although this measurement technique is rough and somewhat subjective, it helps an organization obtain a clearer idea of its portrayal by the media.

Handling Interviews

Another primary task of public relations people is to coordinate interviews for their executives with the media.

Most executives are neither familiar with nor comfortable in such interview situations. For one thing, reporters ask a lot of searching questions, some of which may seem impertinent. Executives aren't used to being put on the spot. Instinctively, they may resent it, and thus the counseling of executives for interviews has become an important and strategic task of the in-house practitioner, as well as a lucrative profession for media consultants.

In conducting interviews with the media, the cardinal rule to remember is that such interviews are not "intellectual conversations." Neither the interviewee nor the interviewer seek a lasting friendship. Rather, the interviewer wants only a "good story," and the interviewee wants only to convey his or her key messages.

Accordingly, the following 10 do's and don'ts are important in newspaper, magazine, or other print interviews:

1. **Do your homework in advance.** An interviewee must be thoroughly briefed—either verbally or in writing—before the interview. Know what the interviewer writes, for whom, and his or her opinions. Also, determine what the audience wants to know.

2. **Relax.** Remember that the interviewer is a person, too, and is just trying to do a good job. Building rapport will help the interview.

3. **Speak in personal terms.** People distrust large organizations. References to "the company" and "we believe" sound ominous. Use "I" instead. Speak as an individual, as a member of the public, rather than as a mouthpiece for an impersonal bureaucracy.

4. **Welcome the naive question.** If the question sounds simple, it should be answered anyway. It may be helpful to those who don't possess much knowledge of the organization or industry.

5. **Answer questions briefly and directly.** Don't ramble. Be brief, concise, and to the point. An interviewee shouldn't get into subject areas about which he or she knows nothing. This situation can be dangerous and counterproductive when words are transcribed in print.

6. **Don't bluff.** If a reporter asks a question that you can't answer, admit it. If there are others in the organization more knowledgeable about a particular issue, the interviewee or the practitioner should point that out and get the answer from them.

7. **State facts and back up generalities.** Facts and examples always bolster an interview. An interviewee should come armed with specific data that support general statements. Again, the practitioner should furnish all the specifics.

8. **If the reporter is promised further information, provide it quickly.** Remember, reporters work under time pressures and need information quickly to meet deadlines. Anything promised in an interview should be granted soon. Forgetting (conveniently) to answer a request may return to haunt the organization when the interview is printed.

9. **There is no such thing as being off the record.** A person who doesn't want to see something in print shouldn't say it. It's that simple. Reporters may get confused as to what was off the record during the interview. Although most journalists will honor an off-the-record statement, some may not. It's not

generally worthwhile to take the risk. Occasionally, reporters will agree not to attribute a statement to the interviewee but to use it as background. Mostly, though, interviewees should be willing to have whatever they say in the interview appear in print.

10. **Tell the truth.** It sounds like a broken record but telling the truth is the key criterion. Journalists are generally perceptive; they can detect a fraud. So don't be evasive, don't cover up, and, most of all, don't lie. Be positive, but be truthful. Occasionally, an interviewee must decline to answer specific questions but should candidly explain why. This approach always wins in the long run. Remember, in an interview, your integrity is always on the line. Once you lose your credibility, you've lost everything.[15]

Press Conferences

Press conferences, the convening of the media for a specific purpose, are generally not a good idea (Figure 14-5).

Unless an organization has real news to communicate, press conferences can flop. Reporters don't have the time for meetings that offer little news. They generally don't like to shlep across town to hear news they could have received through a release. They also don't like learning of the news at the same time as their competitors.

BACKGROUNDER

Confessions of a Media Maven

Dealing with the media for fun and profit, even for an experienced public relations hand, is a constant learning experience. Often, such learning is achieved the hard way. Consider the real-life case of an up-and-coming, daring, but wet-behind-the ears public relations trainee.

In the 1980s, many of the nation's largest banks were a bit jittery about negative publicity on their loans to lesser developed countries. One of the most vociferous bank bashers was Patrick J. Buchanan, a syndicated columnist who later became President Reagan's communications director and still later ran for president.

After one particularly venomous syndicated attack on the banks, the young and impetuous bank public affairs director wrote directly to Buchanan's editor asking whether he couldn't "muzzle at least for a little while" his wild-eyed columnist. The letter's language, in retrospect, was perhaps a bit harsh.

Some weeks later, in a six-column article that ran throughout the nation, Buchanan wrote in part:

> Another sign that the banks are awaking to the reality of the nightmare is a screed that lately arrived at this writer's syndicate from one Fraser P. Seitel, vice president of Chase Manhattan.
> Terming this writer's comments "wrong," "stupid," "inflammatory," and "the nonsensical ravings of a lunatic," Seitel nevertheless suggested that the syndicate "tone down" future writings, "at least 'til the frenetic financial markets get over the current hysteria."*

The columnist went on to describe the fallacy in bankers' arguments and ended by suggesting that banks begin immediately to cut unnecessary frills—such as "directors of public affairs"!

Moral: Never get into a shouting match with somebody who buys ink by the barrel.

Secondary moral: Just because you write a textbook doesn't mean you know everything!

*Patrick J. Buchanan, "The Banks Must Face Up to Losses on Third World Loans," New York Post (July 12, 1984): 35.

"*Just tell the press the Ambassador feels it would be inappropriate to comment until he's had time to study the complete text.*"

FIGURE 14-5 **Enter laughing.** For some executives, "meeting the press" is their least-favorite pastime.

Before attempting a conference, ask this question: Can this information be disseminated just as easily in a news release? If the answer is yes, the conference should be scratched.

Eventually, though, every organization must face the media in a conference—in connection with an annual meeting or a major announcement or a presentation to securities analysts. The same rules and guidelines that hold true for a one-on-one interview hold true for dealing with the press in conference. Be honest, forthright, and fair. Follow these additional guidelines in a press conference:

1. **Don't play favorites.** Invite representatives from all major news outlets. Normally, it makes sense to alert wire services, which in turn may have the resources to advise their print and broadcast subscribers. For example, the AP carries daily listings, called the "Daybook," of news events in major cities.
2. **Notify the media by mail well in advance.** Ordinarily, the memo announcing the event should be straightforward and to the point, listing the subject, date, time, and place. If possible, the memo should reach the editor's desk at least seven to 10 days before the event.
3. **Follow up early and often.** Journalists are notorious "no shows." They say they'll be somewhere and they don't make it. So follow up frequently to get an accurate expected count.

4. **Schedule the conference in mid-morning.** Journalists get to work late and leave work later. They are on deadline in the afternoon. So 11:00 A.M. to noon is about right for most press conferences.

5. **Hold the conference in a meeting room, not someone's office.** You want enough space, but not too much space. There's nothing worse than a sparsely attended event in an oversized room.

6. **The time allotted for the conference should be stated in advance.** Reporters should be told at the beginning of the conference how much time they will have. That will help avoid people drifting out at various intervals.

7. **Keep the speaker away from the reporters before the conference.** Mingling prior to the conference will only give someone an edge. Keep all reporters on equal footing in their contact with the speaker.

8. **Prepare materials to complement the speaker's presentation.** Just because journalists are there doesn't mean they'll write the story the way you'd like it. Therefore, press kits and releases are a must.

9. **Remember TV.** This means prepare your executives for the entry of the Cro-Magnon man. TV reporters, light men, and soundmen are notorious for knocking things over, disrupting organized proceedings, and generally being slobs. Prepare for the worst if you want TV coverage. (And you do!)

10. **Let the reporters know when the end has come.** Just before the stated time has elapsed, the practitioner should announce to the reporters that the next question will be the last one.

11. **Cue the reinforcements.** The worst thing that can happen to you is that 10 minutes before the press conference, there is one bored reporter sitting among 30 empty chairs. When that happens (and, alas, it will), get on the phone to the public relations department and summon every last man, woman, and child to get upstairs with pads, pens, and trench coats to save your job.

S U M M A R Y

When journalists were asked in 1999 "how much respect" they had for public relations people, less than half answered in the affirmative. That's the bad news. The better news is that the scores accorded public relations professionals ranked higher in the eyes of these scribes than did lawyers, salespeople, celebrities, or politicians.[16] So there's always hope. On the other hand, it must be acknowledged that journalists still regard public relations people with suspicion (Figure 14-6).

As is true of any other specialty in public relations work, the key to productive media relations is professionalism. Because management relies principally on public relations professionals for expertise in handling the media effectively, practitioners must not only know their own organization and management, but must also be conversant in and respectful of the role and practice of journalists.

This means all that has been discussed in this chapter must be practiced: sending journalists information that is "newsworthy," knowing how to reach reporters most expeditiously, and understanding that journalists have become more pressured to produce material that is "entertaining" and therefore more potentially flammable for most organizations.

FIGURE 14-6 **Nothing but news.** Journalists sometimes question the newsworthy instincts of public relations people. But somehow, announcements like this one, concerning the Swedish Bikini Team's return to the United States to launch its annual calendar, always seem to make the news.

At the same time, all public relations practitioners should understand that their role in the news-gathering process has become more respected by journalists. As Fred Andrews, the former business/finance editor of the *New York Times,* once said:

> PR has gotten more professional. PR people can be a critical element for us. It makes a difference how efficiently they handle things, how complete the information is that they have at hand. We value that and understand all the work that goes into it.[17]

Indeed, the best public relations-journalist relationship today—the only successful one over the long term—must still be based on mutual understanding, trust, and respect.

Discussion Starters

1. What is the difference between advertising and publicity?
2. What is the current state of the newspaper industry?
3. Why should public relations professionals be familiar with newspaper deadlines?
4. How has dealing with the media changed in the new millennium?
5. What is the difference between public relations and publicity?
6. What are the general interest, financial, and commercial wire services?
7. How can public relations professionals keep track of the publicity they receive for their organizations?
8. What are the several dos and don'ts of interviews?
9. Are press conferences advisable in most cases?
10. What are five recommended ways to work with the media?

Notes

1. Ed Shanahan, "A Travel Tale's Crash Landing," *Brill's Content* (September 1999): 36.
2. Evelyn Tan Powers, "Journal Editor," *USA Today* (October 11, 1999): D1.
3. Alex Kuczynski, "Several Media Companies Form Web Site Partnership," *New York Times* (February 2, 2000): C6.
4. "Top Daily Newspapers in the U.S." *The Luce Report,* www.lucepress.com, March 1999.
5. "World Newspaper Sales Also Falling Like the U.S.," *Business Wire Newsletter* (January 1999): 1.
6. Survey on the Media, Freedom Forum and Newseum, www.newseum.org/survey/about.html, March 1997.
7. Koh Boon Pin, "More Reading Papers Despite Competition," *The Straits Times* (October 7, 1999): 32.
8. "Top Daily Newspapers in the U.S," ibid.
9. Jo-Ann Barnas, "The Drive Never Ends," *The Sporting News* (April 14, 1997): 21.
10. Peter Truell, "Investor Settles Libel Suit Against *Business Week,*" *New York Times* (December 18, 1997): D3.
11. "Ink and Air," *PR Tactics* (November 1997): 4.
12. David T. Z. Mindichi, "The New Journalism," *Wall Street Journal* (July 15, 1999): A18.
13. Lee Berton, "Avoiding Media Land Mines," *The Public Relations Strategist* (Summer 1997): 16.
14. "Online Media Relations: How to Take Full Advantage," *Ragan's Interactive Public Relations* no. 5, no. 6 1999.
15. Robert T. Gilbert, "What to Do When the Press Calls," *Wall Street Journal* (June 17, 1996).
16. Adam Leyland, "Journalists Grudging Respect for PR Execs," *PR Week* (September 20, 1999): 1.
17. "Getting into the Times: How Andrews Views PR," *Across the Board* (August 1989): 21.

Suggested Readings

American Society of Journalists and Authors Directory (1501 Broadway, New York, NY 10036). Freelance writers.

Bacon's Media Alerts. Chicago: Bacon Publishing Co. (332 S. Michigan, Chicago 60604). Bimonthly.

Buchs, Jerry. "Companies Must Be Publicity Hounds: A Consultant Says Getting Media Interest Can Be Easier, and Cheaper, Than Buying an Ad." *Journal of Commerce and Commercial* (September 9, 1998): 1 cff. PR expert Jerry Buchs shows how a well-prepared publicity kit can lead to news reports.

Caruthers, Dewey. "Media Placement: An Art That Gets No Respect." *Public Relations Tactics* (October 1998): 23 ff.

Chancellor, John, and Walter R. Mears. *The New News Business: A Guide to Writing and Reporting*. New York: HarperCollins, 1995.

Charity, Arthur. *Doing Public Journalism*. New York: Guilford Press, 1995.

Downing, John, et al. *Questioning the Media,* 2nd ed. Thousand Oaks, CA.: Sage Publications, 1995.

Easley, Lisa. "Using Media Relations (Instead of Investor Relations)." *Public Relations Quarterly,* (Summer 1998): 39 ff. Outlines the steps one PR firm took to attract attention and investors for a new bioscience product.

Edelstein, Alex. S. *Total Propaganda: From Mass Culture to Popular Culture*. Mahwah, NJ: Lawrence Erlbaum Associates Inc., 1997.

Fischer, Rick. "Free Media Lists." *Public Relations Quarterly* (Fall 1999): 43 ff. A guide to media sites, with a chart listing and describing 20 media directory Web sites.

Gamson, Joshua. *Claims to Fame: Celebrity in Contemporary America*. Berkeley, CA: University of California Press, 1994.

Helitzer, Melvin. *The Dream Job: Sports Publicity, Promotion and Marketing,* 3rd edition. Mansfield, OH: University Sports Press Inc., 1999.

International Directory of Special Events and Festivals. Chicago: Special Events Reports (213 W. Institute Place, Chicago 60610).

Lichter, Robert, and Robert Noyes. *Good Intentions Make Bad News*. Lanham, MD: University Press of America, 1995. Outlines how campaign journalism has evolved in the last quarter century.

Lubove, Seth. "Get Smart: A Reporter's Take on Good PR Practices." *Public Relations Tactics* (October 1998): 20. A Forbes reporter lists the best of PR practices he has seen.

Marconi, Joe. *The Complete Guide to Publicity: Maximize Visibility for Your Product, Service or Organization*. Lincolnwood, IL: NTC Business Books, 1999.

Martin, Aimee, and Carter H. Griffin. "Creatively Measuring Media Relations." *Public Relations Strategist* (Spring 1998): 36 ff.

Merritt, Davis "Buzz." *Public Journalism and Public Life: Why Telling the News Is Not Enough*. Mahwah, NJ: Lawrence Erlbaum Associates, 1997.

National Research Bureau. *Working Press of the Nation*. (Available from the author, 242 N. 3rd St, Burlington, IA 52601.) Each volume covers a different medium: newspapers, magazines, radio-TV, feature syndicates, and in-house newsletters.

Nelson, Joyce. *Sultans of Sleaze: Public Relations and the Media*. Monroe, ME: Common Courage Press, 1992. A different—purists would say "jaundiced"—view of public relations and the media.

Network Futures (Television Index, 40–29 27th St., Long Island City, New York 11101). Monthly.

Newsletter on Newsletters (P.O. Box 348, Rhinebeck, NY 12572). Semimonthly.

O'Dwyer, Jack, ed. *O'Dwyer's Directory of Corporation Communications.* New York: J. R. O'Dwyer, 1999. This guide provides a full listing of the public relations departments of thousands of public companies and shows how the largest companies define public relations and staff and budget for it.

O'Dwyer, Jack, ed. *O'Dwyer's Directory of PR Firms.* New York: J. R. O'Dwyer, 1999. This directory lists thousands of public relations firms. In addition to providing information on executives, accounts, types of agencies, and branch office locations, the guide provides a geographical index to firms and cross indexes more than 8,000 clients.

Rein, Irving, Philip Kotler, and Martin Stoller. *High Visibility: The Making and Marketing of Professionals into Celebrities.* Lincolnwood, IL: NYC Business Books, 1997.

Rodgers, Joann Ellison, and William C. Adams. *Media Guide for Academics.* Los Angeles: Foundation for American Communications, 1994.

Salzman, Jason. *Making the News: A Guide for Non-Profits and Activists.* Boulder, CO: Westview Press, 1998.

Schudson, Michael. *The Power of News.* Cambridge: Harvard University Press, 1995. Describes news coverage as a culture with its own conventions.

Silverblatt, Art. *Media Literacy.* Westport, CT: Praeger Publishers, 1995.

Sohn, Ardyth, et al. *Media Management: A Casebook Approach,* 2nd edition. Mahwah, NJ: Lawrence Erlbaum Associates, 1998.

Surmanek, Jim. *Media Planning: A Practical Guide.* Lincolnwood, IL: NTC Business Books, 1995.

Van Ginneken, Jaap. *Understanding Global News: A Critical Introduction.* Thousand Oaks, CA: Sage Publications, 1998.

Veciana-Suarez, Ana. *Hispanic Media: Impact and Influence.* Washington, D.C.: The Media Institute, 1990.

Weiner, Richard. *Webster's New World Dictionary of Media and Communications.* Foster City, CA: IDG Books Worldwide, 1996.

"What to Do When the Media Contact You." (New York State Bar Association, Department of Communications and Public Affairs, One Elk St., Albany, NY 12207).

Whetsel, Tripp. "Nothing Beats a Good Pitch Letter." *Public Relations Tactics* (October 1998): 18 ff.

Yale, David R. *Publicity and Media Relations Checklists: 59 Proven Checklists to Save Time, Win Attention, and Maximize Exposure with Every Public Relations and Publicity Contact.* Lincolnwood, IL: NTC Business Books, 1995.

CASE STUDY

Of Mankind, Stone Cold, and the Rock: The Media Phenomenon of the WWF

In the winter of 1999, three initials were enough to warm the cockles of even the hardest corporate heart: IPO. This stood for "Initial Public Offering," the magic status that signaled a hot new company was about to go public and its principal stockholders were about to get rich.

top of the shelf

Carole M. Howard and Wilma K. Matthews

On Deadline: Managing Media Relations, 3rd edition.
Prospect Heights, IL: Waveland Press Inc., 2000.

The best media relations guidebook available.

This new, expanded edition of *On Deadline* includes the latest on Internet and e-mail media relations. The first chapter sets the new tone: "Technology and Tabloids: How the New Media Is Changing Your Job."

Throughout the book the authors give hints on taking advantage of the Internet. For example, in crisis situations establish a crisis update center on-line, put spokespersons in chat rooms, create multilingual sites if reporters covering the news speak other languages than English, and do keyword searches regularly so that you are not sabotaged by negative or erroneous information that could have been corrected or explained.

This expanded edition also presents strategy and practical guidelines on all aspects of developing and implementing a successful media relations program, drawing on case histories and the authors' extensive experience practicing media relations in the United States and around the world.

In October 1999, amidst all the dotcom companies and spinoffs of major corporate behemoths, one unique enterprise stood out among all of the other IPOs: the World Wresting Federation the WWF.

How an operation, built on the premise of 400-pound Goliaths battering themselves into oblivion, became a national pastime and a $1 billion public company, with $350 million in sales, is testimony to how an entrepreneur with *a questionable* vision but *unquestioned* chutzpah can create a multimedia empire, using every available communications channel to get there.

EMERGING FROM THE HAYSTACK

In its infancy, professional wrestling was a regional phenomenon, where strange-looking men—a few midgets, a few bodybuilders, and one Haystacks Calhoun—would travel from town to town in a caravan of cars, pretending to hurt each other in a different ring every night.

From these humble beginnings, today's WWF is the biggest of big media business—the very opposite of what it appears to be: a dopey spectacle where big men in tights pretend to hurt each other. Consider the following:

- WWF's *Raw Is War,* viewed by five million people weekly, is the highest-rated program on cable TV
- WWF's *SmackDown!* seen by another five million weekly, is the top-rated show on the UPN network
- WWF's home videos routinely rank number one in sports
- WWF's action figures outsell Pokemon
- WWF's Web site was one of the first outlets to turn streaming video into profits
- (If you can believe it) the autobiographies of two WWF star performers, Mick Foley aka Mankind and Dwayne Johnson aka The Rock, both topped the *New York Times* best-seller list (Figure 14-7).

FIGURE 14-7 **Prize-winning author.** Best-selling author Dwayne Johnson aka "The Rock" outside the WWF New York City theme restaurant.

MULTIMEDIA MCMAHON FORMULA

The WWF is the creation of Vince McMahon, a third generation, take-no-prisoners wrestling promoter, who thought big enough to take professional wrestling out of local gyms and put it into the national spotlight. One way he did it, according to *Newsweek,* was with a "scorched-earth" initiative that put smaller wrestling promoters out of business by signing up their performers, including announcers.

McMahon's formula is one part high-flying theatrics, one part wacky story line and many parts media to maximize exposure:

1. The first ingredient is a group of athletic performers, most of whom have undergone six to eight months of training in the art of giving and getting hits, learning how to fall, and being able to take a punch—sucker though it may be.
2. Next comes the story line. Every one of McMahon's wrestlers has a soap opera story. Even his own family participates. When daughter Stephanie announced she was in love with archvillain Triple H, her father set out to get revenge and almost did on a special pay-per-view match watched by millions. What stopped him was that daughter Stephanie jumped into the ring with a sledgehammer, and HHH coldcocked the boss.

   Wide World of Disney this ain't.
3. Third comes the media—lots of it in every conceivable form.

   TV: WWF bouts air four nights a week with no reruns and no stoppage in action. Beyond broadcast and cable, more than half a million fans pay $30 per month for WWF pay-per-views.

Web site: More than one million people visit the WWF Web site monthly. The Web site is multipurpose, offering bios on the wrestlers, fan club news, newsletters for the faithful, and lots of merchandise.

Merchandise: From stuffed bears and dog tags to Vince McMahon action figures, retail sales from WWF consumer products total in excess of $400 million.

Videos, CDs, video games: WWF boasts eight of the top 10 sports videos, two platinum CDs, and a million-selling video game.

QUICK RESPONSE TO CRISIS

Vince McMahon and his media phenomenon may appear dopey, but when challenged in the court of public opinion, the WWF has responded quickly:

- ☑ In the early 1990s, after a steroid scandal and allegations of sexual misconduct cast a pall over the entire proceedings, McMahon acknowledged what even the diehard fans had suspected: that each match was choreographed, competing wrestlers worked as a team rather than being in "competition," and WWF matches were, in fact, "entertainment," or rigged.

  If anyone minded that the WWF was acknowledging the "fixed" nature of its programs, it sure didn't affect the ratings.

- ☑ In the winter of 1999, when Coca-Cola, the U.S. Army, and the Coast Guard all announced they would stop advertising on *SmackDown!* because of its questionable content. The *New York Post* reported that other big companies, such as AT&T, Mars, Inc., and Wm. Wrigley Jr., Company also were pulling their advertising. The WWF, obviously aware that such advertising bailouts were not good for stockholders, responded in most unmacho-like fashion: It cried "Uncle" immediately. "As good business people," said the WWF marketing head, "we are willing to initiate change." Sure enough, the act was toned down so that important advertisers could save face.

  In early 2000, when a California man registered the domain name, www.worldwrestlingfederation.com, the WWF took its case to the World Intellectual Property Organization, which ruled that the man's only purpose was "to sell the name back to the World Wrestling Federation at a substantial profit." The name was returned to the WWF, the first case testing the new forum for resolving disputes over Internet domain names.

GUERILLA ATTORNEYS

While wrestling has waxed and waned over time in terms of popularity, Vince McMahon and his media-savvy organization don't intend to die on the vine.

In early 2000, on the heels of the Super Bowl, the media maven and his colleagues announced plans to start their own professional football league, the XFL or Extreme Football League, vowing to offer "real rock 'em, sock 'em football," as opposed to the sissy stuff offered by the National Football League (Figure 14-8).

One couldn't help but wonder, though, about the new league's "toughness" in light of the following. When an admittedly wimpy public relations textbook author inquired as to whether he might have permission to use WWF photos to accompany a much kinder draft of what you have just read, he was told by a very nice public relations lady that the WWF legal department had decided it "will not agree to participate."

Thank goodness AP Wide World Photos wasn't equally fraidy-scared of the big bad book.

FIGURE 14-8 **Prize-winning promoter.** WWF impresario Vince McMahon announcing his eight-team football league, the XFL.

Questions

1. How has use of the media helped propel pro wrestling into the national spotlight?
2. How do you explain books by pro wrestlers topping the best-seller lists?
3. How would you characterize the WWF's handling of the crisis involving its advertisers? What other actions might it have taken?
4. Why did the WWF challenge the use of someone else's domain name?
5. How would you characterize the "ethics" of the WWF, particularly regarding children?
6. How could a textbook be able to publish a case study of the WWF, even though the company refused to grant its "permission?" (Hint: See First Amendment.)
7. Visit the WWF home page (www.wwfei.net/splash) and follow the "News" link. How do the headlines on this Web page demonstrate McMahon's savvy use of media?

For further information, see Jeri Clausing, "Wrestling Group Wins Back Use of Its Name on Internet," *New York Times,* January 17, 2000, C4; Don Kaplan, "Wrestlers Cry Uncle," *New York Post,* December 1, 1999, 3; John Leland, "Why America's Hooked on Wrestling," *Newsweek,* February 7, 2000, 46–55; "WWFE Goes Mainstream," *O'Dwyer's PR Services Report,* December 1999, 1,10.

O V E R   T H E   T O P

An Interview with Sheila E. Widnall

Dr. Sheila E. Widnall was appointed the nation's first female Secretary of the Air Force in 1993. In 1996, the nation's first female bomber pilot, Lieutenant Kelly Flinn, was charged with, among other things, having an affair with a married man. In the end, the first woman to head a branch of the military decided to grant the nation's first female B-52 pilot "a general discharge." It was among the Air Force's most public hours in history.

How did you help shape the public image of the Air Force?

The American people are our board of directors. We want to be very forthcoming, so we try to communicate with them in many different ways. I come from a background as an educator, and if there's one thing I've learned is that in dealing with students, you have to say it over and over again. And I suspect that that translates into the public realm as well. There is a continuing need to keep the issues in front of the American people.

How did you promote the role of women in the military?

I took every advantage to talk about that topic, because I thought I was uniquely qualified and was likely to get more attention for that topic than any other service secretary. So I used that as an edge to get access to media that had never been accessed, magazines like *Harper's Bazaar, Working Woman* and others which hardly know what a service secretary is.

When did you learn about Kelly Flinn's problems?

I learned about them during the North Dakota blizzard, because basically we had shut down North Dakota, and our Air Force people had been on the road for 20 days snowplowing the state. I went out there with the congressional delegation to thank the people at Minot and Grand Forks for their service to the state. And I learned that we had just begun to get inquiries from the Minot media about this Kelly Flinn case. My heart kind of sunk.

Did you try to talk to her at all?

Oh no, no. I am the senior convening authority for the military justice system. So I must absolutely keep myself out of any of these cases until they actually reach my desk.

What about the criticism that the Air Force uses a double standard in dealing with adultery?

In fact it's exactly the opposite. If you changed the sex of everybody involved in the Kelly Flinn case, I don't think there's any question of what would have happened. A man would have been court martialed. No base would put up with the kind of disruption that was involved.

What about the negative publicity for the Air Force?

What can I say? It was a sex case. I mean she's a gorgeous gal, and she hired a public relations firm, and they played it to the hilt. I probably missed it. I mean I probably didn't realize how the notion that a female could commit adultery was going to titillate the public.

What did you do when the media came roaring in?

We tried to ensure that at least the facts of the case were known. We would respond to queries but did not put out press releases nor hold press conferences nor respond to things on *60 Minutes*.

Looking back, what are the public relations lessons from the Kelly Flinn situation?

What I really believe is that you have to get the substance and values "right" before taking the various steps and making the ultimate decisions.

Chapter 15

Electronic Media

By the World Series of 1999, television sportscaster Jim Gray had earned justifiable recognition as one of the best in the business. It was Gray, after all, who won an Emmy in 1998 for his fearless interview of Mike Tyson, after the former champ bit off part of Evander Holyfield's ear. Similar relentless reporting by Mr. Gray distinguished him in his field.

It was only fitting, therefore, that Mr. Gray be chosen to conduct a live interview with baseball great Pete Rose before Game 2 of the World Series at Yankee Stadium (Figure 15-1). It was the first time Mr. Rose, who was being honored as a member of baseball's All Century Team, had been permitted to set foot on a Major League Baseball field since he was banned from the sport for gambling in 1989.

The interview went downhill from the get-go.

Gray: *Pete . . . are you willing to show some contrition, admit that you bet on baseball, and make some sort of apology to that effect?*

Rose: *Not at all, Jim. I'm not going to admit to something that didn't happen.*

Gray: *With the overwhelming evidence in that report, why not make that step?*

Rose: *No, I don't know what evidence you're talking about. I'm surprised you're bombarding me like this.*

Gray: *Well, I bring it up because people would like to see you get it on.*

Rose: *This is a prosecutor's brief, not an interview, and I'm very surprised at you.*

"Charley Hustle" wasn't the only one surprised at newscaster Gray. The NBC veteran was pilloried in editorials, chat rooms, and bars throughout the land for ambushing Rose on what was supposed to be an occasion for celebration. The New York Yankees, out of solidarity with their comrade, refused to be interviewed by Mr. Gray. One Series hero, Chad Curtis, after dedicating his game-winning home run to his grandmother, walked away from Gray's questions, embarrassing everybody.

FIGURE 15-1 **Rose Bawl.**
Sportscaster Jim Gray barked up the wrong tree when he tried to pin down baseball great Pete Rose prior to the 1999 World Series.

In subsequent days, things got so bad that the chief of NBC Sports had to publicly defend his fallen star. The reality was that Jim Gray's reputation, painstakingly built up over many years, had been pulverized, perhaps irreparably, because of a few careless minutes of intense questioning.[1]

Such is the power in our society of the electronic media.

In the 21st century, few communications forces are more pervasive and prominent than the electronic media.

Television and radio are everywhere, which is both good and bad for society.

☑ *Once, three TV news networks dominated the airwaves; today, in addition to NBC, CBS, and ABC, CNN, Fox News Channel, and MSNBC all hum along 24/7, keeping the nation and the world posted on the breaking news of the day.*

☑ *The effect is that Americans are provided with a continuous loop of unrelated national events that seem to all run together in perpetual images, from the O. J. Simpson trial and the tragedy of Princess Diana to the Bill Clinton-Paula Jones-Monica Lewinsky travails and the presidential election campaign.*

☑ *Specialized cable networks, offering everything from food and fashion to weather and history, beam nonstop across the land. In the financial area alone, CNBC, CNNfn, Bloomberg Television,*

> *PBS* Nightly Business Report, *and other similar efforts have become enormously popular barometers of the nation's stock market appetite.*
>
> ☑ *By the time the average child graduates from elementary school, he or she will have witnessed at least 8,000 murders and more than 100,000 other assorted acts of violence on television.[2]*
>
> ☑ *Meanwhile, talk radio has become an enormous political and social force. Each week, tough-love advocate Dr. Laura Schlessinger spews out take-no-prisoners advice, infantile "shock jock" Howard Stern unleashes trash-mouth venom, and political pundit Rush Limbaugh lets fly conservative bombast—all to approximately 18 million loyal listeners.[3]*

In other words, the power of the electronic media is awesome. According to a 1997 Roper Center for Public Opinion Research study, 50 percent of the nation gets most of its news from TV, as opposed to 24 percent from newspapers and 14 percent from radio.[4]

What makes TV's news dominance so disconcerting—some would say scary—is that the average 30-minute TV newscast would fill, in terms of words, only one-half of one page of the average daily newspaper!

Moreover, in recent years, TV news has been wracked by scandals—NBC Dateline's exploding General Motors trucks, discussed in chapter 6; ABC Prime Time Live's contaminated Food Lion supermarket story, which used hidden cameras and deception; and journalists serving as "pitchmen" for products. The state of television reporting has caused at least one veteran newsman to decry, "Soft news is in, and ratings are all powerful."[5]

The convergence of media, particularly the incursion of the Internet, is another factor that has challenged the supremacy of television. One survey of 6,500 adult cable and satellite subscribers ranked America Online ahead of all the TV networks in terms of "highly regarded media."[6]

Despite its problems, the electronic media will remain a force in the new millennium. Given the extent to which the electronic media dominate society, it is incumbent upon public relations people to become more resourceful in understanding how to deal with them.

TV News—Pervasive, Investigative, Inflammatory

Video news, in particular, has overwhelmed society.

In the 21st century, no situation comedy, ensemble drama, miniseries, movie, or documentary—not even programs about becoming or marrying a millionaire!—dominate American TV the way news and talk do.

In the daytime, it's wall-to-wall stock market coverage on CNBC and Bloomberg TV and sports coverage on ESPN. In the evening, it's the nightly network news on ABC, CBS, and NBC; the perpetual news cycle on CNN, MSNBC, and Fox News; the news-oriented gabfests of *Crossfire, Hardball,* and *Geraldo Live;* and the news magazines of *60 Minutes, 20/20* and *NBC Dateline.* Even the weekends are loaded with news/talk, such as *Meet the Press, Face the Nation, Movers,* and *Pinnacle.* Moreover, in times of national crisis—the trial of a football star accused of murder, a terrorist attack in a major city, an airplane crash—TV news is there immediately and nonstop.

Most instrumental in the rise of TV news around the world has been the growth of the Cable News Network (CNN). Entrepreneur Ted Turner's brainchild—which competitors mocked as "Chicken Noodle Network" when it began more than a decade ago—today reaches hundreds of millions of people around the world and is part of Time Warner, the world's largest media empire.

The growth of cable television has created enormous new publicity placement possibilities for public relations professionals. Cable networks offer so-called "narrowcasting" opportunities for everyone—on the Food Channel, the Game Show Channel, the History Channel, the Black Entertainment Television, and National Empowerment Television.

On the other hand, the push toward investigation and more inflammatory reporting on television has created additional problems for public relations professionals assigned to ensure their organizations are treated with fairness.

- Newsmagazine programs have been attacked in recent years for occasional bias and distortion. In one of the most celebrated cases, ABC's *Prime Time Live* drew great fire for using devious methods, including falsified employee applications and hidden cameras, to infiltrate Food Lion stores in the Carolinas in 1992. More recently, the case of CNN's "Tailwind" report (see "A Question of Ethics" this chapter) raised serious questions about investigative TV reporting.

- Talk shows, such as *The Oprah Winfrey Show, Sally Jesse Raphael Show, The O'Reilly Factor, Politically Incorrect,* and *Larry King Live,* have become standard stomping grounds for politicians, authors, and anyone else seeking to sell a product or an issue.

- Talk show knockoffs, specializing in sleaze, such as offerings from Jerry Springer, Howard Stern, and Jenny Jones, have proliferated.

- Reality-based shows, such as *Unsolved Mysteries, Cops* and *Rescue 911,* which stage reenactments of real-life events, have appeared. One step removed is the wave of "millionaire" TV shows, where so-called "real people" can hook up with a million dollars. In early 2000, such shows lost a step, when questions arose about a man, who had presented himself as a millionaire and married a woman on a highly rated Fox TV show.

The man turned out to be a fringe comedian, who did have money but also had received a restraining order in 1991 after threatening a former fiance.

Also gaining in popularity are "screaming commentary" programs, such as the terminally inane *McLaughlin Group* and *Crossfire.* Mercifully, tabloid TV programs popular in the late 1990s, such as *Hard Copy, A Current Affair,* and *Inside Edition* have waned.

As NBC's *Today Show* moderator Katie Couric put it, "Some news coverage has become more salacious, more sensationalistic, less intelligent, more giving people what they want to hear or what you think they want to hear, rather than what you think they need to or should ideally hear."[7] Organizations have gone to great lengths

A QUESTION OF ETHICS

An Ill Tailwind Botches a Broadcast

On July 13, 1998, *Time* magazine, for perhaps the first time in its illustrious history, apologized to its readers.

The subject of *Time*'s embarrassment was a companion article it ran in conjunction with the launch of its CNN affiliate's investigative news show, *NewsStand*.

The new show, announced with much ballyhoo and fanfare by both CNN and *Time*, broadcast an expose that illegal and lethal sarin nerve gas was used by U.S. forces in a secret operation in Laos, known as "Tailwind." Even worse, the story alleged that U.S. defectors were intentionally killed.

To add credibility to the CNN revelation, "Did the U.S. Drop Nerve Gas?" was narrated by famed Pulitzer Prize-winning war correspondent Peter Arnett (Figure 15-2).

FIGURE 15-2 Out the door. Pulitzer Prize-winning former CNN correspondent Peter Arnett.

Predictably, the story sent shockwaves throughout the U.S. government and military. It was riveting journalism, inflammatory, controversial, and, as it turned out, completely untrue.

As *Time* reluctantly concluded, after launching an investigation, "The allegations about the use of nerve gas and the killing of defectors are not supported by the evidence."

How could such a thing happen to the world's most well-known news network?

- One on-the-record source was a former Vietnam lieutenant, who said he had seen two American defectors and vividly described the use of nerve gas. But in his own book on Tailwind, the same former soldier had failed to make a similar charge. After the story ran, the man was ambiguous about his knowledge of the gas and couldn't recall whether the defectors he cited were Americans or Russians.

- Another source was Admiral Thomas Moorer, former chairman of the Joint Chiefs of Staff. Admiral Moorer indicated that sarin gas was "available," and CNN producers took that to be a confirmation that the deadly gas was used.

- Retired Major General John Singlaub was also quoted in a way that seemed to confirm that American defectors were intentionally killed. However, when questioned after the program, the general acknowledged he wasn't involved in the Tailwind mission and had no knowledge of the events there.

- CNN also conducted telephone interviews with a former senior military official, who refused to identify himself, but seemed to confirm the use of sarin gas. His statements, however, were not based on first-hand knowledge, and he, too, denounced the broadcast after the fact.

- After the broadcast ran, a pilot of one of the planes involved in the Tailwind mission came forward and reported that although gas was dropped that day in Laos, it was actually tear gas. "My eyes burned slightly, and maybe it was a little bit difficult to breathe, but not so it should have rendered anyone ineffective," he said.

In the aftermath of Tailwind, the executive producer on the project resigned and the two producers under her were fired. Mr. Arnett, the award-winning journalist, admitted that while he narrated the program, he was an "insignificant contributor" and added "not one comma" to it. Shortly thereafter, Mr. Arnett, too, vanished from the network he had worked at for 18 years.

In its apology, *Time* acknowledged:

"Our credibility is our most important asset. When we make mistakes, it's important to be open and honest about them, get all the facts out as quickly as possible and try to set the record straight. And to say we're sorry. We are."*

*For further information, see Felicity Barringer, "Critic of Flawed CNN Report Is Named as a Source for It," New York Times, May 8, 1999, A10; Bill Carter, "CNN Excludes Arnett from War and Future," New York Times, April 19, 1999, C1, 2; Walter Issacson, "To Our Readers, Tailwind: An Apology," Time, July 13, 1998, 6; Robin Pogrebin and Felicity Barringer, "CNN Retracts Report That U.S. Used Nerve Gas," New York Times, July 3, 1998, A1, 14; Evan Thomas and Gregory L. Vistica, "Fallout from a Media Fiasco," Newsweek, July 20, 1998, 24–26.

to protect themselves from "ambush interviews" and unfair exposure on national television. The most famous case in public relations history occurred in 1979, when Illinois Power Company followed *60 Minutes* reporter Harry Reasoner with its own camera and produced a video that clearly indicated the CBS program's one-sided presentation (see "Case Study," chapter 12).

Today, the "dumbing down" of TV news has put added pressure on public relations people to deal cautiously when contemplating coverage of the organizations they represent.

Handling TV Interviews

Although appearing on television may indeed be dangerous for one's health, it nonetheless can also be most persuasive. Accordingly, as television has become a more potent channel of news, executives from all fields are being called on to air their views on news and interview programs. For the uninitiated and the unprepared, a TV interview can be a harrowing experience. This is particularly true now, when even TV veterans like Dan Rather warn of "sleaze and glitz replacing quality and substance" on the airwaves.[8] To be effective on TV takes practice. Executives must accept guidance from public relations professionals on how to act appropriately in front of a camera that never blinks. The following do's and don'ts may help:

1. **Do prepare.** Preparation is the key to a successful broadcast appearance. Executives should know the main points they wish to make before the interview begins. They should know the audience. They should know who the reporter is and something about the reporter's beliefs. They should also rehearse answering tough hypothetical questions before entering the studio.
2. **Do be yourself.** Interviewees should appear relaxed. Smiles are appropriate. Nonverbal signs of tension (clenching fists, gripping the arms of a chair, or tightly holding one hand with the other) should be avoided. Gesturing with the palms opened, on the other hand, suggests relaxation and an eagerness to discuss issues. Giggling, smoking, or chewing gum should be avoided (unless you are ex-quarterback Terry Bradshaw!). Proper posture also is important.

3. **Do be open and honest.** Television magnifies everything, especially phoniness. If facts are twisted, it will show. On TV, a half-truth becomes a half-lie. Credibility must be established early.

4. **Do be brief.** TV and radio have no time for beating around the bush. Main points must be summarized at the beginning of sentences. Language must be understandable. Neither the reporter nor the public is familiar with technical jargon, so avoid it.

5. **Do play it straight.** An interviewee can't be giddy, vacuous, or irreverent. Attempts to be a comic may be interpreted as foolishness. Natural and relaxed use of appropriate humor may be a big plus in getting a point across. If humor doesn't come naturally, interviewees should play it straight. That way, they won't look stupid.

6. **Do dress for the occasion.** Bold patterns, checks, or pinstripes should be avoided; so should jewelry that shines or glitters. Skirts should fall easily below a woman's knees. Men's socks should be high enough to prevent a gap between socks and pants. Colors of shirts, socks, suits, and accessories generally should be muted.

7. **Don't assume the interviewer is out to get you.** Arguments and hostility come through clearly on TV. In a discussion on a controversial subject with a professional interviewer, the guest frequently comes out looking like the villain. Therefore, all questions, even naive ones, should be treated with respect and deference. If an interviewee becomes defensive, it will show.

8. **Don't think everything you say will be aired.** TV is a quick and imperfect medium. A guest might be interviewed for 45 minutes and appear as a 10-second segment on a newscast. That's why an interviewee must constantly hammer home his or her main points.

9. **Don't let the interviewer dominate.** Interviewees can control the interview by varying the length and content of their responses. If a question requires a complicated answer, the interviewee should acknowledge that before getting trapped in an incomplete and misleading response. If interviewees make mistakes, they should correct them and go on. If they don't understand the question, they should ask for clarification.

10. **Don't say "No comment."** "No comment" sounds evasive, and most Americans assume it means "guilty." If interviewees can't answer certain questions, they should clearly explain why. Begging off for competitive or proprietary reasons is perfectly all right as long as some explanation is offered.

11. **Do stop.** One common broadcast technique is to leave cameras running and microphones open even after an interviewee has responded to a question. Often the most revealing, misleading, and damaging statements are made by interviewees embarrassed by the silence. Don't fall for the bait. Silence can always be edited out later. Interviewers know this and interviewees should, too, especially before getting trapped.

These are just a few hints in dealing with what often becomes a difficult situation for the uninitiated. The best advice for a TV interviewee is to be natural, straightforward, and, most of all, prepared.

BACKGROUNDER

Acting on Instinct

In the summer of 1999, the nation was shocked once again by reports from Atlanta that a crazed former day-trader had opened fire on coworkers at the All Tech Company, killing several people.

How could this happen? Was it the high-pressured world of day trading that caused the man to snap? These were the kinds of questions that reporters wanted to know from the CEO of All Tech. So they stormed his suburban New Jersey headquarters, just hours after the Atlanta rampage.

The CEO, Harvey Houtkin, dubbed "the father of day trading," was obviously not prepared for the onslaught. But he had done his homework, so he was ready to face the press. How he handled the media is instructive for any student. Here's what he did.

- *First, get the facts.* Research quickly. That's the first and most immediate challenge. Get as many facts as quickly as possible, before going public with the media. This is precisely what Mr. Houtkin and All Tech did before responding to questions.
- *Second, get it on the Web.* The Internet has become any organization's most direct communications vehicle with the widest number of people. Accordingly, All Tech issued a lengthy, fact-

finding statement on the Web, and this gave reporters something to draw from.
- *Third, get the CEO out front.* In a crisis of the magnitude of shooting deaths, it is important to get the top person out front to underscore corporate concern. Mr. Houtkin, not particularly Brad Pitt-ish in appearance and demeanor, nonetheless made himself immediately available to any and all media. Although he was understandably shocked at the awful events, he acquitted himself well.
- *Fourth, express shock and sadness.* The most important thing to remember in such a horrible situation, as that which Mr. Houtkin and his firm faced, is to first acknowledge the human tragedy. The public must understand that you and the company are profoundly and sincerely sorry. Mr. Houtkin's response was appropriately concerned.

He and his company had performed splendidly when faced with the hot lights of national TV exposure.*

*For further information, see Jill Lieber, "Atlanta Gunman Dead," USA Today, July 30, 1999, 1; and Fraser P. Seitel, "Acting on Instinct," The Ragan Report, August 6, 1999, 2.

Video News Releases

If it is true that most Americans get most of their news from television—and it is—then public relations people must try to get their organizations covered on the tube.

News releases in video form, known as video news releases (VNRs), have become standard tools in the practice of public relations. The best VNRs are those that cover "breaking" news—a press conference or news announcement that broadcasters would cover themselves if they had the resources. Such "breaking" news VNRs are delivered by satellite directly to TV newsrooms.

Satellite feeds of unedited footage, called B-roll, include a written preamble-story summary and sound bites from appropriate spokespersons. The TV stations then assemble the stories themselves, using as much or as little of the VNR footage as they see fit.

The second method of VNR delivery is for stories without a breaking news angle. These "evergreen" VNRs are usually delivered by cassette to broadcasters and are more timeless in terms of content. Public relations professionals should keep in mind that larger stations, which pride themselves on doing original work, generally refuse to use pre-edited, nonbreaking news features.

On the other hand, VNRs have proliferated because of the growth of local news and cable news programming. News programming is generally less expensive than entertainment, thus the increase in news and talk programming. With news programs hungry for information, the VNR business has become a booming industry. Today, as VNRs have proliferated, the competition to place them on the air has increased. Indeed with upward of 150 video firms producing VNRs, the "hit rate" of VNR placements has declined measurably.

What does promise to become increasingly popular is the on-line VNR, in which a VNR is downloaded directly to the Internet. More and more, organizations will produce video news for the Net.

VNR Protocol

VNRs are not for everyone. Indeed, with the competition to penetrate the public airwaves so intense today, many VNRs may prove a wasted expense.

Before a VNR is attempted then, the following questions must be considered:

1. **What is a reasonable expectation of a VNR?** A well-done, timely VNR should receive 40–50 station airings with an audience of 2.5 to 3 million viewers. Some may reach more; others may not be used by stations at all.
2. **How should a VNR be distributed?** The answer is the same as with a print news release: any way the reporters want it. If a station prefers satellite or hard copy cassette, give them what they want.
3. **Are you out of luck if a VNR doesn't get picked up?** Not necessarily. It can be lightly edited, removing the "breaking news" aspect and redistributed as an "evergreen."
4. **How important is it to localize a VNR?** Localization—tailoring for local interest—is quite important. Anything that can be done to include local personalities, contacts, or statistics will help potential usage.
5. **Do all stations use VNRs?** Some say they don't. But virtually every TV station nationwide will use a VNR, at least in part. Much depends on the subject matter.
6. **What makes a good VNR?** It has to tell a story and tell it in television format: effective sound bites, graphics, and a short, punchy style. In other words, it has to look and feel just like the evening news.
7. **What kinds of subjects should a VNR treat?** The short answer is anything newsworthy and visual—a legitimate medical, scientific, or industrial breakthrough where the video will clarify or provide a new perspective and help a news department create a better story.
8. **When is a VNR not appropriate?** If a story has no visuals to complement it, save your money. Television is a visual medium. Without the pictures, you have little chance for making the airwaves. Also, you need a wide enough audience and a large enough budget.

9. **How much should a VNR cost?** They're not cheap. A nationally distributed VNR should cost $20,000 at a minimum. So the point is, it must be worth the expense.[9]

VNR Caveats

As noted, VNRs are not without risks.

For one thing, they are expensive. They must be created, produced, packaged, and distributed professionally. Before one creates a VNR—and because a good one is expensive—the following questions must be asked:

- ☑ Is this VNR needed?
- ☑ How much time do we have?
- ☑ How much do we have to spend to make the VNR effective?
- ☑ What obstacles must be considered, including bad weather, unavailability of key people, and so on?
- ☑ Is video really the best way to communicate this story?

Then, too, there is the controversy surrounding VNRs in general. In 1992, *TV Guide,* angered primarily by the Kuwaiti VNR distributed by Hill & Knowlton to build support for the Desert Storm offensive, labeled VNRs "fake news—all the PR that news can use." *TV Guide*'s researchers reported that although broadcasters used elements from VNRs, rarely were they labeled so that viewers could know their sponsor's identity.

On the heels of the *TV Guide* controversy, the PR Service Council for VNR Producers issued a "Code of Good Practice" for VNRs, which called for putting the source of the material on every VNR issued. Still, the controversy persists.

Despite their problems, the fact remains that if an organization has a dramatic and visual story, using VNRs may be a most effective and compelling way to convey its message to millions of people.

Satellite Media Tours

The 21st-century equivalent to the sit-down, in-studio interview is the satellite media tour (SMT), which is a series of preset interviews, conducted via satellite, between an organization's spokesperson and TV station personalities across the nation or around the world.

An SMT originates with a subject speaking from one location, who is then whisked electronically from station to station where he or she enjoys on-air, one-on-one discussions. A derivative of the in-studio SMT is a remote SMT, which originates on location from a site outside the studio.

Corporate executives, celebrities, and "experts" of every stripe have taken advantage of the privatization of satellites and downlink dishes at local TV stations by conducting these rapid-fire "personalized" television interviews.

A successful SMT relies on the immediate relevance of an organization's issue and message. In addition, several steps must be taken to ensure the viability of an SMT:

1. **Defining objectives.** As in any public relations program, the organization's objectives must first be considered. What is the "news hook" required to

interest stations? Who is the target audience? In which markets do we want interviews? What stations do we prefer? Within which programs on these stations will our interviews play best?

2. **Pitching the SMT.** Television producers must be contacted, first by letter and then by phone, about the availability of the organization's spokesperson. The key issue that must be stressed is news value. Press kits and background material should be sent to the stations at least two weeks in advance of the interview.

3. **Last-minute juggling.** Stations often request time changes. Maintain contact with station personnel, even when placed on a waiting list, so that any scheduling "holes" can be filled if a station cancels an interview close to the SMT date.

4. **Satellite time.** Satellite time needs to be contracted for well in advance to ensure that the SMT is aired when the organization wants.

5. **B-roll. Background footage.** B-roll video should be available to further illustrate the topic and enhance the interest of stations.

6. **Availability of dedicated phone lines.** Several dedicated phone lines to communicate with stations should be available, especially in case of interrupted feedback audio—in other words, static.

7. **Spokespeople briefing.** It is essential to brief spokespersons to avoid potential confusion on the names and locations of interviewers during an SMT. All names should be written out on a studio teleprompter or on large cue cards, which the spokesperson should refer to before the interview. In addition, the spokesperson should become accustomed to the earpiece, because the director's voice can be distracting initially.

8. **Consider controversy.** Don't worry about stirring up a storm; it often makes news.

9. **Avoid becoming too commercial.** Of course the spokesperson is there to "plug" the organization or product, but don't overdo it or you won't be invited back. SMTs can save time and streamline logistics for any organization. But they are expensive—costing $9,000 for a two-hour studio-produced tour reaching 12 to 14 outlets.[10]

Public Service Announcements

The public service announcement (PSA) is a TV or radio commercial, usually 10 to 60 seconds long, that is broadcast at no cost to the sponsor. Nonprofit organizations are active users of PSAs. Commercial organizations, too, may take advantage of PSAs for their nonprofit activities, such as blood drives, voter registration drives, health testing, and the like. The spread of local cable TV stations has expanded the opportunity for placing PSAs on the air.

Unlike news releases, PSAs are generally written in advertising-copy style: punchy and pointed. The essential challenge in writing PSAs is to select the small amount of information to be used, discard extraneous information, and persuade the listener to take the desired action. The following is a typical 30-second PSA:

> The challenge of inflation has never been more serious than it is today. The need for strong national leadership has never been more pressing than it is today.
>
> Americans must tell their elected leaders to stop spending and regulating and start listening to the people.

But they won't until you demand it.

Until you demand that they stop overspending, stop crippling our economy with needless regulation, stop suffocating America with outrageous taxes.

You can make a difference.

This message brought to you by Seattle City Coffee.

According to survey research, broadcasters use three primary criteria in determining which PSAs make the air: (1) sponsorship, (2) relevance of the message to the community, and (3) message design. In terms of sponsorship, the reputation of the sponsor for honesty and integrity is critical.

As to the relevance of the message, urgent social problems, such as health and safety issues and education and training concerns, all rank high with broadcasters. In message design, the more imaginative, original, and exciting the message, the better the chance of its getting free play on the air.

Video Conferences

A more recent phenomenon of the video revolution is the video conference, which connects audiences throughout the United States or around the world in a satellite-linked meeting.

Long-distance meetings via video conferences are now becoming much more popular. Video conferences may originate from hotel ballrooms or offshore oil platforms, from corporate headquarters or major trade shows. They can be used for information or motivation. All have the benefit of conveying a message—internally to employees or externally to the news media, investors, or consumers—instantly.

In considering a video conference, the following factors should be addressed:

- **Origination site.** Video conferences may originate from a broadcast studio. However, their impact can be increased by choosing a remote location that adds authenticity to the proceedings.
- **Visuals.** Because a video conference is a live TV show, graphics must be considered, to heighten the visual excitement of the presentation. In 1993, when General Motors exposed *Dateline NBC*'s fraudulent reporting of its trucks, the company used a host of visuals at its media video conference. GM not only made use of extensive video at the conference, it also displayed one of the actual trucks used in the bogus broadcast.
- **Interactivity.** A video conference also may be enhanced by allowing viewers to ask questions. Two-way audio linkups are now common in video conferences. Again, these add a note of immediacy and spontaneity that enhances the interest and impact of the video conference.

Growth of Talk Radio

Talk radio has become an influential communications medium in contemporary America. Half of all U.S. adults regularly listen to the radio.

With many downsized and outsized Americans working from home and many others on the road, the radio has returned as a primary communications medium. All-news, all-sports, and talk have become a steady communications diet for many Americans.

Part of the appeal of talk radio is that it offers almost every shade of opinion. And it's unfiltered; that is, talk radio cuts out the "middle man." There is no reporter interceding between the listener and the speaker. Communication on talk radio, then, can be considered "purer" than other methods.

Talk radio is also among the only media in which the voices of "everyday people" can be heard immediately. No wonder: Talk radio must fill 24 hours of air time each day, 189 hours a week, 2,555 hours a year. That's a lot of talk! Says talk show host and former Ronald Reagan associate Oliver North, himself no stranger to controversy, "Talk radio is interactive. Listeners know that what they're hearing is authentic."[11]

With FM radio dominated by music, talk radio has resurrected AM radio. Talk radio is still dominated by conservative viewpoints; it's estimated that 70 percent of talk radio hosts nationally are conservatives.[12] But for every Rush Limbaugh "ditto head," there is a devoted lovelorn fan of Dr. Laura Schlessinger or Dr. Joy Browne, or a hormone-happy, loyal leering listener of Howard Stern. The medium is nothing if not controversial. But controversy sells, and talk radio is booming.

Penetrating the Radio Marketplace

What makes radio especially effective for public relations people is the sheer number of radio outlets in the United States: There are 11,000 radio stations versus 400 to 600 TV outlets.

Four aspects must be considered paramount in penetrating the radio market.

1. **Strong, focused message.** Stations must be given valuable information that will enhance the lives of listeners.
2. **Localization.** The local angle is key. The message must be tailored to suit the needs of targeted listeners.
3. **Positive spokespeople.** Spokespeople must radiate enthusiasm and goodwill. They, after all, are representing the organization and must reflect on it positively.
4. **Timeliness.** Finally, the message must be timely and topical. Or else, a radio station won't be interested.

Although radio, broadcasting 24 hours a day, is difficult to monitor, the growth in listenership makes the medium a prime choice for public relations professionals.

BACKGROUNDER

A Star Is Morphed

Move over Dan and Peter and Tom and Rush and Barbara: Ananova Ltd., the interactive services division of the Press Association of Great Britain, has developed a computer-generated newscaster—part bombshell, part Max Headroom.

The newscaster, also named Ananova, began broadcasting news from www.ananova.com in the spring of 2000. According to the Press Association's director of new media, "We were sort of faceless, so we decided to create a virtual face, a virtual star."

In order to distinguish the new Internet broadcaster from her TV counterparts, Ananova has blue-green hair.

S U M M A R Y

The growth of electronic media has made it even more important for public relations professionals to be conversant with TV and radio. Adding to the challenge is the afore-mentioned trend of "softer news" and heightened "sensationalism."

As generations weaned on TV enter the public relations field, familiarity with broadcast methods will increase. As cable television stations in particular proliferate, the need for additional programming—for more material to fill news and interview holes—also will expand. Finally, the growth of streaming audio and video on the Internet only adds to the necessity that public relations professionals master the electronic media.

This will open the door to a new breed of public relations professional, comfortable with and proficient in the nuances of writing for, dealing with, and mastering the art of electronic communication.

Discussion Starters

1. Why has video become more important for public relations professionals?
2. How has the definition of news changed because of video?
3. Is it a good idea for an executive to be spontaneous in a TV interview?
4. How comprehensive should answers be on TV?
5. When should an organization consider using a VNR?
6. Why are VNRs considered controversial?
7. What are the key facets of a PSA?
8. What is a Satellite Media Tour and when does it make sense?
9. What factors must be considered in arranging a video conference?
10. Why is talk radio more important to public relations professionals today?

Notes

1. Jonathan Lesser, "The Rose Bawl: What We Learned from Rose Vs. Gray," *Public Relations Tactics* (January 2000): 1,15.
2. William F. Baker, "The Lost Promise of American Television," *Vital Speeches of the Day* (June 5, 1998): 684.
3. Ruth Bayard Smith, "Absolute Talk on the Radio," *Media Studies Journal* (Spring/Summer 1998): 73.
4. "How Americans Use the News," *Roper Center for Public Opinion Research,* The Freedom Forum Media Studies and the Newseum, January 1997.
5. Remarks by Ken Bode, Ragan Corporate Communicators Conference, Chicago, IL, September 21, 1999.
6. David Lieberman, "AOL Tops the TV Networks," *USA Today* (November 11, 1999): 1.
7. Peter Johnson, "NBC's Couric Reflects on the State of TV News," *USA Today* (February 19, 1997): D3.
8. "Rather to TV News Heads: Fight 'Sleaze and Glitz,' " *O'Dwyer's PR Services Report* (November 1993): 1, 22–26.

9. "Answers to the Most Frequently Asked VNR Questions," *PR Tactics* (June 1999): 21.

10. "The Experts Reveal the Secrets to Successful Satellite Media Tours," *Interactive Public Relations* (September 1, 1995): 1.

11. "Radio is One Way PR Pros Can Reach a Lot of People," *Interactive Public Relations* (August 1, 1995): 8.

12. Ruth Bayard Smith, "Absolute Talk on the Radio," 73.

Suggested Readings

Associated Press. *Broadcast News Stylebook*. (Available from the author, 50 Rockefeller Plaza, New York, NY 10020.) This has a more generalized style than that presented in the UPI stylebook. Suggestions of methods and treatment for the preparation of news copy and information pertinent to the AP broadcast wire operations are given.

Broadcasting Publications. *Broadcasting*. (Available from the author, 1735 DeSales St., NW, Washington, D.C. 20036; published weekly on Mondays.) This basic news magazine for the radio, TV, and cable TV industries reports all activities involved in the entire broadcasting field.

Campbell, Christopher P. *Race, Myths, and the News*. Thousand Oaks, CA: Sage Publications, 1995.

Common Sense Guide to Making Business Videos. (Available from Creative Marketing Corporation, 285 S. 171 St., New Berlin, WI 53151-3511.) Anyone not familiar with business videos will benefit from this booklet, which zeros in on the planning needed to make a successful video.

Critchlow, James. *Radio Hole-in-the-Head/Radio Liberty: An Inside Story of Cost War Broadcasting*. Lanham, MD: University Press of America, 1995. Traces the evolution of Radio Liberty onto the international scene.

Cronkite, Walter. *A Reporter's Life*. New York: Knopf, 1996. Reminiscences of the "most trusted man in America."

Daily Variety. (Available from 1400 N. Cahuenga Blvd., Hollywood, CA 90028.) This trade paper for the entertainment industries is centered mainly in Los Angeles, with complete coverage of West Coast production activities; it includes reports from all world entertainment centers.

Jankowski, Gene F., and David C. Fuchs. *Television Today and Tomorrow*. New York: Oxford University Press, 1995.

Lewis, Lidj Ernest. "When Two Tours Are Better Than One." *Public Relations Tactics*. (July 1997): 20 ff. Combine satellite and radio media tours—twice the exposure for one reasonable price.

Marconi, Joe. *The Complete Guide to Publicity: Maximize Visibility for Your Product, Service or Organization*. Lincolnwood, IL: NTC Business Books, 1999.

Shingler, Martin. *On Air: Methods and Meanings of Radio*. New York: Oxford University Press, 1998.

www.Gebbieinc.com. Web sites listing an estimated 4,600 radio stations with Web sites and an estimated 1,020 TV stations with Web sites.

www.MediaPost.com. Web site listing of 4,993 radio stations in 260 markets, 2,188 TV stations in 21 markets, and 125 cable networks.

www.NewsDirectory.com. Web site listing 1,070 TV stations.

top of the shelf

60 Minutes

CBS Television News magazine program www.sixtyminutes.com.

For decades, the most widely watched TV program in the nation has been a Sunday night news magazine program that is the subject of fear and loathing of politicians, presidents, and corporate potentates.

60 Minutes, as the saying goes, has been often imitated, never duplicated—although weekdays, *60 Minutes II* now appears. The brainchild of news producer Don Hewitt, the show and its correspondents—Mike Wallace, Morley Safer, Dan Rather, Diane Sawyer, Lesley Stahl, Steve Croft, the late Harry Reasoner, Ed Bradley, and others—have become synonyms for investigative TV journalism.

In its first decade, *60 Minutes* was despised and avoided by most business organizations. They feared the consequences of a national TV skewering, and most refused to be interviewed. Invariably, this cost them, because *60 Minutes* correspondents ordinarily don't accept "not available" or "no comment" for an answer.

In recent years, smart organizations have realized that, in some cases, it makes sense to cooperate with *60 Minutes.* Adolph Coors Company and Johnson & Johnson, for example, found that the program treated them fairly in the midst of terrible crisis.

In the new century, with the plethora of *60 Minutes* copycats on the broadcast and cable landscape, it is incumbent upon public relations students to make the viewing of *60 Minutes* a required Sunday evening ritual.

CASE STUDY

They're Heeere!

Suppose you gave a party and *60 Minutes* showed up at the door. Would you let them in? Would you evict them? Would you commit hara-kiri?

Those were the choices that confronted The Chase Manhattan Bank at the American Bankers Association convention, when *60 Minutes* came to Honolulu to "get the bankers."

The banking industry at the time was taking its lumps. Profits were lagging. Loans to foreign governments weren't being repaid. And it was getting difficult for poor people to open bank accounts.

Understandably, few bankers at the Honolulu convention cared to share their thoughts on camera with *60 Minutes.* Some headed for cover when the cameras approached. Others barred the unwanted visitors from their receptions. In at least one case, a *60 Minutes* cameraman was physically removed from the hall. By the convention's third day, the *60 Minutes* team was decrying its treatment at the hands of the bankers as the "most vicious" it had ever been accorded.

By the third night, correspondent Morley Safer and his *60 Minutes* crew were steaming and itching for a confrontation.

That's when *60 Minutes* showed up at our party.

For 10 years, with your intrepid author as its public affairs director, Chase Manhattan had sponsored a private convention reception for the media. It combined an informal cocktail party, where journalists and bankers could chat and munch hors d'oeuvres, with a more formal, 30-minute press conference with the bank's president. The press conference was on the record, no holds barred, and frequently generated news coverage by the wire services, newspapers, and magazines that regularly sent representatives. No TV cameras were permitted.

But when we arrived at Honolulu's scenic Pacific Club, there to greet us—unannounced and uninvited—were Morley and the men from *60 Minutes,* ready to do battle.

The ball was in our court. We faced five questions that demanded immediate answers.

☑ **First, should we let them in?** What they wanted, said Safer, was to interview our president about "critical banking issues." He said they had been "hassled" all week and were "entitled" to attend our media reception.

But we hadn't invited them. And they hadn't had the courtesy to let us know they were coming. It was true that they were members of the working press. It was also true that our reception was intended to generate news.

So we had a dilemma.

☑ **Second, should we let them film the press conference?** Chase's annual convention press conference had never before been filmed. TV cameras are bulky, noisy, and intrusive. They threatened to sabotage the normally convivial atmosphere of our party. Equally disconcerting would be the glaring TV lights that would have to be set up. The *60 Minutes* crew countered that their coverage was worthless without film. Theirs, after all, was a medium of pictures, and without pictures, there could be no story.

As appetizing as this proposition sounded to us, we were worried that if we refused their cameras, what they might film instead would be us blocking the door at an otherwise open news conference. So we had another problem.

☑ **Third, should we let them film the cocktail party?** Like labor leader Samuel Gompers, TV people are interested in only one thing: "More!" In the case of our reception, we weren't eager to have CBS film the cocktails and hors d'oeuvres part of our party. We were certain the journalists on hand would agree with us. After all, who wants to see themselves getting sloshed on national television when they're supposed to be working?

☑ **Fourth, should we let them film a separate interview with our president?** Because few top people at the convention were willing to speak to CBS, *60 Minutes* was eager to question our president in as extensive and uninterrupted a format as possible. Safer wanted a separate interview before the formal press conference started.

So we also had to deal with the question of whether to expose our president to a lengthy, one-on-one, side-room interview with the most powerful—and potentially negative—TV news program in the land.

☑ **Fifth, should we change our format?** The annual media reception/press conference had always been an informal affair. Our executives joked with the journalists, shared self-deprecating asides, and generally relaxed. Thus, in light of the possible presence of *60 Minutes,* we wondered if we should alter this laid-back approach and adopt a more on-guard stance.

We had 10 minutes to make our decisions. We also had splitting headaches.

Questions

1. Would you let *60 Minutes* in?
2. Would you let them film the press conference?
3. Would you let them film the cocktail party?
4. Would you let them film a separate interview with the president?
5. Would you change the format of the party?
6. How does the American Bankers Association deal with the media today? Visit its on-line press room (www.aba.com/aba/PressRoom/PR_mainmenu.asp). What resources can members of the press access on this site? How does ABA make it easy for reporters to make contact?

OVER THE TOP

An Interview with Michael Jordan

No, not that Michael Jordan! This Michael Jordan was chairman and CEO of CBS from 1995 through 1998. As CEO of Westinghouse, he orchestrated the acquisition of CBS and its ailing network for $5.4 billion. In 1996, Westinghouse shed its industrial business, and Mr. Jordan concentrated his attention on the network made famous by, among other things, David Letterman, Don Imus, Howard Stern, and *60 Minutes*.

Can journalists and corporate broadcast executives coexist?

I think there is a conflict. Some CBS news programs and competitors' news programs are very anti-establishment, and good, bad or indifferent, we happened to be part of the establishment, the corporate establishment.

If there were things that *60 Minutes* presents that you don't like, as CEO how did you deal with it?

I tried to stay out of editing their work as long as we were not in violation of some law or something like that. If it was something in really bad taste or stupid, I guess we would all raise objections to it, but *60 Minutes*, for example, is the most successful of its genre and it takes shots at lots of people. I think that's life.

How would you defend *60 Minutes* to a CEO friend whose company got hammered?

I'd tell him, "Welcome to the NFL."

What did you do when someone called you to complain about an Imus or a Stern?

We got lots and lots of different complaints, whether television or Imus or Stern. Some people object to violence. Some people will object to *NYPD Blue*. Actually, network television and CBS are much cleaner, very clean, compared to the cable people.

What was your attitude toward the V-Chip to block out offensive programming?

We didn't think the V-Chip was a good idea. I prefer a voluntary rating system.

What did you consider your role in regard to censorship?

Our role was to try to give parents information about what's on, but we were not going to censor our broadcast just to meet the feelings of a particular group of people. We wanted it to be in good taste, we wanted it to be controlled, but I don't think what's on the air in television is really offensive. It may not be like the '50s, but I think it is in good taste.

What was your reaction when David Letterman publicly taunted you on his late-night program?

Well, first of all, you have to joke about it because it's his "trade." He did a bigger number on Jack Welch (CEO of General Electric) when he worked at NBC. After a particularly rough show, I sent David a videotape on how to box.

Chapter 16

Employees

According to Fortune *magazine, the top 200 "most admired" corporations in America spent a significantly larger share of their communications budgets—more than 50 percent—on employee communications. These firms spent three times as much on communicating with employees, in fact, as the 200 companies ranked "least admired."*[1]

In the 21st century, employee communications matters—a lot. This was not always the case. For years, internal communications was considered a "stepchild" to the more glamorous and presumably "more critical" functions of media, government, and investor relations. No more. For a variety of reasons, communicating with employees has become increasingly important for organizations in the new millennium.

■ *First, the wave of downsizings and layoffs that dominated business and industry both in the United States and worldwide during the latter half of the 1990s and continuing into the new century has taken its toll on employee loyalty.*

Where once, employees implicitly trusted their organizations and superiors, today they are much more "brittle," hardened to the realities of a job market dominated by technological change that reduces human labor. Today, when companies lay off workers, they are rewarded by the stock market for becoming more productive and efficient. This phenomenon has caused employees to understand that in today's business climate, every employee is expendable and there is no such thing as "lifetime employment."

Consequently, companies must work harder at honestly communicating with their workers.

■ *The widening gulf between the pay of senior officers and common workers is another reason why organizations must be sensitive to employee communications.*

One 1999 study of CEO compensation found that "the line between pay and any objective standard of performance has been all but severed."[2] *Some examples of bloated CEO pay are scandalous.*

Occidental Petroleum CEO Ray Irani received $101.5 million in total 1997 compensation, after the company lost—lost!—$390 million.

Foundation Health Systems CEO Malik Hasan collected more than $28 million during a five-year period, during which the company's stock declined by 2 percent.

Engelhard Corporation recorded a return of −7 percent for 1997, but CEO Orin Smith's bonus of $800,000 was unchanged from the previous year.

Examples like these can't help but breed contempt among rank-and-file employees.

☑ *Not surprisingly, the notion of "job stability" for most workers has disappeared in the 21st century. Most employees no longer expect cradle-to-grave employment. They're eager to develop work skills to pursue more money, better hours and greater job satisfaction, but not necessarily at the same company.*

The name of the game today is job mobility. New employment opportunities fueled by the high-tech revolution, coupled with labor shortages in many industries, has led to unprecedented mobility among workers. So in the new century, the notion of employee loyalty is as outmoded as a manual typewriter.[3] Companies must communicate to keep employees interested.

☑ *The move toward globalization, including the merger of geographically dispersed organizations, is another reason for increased focus on internal communications.*

Technology has hastened the integration of business and markets around the world. Customers on far-away continents are today but a mouse click away. Alliances, affiliations and mergers among far-flung companies have proliferated. Organizations have become much more cognizant of the importance of communicating the opportunities and benefits that will enhance support and loyalty among worldwide staffs.[4]

☑ *In light of these phenomena, the value of "intellectual capital" has increased in importance. In the new information economy, business managers have realized that the assets of their companies exist "very much in the heads of their employees."[5] Employee communications, then, has become a key way to nourish and transfer that intellectual capital among workers.*

All of these changes pose a significant challenge for employee communicators.

Consequently, internal communications has become a "hot ticket" in public relations. With fewer employees expected to do more work, staff members are calling for empowerment—for more of a voice in decision making. Just about every researcher who keeps tabs on employee opinion finds evidence of a "trust gap" that exists between management and workers.

One Roper Starch Worldwide study for the Public Relations Society of America found that attitudes toward work have declined over time, just as morale has gotten worse. In response, one CEO suggests, "If employees are to share in greater risk, they should also have a greater share of the rewards."[6] Whatever the solution, increased employee communications must play a pivotal role.

AKA "You're Outta' Here"

Nobody these days gets "fired" or even "laid off." Rather, companies describe their attempts to pare the staff in the following more palatable terms:

- Strengthening global effectiveness—Procter & Gamble
- Focused reduction—Tandem Computer

- Career transition program—General Motors
- Reshaping—National Semiconductor
- Release of resources—Bank of America
- Normal payroll adjustment—Wal-Mart
- Schedule adjustments—Stouffer Foods Corp.
- Involuntarily separated from the payroll—AT&T

Dealing with the Employee Public

Just as there is no such thing as the "general public," there is also no single "employee public."

The employee public is made up of numerous subgroups; senior managers, first-line supervisors, staff and line employees, women and minority workers, union laborers, per diem employees, contract workers, etc. Each group has different interests and concerns. A smart organization will try to differentiate messages and communications to reach these segments.

Indeed in a general sense, today the staff is younger, increasingly female, more ambitious and career-oriented, less complacent, and less loyal to the company than in the past. Today's more hard-nosed employee demands candor in communications. Internal communications, like external messages, must be targeted to reach specific subgroups of the employee public.

According to research, communications must be continuous, respectful, and candid to reinforce a consistent management message.

- A survey of 700 employees at 70 companies found that 54 percent felt they didn't get decisions explained well, and another 64 percent said they didn't believe what management told them.[7]
- A survey by Deloitte & Touche found that 81 percent of health care respondents said "employee morale" was the top human resources issue in hospitals today—compared to 75 percent only one year earlier.

◪ A survey of American Management Association member companies that cut jobs revealed that declining morale was a problem for three out of four of them.[8]

Clearly, organizing effective, believable, and persuasive internal communications in the midst of organizational change is a core critical public relations responsibility in the 21st century.

Communicating Effectively in a Sea of Doubt

An organization truly concerned about "getting through" to its employees in an era of downsizing, displacement, and dubious communications must reinforce five specific principles:

◪ **Respect.** Employees must be respected for their worth as individuals and their value as workers. They must be treated with respect and not as interchangeable commodities.

◪ **Honest feedback.** By talking to workers about their strengths and weaknesses, employees know where they stand. Some managers incorrectly assume that avoiding negative feedback will be helpful. Wrong. Employees need to know where they stand at any given time. Candid communications will help them in this pursuit.

◪ **Recognition.** Employees feel successful when management recognizes their contributions. It is the duty of the public relations professional to suggest mechanisms by which deserving employees will be honored.

◪ **A voice.** In the era of talk radio and television talk shows, almost everyone wants their ideas to be heard and to have a voice in decision making. This growing "activist communications" phenomenon must be considered by public relations professionals seeking to win internal goodwill for management.

◪ **Encouragement.** Study after study reveals that money and benefits motivate employees up to a point, but that "something else" is generally necessary. That something else is encouragement. Workers need to be encouraged. Communications programs that can provide encouragement generally produce results. What distinguishes the communication effort at a "better place to work"? According to Milton Moskowitz, co-author of the *100 Best Companies to Work For,* six criteria, in particular, are important:

1. **Willingness to express dissent.** Employees, according to Moskowitz, want to be able to "feed back" to management their opinions and even dissent. They want access to management. They want critical letters to appear in internal publications. They want management to pay attention.

2. **Visibility and proximity of upper management.** Enlightened companies try to level rank distinctions, eliminating such status reminders as executive cafeterias and executive gymnasiums. They act against hierarchical separation, says Moskowitz. He adds that smart CEOs practice MBWA— "management by walking around."

3. **Priority of internal to external communication.** The worst thing to happen to any organization is for employees to learn critical information about the company on the 10 o'clock news. Smart organizations always release pertinent information to employees first and consider internal communication primary.

4. **Attention to clarity.** How many employees regularly read benefits booklets? The answer should be "many" because of the importance of benefit programs to the entire staff, but most employees never open them. Good companies will write such booklets with clarity—to be readable for a general audience rather than for human resources specialists.

5. **Friendly tone.** According to Moskowitz, the best companies "give a sense of family" in all that they communicate. One high-tech company makes everyone wear a name tag with the first name in big block letters. These little things are most important, declares Moskowitz.

6. **Sense of humor.** People are worried principally about keeping their jobs. Corporate life for many is grim. Moskowitz says this is disastrous. "It puts people in straitjackets, so they can't wait to get out at the end of the day."[9]

What internal communications comes down to—just like external communications—is, in a word, credibility. The task for management is to convince employees that it not only desires to communicate with them, but also wishes to do so in a truthful, frank, and direct manner. That is the overriding challenge that confronts today's internal communicator.

Credibility: The Key

The employee public is a savvy one. Employees can't be conned because they live with the organization every day. They generally know what's going on and whether management is being honest with them. That's why management must be truthful.

Employees want managers to level with them. They want facts, not wishful thinking. The days when management could say "Trust us, this is for your own good" are over. Employees like hearing the truth, especially in person. Candor works best when it's "not slipped inside a memorandum or—worst of all—in an e-mail or voice mail message broadcast to the troops."[10]

Employees also want to know, candidly, how they're doing. Research indicates that trust in organizations would increase if management (1) communicated earlier and more frequently, (2) demonstrated trust in employees by sharing bad news as well as good, and (3) involved employees in the process by asking for their ideas and opinions. The fact is, employees desperately want to know in what direction an organization is headed and what their own role is in getting it there. Without management feedback, employees are left to gauge for themselves how they are doing, which ultimately creates the feeling that "they must not care so I must not be meeting expectations."[11]

Today, smart companies realize that well-informed employees are the organization's best goodwill ambassadors. Managements have become more candid in their communications with the staff. Gone are the days when all the news coming from the communications department was good. In today's environment, being candid means treating people with dignity and giving them the opportunity to understand the realities of the marketplace.[12]

IBM, for example, gutted its award-winning, four-color magazine, *Think,* with the arrival of new CEO Lou Gerstner in 1993. The new *Think* was smaller and more candid than its predecessor, discussing such formally taboo topics as "avoiding getting swallowed up in bureaucracy" and "working without the warmth of a corporate security blanket." The new *Think* was most successful.

FIGURE 16-1 **Snuffing a spark.** *The (ARCO) Spark*, discontinued after a 1999 merger, was legendary among employee publications for its candor and openness. *The Spark* freely published taboo subjects—everything from photos of refinery fires to employee letters criticizing management. Few similar publications would have had the chutzpah to feature their own employees in a *National Enquirer* "Lifestyles of the Rich and Famous" motif.

So, too, was the no-holds-barred *The Spark,* the monthly publication of ARCO (Figure 16-1). *The Spark* poked fun at the company, encouraged blunt feedback from employees, and generally promoted an environment of candor and openness at ARCO. Alas, when BP Amoco purchased ARCO in 1999, *The Spark* was replaced by BP Amoco's less lively *Horizon*.[13]

With the growth of e-mail and Intranets, organizations have an even greater opportunity today to increase the frequency and candor of communications. A major part of the challenge that confronts internal communicators is to reflect a credibility in communicating that underscores the level of "respect" with which employees should be held by management.

There is little worse than management being condescending to employees. For example, when the former CoreStates Financial Corporation downsized 7,000 people in 1998, it treated the wrenching event like a high school graduation—distributing going-away yearbooks and disposable cameras to take parting snapshots. The imbecilic attempt to assuage feelings failed miserably.[14]

The point is most employees desperately want to be treated as important parts of an organization; they should not be taken for granted, nor should they be shielded from the truth. Thus, the most important ingredient of any internal communications program must be credibility.

Employee Communications Strategies

Enhancing credibility, being candid, and winning trust must be the primary employee communications objectives in the new century. Earning employee trust may result in more committed and productive employees. But scraping away the scar tissue of distrust that exists in many organizations requires a strategic approach. Five elements are key in any strategic program:

1. **Survey employees' attitudes regularly.** Ironically, it is organizations that audit their financial resources on a daily basis that regularly fail to take the temperature of their own employees. They "fly blind." Attitude surveys can identify problems before they become crises. Employees who are surveyed about their attitudes, consulted on what the surveys reveal, and then shown action as a result of the survey findings will be much more willing to accept management's policies.
2. **Be consistent.** Management that promises open and honest communications must practice it. An open door must remain open—not just partly open part of the time. Communications must be consistent to be believed. That means conveying both good and bad news on a regular basis.
3. **Personalize communications.** One study found that 80 percent of corporate chief executives believed that "personally communicating with employees benefits the bottom line." But only 22 percent of them did it on a regular basis. Workers want personal attention from those for whom they work, particularly their immediate supervisor. Given this, companies like Navistar conduct "town meetings" at which senior managers travel to plant locations to speak directly to the rank and file (see "Over the To's" at the end of this chapter).
4. **Be candid.** Employees today are younger, less well-educated, less loyal, and include more women, minorities, and immigrants than workers of the past. These new, more skeptical, less-trusting employees demand honesty in everything management says.
5. **Be innovative.** New employees in the work force and increased skepticism in the workplace demand new communications solutions. This means resorting to the new technology—voice, video, data transmission on PCs, and so on—to reach workers. Today's work force, fiercely loyal to the Internet, and

weaned on a daily diet of high-resolution, mind-numbing television, demands innovative solutions to counteract the trust gap.[15]

Employee Communications Tactics

Once objectives are set, a variety of techniques can be adopted to reach the staff. The initial tool again is research. Before any communications program can be implemented, communicators must have a good sense of staff attitudes.

Perhaps the most beneficial form of research on which to lay the groundwork for effective employee communications is the internal communications audit. Basically, this consists of old-fashioned personal, in-depth interviews to determine staff attitudes about their jobs, the organization, and its management, coupled with an analysis of existing communications techniques. The findings of such audits are often startling, always informative, and never easily ignored.

Once internal communications research is completed, the public relations practitioner has a clearer idea of the kinds of communications vehicles that make sense for the organization. Today, such internal communications vehicles are dominated by on-line delivery.

On-Line Communications: Up and Coming

The age of on-line communication has ushered in a whole new set of employee communications vehicles—from e-mail to voice mail to tailored organizational intranets. Such vehicles are more immediate than earlier print versions. They reach employees at their desks and are more likely to be read, listened to, and acted upon.

As print publications become fewer and fewer, tailored on-line newsletters have begun to replace them. Every Friday, for example, *Honeywell International* dispatches an electronic publication called *Honeywell Headlines,* a roundup of key news and events involving the firm. Honeywell also issues "e-mail on demand" to employees wishing to keep abreast of changing corporate information and developments, for example, by summary reports of management meetings.[16]

Many organizations, from traditional companies such as Xerox, Exxon and Ford, to the new high-tech giants such as Cisco Systems, Intel and Oracle, increasingly rely on intranets to exchange information quickly and effectively. Miller Brewing Company's intranet, "Miller Time," sponsors an interactive forum, through which employees offer suggestions to and ask questions of management. Everyone who offers an idea through the Miller intranet is guaranteed a response, such feedback being critical to corporate credibility.[17]

Perfecting the Intranet

According to Forrester Research, the vast majority of American companies either have an intranet or plan to have one soon. It is likely that in the first few years of the new century, every major company will have intranet capability.[18]

But having an intranet site doesn't mean employees will necessarily go there for information. Sites high in visual appeal but low in usefulness will likely be ignored. To prevent that, intranet creators should keep in mind several important considerations:

1. **Consider the culture.** If the organization is generally collaborative and collegial, it will have no trouble getting people to contribute information and

materials to the intranet. But, if the organization is not one that ordinarily shares, a larger central staff may be necessary to ensure that the intranet works.

2. **Set clear objectives, then let it evolve.** Just as in setting up a corporate Web site, intranets must be designed with clear goals in mind: to streamline business processes, to communicate management messages, etc. Once goals are established, however, site creators ought to allow for growth and evolution as new intranet needs become apparent.

3. **Treat it as a journalistic enterprise.** Company news gets read by company workers. That's a truism throughout all organizations. Employees must know what's going on in the company and complain bitterly if they are not given advanced notice of important developments. In this way, the intranet can serve as a critical journalistic communications tool within the organization.

4. **Market, market, market.** The intranet needs to be "sold" within the company. Publicize new features or changes in content. Weekly e-mails can be used to highlight noteworthy additions and updates. Just as with any other internal communications vehicle, the more exposure the site gets, the more frequently it will be used.

A QUESTION OF ETHICS

E-mail Makes a Great Gray Lady Blush

The *New York Times* prides itself on its reputation as "the great gray lady"—the most serious, understated, comprehensive, and objective daily newspaper in the world.

That's why *Times'* management probably could be forgiven for going ballistic in November 1999, when it discovered internal e-mail images in its Norfolk, Virginia, office of an obese woman in a bikini, an adult version of a Peanuts cartoon, and a video depicting a clown being shot out of a cannon into a donkey's posterior.

Management immediately launched an internal investigation. When the dust had settled, nearly two dozen employees—10 percent of the Norfolk workforce—were fired for sending e-mail that violated *New York Times* standards.

Times' management thought the situation so serious that the CEO himself, Arthur O. Sulzberger Jr., flew to Norfolk to discuss the reasons for the firings with the remaining staff. The executives explained that the offending e-mails included sexual images and jokes that wouldn't be tolerated in the workplace.

The *Times* allows employees "reasonable" personal use of company e-mail. But company policy also states:

Computer communications must be consistent with conventional standards of ethical and proper conduct, behavior and manners and are not to be used to create, forward or display any offensive or disruptive messages, including photographs, graphics and audio materials.

So the *Times* fired the offenders, en masse.

Some of the fired employees raised ethical questions about their former employer's right to invade their personal e-mail and extract the offending material. Others wondered how an institution so committed to the First Amendment could so blatantly act against its own employees' "freedom of speech."

To this charge, the *Times* responded, "There is no First Amendment right to transmit pornography over the company's e-mail system or to view the pornography in the workplace."

Perhaps not. But the questions of e-mail, an individual's right to privacy, and an employer's ability to monitor its own internal communications did not promise to be easily solved.

One of the fallen Norfolk employees offered some simple advice to her former employer. The *New York Times*, she said, ought to "chill out."*

For further information, see Ann Cairns, "Those Bawdy E-Mails Were Good for a Laugh—Until the Ax Fell, " Wall Street Journal, February 4, 2000, A1,8.

5. **Link to outside lives.** Some CEOs may not recognize it, but employees have lives outside the corporation. An intranet site that recognizes that simple fact can become quite popular. Links to classified ads, restaurant and movie reviews, and information on local concerts is one way to reinforce both the intranet's value and the organization's concern for its staff.
6. **Senior management must commit.** Just like anything else in an organization, if the top man or woman is neither interested nor supportive, the idea will fail. Ergo, the perceived value of an organization's intranet will increase dramatically if management actively supports and uses it.[19]

Print Publications: Not Dead Yet

The advent of on-line internal communications has been hard on print publications.

It's happening all over corporate America: Print editors are being told to either kill their publication entirely or move it onto the company's intranet.[20]

- ☑ At Tennessee's Eastman Chemical Company, for example, the CEO's drive to convert the firm to a Web-based organization tolled the death knell in 1999 for the *Inside Eastman* newsletter, after 50 years of publication.
- ☑ At another Eastman, New York's Eastman Kodak Company, the internal publication was not used when the company announced in 1998 that it would lay off 16,600 workers and save $1 billion. Supervisors were briefed by special e-mails and then directed to personally relay the bad news to their subordinates.
- ☑ That same year, when Michigan's Fel-Pro Inc. agreed to be acquired by Federal-Mogul Corporation, it "cascaded" the information down from departmental managers to supervisors to staff.

To print critics, what all these instances suggest is that "the time-honored or worn corporate newsletter with its stiff 'message from the chairman' and months-old articles is becoming passé."[21]

Thus sayeth the critics.

Print defenders, on the other hand, argue that there is still a complementary role for a management-driven publication that unites employees within divisions or around the world (Figure 16-2).

Indeed, a traditional first job for an entry-level public relations professional is working on the employee newsletter. Whether print or on-line, in approaching the writing or editing of an employee newsletter, the professional should ponder the following questions:

1. Who is this publication designed to reach?
2. What kinds of articles should be featured?
3. What is the budget for the newsletter?
4. What is the appropriate format for the newsletter?
5. How frequently should the newsletter be published?
6. What is the desired approval process for the newsletter?

The answers to these questions, of course, vary from one organization to another, but all should be tackled before approaching the assignment. Whether print or on-line, employee newsletters should appear regularly, on time, and with a consistent format. Employees should expect them and even look forward to them.

FIGURE 16-2 **First line of defense.** Print is by no means dead in a besieged company like cigarette manufacturer Philip Morris, which used its international newsletter to rally the troops.

One reason that such publications will likely survive, at least in a periodic state, is that they serve as a ready vehicle for management to explain the company's philosophy and policies. In the 21st century, it is especially important that such newsletters provide two-way communications, expressing not only management wishes but staff concerns as well.

Emergence of Desktop Publishing

One reason print publications won't go the way of the buggy whip and Vanilla Ice so quickly is the emergence of desktop publishing.

Desktop publishing enables a public relations professional to produce a newsletter at his or her own desk.

Introduced in 1985, desktop publishing allows an editor to write, lay out, and typeset a piece of copy. (The term *desktop publishing* is a misnomer; *desktop layout* or *desktop page layout* is more accurate.) Desktop publishing requires a personal computer, a laser printer, and software for word processing, charts, drawings, if desired, and publishing applications such as layout.

Desktop publishing allows a user to control the typesetting process in-house, provides faster turnaround for clients, and saves money on outside design. The desktop operation allows scanning photos and drawings, incorporating those images into page layouts, using the computer to assign color in design elements, and producing entire color-separated pages of film, from which a printer can create plates for printing.

Most who have switched to desktop publishing to gain control and curb the costs of printed materials combine the new technology with more conventional editing methods.

Specifically, a typical newsletter editor must consider the following steps in approaching the task:

1. **Assigning stories.** Article assignments must focus on organizational strategies and management objectives. Job information—organizational changes, mergers, reasons behind decisions, and so on—should be stressed.
2. **Enforcing deadlines.** Employees respect a newsletter that comes out at a specific time. An editor, therefore, must assign and enforce rigid copy deadlines. Deadline slippage can't be tolerated if the newsletter is to be respected.
3. **Assigning photos.** People like photographs. Because internal publications compete with glossy, high-tech newspapers and magazines and the Internet, organizational photos can't be dull (Figure 16-3).
4. **Editing copy.** An editor must be just that: a critic of sloppy writing, a student of forceful prose, a motivator to improve copy style. This is especially

FIGURE 16-3 **Alien crowd.** Publicity photos don't have to be mundane. At least that's the view of Sue Bohle Public Relations and Infogrames Entertainment, which decked out these Southwest Airlines passengers in out-of-this-world masks on the way to the E3 Entertainment Trade Show.

true now that the computer does at least part of the job for you. However, Spell-Check isn't foolproof, especially when it comes to context.

5. **Formatting copy.** An editor, particularly a desktop editor, must also make the final decisions on the format of the newsletter: how long articles should run, where to put photos, how to crop artwork, what headlines should say, and so on.

6. **Ensuring on-time publication.** In publishing, timeliness is next to godliness. It is the editor's responsibility to ensure that no last-minute glitches interfere with on-time publication.

7. **Critiquing.** After the fact, the editor's job must continue. He or she must scrupulously review copy, photos, placement, content, philosophy, and all the other elements to ensure that the next edition will be even better.

One organization devoted originally to internal communications, the International Association of Business Communicators, has come to rival the older Public Relations Society of America. With more than 13,000 members throughout the United States and in 40 countries, this association helps set journalistic standards for communicators for both print and on-line publications.[22]

Employee Annual Reports: On the Rise

It often makes sense to print a separate annual report just for employees. Frequently, the lure of this report—published in addition to the regular corporate shareholder annual report—is that it is written for, about, and by the employees.

Most employees do care about how their organization functions and what its management is thinking. The annual report to the staff is a good place to discuss such issues informally, yet candidly. The report can be both factual, explaining the performance of the organization during the year, and informational, reviewing organizational changes and significant milestones during the year. It can also be motivational in its implicit appeal to team spirit and pride. Southwest Airlines does perhaps the best job in America in keeping its staff loose and making it feel special through a constant barrage of innovative and fun communications (Figure 16-4).

Staff reports observe few hard-and-fast rules about concept and format. Staff annuals can be as complex as the shareholder annual report itself or as simple as a brief outline of the company's highlights of the year. Typical features of the employee annual report include the following:

1. **Chief executive's letter:** a special report to the staff that reviews the performance and highlights of the year and thanks employees for their help
2. **Use-of-funds statement:** often a graphic chart that describes how the organization used each dollar it took in
3. **Financial condition:** frequently a chart that describes the assets and liabilities of the corporation and the stockholders' equity
4. **Description of the company:** simple, graphic explanation of what the organization is and where its facilities are located
5. **Social responsibility highlights:** discussion of the organization's role in aiding society through monetary assistance and employee participation during the year
6. **Staff financial highlights:** general description, usually in chart form, of salaries, benefits, and other staff-related expense items

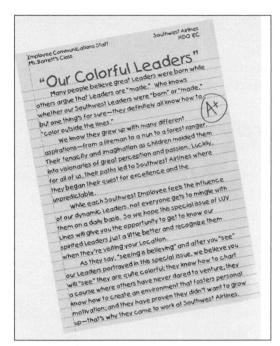

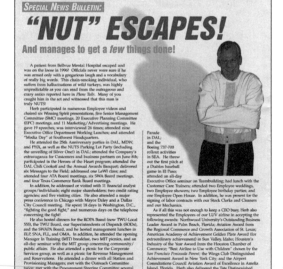

FIGURE 16-4 **One-of-a-kind.** Southwest Airlines is "another" kind of company. Its irrepressible founder and chairman, Herb Kelleher, has created a climate of creativity and productivity through spirited communications that encourage airline employees to adopt a "happy family" attitude. Southwest's success suggests the approach pays bottom-line dividends.

7. **Organizational policy:** discussion of current issues about which management feels strongly and for which it seeks employee support
8. **Emphasis on people:** in-depth profiles of people on the job, comments from people about their jobs, and/or pictorial essays on people at work to demonstrate, throughout the report, the importance of the people who make up the organization.

Employees appreciate recognition. The special annual report is a measure of recognition that does not go unnoticed—or unread—by a firm's workers.

Bulletin Boards: Coming Back

Bulletin boards, among the most ancient of employee communications vehicles, have made a comeback in recent years.

For years, bulletin boards were considered second-string information channels, generally relegated to the display of federally required information and policy data for such activities as fire drills and emergency procedures. Most employees rarely consulted them. But the bulletin board has experienced a renaissance and is now being used to improve productivity, cut waste, and reduce accidents on the job. Best of all, employees are taking notice.

How come? For one thing, yesterday's bulletin board has become today's news center. It has been repackaged into a more lively visual and graphically arresting medium. Using enlarged news pictures and texts, motivational messages, and other company announcements—all illustrated with a flair—the bulletin board has become an important source of employee communications (Figure 16-5). Hospitals, in particular, have found that a strategically situated bulletin board outside a cafeteria is a good way to promote employee understanding and cooperation.

One key to stimulating readership is to keep boards current. One person in the public relations unit should be assigned to this weekly task.

Internal Video: Up and Down

As omnipresent as broadcast and cable TV are in society today, video has had an up-and-down history as an internal communications medium.

On the one hand, internal television can be demonstrably effective. A 10-minute videotape of an executive announcing a new corporate policy imparts hundreds of times more information than an audiotape of that same message, which, in turn, contains hundreds of times more information than a printed text of the same message.

A number of organizations work skillfully with internal video:

- Burger King produces video in an in-house studio and sound stage to train workers in its 5,000 restaurants.
- Miller Brewing Company produces a 20-minute video magazine, distributed to all company locations. It features new company commercials, brand promotions, happenings at Miller plants, and employee human interest stories.
- The Ford Motor Company has taken the unprecedented step of stopping work on assembly lines to show videotapes to workers.
- The most unique internal video ever produced was the legendary "Southwest Shuffle," in which the employees of Southwest Airlines—from maintenance

ETHICS
QUESTIONS OR CONCERNS

For help...

STEP 1

Contact your supervisor. If necessary, take it up the chain of command at your location.

STEP 2

Contact your Company Ethics Officer in person, by phone, or by mail.

LMASC Ethics Director:	Tom Salvaggio
Location:	B-2, 2nd Floor, Col. 28
Phone:	Helpline Coordinator, (770) 494-3999
Mailing Address:	LMASC Ethics Office
	P O Box 1771
	Marietta, GA 30061

STEP 3

If the first two steps do not resolve the matter, contact the Corporate Office of Ethics and Business Conduct for confidential assistance:

Helpline:	800 LM ETHIC (800 563-8442)
Fax:	(818) 876-2082
Or Write:	Corporate Office of Ethics and Business Conduct
	Lockheed Martin Corporation
	P O Box 34143
	Bethesda, MD 20827-0143

STEP 4

Contact the Department of Defense Hotline to report fraud, waste and abuse, and/or security violations.

Hotline:	800 424-9098
Or Write:	Defense Hotline
	The Pentagon
	Washington, DC 20301-1900

IDENTITIES OF WRITERS AND CALLERS ARE FULLY PROTECTED.

LOCKHEED MARTIN

FIGURE 16-5 Comeback kid. Among important announcements included on organizational bulletin boards are updates on key corporate issues such as ethical questions and concerns.

crews to pilots—chimed in on a rap video extolling the virtues of their innovative carrier. Deejay for the rap extravaganza was—who else?—Southwest CEO Herb Kelleher!

On the downside, internal video is a medium that must be approached with caution. Unless video is of "broadcast quality," few will tolerate it—especially an audience of employees weaned on television. Consequently, a public relations professional must raise at least a dozen questions before embarking on an internal video excursion:

1. Why are we doing this video?
2. Whom are we trying to reach with this video?
3. What's the point of the video?
4. What do we want viewers to do after seeing the video?

5. How good is our video script?
6. How sophisticated is the quality of our broadcast?
7. How innovative and creative is the broadcast? Does it measure up to regular television?
8. How competent is our talent?
9. How proficient is our crew?
10. Where will our viewers screen the video?
11. With what communications vehicles will we supplement the video?
12. How much money can we spend?

The keys to any internal video production are, first, to examine internal needs; then to plan thoughtfully before using the medium; and, finally, to reach target publics through the highest-quality programming possible. Broadcast quality is a tough standard to meet. If an organization can't afford high-quality video, it shouldn't get involved.

Supervisory Communications: The Key Vehicle

First and foremost, employees want information from their supervisors. Supervisors, in fact, are the preferred source for 90 percent of employees, making them the top choice by far. The reason is obvious. You report to your supervisor, who awards your raise, promotes you, and is your primary source of corporate information.

That's the good news.

The bad news is that despite paying attention to enhanced supervisory communications, most companies still come up inconsistent when it comes to supervisors relaying important information. Thus, even though most employees vastly prefer information from their supervisor over what they learn through rumors, many still rely on the grapevine as a primary source of information.

What can public relations departments do to combat this trend?

Some departments formalize the meeting process by mixing management and staff in a variety of formats, from gripe sessions to marketing/planning meetings. Many organizations embrace the concept of skip-level meetings, in which top-level managers meet periodically with employees at levels several notches below them in the organizational hierarchy. As with any other form of communication, the value of meetings lies in their substance, their regularity, and the candor managers bring to face-to-face sessions. In any event, one key to improved internal communications clearly is increased face-to-face communications between supervisor and subordinate.[23]

Dealing with the Grapevine

In many organizations, it's neither the Internet nor cyberspace that dominates communications but rather the company grapevine. The rumor mill can be devastating. As one employee publication described the grapevine:

> It's faster than a public address announcement and more powerful than a general instruction. It's able to leap from LA to San Francisco in a single bound. And its credibility is almost beyond Walter Cronkite's.

Rumors, once they pick up steam, are difficult to stop. Because employees tend to distort future events to conform to a rumor, an organization must work to correct rumors as soon as possible.

BACKGROUNDER

The Newest Employee Benefit: PCs/Internet

One way to beat the rumor mill and keep the grapevine to a low rumble is for a company to offer liberal employee benefits.

In February 2000, the Ford Motor Company introduced a particular employee benefit never before offered: a high-speed desktop computer, color printer, and unlimited Internet access for just $5 a month.

Not only that, but Ford offered the benefit to every one of its 350,000 employees worldwide. Ford said the initiative would improve both employee computer literacy and employee communications. It was also

sure to benefit labor relations and boost morale in a company and industry that suffered periodic employee layoffs and division divestitures.

For the 190,000 Ford workers who lived outside the United States, Ford said it would offer Internet home pages in 14 languages and subsidize computer training.

The question of whether any other employer might resort to a similar employee benefit was answered the day after the Ford announcement. Delta Air Lines said it would offer its 72,000 employees PCs and Web access for $12 a month.

Identifying the source of a rumor is often difficult, if not impossible, and it's usually not worth the time. However, dispelling the rumor quickly and frankly is another story. Often a bad-news rumor—about layoffs, closings, and so on—can be dealt with most effectively through forthright communication. Generally, an organization makes a difficult decision after a thorough review of many alternatives. The final decision is often a compromise, reflecting the needs of the firm and its various publics, including, importantly, the work force.

In presenting a final decision to employees, management often overlooks the value of explaining how it reached its decision. By comparing alternative solutions so that employees can understand more clearly the rationale behind management decisions, an organization may make bad news more palatable.

As diabolical as the grapevine can become, it shouldn't necessarily be treated as the enemy of effective communications with employees. Management might even consider using it as a positive force. A company grapevine can be as much a communications vehicle as internal publications or employee meetings. It may even be more valuable because it is believed, and everyone seems to tap into it.

SUMMARY

The best defense against damaging grapevine rumors is a strong and candid communications system. Employee communications, for years the most neglected strategic opportunity in corporate America, is today much more appreciated for its strategic importance. Organizations which build massive marketing plans to sell products have begun today to apply that same knowledge and energy to communicating with their own employees.

In the 21st century, organizations have no choice but to build rapport with and morale among employees. The shattering of morale that accompanied the massive downsizings of the 1990s will take time to repair. Building back internal credibility is a long-term process that depends on several factors—among them, listening to employees, developing information exchanges to educate employees about changing technologies and processes, providing the strategic business information that employees require, and adapting to the new culture of job "mobility" replacing job "stability."[24]

Most of all in this new century, effective employee communications requires openness and honesty on the part of senior management. Public relations professionals must seize this initiative to foster the open climate that employees want and the two-way communications that organizations need.

Discussion Starters

1. What societal factors have caused internal communications to become more important?
2. What one element is key to organizational communication?
3. What characteristics constitute the best employee communicators?
4. What is the status of internal print communications?
5. What is the status of on-line internal communications?
6. What are the primary tasks of an employee newsletter's editor?
7. What questions should be raised before communicating through internal video?
8. What is the preferred channel of communications among most employees?
9. What is the best way to combat the grapevine?
10. Why haven't most organizations convinced their employees of top management's sincerity?

Notes

1. "Employee Communications Today: It's New, It's Different, and It Has Bottom Line Impact," *Positioning Newsletter* 10, no. 2, (1999). Heyman Associates, Inc., 11 Penn Plaza, Suite 1105, New York, NY 10001.
2. Denis B. K. Lyons, "CEO Compensation: The Whole Truth," (1999), Spencer Stuart, 401 N. Michigan Ave., Chicago, IL.
3. Erin Arvedlund, "Jumping Careers," *Kinko's Press* 1 (2000): 22.
4. Jeffrey Ball, "Daimler Chrysler's Transfer Woes," *Wall Street Journal* (August 24, 1999): B1, 12.
5. "Employee Communications Today: It's New, It's Different, and It Has Bottom Line Impact," *Positioning Newsletter* 10, no. 2. (1999). Heyman Associates, Inc., 11 Penn Plaza, Suite 1105, New York, NY 10001.
6. "The Dream in Danger," *Public Relations Strategist* (Spring 1995): 43.
7. Steve Rivkin, "Mutiny in the Cafeteria," *Public Relations Strategist* (Winter 1998): 20.
8. Bryan W. Armentrout, "The Five Best Gifts to Give Your Employees," *HR Focus* (December 1995): 3.
9. "An Employee's-Eye View of Business," *Ragan Report* (November 25, 1991): 1, 2.
10. Rivkin, *Mutiny in the Cafeteria."*
11. Thomas W. Hoog, "A Strategy to Retain Your Best People," *Public Relations Strategist* (Summer 1999): 16.
12. Fraser P. Seitel, "Leaping the 'Trust Gap,' " *U.S. Banker* (November 1990): 61.

13. "After More than 25 Years, the Arco *Spark* is Snuffed," *Ragan Report* (November 15, 1999): 4.

14. "Putting the Fun Back in Downsizing," *Ragan Report* (May 18, 1998): 1.

15. Fraser P. Seitel, "Leaping the Trust Gap," *U.S. Banker* (November 1990): 61.

16. Karen Bachman, "Does Anybody Do It Better?" *Across the Board* (January 1997): 55.

17. "Two Ways to Pull People to the Intranet," *Ragan Report* (October 18, 1999): 6.

18. Scott Rodrick, "Use Intranets" to Connect Employee Owners," *Interactive Investor Relations* (January 1997): 3.

19. John R. Kessling, "Maintaining a Successful Intranet: The KGN Experience," *PR Tactics* (November 1999): 20.

20. "Kissing Off Your Print Publication," *Ragan Report* (October 11, 1999): 6.

21. Joanne Cleaver, "An Inside Job," *Marketing News* (February 16, 1998): 1,14.

22. For further information about the International Association of Business Communicators, write to IABC, One Hallidie Plaza, Suite 600, San Francisco, CA 94102, www.iabc.com, phone 800-776-4222, fax 415-544-4747.

23. Wilma K. Mathews, "What the CEO Can Do About It," *The Public Relations Strategist* (Spring 1995): 49.

24. "Employee Communications Today: It's New, It's Different, and It Has Bottom Line Impact," *Positioning Newsletter* 10, no. 2. (1999). Heyman Associates, Inc., 11 Penn Plaza, Suite 1105, New York, NY 10001.

Suggested Readings

"Best Practices in Internal Communications," *Public Relations Tactics,* (May 1998): 10 ff.

Bishop, Larry A. "Merging with Employees in Mind." *Public Relations Strategist,* (Spring 1998): 46 ff.

Cohen, Allan. *Effective Behavior in Organizations.* Burr Ridge, IL: Irwin Professional Publishing, 1995.

Ferguson, Gary. "Give Your Employees the Business." *Public Relations Tactics,* (August 1998): 6. Employees should be told about significant corporate events before they read them in the newspaper.

Flannery, Thomas P. *People, Performance and Pay: Dynamic Compensation for Changing Organizations.* New York: The Free Press, 1995. Traditional methods of compensation may simply not cut it in an era of employee skepticism and quest for empowerment.

Freeland, David B. *Company Policy Manual Special Report: Effective Communication Strategies.* New York: Aspen Publishers, 1998. Discusses the rising skepticism of employees and offers solutions.

Hammer, Michael, and Steven Stanton. *The Reengineering Revolution.* New York: Harper Business, 1995. Reengineering gurus explain why work and workers will differ materially in the 21st century.

Kreitner, Robert, and Angelo Kinicki. *Organizational Behavior,* 3rd ed. Burr Ridge, IL: Irwin Professional Publishing, 1995. How to manage change in a learning culture.

Penzias, Arno. *Harmony: Business Technology and Life After Paperwork.* New York: Harper Business, 1995. Deals with the uncertainty resulting from technology replacing people and the challenges of the technical work force.

Ragan's Intranet Report. Chicago: Ragan Communications Inc. Monthly newsletter.

www.ReportGallery.com. This Web site features annual reports for more than 1,000 publicly traded companies, including most of the Fortune 500 companies. Also links to the companies' home pages.

Rivkin, Steve. "Mutiny in the Cafeteria." *Public Relations Strategist,* (Winter 1998): 20 ff. How to rebuild trust and loyalty after employee demoralization.

Sack, Steven Mitchell. *From Hiring to Firing: The Legal Survival Guide for Employers in the '90s.* New York: Legal Strategies Inc., 1995. The first, best defense for a public relations professional: Know the law.

Winkler, Donald. "Breaking Through Gray-Flannel Barriers." *Public Relations Strategist,* (Spring 1998): 29 ff. Encourages new types of communications.

top of the shelf

Jim Harris

Getting Employees to Fall in Love with Your Company.
New York: AMACOM, 1996.

Author Jim Harris asks, "What's love got to do with it?"

Here's what: Airline pilots voluntarily cleaning their planes on their days off! Employees voluntarily giving back their bonuses to pay down corporate debt! Hard to believe in today's cynical, bottom-line, downsizing, job-shifting environment?

Harris says, "Believe it! Learn how over 140 of today's most profitable and progressive organizations go beyond the bottom line to build commitment, trust . . . and even love with their employees."

Every supervisor should read *Getting Employees to Fall in Love with Your Company.*

CASE STUDY

CEO Trial by Fire

On the night of December 11, 1995, a fire engulfed much of the Malden Mills Industries complex in Lawrence, Massachusetts.

Twenty-four people were injured, and the company's manufacturing facilities were substantially affected. It was one of the largest factory fires in New England history. The next day, as the embers still smoldered, company CEO Aaron Feuerstein vowed, "The tragedy will not derail Malden Mills' leadership position in either the local community or the world textile market".

Most people probably took the CEO's vow with a grain of salt. At 70 years old and his factory fully insured, the Malden Mills chief could have been excused for taking the insurance money and retiring to a warmer climate.

PAY TO STAY

However high the factory flames and devastating the loss, since no one died in the fire, attention to Malden Mills quickly dissipated, and the story disappeared from the headlines.

The world began to take notice a week later.

Addressing 1,000 of the company's 2,400 workers in a local high school gym, CEO Feuerstein declared, "At least for the next 30 days, all our hourly employees will be paid their full salaries." He also promised to quickly build a new plant in Lawrence.

He concluded his remarks by promising, "We will be 100 percent operational in 90 days."

The CEO was adamant. The crowd was on its feet. The journalists shook their heads in disbelief.

After all, the 1990s were the days of downsizing and layoffs. No CEO in his right mind would actually pay workers who weren't working. How would the stockholders stand for it?

COMMITTED TO THE CHIEF

In the case of Malden Mills, the only stockholders were CEO Feuerstein and his family. They would be the ones who would have to come up with the $15 million calculated to keep paying salaries and benefits to Malden Mills employees.

Malden Mills workers, meanwhile, stayed loyal to their company and its CEO. In a day of diminishing worker trust, Malden Mills retained 95 percent of its employees and paid them on average, $3 more per hour than the industry average.

As it turned out, the CEO paid his employees not for 30 days of no labor but for the full 90 days it took to get the factory back to speed.

When the employees returned, their productivity skyrocketed. Before the fire, 6 to 7 percent of the company's production was adjudged "off quality." After the fire, "off quality" production dipped to 2 percent—a significant improvement.

A NATIONAL HERO

Less than a year later, the company began constructing a new $120 million, 500,000-square-foot plant on the site of the fire. Best of all, all but a handful of Malden Mills employees had returned to work.

Aaron Feuerstein became a national hero. President Clinton invited the CEO to the State of the Union address. The Malden Mills fire became a legendary event in the annals of employee relations.

Summarized the hero CEO:

> Today there's some kind of crazy belief that if you discard the responsibility to your country, to your city, to your community, to your workers, and think only of the immediate profit, that somehow not only your company will prosper but the entire economy will prosper as a result.
> I think it's dead wrong.

Questions

1. What were the corporate values represented by Malden Mills and its CEO?
2. Was there a relationship between the CEO's actions and his employees performance?
3. Some companies use an employee relations philosophy of "command, control and compliance." How would you describe the Malden Mills philosophy?
4. Could you foresee a time when CEO Feuerstein would cut hundreds of employees?
5. For the employees' view of their CEO, visit the Malden Mills Web site (www.polartec.com) and follow the link to "Malden Mills." Click on the link to "Articles" and then click to read "They Call Their Boss a Hero." What effect has Feuerstein's decisions and actions had on his employees?

OVER THE TOP

An Interview with John Horne

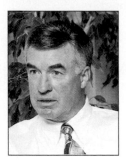

By his own admission, when John Horne was named chief operating officer of Navistar International Corporation in 1992, things were "horrible." Navistar was one of the nation's great producers of highway trucks, school buses, and diesel engines, but it had suffered its share of problems. Reeling from losses in the 1980s, the Chicago company—formerly known as International Harvester—was perhaps most well known for its difficult labor and employee relations. Named CEO in 1995, Mr. Horne engineered a business and cultural change at Navistar that resulted in a total stock market return of 172 percent.

What was the state of public relations when you took over as chief executive officer in 1995?

When I became CEO, we were still coming out of crisis communications. We really didn't have a good relationship with the press. We didn't have good communication with our employees, who told us on surveys that there was "no vision, no strategy, no leadership." It wasn't exactly what we wanted to hear.

How did you go about repairing the acrimonious relationship with the union?

It took us a long time. I think that's how we really got into communications. When I became CEO, we felt that we were not communicating adequately to our people on the front line. And when we did these surveys and they said, "We don't trust you," we knew we had a problem.

When you decided to change the corporate culture, how did you get management to buy in to the new approach?

We did our first leadership conference in 1995. We debated about how many people to bring in, and we finally decided to bring in everybody on direct incentive program—450 people. Sounds like an unmanageable group. But we wanted every one of them informed.

What did you learn about employee communication?

One thing we learned is that the good old American way of cascading information down is a totally flawed process, like the telephone game in grade school. By the time the story gets to the second or third kid, the subject's not even the same. Yet, as a company, we had these plans up at the top level and we were cascading them, and they never got down. So we started these leadership conferences for direct communication.

How did you integrate communications into the role of supervisors?

One of the key values is communication. We set up a communication schedule in the company, where senior executives visit plants every month. I'm probably at four plants a month.

As CEO, how important to you is the public relations function?

It's probably in the top five things you must know to run a company. It's in the top five for sure.

Why has it become so important in your view?

We want people to understand what we're trying to accomplish and achieve. We want customers to understand that; we want investors to understand that; we want employees to understand that. The worst thing about "bad communications" is the people trying to accomplish the plans who don't know what they're doing. So that is where it all starts.

Chapter 17

Community Diversity

Most people overlooked the story in August 1998, but it was very big news nonetheless. Fortune *magazine had just announced its selection of "The 50 Best Companies for Asians, Blacks and Hispanics." There, incredibly, at no. 2 on the list of corporate models of diversity, was Advantica Restaurant Group, parent of Denny's.[1]*

Six years earlier, both Denny's and its sister company Shoney's were synonymous with mistreatment of minorities and bigotry. In 1992, Shoney's paid $132.8 million to settle a class-action discrimination suit brought by 20,000 employees and rejected job applicants. Two years later, Denny's paid $54.4 million to settle two class-action suits brought by black customers who claimed some restaurants refused to seat or serve them (see "Case Study" at the conclusion of this chapter).

Fortune's recognition of the Denny's/Advantica turnaround epitomized how seriously organizations today consider multicultural communities.

Women, senior citizens, African Americans, Latinos, gays, and other groups formerly overlooked are today focused on, marketed to, and targeted by organizations of all types, especially mainstream corporations.

In today's society, multiculturalism has become big business.

America has always been a melting pot, attracting freedom-seeking immigrants from countries throughout the world. Never has this been more true than today, as America's face continues to change. Consider the following:

■ *In 1990, the U.S. population was 76 percent Anglo, 12 percent African American, 9 percent Latino, and 3 percent Asian. By the year 2050, the breakdown is projected to be 52 percent Anglo, 16 percent African American, 22 percent Latino, and 10 percent Asian. Today ethnic minorities spend $600 billion a year out of a total U.S. consumer economy of $4.4 trillion. This amount is certain to increase substantially.[2]*

■ *In 1940, 70 percent of U.S. immigrants came from Europe; today the vast majority of immigrants arrive from Asia, Latin America, and the Caribbean.*

■ *In 1976, there were 67 Spanish-language radio stations in the United States; today, that number has increased fivefold. There are also 100 Spanish-language TV stations, 350 Spanish-language newspapers, and a potential audience of 30 million.*

☑ *In New York City alone, 12 percent of the population under 18 is foreign-born, and that percentage continues to increase.*

☑ *The Internet, a broad canvass of interactive communities uniting the world, has spawned numerous micro-community sites, such as iVillage for women, NetNoir for blacks, SeniorNet for senior citizens, and CollegeClub for Generation Xers.*

Such is the multicultural diversity enjoyed today by America and the world. The implications for organizations are profound. Almost two-thirds of the new entrants into the workforce now are women. People of color make up nearly 30 percent of these new entrants. For the first time since World War I, immigrants will represent the largest share of the increase in the population and the workforce.[3]

In light of the increasing diversity of U.S. society, both profit and nonprofit organizations must themselves become more diverse and learn to deal and communicate with those who differ in work background, education, age, gender, race, ethnic origin, physical abilities, religious beliefs, sexual orientation, and other perceived differences.

Those organizations that waver in responding to the new multicultural communities do so at their own peril. Community activism, so prominent in prior decades, has returned. To wit:

☑ *In 2000, the New York City Police Department was attacked by the African American community and its leaders, after four officers were acquitted in the killing of an unarmed African immigrant, Amadou Diallo. The community refused to accept the court's verdict and kept the issue alive as a police brutality cause célèbre.*

☑ *In 1992, the chief of the Los Angeles Police Department was forced to step down and police officers were jailed, after an African American motorist, Rodney King, was beaten following a high-speed chase. The King beating triggered a massive riot and focused attention on the department's problems in dealing with minorities (Figure 17-1). In 2000, the LAPD once again came under scrutiny in terms of its treatment of minorities.*

☑ *In 1996, Texaco devoted $176 million to settle an antidiscrimination suit, after incriminating tapes, in which executives disparaged minorities, were made public. The company's CEO, Peter Bijur, settled the suit, he said, so that the offensive comments of the executives would not be construed to represent Texaco.[4]*

As the arbiters of communications in their organizations, public relations people must be sensitive to society's new multicultural realities. Dealing in an enlightened manner with multicultural diversity and being sensitive to nuances in language and differences in style are logical extensions of the social responsibility that has been an accepted part of American organizational life since the 1960s.

FIGURE 17-1 **Healing community conflicts.** Los Angeles was sorely tested in the spring of 1992, when the Rodney King beating led to riots. Southern California Edison published a special issue of its SCE News to report on the company's response to the disturbances and to salute employees who worked through the crisis. The issue was called "Time to Heal."

Social Responsibility in the Community

More and more, companies and other organizations acknowledge their responsibilities to the community: helping to maintain clean air and water, providing jobs for minorities, enforcing policies in the interests of all employees, and, in general, enhancing everyone's quality of life. This concept of social responsibility has become widely accepted among enlightened organizations.

For example, most companies today donate a percentage of their profits to nonprofit organizations—schools, hospitals, social welfare institutions, and the like. After "feeling their way" in terms of such philanthropy, high-tech companies have responded admirably to the challenge. The Bill Gates Foundation, an initiative of the Microsoft founder and arguably world's richest man, has vowed to donate computers to poorer school districts throughout the nation.

One of the most socially responsible of the new breed is Lucent Technologies, whose annual foundation budget is upwards of $50 million (Figure 17-2). Lucent's philanthropic mission is to "live up to our responsibilities to serve and enhance the communities in which we work and live and the society on which we depend."[5] Like most companies, Lucent focuses its giving on business-related areas, particularly technology. It provides donations to improve such areas as science education in public schools,

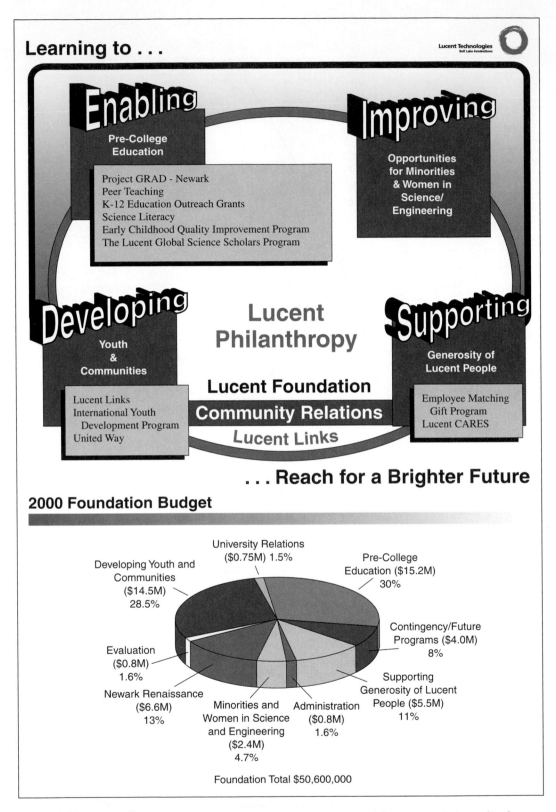

FIGURE 17-2 **Enlightened self interest.** Lucent Technologies is one of the most "enlightened" of corporations, annually donating more than $50 million to a wide variety of worthwhile charitable endeavors in the fields of education and youth development.

FIGURE 17-3 **America's promise.** General Colin Powell, George W. Bush, and the symbol of America's Promise—The Alliance for Youth, the little red wagon.

math and science education in American Indian schools, and technology training in minority colleges.

An important part of corporate social responsibility programs is the aspect of voluntarism. Many firms, which have given generously to their communities, have begun to become more directly involved, actively encouraging executives and employees to roll up their sleeves and volunteer to help out in their communities.[6] At The Walt Disney Company, for example, Disney VoluntEARS spent more than 800,000 hours in volunteer services over a two-year span. A national effort to spur voluntarism was launched in 1998, under the leadership of General Colin Powell. Called "America's Promise—The Alliance for Youth," General Powell's initiative was designed to "give back" to the community by connecting two million children from poorer neighborhoods with adult mentors and "hope for a brighter future" (Figure 17-3).[7]

Such initiatives reject the notion, made famous by economics professor Milton Friedman, that a corporation's only responsibility is to make money and sell products, so that people can be hired and paid. It is the job of the individual, Professor Friedman argued, to serve society through philanthropy. Accordingly, enlightened self-interest among executives has taken time to develop:

- The social and political upheavals of the 1960s forced organizations to confront the real or perceived injustices inflicted on certain social groups
- The 1970s brought a partial resolution of those problems as government and the courts moved together to compensate for past inequities, to outlaw current abuses, and to prevent future injustice
- In the 1980s, the conflict between organizations and society became one of setting priorities—of deciding which community group deserved to be the beneficiary of corporate involvement

☑ In the resurgent 1990s, corporations realized that they would have to "give back" to society for the unprecedented wealth of the latter part of the decade

☑ Today, in the 2000s, most organizations accept their role as an agent for social change in the community

For an organization to coexist peacefully in its community, three skills in particular are required: (1) determining what the community knows and thinks about the organization, (2) informing the community of the organization's point of view, and (3) negotiating or mediating between the organization and the community and its constituents, should there be a significant discrepancy.

Basically, every organization wants to foster positive reactions in its community. This becomes increasingly difficult in the face of protests from and disagreements with community activists. Community relations, therefore—to analyze the community, help understand its makeup and expectations, and communicate the organization's story in an understandable and uninterrupted way—is critical.

Community Relations Expectations

The community of an organization can vary widely, depending on the size and nature of the business. The mom-and-pop grocery store may have a community of only a few city blocks, the community of a Buick assembly plant may be the city where the plant is located, and the community of a multinational corporation may embrace much of the world.

What the Community Expects

Communities expect from resident organizations such tangible commodities as wages, employment, and taxes. But communities have come to expect intangible contributions, too:

☑ **Appearance.** The community hopes that the firm will contribute positively to life in the area. It expects facilities to be attractive, with care spent on the grounds and the plant. Increasingly, community neighbors object to plants that belch smoke and pollute water and air. Occasionally, neighbors organize to oppose the entrance of factories, coal mines, oil wells, drug treatment centers, and other facilities suspected of being harmful to the community's environment. Government, too, is acting more vigorously to punish offenders and to make sure that organizations comply with zoning, environmental, and safety regulations.

☑ **Participation.** As a citizen of the community, an organization is expected to participate responsibly in community affairs, such as civic functions, park and recreational activities, education, welfare, and support of religious institutions.

☑ **Stability.** A business that fluctuates sharply in volume of business, number of employees, and taxes paid can adversely affect the community through its impact on municipal services, school loads, public facilities, and tax revenues. Communities prefer stable organizations that will grow with the area. Conversely, they want to keep out short-term operations that could create temporary boom conditions and leave ghost towns in their wake.

☑ **Pride.** Any organization that can help put the community on the map simply by being there is usually a valuable addition. Communities want firms that are proud to be residents. For instance, to most Americans, Battle Creek, Michigan, means cereal; Hershey, Pennsylvania, means chocolate; and Armonk, New York, means IBM. Organizations that help make the town usually become symbols of pride.

What the Organization Expects

Organizations expect to be provided with adequate municipal services, fair taxation, good living conditions for employees, a good labor supply, and a reasonable degree of support for the business and its products. When some of these requirements are missing, organizations may move to communities where such benefits are more readily available.

Inner cities, such as New York, for example, experienced a substantial exodus of corporations during the 1970s, when firms fled to neighboring Connecticut and New Jersey, as well as to the Sun Belt states of the Southeast and Southwest. New York's state and city legislators responded to the challenge by working more closely with business residents on such issues as corporate taxation. By the new century, not only had the corporate flight to the Sun Belt been arrested, but many firms reconsidered the Big Apple and returned to the now more business-friendly city and state.

The issue for most urban areas faced with steadily eroding tax bases is to find a formula that meets the concerns of business corporations while accommodating the needs of other members of the community.

Community Relations Objectives

Research into community relations indicates that winning community support for an organization is no easy matter. Studies indicate difficulty in achieving rapport with community neighbors, who expect support from the company but object to any dominance on its part in community affairs.

One device that is helpful is a written community relations policy that clearly defines the philosophy of management as it views its obligation to the community. Employees, in particular, must understand and exemplify their firm's community relations policy; to many in the community, the workers are the company.

Typical community relations objectives may include the following:

1. To tell the community about the operations of the firm: its products, number of employees, size of the payroll, tax payments, employee benefits, growth, and support of community projects
2. To correct misunderstandings, reply to criticism, and remove any disaffection that may exist among community neighbors
3. To gain the favorable opinion of the community, particularly during strikes and periods of labor unrest, by stating the company's position on the issues involved
4. To inform employees and their families about company activities and developments, so that they can tell their friends and neighbors about the company and favorably influence opinions of the organization
5. To inform people in local government about the firm's contributions to community welfare and to obtain support for legislation that will favorably affect the business climate of the community

FIGURE 17-4 Cooperative citizenship. Florida International University's Public Relations Student Society of America teams with Amoco and others each year to provide a valuable "Hurricane Alert Program" to the community.

6. To find out what residents think about the company, why they like or dislike its policies and practices, and how much they know of its policy, operations, and problems
7. To establish a personal relationship between management and community leaders by inviting leaders to visit the plant and offices, meet management, and see employees at work
8. To support health programs through contributions of both funds and employee services to local campaigns
9. To contribute to culture by providing funds for art exhibits, concerts, and drama festivals and by promoting attendance at such affairs
10. To aid youth and adult education by cooperating with administrators and teachers in providing student vocational guidance, plant tours, speakers, films, and teaching aids and by giving financial and other support to schools
11. To encourage sports and recreational activities by providing athletic fields, swimming pools, golf courses, or tennis courts for use by community residents and by sponsoring teams and sports events
12. To promote better local and county government by encouraging employees to run for public office or to volunteer to serve on administrative boards; by lending company executives to community agencies or to local government to give specialized advice and assistance on municipal problems; and by making company facilities and equipment available to the community in times of emergency (Figure 17-4)
13. To assist the economy of the community by purchasing operating supplies and equipment from local merchants and manufacturers whenever possible
14. To operate a profitable business in order to provide jobs and to pay competitive wages that increase the community's purchasing power and strengthen its economy
15. To cooperate with other local businesses in advancing economic and social welfare through joint community relations programs financed and directed by the participating organizations

Community Relations on the Internet

At the heart of the Internet is a sense of "community." Indeed, the Internet links people of like-minded interests in a virtual community, although "community members" may live continents away.

From this concept of community has emerged an effort to use the Internet for social good, to expand educational and commercial opportunities for minority communities as well as provide a philanthropic forum for the less fortunate. For example:

◪ Black Entertainment Television created BET.com to bring "connectivity, content, and commerce" to African Americans, a community decidedly underrepresented in cyberspace. While 74 percent of white college and high school students own computers, only 32 percent of African American students own computers. So armed with $35 million, the largest on-line investment ever aimed at African Americans, BET.com hopes to help African Americans become more computer-savvy, and, armed with $35 million—the largest on-line investment ever aimed at the African Americans community—the Bet.com on-line community brings connectivity, content and commerce to the global Black on-line population.[8]

☑ In a more global community effort, Cisco Systems launched "NetAid" in 1999 to raise awareness of and cash for the one billion people living in extreme poverty throughout the world. NetAid's initially webcasted live concerts from New Jersey with the Black Crowes and Mary J. Blige, London with David Bowie and the Eurythmics, and Geneva with Bryan Ferry and Ladysmith Black Mambazo, among others. Cisco kicked in $22 million to make sure that "the Internet would serve as a bootstrap mechanism to improve people's lives."[9]

☑ Perhaps the most ambitious socially responsible undertaking on the Internet is GreaterGood.com, one of a number of Internet firms that have introduced a cause orientation to e-commerce. GreaterGood.com is aimed at America's 650,000 registered not-for-profit charities. It helps fund these charities by arranging the sale of name-brand retail items on not-for-profit Web sites and then donating part of the purchase price back to the charity.[10]

While the Internet may be characterized by some as metallic and heartless, efforts like these underscore the Internet's immense potential in furthering human relations and progress—across common communities and for the larger society.

Serving Diverse Communities

What were once referred to as "minorities" are rapidly becoming the majority.

The U.S. Census Bureau's long-term population projections estimate that by the year 2050, Asians, Latinos, and African Americans will represent as much as 47 percent of the total population of the United States, compared to less than 25 percent today.

According to the Census Bureau, Latinos will soon overtake African Americans as the largest minority group, but the fastest-growing segment of minorities will be Asians and Pacific Islanders, whose numbers will increase fivefold.[11]

For many years, women were considered a minority by public relations professionals. This is no longer the case; women now dominate not only the public relations field but also many service industries. Women, African Americans, Latinos, Asians, gays, and a variety of other groups have become not only important members of the labor force but also important sources of discretionary income.

Public relations professionals must be sensitive to the demands of all for equal pay, promotional opportunities, equal rights in the workplace, and so on. Communicating effectively in light of the multicultural diversity of society has become an important public relations challenge.

Women

In the 21st century, women have made great strides in "leveling the playing field" between their roles and compensation schedules and those of their male counterparts. The days of "mommy tracks" and "mommy wars," glass ceilings, and pink-collar ghettos are rapidly falling by the wayside.

Women today head large corporations, including the high-tech area, where Carly Fiorina was recruited in 1999 to become CEO of powerful Hewlett-Packard. In public relations as well, women have increasingly graduated into middle-management and upper-management positions, particularly at public relations agencies. In the corporate area, there is still a disparate number of men holding top public relations jobs.

While some disparities also may linger in compensation schedules in public relations and other fields, nonetheless equality of the sexes in the workplace is clearly an imminent reality.[12]

African Americans

Today, 25 of the nation's largest cities—including Chicago, Detroit, and Los Angeles—have a majority population of African Americans, Latinos, and Asians. The socioeconomic status of African Americans has improved markedly, with disposable income increasing fivefold over the past decade.

Despite their continuing evolution in the white-dominated workplace, African Americans can still be reached effectively through special media:

- Black Entertainment Television is a popular TV network that has done well.
- Local African American radio stations have prospered.
- Pioneering Internet sites, such as BlackFamilies.com, Blackvoices.com, NetNoir.com, and The Black World Today (www.tbwt.com) have created a culture of acceptance and desirability for Web access among African Americans.
- Magazines such as Black Enterprise and Essence are natural vehicles. Ebony, the largest African American-oriented publication in the world, has a circulation of 1.3 million.
- Newspapers such as the *Amsterdam News* in New York City and the *Daily Defender* in Chicago also are targeted to African Americans. Such newspapers are controlled by active owners whose personal viewpoints dominate editorial policy.

All should be included in the normal media relations functions of any organization. In recent years, companies have made a concerted effort to understand the family structure, traditions, and social mores of the black community, through sponsorship of programs targeted to pressing community needs (Figure 17-5).

One area of frustration in improving the livelihood of African Americans is the practice of public relations. The field has failed to attract sufficient numbers of African American practitioners to its ranks. This remains a great challenge to public relations leaders in the new century.

Latinos

There is little question why companies need to reach Latinos. Currently 30 million strong, the group is growing three times faster than the rest of the country. The Census Bureau predicts that the Latin population will jump from 11 to 14 percent in the next 10 years. At the same time, the African American population is expected to level off at approximately 12.5 percent. Thus, Latinos will soon be the nation's most prominent minority group, and by 2050, Latinos will comprise one-quarter of the population.[13]

Latinos also comprise a potent political and economic force. Between 1994 and 1998, Latino voting in nationwide midterm elections jumped 27 percent, even as overall voter turnout dropped. In terms of commerce, U.S. Latinos pump $300 billion a year into the economy.[14]

More than 70 percent of all U.S. Latinos reside in California, Texas, New York, and Florida. New York City has the largest Latin population with 1.8 million residents. Los Angeles rates second with more than one million.[15] The majority of U.S. Latinos—

TAKING CONTROL

FOR IMMEDIATE RELEASE
April 2, 1996

NEWS RELEASE
Contact: Katherine Gill
212/213-7047

**COMMUNITY LEADERS MEET TO CONFRONT ISSUES OF
UNINTENDED PREGNANCY AMONG AFRICAN AMERICANS AND LATINOS**

Dr. Joycelyn Elders Convenes "Taking Control" Conference

(NEW YORK, NY) -- Dr. Joycelyn Elders, former U.S. Surgeon General, will lead an expert roundtable
called *Taking Control: Contraceptive Issues in African American and Latino Communities* on
Wednesday, April 10 in New York City. The event, an unprecedented collaborative effort of leading
healthcare and grassroots organizations to reduce the unintended pregnancy rate among African
Americans and Latinos, will be held at the Equitable Center from 11 a.m. to 2 p.m. and is co-sponsored
by Planned Parenthood Federation of America, the National Medical Association, the National Council
of La Raza, *Essence* and *Latina* Magazines, and Pharmacia & Upjohn, Inc.

In a major effort led by the private sector, leading grassroots organizations will cross cultural
boundaries to openly examine the unique factors that inhibit the use of contraception in these
communities. They will make practical, culturally appropriate recommendations for an evolving model
of reproductive health care for African American and Latina women.

"It's time we intervene and break the recurring pattern of unintended pregnancy from one
generation to the next," said *Taking Control* moderator Dr. Joycelyn Elders. "We're coming together to
be honest about the factors that contribute to this pattern, so our children's children will have tools they
understand and can use to help them make better choices."

FIGURE 17-5 Aiding minority health care. Pharmaceutical giant
Pharmacia & Upjohn, Inc. was typical of companies that sponsored
health care programs for minority communities. In this case, the
company recruited former U.S. Surgeon General Joycelyn Elders to lead
a roundtable on contraceptive issues.

62 percent—are of Mexican origin. About 13 percent are of Puerto Rican origin, and
5 percent are of Cuban origin. In Los Angeles, Latino kindergarten enrollment is 66
percent and rising. The Anglo enrollment is 15 percent and falling.

Latinos are voracious media consumers, relying heavily on TV and radio to keep
them informed (Figure 17-6).[16] Two large Spanish-programming networks, Univision
and Telemundo, dominate the airwaves, with Univision drawing 83 percent of the
country's adult prime-time, Spanish language viewing audience.[17] CNN also offers a
daily program in Spanish for its Latin American viewers.

FIGURE 17-6 **Todas las Noticias.**
Television is a key medium for reaching Latinos. News anchors Edwardo Quezada and Andrea Kutyas delivered "Noticias 34" for KMEX-TV.

Magazines also are a great source of entertainment to the Latino community, so recent years have seen a plethora of new offerings, from *LatinCEO* for top executives to *Latina* magazine for teenage girls to *Healthy Kids en Español* for parents.

In addition, radio stations and newspapers that communicate in Spanish, such as New York City's *El Diario* and *La Prensa,* are prominent voices in reaching this increasingly important community.

Other Ethnic Groups

Beyond Latinos, other ethnic groups—particularly Asians—have increased their importance in the American marketplace.

Japanese, Chinese, Koreans, Vietnamese, and others have gained new prominence as consumers and constituents. Asians and Pacific Islanders account for 4 percent of the U.S. population, and that number is expected to increase significantly by 2050.[18]

The formation of the Asian American Advertising and Public Relations Alliance in California underscored the increasing prominence of Asian Americans in the public relations profession.

Gays, Seniors, and Others

In the 21st century, a diverse assortment of special communities have gravitated into the mainstream of American commerce.

BACKGROUNDER

Que Lastima

The following editor's box appeared in the March 29, 1999, *New York Daily News*.

To Our Readers:

On Monday, March 22, on page 7 of the newspaper, in the context of a review of the fashions at the Academy Awards, the *Daily News* made an editorial error and captioned a photo of Jennifer Lopez (Figure 17-7) with the wording "Reformed Tramp."

The caption was intended to refer to her change in dress from her former look to her new look, but that was not clearly explained by the caption. We sincerely apologize to Ms. Lopez for any inadvertent inferences that might be drawn from the inappropriate caption, and to any readers we may have offended.

We have taken steps to insure that such occurrences will not happen again. The newspaper operates under deadline time pressure and in circumstances particularly such as these, the choice of wording could have been more thoughtful.

The *News* has had a long-standing cooperative partnership with the Latino community and is a major co-sponsor of the National Puerto Rican Day Parade. We greatly appreciate the responsible way in which the leaders of the Latino community have brought this problem to our attention and worked toward a constructive resolution.

Fred Drasner

CEO and Co-Publisher

FIGURE 17-7 **The lady is not a "tramp."** Subject of the *Daily News* apology—Jennifer Lopez.

One such group is the gay market. To some, homosexuality may remain a target of opprobrium, but in the new century, the gay market, estimated at 12 to 20 million Americans, comprises a major target of opportunity.

An increasing number of marketers, including IBM, United Airlines, and Anheuser-Busch, run ads with gay themes. Generally, marketers confine such advertising to the gay press. However, in 2000, Gfn.com devoted $6 million to advertise its Gay Financial Network Internet Web site in the mainstream media. This groundbreaking campaign indicated that gay advertising was ready to cross over into the more widely read and seen media.[19]

The clear conclusion is that the gay market—average age 36, household income six times higher than the national average and with more discretionary income than average, three times more likely to be college graduates than the national average, and 86 percent of whom saying they would purchase products specifically marketed to them—has become extremely attractive to all kinds of marketers.

In addition to gay men and women, senior citizens also have become an important community for public relations professionals and the organizations they represent. The

A QUESTION OF ETHICS

Cutting Off Gay Partners

The merger of the huge oil giants Exxon and Mobil in 1999 got off to an unexpectedly rocky start, after the new company revoked a long-standing Mobil policy that provided health care coverage to the partners of newly hired gay employees.

The move outraged gay rights advocates, who said the reversal was a step back for gay employees and went against the trend of other companies and municipalities to extend benefits to gay employees.

An Exxon Mobil spokesman tried to kabuki dance around the revised policy by stating, "It's our opinion that basing benefits coverage on a legally recognized relationship eliminates the need for the company to establish criteria of its own for which to assess the legitimacy of any relationship, whether it's straight or gay." (Whew!)

Gay right advocates weren't impressed.

Said the communications director of the gay rights group, Human Rights Campaign, "It's smoke. They're basically trying to justify what they have done. The fact is, no jurisdiction recognizes marriages between same-sex couples. These benefits have proliferated throughout corporate America as a way for companies to offer equal pay for equal work."

When Exxon Mobil made its decision, 74 of the Fortune 500 companies offered same-sex benefits to gay employees. Ironically, one of the most progressive of former members of this group was Mobil Corporation.*

*Richard A. Oppel Jr., "Exxon to Stop Giving Benefits to Partners of Gay Workers," New York Times (December 7, 1999): D1, 19.

baby-boomer generation has passed 50 years of age. Together, the over-50 crowd controls more than 50 percent of America's discretionary income.

As the American population grows older, the importance of senior citizens will increase. Public relations professionals must be sensitive to that reality and to the fact that other special communities in the society will increasingly demand specialized treatment and targeted communications. Nowhere was this fact more apparent than when actor Christopher Reeve was paralyzed in 1996 after falling off a horse. Mr. Reeve, who gained fame as the movie hero Superman, became an effective and outspoken advocate for the disabled, calling for an additional $40 million a year in congressional funding.[20]

Growing Community Advocacy

One outgrowth of the increased voice in society of minority groups and other special communities is a willingness to speak out and object to what they perceive as wrongs.

One popular tactic in raising public awareness, particularly among community groups, is so-called "media advocacy." Media advocacy is public relations without resources. It is using the media to attract attention and shake the established order.[21] Examples abound:

◪ In 1999, antibiotech activists around the world used the Internet and the media to challenge genetically modified foods. In the face of the attack, the world's biggest biotech companies mounted a massive public relations campaign to counter a campaign that vilified firms like Monsanto, labeling it "Mutanto" and "Monsatan."[22]

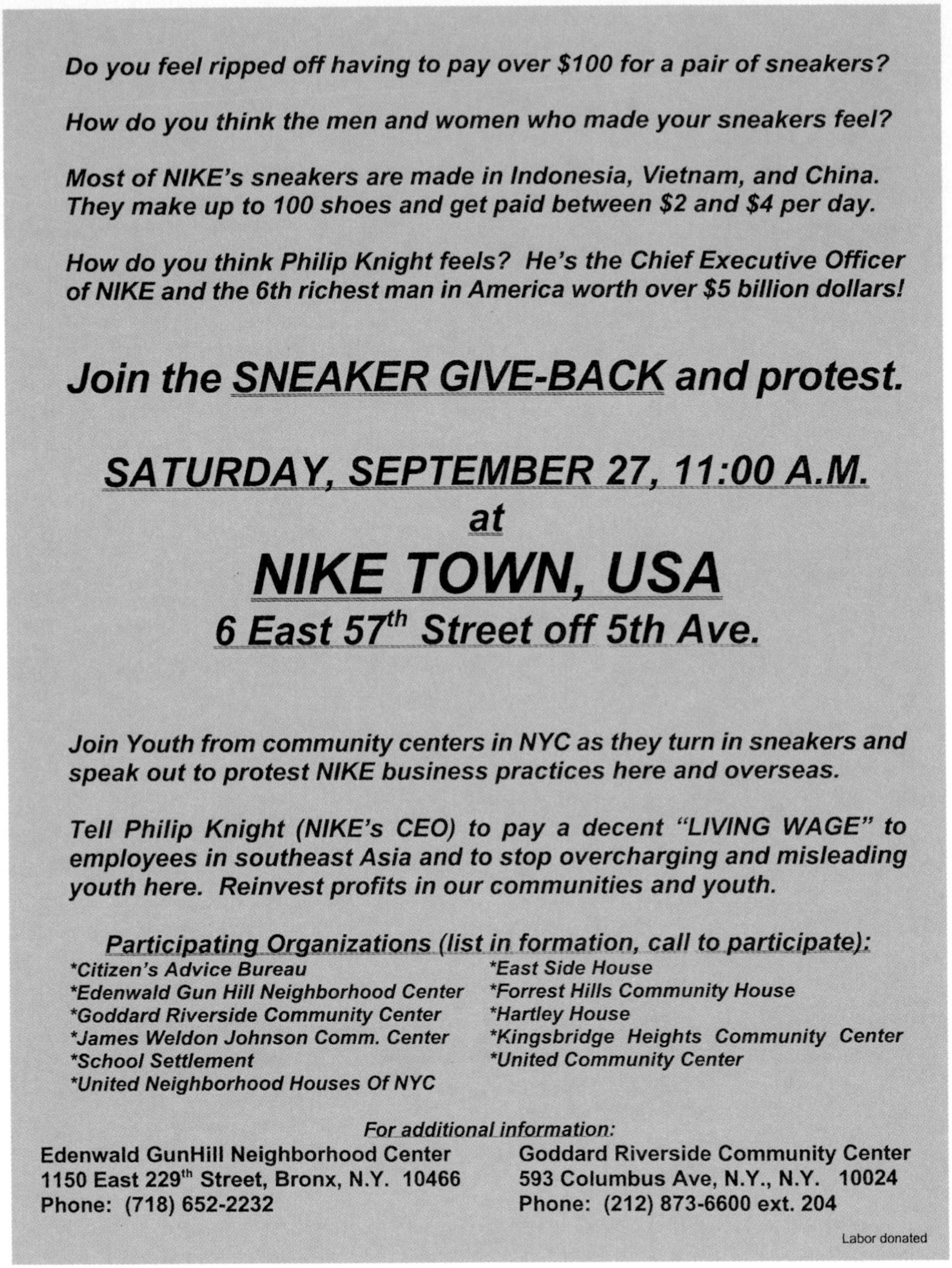

Do you feel ripped off having to pay over $100 for a pair of sneakers?

How do you think the men and women who made your sneakers feel?

Most of NIKE's sneakers are made in Indonesia, Vietnam, and China. They make up to 100 shoes and get paid between $2 and $4 per day.

How do you think Philip Knight feels? He's the Chief Executive Officer of NIKE and the 6th richest man in America worth over $5 billion dollars!

Join the SNEAKER GIVE-BACK and protest.

SATURDAY, SEPTEMBER 27, 11:00 A.M.
at
NIKE TOWN, USA
6 East 57th Street off 5th Ave.

Join Youth from community centers in NYC as they turn in sneakers and speak out to protest NIKE business practices here and overseas.

Tell Philip Knight (NIKE's CEO) to pay a decent "LIVING WAGE" to employees in southeast Asia and to stop overcharging and misleading youth here. Reinvest profits in our communities and youth.

Participating Organizations (list in formation, call to participate):

*Citizen's Advice Bureau	*East Side House
*Edenwald Gun Hill Neighborhood Center	*Forrest Hills Community House
*Goddard Riverside Community Center	*Hartley House
*James Weldon Johnson Comm. Center	*Kingsbridge Heights Community Center
*School Settlement	*United Community Center
*United Neighborhood Houses Of NYC	

For additional information:

Edenwald GunHill Neighborhood Center	**Goddard Riverside Community Center**
1150 East 229th Street, Bronx, N.Y. 10466	**593 Columbus Ave, N.Y., N.Y. 10024**
Phone: (718) 652-2232	**Phone: (212) 873-6600 ext. 204**

Labor donated

FIGURE 17-8 Power to the people. Huge corporations such as Nike are sensitive when their policies and public image are questioned by protests and placards.

That same year, environmental activists in New York City, led by entertainer Bette Midler, loudly protested the Giuliani administration's plan to sell off city-owned lots that had been transformed into community gardens. The media effort resulted in encouraging the mayor to compromise.[23]

Settlement House Youth
NIKE Give Back Campaign

Its a New Year, We're Still Here

It's 1998 and Nike has not changed:
-Your still being charged $75 - $200 for $6 sneakers.
-Nike workers are still underpaid.
-They're still not giving back to your community.

In the spirit of Martin Luther King Jr. we protest
these practices!

January 19, 1998
12:00 noon - 1:00 pm
at Niketown
6 East 57th Street

Bring your old Nike sneakers and apparel.

For more information:

Edenwald - Gun Hill	Goddard Riverside
Neighborhood Center	Community Center
(718) 652-2232	(212) 873-6600, ext. 204

Labor donated

FIGURE 17-8 Continued.

☑ Even the mighty Nike Corporation came under attack for selling astronomically priced sneakers while underpaying its workers (Figure 17-8). The protest centered on the company's flagship retail outlet, Nike Town USA in New York City.

Undoubtedly enhancing the spread of activism in the years ahead will be the increased access to and proficiency with the Internet as a tool of social discontent.

Nonprofit Public Relations

Among the most important champions of multiculturalism in any community are nonprofit organizations. Nonprofit organizations serve the social, educational, religious, and cultural needs of the community around them. So important is the role of public relations in nonprofit organizations that this sector is a primary source of employment for public relations graduates.

The nonprofit sector is characterized by a panoply of institutions: hospitals, schools, social welfare agencies, religious institutions, cultural organizations, and the like. The general goals of nonprofit agencies are not dissimilar to those of corporations. Nonprofits seek to win public support of their mission and programs through active and open communications. Unlike corporations though, nonprofits also seek to broaden volunteer participation in their efforts (Figure 17-9).

Because America is a nation of joiners and belongers, nonprofit organizations in our society are encouraged to proliferate. As the number of nonprofit agencies has grown, it has become increasingly difficult to find funding sources. Most nonprofits depend on a combination of government funding and private support.

The booming stock market into the new century has encouraged wealthy individuals to increase their contributions to nonprofit organizations. Nonetheless, for public relations professionals at nonprofits, in addition to writing speeches, dealing with the media, communicating with employees, and counseling managements, another key component of the job is to assist in fund-raising.

FIGURE 17-9 Nonprofit communicators. The Campaign for Tobacco Free Kids was chaired by former public relations executive William Novelli, who aggressively spoke out about the evils of cigarette smoking.

Fund-Raising

Fund-raising—the need to raise money to support operations—lies at the heart of every nonprofit institution. Schools, hospitals, churches, and organizations—from the mighty United Way to the smallest block association—can't exist without a constant source of private funds. Frequently, the fund-raising assignment becomes the province of public relations professionals. Like other aspects of public relations work, fund-raising must be accomplished in a planned and programmatic way.

A successful fund-raising campaign should include the following basic steps:

1. **Identify campaign plans and objectives.** Broad financial targets should be set. A goal should be announced. Specific sectors of the community, from which funds might be extracted, should be targeted in advance.
2. **Organize fact finding.** Relevant trends that might affect giving should be noted. Relations with various elements of the community should be defined. The national and local economies should be considered, as should current attitudes toward charitable contributions.
3. **Recruit leaders.** The best fund-raising campaigns are ones with strong leadership. A hallmark of local United Way campaigns, for example, is the recruitment of strong business leaders to spearhead contribution efforts. It is the responsibility of the nonprofit itself to direct its leaders, particularly outside directors, so that their efforts can be targeted in the best interests of the organization.[24]
4. **Plan and implement strong communications activities.** The best fund-raising campaigns are also the most visible. Publicity and promotion must be stressed. Special events should be organized, particularly featuring national and local celebrities to support the drive. Updates on fund-raising progress should be communicated, particularly to volunteers and contributors.
5. **Periodically review and evaluate.** Review the fund-raising program as it progresses. Make mid-course corrections when activities succeed or fail beyond expectations. Evaluate program achievements against program targets. Revise strategies constantly as the goal becomes nearer.

Because many public relations graduates enter the nonprofit realm, a knowledge of fund-raising strategies and techniques is especially important. Beginning practitioners, once hired in the public relations office of a college, hospital, religious group, charitable organization, or other nonprofit organization, are soon confronted with questions about how public relations can help raise money for the organization.

SUMMARY

The increasing cultural diversity of society in the 21st century has spawned a wave of "political correctness," particularly in the United States. Predictably, many have questioned whether sensitivity to women, people of color, the physically challenged, seniors, and other groups has gone too far. One thing, however, is certain. The makeup of society—of consumers, employees, political constituents, and so on—has been altered inexorably. The number of discrete communities with which organizations must be concerned will continue to increase.

Intelligent organizations in our society must be responsive to the needs and desires of their communities. Positive community relations must begin with a clear understanding of community concerns, an open door for community leaders, an open and honest flow of information from the organization, and an ongoing sense of continuous involvement and interaction with community publics.

Community relations is only as effective as the support it receives from top management. Once that support is clear, it becomes the responsibility of the public relations professional to ensure that the relationship between the organization and all of its multicultural communities is one of mutual trust, understanding, and support.

Discussion Starters

1. How is the atmosphere for community relations different today than it was in the 1960s?
2. What is meant by the term *multicultural diversity?*
3. In general terms, what does a community expect from a resident organization?
4. What are typical community relations objectives for an organization?
5. What was the philosophy of corporate responsibility espoused by economist Milton Friedman?
6. What is meant by the term *media advocacy?*
7. What is the significance of dealing with the gay community?
8. What communications vehicles should be used in appealing to Latinos?
9. What is meant by the term *corporate social responsibility?*
10. What internal factor does community relations most depend on?

Notes

1. Anne Faircloth, "Guess Who's Coming to Denny's," *Fortune* (August 3, 1998).
2. Bob Weinstein, "Ethnic Marketing: The New Numbers Game," *Profiles* (May 1994): 51–52.
3. Paul Holmes, "Viva la Difference," Inside PR (March 1994): 13–14.
4. Robert A. Bennett, "Texaco's Bijur: Hero or Sellout?" *The Public Relations Strategist* (Winter 1996).
5. Lucent Technologies Foundation Programs 2000 report, Lucent Technologies, January 2000, 600 Mountain Avenue, Murray Hill, NJ 07974, *foundation@lucent.com.*
6. Dayton Fandray, "Corporate Volunteerism," *Continental* (December 1999): 58.
7. Hal Gordon, "Colin Powell's Grand Experiment—'Franchising Voluntarism,'" *The Public Relations Strategist* (Winter 1998): 30.
8. Ann Marie Gothard, "The African-American Online Community: A Portal to the Global Black Diaspora," *Public Relations Tactics* (November 1999): 18.
9. "Cisco Enlists Net in War on Poverty," *O'Dwyer's PR Services Report* (November 1999): 8.
10. Peter Santucci, "Giving a Heart to E-Commerce," *Washington CEO* (October 1999).
11. "The First Black Face I Ever Saw in Public Relations Was in the Mirror," *Inside PR* (March 1993): 25.
12. Elizabeth L. Toth, "Confronting the Reality of the Gender Gap," *The Public Relations Strategist* (Fall 1996): 51.

13. "Reaching the Hispanic Audience," *fastforward* (Fall 1999): 1.

14. Brook Larmer, "Latino America," *Newsweek* (July 12, 1999): 49.

15. Ignasi B. Vendrell, "What is Hispanic Public Relations and Where is it Going? *Public Relations Quarterly* (Winter 1994–95): 33.

16. "Study Shows Hispanic Trends," *Jack O'Dwyer's Newsletter* (January 26, 2000): 3

17. Dana Calvo, "As the Channels Turn: Soaps Draw Viewers to Telemundo," *Washington Post* (December 25, 1999): C2.

18. "USA: The Way We'll Live Then," *Newsweek* (January 1, 2000): 34.

19. Ronald Alsop, "Web Site Sets Gay-Themed Ads for Big, National Publications," *Wall Street Journal* (February 17, 2000): B4.

20. Kendall Hamilton, "Fighting to Fund an 'Absolute Necessity,'" *Newsweek* (July 1, 1996): 56.

21. Michael Pertschuk, "Progressive Media Advocacy," *The Public Relations Strategist* (Winter 1995): 55.

22. David Barboza, "Biotech Companies Take On Critics of Gene-Altered Food," *New York Times* (November 12, 1999): A1, 12.

23. Dan Barry, "Sudden Deal Saves Gardens Set for Auction," *New York Times* (May 13, 1999): B1, 6.

24. Robert S. Cole, "Replacing Directionless Directors," *The Public Relations Strategist* (Spring 1999): 30.

Suggested Readings

Dines, Gail, and Jean M. Humez. *Gender, Race and Class in Media*. Thousand Oaks, CA: Sage Publications, 1995.

Ferguson, Robert. *Representing Race: Ideology, Identity and the Media*. London: Oxford University Press Inc., 1998.

Godfrey, Joline. *No More Frogs to Kiss*. New York: HarperBusiness, 1995. Offers a guide to empowering women economically and avoiding economic dependence on men.

Gothard, Ann Marie. "Black Newspapers: An Overlooked PR Opportunity." *Public Relations Tactics,* (October 1998): 24.

"How Public Relations Can Foster Better Communications with Women." *Media Report to Women* (Fall 1998): 1 ff.

Kalbfleisch, Pamela J., and Michael J. Cody. *Gender Power and Communications in Human Relationships*. Hillsdale, NJ: Lawrence Erlbaum Associates, 1995. Focuses on understanding differences in uses of communication by males and females.

Kelly, Kathleen S. *Effective Fund-Raising Management*. Mahwah, NJ: Lawrence Erlbaum Associates, 1998.

Kelly, Kathleen S. *Fund Raising and Public Relations: A Critical Analysis*. Mahwah, NJ: Lawrence Erlbaum Associates, 1991.

Lukenbill, Grant. *Untold Millions: Secret Truths about Marketing to Gay and Lesbian Consumers*. New York: Haworth, 1999. Uncovers truths and debunks myths behind the gay and lesbian consumer patterns and lifestyles.

Newsom, Doug A., and Bob J. Carrell. *Silent Voices*. Lanham, MD: University Press of America, 1995. A collection of articles examining issues concerning the status of women worldwide.

Source Book of Multicultural Experts, 1999–2000. New York, NY: Multicultural Marketing Resources Inc., 1999. Lists hundreds of resources and experts in the African-American, Asian-American, Hispanic, gay and lesbian, women's, and multicultural markets.

St. John, Burton. "Public Relations as Community-Building: Then and Now." *Public Relations Quarterly* (Spring 1998): 34 ff.

Svoboda, Sandra A. "Promoting Detroit's African-American Cultural Sites." *Public Relations Tactics* (April 1998): 21. A campaign that takes a special sensitivity to history, culture, and race.

Tingley, Judith C. *Genderflex: Men and Women Speaking Each Other's Language at Work*. New York: AMACOM, 1995. Author refers to the phenomenon of adapting to the language gap between men and women as "genderflexing."

Valdivia, Angharad L. *Feminism, Multiculturalism and the Media*. Thousand Oaks, CA: Sage Publications, 1995.

Wilson, Clint C. II. *Race, Multiculturalism and the Media: From Mass to Class Communication*. Thousand Oaks, CA: Sage Publications, 1995. Examines the historical relationship between the four largest racial groups and the mainstream media in the United States.

top of the shelf

Saul D. Alinsky

Rules for Radicals: A Practical Primer for Realistic Radicals.
New York: Vintage Books, 1989.

As ancient as it is, Alinsky's *Rules for Radicals* is still the classic handbook for those bent on organizing communities, rattling the status quo, and effecting social and political change as well as for those who wish to learn from a legendary master.

Alinsky, a veteran community activist who fought on behalf of the poor from New York to California, provides strategies for building coalitions and for using communication, conflict, and confrontation advantageously.

In "Of Means and Ends," Alinsky lists 11 rules of ethics that define the uses of radical power. His discussion of tactics suggests 13 ways to help organizers defeat their foes. Rule three, for instance, tells activists to go outside the experience of their enemy to "cause confusion, fear, and retreat."

Alinsky supports his principles with numerous examples, the most colorful of which occurred when he wanted to draw attention to a particular cause in Rochester, New York. To do so, Alinsky and his group attended a Rochester Symphony performance—after a meal of nothing but beans. The results were hilarious.

Alinsky died in 1972, but his lessons endure in this offbeat guide to seizing power. Whether your goal is to fluster the establishment or defend it, *Rules for Radicals* is must reading. So read it!

CASE STUDY

Guess Who's Coming to Denny's

Few allegations are more damaging to a company's reputation than charges of racism.

When systemic racism is revealed in the ranks, strong—and often momentarily painful—remedial action must be taken. This is precisely what Denny's restaurants did—to the tune of $54 million—in the spring of 1994.

Denny's was vilified as a symbol of racial discrimination. But in the years immediately following the company's embarrassing and painful publicity, Denny's became a model of progressive diversity.

PAINFUL BREAKFAST AT DENNY'S

With more than 1,500 company and franchise restaurants located throughout the United States, Denny's is the nation's largest full-service family restaurant chain. On April Fool's Day 1993, 21 members of the Secret Service, preparing for a Naval Academy visit by President Clinton, stopped for breakfast at a Denny's outside Annapolis, Maryland.

Fifteen of the officers were served quickly, but one table of six uniformed men—all black—never received the food they had ordered. As it turned out, although their food was ready for a full 20 minutes, neither the waitress nor her manager felt compelled to serve the black agents until they got around to it.

The officers' subsequent discrimination suit unleashed a tidal wave of damning national publicity and legal actions against the 43-year-old company. Dan Rather summarized the situation on the *CBS News*: These agents "put their lives on the line every day, but they can't get served at Denny's."

Denny's paid $54 million to settle all suits and adopted a far-reaching affirmative action program to hire minority managers, recruit minority franchise owners, and roust out racists in its ranks (Figure 17-10).

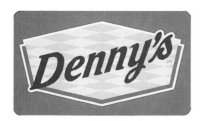

STATEMENT BY C. RONALD PETTY
DENNY'S PRESIDENT AND CHIEF EXECUTIVE OFFICER

As the settlement payout process is completed, Denny's, our managers and our employees will be able to look ahead. We will be able to focus our attention on providing all our restaurant guests with quality, value and excellent service.

All of us at Denny's regret any mistakes made in the past. But I want to emphasize that Denny's does not tolerate racial discrimination. Our company policy is clear and simple: If employees discriminate, they will be fired. If franchisees discriminate, they will lose their franchises.

I am proud to say Denny's and our parent company, Flagstar, have already made important strides in recent years. In fact, Denny's is becoming a model in our industry.

Let me be specific:

Dr. Vera King Farris, an African-American, president of Richard Stockton College in Pomona, N.J., joined the Flagstar board of directors two years ago. Mr. Michael Chu, a Hispanic and Asian-American, has been a board member since 1992. Minorities hold 27 percent of Flagstar restaurant and multi-restaurant supervisory positions. Almost half of Flagstar's 94,000 employees are minorities.

FIGURE 17-10 **Cleansing the company.** Denny's confronted charges of blatant racism at its restaurants with a comprehensive and well-publicized program.

FIGURE 17-11 Lessons learned. Advantica CEO James Adamson announced a series of diversity ads to symbolize the hard lessons that Denny's learned about diversity.

ADVANTICA
restaurant group

STATEMENT BY JAMES B. ADAMSON
CHAIRMAN & CEO ADVANTICA RESTAURANT GROUP, INC.
NATIONAL PRESS CLUB

We will begin this week to air three television messages on the topic of racial diversity, spending nearly $2 million between now and June to get these important messages out to the American public. The messages are intended to spark thinking and honest discussion about the importance of America's racial diversity. We at Denny's have learned some difficult, but valuable, lessons about race in the last few years and are committed to spending our time and money sharing those lessons with America.

Contact: Karen Randall
             864-597-8440

1/12/99

• ADVANTICA RESTAURANT GROUP, INC. •
203 East Main Street • Spartanburg, South Carolina 29319 • 864-597-8000

Citigate
communications

TV 30:   I'm Black

I want to let you in on a little secret. I'm black.

There are some people who never notice another person's color.

But most of us do. And that's OK. Don't feel guilty. Noticing a person's color doesn't make you a racist. Acting like it matters does.

Some flowers are roses. Some are daisies.

One's not automatically better than another. Just different.

America is a garden. The more variety, the better.

AVO: Diversity. It's about all of us.

LESSONS LEARNED

"All of us at Denny's regret any mistakes made in the past," said C. Ronald Petty, president and chief executive officer, when Denny's announced its settlement (Figure 17-11).

"Our company policy is clear and simple: If employees discriminate, they will be fired. If franchisees discriminate, they will lose their franchises."

After the flare-up, Denny's worked at becoming "a model in the industry." It recruited an African-American woman to join its parent company board of directors. It promoted minorities to supervisory positions, and it introduced a "Fast Track" program to help prepare minority candidates for restaurant ownership. In 1993, there was only one Denny's restaurant owned by an African American. By 1995, the number had risen to 26, with plans to reach 65 within two years.

Said Karen Randall, public relations director of Denny's new parent Advantica Restaurant Group, "We decided to look inside the organization and focus on 'substance' and change our makeup and management philosophy and the way we serve our customer base. In just a few years, this effort has changed the company."

DIVERSITY ROLE MODEL

When Advantica CEO Jim Adamson took over Denny's in 1995, he made no secret of his intent. "I am a complete supporter of affirmative action because I don't believe the playing field is level." To ensure that a diverse slate of candidates is presented for every senior Advantica job, Adamson employs minority-owned search firms in addition to more traditional companies.

In 1992, there were no Asians, blacks, or Latinos in top corporate management and only one minority on the company's board. Today, minorities account for a third of its directors. Nearly one of three Advantica officers and managers are minorities.

Purchases from minority suppliers accounted for less than $2 million in 1989. By 1997, that number had increased to more than $36 million. In terms of franchises, minorities own 35 percent of the 737 franchised restaurants. An African American, Akin Olajuwon (brother of professional basketball player Hakeem Olajuwon), is the company's second-largest franchisee.

The company's chief diversity officer coaches diversity training sessions, specifically geared toward serving customers and managing Denny's restaurants. Managers are required to attend two-day sessions to learn how to communicate to their employees about diversity issues and to better meet the needs of customers.

Has it worked? Well, *60 Minutes* was impressed enough to give Denny's glowing marks in 1999. And *Fortune* magazine, in compiling its "50 Best Companies for Asians, Blacks and Hispanics" in 1998, ranked Denny's first in contributions to minority organizations, second in spending with minority vendors, and second in overall diversity consciousness.

It was, indeed, a miraculous turnaround.

Questions

1. Should Denny's have capitulated so quickly to charges of racism in its restaurants?
2. How would you assess the company's response to the accusations?
3. How wise was Denny's to appoint a chief diversity officer?
4. With Denny's now having proven itself relative to diversity efforts, can it feel free to devote less resources to the effort?
5. Read the company philosophy posted on its Web site (www.dennysrestaurants. com/who/philosophy_main.html). Why would Denny's use the Internet to publicize its approach to diversity?

OVER THE TOP

Three Perspectives on Diversity and Community Relations

I. *The African American: An Interview with Terrie M. Williams*

Terrie M. Williams is president of The Terrie Williams Agency, called by *New York* magazine "the most powerful black [owned] public relations firm in the country." Williams graduated from social worker to adviser to the stars when she landed her first client, Eddie Murphy, in 1988. She has been featured in many national magazines, is a sought-after lecturer on self-development topics, and is author of *The Personal Touch: What You Really Need to Succeed in Today's Fast-Paced Business World.*

How did you get started in public relations?
I am a strong believer in destiny. I was a practicing medical social worker at New York Hospital and was very deeply affected by my inability to really change a lot of people's circumstances. It was just very, very depressing. I saw an advertisement in the *Amsterdam News,* New York's largest black-owned newspaper, and there was a one-paragraph article about a public relations course being taught at the Y on Lexington and 51st. And the idea of it just seemed intriguing. I didn't know anyone in the field, but it sounded like something I should check out. I did. And that was really it.

What's been your most difficult challenge?
Running a business. It's one thing to be good at what you do and quite another to run a business. It's also hard to find good, strong, talented, intelligent, creative people who have a strong, strong work ethic and integrity. That, I think, is very challenging.

What is the future of public relations practice for minorities?
We have a long way to go. But we're making progress. People need to understand the importance of stretching themselves, to do business and interact with people with whom you're not most comfortable. That's probably the single biggest reason why our numbers are not great. It really blows me away when I hear mainstream PR firms and executives say, "There are

not qualified minorities out there." I receive two or three resumes a day and an equal number of phone calls, which range from experienced practitioners to entry-level candidates. Many mainstream firms overlook the fact that minority PR professionals bring a much more well-rounded perspective to the table. As a member of an ethnic group, the ability to operate effectively with both majority and minority publics is second nature. Majority practitioners often are without the benefit of being exposed to an ethnically diverse population. We, on the other hand, have to know how to make it, how to be conversant and survive in our own world and the world of the majority. We've got to be culturally aware and sensitive. It's a matter of necessity. And if the numbers are low now—and they are—it's really because nobody has made a real effort to reach out to this segment of PR professionals.

How do you handle this at your agency?
We make it a priority here at our agency that anybody who wants to get into it, or wants to change careers or whatever, has an opportunity to work with us. They hang out with us for a day or assist us in the evening on an event. That's the only way that we are going to increase our numbers in this business.

What's the secret of individual success in public relations?
I don't believe in using race or sex or anything of any kind as an obstacle or a barrier to being able to accomplish great things. If you perfect your craft, treat people correctly, have a strong work ethic, believe in passing it on and giving it back to the community, if you're detail oriented, do the things you say you're going to do, there's no way you can lose. You will, in fact, excel.

II. *The Latino: An Interview with Ray Durazo*
Ray Durazo is president of Los Angeles-based Durazo Communications and a nationally recognized authority on Latino public relations. Before forming his own firm, Durazo was a partner in the Latino public

relations firm of Moya, Villanueva & Durazo. Earlier, he headed the Los Angeles office of Ketchum Public Relations. Before returning to his native Southern California, Durazo headed Ketchum's Washington, D.C., office.

How important is the ethnic market in the United States?

The United States receives two-thirds of the world's immigrants. Two-thirds of those immigrants will settle in California and Texas. Soon "minorities" will be the "majority" in Los Angeles, Dallas, Denver, Houston, and 23 other major U.S. cities. In Los Angeles, the Latino kindergarten enrollment is 66 percent and rising; Anglo enrollment is 15 percent and falling. Latino, Asians, and African Americans constitute more than half the population of Los Angeles County. In short, the U.S. ethnic market has become too large to ignore.

Why deal specially with ethnic markets?

Addressing ethnic audiences is simply another form of market segmentation, a recognition that the lifestyles, the life experiences, and the attitudes and outlooks of ethnic persons may influence their receptivity to certain messages, to the way in which products and ideas are presented to them. As to why it's worth doing, all you have to do is look at the numbers, the buying power, the proportion of the population made up by ethnics, and you conclude that it's worth the effort.

What should a practitioner do to become conversant with the ethnic market?

The market isn't going to come to you. You have to go out and find it, experience it, learn it. And it isn't hard. Next time there's a Cinco de Mayo festival, or a Chinese New Year celebration, or an African-American heritage celebration, or any other ethnic event in your community, get out of your home or office, get in your car, drive over there, and participate!

What is the future of minority-oriented public relations?

The world is becoming a more competitive place every day. Recent history has shown that only the strong, the smart, the courageous will survive in this new international arena. If you are too timid even to venture into your own back yard to reach important new audiences, I hate to think what will happen to you in the future! Aggressive, progressive companies have already concluded that the U.S. ethnic audience is too big to ignore. It isn't about being politically correct. It isn't about being touchy-feely. It's about the bottom line, about profits, about market share, about winning.

Wake up and smell el cafe!

III. *The CEO: An Interview with Dave Checketts*

Dave Checketts is president and chief executive officer of New York City's Madison Square Garden, the world's most famous arena. Mr. Checketts came to New York in 1991 as president of the New York Knicks. As Madison Square Garden CEO, he presides over two of the most visible sports franchises in the country, the Knicks and Rangers; an emerging women's basketball franchise, the Liberty; two sports networks, MSG and FOX Sports Net New York; and a host of high-visibility entertainment properties.

When you came to the Knicks, the team was in disarray, dull, losing. What was your thinking when you took over?

I saw what went on on a daily basis: the losing, the criticism, the internal debates, the lack of credibility in such a major market. I just really didn't understand that. I just thought the lack of communication with the press, almost a fear of New York, of criticism—I thought that looked terrible for the organization.

What attitude were you seeking?

The attitude should be that we are committed to excellence as an organization. We're going to be the best-run franchise in all of professional sports. We must expect that of ourselves, and if we expect that of ourselves, then our players will inherit that same attitude. We may not win the world championship every year, but we will be perceived as a strong, solid, fan-based organization.

How do you enhance your image in the community?

That first year we started the Knicks Junior League with the YMCA, and before we knew it we had 12,000 kids signed up to play basketball that was sponsored by the Knicks. As part of that, they were going to get a ticket to come to the Garden for a game, and they were going to get a Knicks jersey, and, most important, at some place in their neighborhood, at their local Y, a player was going to come and give them a clinic during the year. We started going to schools, making appearances. On the first day of school every year, we've gone out with our players and coaches.

What impact has this had?

In 1991, Madison Square Garden was the only arena, even to this day, to not sell out a playoff game that involved Michael Jordan. In fact, we were 6,000 seats short of a sellout. Today, we have a waiting list of 30,000 people for season tickets. We have over 300 straight sellouts. The record number of sellouts prior to that was 31.

What happens now that you don't have to worry about making your numbers?

We actually have to do more. It has to be more of a priority for us. Suddenly there is all this pressure on tickets—with the notion there is no way you can get into the Garden. A kid growing up on the streets of the Bronx or Brooklyn will never get to see the Knicks in person. So we have to step up the community relations effort. Yesterday, in this building, we had a practice open to the public. We had 3,000 people come, just at the drop of a hat. They came, they cheered, and we picked 17 people out of the audience and took them down to center court while a player autographed a basketball for them. We've got to provide more access this way.

Is it realistic to think, in this day of highly paid athletes and highly charged fans, that sports figures can be role models?

Sports has a way of stirring people's allegiance and emotion. Sports figures can and should be heroes to kids. When somebody puts a Knicks shirt on, they are showing their loyalty and demonstrating an emotional commitment, which gives them strength. That is why we give away thousands of T shirts and hats. So again, we've got to get to the point where there is a relationship between the community and the players.

Chapter 18

Government

In the 2000 Republican presidential primary campaign, candidate Senator John McCain of Arizona hit upon a novel public relations concept that literally took the nation by storm.

McCain's concept?

Openness. Candor. Full disclosure about anything anybody wanted to talk about.

While front-runner George W. Bush drew on a campaign war chest of countless millions, Senator McCain countered him with the oldest weapon in the book: free publicity. With his freewheeling "town meetings" with the public and anything-goes news conferences aboard his campaign bus, "the Straight Talk Express," Senator McCain became the "darling of the press corps" and a serious challenger for the nomination, perhaps setting the tone for political campaigns to come.[1]

The senator's openness came just in time. Increasingly, the political system, for a variety of reasons—a lack of candor high among them—was losing its relevance for many Americans.

- ☑ *President Clinton's notorious conduct in the Oval Office may have soured the masses. Indeed, the president's 2000 State of the Union address drew about 10 million U.S. household viewers. However, one show that immediately preceded the address, "Who Wants to Be a Millionaire?" drew an audience of 19 million households.[2]*
- ☑ *Even though spirited opposition spruced up both the Republican and Democratic primary campaigns, a Harvard University study on "The Vanishing Voter," found that 50 percent of Americans considered the campaign "boring."[3]*
- ☑ *The line between political operatives and journalists seemed to be blurring like never before. Clinton aide George Stephanopoulos became an ABC commentator. Clinton counselor Dick Morris went to work for* Fox News, *which also hired former Republican House Speaker Newt Gingrich and Senator Alfonse D'Amato.[4] Even former White*

House press secretaries got into the act, with Republican Marlin Fitzwater and Democrats Mike McCurry and Dee Dee Myers appearing regularly on cable networks.

Senator McCain's effort to use the media to speak directly to the people was a timely reminder. The fact is the government serves at the will of the people and therefore largely depends on the media to communicate its messages.

The smartest politicians, therefore, recognize the importance of the practice of public relations to their own success in getting themselves elected, their programs supported, and their policies adopted.

Public Relations in Government

The growth of public relations work both with the government and in the government has exploded in recent years. Although it is difficult to say exactly how many public relations professionals are employed at the federal level, it's safe to assume that thousands of public relations–related jobs exist in the federal government and countless others in government at state and local levels. Thus, the field of government relations is a fertile one for public relations graduates.

Since 1970, some 20 new federal regulatory agencies have sprung up—including the Environmental Protection Agency, the Consumer Product Safety Commission, the Department of Energy, the Department of Education, and the Drug Enforcement Agency. Moreover, according to the Government Accounting Office (GAO), 116 government agencies and programs now regulate business.

Little wonder that today, American business spends more time calling on, talking with, and lobbying government representatives on such generic issues as trade, interest rates, taxes, budget deficits, and all the other issues that concern individual industries and companies. Also, little wonder that political interest groups of every stripe—from Wall Street bankers to Asian influence seekers to friends of the earth—contribute more to political coffers than ever before. Thus, today's organizations continue to emphasize and expand their own government relations functions.

Beyond this, the nation's defense establishment offers thousands of public relations jobs in military and civilian positions. Indeed, with military service now purely voluntary, the nation's defense machine must rely on its public information, education, and recruiting efforts to maintain a sufficient military force. Thus, public relations opportunities in this realm of government work should continue to expand.

Ironically, the public relations function has traditionally been something of a stepchild in the government. In 1913, Congress enacted the Gillette Amendment, which almost barred the practice of public relations in government. The amendment stemmed from efforts by President Theodore Roosevelt to win public support for his programs through the use of a network of publicity experts. Congress, worried about the potential of this unlimited presidential persuasive power, passed an amendment stating: "Appropriated funds may not be used to pay a publicity expert unless specifically appropriated for that purpose."

BACKGROUNDER

Today's Military Public Relations: Sports Information and Hollywood Liaison

The U.S. Air Force Office of Public Affairs is a far cry from the days of issuing dry and formal news releases about troop deployments and officer promotions.

Today, more likely, the end result of Air Force public affairs activity is just as likely to be a marketing arrangement with the National Football League, an interactive Web site for schoolchildren, or a counseling role in the latest Harrison Ford feature film.

All in all, Air Force public affairs consists of 2,440 individuals around the world, from internal communicators to external broadcasters to members of the Air Force band.

Among the more innovative aspects of Air Force headquarters public affairs are the following:

- *Hollywood liaison.* A Los Angeles public affairs office is responsible for communicating with the motion picture and television industries, to advise them on the appropriateness of using Air Force resources in television programs, documentaries, and commercial films, such as Harrison Ford's "Air Force One."

- *Sports marketing.* The responsibility of this operation is to work with the professional sports leagues to collaborate in the use of Air Force resources, such as the scheduling of the USAF Thunderbirds precision flying squad at National Football League games.

- *Children's Web site.* The creation of www.af.mil/aflinkjr, a Web site designed to provide children with an entertaining and educational introduction to the Air Force, is the latest wrinkle in Air Force public affairs. The result of a partnership with American University, much of the original art and programming for this was contributed by interns, summer hires, and volunteers.

So even when it comes to "hiring cheap labor," Air Force public affairs is every bit as potent as the most advanced corporate public relations operations.*

*"Today's Air Force Public Affairs: Sports Information and Hollywood Liaison," The Public Relations Strategist (Winter 1998): 12.

Several years later, still leery of the president's power to influence legislation through communication, Congress passed the gag law, which prohibited "using any part of an appropriation for services, messages, or publications designed to influence any member of Congress in his attitude toward legislation or appropriations." Even today, no government worker may be employed in the "practice of public relations." However, the government is flooded with "public affairs experts," "information officers," "press secretaries," and "communications specialists."

Government Practitioners

Most practitioners in government communicate the activities of the various agencies, commissions, and bureaus to the public. As consumer activist Ralph Nader has said, "In this nation, where the ultimate power is said to rest with the people, it is clear that a free and prompt flow of information from government to the people is essential."

It wasn't always as essential to form informational links between government officials and the public. In 1888, when there were 39 states in the Union and 330 members in the House of Representatives, the entire official Washington press corps consisted of 127 reporters. Today there are close to 4,000 full-time journalists covering the capital.

In 1990, the U.S. Office of Personnel Management reported nearly 15,000 public relations–related jobs in the federal government. More recently, the National Association of Government Communicators, which has members from all levels of government, estimated there were about 40,000 government communicators in the United States.[5] The vast majority of government communicators are engaged in public affairs tasks, such as dealing with the media and other layers of government, as well as writing, editing, and the other classical public relations tasks.

The closest thing to an audit of government public relations functions came in 1986 when former Senator William Proxmire, a notorious gadfly, asked the GAO to tell him "how much federal executive agencies spend on public relations."

The GAO reported that the 13 cabinet departments and 18 independent agencies spent about $337 million for public affairs activities during fiscal 1985, with almost 5,600 full-time employees assigned to public affairs duties. In addition, about $100 million was spent for congressional affairs activities, with almost 2,000 full-time employees assigned. Also, about $1.9 billion—that's $1.9 billion—was spent, primarily in the Department of Defense, "for certain public affairs–related activities not classified as public affairs." These included more than $65 million for military bands, $13 million for aerial teams, $11 million for military museums, and more than $1 billion for advertising and printing regarding recruitment.

Increasing Voice of the State Department

In recent years, the most potent public relations voice in the federal government, exclusive of the president, has been the U.S. Department of State.

The State Department, like other government agencies, has an extensive public affairs staff, responsible for press briefings, maintaining Secretary of State home page content, operating foreign press centers in Washington, New York, and Los Angeles, as well as managing public diplomacy operations abroad.

In October 1999, as part of the Foreign Affairs Reform and Restructuring Act of 1998, the State Department inherited the United States Information Agency (USIA), for many years the most far-reaching of the federal government's public relations arms. USIA had been an independent foreign affairs agency within the executive branch. Its job was to explain and support American foreign policy and promote U.S. national interests through a wide range of overseas information programs and educational and cultural activities.

The State Department consolidated USIA's 1,800 U.S. personnel and 2,000 foreign employees, maintaining 190 posts in 142 nations. Overseas, USIA had been known as the United States Information Service. The director of the USIA had reported directly to the president and received policy guidance from the secretary of state. Under the 1999 integration plan, an undersecretary for public diplomacy and public affairs, within the State Department, was chosen to head the operation.[6] The USIA's annual appropriation has exceeded $1 billion since the late 1980s.

In the 21st century, with democracy spreading throughout the world, the former USIA's mission—"to support the national interest by conveying an understanding abroad of what the United States stands for"—has been modified to include new challenges:

- Build the intellectual and institutional foundations of democracy in societies around the globe
- Support the war on drugs in producer and consumer countries
- Develop worldwide information programs to address environmental challenges

☑ Bring the truth to any society that fails to exercise free and open communication

In its 46-year history, USIA was a high-level public relations operation, not without controversy. Under the direction of such well-known media personalities as Edward R. Murrow, Carl Rowan, Frank Shakespeare, and Charles Z. Wick, the agency prospered. Among its more well-known communications vehicles are the following.

1. **Radio.** Voice of America broadcasts 660 hours of programming weekly in 52 languages, including English, to an international audience. In addition to Voice of America, the USIA in 1985 began Radio Marti, in honor of José Marti, father of Cuban independence. Radio Marti's purpose is to broadcast 24 hours a day to Cuba in Spanish and "tell the truth to the Cuban people" about ruler Fidel Castro and communism. TV Marti telecasts four-and-a-half hours daily. While some in Congress claim that the latter is a waste, since the Castro government blocks its signal, the effort continues.
2. **Film and television.** The agency annually produces and acquires an extensive number of films and videocassettes for distribution in 125 countries.
3. **Media.** About 25,000 words a day are transmitted to 214 overseas posts for placement in the media.
4. **Publications.** Overseas regional service centers publish 16 magazines in 18 languages and distribute pamphlets, leaflets, and posters to more than 100 countries.
5. **Exhibitions.** Approximately 35 major exhibits are USIA-designed annually for worldwide display, including in Eastern European countries and the former Soviet Union.
6. **Libraries and books.** The agency maintains or supports libraries in more than 200 information centers and binational centers in more than 90 countries and assists publishers in distributing books overseas.
7. **Education.** The agency is also active overseas in sponsoring educational programs through 111 binational centers where English is taught and in 11 language centers. Classes draw about 350,000 students annually.
8. **Electronic information.** Electronic journals were created to communicate with audiences overseas on economic issues, political security and values, democracy and human rights, terrorism, the environment, and transnational information flow. The journals are transmitted in English, French, and Spanish. They are also transmitted on a domestic World Wide Web site: http:/www.usia.gov.[7]

Government Agencies

Nowhere has government public relations activity become more aggressive than in federal departments and regulatory agencies. Many agencies, in fact, have found that the quickest way to gain recognition is to increase their public relations aggressiveness.

The Federal Trade Commission (FTC), which columnist Jack Anderson once called a "sepulcher of official secrets," opened up in the late 1970s to become one of the most active government communicators. In an earlier heyday, a former FTC director of public information described the agency's attitude: "The basic premise underlying the commission's public information program is the public's inherent right to know what the FTC is doing."[8] When the FTC found a company's products wanting in standards of safety or quality, it often announced its complaint through a press conference.

Although corporate critics branded this process "trial by press release," it helped transform the agency from a meek, mild-mannered bureau into an office with real teeth.

The late 1990s successor to the FTC was the Food and Drug Administration, particularly under President Clinton appointee Dr. David Kessler. Dr. Kessler was an unbridled critic of products from fat substitutes and cigarettes to silicone breast implants. When he stepped down in 1997, consumer advocates groaned while business groups cheered.

Other government departments also have stepped up their public relations efforts. The Department of Defense has more than 1,000 people assigned to public relations–related work. The Air Force alone answers about 35,000 letters annually from schoolchildren inquiring about this military branch. The Department of Health and Human Services has a public affairs staff of 700 people. The departments of Agriculture, State, and Treasury each have communications staffs in excess of 400 people, and each spends more than $20 million per year in public relations–related activities. Even the U.S. Central Intelligence Agency has three spokesmen. Out of how many CIA public relations people? Sorry, that's classified.

The President

Despite early congressional efforts to limit the persuasive power of the nation's chief executive, the president today wields unprecedented public relations clout. The president controls the "bully pulpit." (Figure 18-1) Almost anything the president does or says makes news. The broadcast networks, daily newspapers, and national magazines follow his every move. His press secretary provides the White House press corps (a group of national reporters assigned to cover the president) with a constant flow of announcements supplemented by daily press briefings. Unlike many organizational

FIGURE 18-1 Bully pulpit. The most powerful public relations soapbox in the land was the one occupied by Presidents Bush, Clinton, and Carter and soon (at least he hoped so!) Vice President Al Gore.

press releases that seldom make it into print, many White House releases achieve national exposure.

Ronald Reagan and Bill Clinton were perhaps the most masterful presidential communicators in history. Reagan gained experience in the movies and on television, and even his most ardent critics agreed that he possessed a compelling stage presence. As America's president, he was truly the "Great Communicator." Mr. Reagan and his communications advisors followed seven principles in helping to "manage the news":

1. Plan ahead
2. Stay on the offensive
3. Control the flow of information
4. Limit reporters' access to the president
5. Talk about the issues you want to talk about
6. Speak in one voice
7. Repeat the same message many times[9]

So coordinated was Reagan's effort to "get the right story out" that even in his greatest public relations test—the accusation at the end of his presidency that he and his aides shipped arms to Iran and funneled the payments to support Contra rebels in Nicaragua, in defiance of the Congress—the president's "Teflon" image remained largely intact. The smears simply washed away.

George Bush was not as masterful as his predecessor in communicating with the American public. Indeed, Mr. Bush met his communications match in 1992, when Bill Clinton beat him soundly in the presidential race.

The press had a love-hate relationship with President Clinton. On the one hand, Mr. Clinton's easygoing, "just folks" demeanor, combined with an unquestioned intelligence and grasp of the issues, was praised by the media. On the other hand, the president's legendary "slickness," accentuated by his false statements and downright lying to the American people during the Lewinsky affair caused many journalists to treat him warily.[10]

Next to the booming economy, President Clinton's accessibility to the media—except during the Lewinsky saga—and his commonsense approach to dealing with media were greatly responsible for his popularity, despite a series of embarrassing scandals afflicting his administration during both terms of his presidency.

Beginning with the presidency of Lyndon Baines Johnson, the president's wife, the first lady, also has borrowed the "bully pulpit" of public relations to promote pet causes. In Lady Bird Johnson's case, it was national beautification. Betty Ford promoted mental health, Nancy Reagan fought drug abuse, and Barbara Bush spoke against illiteracy. First Lady Hillary Clinton, however, superseded all of her predecessors by taking an active role in education and health care policy, as an agent of the president, eventually running for the U.S. Senate in New York in 2000.

The President's Press Secretary

Some have called the job of presidential press secretary the second most difficult position in any administration. The press secretary is the chief public relations spokesperson for the administration. Like practitioners in private industry, the press secretary must communicate the policies and practices of the management (the president) to the public. Often, it is an impossible job.

In 1974, Gerald terHorst, President Ford's press secretary, quit after disagreeing with Ford's pardon of former President Richard Nixon. Said Mr. terHorst, "A

Bye Bye Bluebird

In 2000, First Lady Hillary Clinton made the unprece-dented announcement of her intention to run for sen-ate in the state of New York. A resident of Arkansas, the first lady and her husband bought a house in Westchester and set out for the senate (Figure 18-2).

But to do it, she had to face up to one of New York's most feared political analysts, David Letterman. Mr. Letterman, the lovable, goofy, acid-tongued late-night TV host was all ready for the candidate when she arrived to boost her candidacy.

And she, evidently, was ready for him.

So ready, in fact, that she scored 100 percent on a "pop quiz" that supposedly was sprung on her at the last minute.

Or was it?

One question she was asked: "What is New York's state bird?"

"The bluebird," she replied without hesitation.

New Yorkers were stunned and also suspicious. Few residents could have even guessed "the bluebird" as the New York State bird. The pigeon, maybe. Or the sparrow. Or even the herring! But the bluebird??

"Was Hillary given the questions in advance?" her spokesman was asked.

The sheepish answer—tantamount to "not exactly"—underscored the fact that just as in war, in political public relations, anything goes.

FIGURE 18-2 **The candidate.** First Lady Hillary Clinton was history's most visible first lady, lending her name and presence to a variety of causes, such as helping children fight asthma.

spokesman should feel in his heart and mind that the chief's decision is the right one, so that he can speak with a persuasiveness that stems from conviction."[11] A contrasting view of the press secretary's role was expressed by terHorst's replace-ment in the job, former NBC reporter Ron Nessen. Said Mr. Nessen, "A press secre-tary does not always have to agree with the president. His first loyalty is to the pub-lic, and he should not knowingly lie or mislead the press".[12] A third view of the proper role of the press secretary was offered by a former public relations profes-sional and Nixon speechwriter who became a *New York Times* political columnist, William Safire:

> "A good press secretary speaks up for the press to the president and speaks out for the president to the press. He makes his home in the pitted no-man's-land of an adver-sary relationship and is primarily an advocate, interpreter, and amplifier. He must be more the president's man than the press's. But he can be his own man as well."[13]

In recent years, the position of press secretary to the president has taken on increased responsibility and has attained a higher public profile. Jimmy Carter's press secretary, Jody Powell, for example, was among Carter's closest confidants and frequently advised the president on policy matters. He went on to found his own Washington public relations agency. James Brady, the next press secretary, who was permanently paralyzed in 1981 by a bullet aimed at President Reagan, later joined his wife, Sarah, to lobby hard for what would be called the "Brady Bill," establishing new procedures for licensing handguns, which was passed by Congress.

In addition, the position of press secretary has been awarded more to career public relations people rather than to career journalists. Larry Speakes, who followed Mr. Brady, was a former Hill & Knowlton executive and was universally hailed by the media for his professionalism. During President Reagan's second term, Mr. Speakes apparently was purposely kept in the dark by Reagan's military advisors planning an invasion of the island of Grenada. The upset press secretary later apologized to reporters for misleading them on the Grenada invasion.

The next press secretary was a low-key, trusted, and respected lifetime government public relations professional, Marlin Fitzwater. His successor was another career political public relations professional, Dee Dee Myers, who was respected by the media and brought a refreshing perspective to her role as President Clinton's press secretary. She went on to become a cable talk show host and magazine editor.

The trend toward retaining experienced communications people continued in the second Clinton White House, with the president hiring political public relations veteran Mike McCurry. When Mr. McCurry left in 1998 to help form a new Washington public affairs agency, he was replaced by another public relations veteran, Joe Lockhart (see "Over the Top" at the end of this chapter).

Over the years, the number of reporters hounding the presidential press secretary—dubbed by some an imperial press corps—has grown from fewer than 300 reporters during President Kennedy's term to around 3,000 today. Salaries approaching six figures, rare in most media offices in prior years, are today common in Washington bureaus. TV network White House correspondents command higher incomes, with each major network assigning two or three correspondents to cover the White House simultaneously. Dealing with such a host of characters is no easy task. And the role of press secretary is neither easy nor totally satisfactory. As former press secretary McCurry put it, "Having a single person standing at a podium and answering questions and trying to explain a complicated world is not a very efficient way to drive home the idea that government can make a difference."[14] Perhaps President Johnson, the first chief executive to be labeled an "imperial president" by the Washington press corps, said it best when asked by a TV reporter what force or influence he thought had done the most to shape the nature of Washington policy. "You bastards," Johnson snapped.[15]

Lobbying the Government

The business community, foundations, and philanthropic and quasi-public organizations have a common problem: dealing with government, particularly the mammoth federal bureaucracy. Because government has become so pervasive in organizational and individual life, the number of corporations and trade associations with government relations units has grown steadily in recent years.

Snow Job on a Slippery Slope

Dealing with the press corps on a national level is not an assignment for the timid. That's what Republican presidential candidate George W. Bush found out in 1999, when he got cornered on questions about possible cocaine use.

After refusing for months to respond to questions about drugs, Mr. Bush told a Texas newspaper that he hadn't used illegal drugs in the past seven years, as is asked on a White House background check form. Later, when pressed, he acknowledged that he "could have passed" a background check inquiring about drug use in the prior 15 years, at the time his father became president in 1989.

And prior to that?

"I'm not playing that game," said the candidate.

But it was too late. By half answering the question, the candidate left the door open to media speculation. With Mr. Bush calling for a "responsibility era" in contrast to the scandal-plagued Clinton administration, the selective handling of the question didn't sit well with supporters and critics alike.

"Candor and honesty would probably be his best call," said one opponent. Mr. Bush, said a supporter, had placed himself on a "slippery slope" on the drug question, particularly if it was found that he had used cocaine, without he himself admitting it.

Political strategists debated whether the "most ethical course" was for Mr. Bush to confront the issue, either confirming or denying use; either way, he had to get the speculation behind him.

In 1998, the nation's 20,500 lobbyists were collectively paid a whopping $1.42 billion to speed up or slow down legislation. Tobacco companies alone spent more than $67 million on lobbying.[16]

Government relations people are primarily concerned with weighing the impact of impending legislation on the company, industry group, or client organization. Generally, a head office government relations staff complements staff members who represent the organization in Washington, D.C., and state capitals. These representatives have several objectives:

1. To improve communications with government personnel and agencies
2. To monitor legislators and regulatory agencies in areas affecting constituent operations
3. To encourage constituent participation at all levels of government
4. To influence legislation affecting the economy of the constituent's area, as well as its operations
5. To advance awareness and understanding among lawmakers of the activities and operations of constituent organizations

Carrying out these objectives requires knowing your way around the federal government and acquiring connections. A full-time Washington representative is often employed for these tasks.

To the uninitiated, Washington (or almost any state capital) can seem an incomprehensible maze. Consequently, organizations with an interest in government relations usually employ a professional representative, who may or may not be a registered lobbyist, whose responsibility, among other things, is to influence legislation. Lobbyists are required to comply with the federal Lobbying Act of 1946, which imposed certain reporting requirements on individuals or organizations that spend a significant amount of time or money attempting to influence members of Congress on legislation.

In 1996, the Lobbying Disclosure Act took effect, reforming the earlier law. The new act broadened the activities that constitute "lobbying" and mandated government registration of lobbyists. Under the new law, a "lobbyist" is an individual who is paid by a third party to make more than one "lobbying contact," defined as an oral or written communication to a vast range of specific individuals in the executive and legislative branches of the federal government. In addition, lobbyists are prohibited from paying for meals for members of Congress or their aides. The law also broadened the definition of "lobbying activities" to include research and other background work prepared for a lobbying purpose.[17]

In fact, one need not register as a lobbyist in order to speak to a senator, congressional representative, or staff member about legislation. But a good lobbyist can earn the respect and trust of a legislator. Because of the need to analyze legislative proposals and to deal with members of Congress, many lobbyists are lawyers with a strong Washington background. Lobbying ranks are loaded with former administration officials and congressional members, who often turn immediately to lobbying when they move out of office.

Lobbyists, at times, have been labeled everything from influence peddlers to fixers to downright crooks. In 1999, in fact, the American League of Lobbyists—the lobbyist's lobby—sent out an open letter asking for "kinder treatment."[18] Fat chance!

Despite the slings and arrows, the fact is that today's lobbyist is likely to be a person well informed in his or her field, who furnishes Congress with facts and information necessary to make an intelligent decision on a particular issue. This task—the lobbyist's primary function—is rooted in nothing less than the First Amendment right of all citizens to petition government.

What Do Lobbyists Do?

The number of lobbyists registered with the U.S. Senate has increased from just over 3,000 in 1976 to upwards of 40,000 today. Lobbying has become big business.

But what exactly do lobbyists do?

In the spring of 1994, the Treasury Department issued a 30-page definition of lobbying that confounded most of those engaged in the arcane profession. Among other decisions, the department ruled that anyone employed to "follow" federal or even state issues—say, by reading newspapers or magazines—is not engaged in lobbying. However, if the articles are clipped and filed as part of research intended to influence legislation, then that, the department ruled, is lobbying.[19]

The fact of the matter is, the essence of a lobbyist's job is to inform and persuade.

The contacts of lobbyists are important, but they must also have the right information available for the right legislator. The time to plant ideas with legislators is well before a bill is drawn up, and skillful lobbyists recognize that timing is critical in influencing legislation. The specific activities performed by individual lobbyists vary with the nature of the industry or group represented. Most take part in these activities:

1. **Fact finding.** The government is an incredible storehouse of facts, statistics, economic data, opinions, and decisions that generally are available for the asking.

2. **Interpretation of government actions.** A key function of the lobbyist is to interpret for management the significance of government events and the potential implications of pending legislation. Often a lobbyist predicts what can be expected to happen legislatively and recommends actions to deal with the expected outcome.

3. **Interpretation of company actions.** Through almost daily contact with congressional members and staff assistants, lobbyist conveys how a specific group feels about legislation. The lobbyist must be completely versed in the business of the client and the attitude of the organization toward governmental actions.

4. **Advocacy of a position.** Beyond the presentation of facts, a lobbyist advocates positions on behalf of clients, both pro and con. Often, hitting a congressional representative early with a stand on pending legislation can mean getting a fair hearing for the client's position. Indeed, few congressional representatives have the time to study—or even read—every piece of legislation on which they are asked to vote. Therefore, they depend on lobbyists for information, especially on how the proposed legislation may affect their constituents.

5. **Publicity springboard.** More news comes out of Washington than any other city in the world. It is the base for thousands of press, TV, radio, and magazine correspondents. This multiplicity of media makes it the ideal springboard for launching organizational publicity. The same holds true, to a lesser degree, in state capitals.

6. **Support of company sales.** The government is one of the nation's largest purchasers of products. Lobbyists often serve as conduits through which sales are made. A lobbyist who is friendly with government personnel can serve as a valuable link for leads to company business.

In recent years, there has been no shortage of controversy surrounding lobbyists and influence peddling in Washington. A number of close advisors to President Clinton, including the late Secretary of Commerce Ron Brown and former Justice Department official Webster Hubbell, were accused of courting influence in a questionable manner. The former was killed in a Bosnian air crash, and the latter went to jail. Meanwhile, a key aide to Vice President Gore was indicted in 2000 for a fundraising scandal at a California Buddhist temple.

With the stakes of political power so high, the temptation to abuse the privileges of lobbying remains a risk in our democratic society.

Emergence of E-Lobbying

As it has in every other area of society and public relations work, the Internet has influenced the practice of lobbying as well.

In 1999, disgraced former Clinton advisor Dick Morris, a veteran of old-fashioned political hardball, turned his attention to the new area of e-politics to get across his messages.

Mr. Morris' company, Vote.com, asked Web site visitors to vote "yes" or "no" on particular issues. The votes were then converted into e-mail messages sent to elected officials. In its early days out of the box, the technique created an uproar among elected officials and Internet experts, because Mr. Morris—and not the visitors to his site—set the question agenda and then flooded politicians' e-mail with his votes. In one barrage of 82,000 such messages to the White House, Mr. Morris' former employer effectively blocked the correspondence from getting through.[20]

In terms of political campaigning and grassroots lobbying, the presidential primary campaign of 1999 indicated that the role of the Web was growing. All the candidates mounted sophisticated Web sites to discuss issues, provide biographies, offer campaign schedules, solicit funds, and recruit volunteers and support. The Web proved so effective in raising donations that Texas Governor George W. Bush and Arizona Senator John McCain plastered banner ads on other Web sites to solicit funds.[21]

Wealthy publisher Steve Forbes, who tried and tried—and spent and spent—to make an impact as a Republican challenger did achieve one distinction: He became the first candidate to declare his candidacy on the Internet and conduct his campaign largely over the Web by organizing supporters and prodding them to opinion polls.

Beyond these measures, the Internet since the mid-1990s, has served as a tool to inform voters about election issues. Such election-oriented sites as FAQvoter.com promise to proliferate in the years ahead, as the World Wide Web becomes a more prominent tool in the election process.

Political Action Committees

The rise of political action committees (PACs) has been among the most controversial political developments in recent years. Thirty years ago, there were about 600 PACs. Today, the number is well in excess of 4,000 representing labor unions, business groups, corporations, nonprofit organizations, and so on.

Each PAC can give a maximum of $5,000 to a federal candidate in a primary election and another $5,000 for the general election. An organization with many individual PACs, then, can have a tremendous monetary influence on an election. In the 1996 presidential campaign, the AFL-CIO labor union spent about $35 million through its various PACs.[22] Indeed, this was one of the issues—campaign finance reform—that Senator McCain used to captivate the interest of Americans in his quest for the 2000 Republican presidential nomination.

The increased influence of such groups on candidates is one reason why Senator McCain and others would like to see PACs severely curtailed or even banned. Indeed, in 1994, Congress limited what its members could accept in the form of trips and other niceties from the sponsors of PACs.

Campaign finance reform will continue to be a national political concern, particularly as the influence wielded through PAC contributions grows in intensity. The evidence thus far is inconclusive. The tobacco industry, for example, was one of the most prominent PAC contributors to Congress, but the industry still got hammered. Although the number and size of PACs have increased, evidence of PAC-inspired indiscretions or illegalities has been minimal. Nonetheless, the furor over the heightened role of PACs in funding elections is bound to continue until campaign reform becomes reality.

The "Be" List of Getting Through to Legislators

One Washington lobbying veteran offered the following most sensible "be" list for anyone wishing to get through to legislators:

- **Be independent.** Policymakers value an independent view.
- **Be informed.** Government thrives on information. Timely facts, a deep knowledge of the subject, and specific examples are invaluable.
- **Be bipartisan.** Matters are more likely to be addressed on merit if approached in a bipartisan manner. Although it is necessary to be sensitive to political nuances, politics is best left to the politicians.
- **Be published.** Clear and cogent thinking, in articles and op-ed pieces, is noticed in Washington and at the state house.

- **Be broad-minded.** Don't peddle petty self-interest. Address the broader interests, and your counsel will be sought.
- **Be persistent.** A long-term, persistent commitment of time is mandatory in dealing with legislators.
- **Be practical.** Politicians value practical recommendations they can defend to their constituents.
- **Be honest.** Politicians and the press are skilled at spotting phonies. Honesty is the best policy. It works.

Source: Cindy Skrzycki, "Possible Leaders Abound in Business Community," Washington Post (January 24, 1988): D2.

Dealing with Local Government

In 1980, Ronald Reagan rode to power on a platform of New Federalism, calling for a shift of political debate and public policy decisions to state and local levels. Presidents Bush and Clinton picked up the same initiative when they assumed power. Senator McCain seized the grassroots spirit when he won the New Hampshire Republican primary in 2000 and made the nomination a horserace. Thus, it has become more important for public relations people to deal with local, state, and regional governments.

Dealing with local entities, of course, differs considerably from dealing with the federal government. For example, opinion leaders in communities (those constituents with whom an organization might want to affiliate to influence public policy decisions) might include such sectors as local labor unions, teachers, civil service workers, and the like. Building a consensus among such diverse constituents is pure grassroots public relations. The very nature of state and local issues makes it impossible to give one, all-encompassing blueprint for successful government relations strategies.

Although the federal government's role—in wielding power and employing public relations professionals—is significant, state and local governments also are extremely important. Indeed, one viable route for entry-level public relations practitioners is through the local offices of city, county, regional, and state government officials.

In local government offices themselves, the need for public relations assistance is equally important. Local agencies deal directly—much more so than their counterparts in Washington—with individuals. State, county, and local officials must make themselves available for local media interviews, community forums and debates, and even door-to-door campaigning. In recent years, local and state officials have found that direct contact with constituents—often through call-in radio programs—is invaluable, not only in projecting an image, but also in keeping in touch with the voters.

Such officials, assigned to ensure the quality of local schools, the efficiency of local agencies, and the reliability of local fire and police departments, increasingly require smart and experienced public relations counsel. State and local information officer positions, therefore, have become valued and important posts for public relations graduates.

S U M M A R Y

The pervasive growth of government at all levels of society may not be welcome news for many people. However, government's growth has stimulated the need for increased public relations support and counsel.

The massive federal government bureaucracy, organized through individual agencies that seek to communicate with the public, is a vast repository for public relations jobs. The most powerful position in the land—that of president of the United States—has come to rely on public relations counsel to help maintain a positive public opinion of the office and the incumbent's handling of it.

On state and local levels, public relations expertise also has become a valued commodity. Local officials, too, attempt to describe their programs in the most effective manner. In profit-making and nonprofit organizations alike, the need to communicate with various layers of government also is imperative.

Like it or not, the growth of government in our society appears unstoppable. As a result, the need for public relations support in government relations will clearly continue to grow in the 21st century.

Discussion Starters

1. Why is the public relations function regarded as something of a stepchild in government?
2. What is the current status of the USIA and what are its responsibilities?
3. What is meant by "trial by press release"?
4. Why was Ronald Reagan called the "Great Communicator?"
5. What is the function of the White House press secretary?
6. What are the objectives of government relations officers?
7. What are the primary functions of lobbyists?
8. What is the role of the Internet on lobbying?
9. What are the pros and cons of PACs?
10. What was John McCain's strength as a communicator in the 2000 campaign?

Notes

1. Alison Mitchell, "McCain Embraces the Press and Open Campaigns of Old," *New York Times* (February 15, 2000): A1, 22.
2. Alex Kuczynski, "TV Viewers Want $1 Million, Not a Million Clinton Words," *New York Times* (January 29, 2000): A8.

3. Frank Rich, "Everybody into the Mudfight," *New York Times* (February 26, 2000): A31.

4. Bill Carter, "Newt Gingrich to Fox News," *New York Times* (October 27, 1999): E8.

5. Robin-Pan Lener, "There's Room to Grow," *Government Communications,* National Association of Government Communicators (March 1992): 3.

6. Press statement by James P. Rubin, U.S. Department of State, October 1, 1999.

7. "Fact Sheet," November 1996, United States Information Agency, 301 4th Street, S.W., Room 602, Washington, D.C. 20647.

8. David H. Buswell, "Trial by Press Release?" *NAM Reports* (January 17, 1972): 9–11.

9. Mark Hertsgaard, "Journalists Played Dead for Reagan—Will They Roll Over Again for Bush?" *Washington Journalism Review* (January–February 1989): 31.

10. "Give Him an 'F'," *The Scudder Media Report* (October 1998): 1,6.

11. Robert U. Brown, "Role of Press Secretary," *Editor & Publisher* (October 19, 1974): 40.

12. I. William Hill, "Nessen Lists Ways He Has Improved Press Relations," *Editor & Publisher* (April 10, 1975): 40.

13. William Safire, "One of Our Own," *New York Times* (September 19, 1974): 43.

14. Remarks by Mike McCurry, "A View from the Podium," New York, NY, May 5, 1999.

15. Michael J. Bennett, "The 'Imperial' Press Corps," *Public Relations Journal* (June 1982): 13.

16. "$1.42 Billion Spent on Lobbying in 98," *O'Dwyer's Newsletter* (March 7, 1999): 5.

17. "PR Is Lobbying? Read the New Law," *Next,* no. 2 1996, Edelman Public Relations Worldwide, 1500 Broadway, New York, NY 10036.

18. "Spin Doctors Try to Spin New Image Despite All Evidence to the Contrary," *Modern Healthcare* (December 20–27. 1999): 84.

19. Robert D. Hershey Jr. "In Very Fine Print the Treasury Defines a Lobbyist," *New York Times* (May 11, 1994): A16.

20. Rebecca Fairley Raney, "In E-Politics, Clinton's Ex-Adviser Still Plays by His Rules," *New York Times* (November 12, 1999): A16.

21. Glenn R. Simpson and Bryan Gruley, "Far-Flung Volunteers Gave Forbes a Boost In Iowa via Internet," *Wall Street Journal* (January 26, 2000): A1, 8.

22. Dennis L. Wilcox, Phillip H. Ault, and Warren K. Agee. *Public Relations Strategies and Tactics* (New York, NY: Addison-Wesley Educational Publishers, 1998): 329.

Suggested Readings

Bodensteiner, Carol A. "Special Interest Group Solutions: Ethical Standards for Broad-Based Support Efforts." *Public Relations Review,* (Spring 1997): 31–46.

Browning, Graeme. *Electronic Democracy: Using the Internet to Influence American Politics.* Information Today Inc., 1996.

Dennis, Lloyd. *Practical Public Affairs in an Era of Change.* New York: The Public Relations Society of America, 1995. A comprehensive guide to contemporary public affairs practice, offering the latest thinking and action programs impacting government and public policy.

Eggers, William D., and John O'Leary. *Revolution at the Roots: America's Quest for Smaller, Better Government*. New York: The Free Press, 1995. Maintains that a revolution is sweeping across America to return power and influence to states and municipalities.

Elster, Jon, ed. *Local Justice in America*. New York: Russell Sage Foundation, 1995. Justice plays a central role in public relations practice, and this book examines aspects of justice, including government relations principles.

Fitzwater, Marlin. *Call the Briefing! Reagan and Bush, Sam and Helen: A Decade with Presidents and the Press*. New York: Times Books, 1995. The trials and tribulations of a longtime political press secretary, done occasionally humorously but also with deadly seriousness in other spots.

Greenberg, Mike. *The Poetics of Cities: Designing Neighborhoods That Work*. Columbus: Ohio State University Press, 1995. Examines the politics of municipalities, including communications aspects on the local level.

Grossman, Lawrence K. *The Electronic Republic: Reshaping Democracy in the Information Age*. New York: Penguin USA, 1996. A discussion of government relations in a democracy rooted in information technology. How times will change.

Howard, Philip K. *The Death of Common Sense: How Law is Suffocating America*. New York: Warner Books, 1996. Posits the view that regulation at all levels is breeding contempt for the governmental system of the United States.

Kauffman, James. "NASA in Crisis: The Space Agency's Public Relations Effort Regarding the Hubble Space Telescope." *Public Relations Review* (Spring 1997): 1–10.

Pratkanis, Anthony, and Elliot Aronson. *Age of Propaganda: The Everyday Use and Abuse of Persuasion*. New York: W. H. Freeman and Company, 1996. This book focuses on the peculiar persuasion proclivities of politicians in the midst of running for office.

Rash, Wayne Jr. *Politics on the Nets: Wiring the Political Process*. W. H. Freeman & Company, 1997.

Somerby, Bob. www.dailyhowler.com. This Web site features The Daily Howler, comedian and former *Baltimore Sun* reporter Bob Somerby, who comments on the Washington news corps' "astonishing combination of dishonesty and foolishness."

Susskind, Lawrence, and Patrick Field. *Dealing with an Angry Public: The Mutual Gains Approach to Resolving Disputes*. New York: The Free Press, 1996. Outlines the six key elements of the "mutual gains approach" to help business and government get along.

Walsh, Kenneth T. *Feeding the Beast: The White House Versus the Press*. New York: Random House, 1996. The press that covers the executive branch of government is characterized by a surly, snarling bunch of pit bulls. And those are the pleasant ones! Or at least that's what Kenneth Walsh argues in this book. A former senior correspondent for *U.S. News and World Report,* he knows whereof he speaks.

Yinger, John. *Closed Doors, Opportunities Lost: The Continuing Costs of Housing Discrimination*. New York: Russell Sage Foundation, 1995. Another aspect of government relations—dealing with the important issue of housing and the lack thereof among certain groups in society.

top of the shelf

www.crp.org/diykit. Washington, D.C.:
The Center for Responsive Politics.

Before the greedy 1990's mantra, "Show me the money," there was the investigative reporters' dictum, "Follow the money."

That is what this Web site offers: the Do-It-Yourself Congressional Investigation Kit lets you see who is handing out the lobbyist money.

- Who's getting tobacco money?
- Who's getting gun-lobby money?

- How about tracking the funding of special interests in gambling, phone rates, or health care?

It's all on this free on-line service of The Center for Responsive Politics. You can log into "The Issues" or "The Money" or "The Votes." You can even use the site to look up soft money by individual donors and recipients.

Check it out. Follow the money.

CASE STUDY

Electing Jesse "The Body" Governor

The election of former professional wrestler Jesse "The Body" Ventura in 1999 as governor of Minnesota was a stirring victory for public relations.

Governor Ventura's election, defying all odds, was the work of a group of volunteers, mainly working out of home offices, who combined creativity, enthusiasm, and persistence to overcome a minuscule budget, voter skepticism, and negative media portrayals.

Here's how they did it.

ACCENTUATE THE POSITIVE

The best thing about Jesse Ventura was his name recognition. Everybody knew him—pictured him in tights with a boa, perhaps, but knew him nonetheless. And in today's America, there is no substitute for ready name recognition.

Jesse "The Body," through years of bombastic preparation on wrestling broadcasts, was a charismatic, telegenic performer. He was comfortable with the media, after having experience as a sports announcer, radio talk-show host, and former city mayor. So, billing their candidate as a "nonprofessional politician," the team had no qualms about maximizing the candidate's media exposure.

Jesse—as everybody called him—also had the great appeal of being the underdog in the race. He represented neither the Republicans nor the Democrats, but rather the Reform Party. Because the Reform Party is recognized as a major party in Minnesota, the candidate was included in most major debates. Nevertheless, he was the clear underdog, and that helped.

ELIMINATE THE NEGATIVE

The "negatives" faced by candidate Ventura were formidable:

☑ First, his opponents argued, "a vote for a third-party candidate is a wasted vote"

FIGURE 18-3 **From "The Body" . . .**

☑ Second, he was running against well-known and popular candidates from the two major parties
☑ Third, he was more well known as a wrestler than a mayor or a political force
☑ Fourth, he agreed to take no PAC money, so the campaign coffers were limited
☑ Fifth, early polls showed he suffered from a severe "gender gap," with many more men supporting him than women
☑ Sixth, he had no office and little staff support or organization

Jesse's response to all these negatives? No sweat.

In almost every talk, the candidate told voters that "not voting your conscience is a wasted vote." The staff continually urged reporters and announcers to identify him as a former mayor, not as a former wrestler. At the same time, the candidate emphasized that he was by no means a "professional politician."

The campaign raised money from grassroots events, including T-shirt sales. The candidate chose an experienced schoolteacher, Mae Schunk, as his running mate, effectively closing the gender gap. Using an extensive network of e-mails and faxes, an effective Internet campaign was developed to identify Ventura volunteers across the state.

CANDIDATE INFANTRY

The most effective public relations weapon in the campaign was the candidate himself, a charismatic celebrity figure. Every time he talked to voters, he transformed skeptics into supporters. So the campaign emphasized direct campaigning.

☑ The candidate addressed 287 meetings of service clubs and veterans' organizations. Mr. Ventura, one of the few military veterans in the campaign, was a great hit.

- He attended more than 30 union and organizational screenings. Although union leaders did not endorse his candidacy, the fact that both Mr. Ventura and Ms. Schunk were union members probably swayed great rank-and-file support.
- He walked in countless parades and met voters at many county fairs, such as the Minnesota State Fair.
- He participated in 39 debates and forums.
- One volunteer produced *The Governing Body* cable TV shows.
- The campaign concluded with a three-day RV tour of the state, where the candidate met thousands of voters in their hometowns.

MEDIA AIR CORPS

While the candidate himself did the heavy public relations lifting, the media was used as air support. At first, the campaign received many more out-of-state, even international, media calls than local ones. These national and international stories helped fuel in-state media attention. Interviews were scheduled with an eye toward their impact on the vote, such as national shows heard within Minnesota.

The campaign issued 52 substantive news releases and held 14 news conferences during the campaign. In all, 260 print, radio, and TV interviews were conducted.

INTERNET ARTILLERY

The jesseventura.org Web site played a critical role in the campaign's success. The candidate's positions on more than 60 issues were summarized on the site. All news releases and biographies were posted, as was the campaign schedule.

JesseNet, a two-way communications vehicle, was most effective. Anyone interested could join, including members of the media. Members received important local and statewide information during the campaign. JesseNet members contributed more than $50,000 to the campaign and donated countless volunteer hours. The RV tour was a JesseNet event, and members made it a resounding success.

VICTORY

In the end, the Republican and Democratic parties spent a combined estimated total of $15 million on the campaign. The Jesse Ventura for Governor Committee spent a grand total of $626,000.

The election results read as follows:

- Jesse Ventura, Reform Party, 37 percent
- Norm Coleman, Republican, 34 percent
- Skip Humphrey, Democrat, 28 percent*

*Based on remarks by Geraldine Drewry, Drewry Communications and media chair—Jesse Ventura for Governor Volunteer Committee, at Ragan Corporate Communicators Conference, Chicago, IL, September 21, 1999.

FIGURE 18-4. . . To the arbiter . . .

FIGURE 18-5... **To the ultimate authority (sort of!).**

From around the country and around the world, people marveled at the unlikely, unpredictable, and uncanny election of Governor Jesse Ventura.

Questions

1. What obstacles did the Ventura for Governor Committee face at the outset of the campaign?
2. What alternatives did the campaign have in how it "positioned" its candidate?
3. What other public relations tactics might the campaign have used? Advertising? Direct mail? Phone solicitation? Other?
4. In light of the money spent on the campaign, what implications can be drawn relative to spending money and getting elected?
5. The JesseNet is still operating. Visit its Web site (www.jesseventura.org/jessenet/joinjnet.htm). What are the current goals of this communication vehicle? What publics are being targeted by JesseNet?

An Interview with Joe Lockhart

Joseph P. Lockhart was the final assistant to the president and press secretary at the Clinton White House. Before joining the White House in 1997, he was national press secretary for the Clinton/Gore 1996 reelection campaign. A public relations and television news veteran, Mr. Lockhart was previously a senior vice president of Robinson Lerer Sawyer Miller, where he brought an international media and U.S. political background to the management of sensitive communications issues.

What is your primary mission as presidential press secretary?

First and foremost, to provide information to the press in a truthful, timely, and straightforward manner. As a press secretary, I am in the unique position of serving both the press and the president. I spend a good portion of my day mediating the relationship between both entities. The press office staff also writes press releases, handles interviews, answers reporters' inquiries, and assists the press at presidential events.

What is your daily access to the president?

I participate in many White House meetings and events that the president attends, and I usually drop by the president's office to update him before his important events. The best White House press secretaries have access to the president, the president's top aides, and any presidential meetings and events.

What is your relationship with the president?

I have spent some of the most fulfilling years of my professional life working for President Clinton. We have a strong professional relationship, and I enjoy being a member of his staff. President Clinton has an open mind and a wonderful sense of humor that he combines with a genuine interest in his staff's opinions and personalities.

How do you regard the White House press corps?

The White House press corps serves an important function in bringing the work of this administration to the American people. Even though we sometimes have different objectives, I am proud of the amicable relationship I have developed with the press, and I value their role in giving the American people an eye on the presidency. A free, democratic press is one of the most fundamental elements of our society.

What should be the proper relationship between the president and the press?

The White House press corps should be a close, constant check on any presidency. When I bring visitors to the White House, they are often surprised that the press work literally right next to the Oval Office. This proximity is absolutely necessary in a democracy that encourages the free flow of information from its leaders to its citizens.

What are the most important attributes of a presidential press secretary?

Honesty and accuracy are the two most important traits that any White House press secretary must possess. A press secretary must be able to advance the objectives of the president in a manner that supports both the needs of the president and the press, a balance that is often difficult to achieve. White House press secretaries must have a solid understanding of administrative policy and must be able to keep pace with the flood of new issues that arise every week. Modern press secretaries must also be sensitive to deadlines, to the 24-hour news cycle, and to the impact of the Internet.

What has been your toughest assignment?

There are obviously many tough days and many tough assignments, but my travel with President Clinton to Kosovo was particularly challenging. We had just completed a fulfilling, but lengthy trip to Turkey, Greece, Italy, and Bulgaria, with Kosovo added to the end of the trip a few days before we actually departed. The area that we traveled into was extremely remote, the press corps was skeptical of what we could accomplish, and the language barrier made communication with local citizens difficult. In the end, though, the experience of seeing an American president touch so many people who had gone through so much made the trip one of my most rewarding.

How does President Clinton feel about the media?
President Clinton has great respect for the media and the role that it plays in the United States and around the world. He has grown to know many of the hardworking members of the press corps through their close proximity and travel together. Like myself, the president believes in the important check that the press provides and their ability to keep the American people informed on important issues.

What is the most rewarding part of your job?
More than anything, I love dissecting complicated issues presented to our administration and then conveying those issues to the press corps in a way that will facilitate their coverage. I spend much of my morning reading the papers and studying my daily briefing book, which details recent developments that may prompt questions from the press.

How does one become press secretary at the White House?
All White House press secretaries have achieved their positions through hard work, perseverance, and a strong level of commitment to their bosses. I personally traveled a long road before I took my current job. I started in politics as a volunteer in the 1980 Carter campaign. I worked for the 1984 Mondale campaign and worked as press secretary for the Clinton-Gore reelection campaign in 1996. Before joining the White House, I also gained invaluable experience working for ABC, NBC, CNN, and SKY Television News of London.

Overall, it is critical for any presidential press secretary to have a sense of humor, a thorough understanding of the president's agenda, and the ability to be quick on one's feet.

Chapter 19

Consumers and Investors

Dear Amazon.com Customer,

On behalf of everyone here at Amazon.com, I'd like to thank you for ordering from us in the last few months. To put it simply, Amazon.com wouldn't be Amazon.com without customers like you.

If you're like me, you're always keeping your eye out for your next great read. We think we might be able to help. . . . .[1]

Thus began the 2000 e-mail from one of the most savvy—if not the most profitable—of the e-commerce marketers: a subtle, soft-sell, yet successful direct e-mail attempt to sell books to a targeted consumer. Pure, positive, pointed public relations.

- *In the spring of 1997, the* Wall Street Journal's *lead story proclaimed, "Old-Fashioned PR Gives General Mills Advertising Bargains." The story chronicled how the venerable General Mills, Inc. had hearkened back to tried and true public relations techniques—Betty Crocker Cook-Offs, newspaper Q&A food columns, pancake breakfasts for presidential candidates—to win recognition. One expert quoted in the story concluded that "a third-party endorsement is almost always more effective than a paid commercial."*[2]
- *That same year, the nation's most powerful marketer of mutual funds for investment, mighty Fidelity Investments, stung by criticism over the performance of its products, announced it would take its case directly to the people by having fund managers meet around the nation with prospective clients.*[3]

As Bruce Springsteen has put it, with "500 channels and nothing on," all offering commercial after commercial, it has become increasingly difficult for consumers to penetrate the clutter to identify winning products and services. Likewise, with the stock market becoming the nation's number one sport and companies, both new and old, clamoring for each investment dollar, it is equally difficult to get through to investors.

As a consequence, many companies enter the 21st century with a new regard for using public relations techniques to get through to two critical publics: consumers and investors.

This chapter will examine how public relations helps attract, win, and keep consumers and also how the practice helps enhance a company's standing in the eyes of its investors. Both consumer and investor relations have become prominent aspects of the overall practice of public relations.

In an era overwrought with advertising "noise"—tens of thousands of blaring messages beamed in the direction of a single consumer—public relations solutions can help cut through the clutter and distinguish one company from the next, both in enhancing the sale of a firm's products or the purchase of its stock.

The Consumer Movement

Although consumerism is considered to be a relatively recent concept, legislation to protect consumers first emerged in the United States in 1872, when Congress enacted the Criminal Fraud Statute to protect consumers against corporate abuses. In 1887, Congress established the Interstate Commerce Commission to curb freewheeling railroad tycoons.

However, the first real consumer movement came right after the turn of the century when journalistic muckrakers encouraged legislation to protect the consumer. Upton Sinclair's novel *The Jungle* revealed scandalous conditions in the meat-packing industry and helped usher in federal meat inspection standards as Congress passed the Food and Drug Act and the Trade Commission Act. In the second wave of the movement, from 1927 to 1938, consumers were safeguarded from the abuses of manufacturers, advertisers, and retailers of well-known brands of commercial products. During this time, Congress passed the Food, Drug, and Cosmetic Act.

By the early 1960s, the movement had become stronger and more unified. President John F. Kennedy, in fact, proposed that consumers have their own bill of rights, containing four basic principles:

1. **The right to safety:** to be protected against the marketing of goods hazardous to health or life
2. **The right to be informed:** to be protected against fraudulent, deceitful, or grossly misleading information, advertising, labeling, or other practices and to be given the facts needed to make an informed choice
3. **The right to choose:** to be assured access, whenever possible, to a variety of products and services at competitive prices
4. **The right to be heard:** to be assured that consumer interests will receive full and sympathetic consideration in the formulation of government policy

Subsequent American presidents have continued to emphasize consumer rights and protection. Labeling, packaging, product safety, and a variety of other issues continue to concern government overseers of consumer interests.

Tyco Tickled with Tickle Me Momentum

Parents who vowed to pay anything to secure a Tickle Me Elmo doll in the winter of 1996 wouldn't believe it, but Tyco Toys Inc., the manufacturer of the hottest toy of the year, was originally concerned with Elmo's potential popularity (Figure 19-1).

So, together with Freeman Public Relations, Tyco devised a carefully planned campaign that ultimately had difficulty coping with its own success.

The strategy called for getting the $28 red and furry creature into the hands of key members of the print and TV media. Elmo's launch began with a Toy Fair breakfast for 15 toy trade publication editors. One of the guests was so impressed with Elmo that he brought it with him to the *Today Show,* where jolly weather man Al Roker played with it on the air.

Next was a special activity day for the media at Sesame Place, a kids amusement and theme park in Pennsylvania. Editors were invited with their children, and Tickle Me Elmo was the star of the day.

Then came the biggest breakthrough. The company sent a doll to talk show host Rosie O'Donnell, who promptly awarded it to her young son. Alas, the boy dropped the doll down the toilet, and O'Donnell announced on the show one day that she desperately needed another.

Tyco obliged with an offer to supply enough Elmos for the whole O'Donnell audience. O'Donnell's producers responded with a "secret word" contest. If one of O'Donnell's guests mentioned the "secret word," known only to the audience, hundreds of Tickle Me Elmos would cascade from the rafters, one for each audience member. On cue, the last guest of the morning mentioned the word. A sea of Elmos came streaming down into the hands of the wildly cheering audience. And the rest, as they say, is toy history.

Demand for the doll overwhelmed the supply. Tyco had to scramble to produce enough Elmos, eventually pulling its advertising when skirmishes erupted among customers fighting for the last doll in stock. With 15,000 media mentions of the doll and sales exceeding projections by 500 percent, Tickle Me Elmo had ridden its publicity to become one of the most sought-after and talked-about toys ever produced.

FIGURE 19-1 **Mega success.** He was cute. He was cuddly. He was the hottest toy in *Sesame Street* history.

Federal Consumer Agencies

Today a massive government bureaucracy attempts to protect the consumer against abuse: upwards of 900 different programs, administered by more than 400 federal entities. Key agencies include the Justice Department, Federal Trade Commission, Food and Drug Administration, Consumer Product Safety Commission, and Office of Consumer Affairs.

- ☑ **Justice Department.** The Justice Department has had a consumer affairs section in its antitrust division since 1970. Its responsibilities include the enforcement of such consumer protection measures as the Truth in Lending Act and the Product Safety Act. Most recently, the department has focused on the computer industry, going after the biggest of them all, Microsoft, for alleged monopolistic practices.
- ☑ **Federal Trade Commission.** The FTC, perhaps more than any other agency, has vigorously enforced consumer protection. Its national advertising division covers television and radio advertising, with special emphasis on foods, drugs, and cosmetics. Its general litigation division covers areas not included by national advertising, such as magazine subscription agencies, door-to-door sales, and income tax services. Its consumer credit and special programs division deals with such areas as fair credit reporting and truth in packaging.
- ☑ **Food and Drug Administration.** The FDA is responsible for protecting consumers from hazardous items: foods, drugs, cosmetics, therapeutic and radiological devices, food additives, and serums and vaccines.
- ☑ **Consumer Product Safety Commission.** This bureau is responsible for overseeing product safety and standards and has been particularly aggressive in recent years in the area of seat belt restraints, strollers, blankets, and other products for small children.
- ☑ **Office of Consumer Affairs.** This agency, the central point of consumer activities in the government, publishes literature to inform the public of recent developments in consumer affairs.

The Justice Department's Microsoft offensive notwithstanding, perhaps the government's most vigilant attack has been against the forces of tobacco. Under Dr. David Kessler, the FDA waged an all-out war against cigarette advertising to children, in particular. After years of fighting, the industry finally capitulated and removed its teenager-drawing Joe Camel symbol from the airwaves (Figure 19-2).

In the 21st century, clearly the best policy for any public company is to communicate directly and frequently with regulators in Washington, ultimately to win their understanding and support.

Consumer Activists on the Internet

The consumerist movement has attracted a host of activists in recent years. While private testing organizations—which evaluate products and inform consumers about potential dangers—have proliferated, the most significant activity to keep "companies honest" has occurred on the Internet.

Perhaps the best-known testing group, Consumers Union, was formed in 1936 to test products across a wide spectrum of industries. It publishes the results in a monthly magazine, *Consumer Reports,* which reaches about 3.5 million readers. Often

Does RJR Nabisco Lie About Marketing To Kids?

In public they say:

"I do not want to sell tobacco to children. I'd fire anyone on the spot if I found they were doing it." (Steven Goldstone, CEO, RJR Nabisco Holdings Corp., 12/6/96).

But a 1976 RJR internal memo stated:

"Evidence is now available to indicate that the 14-to-18-year-old group is an increasing segment of the smoking population. RJR-T must soon establish a successful new brand in this market if our position in the industry is to be maintained over the long term."

You Decide.

In 1988, RJR introduced Joe Camel. Subsequently, Camel's share of the kids' market quadrupled. Camel is now the second most popular cigarette among children, and kids were found to be as familiar with Joe Camel as Mickey Mouse.

Tell your elected officials to support restrictions on tobacco marketing to children, including the Food and Drug Administration rule.

Tobacco vs. Kids. Where America draws the line.

CAMPAIGN for TOBACCO-FREE Kids

To learn more, call 1-800-284-KIDS.

This ad supported by: American Cancer Society; American Lung Association; American Heart Association; Center for Women Policy Studies; National Federation of State High School Associations; Committee for Children; Intercultural Cancer Council; Interreligious Coalition on Smoking OR Health; Youth Service America; American College of Preventive Medicine; Girl Scouts USA; Child Welfare League of America; National Association of Secondary School Principals; National Association of Elementary School Principals; American Federation of Teachers; Women's Legal Defense Fund; Association of State and Territorial Health Officials.

The National Center for Tobacco-Free Kids, 1707 L Street NW, Suite 800, Washington, DC 20036

FIGURE 19-2 **Good-bye Joe.** For years, Joe Camel was the too-cool symbol that helped lure teenage smokers. Ultimately, the industry, at the government's insistence, killed old Joe.

an evaluation in *Consumer Reports,* either pro or con, greatly affects how customers view particular products. Consumers Union also produces books, a travel newsletter, a column for 450 newspapers, and monthly features for network television. It has an annual budget of $70 million.

The Consumer Federation of America was formed in 1967 to unify lobbying efforts for pro-consumer legislation. Today the federation consists of 200 national, state, and local consumer groups, labor unions, electric cooperatives, and other organizations with consumer interests.

Probably most effective, though, in actively dealing with corporate abuse is the emergence of the Internet. From the Yahoo! Boycott Board, which lists actions being taken against organizations; to so-called rogue Web sites, which air the gripes of dissatisfied consumers; to wildfire e-mail campaigns and discussion groups directed at product abuse—the Internet has become a prime source of consumer activism.

Smart companies take Internet challenges seriously and act on them immediately. When a disgruntled Buy.com customer began a Web site in 1999, www.buycrap.cjb.net, to complain about purchasing a wrongly priced computer, the company flew him across the country to meet top executives.[4] Accordingly, companies have found that word-of-mouth criticism, aided and abetted by the Internet, must be dealt with—quickly.

Although companies often find such activists' criticism annoying, the emergence of the consumer watchdog movement has generally been a positive development for consumers. Ralph Nader, the dean of consumer activists, and others have forced organizations to consider, even more than usual, the downside of the products and services they offer. Smart companies have come to take seriously the pronouncements of consumer activists.

Business Gets the Message

Obviously, few organizations can afford to shirk their responsibilities to consumers. Consumer relations divisions have sprung up, either as separate entities or as part of public relations departments. The title of vice president for consumer relations is showing up with more frequency on corporate organization charts.

In many companies, consumer relations began strictly as a way to handle complaints, an area to which all unanswerable complaints were sent. Such units have frequently provided an alert to management. More recently, companies have broadened the consumer relations function to encompass such activities as developing guidelines to evaluate services and products for management, developing consumer programs that meet consumer needs and increase sales, developing field-training programs, evaluating service approaches, and evaluating company effectiveness in demonstrating concern for customers.

The investment in consumer service apparently pays off. Marketers of consumer products say that most customer criticism can be mollified with a prompt, personalized reply—and a couple of free samples (Figure 19-3). Failing to answer a question, satisfy a complaint, or solve a problem, however, can result in a blitz of bad word-of-mouth advertising. More typical of the increased concern shown today by most business organizations are the following:

> ◪ In 1999, a revitalized Apple Computer, Inc. backed off a decision to retroactively raise prices on some computers that customers already had ordered and paid for.[5]

Continental

Continental Airlines, Inc.
Customer Care Department
Suite 500
3663 N Sam Houston Parkway E
Houston TX 77032

Tel 800 WE CARE 2
Fax 1 800 214 0506

October 24, 1998

Mr. Fraser Seitel
Emerald Partners
177 Main St., Ste. 215
Fort Lee, NJ 07024

Dear Mr. Seitel:

Thank you for contacting us regarding the problems you encountered on Continental Airlines. I sincerely apologize for the inconvenience you experienced on your trip.

When we fail to provide our customers with the service they expect, we are disappointed. At Continental, we are aware that to maintain our continued growth, customer service must remain a top priority, such as that provided by Kelly Cline in Houston who will be commended. However, the ensuing situation with your luggage is very disconcerting and below our standards. I have forwarded your comments to our senior management staff to ensure corrective measures are taken.

I realize that an apology after the fact does little to alleviate an unpleasant experience. Therefore, in an effort to regain your confidence, I have enclosed compensation, as a gesture of goodwill.

Given the opportunity to serve you in the future, I am confident we will warrant a better report. Your business is appreciated, and thank you for choosing Continental.

Sincerely,

K. D. Tyler

Keith D. Tyler
Manager

KT/mh

Enclosures

FIGURE 19-3 **Positive activism.** In the 21st century, smart companies value their customers and take their complaints seriously.

- ◪ When Alamo Rent A Car experienced a shortage of vehicles in a busy vacation season at certain locations, it eagerly reimbursed customers for the difference between their reserved Alamo rate and the upgraded one they were forced to pay.
- ◪ When the Swingline Company received numerous complaints about its Tot Stapler, it reconstituted the product and sent new models, free of charge, to people who complained.
- ◪ When Newman's Own Microwave Popcorn received complaints that its bags were leaking, it hired a technical consulting organization to reevaluate the bag sealing system. It also refunded the cost of the purchase.

In adopting a more activist consumerist philosophy, firms like these have found that consumer relations need not take a defensive posture. Consumer relations professionals must themselves be "activists" to make certain that consumers understand the benefits and realities of using their products.

The consumer philosophy of the Chrysler Corporation is typical of the more enlightened attitude of most companies today. Its "Car Buyer's Bill of Rights" states:

1. Every American has the right to quality
2. Every American has the right to long-term protection
3. Every American has the right to friendly treatment, honest service, and competent repairs
4. Every American has the right to a safe vehicle
5. Every American has the right to address grievances
6. Every American has the right to satisfaction

Consumerist Objectives

Building sales is the primary consumer relations objective. A satisfied customer may return; an unhappy customer may not. Here are some typical goals:

- ◪ **Keeping old customers.** Most sales are made to established customers. Consumer relations efforts should be made to keep these customers happy. Pains should be taken to respond to customers' concerns. For example, telephone companies will typically suspend normal charges in areas of natural disasters to make calls to loved ones.
- ◪ **Attracting new customers.** Every business must work constantly to develop new customers. In many industries, the prices and quality of competing products are similar. In choosing among brands, customers may base decisions on how they have been treated.
- ◪ **Marketing new items or services.** Customer relations techniques can influence the sale of new products. Thousands of new products flood the market each year, and the vast array of information about these products can confuse the consumer. When General Electric's research revealed that consumers want personalized service and more information on new products, it established the GE Answer Center, a national toll-free, 24-hour service that informed consumers about new GE products and services. Building such company and product loyalty lies at the heart of a solid consumer relations effort.

■ **Expediting complaint handling.** Few companies are free of complaints. Customers protest when appliances don't work, errors are made in billing, or deliveries aren't made on time. Many large firms have established response procedures. Often a company ombudsman can salvage a customer relationship with a speedy and satisfactory answer to a complaint.

■ **Reducing costs.** To most companies, an educated consumer is the best consumer. Uninformed buyers cost a company time and money—when goods are returned, service calls are made, and instructions are misunderstood. Many firms have adopted programs to educate customers about use of their products.

Office of the Ombuds Officer

Research indicates that only a handful of dissatisfied customers—4 percent—will ever complain. But that means that there are many others with the same complaint who never say anything. And the vast majority of dissatisfied customers won't repurchase from the offending company.

In the old days, a frequent response to complaint letters was to dust off the so-called "bed bug letter." This stemmed from occasional letters to the railroads complaining about bed bugs in the sleeper cars. To save time, railroad consumer relations personnel simply dispatched a prewritten bed bug letter in response. Today, with the volume of mail and e-mail and faxes at a mountainous level, an occasional bed bug letter still appears from time to time (Figure 19-4).

At many companies the most immediate response to complaints has been the establishment of ombudsman offices. The term *ombudsman* originally described a govern-

---

A QUESTION OF ETHICS

Du-ude! Chill! Back to School Drinking 101

Abercrombie & Fitch became hugely profitable in the late 1990s, largely due to its success with the fickle college crowd. Abercrombie's sales soared and its share price doubled as it nursed an image of "Ralph Lauren Meets Animal House."

Then it went too far.

In the summer of 1998, the *A&F Quarterly*, a magazine the company described as "chronicling the college experience," featured an article titled, "Drinking 101." The piece offered recipes for 10 unsubtly named liquor and fruit juice cocktails, such as Dirty Girl Scout Cookie, Orgasm, Woo-Woo, Sex on the Beach, and the ever-popular Brain Hemorrhage. "Rather than the standard beer binge, indulge in some creative drinking this semester," the article urged.

Consumer groups weren't amused. Among them, Mothers Against Drunk Driving (MADD) was especially outraged. Citing statistics that 2,315 Americans

between the ages of 15 and 20 died in alcohol-related car crashes in the prior year, MADD's national president said, "This is a blatant example of a big corporation putting its profits ahead of the health and safety of their consumers."

At first, Abercrombie was unapologetic. "College is a major rite of passage for all of us in terms of accepting responsibility," an A&F spokesman said, "and this topic falls within the range of editorial content of a magazine that writes about college life."

But then, stung by the criticism, the company buckled. It announced it would pull all available issues of the magazine—at a cost of $200,000—and redistribute them with a sticker on the front cover that read:

"We don't want to lose anybody to thoughtlessness and stupidity. For some, part of college life involves partying and drinking—be smart and be responsible."

12 King Place
Closter, New Jersey
07624
June 2, 1993

President Clinton
The White House
Washington, D.C. 205000

Dear President Clinton:

My name is David Seitel, and I am a sixth grader. I'm writing about a very important topic. This topic is SMOKING. Our tobacco companies in the U.S. are setting a bad example for us kids today. They are going to other countries, and encouraging people in their teens especial my age, to smoke.

Please, won't you try to help stop American tobacco companies from addicting the world's children. Thank you.

Sincerely,
David Seitel

Thank you for writing to me. I enjoy hearing from young people because you are the future of our country. I am honored to be your President.

Bill Clinton

FIGURE 19-4 **Bedbug letter.** Even in these days of direct-mail sophistication, a young consumer still risks the disappointment of his sincere missive being answered with a cursory bed bug letter.

ment official—in Sweden and New Zealand, for example—appointed to investigate complaints about abuses made by public officials. In most firms, the office of the ombuds officer investigates complaints made against the company and its managers. Such an office generally provides a central location that customers can call to seek redress of grievances.

Typically, the ombuds officer monitors the difficulties customers are having with products. Often, he or she can anticipate product or performance deficiencies. Ombuds officers are in business to inspire customer confidence and to influence an organization's behavior toward improved service. They accomplish this by responding, more often than not, in the following manner:

- "We'll take care of that for you"
- "We'll take full responsibility for that defect"
- "We want your business"
- "Thank you for thinking of us"
- "Consider it done"

Alas, in these days of voice mail and e-mail and recorded sequential answering systems, such personalized "magic words" seem to be in short supply. Pity. The companies that express such understanding and courtesy will be the ones that keep the business.

Dealing with Investors

Investor relations—or just IR—has increased in importance as the stock market of the late 1990s and early 2000s climbed ever higher.

Investor relations was born in the mid-1930s, shortly after the passage of the Securities Act of 1933 and the Securities Exchange Act of 1934, which attempted to protect the public from abuses in the issuance and sale of securities.

What exactly is IR?

Basically, it is the effort to narrow the gap between the perception of a company and the reality—in other words, helping the firm's securities reach their appropriate market price. To do this, IR professionals must encourage stockholders to buy and hold company shares and persuade Wall Street financial analysts and institutions to take an interest.

A company's stock price is its currency. Premium stock prices allow an organization to acquire others, whose low stock prices encourage raids from competitors. For example, in the most talked-about venture of the new century, upstart America Online announced in 2000 that it would merge with venerable Time Warner Inc., owner of Time and Warner Brothers and CNN. The $120 billion deal was the biggest combination ever of a major Internet company with a traditional company.[6]

If a company's shares are fairly priced in relation to current or future expectations, the company has a better chance of raising money for future expansion. Internet companies, whose valuations have shocked traditional investors, have used sky-high stock prices to acquire others. In any event, a strong shareholder base is necessary to support management's objectives. One way to win shareholder support is through timely and valuable communications. This is the job of investor relations.

Investor Relations Philosophy

The essence of investor relations lies in a public company's obligation to disclose information that may impact an investor's decision to buy, sell, or hold a stock.

This means that a company must disclose information that is adjudged to be "material." The legal standard of what is "material" is any fact that "would be important to an investor making an investment decision." Typical examples of "material" material are the following:

- Proposed mergers or acquisitions
- Change in dividend policy
- Determination of earnings
- Acquisition or loss of a significant business contract
- Major management changes
- Significant change in capital investment plans
- Purchase or sale of a significant asset
- Incurring a significant debt or sale of a significant amount of equity securities
- Pending significant legislation
- A major discovery or invention
- The marketing of significant new products.[7]

When such realities exist, the law expects the company to release the information as fully and fairly and quickly to the widest audience, in order that all market participants be given the same opportunity to act on the news.

Today, with the ability of the Internet to disseminate material news immediately, the SEC has expressed great concern about "selective disclosure" to some investors and not to others. In particular, corporate "conference calls" with securities analysts increasingly let out news not known to the wider investing public. This is the practice that the SEC has vowed to stop.[8]

Investor Relations Activities

Investor relations professionals are responsible for a variety of communications activities.

- **Annual report.** The annual report is a company's key financial communications tool. The annual report, both in printed and on-line versions, generally include the following elements:
- **Company description.** This includes the company's name, headquarters address, description of its overall business, and a summary of operations.
- **Letter to shareholders.** This incorporates a photo of the firm's CEO, an account of last year's performance, and a forward-looking view of the industry, environment, and company's prospects for the future. The best shareholders letters are those that are frank, fun, and straightforward.
- **Financial review.** In light of the SEC's increased demand for financial disclosure, companies have expanded financial sections to include required filings and registration statements.
- **Explanation and analysis.** This complement to the financial review is a general discussion of the factors influencing the financial results.
- **Management/marketing discussion.** The annual report has a narrative section that allows the company to expand on its products and prospects.
- **Graphics.** Photos and charts are critical to help bring to life the company and its performance.
- **Quarterly reports.** Quarterlies or interim reports are issued every quarter to keep shareholders abreast of corporate developments, particularly earnings, between annual reports. In general, companies compare their performance during the current quarter with their performance over the same period of time in the previous year.
- **Annual meeting.** Once a year, the management of public companies is obligated to meet with the shareholders, in person, to discuss the firm. Occasionally, this annual "mating dance" between management and shareholders is greeted with fear and loathing by CEOs, particularly if the company has had problems. Nonetheless, shareholders are the "owners" of the company and deserve answers. In addition to question-and-answer sessions, the annual meeting also consists of management speeches updating the shareholders on corporate performance and stockholder voting on proposals spelled out in previously mailed proxy statements.
- **Conference calls.** An increasing number of companies—73 percent according to one survey—are releasing quarterly corporate earnings information with a conference phone call to analysts and institutions. Top management conducts the call, explains earnings, and answers tough questions.[9]

Companies must be careful about making forecasts on sales and earnings during such calls. Such forecasts require immediate disclosure, so that those not on the call have an equal opportunity to act on the material information. Likewise, firms should consider including members of the media on the call, so that charges of "selective disclosure" can be rebutted.

☑ **Media contact and monitoring.** Visit a business establishment or a doctor's office or even a health club anywhere in America these days, and a television set is tuned—often with sound off—to CNBC, CNNfn, or Bloomberg TV. These financial news networks, which broadcast live during each business day, keep investors aware of current market developments. Savvy investor relations specialists must also keep as current, through regular contact with and monitoring of these important financial news outlets.

Internet Investor Relations

Just as it has affected most areas of public relations work, the Internet has revolutionized investor relations.

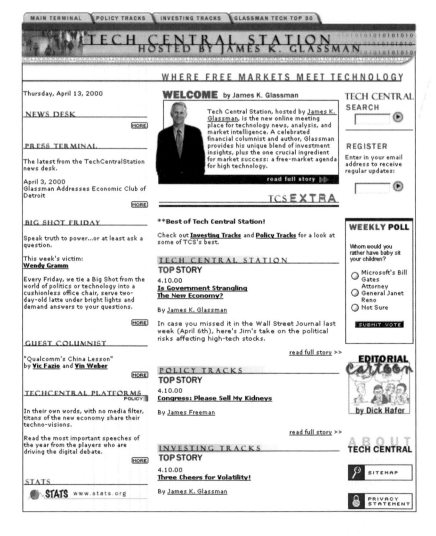

FIGURE 19-5 **Investing in sites on-line.** In 2000, Tech Central Station.com was launched, sponsored by AT&T. Hosted by stock market author James Glassman, it provided commentary and insights on issues of interest to tech investors, policy makers, and consumers.

In the 21st century, companies must use the Internet to reach investors.

- ☑ It has become expected of a forward-looking company to have a home page providing investment information.
- ☑ A well-designed Web site provides a service to investors and potential investors they can receive nowhere else. At any time of day, anywhere in the world, a potential investor can learn about the company as an investment.
- ☑ The firm can better control its messages to investors through an integrated Web site than it can through randomly distributed news releases and investor packets.
- ☑ Today's investor not only often invests by using on-line mechanisms, but also prefers to research personal investments on the Internet (Figure 19-5).[10]

A strong investor site will include all of the staples of investor relations work: news releases, SEC documents, executive profiles, annual and quarterly reports, even analyst recommendations and stock price data. In addition, a section of frequently asked questions (FAQs) should be linked to financial data within tables on the site. All material should be able to be downloaded, and a feedback e-mail mechanism should be incorporated to hear from investors.[11]

Beyond the Web site itself, investor relations professionals must monitor and be in contact with the most widely consulted on-line investor sites. MarketWatch.com, Fool.com, CNNfn.com, Thestreet.com, and CNBC.com are just some of the sites to which investors turn on a daily basis to learn what's going on in the market. A sudden report or rumor broadcast on-line on one of these services could torpedo a company's securities. That's why they must be monitored.[12]

Once a firm's Web site has been established satisfactorily, Internet search services, such as Yahoo! and Lycos, should be notified, so that the company can be included in their directories. Finally, great care should be taken with keeping information and technology current. On-line investor relations is a good way to showcase one's firm and differentiate it from all others. That's why the data must be fresh and the technology state-of-the-art.

SUMMARY

Consumers and investors are among a public company's most important publics. Without either, there would be no company.

In terms of consumers, despite periodic legislative setbacks and shifting consumerist leadership, the cause of consumerism seems destined to remain strong. The increasing use of seat belts and air bags, increased environmental concerns about packaging and pollution, rising outrage about secondhand smoke and all smoking in general, and numerous other causes indicate that the push for product safety and quality will likely increase in the years ahead.

In terms of investors, the nation—and much of the world for that matter—has never been more heavily invested in the stock market than is the case today. Investors therefore will demand ever-increasing amounts of information from which to make intelligent investment choices. The government, cognizant of the pervading interest in the markets, will certainly increase its scrutiny of disclosure and other practices designed for investors.

Both of these phenomena suggest that in the new century, communications to consumers and investors will become even more important, a primary task for public relations practitioners.

Discussion Starters

1. Why has dealing with consumers and investors become so important for public relations?
2. What key federal agencies are involved in consumerism?
3. What is a consumer bill of rights?
4. What are typical consumerist objectives?
5. What is the office of the ombuds officer?
6. What is meant by the term *materiality*?
7. How does the SEC define "full disclosure?"
8. What are the principle activities of an investor relations professional?
9. What is the problem with investor conference calls?
10. What is the role of the Internet with respect to investor relations?

Notes

1. Customer e-mail from Allison Demeritt, product manager, Amazon.com, January 19, 2000.
2. Kevin Helliker, "Old-Fashioned PR Gives General Mills Advertising Bargains," *Wall Street Journal* (March 20, 1997): 1.
3. Edward Wyatt, "Fidelity Will Take Its Case Directly to Its Fund Investors," *New York Times* (January 14, 1997): D2.
4. Rachel Beck, "On-line Gripe Pays Off," *The Record* (May 6, 1999): B1, 2.
5. "Apple's Selling Practices Called Rotten to Core," *Boston Herald* (October 18, 1999): 31.
6. Alex Berenson, "Minimal Research Prepared on AOL-Time Warner Deal," *New York Times* (February 18, 2000): C2.
7. Alan J. Berkeley, "Some FAQs and Answers about Corporate Disclosure," Kirkpatrick & Lockhart, LLP, Washington, D.C., August 1998.
8. "SEC Proposes New Disclosure Rules," *Jack O'Dwyer's Newsletter* (January 26, 2000): 6.
9. Charles Nekvasil, "Getting the Most Out of Your Investor Relations Conference Calls," *PR Tactics* (August 1999): 10, 11.
10. Allan Feinstein, "Investor Relations on the Internet: A Step-by-Step Guide to Getting Started," *Interactive Investor Relations* (July 1999): 8.
11. "24 Items to Supplement Your Online Annual Report," *Interactive Investor Relations* (July 1999): 9.
12. Felicity Barringer, "Financial Sites Are Said to Seek Merger," *New York Times* (February 17, 2000): C11.

Suggested Readings

Barlow, Janelle, and Claus Moller. *A Complaint Is a Gift*. San Francisco: Berett-Koehler, 1996. Provides feedback mechanisms.

"Best Practices in Customer Service Communications." *Public Relations Tactics* (July 1998): 10.

Caywood, Clarke L., ed. *The Handbook of Strategic Public Relations and Integrated Communications.* New York, NY: McGraw-Hill, 1997.

Crego, Edwin T., Jr., and Peter D. Schriffin. *Customer-Centered Reengineering Remapping for Total Customer Value.* Burr Ridge, IL: Irwin Professional Publishing, 1995. Focuses on the failures of many reengineering efforts to make effective long-range change.

Dickman, Steven. "Catching Customers on the Web." *Inc.* (Summer 1995): 56–61. How to turn browsers into customers.

Elsasser, John, ed. "Buyer's Choice Consumer Test Brims with Effective PR Methods." *Public Relations Tactics* (April 1997): 22. A case study.

Hagel, John, III, and Jeffrey F. Rayport. "The Coming Battle for Customer Information." *Harvard Business Review* (January–February 1997): 53–60, 64–65. Claims customers are going to take ownership of information about themselves and demand value in exchange for it.

Hartman, Jason. *Become the Brand of Choice: How to Earn Millions Through Relationship Marketing.* Greensboro, NC: Lifestyles Press.

Hennies, Jack. "Relationship Marketing in New Product Launches." *Journal of Corporate Public Relations* (1996–97): 28–29.

Lewis, Jordan D. *The Connected Corporation: How Leading Companies Win Through Customer-Supplier Alliances.* New York: The Free Press, 1995. Finds customers and suppliers forming alliances for their mutual benefit instead of engaging in adversarial wrangling.

Peppers, Don, and Martha Rogers. *The One to One Future: Building Relationships One Customer at a Time.* New York: Bantam Doubleday Dell Publishers, 1997.

Pertschuk, Michael. "Progressive Media Advocacy." *The Public Relations Strategist* (Winter 1995): 52–55. Former head of the Federal Trade Commission calls for consumer groups to use the media more readily in forwarding their cause.

Speer, Tibbett. "How to be a Friend to Your Customers." *American Demographics* (March 1995): 14–16.

Stewart, Thomas A. "After All We've Done For You, Why Are You Still Not Happy?" *Fortune* (December 4, 1995): 178–81. Reports study that shows customer satisfaction down, despite rising expectations.

top of the shelf

Del Vecchio, Gene

Creating Ever-Cool: A Marketer's Guide to a Kid's Heart.
Gretna, LA: Pelican Publishing Co. Inc., 1997.

You don't want to know how many billions of dollars kids 14 and under spend each year.

But if your company or client's publics include children, you do want to know what Gene Del Vecchio has to say in *Creating Ever-Cool.* As senior partner for planning and research, he is the resident "kid expert" in the Los Angeles office of Ogilvy & Mather.

What's "cool" one year is probably not the next year, unless the product—like the Barbie doll—has reached "Ever-Cool" status. In this book Mr. Del Vecchio reveals "the Ever-Cool formula as the beginning of true knowledge and as a beacon that will show marketers the path to creating long-term brands. . . . It is the critical step toward winning a kid's heart."

CASE STUDY

Tobacco Wars

The manufacturers of cigarettes are engaged in nothing short of war.

In the last years of the last century and the first years of this one, cigarette companies have seen their products and advertising restricted, their executives denigrated before national panels, and their reputations tarnished with accusations of lying and worse.

The enemies of smoking have recast the pastime as nothing short of sin. Today, smokers can no longer light up on airplanes, in restaurants, offices, or stadiums. They have been branded as outcasts, forced to vacate the premises if they wish to have a light up.

As recently as the 1980s, congressional and business deals were still made in smoke-filled rooms. Even the first Americans, Christopher Columbus wrote, carried a "fire brand in the hand, and herbs to drink the smoke thereof, as they are accustomed."

Smoking had always been politically sacrosanct, like guns. Tobacco companies produced jobs for workers and profits for shareholders and, not coincidentally, also financed political campaigns. Tobacco was untouchable, right up until 1994.

And then the roof caved in.

PERMANENT POLITICAL SHIFT

As more activist politicians spoke out against the dangers of smoking, particularly to young people, the political landscape began to shift. Some believe the shift is irreversible.

- President Clinton proposed steep excise taxes on cigarettes as part of health care reform efforts.
- The Environmental Protection Agency classified secondhand smoke as a serious health risk. The House approved legislation barring smoking from most public places. The Department of Defense prohibited smoking in its workplaces worldwide.
- FDA Commissioner Dr. David A. Kessler, considered public enemy number one by tobacco companies, proposed treating tobacco products as drugs, based on "accumulating evidence" that the industry was using unnecessarily high levels of nicotine to create and maintain smokers' addiction.
- Lawsuits began to be filed around the country, including one by Mississippi's attorney general, seeking reimbursement for the estimated tens of millions of dollars that the state spent on medical care for tobacco-related illness. Other states, like Florida, initiated similar efforts.

The major manufacturers of tobacco products increasingly found themselves under pressure and under the spotlight.

FATAL CONGRESSIONAL TESTIMONY

In February of 1994, tobacco makers appeared before Congress, denying that nicotine is addictive and that cigarettes have been proved to cause disease and more than 400,000 deaths a year. It was the first of many bitter confrontations.

As part of the hearing process, internal company documents were made public that shed light on the approach of cigarette companies in selling their product.

Among the documents was one detailing minutes of a meeting of Brown & Williamson executives held just before tobacco advertising was banned from radio and television in 1971. Code-named "Project Truth," the text of the presentation made at the meeting read in part:

> Doubt is our product, since it is the best means of competing with the "body of fact" that exists in the minds of the general public. With the general public, the consensus is that cigarettes are in some way harmful to their health.
>
> Unfortunately, we cannot take a position directly opposing the anti-cigarette forces and say that cigarettes are a contributor to good health. No information that we have supports this claim.

The objective of Project Truth was to "lift the cigarette from the cancer identification as quickly as possible and restore it to its proper place of dignity and acceptance in the minds of men and women in the marketplace of American free enterprise."

By the mid-1980s, according to the documents revealed at the hearing, the companies had forsaken attempts to exonerate smoking as a health hazard and seemed to shift to a legal concern "about what would happen if the years of studies on biological hazards of cigarettes were to become available to plaintiffs in court cases."

In later testimony, Commissioner Kessler revealed information that Brown & Williamson developed a genetically engineered tobacco that would more than double the amount of nicotine delivered in some cigarettes. The company responded by calling Dr. Kessler's testimony "exaggerated."

PUBLIC PERCEPTION GROWS NEGATIVE

The confusion and disputes resulting from the cigarette manufacturers' testimonies before Congress began to build up.

The American Heart Association, American Cancer Society, American Lung Association, and American Medical Association began to work together to win smoking bans. Activists began to get access to caches of internal tobacco industry documents through lawsuits, such as the one filed by the family of Rose Cipollone, who died in 1984 at age 58. Her family won initially but dropped its suit in 1992 after years of costly litigation. The cigarette companies refused to acquiesce.

Perhaps the most damning report was the EPA document on secondhand smoke, which said that environmental tobacco smoke causes 3,000 lung cancer deaths each year. When incoming Clinton administration EPA Administrator Carol Browner was apprised of the findings, she said, "Let that thing rip," and she began promoting the report heavily.

In the latter years of the 1990s, tobacco manufacturers slid further into the public abyss:

- ☑ In February 1997, the FDA implemented regulations that forbade merchants from selling tobacco to minors.
- ☑ Cigarette advertising was the next to be attacked, with critics vowing to rid such advertising from the airwaves, where minors are exposed to it. Primary target was R. J. Reynolds' Joe Camel advertising campaign. Joe Camel, it was charged, represented a seductive appeal to young people.
- ☑ The Campaign for Tobacco-Free Kids was begun with a vigorous public relations and advertising barrage that mobilized children in the pursuit against big tobacco (Figure 19-6).

FIGURE 19-6　Kids against cancer.
The Campaign for Tobacco-Free Kids was relentless in its attacks on smoking.

FIGURE 19-7　Smoking kills. Warnings posted on cigarettes sold in Great Britain left nothing to the imagination in terms of the relative danger.

■ Cigarette package labeling became more restrictive. U.S. legislators looked toward Great Britain, where cigarette advertising is more tightly regulated and packs are labeled with dire warnings (Figure 19-7).

■ In 1997, the Liggett Group tobacco company agreed that its tests had indicated that cigarette smoking was in fact harmful to health and agreed to label its products accordingly. Liggett also acknowledged that it had consciously marketed its products for children.

COMPANY CAPITULATION

For their part, the cigarette companies themselves remained adamant in their fight—at least at first. Said the Philip Morris public affairs director, "There are risk factors in smoking. But 50 million adults have chosen to smoke, and they have the right to make that decision."

In the wake of the Liggett bombshell, however, the industry was on shaky ground. In 1998, the tobacco industry settled a battery of legal cases with 46 individual states attorneys general for $206 billion. As part of the settlement with the states, $1 billion was devoted to a multiyear public relations program to fight tobacco use. Nonetheless, more suits loomed, and the Justice Department readied further litigation as the drumbeat against tobacco increased (Figure 19-8).

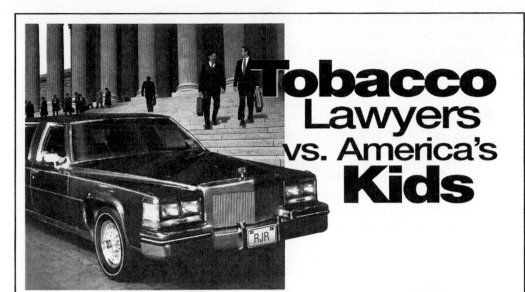

Tobacco companies claim they don't target kids. Yet they're in court, right now, trying to block a sensible Food and Drug Administration rule to protect kids from tobacco marketing and sales.

Three thousand children start smoking every day. One-third will eventually die from their addiction. If the tobacco industry's lawyers get their way in court, thousands of kids will be sentenced to an early death.

Where's the justice in that?

**Tobacco vs. Kids.
Where America draws the line.**

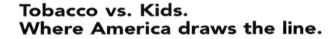

CAMPAIGN for TOBACCO-FREE Kids

To learn more, call 1-800-284-KIDS.

This ad sponsored by: American Cancer Society; American Heart Association; American Lung Association; Association of Black Cardiologists, Inc.; YWCA of the U.S.A.; American Federation of Teachers; General Board of Church and Society of the United Methodist Church; Intercultural Cancer Council; Women's Legal Defense Fund; Committee for Children; Interreligious Coalition on Smoking OR Health; National Middle School Association; American College of Preventive Medicine; Association of State and Territorial Health Officials; American College of Cardiology.

The National Center for Tobacco-Free Kids,
1707 L Street, NW, Suite 800, Washington, DC 20036

FIGURE 19-8 **Pitched battle.** The wave of antismoking advertising continued, even after huge industry class-action settlements.

In 1999, Philip Morris, the largest tobacco company, announced plans to repair its tarnished image. Centerpiece was a $100 million Philip Morris Youth Smoking Prevention Initiative public relations program. By 2000, the Philip Morris stock, once one of the bluest of all blue chips, had plunged by more than half.

Faced with an unprecedented loss of public opinion and a tide against cigarettes that now swept around the world, the companies could have but one overriding objective as they faced the new century: to restore their public image.

It would not be an easy task.

Questions

1. How would you assess the credibility of the cigarette industry today?
2. If you were hired as public relations counsel to the tobacco industry, what would you advise it to do?
3. Visit the Philip Morris tobacco Web site (www.philipmorris.com/tobacco_bus/index.html). Read the home page and then follow the link to "Tobacco Issues." How is Philip Morris using this Web site to boost its credibility?

For further information on the Tobacco Wars, see "Defending an Embattled Industry," *The Public Relations Strategist* (Summer 1999): 7; Stuart Elliott, "When the Smoke Clears, It's Still Reynolds," *New York Times* (September 13, 1995): D1; Suein L. Hwang, "Philip Morris Plans to Take Steps to Mend Its Image," *Wall Street Journal* (June 29, 1999): B9; Youssef M. Ibrahim, "Cigarette Makers Cope with British Ad Restrictions," *New York Times* (April 18, 1997): D5; Mary Kuntz and Joseph Weber, "The New Hucksterism," *Business Week* (July 1, 1996); William D. Novelli, "Waging War on Tobacco," *The Public Relations Strategist* (Fall 1999): 15; Tara Parker-Pope, "Danger: Warning Labels May Backfire," *Wall Street Journal* (April 28, 1997): B1; "Philip Morris Launches $100M Anti-Smoking Pitch," *O'Dwyer's PR Services Report* (January 1999): 1, 20; Eben Shapiro, "RJR Nabisco's Tobacco Unit Escapes Fight with FTC Over Joe Camel Ads," *Wall Street Journal* (June 2, 1994); John Schwartz, "Double Blow for Tobacco Industry: Waxman Assails Research Council, Justice Dept. Probe Sought," *Washington Post* (May 27, 1994): A1.

O V E R   T H E   T O P

An Interview with Murray H. Bring

Murray H. Bring was vice chairman for external affairs and general counsel of Philip Morris Companies Inc. In addition to being the top lawyer at the world's leading cigarette manufacturer, Mr. Bring was also responsible for the company's public affairs function.

The industry has lost a number of court cases. Why do you think these cases have gone against you?

It's hard to say. It's probably a combination of things, which started in 1994 with Commissioner David Kessler's congressional testimony before the Waxman Committee, and a series of events that transpired at about that time, including a program in which *ABC Day One* made the false allegation that the tobacco companies spiked their cigarettes with additional nicotine to keep smokers hooked.

What was your response to that broadcast?

We sued ABC for libel. We ended up settling after ABC agreed to pay all of our costs and issued a retraction and apology indicating their allegation was inaccurate.

Isn't the industry to blame to some degree for its willingness to remain silent?

That's an interesting question and a subject of discussion internally. We try very hard to counteract these false allegations whenever we can.

What about your approach toward litigation public relations?

For many years, we refused to engage in a public relations discussion of the issues that were involved in litigation. That began to change in the *Cipollone* case in New Jersey in 1988, when the other side was offering things to the press virtually every day at the end of court. So we decided we needed to be a player in that arena.

We hired a public relations consultant to work with the lawyers in that case, and he was an integral part of the effort by the industry to get our side of the story across—to the public at large, who was reading about the case.

And your public relations strategy today?

From that point forward, we have concluded that it is important to have a public relations component to our litigation activities. We now have public relations people in the company who have experience in the media and work with the trial lawyers. We also have outside consultants present during the course of important trials and make an effort on a daily basis to communicate to the press about what's going on in the courtroom from our perspective. We now realize this is an important function for us.

What's the Philip Morris approach to its adversaries?

We've had critics and adversaries out there for a long time. We obviously have to be mindful of what they're saying. I think we need to correct the record when we can if we think what they're saying is inappropriate. But I think it's important for us to try and develop a dialogue. In the earlier days of this industry, there was probably not enough of an effort made to try to communicate with our critics and to try to find common ground.

What lessons have you learned from being in the spotlight in recent years?

I think we have learned that when you are in the spotlight and subject to intense scrutiny, you have to listen to others, including your critics. You need to try to engage in a dialogue and work with others to find common ground and reasonable solutions.

The Future
Part VI

Chapter 20

The Golden Age

Even without the Internet, the 21st century would still be the "Golden Age of Public Relations." With the Internet, the age will mean pure growth for the field.

Personnel recruiters from around the country report that high-tech and dot.com companies are creating public relations positions faster than they can fill them.[1] The demand in the public relations job market is unprecedented.

Why? A number of reasons.

- ☑ *A booming economy and seemingly endless supply of venture capital has fueled the creation of a steady weekly stream of new high-tech and dot.com companies. All are fighting for recognition and identity. In other words, they need public relations help to get noticed.*

- ☑ *Competition has caused companies to turn more toward outsourcing services, including public relations. This, in turn, has led to a boom time for public relations agencies. For the first time in history, agencies—particularly those in the white-hot areas of high tech and health care—are using unheard-of inducements, from paid sabbaticals to free legal aid to weekly massages, to attract public relations talent.[2]*

- ☑ *On the other hand, after years of downsizing, corporations have begun to gradually increase communications budgets and reward communications executives. One global survey found public relations budgets growing at a rate of about 7 percent in 2000, after years of staying flat.[3]*

- ☑ *Public relations agencies meanwhile have never been more flush. A decade ago, there were few firms knowledgeable about technology. Today, public relations agencies specializing exclusively in high tech record annual fee incomes in excess of $40 million (Table 20-1).*

- ☑ *Meanwhile, the communications media around the world have truly converted the globe into one large "village," united by satellite and*

TABLE 20-1

1998 Fee Income of High-Tech PR Firms

1	Porter Novelli	$54,981,000	39. Cone Communications	1,807,000
2.	Shandwick	48,911,000	40. KCSA PR Worldwide	1,800,000
3.	Edelman PR Worldwide	41,139,676	41. Earle Palmer Brown PR	1,719,183
4.	Waggener Edstrom	40,900,000	42. McKinney Adv. & PR	1,400,000
5.	Fleishman-Hillard	31,989,000	43. Imagio Technology Adv. & PR	1,349,009
6.	Copithorne & Bellows	26,705,427	44. Price/McNabb	1,115,355
7.	Weber Group of WPRW	26,633,215	45. Smith Public Relations	1,100,000
8.	Ogilvy PR	24,829,400	46. Environics Communications	1,062,091
9.	Ketchum	22,988,000	47. PepperCom	1,000,000
10.	Manning Selvage & Lee	22,811,000	48. LobsenzStevens	1,000,000
11.	GCI/APCO	21,211,295	49. PRx	994,200
12.	Cunningham Comm.	20,437,000	50. M Booth & Assocs	972,482
13.	TSI Communications of WPRW	15,907,144	51. KMC Group	959,014
14.	BSMG Worldwide	15,900,000	52. Stanton Crenshaw Comms.	900,000
15.	Schwartz Communications	15,019,646	53. Gibbs & Soell	867,200
16.	Lois Paul & Partners	13,482,032	54. Kratz & Jensen	846,628
17.	Golin/Harris Int'l	12,209,150	55. Vollmer PR	846,000
18.	Burson-Marsteller	11,674,000	56. Tierney Group	725,388
19.	Ruder Finn	9,231,500	57. Kamber Group	650,000
20.	Blanc & Otus	8,091,587	58. Clay Marketing & PR	615,923
21.	Niehaus Ryan Wong	7,731,041	59. HLB Communications	600,000
22.	Hawthorn Group	7,408,743	60. Spring O'Brien	568,000
23.	Access PR	6,799,618	61. Carter Ryley Thomas	565,182
24.	Wilson McHenry Co.	6,425,752	62. Levenson PR	504,385
25.	MWW Group	6,015,406	63. Charleston/Orwig	426,078
26.	Hoffman Agency	5,514,271	64. McNeely Pigott & Fox	404,544
27.	The Horn Group	4,373,141	65. Tattar Cutler-LD&B PR	409,573
28.	Applied Communications	4,093,128	66. MGA Communications	390,000
29.	Phase Two Strategies	4,047,557	67. Paine & Assocs.	358,870
30.	Makovsky & Co.	3,378,000	68. Emmanuel Kerr Kilsby	300,000
31.	Bohle Company	3,133,413	69. ACS Communications	296,888
32.	PR21	2,671,045	70. DCS Group	288,804
33.	Padilla Speer Beardsley	2,497,372	71. Aviso	268,150
34.	Middleberg + Assocs.	2,482,371	72. Hager Sharp	261,510
35.	Rowland Worldwide	2,468,000	73. Bader Rutter & Assocs.	250,000
36.	Interactive PR	2,132,000	74. Dome Newmark Wolf Comms.	250,000
37.	Townsend Agency	1,982,000	75. Star/Rosen PR	207,000
38.	Publicis Dialog	1,932,711	76. Dragonette	200,003

Source: *O'Dwyer's PR Services Report,* November 1999. Used with permission.

High-tech bonanza. Public relations agencies specializing in high tech are thriving in the dot.com environment.

Internet technology. What happens in one corner of the globe is instantly transmitted to another. Organizations, therefore, need professional communicators to navigate through this "brave new world" of instantaneous communication.

☑ *As organizations internationally have merged and affiliated and combined forces, the need to accurately "interpret" management's philosophies, policies, and programs to its customers, employees, the government, and other key constituent groups has intensified.*

☑ *As society has gotten more technologically savvy and automated, the human factor has diminished. The less-appealing facet of voice mail and e-mail and the World Wide Web is its impersonal nature. Again, organizations need communications specialists today, just as John D. Rockefeller needed Ivy Lee at the start of the last century, to help them "humanize" their approach to their markets and their publics.*

All of these factors signal one clear conclusion: the 21st century promises to be the Golden Age of Public Relations.

Issues of the Millennium

Undeniably, the people who practice public relations today must be better than those who came before them. Institutions operate in a pressure-cooker environment and must keep several steps ahead of the rapid pace of social, economic, and political change. The environment is being shaped by many factors:

☑ **Economic globalization.** This is affecting all organizations, even nonmultinational companies. The world is getting smaller. Communism is dead or dying. Democracy and free enterprise reign supreme. Competition will intensify, and so will communications, making it easier to communicate around the world but much more difficult to be heard. Public relations has become a growth industry around the world.

☑ **Shifting public opinion.** Sudden shifts in public opinion are being ignited by instantaneous communications, challenging the ability of communicators to respond to fast-moving events. Interest groups of every stripe are jockeying for position on the public stage.

☑ **Aging of society.** Baby boomers have turned 50 and dominate society. Households headed by people over 55 are the fastest-growing segment of the consumer market in America, and this group controls an increasing percentage of all personal income.

☑ **Leanness and meanness.** The new reality of employment is that "nothing lasts forever." Lifetime employment is no longer possible in most organizations. With downsizing, companies are continuing to pare overhead and trim

A QUESTION OF ETHICS

Bugs in the Belfry

As much as "technology rules" in the new century, that doesn't mean that every public relations move made by high-tech firms is the right one.

Consider the dumb dumb stunt planned by Sun Microsystems to disrupt the launch of Microsoft's Windows 2000 operating system.

In February 2000, on the day Microsoft was scheduled to unveil its new system in San Francisco, Sun marketing executives hired a fleet of 20 bright yellow trucks used by a pest-control company. The plan was to pay the drivers to circle the Moscone Convention Center during the Microsoft event inside. The idea was to draw attention to news reports,

denied by Microsoft, that there were still "bugs" in the new Microsoft program.

Get it?

Near the appointed hour, the trucks were lined up a few blocks from their target, when the manager of the extermination company learned that it was Sun and not Microsoft that had hired his company's trucks. He immediately aborted the stunt.

He was worried about the fairness of such a prank and, more than that, concerned about the reaction of one Bill Gates if he heard about it. "He could buy the company and close it," the manager was reported as saying.

staff to become more competitive. Incoming employees understand that "job hopping" is much more a reality today than in years past. The effect on business and employee morale is profound, and the need for good internal communications is critical.

- **Corporate responsibility.** This buzzword of the 1960s and 1970s has become critical in the 2000s, especially during years of economic plenty. Organizations today—particularly those in the fertile area of technology—must "give back" to society.
- **Technology.** The overwhelmingly important phenomenon of today. Knowledge of the Internet is an imperative, not only in the practice of public relations but in virtually every field of endeavor.
- **Bigness is back.** The trend toward linkages and mergers among huge industrial corporations, hospitals, banks, telecommunications firms, media companies, and others is unstoppable. The AOL-Time Warner merger may have ushered in a merger wave in the Internet industry.
- **So is accountability.** With larger and larger companies delivering products, consumers and politicians are demanding more accountability from all institutions, as well as higher standards of ethical conduct.

In the face of all these changes, it is understandable that management today is giving greater attention than ever before to the public's opinions of its organization and to public relations professionals who can help deal with these opinions.

21st Century Public Relations Challenges

As the significance of the practice of public relations intensifies, so will the challenges confronting the public relations profession. The challenges will be worldwide, just as the field itself has become worldwide. The power of communication, especially global communication, will no longer be an American domain. Among the significant challenges confronting public relations professionals are the following:

- **Need for tailored approaches.** Demographic changes will affect the way professionals communicate. Public relations practitioners will have to target messages across cultural lines to special groups within the population. This will involve narrowcasting, as opposed to broadcasting. The mass media will play a less important role, and public relations professionals will have to deal with increased media fragmentation.[4]

- **Creativity.** As technology continues to advance, new and exotic forms of information dissemination will evolve. These media will capture public attention in the most creative ways—interactive video, talking billboards, blimps, in-flight headsets, and myriad others. Public relations will have to be equally creative to keep up with the new media and harness them for persuasive purposes.

- **Increased specialization.** Public relations professionals will have to be much more than a conduit between an organization and the public. They will have to be much more fully informed about company policy and activities. They will have to be specialists—experts in dealing with, for example, the media, consumers, and investors—possessing the sophisticated writing ability that management demands. At the same time, public relations will have to avoid what some have called the "balkanization" of the practice into discrete functions and away from management counseling.[5]

- **Globalization.** As companies expand internationally, media coverage transcends national borders, and the practice of public relations becomes more accepted and coveted across national borders, the globalization of public relations will accelerate.

- **Technology.** Public relations professionals, as noted, will be blessed with an expanding array of technological tools to cope with the speed and impact of rapid, more global communications. Professionals must not only understand but stay current with and even ahead of the new technology if the field is to continue to develop.

- **Research/results orientation.** The growth of research to measure and evaluate public relations results will continue. Public relations professionals must find ways to improve their measurement capability and justify their performance—that is, the results of their actions—to management.

- **Decreased sexism.** Women are becoming more dominant in public relations and, in fact, outnumber their male counterparts—women make up more than 60 percent of the practice. The salary gap with men, although not yet acceptable to many, is nonetheless narrowing. This marks another challenge for the field in the new century.

- **Minority recruitment.** While women continue to move in and up in public relations, minorities—particularly African Americans—have not made significant strides. This is a challenge that the field and its associations must confront and solve.

- **Education.** The importance of public relations education, so vital if the field is to fulfill the jobs and promise of the new millennium, will also become more important. As management consultants, accountants, and lawyers all move to invade the influential turf that public relations has occupied, it will become more vital to train public relations leaders of the future.[6]

☑ **Ethics and reputation.** If public relations is truly to distinguish itself in the 21st century, it must represent the very highest values. Reputation matters, and public relations professionals are often "the keepers of the reputation." Most corporate CEOs look to their public relations professionals to oversee the firm's reputation.[7] In the 21st century, no challenge will be more important or critical to the field.

Internationalization of Public Relations

In the 21st century, public relations has become a global phenomenon.

Major political shifts toward democracy throughout the world, coupled with the rapidity of worldwide communications and the move to form trading alliances of regional nations, have focused new attention on public relations. The collapse of communism, the coming together of European economies, and the outbreak of democracy everywhere from Eastern Europe to South Africa have brought the global role of public relations into a new spotlight.

Canada

Canadian public relations is the rival of American practice in terms of its level of acceptance, respect, sophistication, and maturity. The Canadian Public Relations Society, formed in 1948, is extremely active. Canadian public relations professionals must be conversant not only in the English-speaking parts of their country, but also in the French-speaking markets, such as Quebec. Also, Canada in recent years has become a nation of nations, with a great many people speaking a Chinese dialect or Hindi.[8]

Latin America

In Latin America, the scene is more chaotic. The field is most highly developed in Mexico, where public relations practice began in the 1930s. Mexican corporations all have communications and public relations departments, and many employ local or U.S. public relations agencies. Mexican schools of higher learning also teach public relations. The passage of the North American Free Trade Agreement (NAFTA) means increasing opportunities for U.S.–Mexican trade and therefore for public relations growth. In the other countries of Latin America, public relations is less well-developed. However, the expanding economies of Argentina, Brazil, Venezuela, and Chile, in particular, indicate clearly that Latin American public relations will grow in the years ahead. Chile, with its booming economy and approach to capitalism, is a particularly prominent candidate for increased public relations activity in the initial years of the new century.

The New Europe

Like Canada, public relations developed more or less simultaneously in Europe and the United States during the 19th century. In Germany, in particular, public relations writings appeared in the early 1900s.

In the new century, privatization and the synthesis of the European Community into a more unified bloc have spurred increased public relations action in many European countries. For example, public relations has experienced tremendous growth in Great Britain. The largest U.K.-based public relations operation is one of the world's largest independent agencies, the Shandwick Group.

The Institute of Public Relations, headquartered in London, is the largest professional organization in Europe for public relations practitioners. It encompasses 13 regional groups located throughout Britain, has a Web site at www.ipr.org.uk and produces a monthly magazine called *Profile*. It maintains close relations with another group, the European Confederation of Public Relations Associations, with branches in 19 European countries.

As European organizations pay increased attention to their reputations and how they are perceived, public relations is certain to be at the forefront of European commercial concern in the years ahead.

Asia

Although public relations has evolved slowly in Asia, it has experienced sharp growth in recent years:

- ◪ In Japan, the public relations profession was established after World War II. Although the Japanese take a low-key approach to public relations work—especially self-advocacy—the field is growing, particularly as the media—six major national newspapers and four national networks—becomes more aggressive in investigating a proliferation of national scandals. Japanese public relations differs markedly from that of the West. For example, Keiretsu business associations—which bring together individual firms—operate with enormous influence as intermediaries in arranging press events. In recent years, television in general and talk shows in particular have become increasingly popular in Japan.

- ◪ Elsewhere in Asia, public relations also has begun to take root. Korea has an active public relations community, as do Indonesia, Taiwan, and Singapore. In Singapore, for example, public relations is dominated by new companies raising funds through a booming stock market and active economy. Technology, financial services, and real estate development also are burgeoning areas of public relations growth.[9]

- ◪ China, after a number of false starts, holds great potential for public relations expansion. By 2020, some predict that 70 percent of the world will name Mandarin as their principal language. China is the world's fastest-growing economy, second only to the United States, which it should pass soon. As the nation with the largest consumer population, China ranks eleventh in world trade and holds magnificent promise. Even with government control, some 150,000 Chinese log onto the Internet every day.[10]

The China Public Relations Association attracted more than 300 practitioners to its 1998 meeting in Beijing. There are 1,200 public relations firms in China, employing upwards of 30,000 people, including more than 5,000 professionals.[11] Public relations courses are offered at leading universities, such as China's Institute of International Relations in Beijing, Nankai University in Tianjin, and Zhongshan University in Guangzhou. In addition, major U.S. public relations agencies have moved into the country (Figure 20-1). All of this suggests that the public relations business in China has a bright future in the 21st century.

- ◪ In Vietnam, opportunities for public relations work also will emerge, as it rejoins the world community. Indeed, a major U.S. business and trade mission to Hanoi in 1993 and the return of a U.S. ambassador to the country in 1997 suggest the public relations potential of a newly rediscovered Vietnam.

FIGURE 20-1 **Entry celebration.** Edelman Worldwide's entry into China was celebrated at a gala Beijing banquet honoring the Chicago-based firm.

Eastern Europe

There are 370 million consumers in recently democratized Eastern Europe. The prospects for public relations expansion are enticing.

- More than 80 percent of all Eastern Europeans watch television daily. Nearly 100 percent watch several times a week.
- In Hungary, about 20 percent of the population have TV sets connected to satellite dishes.
- In Poland, 13 percent of the population report owning VCRs.
- In Hungary, Serbia, and Croatia, about two-thirds of the population read newspapers daily.

Russia

Although newly capitalist Russia has suffered fits and starts—not to mention scandals and bloody internal conflicts—the practice of public relations will likely build in the years ahead. AT&T, Intel, Coca-Cola, and many other companies are already ensconced in Russia. Large American public relations firms have also set up bases. PR Newswire, in combination with the news agency TASS, distributes news releases from U.S. companies to locations in the Commonwealth of Independent States. Releases are translated into Russian and reach 40 newspapers in Moscow alone.

Australia

The Public Relations Institute of Australia is an extremely active organization and the practice is widespread, particularly in the country's two commercial centers,

Melbourne and Sydney. Australian public relations practice, like Australians them-selves, is more low key and less flashy than American practice.

Middle East

Although the public relations profession is less active in the Middle East, the power of public relations is well known and understood. Indeed, during the 1990 invasion of Kuwait, Iraq's leader Saddam Hussein was quick to harness the world's communica-tions apparatus to spread his views. The Kuwaitis responded by hiring Hill & Knowlton to represent the country in an appeal for American support. Even in coun-tries as traditional as Saudi Arabia, public relations work has begun to carry increased significance.[12] One positive sign of growth in the field was the admission of 20 women students into the public relations major program at the United Arab Emirates University in Al-Ain in 1995.[13]

Africa

In Africa, too, the practice of public relations is growing. In 1990, the largest public relations meeting in the history of the continent was held in Abuja, Nigeria, with 1,000 attendees from 25 countries. In 1994, as a result of an extensive worldwide com-munications and public relations campaign, Nelson R. Mandela became the first demo-cratically elected president of the nation of South Africa. Africa, too, has discovered the power of public relations.

BACKGROUNDER

Think Multilingual—Or Else

According to America's foremost "nameologist," Steve Rivkin, organizations dealing overseas better think multilingual—or else.

Or else what? Or else this:

- A food company named its giant burrito a "Burrada." Big mistake. The colloquial meaning of that word in Spanish is "big mistake."
- Estee Lauder was set to export its "Country Mist" makeup when German managers pointed out that "mist" is German slang for "manure." (The name became "Country Moist" in Germany.)
- General Motors introduced the Chevrolet "Nova" in South America and was shocked to learn that "no va" is Spanish for "does not go." After GM realized it wouldn't sell many of the "go-less" cars, it renamed the vehicle "Caribe" in Spanish markets.
- Ford had a similar problem in Brazil when it introduced the "Pinto." The name turned out to be Brazilian slang for "tiny male genitals." Red-

faced Ford pried off all the nameplates and renamed the car "Corcel," which means "horse."
- Colgate introduced a toothpaste in France called "Cue," the name of a notorious French porno magazine.
- The name "Coca-Cola" in China was first ren-dered as "ke-kou-ke-la." Unfortunately, Coke did not discover until after thousands of signs had been printed that the phrase means "bite the wax tadpole." Coke then researched 40,000 Chinese characters and found a close phonetic equivalent, "ko-kou-ko-le," which loosely trans-lates as "happiness in the mouth." Much better.
- A leading brand of car de-icer in Finland will never make it to America. The brand's name: "Super Piss."
- Ditto for Japan's leading brand of coffee creamer. Its name: "Creap."*

Courtesy of Rivkin & Associates, 233 Rock Road, Glen Rock, NJ 07452

Counseling Top Management

In the new century, no challenge for public relations professionals is more important than counseling senior management.

Top managers in companies, hospitals, associations, governments, educational institutions, and most other organizations need counsel. Most CEOs think in terms of "tangibles"—revenue, income, costs per thousands, etc. Public relations professionals think in terms of "intangibles"—attitudes, opinions, motivation, tomorrow morning's headline, and the like. Top management needs advice in these areas, and public relations practitioners must provide it.

Public relations people in the years ahead must be willing and eager to provide a counseling role to management. Accomplishing such a task will depend on the following 10 characteristics:

1. **Intimate knowledge of the institution.** A public relations professional may be an excellent communicator, but without knowledge of the industry or institution represented, his or her ultimate value will be limited.
2. **Access to and respect for management.** The public relations professional who acquires the respect of top management is a powerful force in an organization. Respect comes only from exposure. Thus, it is essential that the public relations professional have ready access to the most senior managers in an organization.
3. **Access to an intelligence network.** Public relations professionals need their own intelligence network to give them the unvarnished truth about programs and projects. If the executive vice president is an idiot, if the employee incentive program isn't working, or if the chairman's speech was terrible, the public relations professional must be able to tap a team of candid employees who will tell the truth so that the practitioner can tell the unvarnished truth to top management—unexpurgated, uncensored, between the eyes.
4. **Familiarity with the reporter on the beat.** A public relations professional, no matter how high up in an organization, should keep in touch with the reporters and analysts who follow the organization. Valuable information can be gleaned from such observers and can be most helpful to top management.
5. **Solid skills base.** The most competent public relations counselors don't just give orders, they demonstrate skills. They are generally good writers who don't mind pitching in to complete a job competently. In public relations, communications competence is a prerequisite for counseling competence.
6. **Propensity toward action.** In working for top management, results and performance are all that count. Certainly, planning and setting strategies are critical aspects of public relations. But practitioners, especially those who counsel management, must be inclined toward action. They must be doers. That's what management demands.
7. **Knowledge of the law.** Public relations work today confronts legal issues: privacy, copyright, lobbying, securities laws, broadcasting regulations, and so on. Although public relations professionals need not be trained lawyers, they must at least be conversant in the general concepts of the law in order to counsel management effectively and to deal with legal counselors.

8. **Knowledge of technological change.** The Internet, the World Wide Web, cyberspace—all must be part of the purview of the savvy public relations counselor. Harnessing the new technology is imperative for communications in this new century.

9. **Strong sense of integrity and confidence.** As noted throughout these pages, public relations professionals must be the ethical conscience of organizations. Their motives and methods must be above reproach. It's also important that public relations counselors demonstrate confidence in their own positions and abilities. They must surround themselves with the highest-caliber performers to enhance the status of the public relations function within the organization.

10. **Contentment with anonymity.** Public relations counselors must understand that they are exactly that—counselors to top management. It is the chief who delivers the speeches, charts the strategies, and makes the decisions. It is the chief, too, who derives the credit. Public relations counselors must remain in the background and should try to stay anonymous. Today, with newspapers demanding the names of spokespersons, with some public relations practitioners attaining national celebrity status, and with the field itself becoming more and more prominent, the challenge of anonymity becomes increasingly more difficult.[14]

Implications for Beginners

The reality of a more respected and, therefore, more competitive public relations profession has numerous implications for people just starting out in the field.

While public relations professionals are highly sought today, competition for good jobs remains stiff. Experience is the great equalizer, and smart beginners can optimize their potential for employment by getting a jump on the competition through early experience. How?

BACKGROUNDER

Rapping in the Millennium

One of the communications challenges of the new century is understanding the current language, as spoken by the "leaders" of our society—from Puff Daddy to Pfish to Bela Fleck & the Flecktones. Toward that end, here is the updated lexicon of hip (but perhaps not hop)—which may or may not be obsolete by the time you read this!

- No diggity: That's the truth
- Props: Kudos, respect

- Peeps: Friends
- Butter: Smooth, nice
- Shorty: Girlfriend
- Playa hater: A person jealous of another's success
- Floss: Bragging and boasting
- Mad: Great
- Flava: Style
- Sweat: Harass
- Cronkite: News

- ☑ By becoming involved with and active in student public relations organizations
- ☑ By securing—through faculty or others—part-time employment that uses the skills important in public relations work
- ☑ By attending professional meetings in the community, learning about public relations activities, and meeting public relations practitioners who might prove to be valuable contacts later on
- ☑ By seizing every opportunity—informal internships, voluntary work for non-profit associations or political candidates, service on the school newspaper, merchandising in-class projects to local merchants

The key to finding and securing a good job in public relations is experience. So, rather than bemoan the catch-22 reality of a field in which you must have worked first in order to land a job, full-time students should use their college days to begin to acquire working knowledge in public relations. That way, when they look for that first job, they already have experience.

BACKGROUNDER

The Moral Collapse of the Media . . . .

FIGURE 20-2 Dead end. It was admittedly difficult for public relations people to maintain ethical standards when the media felt obliged to record and broadcast grotesque situations like this unidentified man who committed suicide on a Los Angeles Freeway in 1998.

S U M M A R Y

Most professions undergo constant change, but few experience more critical or frequent change than public relations.

In the latter years of the 1990s, practitioners were introduced to a tidal wave of primary concerns: consumerism, environmentalism, government relations, and public policy forecasting. Areas of public relations opportunity shifted from marketing publicity to financial relations to employee communications to public issues management. Steadily, the field has expanded its horizons and increased its influence.

In the 21st century, the field has encountered the Internet and the World Wide Web. High technology rules. And the practice of public relations stands at the threshold of its golden age. To get there, however, public relations professionals must exhibit certain qualities. Among them are the following:

- **Professionalism.** Practitioners must recognize that every time someone in public relations is accused of bending the truth, all in the practice suffer. The cardinal rule must always be: "Tell the truth." Being professional also means standing for something. At base, public relations people are professional communicators. Communications standards, therefore, must remain high, and practitioners must take pride in the communications products for which they are responsible.

- **Generalized specialization.** The old notion that people in public relations must be generalists rather than specialists simply won't wash in the new century. As noted, the competition today is ferocious. Public relations people must have an edge to differentiate themselves from others. Clearly, a solid general base of communications knowledge is still obligatory for public relations work. But at the same time, it has become more urgent today to master a specialty—to become conversant in and knowledgeable about a specific aspect of public relations work—investor relations, government relations, or speechwriting, for example—or about a particular industry—such as computers, health care, sports, insurance, banking, or the arts. Public relations people must become generalized specialists.

- **Guts.** Public relations people also must be willing to stand up for what they stand for. Too often, public relations managers are posturers rather than practitioners, politicians rather than professionals, corporate lap dogs rather than leaders. Such faint-hearted communications counsel won't be sufficient in the 21st century. As top management gets better, public relations must also improve its standing.

- **Ethics.** The public relations professional must be the most ethical individual in the organization. Public relations must be the conscience of the organization, the standard bearer for honor and ethics and integrity. Public relations people should never compromise their values. This may not be easy in a society where ethics and standards are often sacrificed (Figures 20-3 and 20-4). Nonetheless, the first question the public relations professional must ask is, "Are we doing the right thing?" Few others in the organization will ever pose this question.

. . . The REAL Moral Collapse of the Media

FIGURE 20-3 **REAL dead end.** And just when you thought media standards couldn't sink any lower, along came Fox TV's "Who Wants to Marry a Multimillionaire?" featuring an immediate on-air marriage, followed by disclosure of questionable biographical details, quickie annulment, and cancellation of the show.

◪ **Leadership.** Finally, public relations professionals must be leaders, particularly those who embrace the new technology and master the new media. But to accomplish leadership, they must have the vision, courage, and character to lead themselves, their organizations, and their profession into the next golden century.

This is the challenge that awaits the new and future leaders entering the exciting, expanding, and ever-changing practice of public relations.

THE LAST WORD

FIGURE 20-4 Jack O'Dwyer

Commentary from Jack O'Dwyer

For three decades, Jack O'Dwyer has been observing, critiquing, and tweaking the practice of public relations. A former business reporter for the late New York Journal American *and advertising reporter for the* Chicago Tribune, *Mr. O'Dwyer is publisher and editor of* O'Dwyer's Newsletter, *the weekly "bible" of what's happening in public relations. He also publishes, among other periodicals, the field's foremost directories of agency and corporate public relations.*

As a "parting shot," O'Dwyer offers his own unique commentary on the contemporary and future practice of public relations.

SPECIALIST VERSUS GENERALIST

Public relations, like other professions, is becoming more and more specialized. Clients are looking for PR firms with expertise in high tech, health care, financial, foods/beverages, beauty/fashion, and travel, to mention a few of these areas. Public relations people like to position themselves as communicators of "anything." But savvy users of public relations are not buying this. If you hired a lawyer or doctor, you would go to a specialist if you had anything more than a routine problem.

HOTTEST AREAS

The three fastest-growing areas of public relations, according to the statistics we collect annually from more than 150 public relations firms—including all but three or four of the 50 largest firms—are high-tech, financial, and health care. Public relations people need lots of specialized knowledge in each area to succeed. The National Investor Relations Institute is the fastest-growing national public relations association. It has doubled to 3,500 members in the past 10 years and has been able to raise dues 55 percent to $425 annually. The Public Relations Society of America, with 18,000 members, and the International Association of Business Communicators, with 12,500 members, haven't been able to raise dues for nearly 10 years. Public relations people will be respected by clients and the press to the extent they have specialized market knowledge.

INTERFACE WITH ADVERTISING/MARKETING

They should be interfacing with reporters and analysts and staying away from marketing and advertising people, who mostly deal in positive facts and news about companies and products. Public relations people must be able to handle negative developments with the same zeal they bring to positive developments. The investor relations pros do this, and their practice has thrived.

Advertising and public relations can work well together but in tandem, rather than at the same time. Advertising is like the bombing that precedes a landing by soldiers. Advertising softens up the prospect and glamorizes a product, but public relations does the actual work of the sale. Few people buy anything anymore just based on what they see in ads. They ask friends, get specialized publications, check the Internet, etc.

The Internet/Employee Communications

Product knowledge and good debating skills are needed by anyone using the Internet. It's the public forum. Public relations people in recent years have been stressing employee communications. What works with employees will often be savaged in the public arena. Public relations and employee relations are two completely different things.

Agency Versus Corporate

The trend is for most public relations to be in the agencies. Corporate public relations units have been downsizing for many years. Information trading with the press is simply too dangerous an activity for corporate public relations people. When a crisis comes up, a public relations firm is called in. If the wrong advice is given, it is the firm that is fired, not the internal public relations director.

The advertising business went external many years ago. Companies used to have big advertising departments. But advertising is 99 percent in the agencies these days.

What Clients/Employers Want

Clients want public relations firms that are knowledgeable about their practice areas. Intelligence gathering is one of the main functions of public relations, but one that is rarely mentioned. Both corporate and agency public relations people should spend most of their time in the field talking to reporters, analysts, the public, and other information sources so that their advice will have relevance.

There's too much emphasis these days on putting out a "message" rather than finding out what's going on.

Discussion Starters

1. What evidence can you point to that indicates the increased stature of public relations practice?
2. What factors are shaping the new environment?
3. What are the primary challenges for public relations into the next century?
4. What are the skills requisite for counseling management?
5. How should a public relations professional regard anonymity?
6. Where are the areas of greatest international growth in the field?
7. What is the outlook for women in public relations?
8. How important is technological knowledge for public relations practitioners?
9. What is the key challenge for entry-level public relations professionals in the 1990s?
10. What is the outlook for public relations practice?

Notes

1. Katie Sweeney, "Dot.Com Frenzy Fuels Red-Hot Job Market, *Public Relations Tactics* (March 2000): 1, 24.
2. Joan Stewart, "Unusual Benefits Help Attract and Keep PR Pros," *Public Relations Tactics* (March 2000): 1, 10.
3. Adam Leyland, "Corporate PR Gaining in Stature and Budget," *PR Week* (February 28, 2000): 1, 25.
4. "PR Heads Into a Golden Age as Advertising's Pitch Falters," *Business Wire Newsletter* (July 1999): 2.

5. Philip Lesly, "The Balkanizing of Public Relations," *The Public Relations Strategist* (Fall 1996): 41.

6. "Consultants, Accounting Firms Take 'Dead Aim' at PR Biz," *O'Dwyer's PR Services Report* (November 1999): 1, 62.

7. "Ten Predictions for PR in the New Millennium," *PR Week* (January 10, 2000): 29.

8. Carole M. Howard, "Going Global: Tips to Help Avoid the 'Ugly American' Label," remarks at Ragan Communicators Conference, Chicago, IL, September 16, 1997.

9. "Gavin Anderson Moves into Growing Singapore Market," *PR News* (February 10, 1997): 1.

10. Steven L. Lubetkin, "China's Growth Makes Understanding of Media Crucial," *Public Relations Tactics* (December 1996): 18.

11. James B. Strenski and Kung Yue, "China: The World's Next Public Relations Superpower," *Public Relations Quarterly* (Summer 1998): 25.

12. Abdulrahman H. Al-Enad, "Values of Public Relations Conduct in Saudi Arabia," *Public Relations Review* (Summer 1992): 213.

13. Pamela J. Creedon, Mai Abdul Wahed Al-Khaja, and Dean Kruckeberg, "Women and Public Relations Education and Practice in the United Arab Emirates," *Public Relations Review* (Spring 1995): 59.

14. Fraser P. Seitel, "Relevance: The Key to Success in Public Relations." Address before ISDP: Communications Management Program, Syracuse University, August 20, 1995.

Suggested Readings

A Port of Entry: Public Relations Education for the 21st Century. New York: Public Relations Society of America. The Report of the Commission of Public Relations Education.

Basye, Dale. "Why Is PR a Dumping Ground?" *Across the Board* (September 1994): 48–49.

Brody, E. W. *Communication Tomorrow: New Audiences, New Technologies.* Westport, CT: Praeger, 1990.

Brody, E. W., ed. *New Technology and Public Relations: On to the Future.* Sarasota, FL: Institute for Public Relations and Education, 1992.

Careers in Public Relations. (Available from the Public Relations Society of America, 33 Irving Place, New York, NY 10003.)

Cavusgil, Tamer, and Michael R. Czinkota. *International Perspective on Trade Promotion and Assistance.* Westport, CT: Greenwood Press, 1990.

Design for Public Relations Education. (Available from the Public Relations Society of America, 33 Irving Place, New York, NY 10003.)

Drucker, Peter F. *Managing for the Future: The 1990s and Beyond.* New York: Plume, 1993.

European Public Affairs Directory, 1993, 3rd ed. Bristol, PA: International Publications Services, 1993.

Futurist. (Available from World Future Society, 4916 St. Elmo Ave., Washington, D.C. 20014.) This bimonthly journal includes forecasts, trends, and ideas about the future on all topics.

Gates, Bill. *The Road Ahead.* New York: Viking, 1996. The guru of cyberspace gurus describes his vision of the future in which all of us will live (if we make it).

Grates, Gary F. "Seeing Through New Eyes . . . A View on Optimizing the Future." *Public Relations Quarterly* (Summer 1998): 5ff.

Guiniven, John E. "The Golden Age: As PR Programs Grow, More Cooperation Needed Between Practitioners and Teachers." *Public Relations Tactics* (August 1998): 1.

Gustafson, Robert. "Ten Ways You Can Improve Education in Marketing Communications." *Public Relations Quarterly* (Winter 1997–98): 2–27.

International Directory of Business Information Sources and Services, 2nd ed. Chicago: Europa Press, 1996.

Kruckeberg, Dean. "The Future of PR Education: Some Recommendations." *Public Relations Review* (Summer 1998): 235ff.

Mintu-Wimsatt, Alma, and Hector R. Lozada, eds. *Green Marketing in a Unified Europe.* Binghamton, NY: The Haworth Press, 1996. This book gives public relations professionals insights into the opportunities for positioning in an environmentally aware Europe.

Naisbitt, John, and Patricia Aburdene. *Megatrends 2000.* New York: William Morrow, 1990.

Pyle, Jack. "Strategy for the Millennium: Communicating Face-to-Face." *Public Relations Strategist* (Fall 1998): 47–48.

Sparks, Suzanne D., and Patrice Conwell. "Teaching Public Relations—Does Practice or Theory Prepare Practitioners?" *Public Relations Quarterly* (Spring 1998): 41 ff.

Taylor, Jim, and Watts Wacker. *The 500-Year Delta.* New York: HarperBusiness, 1996. The language of the millennium, say the authors, will begin with "re"—reengineering, reclamation, reintermediation, etc., rather than the "dis" that characterized the 1990s.

Thomsen, Steven R. "Public Relations in the New Millennium: Understanding the Forces That Are Reshaping the Profession." *Public Relations Quarterly* (Spring 1997): 11–17.

top of the shelf

Gerald Celente

Trends 2000: How to Prepare for and Profit from the Changes of the 21st Century. New York: Warner Books, 1998.

Here's what some of the biggies say about Gerald Celente and his Trends Research Institute:

- "Those who take predictions seriously might consider The Trends Research Institute."—*Wall Street Journal*
- "The *Standard and Poor's* of Popular Culture."—*Los Angeles Times*
- "Gerald Celente is the best trend forecaster in the business."—*Psychology Today*

Here's what Celente has to say about the coming years: "It's not all doom and gloom. The new millennium is a time of profound transformation—an old order is dying and a new order is taking root. When the chaos clears and the dust settles, it will be a time for a Renaissance—an era of unprecedented artistic, intellectual, philosophical, and scientific achievement."

This from the fellow who predicted the October 1987 stock market crash—in 1986 and the length and depth of the 1990 U.S. recession—in 1988.

Although published in 1998, *Trends 2000* was on the *Wall Street Journal*'s Best Selling Business Books list at the close of 1999. Enlighten yourself, and amaze your friends, read *Trends 2000*.

CASE STUDY

Public Relations Hero of the 20th Century

And the winner is neither man nor woman nor beast for that matter.

None of the above. It's a machine. Not just any machine, mind you. But rather, Deep Blue.

Anybody who doubts the power of public relations in the new technological society evidently never heard of Deep Blue (Figure 20-5).

Deep Blue was IBM's 6-foot, 5-inch, 1.4-ton supercomputer, which took on 5-foot, 10-inch, 176-pound world chess champion Garry Kasparov. Deep Blue's chess playing program was designed by a special IBM team, which included research scientists, engineers, and one chess grand master. By joining special purpose hardware and software with general purpose parallel computing, the team developed a system with a brute force computing speed capable of examining 200 million moves per second—or 50 billion positions in the three minutes allocated for a single move in a chess game.

More than 250 journalists from around the world flocked to New York City in May of 1997 to view the historic showdown between "man and machine." After a bitter struggle, Kasparov threw in the towel, surrendering to the stoic IBM computer. In a blaze of worldwide, front-page publicity, Deep Blue had vanquished archrival Kasparov (Figure 20-6).

FIGURE 20-5 **The winner.** Deep Blue, the world chess—and publicity—champion.

FIGURE 20-6 **The loser.** Russian chess champ Garry Kasparov proved no match for IBM's chess-loving, publicity-generating machine.

The event constituted one of the most extensive publicity barrages in history. More than two billion media impressions were generated by the match—most of the publicity prominently played in worldwide media.

After the match, IBM dedicated the system to solve other complex problems, such as pharmaceutical drug design, financial analysis, and decision support. But a deeply disappointed Kasparov insisted on a rematch with another IBM chess computer. One had to believe that IBM would consider the defeated champ's request, especially in light of all that positive publicity.

If it was any consolation to Kasparov, he probably didn't feel half as badly as the people at Microsoft, Dell, Intel, and Compaq, who also could have produced, but didn't, the internationally renowned supercomputer.

Questions

1. What do you think IBM hoped to prove with its Deep Blue contest? What were its corporate objectives?
2. What would you have advised IBM to say if Deep Blue lost the match?
3. Either way, do you think IBM would have come out the winner? (HINT: You betchy!)
4. Learn more about Deep Blue and the big chess battle on an IBM site (www.research.ibm.com/deepblue/). Why would IBM keep this information on the Internet years after the match?

OVER THE TOP

An Interview with Peter Drucker

FIGURE 20-7 **The great professor.** The eminent Dr. Drucker and a less eminent friend.

Peter Drucker, called "the greatest thinker management theory has produced" by the *London Economist,* has written 29 books, which have been translated into nearly every language in the world; counseled presidents, bishops, baseball managers, CEOs, and symphony conductors on the finer points of management success; and, in his eighth decade, continued to write, lecture, and teach regularly at Claremont College in California.

What would you say have been your greatest contributions to business and society?
One, I made management visible. People say I've discovered management—that's nonsense. I made it into a discipline.

I was also the first one who said that people are a resource and not just a cost, and they have to be placed where they can make a contribution. The only ones who took me up on it were the Japanese for a long time.

The third one is knowledge—that knowledge work would be preeminent.

Four, I was the first to say that the purpose of business is to create the customer and to innovate. That I think is a major contribution. That took a long time to sink in—that management is not this mad dog of internal rules and regulations, that it's a discipline that can be learned and taught and practiced.

I think those four. The rest are secondary.

What is your view of today's public relations practice?
There is no public relations. There's publicity, promotion, advertising, but "relations" by definition are a two-way street. And the more important job and the more difficult is not to bring business and the executives to the outside but to bring the outside to these terribly insulated people. And this will be far more important in the next 20 years, when the outside is going to change beyond all recognition. I'm

not only talking business CEOs, but also university presidents, bishops—several of my charity patients are bishops—all need to know what's going on outside.

Can you elaborate?

With an example. Have you ever heard of Paul Garrett? Paul Garrett came out of journalism. He wanted to build a proper public relations department, to bring to General Motors what the outside was like. He would have been very effective. But GM didn't let him. Alfred Sloan (GM's CEO) brought Garrett in 1930 to keep GM out of *Fortune*. *Fortune* was founded as a muckraking magazine with investigative journalism.

Why didn't Sloan, supposedly one of the greatest managers of all time, want to listen to Garrett?

Neither Sloan nor anybody else in top management of General Motors wanted to hear what Garrett would have told them. And this was still the case much later. Paul Garrett was a professional, who would have told them things they didn't want to hear and wouldn't believe. Killing the messenger is never the right policy.

And in GM's case, the employee relations people totally failed to warn the company of the horrible sitdown strike they would suffer. And then when investor relations became important, it wasn't assigned to the public relations people.

And to this day, most institutions still look upon public relations as their "trumpet" and not as their "hearing aid." It's got to be both.

What do you see as the future of the practice of public relations?

I think there is a need. It is a very complicated and complex function. The media are no longer homogenous and much more critical. But there is a need for an intermediary to tell the truth to management. Public relations people today don't do that because they're scared, because the people they work for don't like to hear what they don't want to hear. Let's face it. There's an old saying, "If I have you for a friend, I don't need an enemy."

APPENDIX A

Code of Professional Standards for the Practice of Public Relations

Public Relations Society of America

This code was adopted by the Assembly of the Public Relations Society of America (PRSA) in 1988. It replaces a Code of Ethics in force since 1950 and revised in 1954, 1959, 1963, 1977, and 1983.

On November 12, 1988, PRSA's Assembly approved a revision of the Society's code for the following reasons:

1. To make the language clearer and more understandable—hence easier to apply and to follow.

   As Elias "Buck" Buchwald, APR, chairman of the Board of Ethics and Professional Standards, explained to the Assembly, the revision introduced no substantive changes to the code; it merely clarified and strengthened the language.

2. To help advance the unification of the public relations profession—part of PRSA's mission.

   The PRSA code's revision was based on the Code of the North American Public Relations Council, an organization of 13-member groups, including PRSA. Eight of the 13 have now revised their own codes in accordance with the NAPRC code—an important step toward unification.

   Code interpretations, as published on pages 17–20 of the 1988–1989 Register, remain in effect. However, the Board of Ethics and Professional Standards is in the process of revising and updating them.

Declaration of Principles

Members of the Public Relations Society of America base their professional principles on the fundamental value and dignity of the individual, holding that the free exercise of human rights, especially freedom of speech, freedom of assembly, and freedom of the press, is essential to the practice of public relations.

In serving the interests of clients and employers, we dedicate ourselves to the goals of better communication, understanding, and cooperation among the diverse individuals, groups, and institutions of society, and of equal opportunity of employment in the public relations profession.

We pledge:

To conduct ourselves professionally, with truth, accuracy, fairness, and responsibility to the public;

To improve our individual competence and advance the knowledge and proficiency of the profession through continuing research and education;

And to adhere to the articles of the Code of Professional Standards for the Practice of Public Relations as adopted by the governing Assembly of the Society.

Code of Professional Standards for the Practice of Public Relations

These articles have been adopted by the Public Relations Society of America to promote and maintain high standards of public service and ethical conduct among its members.

1. A member shall conduct his or her professional life in accord with the public interest.

2. A member shall exemplify high standards of honesty and integrity while carrying out dual obligations to a client or employer and to the democratic process.

3. A member shall deal fairly with the public, with past or present clients or employers, and with fellow practitioners, giving due respect to the ideal of free inquiry and to the opinions of others.

4. A member shall adhere to the highest standards of accuracy and truth, avoiding extravagant claims or unfair comparisons and giving credit for ideas and words borrowed from others.

5. A member shall not knowingly disseminate false or misleading information and shall act promptly to correct erroneous communications for which he or she is responsible.

6. A member shall not engage in any practice which has the purpose of corrupting the integrity of channels of communications or the processes of government.

7. A member shall be prepared to identify publicly the name of the client or employer on whose behalf any public communication is made.

8. A member shall not use any individual or organization professing to serve or represent an announced cause, or professing to be independent or unbiased, but actually serving another or undisclosed interest.

9. A member shall not guarantee the achievement of specified results beyond the member's direct control.

10. A member shall not represent conflicting or competing interests without the express consent of those concerned, given after a full disclosure of the facts.

11. A member shall not place himself or herself in a position where the member's personal interest is or may be in conflict with an obligation to an employer or client, or others, without full disclosure of such interests to all involved.

12. A member shall not accept fees, commissions, gifts, or any other consideration from anyone except clients or employers for whom services are performed without their express consent, given after full disclosure of the facts.

13. A member shall scrupulously safeguard the confidences and privacy rights of present, former, and prospective clients or employers.

14. A member shall not intentionally damage the professional reputation or practice of another practitioner.

15. If a member has evidence that another member has been guilty of unethical, illegal, or unfair practices, including those in violation of this Code, the member is obligated to present the information promptly to the proper authorities of the Society for action in accordance with the procedure set forth in Article XII of the Bylaws.

16. A member called as a witness in a proceeding for enforcement of this Code is obligated to appear, unless excused for sufficient reason by the judicial panel.

17. A member shall, as soon as possible, sever relations with any organization or individual if such relationship requires conduct contrary to the articles of this Code.

INTERNATIONAL CODE OF ETHICS
Code of Athens

English Version
adopted by IPRA General Assembly at Athens on 12 May 1965
and modified at Tehran on 17 April 1968

CONSIDERING that all Member countries of the United Nations Organization have agreed to abide by its Charter which reaffirms "its faith in fundamental human rights, in the dignity and worth of the human person" and that having regard to the very nature of their profession, Public Relations practitioners in these countries should undertake to ascertain and observe the principles set out in this Charter;

CONSIDERING that, apart from "rights", human beings have not only physical or material needs but also intellectual, moral and social needs, and that their rights are of real benefit to them only in so far as these needs are essentially met;

CONSIDERING that, in the course of their professional duties and depending on how these duties are performed, Public Relations practitioners can substantially help to meet these intellectual, moral and social needs;

And lastly, CONSIDERING that the use of techniques enabling them to come simultaneously into contact with millions of people gives Public Relations practitioners a power that has to be restrained by the observance of a strict moral code.

On all these grounds, the undersigned Public Relations Associations hereby declare that they accept as their moral charter the principles of the following Code of Ethics, and that if, in the light of evidence submitted to the Council, a member of these associations should be found to have infringed this Code in the course of his professional duties, he will be deemed to be guilty of serious misconduct calling for an appropriate penalty.

Accordingly, each Member of these Associations:

SHALL ENDEAVOUR

1. To contribute to the achievement of the moral and cultural conditions enabling human beings to reach their full stature and enjoy the indefeasible rights to which they are entitled under the "Universal Declaration of Human Rights";

2. To establish communication patterns and channels which, by fostering the free flow of essential information, will make each member of the society in which he lives feel that he is being kept informed, and also give him an awareness of his own personal involvement and responsibility, and of his solidarity with other members;

3. To bear in mind that, because of the relationship between his profession and the public, his conduct—even in private—will have an impact on the way in which the profession as a whole is appraised;

4. To respect, in the course of his professional duties, the moral principles and rules of the "Universal Declaration of Human Rights";

5. To pay due regard to, and uphold, human dignity, and to recognise the right of each individual to judge for himself;

6. To encourage the moral, psychological and intellectual conditions for dialogue in its true sense, and to recognise the right of the parties involved to state their case and express their views;

SHALL UNDERTAKE

7. To conduct himself always and in all circumstances in such a manner as to deserve and secure the confidence of those with whom he comes into contact;

8. To act, in all circumstances, in such a manner as to take account of the respective interests of the parties involved; both the interests of the organisation which he serves and the interests of the publics concerned;

9. To carry out his duties with integrity, avoiding language likely to lead to ambiguity or misunderstanding, and to maintain loyalty to his clients or employers, whether past or present.

SHALL REFRAIN FROM

10. Subordinating the truth to other requirements;

11. Circulating information which is not based on established and ascertainable facts;

12. Taking part in any venture or undertaking which is unethical or dishonest or capable of impairing human dignity and integrity;

13. Using any "manipulative" methods or techniques designed to create subconscious motivations which the individual cannot control of his own free will and so cannot be held accountable for the action taken on them.

APPENDIX B

Advertising Effectiveness Tracking Study

Contemporary Marketing Research Inc. 6-1-107
1270 Broadway February 1999
New York, NY 10001

ADVERTISING EFFECTIVENESS TRACKING STUDY CARD 1
MAIN QUESTIONNAIRE (11-17Z)

RESPONDENT'S NAME: —————————————————————

1a. Today I am interested in obtaining your opinions of financial institutions. To begin with, I'd like you to tell me the names of all the financial institutions you have heard of. (DO NOT READ LIST. RECORD FIRST INSTITUTION MENTIONED SEPARATELY FROM ALL OTHERS UNDER "FIRST MENTION.") (PROBE:) Any others? (RECORD BELOW UNDER "OTHERS.")

1b. Now, thinking only of <u>banks</u> in the New York area, what (other) banks have you heard of (RECORD BELOW UNDER "OTHERS.")

2. And what financial institutions, including banks, have you seen or heard advertised within the past 3 months? (DO NOT READ LIST. RECORD BELOW UNDER Q.2.)

3. FOR EACH ASTERISKED INSTITUTION LISTED BELOW AND NOT MENTIONED IN Q.1a/1b OR Q.2, ASK:

Have you ever heard of (NAME)? (RECORD BELOW UNDER Q.3.)

4. FOR EACH ASTERISKED INSTITUTION CIRCLED IN Q.1a/1b OR Q.3 AND NOT CIRCLED IN Q.2, ASK:

Have you seen or heard advertising for (NAME) within the past 3 months? (RECORD BELOW UNDER Q.4.)

	Q. 1a/1b		Q.2	Q.3	Q.4
	AWARE OF FIRST MENTION (18) (21)	AWARE OTHERS (24)	OF ADVTG.	AWARE ADVTG. (AIDED)	AWARE (AIDED)
Anchor Savings Bank	1	1	1		
Apple Savings Bank	2	2	2		
Astoria Federal Savings	3	3	3		
Bank of Commerce	4	4	4		
Bank of New York	5	5	5		
Bankers Trust	6	6	6		
Barclays Bank	7	7	7		
Bowery Savings Bank	8	8	8		
*Chase Manhattan Bank	9	9	9	9 (27)	9 (29)
*Chemical Bank	0	0	0	0	0
*Citibank	X	X	X	X	X
Crossland Savings Bank	Y	Y	Y		
*Dean Witter	1 (19)	1 (22)	1 (25)	1 (28)	1 (30)
Dime Savings Bank	2	2	2		

496

	Q. 1a/1b AWARE OF FIRST MENTION (18)	AWARE OTHERS (21)	Q.2 OF ADVTG. (24)	Q.3 AWARE ADVTG. (AIDED)	Q.4 AWARE (AIDED)
Dollar Dry Dock Savings Bank	3	3	3		
*Dreyfus	4	4	4	4	4
Emigrant Savings Bank	5	5	5		
European American Bank	6	6	6		
Fidelity	7	7	7		
Goldome Savings Bank	8	8	8		
*Manufacturer's Hanover Trust	9	9	9	9	9
*Marine Midland Bank	0	0	0	0	0
*Merrill Lynch	X	X	X	X	X
*National Westminster Bank	Y	Y	Y	Y	Y
Prudential Bache	1 (20)	1 (23)	1 (26)		
Shearson-Lehman	2	2	2		
Other (SPECIFY):					
_____	X	X	X		
_____					
_____					

REFER BACK TO Q.2 AND 4. IF RESPONDENT IS AWARE OF ADVERTISING FOR
CHASE MANHATTAN BANK IN Q.2 OR Q.4, ASK Q.5a. OTHERWISE, SKIP TO Q.6.

5a. Today we are asking different people about different banks. In your case, we'd like to
talk about Chase Manhattan Bank. You just mentioned that you remember seeing or
hearing advertising for Chase Manhattan Bank. Please tell me everything you remember seeing or hearing in the advertising. (PROBE FOR SPECIFICS) What else?

_____ (31)

_____ (32)

_____ (33)

_____ (34)

_____ (35)

5b. And where did you see or hear advertising for Chase Manhattan Bank? (Do <u>NOT</u>
READ LIST) (MORE THAN ONE ANSWER MAY BE GIVEN)

	(36)
Television	1
Radio	2
Newspaper	3
Magazine	4
Billboard	5
Other (SPECIFY): _____	X

6. Different banks use different slogans. (START WITH THE X'D QUESTION BELOW AND CONTINUE UNTIL ALL FOUR QUESTIONS (Q.6a-6d) HAVE BEEN ASKED.)

<u>START</u>:

(√) 6a. What slogan or statement do you associate with Chase Manhattan Bank? (DO <u>NOT</u> READ LIST)

(37)

Chase. The Experience Shows	1
You Have a Friend at Chase	2
Ideas You Can Bank On	3
The Chase Is On	4
Other (SPECIFY) _____	X
_____	

( ) 6b. What slogan does Chemical Bank use? (DO <u>NOT</u> READ LIST)

(38)

The Chemistry's Just Right at Chemical	1
Other (SPECIFY) _____X	

(√) 6c .What slogan or statement do you associate with Citibank? (DO <u>NOT</u> READ LIST)

(39)

It's Your Citi	1
The Citi Never Sleeps	2
Other (SPECIFY)_____X	

( ) 6d. What slogan does Manufacturer's Hanover Trust use? (DO <u>NOT</u> READ LIST)

(40)

The Financial Source. Worldwide	1
We Realize Your Potential	2
Other (SPECIFY)_____	X

7. Now, I'd like to know how likely you yourself are to consider banking at several different banks in the future. For each bank I read, please tell me whether you would definitely consider banking there, probably consider banking there, might or might not consider banking there, probably not consider banking there, or definitely not consider banking there in the future. Now, how likely are you to consider banking at (READ X'D BANK) in the future? (REPEAT SCALE IF NECESSARY. OBTAIN A RATING FOR EACH BANK.)

	START: ( ) CHASE MANHATTAN BANK	( ) CHEMICAL BANK	( ) CITIBANK	(√) MANUFACTURER'S HANOVER TRUST
Definitely Consider Banking There	5 (41)	5 (42)	5 (43)	5 (44)
Probably Consider Banking There	4	4	4	4
Might Or Might Not Consider Banking There	3	3	3	3
Probably Not Consider Banking There	2	2	2	2
Definitely Not Consider Banking There	1	1	1	1
(DO <u>NOT</u> READ) l (Currently Bank There)	X	X	X	X

(45-1)

8a. Now, I'd like you to rate one bank on a series of statements—<u>Chase Manhattan Bank</u>. If you have never banked there, please base your answers on what you know about this bank and your perceptions of it. After I read each statement, please tell me whether you agree completely, agree somewhat, neither agree nor disagree, disagree somewhat, or disagree completely that this statement describes <u>Chase Manhattan Bank</u>. (START WITH X'D STATEMENT AND CONTINUE UNTIL ALL ARE RATED.)

START HERE:	AGREE COM- PLETELY	AGREE SOME- WHAT	NEITHER AGREE NOR DIS- AGREE	DIS- AGREE SOME- WHAT	DIS- AGREE COM- PLETELY
[ ] Is Responsive to Your Needs	5	4	3	2	1 (46)
[ ] Offers High Quality Accounts and Services	5	4	3	2	1 (47)
[ ] Deals With Its Customers on a Personalized Level	5	4	3	2	1 (48)
[ ] Helps Make Banking Easier	5	4	3	2	1 (49)
[ ] Has Bank Personnel That Are Concerned About You	5	4	3	2	1 (50)
[ ] Designs Accounts to Meet Your Special Needs	5	4	3	2	1 (51)
[ ] Is Responsive to Community Needs	5	4	3	2	1 (52)
[ ] Makes It Easy to Open an IRA Account	5	4	3	2	1 (53)
[ ] Has a Full Range of Banking and Investment Services	5	4	3	2	1 (54)
[ ] Is a Bank Where You Want to Have Most of Your Accounts	5	4	3	2	1 (55)

START HERE:	AGREE COM- PLETELY	AGREE SOME- WHAT	NEITHER AGREE NOR DIS- AGREE	DIS- AGREE SOME- WHAT	DIS- AGREE COM- PLETELY
[ ] Has Bank Personnel That Are Experienced	5	4	3	2	1 (56)
[ ] Has Innovative Accounts and Services	5	4	3	2	1 (57)
[ ] Understands Your Banking Needs	5	4	3	2	1 (58)
[ ] Has Branches That Are Pleasant to Bank In	5	4	3	2	1 (59)
[ ] Has Accounts to Help People Just Starting Out	5	4	3	2	1 (60)
[ ] Continuously Develops Services to Meet Your Needs	5	4	3	2	1 (61)
[ ] Has Bank Personnel That Are Friendly and Courteous	5	4	3	2	1 (62)
[ ] Has Accounts and Services That Are Right for You	5	4	3	2	1 (63)
[√] Puts Customers' Needs First	5	4	3	2	1 (64)
[ ] Is a Modern, Up-to-Date Bank	5	4	3	2	1 (65)

END CARD 1

APPENDIX C

Definitions of Selected Terms Used in Public Relations Evaluation

Advertising Equivalency—A means of converting editorial space in the media into advertising costs, by measuring the amount of editorial coverage and then calculating what it would have cost to buy that space, if it had been advertising. Most reputable researchers contend that advertising equivalency computations are of questionable validity, since in many cases the opportunity to "buy" advertising in space that has been specifically allocated to editorial coverage simply does not exist.

Attitude Research—Consists of measuring and interpreting the full range of views, sentiments, feelings, opinions, and beliefs that segments of the public may hold toward given people, products, organizations and/or issues. More specifically, attitude research measures what people say (their verbal expressions), what they know and think (their mental or cognitive predispositions), what they feel (their emotions), and how they're inclined to act (their motivational or drive tendencies).

Bivariate Analysis—Examination of the relationship between two variables.

Causal Relationship—A theoretical notion that change in one variable forces, produces, or brings about a change in another.

Circulation—Refers to the number of copies sold of a given edition of a publication, at a given time, or as averaged over a period of time.

Communications Audit—A systematic review and analysis—using accepted research techniques and methodologies—of how well an organization communicates with all of its major internal and external target audience groups.

Confidence Interval—In a survey based on a random sample, the range of values within which a population parameter is estimated to fall. For example, in a survey in which a representative sample of 1,000 individuals is interviewed, if 55% express a preference for a given item, we might say that in the population as a whole, in 95 out of 100 cases, the true pro-portion expressing such a preference probably would fall between 52% and 58%. The plus or minus 3% range is called the *confidence interval*. The fact that we are using 95 out of 100 cases as our guide (or 95%) is our *confidence level*.

Content Analysis—The process of studying and tracking what has been written and broadcast and translating this qualitative material into quantitative form through some type of counting approach that involves coding and classifying of specific messages.

Correlation—Any association or relationship between two variables.

Correlation Coefficient—A measure of association (symbolized as r) that describes the direction and strength of a linear relationship between two variables, measured at the interval or ratio level (e.g. Pearson's Correlation Coefficient).

Cost Per Thousand (CPM)—The cost of advertising for each 1,000 homes reached by radio or television, for each 1,000 copies of a publication, or for each 1,000 potential viewers of an outdoor advertisement.

Cross-Sectional Study—A study based on observation representing a single point in time.

Demographic Analysis—Consists of looking at the population in terms of special social, political, economic, and geographic subgroups, such as a person's age, sex, income-level, race, education-level, place of residence, or occupation.

Ethnographic Research—Relies on the tools and techniques of cultural anthropologists and sociologists to obtain a better understanding of how individuals and groups function in their natural settings. Usually, this type of research is carried out by a team of impartial, trained researchers who "immerse" themselves into the daily routine of a neighborhood or community, using a mix of observation, participation, and role-playing techniques, in an effort to try to assess what is really happening from a "cultural" perspective.

Evaluation Research—Determines the relative effectiveness of a public relations program or strategy, measuring outputs and outcomes against a predetermined set of objectives.

Experiment—Any controlled arrangement and manipulation of conditions to systematically observe specific occurrences, with the intention of defining those criteria that might possibly be affecting those occurrences. An experimental, or quasi-experimental, research design usually involves two groups—a "test" group which is exposed to given criteria, and a "control" group, which is not exposed. Comparisons are then made to determine what effect, if any, exposures to the criteria have had on those in the "test" group.

Factor Analysis—A complex algebraic procedure that seeks to group or combine items or variables in a questionnaire based on how they naturally relate to each other, or "hang together," as general descriptors (or "factors").

Focus Group—An exploratory technique in which a group of somewhere between 8 and 12 individuals—under the guidance of a trained moderator—are encouraged, as a group, to discuss freely any and all of their feelings, concerns, problems, and frustrations relating to specific topics under discussion. Focus groups are ideal for brainstorming, idea-gathering, and concept testing.

Frequency—The number of advertisements, broadcasts, or exposures of given programming or messaging during a particular period of time.

Gross Rating Point—A unit of measurement of broadcast or outdoor advertising audience size, equal to 1% of the total potential audience universe; used to measure the exposure of one or more programs or commercials, without regard to multiple exposure of the same advertising to individuals. A GRP is the product of media reach times exposure frequency. A *gross-rating-point buy* is the number of advertisements necessary to obtain the desired percentage of exposure of the message. In outdoor advertising, GRPs, often used as a synonym for showing, generally refer to the daily effective circulation generated by poster panels, divided by market population. The *cost per gross rating point* (CPGRP) is a measure of broadcast media exposure comparable to the *cost per thousand* (CPM) measure of print media.

Hypothesis—An expectation about the nature of things derived from theory.

Hypothesis-Testing—Determining whether the expectations that a hypothesis represents are, indeed, found in the real world.

Impressions—The number of those who might have had the opportunity to be exposed to a story that has appeared in the media. Sometimes referred to as "opportunity to see." An "impression" usually refers to the total audited circulation of a publication or the audience reach of a broadcast vehicle.

Incidence—The frequency with which a condition or event occurs within a given time and population.

Inquiry Study—A systematic review and analysis, using content analysis or sometimes telephone and mail interviewing techniques, to study the range and types of unsolicited inquires that an organization may receive from customers, prospective customers or other target audience groups.

Judgmental Sample—A type of nonprobability sample in which individuals are deliberately selected for inclusion in the sample by the researcher because they have special knowledge, position, characteristics or represent other relevant dimensions of the population that are deemed important to study. Also known as a "purposive" sample.

Likert Scale—Developed by Rensis Likert, this is a composite measure in which respondents are asked to choose from an ordered series of five responses to indicate their reactions to a sequence of statements (e.g., strongly agree . . . somewhat agree . . . neither agree nor disagree . . . somewhat disagree . . . strongly disagree).

Longitudinal Study—A research design involving the collection of data at different points in time.

Mall Intercept—A special type of in-person interview, in which potential respondents are approached as they stroll through shopping centers or malls. Most mall intercept interviews are based on nonprobability sampling.

Market Research—Any systematic study of buying and selling behavior.

Mean—A measure of central tendency that is the arithmetic average of the scores.

Median—A measure of central tendency indicating the midpoint in a series of scores, the point above and below which 50% of the values fall.

Mode—A measure of central tendency that is the most frequently occurring, the most typical, value in a series.

Multivariate Analysis—Examination of the relationship among three or more variables.

Omnibus Survey—An "all-purpose" national consumer poll usually conducted on a regular schedule—

once a week or every other week—by major market research firms. Organizations are encouraged to "buy" one or several proprietary questions and have them "added" to the basic questionnaire. Those adding questions are usually charged on a per-question basis. Also, sometimes referred to as "piggyback" or "shared-cost" surveys.

Panel Study—(1) A type of longitudinal study in which the same individuals are interviewed more than once over a period of time to investigate the processes of response change, usually in reference to the same topic or issue. (2) Also, a type of study in which a group of individuals are deliberately recruited by a research firm, because of their special demographic characteristics, for the express purpose of being interviewed more than once over a period of time for various clients on a broad array of different topics or subjects.

Probability Sample—A process of random selection in which each unit in a population has an equal chance of being included in the sample.

Psychographic Analysis—Consists of looking at the population in terms of people's nondemographic traits and characteristics, such as a person's personality type, life style, social roles, values and beliefs.

Q-Sort—A personality inventory introduced in the 1950s in which respondents are asked to sort opinion statements along a "most-like-me" to "most-unlike-me" continuum. Q-Sorting allows researchers to construct models of individual respondents' belief systems.

Qualitative Research—Usually refers to studies that are somewhat subjective, but nevertheless in-depth, using a probing, open-end, free-response format.

Quantitative Research—Usually refers to studies that are highly objective and projectable, using closed-end, forced-choice questionnaires. These studies tend to rely heavily on statistics and numerical measures.

Quota Sample—A type of nonprobability sample in which individuals are selected on the basis of prespecified characteristics, so that the total sample will have the same general distribution of characteristics as are assumed to exist in the population being studied.

Range—A measure of variability that is computed by subtracting the lowest score in a distribution from the highest score.

Reach—Refers to the range or scope of influence or effect that a given communications vehicle has on tar-

geted audience groups. In broadcasting, it is the net unduplicated radio or TV audience—the number of different individuals or households—for programs or commercials as measured for a specific time period in quarter-hour units over a period of 1 to 4 weeks.

Regression Analysis—A statistical technique for studying relationships among variables, measured at the interval or ratio level.

Reliability—The extent to which the results would be consistent, or replicable, if the research were conducted a number of times.

Screener Question—One or several questions usually asked in the beginning of an interview to determine if the potential respondent is eligible to participate in the study.

Secondary Analysis—A technique for extracting from previously conducted studies new knowledge on topics other than those that were the focus of the original studies. It does this through a systematic re-analysis of a vast array of already-existing research data.

Situation Analysis—An impartial, often third-party assessment of the public relations and/or public affairs problems, or opportunities, that an organization may be facing at a given point in time.

Standard Deviation—An index of variability of a distribution. More precisely, it is the range from the mean within which approximately 34% of the cases fall, provided the values are distributed in a normal curve.

Statistical Significance—Refers to the unlikeliness that relationships observed in a sample could be attributed to sampling error alone.

Survey—Any systematic collection of data that uses a questionnaire and a recognized sampling method. There are three basic types of surveys: those conducted *face-to-face* (in-person) . . . those conducted by *telephone* . . . and those that are *self-administered* (usually distributed by mail, e-mail, or fax).

Univariate Analysis—The examination of only one variable at a time.

Validity—The extent to which a research project measures what it is intended, or purports, to measure.

Variance—A measure of the extent to which individual scores in a set differ from each other. More precisely, it is the sum of the squared deviations from the mean divided by the frequencies.

APPENDIX D

Audiovisual Supports

Material	Advantages	Limitations
Slide Series A form of projected audiovisual materials easy to prepare with any 35-mm camera	1. Prepared with any 35-mm camera for most uses 2. Requires only filming, with processing and mounting by film laboratory 3. Colorful, realistic reproductions of original subjects 4. Easily revised, updated, handled, stored, and rearranged 5. Can be combined with taped narration for greater effectiveness 6. May be played through remote control presentation	1. Requires some skill in photography 2. Requires special equipment for close-up photography and copying 3. Prone to get out of sequence and be projected incorrectly
Filmstrips Closely related to slides, but instead of being mounted as separate pictures, remain uncut as a continuous strip	1. Compact, easily handled, and always in proper sequence 2. Can be supplemented with captions or recordings 3. Inexpensive when quantity reproduction is required 4. Projected with simple, lightweight equipment 5. Projection rate controlled by presenter	1. Relatively difficult to prepare locally 2. Requires film laboratory service to convert slides to filmstrip form 3. In permanent sequence and therefore cannot be rearranged or revised
Overhead transparencies A popular form of locally prepared materials, requiring an overhead projector for presentation	1. Can present information in systematic, developmental sequences 2. Simple-to-operate projector with presentation rate controlled by presenter 3. Requires limited planning 4. Can be prepared by a variety of simple, inexpensive methods	1. Requires special equipment facilities, and skills for more advanced preparation methods 2. May be cumbersome and lack finesse of more remote processes

APPENDIX E

Defining Key Cyberspace Terms

Understanding the following words and phrases is essential to surviving in cuberspace.

Access—The means of getting into an online system. Different systems require different types of access. For instance, CompuServe access requires an account, a CompuServe access telephone number, a password, and (optionally) special software designed just for CompuServe; however, any old phone line and modem will do. Conversely, a direct Internet connection that provides you with access to the graphical version of the World Wide Web requires a special configuration for your computer called a TCP/IP stack in addition to an Internet access account.

Address—Where somebody can send mail or files to you at an online site. Depending on the type of service you use, the look of an address can vary a great deal. For example, my CompuServe address is ⟨76346,627⟩; my America Online address is ⟨She1H⟩, and my Internet address is ⟨shel@ccnet.com⟩.

ASCII—The American Standard Code for Information Exchange. These are the characters that you type on a computer keyboard. "Low" ASCII refers to those characters available on your keyboard only—Aa through Zz, 0–9, and several symbols: ~'@#$%∧&*()_ +|\{}[]:;"'⟨⟩,.?/. In UNIX applications, including "shell" Internet accounts, Lower ASCII is all there is. Upper ASCII refers to characters available through a combination of keystrokes on higher-level systems and applications, such as ®, ©, and õ.

Baud (or bauds per second or bps)— Refers to the rate of speed at which information travels from computer to computer and is related to the type of communication device you have. A 2400-bps modem sends and receives information at 2400 bauds per second, while a 28,800-bps modem works at more than ten times that speed. Other nonmodem connections (such as ISDN and T1) are much faster.

BBS—Bulletin Board System, an electronic version of the old bulletin boards on which people attached notices with thumb tacks. Generally includes a public message area, a section for the storage of files, live chat, e-mail (either limited to the system's boundaries

or connected to some larger e-mail system, including the Internet), and other features.

Browser—Software designed to allow you to "parse"—or view—documents created specifically for the Internet's World Wide Web. More recent browsers also allow you to access other Internet services, including gopher and FTP. The most popular browsers currently are Netscape and Mosaic.

Chat—Real-time online conversation conducted when two or more people type to one another. Services like America Online provide chat "rooms," while Internet Relay Chat (IRC) is the most notorious chat venue.

Client—A software application used to do something online. A piece of software that allows you to retrieve documents from an FTP site, for example, is an FTP client; one that allows you to search gopher sites is a gopher client.

Commercial Online Service—An online bulletin boardlike service that provides an array of services for a fee. Local dial-ups (a phone number in your area) is another feature of the commercial online services, which include CompuServe, America Online, Prodigy, eWorld, Transom, and Delphi.

Cyberspace—A term that refers to the unreal world in which information passes between computers. Originally coined by cyberpunk novelist William Gibson in his groundbreaking novel, *Neuromancer*, the term has become widely accepted as the geographical name for the place where online conversations, e-mail exchanges, flame wars, spam attacks, and information transfers occur.

Distributed—Computing that exceeds the bounds of a restricted hierarchy. The Internet is a "distributed" network because a message can be sent to any location (or number of locations) on the Internet, generally without limitation. It is its internationally distributed nature that makes the Internet a bit of an anarchy, difficult (make that impossible) to control or regulate.

Download—Move files from a remote computer to your own.

Electronic Newsletter—A newsletter distributed digitally from one computer to many other computers.

E-mail—Short for electronic mail. A message passed from one person to one or more other people via computer, generally using an e-mail program of one kind or another. These programs can reside on the user's computer, or on a "host" computer.

Extension—The last part of an IBM PC-compatible file name. In the file name ⟨program.exe⟩, ⟨exe⟩ is the extension.

FAQ—Frequently Asked Questions, lists of questions about a particular Usenet newsgroup and the newsgroup's particular topic. An FAQ from sci.agriculure.beekeeping would include information about the newsgroup, but also the fundamentals of beekeeping.

File—A single archive of information recognized as an information unit by a computer. A file may store a text document, a graphic image, an executable program that launches an application, a sound, a video, or some indecipherable collection of characters that only the computer understands but requires to execute some function. Most computer programs are comprised of many files.

Flame—An angry response to a posting, usually in a newsgroup.

Flame War—A flurry of flames generated from a single source, usually drawing in several newsgroup participants.

Forum—A gathering place based on a theme, specifically in CompuServe. There are professional forums, special interest forums (including the Public Relations and Marketing Forum), and hobby-oriented forums, where people can leave messages on a public notice area, contribute and download files, and chat.

FTP—File Transfer Protocol, one of the principal means by which you retrieve files from the Internet.

Gopher—A means of finding information on the Internet. Gopher was developed at the University of Minnesota (home of the Minnesota Golden Gophers). Computer systems store information in gopherspace so that people using Gopher software can easily find the information stored there.

Information Retrieval Service—Online services that search databases of information and return references to that information based on user queries. These services include Lexis-Nexis, Dialog, IQuest, and Dow Jones.

Internet—A vast system of computer networks connected together, allowing computers in one part of the world to instantly access computers in another. Used to send e-mail across various systems, to find information stored on various systems, and to engage in person-to-person and many-to-many exchanges.

LAN—Local Area Network, a small system of computers that are linked together by a "server." On a LAN, you can use an application (such as a word processor) that is resident on your own computer to read files that reside on the server, or you can actually run applications that reside on the server. Particularly handy for organizations that desire employees to share information.

Listserv—A program that allows you to maintain an e-mail-based mailing list.

Mailing List—Participants who subscribe to mailing lists receive all posts that are sent to the list. Say you subscribe to a list about people who hate the Los Angeles Rams. You might send a message to the list that asks, "Does anybody actually remember the name of any Rams quarterback?" Even though you only sent your message to one address—the list address—every subscriber would receive the message. If somebody responded, "Come to think of it, I can't think of a single one," everybody on the list would receive *that*, too. Simple commands allow you to cancel subscriptions and, in some cases, to take advantage of other list services, such as accessing files stored in the list archives.

Majordomo—A program that allows you to maintain an e-mail-based mailing list.

Network—Two or more computers linked together comprise a network.

Newsgroup—An area where people can discuss common topics by leaving postings, as on a bulletin board, that others can read when they log on. "Newsgroups" generally refer to discussions on Usenet, which most people access via the Internet. There are over 10,000 newsgroups with topics from journalism and media to mysticism, bondage, holocaust revisionism, gun control, cartoons, photography, horses—if people have an interest in it, there's probably a newsgroup where they get online to discuss it.

Online—Any situation when two computers are talking to each other.

Provider—An entity (university, association, corporation, or private business) that provides you with Internet access.

Service Provider—An organization or institution that provides access to the Internet for people like you.

UNIX—The original language developed by Bell Labs that allows computers of differing platforms to communicate with one another. UNIX is the infrastructure of the Internet. If you have a shell account, you will end up learning some very fundamental UNIX commands in order to get around.

Upload—To send a file from your computer to a remote system, such as a commercial online service, an Internet FTP site, or a BBS file storage area.

URL—Uniform Resource Locator, an address where stuff on the Internet is located.

Usenet—An international meeting place where people gather (but not in real time) to meet their friends, discuss events, keep up with trends, discuss politics or other issues, seek information, or just talk. Over 10,000 newsgroups exist on Usenet, which resides primarily on the Internet. You'll find discussions on engineering, environmental issues, television shows, college classes, O.J. Simpson, and any other subject about which more than one or two people have a passing interest.

Your Guide to Finding PR on the Web

ADI Press Track—http://www.presstrac.com Information about its news and media content analysis; company directory, a search mechanism and links.

Admark Corp—http://www.admarkcorp.com Information on Admark Corp.'s software packages.

Agenda Online—http://www.agendaonline.com Information about event planning including finding hotel rooms, best caterer, locating photographer.

American Association Of Advertising Agencies—http://www.commercepark.com/AAAA/ Information on membership benefits, legislative news, roster of members.

American College Media Directory—http://www.webcom.com/shambhu/acmd/welcome.html Describes the college media directory listing approximately 3,000 college newspapers, radio stations, and TV stations.

Association for Education in Journalism and Mass Communication—http://www.aejmc.sc.edu/online/home.html

Business Wire—http://www.hnt.com/bizwire Information about purchasing a location on site for distribution of releases, corporate profile, quarterly reports; create a virtual media kit.

Canadian Public Relations Society—http://www.cprs.ca Provides information about new services and upcoming events.

Cato Communications—http://www.sidcato.com Site is by publisher of monthly newsletter *Sid Cato's Newsletter on Annual Reports*.

Center for Corporate Community Relations at Boston College—http://www.bc.edu/bc_org/avp/acavp/cccr.

Direct Marketing Association—http://www.the-dma.org. Areas include Business Affairs, Newsstand, Research Observatory.

Delahaye Group—http://www.delahaye.com Devoted to communications measurement; offers case studies, tips, techniques for communications professionals.

Dryden Brown—http://www.dryden.co.uk This marcom firm helps organizations worldwide pinpoint suitable press event locations in major cities in UK and Ireland.

DWJ Television—http://www.dwjtv.com This broadcast PR firm provides a "clip of the week", daybook, client pages, news section as well as a digital media and broadcast report.

Editor & Publisher—http://www.mediainfo.com/edpub E&P provides online newspapers, lists of conferences centers, research, classifieds and a Web edition of the magazine.

Edgar Online—http://www.edgar-online.com Features up-to-the-minute listings of SEC EDGAR corporate filings.

Feature Photo—http://www.featurephoto.com Distributes color and black and white photos to the media, nationwide. Media can download images.

Institute For Crisis Management—http://www.crisis-mgmt.com Information about the center, events and publications.

Institute For Public Relations Research & Education—http://www.jou.ufl.edu/iprre/home-page.htm Information on the latest news, research projects, academic papers, a newsletter, seminars, awards, and competitions.

International Association of Business Communicators—http://www.iabc.com Information about the association, conferences, services, publications, products.

Investor Relations Network Services—http://www.irnetserv.com PR execs can put their company's annual report on this site; educational resources to PR professionals for investor relations.

Journalism Forum—http://www.jforum.org Online resource for journalists to discuss topics about news issues. PR execs also can post news releases on the site.

Luce Press Clippings—http://www.lucepress.com The first national clipping service on Web, has information about print, broadcast coverage, clipping analysis.

Market Place Media—http://www.marketmedia.com. Includes the Media Analysis Tool with access to 3,000-plus publications in four market segments (college, military, minorities, seniors)

Medialink—http://www.medialinkworldwide.com Medialink established a unique classroom on the web that provides video, video production, television station relations, ethical guidelines, and links to useful sites.

MediaMap—http://www.mediamap.com Database of media addresses, editorial opps.

Mediasource—http://www.mediasource.com Source for journalists, information on hundreds of subscriber companies. For a company will develop and promote homepage for you.

NAPS-NET—http://www.napsnet.com Features and graphics from more than 750 companies, associations, PR firms, and government information offices.

National Investor Relations Institute—http://www.niri.org Lists membership information, conferences, and other NIRI resources.

North American Network—http://www.radio-space.com/welcome.html Information on how to use sound files and scripts as well as lists of radio networks, stations, interviews, and news.

PiMS—http://www.pimsinc.com Information about distribution of press kits, media list development, broadcast faxing, and word processing as well as an e-mail book and news and notes.

PR Cybermall—http://www.prgenius.com An open market Web site with a forum section, ideas, publications, products, and research.

PR Newswire—http://www.prnewswire.com/cnoc.html Lets users read news from members, get financial insight from leading commentators.

ProfNet—http://www.vyne.com/profnet Site describes ProfNet, an e-mail, phone, and fax service linking journalists with experts; includes list of sources.

PR Watch—http://users.aol.com/srampton/center/html Information on abuses in public affairs, grassroots programs. Resource for counter-PR research services.

Public Relations Society of America—http://www.prsa.org The world's largest organization for public relations professionals provides information about membership, chapters, accreditation, seminars, and publications.

Southwest Newswire—http://www.swenewswire.com Information about its corporate profile, newsletter, wire services, news releases, headlines, Internet services, and listings.

U.S. Newswire—http://access.digex.net/~usnwire. Lists information about national newswire; including headlines from previous day's evening newscast.

Weick PhotodataBase—http://www.wieckphoto.com View photos in three databases: auto, corporate, and travel; links to various news wires and breaking business news images.

West Glen Communications—http://www.westglen.com Video news release production and distribution company.

APPENDIX F

On-Line Databases

Particularly important for public relations research are on-line databases, which store vast quantities of information on current and historical subjects. Some of the major service information vendors available to public relations practitioners are described here.

CD Plus Technologies
333 Seventh Avenue
4th Floor
New York, NY 10001

For over a decade, this service has supplied a large number of databases, with primary emphasis on medical, engineering, educational, and business-oriented information. Price structure varies according to the type of service selected. The Open Access Plan has an annual password fee of $80, a per connect-hour charge of between $10 and $139, depending on the service, and a telecommunications charge of about $12.

DIALCOM Services, Inc.
2560 N. First Street
P.O. Box 49019
San Jose, CA 95161-9019
800-872-7654

DIALCOM, begun in 1970, was purchased by MCI. It offers gateways to databases such as UPI, the Official Airline Guide, and the Bureau of National Affairs. It also offers gateway services to other on-line vendors, which enable customers to access databases offered on Dow Jones News/Retrieval Service, BRS, and DIALOG. The fee structure is based on the number of hours used, not the databases accessed. Costs for accessing the gateway services are based on the rates charged by other vendors. The service operates 24 hours a day, 7 days a week.

DIALOG Information Services, Inc.
Lockheed Corporation
3460 Hillview Avenue
Palo Alto, CA 94304
800-334-2564

DIALOG was started as a commercial venture in 1972 by the Lockheed Corporation. It is one of the largest on-line services, offering nearly 400 databases that range from business and economics to science and technology. DIALOG charges a $295 initiation fee, $100 of which can be applied to future use, and has a wide variation in connect-hour cost. Each database has a set hourly cost, ranging from $30 to $300. DIALOG is available 24 hours a day, 7 days a week.

Dow Jones News/Retrieval
P.O. Box 300
Princeton, NJ 08543
800-522-3567

This is part of Dow Jones and Company, publisher of *The Wall Street Journal*. More than 60 databases are offered, primarily relating to business and economics, financial and investment services, and general news and information. *The Wall Street Journal* is available in summary form as well as in its entirety. The fee structure for companies is complex. For individuals, costs start with a $29.95 sign-up fee and an $18 annual service fee that kicks in after the first year. Then fees range from $.50 to $2.85 per minute for prime time and from $0.08 to $0.60 per minute for nonprime time. The service is available 24 hours a day.

Facts on File
460 Park Avenue South
New York, NY 10016
212-683-2244

Facts on File summarizes information daily from leading U.S. and foreign periodicals, the publications of Commerce Clearing House, *Congressional Quarterly*, *Congressional Record*, *State Department Bulletin*, presidential documents, and official press releases. Subject areas are as diverse as the news of the day. The annual subscription fee is $680.

Find/SVP
625 Avenue of the Americas
New York, NY 10011
212-645-4500

Find/SVP provides quick consulting and research services by telephone for decision makers as a primary information resource to small and medium-sized companies and as a supplemental service to larger corporations that maintain in-house research and information centers. It has access to more than 3,000 on-line databases, 2,000 periodical subscriptions, tens of thousands of subject company and company files, hundreds of directories and reference works, dozens of cabinets of microfiche, and extensive CD-ROM sources. Its activities are organized into 10 consultant teams: (1) business/financial, (2) consumer products, (3) technical/industrial, (4) human resources/employee benefits, (5) document services, (6) accounting/tax, (7) legal, (8) health care, (9) society and media, and (10) PC help. Hourly rates range from $40 to $175, depending on the complexity of the request. Retainers of $500 to $1,500, plus out-of-pocket expenses, entitle unlimited use. Find/SVP promises that "in most cases, you'll have your answer in less than 48 hours from the time you call."

LEXIS and NEXIS
Mead Data Central
9443 Springboro Pike
P.O. Box 933
Dayton, OH 45401
800-227-4908

LEXIS and NEXIS are two of the information services provided by this division of Mead Corporation. LEXIS is a legal information database containing the full text of case law from state, federal, and international courts; state and federal regulations; and other legal records. NEXIS is a full-text database containing 750 major newspapers, magazines, and newsletters. In 1988, a group of media in the NEXIS databank was organized as the Advertising and Public Relations Library, including news wires and communications-oriented publications. The fee structure is complex, but the range of costs varies from $6 to $50 for the search and $35 per hour for connect charges. Both services are available 24 hours a day on weekdays and all weekend, except from 2 A.M. to 10 A.M. Sunday.

NewsNet, Inc.
945 Haverford Road
Bryn Mawr, PA 19010
800-345-1301

NewsNet was started in 1982 by Independent Publications. It offers primarily newsletters and wire services. There are more than 400 specialized business newsletters and wire services covering more than 35 industries, including telecommunications, publishing, broadcasting, electronics and computers, energy, investment, accounting, and taxation. Prices range from $24 to more than $100 an hour, depending on the newsletter being accessed. There is also a monthly minimum charge of $15. NewsNet is available 24 hours a day.

APPENDIX G

Leading Media Directories

When public relations professionals are asked which media directories they use most often, their answers are as varied as the tasks their firms perform. Publishers have carved such precise market niches for their wares that direct comparison of one directory to another is usually inappropriate. A comprehensive list of media directories begins on this page. Directories are listed by category and then alphabetically. Another list provides complete names and addresses of the publishers cited.

Directories

NEWSPAPERS

E&P International Yearbook. Annual list of U.S. and Canadian daily newspaper personnel and other data. $60. **Editor & Publisher.**

Family Page Directory. $60 for two editions printed at six-month intervals. Contains information about home, cooking, and family interest sections of newspapers. **Public Relations Plus.**

Media Alerts. Data on 200 major dailies as well as 1,900 magazines. $155. **Bacon's.**

National Directory of Community Newspapers. Listings on newspapers serving smaller communities. $35. **American Newspaper Representatives.**

Publicity Checker, Volume 2: Newspapers. $155 when purchased with Volume 1 on magazines. Two volumes list over 7,500 publications. **Bacon's.**

Working Press of the Nation, Volume I: Newspapers. Part of a $260 five-volume set with 25,000 publicity outlets. **National Research Bureau.**

1988 News Bureaus in the U.S. $133. **Larimi.**

MAGAZINES

Media Alerts. Data on 1,900 magazines and 200 major daily newspapers. $155. **Bacon's.**

National Directory of Magazines. Lists basic information on 1,300 magazines in the United States and Canada. $125. **Oxbridge.**

Publicity Checker, Volume 1. Part of a two-volume set (for magazines and newspapers) with over 7,500 listings. $155 for both volumes. **Bacon's.**

Standard Periodical Directory. Has 60,000 titles with 50 fields of data per title, divided into 250 subject areas. $295. **Oxbridge.**

Working Press of the Nation, Volume 2: Magazines. Part of a $260 five-volume set with data on 25,000 publicity outlets. **National Research Bureau.**

TELEVISION

Cable Contacts Yearbook. Lists all cable systems. $184. **Larimi.**

Radio-TV Directory. Over 1,300 TV stations and 9,000 radio stations. $155. **Bacon's.**

Talk Show Selects. Identifies talk show contacts nationwide for both TV and radio. Emphasizes network and syndication programs. $185. **Broadcast Interview.**

Television Contacts. Updated extensive listings. $233. **Larimi.**

TV News. Guide to news directors and assignment editors. $172. **Larimi.**

TV Publicity Outlets. Two editions are printed at six-month intervals. $159.50. **Public Relations Plus.**

Working Press of the Nation, Volume 3: TV and Radio. Part of a $260 five-volume set with 25,000 publicity outlets. **National Research Bureau.**

RADIO

National Radio Publicity Outlets. Two editions are printed at six-month intervals. $159.50 for both. **Public Relations Plus.**

Radio Contacts. Extensive, updated listings. $239. **Larimi.**

Radio-TV Directory. Over 9,000 radio and 1,300 TV stations. $155. **Bacon's.**

Talk Show Selects. Identifies both radio and TV talk show contacts nationwide. Emphasis is on syndicated and network programs. $185. **Broadcast Interview.**

Working Press of the Nation, Volume 3. Includes both radio and TV. Part of a five-volume $260 set that contains data on 25,000 publicity outlets. **National Research Bureau.**

NEWSLETTERS

Directory of Newsletters. Has 13,500 newsletters in the United States and Canada. Publications are divided into 168 categories. $125. **Oxbridge.**

The Newsletter Yearbook Directory. Lists worldwide newsletters available by subscription. $60. **Newsletter Clearinghouse.**

Newsletters Directory. Guide to more than 8,000 subscription, membership and free newsletters. $140. **Gale Research.**

1988 Investment Newsletters. Lists over 1,000 newsletters. $160. **Larimi.**

REGIONAL

Burrelle's Media Directories. Regional directories for New York State ($85), New Jersey ($70), Pennsylvania ($38), New England ($95), Connecticut ($32), Maine ($25), New Hampshire ($25), Massachusetts ($44), Rhode Island ($25), Vermont ($25), and Greater Boston ($29). **Burrelle's.**

Metro California Media. Detailed listing of California media. $89.50 includes semiannual revised edition. **Public Relations Plus.**

Minnesota Non-Metro Media Directory. Guide to the media in the Twin Cities region. $90. **Publicity Central.**

New York Publicity Outlets. Media within a 50-mile radius of New York City. $89.50 includes the semiannual revised edition. **Public Relations Plus.**

New York TV Directory. Lists producers, directors, and others active in the New York market. Published annually. $15. **National Academy.**

Vermont Media Directory. TV, radio, newspaper, and magazine listings. $99. **Kelliher.**

Washington News Media. Detailed listings of wire services, newspapers, magazines, radio-TV, and foreign correspondents. $99. **Hudson's.**

1988 Media Guide and Membership Directory. Chicago media outlets. $75. **Publicity Club of Chicago.**

INTERNATIONAL

International Literary Market Place. $85. **R. R. Bowker.**

International Media Guide. Publishers of *Newspapers Worldwide* and *Consumer Magazines Worldwide.* A four-volume set covers business and professional publications for Asia/Pacific; Middle East and Africa; Latin America; and Europe. Each volume sells for $100. **International Media Guide.**

International Publicity Checker. Lists 10,000 Western European business, trade, and technical magazines and 1,000 national and regional newspapers. $165. **Bacon's.**

Ulrich's International Periodicals Directory. Lists 70,730 periodicals in 542 subject areas in two volumes. Over 40,000 entries from the previous edition have been updated. $159.95. **Ulrich's.**

UNITED KINGDOM

Benn's Media Directory. Available in two books, one for the United Kingdom and the other for international listings. Each is $95; both are $160. Published by Benn Business Information Services. **Nichols.**

Bowdens Media Directory. Updated three times annually, with complete media listings. **Bowdens.**

Editors Media Directories. Series of directories covering journalists, features, and profiles. **Editors.**

Hollis Press and Public Relations Annual. Over 18,000 organizations in the public relations industry, with a full range of media. $36. **Hollis.**

PIMS United Kingdom Financial Directory. Detailed listings. $300 annually or $90 for a single copy. **PIMS U.S.A.**

PIMS United Kingdom Media Directory. Provides detailed access to the total range of U.K. media. $390 annually, $220 quarterly, or $90 for a single issue. **PIMS U.S.A.**

Willing's Press Guide. Extensive U.K. media listings. $105 plus $5 shipping. Published by Thomas Skinner Directories. **Business Press International.**

CANADA

Matthews List. Contains 3,600 media throughout Canada. Updated three times annually. $130 per year. **Publicorp.**

Australia

Margaret Gee's Media Guide. Lists 2,400 Australian media. Updated three times annually. $100. **Margaret Gee.**

Japan

Publishers in English in Japan. Media selection for English-speaking readers. Published by Japan Publications Guide Service. **Pacific Subscription Service.**

Africa

African Book World and Press. Lists over 4,000 publishers. The latest edition is 1983. $78. **K. G. Saur.**

Specialists

Business and Financial News Media. Print, electronic, syndicated columns, and individual writers. $85. **Larriston.**

Business and Technical Media. Available on paper and floppy disk, at $200 total for both. **Ron Gold.**

Computer Industry Almanac. Extensive industry data, as well as a publications directory. $49.50 hardcover; $29.95 softcover. **Computer Industry Almanac.**

Directory of the College Student Press in America. Has 5,000 student newspapers and magazines on 3,600 campuses. $75. **Oxbridge.**

Encyclopedia of Association Periodicals. Three-volume directory sells for $150; individual volumes sell for $60. Vol. I: business and finance. Vol. II: science and medicine. Vol. III: social sciences and education. **Gale Research.**

Medical and Science News Media. Specialized listings with major news contacts. $85. **Larriston.**

Medical Press List. Available on paper and floppy disk at a combination price of $125. **Ron Gold.**

Nelson's Directory of Investment Research. Contact information and areas of specialization for over 3,000 security analysts. $259. **W. R. Nelson.**

TIA International Travel News Directory. Comprehensive travel media listings. $35. **Travel Industry Association.**

Travel, Leisure and Entertainment News Media. Major nationwide contacts. $85. **Larriston.**

1988 College/Alumni/Military Publications. Over 1,150 publications in these three fields. $87. **Larimi.**

Working Press of the Nation, Volume 5. Internal Publications Directory. Describes house organs published primarily for distribution inside companies. Part of a five-volume library selling for $250. **National Research Bureau.**

Ethnic

Black Media in America. $50. **Hall Co.**

Burrelle's Special Directories. Directories of Black, Latino, and women's media are covered in three volumes at $50 each. **Burrelle's.**

Hispanic Media, U.S.A. Provides a narrative description of Spanish-language media. Includes newspapers, radio, and TV stations. $75 plus $1.50 handling. **The Media Institute.**

General

Business Publications Rates and Data. Monthly directory of magazines and newspapers categorized by field. $398 for 12 monthly issues, or $194 for one copy. **Standard Rate and Data Service.**

Directory of Directories. More than 10,000 entries in two volumes. $195. **Gale Research.**

Gale Directory of Publications. Annual directory to newspapers, magazines, journals, and related publications. $135. **Gale Research.**

Gebbie All-In-One Directory. Comprehensive listings of all media. $79.25. **Gebbie Press.**

Market Guide. Has data on population, income, households, and retail sales for markets around the nation. $70. **E&P.**

Print Media Editorial Calendars. Lists 12-month editorial calendars for 4,200 trades, 1,700 newspapers, 1,500 consumer magazines, and 400 farm publications. $195. **Standard Rate and Data Service.**

Experts and Writers

Directory of Experts, Authorities and Spokespersons. Access to over 3,569 experts. $19.95 plus $3.50 shipping. Can be ordered on Rolodex cards for $165. **Broadcast Interview.**

1988 Syndicated Columnists. Over 1,400 columnists listed. $157. **Larimi.**

Syndicate Directory. Lists syndicated features by classification and by-lines, as well as how material is furnished. $6. **E&P.**

Working Press of the Nation, Volume 4: Feature Writer and Photographer Directory. Part of a five-volume set selling for $260. **National Research Bureau.**

Directory of Publishers

Publishers of media directories are presented in alphabetical order in the list that follows.

American Newspaper Representatives
12 South Sixth St., Ste. 520
Minneapolis, MN 55402
612/332-8686
   National Directory of Community Newspapers

Bacon's PR and Media Information Systems
332 S. Michigan Ave.
Chicago, IL 60604
800/621-0561
   International Publicity Checker
   Media Alerts
   Publicity Checker
   Radio-TV Directory

Bowden's Information Services
624 King Street West
Toronto ON M5V 2X9, Canada
416/860-0794
   Bowden's Media Directory

Broadcast Interview Source
2500 Wisconsin Ave., NW
Suite 930
Washington, DC 20007
202/333-4904
   Directory of Experts
   Talk Show Selects

Burrelle's Press Clipping Service
75 East Northfield Ave.
Livingston, NJ 07039
201/992-6600
   Regional Media Directories

Computer Industry Almanac
8111 LBJ Freeway, 13th floor
Dallas, TX 75251-1313
214/231-8735
   Computer Industry Almanac

Editor and Publisher
11 West 19th St.
New York, NY 10011
212/675-4380
   E&P International Yearbook
   Market Guide
   Syndicate Directory

Editors Media Directories
9/10 Great Sutton St.
London EC1 VOBX England
   Editors Media Directories

Gale Research
Book Tower
Detroit, MI 48226
313/961-2242
   Directory of Directories
   Directory of Publications
   Encyclopedia of Association Periodicals
   Newsletters Directory

Gebbie Press
Box 1000
New Paltz, NY 12561
914/255-7560
   Gebbie All-In-One Directory

Hollis Directories
Contact House
Sunbury-on-Thames
Middlesex TW16 5HG, England
   Hollis Press and Public Relations Annual

International Media Guide Enterprises
22 Elizabeth St.
South Norwalk, CT 06856
203/853-7880
   International Media Guide

Kelliher/Samets
130 South Willard St.
Burlington, VT 05401
802/862-8261
   Vermont Media Directory

Larimi Communications Associates
5 West 37th St.
New York, NY 10018
800/634-4020
212/819-9310
   Cable Contacts Yearbook
   1988 News Bureaus in the U.S.
   Radio Contacts
   Television Contacts
   TV News

Larriston Communications
P. O. Box 20229
New York, NY 10025
212/864-0150
   Business and Financial News Media
   Medical and Science News Media Travel
   Leisure and Entertainment News Media

Margaret Gee Media Group
384 Flinders Lane
Melbourne, Victoria 3000 Australia
Information Australia
Margaret Gee's Media Guide

The Media Institute
3017 M Street
Washington, DC 20007
202/298-7512
Hispanic Media, U.S.A.

National Academy of Television
Arts and Sciences
New York Chapter
110 West 57th St.
New York, NY 10019
212/765-2450
New York TV Directory

National Research Bureau
310 S. Michigan Ave.
Chicago, IL 60604
312/663-5580
Working Press of the Nation

W. R. Nelson Co.
1 Gateway Plaza
Port Chester, NY 10573
914/937-8400
Nelson's Directory of Investment
Research

Newsletter Clearinghouse
44 W. Market St.
P. O. Box 311
Rhinebeck, NY 12572
914/876-2081
Hudson's Washington News
Media Newsletter Yearbook
Directory

Nichols Publishing
P. O. Box 96
New York, NY 10024
212/580-8079
Benn's Media Directory

Oxbridge Communications
150 Fifth Ave.
New York, NY 10011
212/741-0231
National Directory of Magazines
Standard Periodical Directory

Pacific Subscription Service
P. O. Box 811
FDR Station
New York, NY 10150
212/929-1629
Publishers in English in Japan

PIMS U.S.A.
1133 Broadway
New York, NY 10010
212/645-5112
United Kingdom Financial Directory
United Kingdom Media Directory

Public Relations Plus
P. O. Drawer 1197
New Milford, CT 06776
203/354-9361
All TV Publicity Outlets
Metro California Media
National Radio Publicity Outlets
New York Publicity Outlets
The Family Page Directory

Publicity Club of Chicago
1441 Shermer Rd. (#110)
Northbrook, IL 60062
1988 Media Guide
Publicity Club of Chicago Membership
Directory

Publicorp Communications
Box 1029
Pointe Claire PQ
W9S 4H9 Canada
Matthews List

Reed Business Publishing
205 E. 42nd St., Ste. 1705
New York, NY 10017
212/867-2080
Willing's Press Guide

Ron Gold, N.A.
1341 Ocean Ave. (#366)
Santa Monica, CA 90401
213/399-7938
Business and Technical Media
Medical Press List

R. R. Bowker
245 West 17th St.
New York, NY 10011
212/645-9700
Ulrich's International Periodicals Directory

Corporate Reporting Requirements

Periodically, the Hill & Knowlton public relations firm updates this compilation of "Disclosure and Filing Requirements for Public Companies." It details the specific requirements of the various exchanges as well as the Securities and Exchange Commission.

DISCLOSURE REQUIREMENTS

Reporting Required for:	Securities and Exchange Commission	New York Stock Exchange	American Stock Exchange	National Association of Securities Dealers	Generally Recommended Publicity Practice, All Companies
Accounting: Change in Auditors	Form 8-K; if principal accountant (or accountants for a subsidiary) resigns, declines to be reelected, or is dismissed or if another is engaged. Disclose date of resignation, details of disagreement (any adverse opinions, disclaimers of opinion, or qualifications of opinion occurring during the audits of the two most recent fiscal (years), comment letters to SEC for former accountant on whether he agrees with the company's statements in the 8-K. See also Regulations S-K, Item 304.	Prompt notice to Exchange, 8-K when filed.	Prompt notification of Listing Representative, prior to filing of 8-K, *and* must state reason for change (Listing Form SD-1, Item 1a).	Prompt notification concurrently with press disclosure (company must file 8-K with SEC, and information may be material enough to warrant trading halt, See NASD Schedule D). Contact NASD's Market Surveillance Section at (202) 728-8187, preferably before public release and when in doubt about "material information."(NASD Schedule D.) Promptly confirm in writing all oral communications to NASD. If public release made after 5:30 p.m. Eastern Standard Time, notify NASD by 9:30 a.m. the following trading day. (NASDSchedule D).	Press release desirable at time of filing 8-K if differences are major. Consider clear statement in annual report or elsewhere on independence of auditors, including their reporting relationship to Board's audit committee; state company policy on rotation/nonrotation of auditors periodically.
Annual (or Special) Meeting of Stockholders	10-Q following meeting, including date of meeting, name of each director elected, summary of other matters voted on.	Five copies of all proxy material sent to shareholders filed with Exchange not later than date material sent to any shareholder. Ten days' advance notice of record date or closing transfer books to Exchange. The notice should	Six copies of all material sent to shareholders should be sent to the Securities Division as soon as mailed to shareholders (Listing Form SD-1, Item 13). Other requirements same as for NYSE (Listing Form SD-1. Item 1H for notice regarding record date).	File 10-Q concurrently with SEC filing.	Press release at time of meeting. Competition for news space minimizes public coverage except on actively contested issues. Check NYSE schedules for competing meetings. Recommended wide distribution of post-meeting report to shareholders.

Reporting Required for:	Securities and Exchange Commission	New York Stock Exchange	American Stock Exchange	National Association of Securities Dealers	Generally Recommended Publicity Practice, All Companies
		state the purpose(s) for which the record date has been fixed. Preferably, notice should be given by TWX (TWX No. 710-581-2801); or, if by telephone, promptly confirmed by TWX, telegram, or letter.			
Annual Report to Shareholders: Contents	Requirements listed under Rule 14a-3 of the 1934 Act. They include audited balance sheets for two most recent fiscal years; audited income statements and changes in financial position for each of three most recent fiscal years; management's discussion and analysis of financial condition and results of financial operations; brief description of general nature and scope of the business; industry segment information; company directors and officers; stock price and dividends. SEC encourages "freedom of management expression."	Include in annual report principal office's address; directors' and officers' names; audit committee and other committee members; trustees, transfer agents, and registrars; numbers of employees and shareholders (*NYSE Company Manual* Section 203.01). Also include the number of shares of stock issuable under outstanding options at the beginning of the year; separate totals of changes in the number of shares of its stock under option resulting from issuance. exercise, expiration, or cancellation of options; and the number of shares issuable under outstanding options at the close of the year, the number of unoptioned shares available at the beginning and at the close of the year for the granting of options under an option plan, and any changes in the price of outstanding options, through cancellation and reissuance or otherwise, except price changes resulting from the normal operation of antidilution provisions of the options (NYSE Listing Agreement, Section 901.01).	Annual report must contain: balance sheets, income statements, and statements of changes in financial position. Financial statements should be prepared in accordance with generally accepted accounting principles, and SEC Regulation S-X.	No specific requirements, but NASD receives 10-K.	Check printed annual report and appropriate news release to ensure that they conform to information reported on Form 10-K. News releases necessary if annual report contains previously undisclosed material information. Trend is to consider report a marketing tool.

Reporting Required for:	Securities and Exchange Commission	New York Stock Exchange	American Stock Exchange	National Association of Securities Dealers	Generally Recommended Publicity Practice, All Companies
Annual Report to Shareholders: Time and Distribution	Annual report to shareholders must precede or accompany delivery of proxy material. State law notice requirements govern the timing of proxy material mailing prior to annual meeting. Form 10-K must be filed within 90 days of close of year.	Published and submitted to shareholders at least 15 days before annual meeting but no later than three months after close of fiscal year. Four copies to Exchange together with advice as to the date of mailing to shareholders. PROMPTEST POSSIBLE ISSUANCE URGED. Recommended release of audited figures as soon as available.	Published and submitted to shareholders at least 15 days before annual meeting but no later than four months after close of fiscal year. PROMPTEST POSSIBLE ISSUANCE URGED. Recommend release of audited figures as soon as available. Six copies of the report to be filed with the Securities division of the Exchange (Listing Form SD-1, Item 17).	File 10-K concurrently with SEC filing.	Financial information should be released as soon as available; second release at time printed report is issued if report contains other material information. NYSE and AMEX urge broad distribution of report—including distribution to statistical services—so that company information is available for "ready public reference."
Annual Report: Form 10-K	Required by Section 13 or 15(d) of Securities Exchange Act of 1934 on Form 10-K. To be filed with SEC no later than 90 days after close of fiscal year. (Some schedules may be filed 120 days thereafter.) Extensive incorporation by reference from annual report to shareholders and from proxy statement now make integration of Form 10-K and report to shareholders more practical (see general instructions G and H of Form 10-K).	Four copies must be filed with Exchange concurrently with SEC filing; also provide notice to Exchange as to date mailed to shareholders. (*NYSE Company Manual* Sections 203.01 and 204.04).	Three copies must be filed with Exchange concurrently with SEC filing. (See *Company Guide*, pp. 12–2.)	File 10-K concurrently with SEC filing.	Publicity usually not necessary unless 10-K contains previously unreported material information.
Cash Dividends (see Stock Split)	All issuers of publicly traded securities are required to give notice of dividend declarations pursuant to Rule 10B-17. Over-the-counter companies must provide the NASD with advance notice of record date for subsequent dissemination to investors, extending comparable stock exchange requirements to OT market. Failure to comply places issuer in violation of	Prompt notice to Exchange and immediate publicity required for *any* action related to dividend, including omission or postponement of dividend at customary time. The NYSE prefers that it be given notice by TWX (TWX No. 710-581-2801) or by telephone promptly confirmed by TWX, telegram, or letter.	Same as NYSE. Notification to Exchange by telephone or telegram, with confirmation by letter (Listing Form SD-1, Item 1g).	Prompt notification 10 days before record date. File one copy of 10b-17 Report (included in "Reporting Requirements for NASDAQ Companies") with officer's signature.	Prepare publicity in advance and release immediately by a designated officer on word of declaration. Publicity especially important when dividend rate changes. Statement of dividend policy now common in annual reports. Statements of "intention" to take dividend policy now common in annual reports. Statements of "intention" to take

Reporting Required for:	Securities and Exchange Commission	New York Stock Exchange	American Stock Exchange	National Association of Securities Dealers	Generally Recommended Publicity Practice, All Companies
	Section 10(b) of the Securities Exchange Act of 1934.	Ten days' advance notice of record date. NYSE manual implies announcement of management intention prior to formal board action may be required in case of a "leak" or rumor. *Notice regarding declaration of a cash dividend should include* declaration date; record date(s) for closing or reopening transfer books (or any other meaningful dates); per share amount of tax to be withheld with respect to the dividend, description of tax, net after-tax fee share dividend; any conditions upon which payment of dividend hinges.			dividend action also becoming common.
Earnings	Form 10-Q required within 45 days of close of each of first three fiscal quarters. Include information outlined in 10-Q plus a narrative management analysis in form outlined in Form S-K, Item 303. Summary of quarterly results for two years in "unaudited" annual report footnote. Form 10-K required to report full year's earnings.	Quarterly. Publicity required. No fourth quarter statement is required, though items of unusual or nonrecurring nature should be reflected in the company's interim earnings statements.	Quarterly. Should be published within 45 days after end of the first, second, and third fiscal quarters. (No statement is required for the fourth quarter, since that period is covered by the annual report.) Five copies of release should be sent to the Exchange. Press release must be sent to one or more New York City newspapers regularly publishing financial news and to one or more of the national newswires.	Prompt notification and press disclosure if earnings are unusual. File 10-Q and 10-K concurrently with SEC filings.	Immediate publicity; do not hold data until printed quarterly report is published and mailed. Release no later than 10-Q filing; annual results as soon as available. Information in news release must be consistent with 10-Q. Breakout of current quarter results together with year-to-date totals desirable in second, third, and fourth quarter releases.
Legal Proceedings	Form 10-Q at start or termination of proceedings and in any quarter when material development occurs (generally damage claims in excess of	No notice to NYSE required unless proceeding bears on ownership, dividends, interest, or principal of listed securities, or start	"Significant litigation." Public disclosure if material. Prompt notice to Exchange.	Prompt notification and public disclosure if material or if company must file report with SEC.	Public disclosure recommended if outcome of legal proceeding could have material effect on company and news of proceeding has

Reporting Required for:	Securities and Exchange Commission	New York Stock Exchange	American Stock Exchange	National Association of Securities Dealers	Generally Recommended Publicity Practice, All Companies
	10% of current assets); also any suit against company by an officer, director, or major stockholder. See Regulation S-K, Item 103. See also appendix entry entitled "environmental matters."	of receivership bankruptcy, or reorganization proceedings.			not already become public. Court filings now commonly distributed to key business media with or without press release.
Merger: Acquisition or Disposition of Assets	Form 8-K if company acquires or disposes of a significant (10% of total assets or whole subsidiary) amount of assets or business other than in normal course of business. Proxy soliciting material or registration statement may also be required. Check application of Rule 145 (b) of Securities Act of 1933, to any such transaction involving exchange of stock (see also Tender Offers).	Form 8-K filed (where assets acquired). Immediate public disclosure. Prompt notice to Exchange where assets disposed of.	Form 8-K if filed, for acquisition or disposition of assets. Immediate public disclosure.	Prompt notification and public disclosure (8-K filed with SEC).	Exchange policy requires immediate announcement as soon as confidential disclosures relating to such important matters are made to "outsiders" (i.e. other than "top management" and their individual confidential "advisers"). Immediate publicity, especially when assets consist of an entire product line, division, operating unit, or a "substantial" part of the business.
Merger: Commenting on Unusual Market Activity	After SEC ruling in *In re Carnation*, and appeals court decision in *Levinson, et al., v. Basic Industries*, company can state "no comment" about merger discussions when stock shows unusual market activity. However, if company comments in response to Exchange or regulatory inquiry, it must do so truthfully and acknowledge that merger discussions are taking place.	Prepare to make immediate public announcement concerning unusual market activity from merger negotiations. Immediate, candid public statement concerning state of negotiations or development of corporate plans, if rumors are correct or there are developments. Make statements as soon as disclosure made to outsiders (from business appraisals, financing arrangements, market surveys, etc.). Public statements should be definite regarding price, ratio, timing, and any other pertinent information	Promptly and publicly disseminate previously undisclosed information contained in any "leak" that resulted in market action. If company unable to determine cause of market action. Exchange may suggest that company issue "no news" release stating that there have been no undisclosed recent developments affecting the company that would account for unusual market activity. Company need not issue public announcement at each state of merger negotiations, but may await agreement in principle	Prompt notification and public disclosure if material or if company must file report with SEC	Either issue "no comment" statement or explain reason for market activity known to company. Comment asserting that company is "unaware of any reason" to explain market activity is a comment. If company knows the reason for market activity but denies its awareness, it has made a false comment and is probably liable.

Reporting Required for:	Securities and Exchange Commission	New York Stock Exchange	American Stock Exchange	National Association of Securities Dealers	Generally Recommended Publicity Practice, All Companies
		necessary to evaluation. Should include disclosures made to outsiders (*NYSE Company Manual*, Sections 202.01 and .03).	on specific terms or point at which negotiations stabilize. However, publicly release announcement setting forth facts to clarify rumor or report material information. (See *Company Guide*, p. 4-7 to 4-8.)		
Projection: Forecast or Estimate of Earnings	See Reg. S-K General Policy (b). SEC policy encourages use of projections of future economic performance that have "a reasonable basis" and are presented in an appropriate format. Obligation to correct promptly when facts change. Should not discontinue or resume projections without clear explanation of action.	Immediate public disclosure when news goes beyond insiders and their confidential advisers.	Exchange warns against "unwarranted promotional disclosure," including premature announcements of products, and interviews with analysts and financial writers that would unduly influence market activity.	Prompt notification and public disclosure if material (NASD Schedule D).	Projections should be either avoided altogether or widely circulated, with all assumptions stated. Projections by others may require correction by company if wrong but widely believed. Once having made projection, issuer has obligation to update it promptly if assumptions prove wrong. Press releases and other communications should include all information necessary to an understanding of the projection. Legal counsel should be consulted.
Stock Split, Stock Dividend, or Other Change in Capitalization	10-Q required for increase or decrease if exceeds 5% of amount of securities of the class previously outstanding. Notice to NASD or exchange 10 days before record date under Securities Exchange Act's antifraud provisions.	Exchange suggests preliminary discussion, Immediate public disclosure and Exchange notification. Issuance of new shares requires prior listing approval. Either "telephone alert" procedure should be followed or, preferably, wire by TWX. Separate confirmation letter to Exchange. Company's notice to Exchange should indicate brokers' and nominees' requirements and date by which they	Immediate public disclosure and Exchange notification. Issuance of new shares requires prior listing approval. Treatment of fractional shares must be announced.	Prompt notification and public disclosure 10 days before record date. File one copy of 10b-17 Report (included in "Reporting Requirements for NASDAQ Companies") with officer's signature. File 10-Q concurrently with SEC filing.	Immediate publicity as soon as proposal becomes known to outsiders, whether formally voted or not. Discuss early whether to describe transaction as a split, dividend, or both and use terminology consistently.

Reporting Required for:	Securities and Exchange Commission	New York Stock Exchange	American Stock Exchange	National Association of Securities Dealers	Generally Recommended Publicity Practice, All Companies
		must notify disbursing agent of full and fractional share requirements. Exchange will publicize this in its *Weekly Bulletin* or special circulars. *Notice regarding stock dividend, split, or distribution should include:* ratio of stock dividend or split; record date for holders entitled to receive distribution; conditions upon which transaction hinges; date for mailing of certificates for additional shares.			
Tender Offer	Conduct and published remarks of all parties governed by Sections 13(d), 13(e), 14(d), 14(e) of the 1934 Act and regulations thereunder. Schedule 14D-1 disclosure required of raider. Target required to file Schedule 14D-9 for any solicitation or recommendations to security holders. (See also *Hart-Scott-Rodino* requirements.)	Consult Exchange Stock List Department in advance. Immediate publicity and notice to Exchange. Deliver offering material to Exchange no later than distribution date to shareholders. Consult Exchange when terms of tender are at variance with Exchange principles regarding tender offers.	Consult Exchange Securities Division in advance. Immediate publicity and notice to Exchange.	Prompt notification and public disclosure (NASD Schedule D).	Massive publicity effort required: should not be attempted without thorough familiarity with current rules and constant consultation with counsel. Neither raider nor target should comment publicly until necessary SEC filings have been made. "Stop, look, listen" letter permitted under Rule 14D-9(e)

APPENDIX I

Annual Meeting Checklist

By Frank Widder

The following annual shareholder's meeting checklist can be adapted to serve as a "preflight" plan for almost any major meeting.

I. Meeting announcement
   A. Shareholder's proxy statement and general notice
   B. Investment houses', major brokers', and institutional investors' notice and invitation
   C. Financial media invitations
   D. Employee notice of meeting
   E. Guests

   Follow-up (by phone or in person)
   A. Investor relations contacts with major shareholders to determine participation, major areas of interest, potential problems
   B. Major investment houses involved with company
   C. Local financial press
   D. Guest relations

II. Management announcement
   A. Notify all key management personnel to make sure they will be there and arrange alternates for those who cannot make it
   B. Notify all members of the board to determine their ability to make the meeting
   C. Arrange flight times and book hotel in advance; guarantee arrival if necessary

III. Management coaching
   A. Draft basic list of shareholders' problems and questions
   B. Arrange meeting with CEO and chairman to prepare answers, with key staff and legal department to run down answers, and practice those answers
   C. Review and practice management speeches

IV. Presentation materials
   A. Review orders for graphs and slides, compare with financial review speech
   B. Screen any films
   C. Review displays

V. Agenda: order of presentations with approximate running times (in minutes)
   A. Introduction—chairman calls meeting to order and introduces board and management (4:00)
   B. Opening comments by chairman and review of overall activities of company (6:00)
   C. President's message (with visuals) (15:00)
   D. Financial report by vice president, finance (with slide highlights) (5:00)
   E. Film (20:00)
   F. Present proposals in proxy (limit each shareholder to one statement per issue; hand out ballots to shareholders at beginning) (20:00)
   G. Voting, collect ballots (3:00)
   H. General discussion (limit shareholders to one question each) (30:00)

    I. Announce voting results (3:00)

    J. Present company awards of appreciation (2:00)

    K. Adjournment (1:00)—total: 1 hour, 49 minutes

Agenda allows 20 additional minutes for discussion or for more questions during presentation of proposals. Final agenda will be printed and passed out by ushers at meeting.

VI. Site preparation

  A. Staff
1. Electrician, lighting, and sound equipment specialists on hand from 8 A.M. to 5 P.M.
2. Supervisor of custodial, security, and equipment staffs
3. Walkie-talkie communications network with equipment staff
4. Waiters for lounge
5. Caterers for lounge

  B. Parking
1. Traffic direction displays at parking lot entrances
2. Parking attendants directing traffic to proper area
3. Signs pointing to meeting entrance in parking lot

  C. Entrance/reception
1. Reception tables with pencils and guest roster
2. Receptionists to staff tables and answer questions about facilities (need to be briefed beforehand)
3. Well-marked rest areas and signs indicating meeting area
4. Unarmed security guards to control crowd and provide protection
5. Armed security guards located in discrete areas of meeting room
6. Name tags for all representatives of company

  D. Display area
1. Displays set up along walls, to avoid impeding foot traffic, and checked for operation 24 hours in advance
2. Representatives to staff each booth and be prepared for questions about display
3. Tables to display necessary financial information—annual report, 10-K, proxy statement, quarterlies

  E. Lounge area
1. Adequate seating for participants and guests
2. Breakfast/luncheon tables

  F. Meeting areas
1. Sound, lighting, and video checks
2. Sound mikes for all stage participants
3. Additional speakers for amplification
4. Alternate hookup in case of failures—sound, lighting, and video; alternate film in case of breakage
5. Large screen for slide and film
6. Slide and film projectors for presentation
7. Audio and lighting mixers
8. Portable, remote mikes with long cords for audience questions
9. Tape-recorder hookup to record proceedings

  G. Construction
1. Podium constructed high enough for everyone to have direct view of all participants
2. Area blocked off for board and management to view film
3. Area blocked off for lighting and sound equipment
4. Exits properly marked
5. Access to podium and all chairs necessary for seating board and management
6. Logo prominently displayed and lighted above podium

H. Staff
   1. Ushers with flashlights at all entrances for seating
   2. Security at far corners of room
   3. Backstage technicians for sound emergencies
   4. Remote mike monitors on both aisles or in front and back of room
   5. Photographer to shoot proceedings, displays, and key presentations
I. Stage seating arrangements
   1. Podium in middle, chairs to either side
   2. Arrange board members in tenure order
   3. Management in hierarchy order
   4. Chairman sits on board side
   5. President on management side
   6. Nameplates for all participants on podium
   7. Glasses, water, and ashtrays
J. Shareholder seating
   1. First-come basis
   2. Areas roped off for invited shareholders and guests
   3. Areas roped off for film viewing by participants
   4. Special area for members not represented on stage—public accountants, special staff, and guests

VII. Final run-through
   A. Day prior to meeting, complete mock session of annual report, with key principals and timing of presentation—including possible questions and responses.
   B. Review slide show and cues four hours before meeting.
   C. Check screening room communications to begin film; make sure time is allowed to clear stage.
   D. Make sure award is ready for presentation.
   E. Hand out scripts to key participants and technical people.

VIII. Day of meeting
   A. Review with supervisor to ensure that all technical checks are okay.
   B. See that all displays are up and working.
   C. Contact board and management people to check for emergencies in transportation; arrange backup accommodations if necessary.
   D. Sit-down breakfast with key participants to go over agenda and cover any last-minute questions.
   E. Go to convention center, check in with supervisor, security head, parking attendant; ensure that copies of scripts are placed at podium.
   F. Greet participants and guide to lounge.
   G. Wait for shareholders and investors, media; be available for questions and arrange interviews.
   H. Sit down and wait.
   I. Guide participants and guests to luncheon in lounge; make sure bar is set up.
   J. Have a drink—and good night.

credits

Chapter 1
(p. 3) AP/World Wide Photos.
(p. 13) Art by Lou Braun.
(p. 19) Courtesy of PR Strategist.
(p. 21) Courtesy of PR Strategist.

Chapter 2
(p. 25) Courtesy of the Anti-Defamation
League ®.
(p. 35) Courtesy of Frankfurt, Gips,
Balkind.
(p. 44) Courtesy of Johnson & Johnson.
(p. 45) Courtesy of Johnson & Johnson.
(p. 46) Courtesy of Johnson & Johnson.
(p. 48) Courtesy of Edward L. Bernays.

Chapter 3
(p. 51) AP/World Wide Photos.
(p. 52) AP/World Wide Photos.
(p. 55) Courtesy of PETA.
(p. 61) Courtesy of United Technologies
Corporation, Hartford, CT.
(p. 63, left) Fulton & Partners, Inc.
(p. 63, right) Courtesy of Xerox.
(p. 64, left) Courtesy of America Online.
(p. 64, right) RealNetworks.
RealNetworks is a trademark of
RealNetworks Inc. All rights reserved.
(p. 70) Courtesy of Pepsi-Cola.
(p. 71) Courtesy of Pepsi-Cola.
(p. 73) Courtesy of Pepsi-Cola.
(p. 74) Courtesy of Pepsi-Cola.
(p. 75) Courtesy of PR Strategist.

Chapter 4
(p. 82) Used with permission of IABC.
(p. 86) Courtesy of Lockheed Martin.
(p. 88) AP/World Wide Photos.
(p. 89) Courtesy of Professional
Journalists.
(p. 91) AP/World Wide Photos.
(p. 92) Courtesy of FineLine.
(p. 95) Courtesy of AP/World Wide
Photos.
(p. 101) AP/World Wide Photos.
(p. 103) Courtesy of Harold Burson.

Chapter 5
(p. 105) Courtesy of
www.walmartsucks.com.
(p. 107) Courtesy of Trout & Partners.
(p. 128) Courtesy of PR Strategist.

Chapter 6
(p. 133) AP/World Wide Photos.
(p. 134) AP/World Wide Photos.
(p. 138) AP/World Wide Photos.
(p. 153) AP/World Wide Photos.

Chapter 7
(p. 162) Courtesy of Trout & Partners.
(p. 163) Global Icons.
(p. 173) Courtesy of PR Strategist.

Chapter 8
(p. 175) Courtesy of Golin Harris PR.
(p. 176) AP/World Wide Photos.
(p. 181) AP/World Wide Photos.
Table 8-1 (p. 188) Courtesy J.R. O'Dwyer
Company, Inc. © 2000. Used with
permission.
Table 8-2 (p. 190) Courtesy of PR
Strategist.
Table 8-3 (p. 191) Courtesy of PR
Strategist.
Table 8-4 (p. 191) Courtesy of PR
Strategist.
(p. 197) AP/World Wide Photos.
(p. 200) AP/World Wide Photos.

Chapter 9
(p. 203) Courtesy of Rose Brooks for
Battered Women and Their Children.
(p. 204) AP/World Wide Photos.
(p. 207) Courtesy of Focus on the Family.
(p. 208) AP/World Wide Photos.
(p. 209) AP/World Wide Photos.
(p. 210) Courtesy of Handgun Control Inc.
(p. 224) Courtesy of PR Strategist.

Chapter 10
(p. 229) AP/World Wide Photos.
(p. 230) Courtesy of Peanut Advisory
Board.

(p. 231) AP/World Wide Photos.
(p. 233) Courtesy of Marketing Works,
Chicago, Illinois.
(p. 237) Courtesy of the Florence Fund.
(p. 239) Courtesy of Xerox Corporation.
(p. 240) Courtesy of Hershey Foods
Corporation.
(p. 241) Courtesy of Zooperstars.
(p. 245) Courtesy of George Washington's
Mount Vernon Estate & Gardens,
Mount Vernon, VA 22121.
(p. 246, all) Courtesy of George
Washington's Mount Vernon Estate &
Gardens, Mount Vernon, VA 22121.
(p. 247, both) Courtesy of George
Washington's Mount Vernon Estate &
Gardens, Mount Vernon, VA 22121.
(p. 248, top) Courtesy of George
Washington's Mount Vernon Estate &
Gardens, Mount Vernon, VA 22121.
(p. 248, bottom) Courtesy of PR
Strategist.
(p. 249) Courtesy of PR Strategist.

Chapter 11
(p. 256) Courtesy of Russell Stover and
Vorhaus Public Relations.
(p. 258) Courtesy of US Postal Services.
(p. 259) Courtesy of US Postal Services.
(p. 261) Courtesy of The New York Times,
November 27, 1992.
(p. 262) Courtesy of Globeset News.
(p. 274) Courtesy of William C. Adams
Florida International University.

Chapter 12
(p. 280) Courtesy of Russell Stover and
Vorhaus Public Relations.
(p. 283, both) Courtesy of National
Lampoon.
(p. 296) Courtesy of Shirley Carter.

Chapter 13
(p. 302) Courtesy of Michael Kaminer
Public Relations, NY, NY.
(p. 306) Courtesy of the Eastern
Paralyzed Veterans Association.

(p. 310) Courtesy of Global Icons.
(p. 312) Courtesy of www.aolsucks.com.
(p. 313) Courtesy of Northern Light Technology Incorporated.
(p. 321) © 1999 Newsweek Inc. All Rights Reserved. Reprinted by permission.
(p. 322) Courtesy of Ron Higgins.

Chapter 14
(p. 325) AP/World Wide Photos.
(p. 329) Courtesy of the Missouri School of Journalism.
(p. 331) AP/World Wide Photos.
(p. 332-33) Courtesy of Chase Manhattan Bank.
(p. 345) © The New Yorker Collection 1979 Lee Lorenz from cartoonbank.com. All Rights Reserved.
(p. 347) Courtesy of Dave Adams Swedish Bikini Team, Inc.
(p. 352) AP/World Wide Photos.
(p. 354) AP/World Wide Photos.
(p. 355) Courtesy of Quebecor Printing Pendell, Inc.

Chapter 15
(p. 357) AP/World Wide Photos.
(p. 360) AP/World Wide Photos.
(p. 373) Courtesy of CBS.

Chapter 16
(p. 379) Courtesy of Arco.
(p. 384) Courtesy Philip Morris Management Corporation.

(p. 385) Courtesy of O'Dwyer's PR Service Report.
(p. 387, all) Courtesy of Southwest Airlines.
(p. 389) Courtesy of Lockheed Martin.
(p. 396) Courtesy of PR Strategist.

Chapter 17
(p. 399) Courtesy of Southern California Edison.
(p. 400) Courtesy of Lucent Technologies.
(p. 401) Courtesy of America's Promise Alexandria, VA.
(p. 404) Courtesy of School of Journalism & Mass Communications/Public Relations Student Society of America.
(p. 408, all) Courtesy of Pharmacia & Upjohn.
(p. 409) Courtesy of O'Dwyer's PR Service Report.
(p. 410) AP/World Wide Photos.
(p. 412) Courtesy of Edenwald GunHill Neighborhood Center.
(p. 413) Courtesy of Edenwald GunHill Neighborhood Center.
(p. 414) Courtesy of Eileen Colton Photography.
(p. 419) Flagstar/Denny's Public Relations Department.
(p. 420) Courtesy of Advantica Restaurant Group.

Chapter 18
(p. 430) AP/World Wide Photos.
(p. 432) Courtesy of O'Dwyer's PR Service Report.

(p. 434) AP/World Wide Photos.
(p. 444) AP/World Wide Photos.
(p. 445) AP/World Wide Photos.
(p. 446) AP/World Wide Photos.

Chapter 19
(p. 450) Courtesy of Freeman Public Relations and Tyco Preschool.
(p. 452) Courtesy of The National Center for Tobacco-Free Kids.
(p. 454) Courtesy of Continental Airlines Inc.
(p. 460) Courtesy of www.techcentralstation.com.
(p. 466) Courtesy of The National Center for Tobacco-Free Kids.
(p. 467) Courtesy of The National Center for Tobacco-Free Kids.
(p. 469) Courtesy of PR Strategist.

Chapter 20
Table 20-1 (p. 471) O'Dwyer's PR Service Report November 1999.
(p. 477) Courtesy of O'Dwyer's PR Service Report.
(p. 481) AP/World Wide Photos.
(p. 483) AP/World Wide Photos.
(p. 484) Courtesy of Jack O'Dwyer.
(p. 488) Courtesy of IBM.
(p. 489) Courtesy of IBM.
(p. 490) Courtesy of PR Strategist.

Appendix C
(pp. 500–2) Courtesy of Guidelines and Standards/The Institute for Public Relations Research and Education.

index